Language Planning and Policy in Europe, Vol. 3

LANGUAGE PLANNING AND POLICY
Series Editors: Professor Richard B. Baldauf Jr., *University of Queensland, Brisbane, Australia*
and Professor Robert B. Kaplan, *University of Southern California, USA*

For more details of these or any other of our publications, please contact:
Multilingual Matters, Frankfurt Lodge, Clevedon Hall,
Victoria Road, Clevedon, BS21 7HH, England
http://www.multilingual-matters.com

LANGUAGE PLANNING AND POLICY

Language Planning and Policy in Europe, Vol. 3
The Baltic States, Ireland and Italy

Edited by

Robert B. Kaplan and Richard B. Baldauf Jr.

MULTILINGUAL MATTERS LTD
Clevedon • Buffalo • Toronto

Library of Congress Cataloging in Publication Data
Language Planning and Policy in Europe/Edited by Robert B. Kaplan and Richard B. Baldauf Jr.
Language Planning and Policy.
Includes bibliographical references.
1. Language planning–Europe. 2. Language policy–Europe. I. Kaplan, Robert B.
II. Baldauf, Richard B. III. Series
P40.5.L352E854 2005
306.44′94–dc22   2005009432

British Library Cataloguing in Publication Data
A catalogue entry for this book is available from the British Library.

ISBN-13: 978-1-84769-028-9 (hbk)

Multilingual Matters Ltd
UK: Frankfurt Lodge, Clevedon Hall, Victoria Road, Clevedon BS21 7HH.
USA: UTP, 2250 Military Road, Tonawanda, NY 14150, USA.
Canada: UTP, 5201 Dufferin Street, North York, Ontario M3H 5T8, Canada.

The articles in this book also appeared in the journal of *Current Issues in Language Planning*
Vol. 5: 3, 2004; Vol. 6: 3, 2005 and Vol.8: 4, 2007.

The policy of Multilingual Matters/Channel View Publications is to use papers that are
natural, renewable and recyclable products, made from wood grown in sustainable forests.
In the manufacturing process of our books, and to further support our policy, preference is
given to printers that have FSC and PEFC Chain of Custody certification. The FSC and/or
PEFC logos will appear on those books where full certification has been granted to the
printer concerned.

Printed and bound in Great Britain.

Contents

Series Overview

Since 1998, when the first polity studies on language policy and planning – addressing the language situation in a particular polity – were published in the *Journal of Multilingual and Multicultural Development*, 27[1] polity studies (and one issue on Chinese character modernization) have been published in that journal and (between 1990 and 2007) in *Current Issues in Language Planning*. These studies have all addressed, to a greater or lesser extent, 22 common questions or issues (Appendix A), thus giving them some degree of consistency. However, we are keenly aware that these studies have been published in the order in which they were completed. While such an arrangement is reasonable for journal publication, the result does not serve the needs of area specialists nor are the various monographs easily accessible to the wider public. As the number of available polity studies has grown, we have planned (where necessary) to update and republish these studies in coherent areal volumes.

The first such volume was concerned with Africa, both because a significant number of studies has become available and because Africa constitutes an area that is significantly under-represented in the language planning literature. Yet it is marked by extremely interesting language policy and planning issues, therefore in the first areal volume, we reprinted four polity studies – Botswana, Malawi, Mozambique and South Africa – as:

- *Language Planning and Policy in Africa, Vol. 1: Botswana, Malawi, Mozambique and South Africa* (2004).

We hope that the first areal volume has served the needs of specialists more effectively. It is our intent to continue to publish other areal volumes as sufficient studies are completed. We will continue to do so in the hope that such volumes will be of interest to areal scholars and others involved in some way in language policies and language planning in geographically coherent regions. We have already been able to produce five areal volumes in addition to Africa 1 and the six areal volumes presently in print cover 20 polities:

- *Language Planning and Policy in Europe, Vol. 1: Hungary, Finland and Sweden* (2005) Robert B. Kaplan and Richard B. Baldauf Jr. (eds)
- *Language Planning and Policy in Europe, Vol. 2: The Czech Republic, The European Union and Northern Ireland* (2006) Richard B. Baldauf Jr. and Robert B. Kaplan (eds)
- *Language Planning and Policy in the Pacific, Vol. 1: Fiji, the Philippines and Vanuatu* (2006) Richard B. Baldauf Jr. and Robert B. Kaplan (eds)
- *Language Planning and Policy in Africa, Vol. 2: Algeria, Côte d'Ivoire, Nigeria and Tunisia* (2007) Robert B. Kaplan and Richard B. Baldauf Jr. (eds)
- *Language Planning and Policy in Latin America, Vol. 1: Ecuador, Mexico and Paraguay* (2007) Richard B. Baldauf Jr. and Robert B. Kaplan (eds)

This volume – Europe 3 – is another such volume:

- *Language Planning and Policy in Europe, Vol. 3: The Baltics, Ireland and Italy* (2007) Robert B. Kaplan and Richard B. Baldauf Jr. (eds)

The areas in which we are planning to produce additional volumes, and some of the polities that may be included are:

- **Europe**, including Cyprus and Luxembourg.
- **Asia**, including Bangladesh, Chinese characters, Hong Kong, Japan, Nepal, Singapore, Sri Lanka, and Taiwan.
- **Africa**, including Cameroon and Zimbabwe.

In the meantime, we will continue to bring out *Current Issues in Language Planning*, and add to the list of polities available for inclusion in areal volumes. At this point, we cannot predict the intervals over which such volumes will appear, since they will be defined by the ability of contributors to complete work on already contracted polity studies.

Assumptions Relating to Polity Studies

We have made a number of assumptions about the nature of language policy and planning that have influenced the nature of the studies presented. First, we do not believe that there is, yet, a broader and more coherent paradigm to address the complex questions of language policy/planning development. On the other hand, we do believe that the collection of a large body of more or less comparable data and the careful analysis of that data will give rise to a more coherent paradigm. Therefore, in soliciting the polity studies, we have asked each of the contributors to address some two-dozen questions (to the extent that such questions were pertinent to each particular polity); the questions were offered as suggestions of topics that might be covered (see Appendix A). Some contributors have followed the questions rather closely, others have been more independent in approaching the task. It should be obvious that, in framing those questions, we were moving from a perhaps inchoate notion of an under-lying theory. The reality that our notion was inchoate becomes clear in each of the polity studies.

Second, we have sought to find authors who had an intimate involvement with the language planning and policy decisions made in the polity they were writing about, i.e. we were looking for insider knowledge and perspectives about the polities. However, as insiders are part of the process, they may find it difficult to take the part of the 'other' – to be critical of that process. But it is not necessary or even appropriate that they should be – this can be left to others. As Pennycook (1998: 126) argues:

> One of the lessons we need to draw from this account of colonial language policy [i.e. Hong Kong] is that, in order to make sense of language policies we need to understand both their location historically and their location contextually. What I mean by this is that we can not assume that the promotion of local languages instead of a dominant language, or the promotion of a dominant language at the expense of a local language, are

in themselves good or bad. Too often we view these things through the lenses of liberalism, pluralism or anti-imperialism, without understanding the actual location of such policies.

While some authors do take a critical stance, or one based on a theoretical approach to the data, many of the studies are primarily descriptive, bringing together and revealing, we hope, the nature of the language development experience in the particular polity. We believe this is a valuable contribution to the theoretical/paradigmatic development of the field. As interesting and challenging as it may be to provide a priori descriptions of the nature of the field based on specific paradigms (e.g. language management, language rights, linguistic imperialism) or to provide more general frameworks (e.g. Hornberger, 2006; Spolsky, 2004) – nor have we been completely immune from the latter ourselves (e.g. Kaplan & Baldauf, 2003: Chapter 12) – we believe that our current state of knowledge about language planning and policy is still partial and that the development of a sufficient database is an important prerequisite for adequate paradigm development.

Furthermore, we recognize that the paradigm, on the basis of which language policy and planning is conventionally undertaken, may be inadequate to the task. Much more is involved in developing successful language policy than is commonly recognized or acknowledged. Language policy development is a highly political activity (see especially the article on the Baltic States in this volume). Given its political nature, traditional linguistic research is necessary but not in itself sufficient, and the publication of scholarly studies in academic journals is really only the first step in the process. Indeed, scholarly research itself may need to be expanded, to consider not only the language at issue but also the social landscape in which that language exists – the ecology of language and its social system. A critical step in policy development involves making research evidence understandable to the lay public; research scholars are not generally the ideal messengers in this context (Kaplan & Baldauf, 2007). We hope this series also may contribute to that end.

An Invitation to Contribute

We welcome additional polity contributions. Our views on a number of the issues can be found in Kaplan and Baldauf (1997); sample polity monographs have appeared in the extant issues of *Current Issues in Language Planning* and in the volumes in this series. Interested authors should contact the editors, present a proposal for a monograph, and provide a sample list of references. It is also useful to provide a brief biographical note, indicating the extent of any personal involvement in language planning activities in the polity proposed for study as well as any relevant research/publication in LPP. All contributions should, of course, be original, unpublished works. We expect to work closely with contributors during the preparation of monographs. All monographs will, of course, be reviewed for quality, completeness, accuracy, and style. Experience suggests that co-authored contributions may be very successful, but we want to stress that we are seeking a unified monograph on the polity, not an edited compilation of various authors' efforts. Questions may be addressed to either of us.

Richard B. Baldauf, Jr.   Robert B. Kaplan
(*rbaldauf4@bigpond.com*)   (rkaplan@olypen.com)

Note

1. Polities in print include: 1. Algeria; 2. The Baltics; 3. Botswana; 4. Cameroon; 5. Côte d'Ivoire; 6. Czech Republic; 7. Ecuador; 8. European Union; 9. Fiji; 10. Finland; 11. Hungary; 12. Ireland; 13. Italy; 14. Malawi; 15. Mexico; 16. Mozambique; 17. Nepal; 18. Nigeria; 19. North Ireland; 20. Paraguay; 21. The Philippines; 22. South Africa; 23. Sweden; 24. Taiwan; 25. Tunisia; 26. Vanuatu; and 27. Zimbabwe. A 28th monograph on Chinese Character Modernization is also available.

References

Hornberger, N.H. (2006) Frameworks and models in language policy and planning. In T. Ricento (ed.) *An Introduction to Language Policy: Theory and Method* (pp. 24–41). Oxford: Blackwell.

Kaplan, R.B. and Baldauf, R.B., Jr. (2007) Language policy spread: Learning from health and social policy models. *Language Problems & Language Planning* 31 (2), 107 – 129.

Kaplan, R.B. and Baldauf, R.B., Jr. (2003) *Language and Language-in-Education Planning in the Pacific Basin.* Dordrecht: Kluwer.

Kaplan, R.B. and Baldauf, R.B., Jr. (1997) *Language Planning From Practice to Theory.* Clevedon: Multilingual Matters.

Pennycook, A. (1998) *English and the Discourses of Colonialism.* London and New York: Routledge.

Spolsky, B. (2004) *Language Policy.* Cambridge: Cambridge University Press.

APPENDIX A

Part I: The Language Profile of . . .

(1) Name and briefly describe the national/official language(s) (*de jure* or *de facto*).

(2) Name and describe the major minority language(s).

(3) *Name and describe the lesser minority language(s) (include 'dialects', pidgins, creoles and other important aspects of language variation).* The definition of minority language/dialect/pidgin will need to be discussed in terms of the sociolinguistic context.

(4) *Name and describe the major religious language(s).* In some polities religious languages and/or missionary policies have had a major impact on the language situation and provide *de facto* language planning. In some contexts religion has been a vehicle for introducing exogenous languages while in other cases it has served to promote indigenous languages.

(5) Name and describe the major language(s) of literacy, assuming that it is/they are not one of those described above.

(6) Provide a table indicating the number of speakers of each of the above languages, what percentage of the population they constitute and whether those speakers are largely urban or rural.

(7) Where appropriate, provide a map(s) showing the distribution of speakers, key cities and other features referenced in the text.

Part II: Language Spread

(8) Specify which languages are taught through the educational system, to whom they are taught, when they are taught and for how long they are taught.

(9) Discuss the objectives of language education and the methods of assessment to determine whether the objectives are met.

(10) To the extent possible, trace the historical development of the policies/ practices identified in items 8 and 9 (may be integrated with 8/9).

(11) Name and discuss the major media language(s) and the distribution of media by socio-economic class, ethnic group, urban/rural distinction (including the historical context where possible). For minority language, note the extent that any literature is (has been) available in the language.

(12) How has immigration effected language distribution and what measures are in place to cater for learning the national language(s) and/or to support the use of immigrant languages.

Part III: Language Policy and Planning

(13) Describe any language planning legislation, policy or implementation that is currently in place.

(14) Describe any literacy planning legislation, policy or implementation that is currently in place.

(15) To the extent possible, trace the historical development of the policies/ practices identified in items 13 and 14 (may be integrated with these items).

(16) Describe and discuss any language planning agencies/organisations operating in the polity (both formal and informal).

(17) Describe and discuss any regional/international influences affecting language planning and policy in the polity (include any external language promotion efforts).

(18) To the extent possible, trace the historical development of the policies/ practices identified in items 16 and 17 (may be integrated with these items).

Part IV: Language Maintenance and Prospects

(19) Describe and discuss intergenerational transmission of the major language(s), and whether this is changing over time;

(20) Describe and discuss the probabilities of language death among any of the languages/language varieties in the polity, any language revival efforts as well as any emerging pidgins or creoles.

(21) Add anything you wish to clarify about the language situation and its probable direction of change over the next generation or two.

(22) Add pertinent references/bibliography and any necessary appendices (e.g. a general plan of the educational system to clarify the answers to questions 8, 9 and 14).

Language Policy and Planning in the Baltic States, Ireland and Italy: Some Common Issues

Robert B. Kaplan
Professor Emeritus, Applied Linguistics, University of Southern California (Mailing Address: PO Box 577, Port Angeles, WA 98362 USA <rkaplan@ olypen.com>)

Richard B. Baldauf Jr.
Professor, TESOL, School of Education, University of Queensland, QLD 4072 Australia <rbaldauf4@bigpond.com>

Introduction

This volume brings together three language policy and planning polity studies related to five countries in Europe.[1] (See the 'Series Overview' for a more general discussion of the nature of the series, Appendix A for the 22 questions each study set out to address, and Kaplan *et al.* 2000 for a discussion of the underlying concepts for the studies themselves.) In this paper, in addition to providing an introductory summary of the material covered in these studies, we want to draw out and discuss some of the more general issues raised by them.

Although the Baltic States, Ireland and Italy do not represent a geographic cluster, they do have in common a number of factors. All three of the polities:

- can be considered European; all are (or aspire to be) members of the European Union;
- have been concerned with spreading literacy as the reason for language policy development;
- have demonstrated the importance of bottom-up development as opposed to top-down planning;
- are experiencing an increasing influence from English as the result of their role in the European Union.
- are also experiencing pressure from the European Union and the various regulations it has espoused in the context of minority languages, in the context of linguistic rights, and in the context of the requirements imposed by membership.

In addition, all three polities are struggling to assert their national languages, but in differing ways. There is among these polities an interesting contrast – Ireland is struggling to resurrect an indigenous language (Irish) which has been overwhelmed by a major language of wider communication (English) (i.e. moving from essentially English monolingualism toward bilingualism in which Irish is a participant), while the Baltic states are struggling to minimise

6

the influence of a major language of wider communication (Russian) on the historical national languages of the several states (Estonian, Latvian, Lithuanian) (i.e. in effect, moving back to a monolingualism – based on the notion of one polity/one language, although bilingualism would certainly be welcome). On the other hand, multilingualism in Italy is rooted in the histori-cal background of a country whose late unification maintained a situation of linguistic diversity that is unique within Europe. Several unofficial languages (still ambiguously called 'dialects') are widely spoken in everyday life and interpenetrate the national language giving it a strong regional flavor in different areas of the peninsula. These linguistic differences are evidence of the heritage of some ten centuries of political division and cultural diversity – a diversity which could not be erased by the official recognition of Tuscan as Italy's national language in 1861. Since then, the interaction between different sectors of the national community has involved a process of language change that is more complex than that found in other European countries. Thus, Italy is struggling to create a national language composed of influences from many linguistic traditions all pulling in different directions, making the official national language a protean structure.

The Baltic States

These three small independent countries, re-emerging from the wreckage of the Soviet Union, have gained a prominence in language policy issues over the past two decades that belies their relatively modest place on the map of Europe. Concerned to undo the political, demographic and social legacies of half a century of Soviet occupation, language issues in these independent polities became one of the key features of separation from the Communist past, but also one of the key features of controversy and at times of conflict. The conflict has been almost entirely with Russia, whose policies have included a linguistic element in defense of significant numbers of 'Russian speakers' who immigrated into the Baltic States during the Soviet occupation. Important differences can also be seen between the Baltic States – particularly Estonia and Latvia – and European and other inter-national bodies with their own views of language, language conflicts and interpretations of language rights.

On the one hand, language issues have threatened relations with geographic and political neighbours, and have also threatened the entry of Estonia and Latvia into the European Union. On the other, all three Baltic States have in varying ways been able significantly to modify previous language regimes, with internal relations being far more accommodating on the part of language minori-ties and the population generally than they have been marked by overt hostility. This apparent contradiction between external strife and internal accommoda-tion may serve to alert scholars to the importance of identifying perceptions and assumptions clearly in the analysis of any language policy situation.

Recent language issues in this region, however, have also represented a con-tinuation of a much longer set of historical changes in language regimes; over the course of the 20th century alone, no fewer than six different major language regimes can be identified as having occurred, ranging:

- from intense Russification followed by brief liberalisation during Tsarist times,
- to the re-assertion of national languages during the first period of independence,
- to the return of a different incarnation of Russification during the first period of Soviet occupation in 1940–1941,
- to the imposition of German during Nazi occupation in 1941–1944,
- to the return of Soviet Russification under the guise of 'the socialist equality of languages' from 1944 to the late 1980s / early 1990s, and
- to the subsequent reinstatement of the three Baltic languages as the sole national languages in their respective territories.

This shifting history of language regimes makes the Baltic States a remarkable laboratory of linguistic change, persistence and language fractures. Also these three countries are small enough to permit the tracing of changes in the linguistic environment with some chance of accurately delineating their complexity. The recent changes in language regimes that the Baltic States have deliberately brought about, the nature of those changes, the opposition they have engendered, and the linguistic, political and social consequences of these changes – both locally and internationally – are the concern of this monograph.

The period of Russian interaction was characterised from the beginning by deportations, repressions and the annihilation of the institutions and civic life of these polities. The full force of totalitarianism followed this repressive era during World War II and its immediate Stalinist aftermath. As the 50 years of occupation changed from overt repression to political, cultural and ideological control and the desire by the Soviet Union to deny national or cultural identity other than Russian, the threats changed to incessant demographic shifts and the steady limiting of the scope of national language use. A number of issues can be identified:

(1)   The situation in the Baltic States represented the defense of *national* languages that had, in the context of Soviet language policy, lost significant sociolinguistic status and functions from the status they had enjoyed in the first period of independence between the World Wars. This was not a situation of the revival, or of the defence of small minority languages; rather, of language reversal. The situation raises the interesting question of how national languages can be threatened, and how they can regain their status.

(2)   Languages are spoken by people; a significant part of the loss of status of the national languages in the Baltic States was due to the massive influx of immigrants from other republics of the Soviet Union, particularly into Estonia and Latvia. Few of those immigrants learned the local languages, thus raising the question of whether demographic changes justify language policies, including the relationship between language and citizenship. An additional issue involves the associated loss of linguistic privilege among previously dominant groups, causing the citizens of the Baltic States to mobilise against the loss of privilege. The issue is whether the loss of

privilege in language status – real or perceived – may act as a source of language conflict.

(3)   In contrast to a much more common issue for language policy where state institutions (i.e. their officials) cannot speak a particular minority language or do not provide education in minority languages, a full set of immigrant minority (Russian) language institutions appeared in which many state employees (or others providing public services) could not communicate in the national language while all significant state institutions and employees could communicate in the minority language (Russian).

(4)   The local language situation in the Baltics has also seen intense internationalisation, with a variety of governments (most prominently Russia) and a host of international organisations involved in an international battle over the status of languages, often cast in terms of language rights. At times the overwhelming interest of international organisations in the Baltic language situation and the stubborn adherence by the Baltic States to their intention to change their language regime significantly has the potential to bring about some profound refinements of understandings of human rights, national rights, and citizenship as well as discrimination and related areas. Moreover, such issues have at times become central to international processes of integration of states (into the EU) and debates on the legitimate roles of governments and the rights of minorities and majorities. These issues raise significant questions about the relation between local and national language imperatives and international organisations.

(5)   No less important has been the intellectual and academic response to the Baltic situation. The range of opinions on Baltic language policy has been arguably more extensive than that of any other language, with debate even more intense than that in Quebec (with which the Baltic States are sometimes compared). The Baltic situation has now engendered a significant literature with contributions deriving even from authors not otherwise concerned with language policy.

(6)   Beyond the macro issues of rights and legitimacy are the details of language initiatives and a range of pertinent technologies; i.e. issues concerning how small languages can be taught, how language assessment may be conducted, how language streams in schools can be maintained, altered or abolished and how streetscapes can be linguistically altered.

(7)   The altered status of national languages and the broader political questions entailed may mask a number of such sociolinguisticly observable issues as language change, language use and language attitudes. The Baltic States demonstrate intriguing shifts in language attitudes among populations sometimes considered embedded in ethnic divisions. Despite repeated accusations of extreme nationalism among the Baltic populations, there is a marked degree of linguistic tolerance, and parallel with such tolerance (while some immigrant minority leaders with their international supporters admittedly claim discrimination) most minority populations have become more pragmatic and as a consequence more supportive of Baltic policies.

(8)   The Baltic States, during the brief period of independence between the wars, managed to cope liberally with minority populations. The long

historical perspective shows that the Baltic States supported policies of cultural autonomy of minorities to a greater extent than any other polities in Eastern Europe. Despite the deep overlay of Soviet (and post-Soviet) attitudes toward minorities, and despite the short memory retention by many observers, the long liberal history in this context still informs Baltic public policy at the present time.

Ireland

Article 8 of the Irish Constitution, *Bunreacht na hÉireann* of 1937 makes the following affirmation:

(1)   The Irish language as the national language is the first official language.
(2)   The English language is recognised as the second official language.

The official languages of Ireland, therefore, are Irish (Gaelic) and English. It would be safe to assume that more than 95% of the population of Ireland speaks English as a first language; Irish, an autochthonous language, is the first official and national language spoken habitually by only about 5% of the population. Ireland, apart from officially being a bilingual country has firm multilingual foundations. An array of myths bedevil discussions of languages in Ireland, conjuring up a monoglot and monolithic English-speaking or a pristine Gaelic-speaking island, disillusioned by the call towards bilingualism and multilingualism and refusing to change from humdrum monolingualism.

The Irish government's strategy for the revival of Irish between 1922 and 1960 comprised a dual policy of maintenance and restoration; i.e. maintenance of the spoken language in areas where it was still a community language (the *aí*) and its restoration through reversal of language shift in all other areas. (Indeed, since the 1920s, State policy of reversing language shift has sought to re-establish the Irish language – possibly defined as a minority language – as a national language.) The latter involved, in particular, a re-introduction of the language into domains from which it had been excluded since the 17th century. The education system was designated as the major institutional means by which such a reversal would be achieved. Over time, this dual policy was overridden by a third, concerned with providing the necessary infrastructure for maintenance and revival.

By the early 1960s, the overall result of this language strategy was an increase in the ratio of Irish speakers outside the *Gaeltacht* and a decrease in the number of indigenous Irish speakers and users in the Irish speaking regions. Preliminary figures for the 2002 census, including questions as to competency and use of the Irish language, revealed that 1.43 million people have some knowledge of the Irish language, with 9.05% of the population professing to use Irish on a daily basis; when school-going children are omitted from this statistic, however, the number of people who habitually use the language drops to 2.6% of the population. Thus, to speak about results in terms of increase and decrease is an oversimplification masking important spatial and social shifts in the designation of what was to constitute an Irish language speech community. The socio-political contextualisation of efforts at Irish language maintenance and revival competing against the predominance of English has long formed the general discourse for language planning in Ireland.

There has never been an official policy in the Irish State as regards the English language. English began to replace Irish as the language of business, trade, education, administration and daily communication in Ireland from the 18th century onwards. At present, Ireland is almost universally English speaking, with no recorded remaining monolingual speakers of Irish. The Irish language mainly gives access to cultural identities, but Irish residents – both citizens and immigrants – know the powerful certainty of the English language as a gateway to all forms of social and economic access. While one may argue that this duality is a consequence of colonisation or of unequal power relations, the reality is that ideas, perceptions and tensions around the competing English–Irish power struggle have influenced perceptions about language status and which have informed and continue to inform decision-making about the Irish language in particular.

Consequently, language planning in Ireland is still largely about the protection and regeneration of Irish, rather than about the implementation of an ecologically-based, articulated and well-labelled language policy that incorporates English, Irish and the other languages of Ireland. Language policy, in so far as it exists at all, tends to be ad-hoc and haphazard rather than being subject to any 'new' socio-political laden ideology. Furthermore, language planning has been excluded to date from national development planning.

At present, there is a call for a language policy based on an extensive analysis of Ireland's present and future language needs – but the call for the articulation of a language policy comes only from the educational and curriculum policy sectors, where an implicit 'acquisition' policy already exists – for example:

- Irish and English are taught in schools for x number of hours per week,
- are taught from the beginning of primary education right through to the end of post-primary education, etc. and
- not from other sectors such as the private sector.

There is evidence on the other hand of a growing consciousness of a new rights-based linguistic mobilisation in the *aí* – for example with an articulated demand that housing in these regions be available only to Irish speakers.

Since the inception of the Irish Free State in 1922, the education system has been seen as a fulcrum of the movement for the revitalisation of Irish; that is, the planning policies for revitalisation were devolved almost entirely on the schools. The government announced its policies on Irish in the schools in 1922 with the aim of immediately including Irish as a core curriculum subject that would gradually replace English with Irish as the sole medium of instruction in all subjects.

Over time, it became apparent that the education sector could not fulfill the role envisioned for it and that language planning was not succeeding across Ireland. Government language promotion through the schools alone was ineffectual without sufficient support, and all areas of society needed to work to maintain and strengthen the language.

The period from 1990 to the present is characterised by a growing and mobilising awareness of linguistic rights, and this awareness includes – as well as Irish – the 'new' languages of migrant communities and the grassroots movements to secure these rights in the several linguistic communities. This function includes the publishing of the Official Languages Act (2003). The evolving role of the media – particularly the broadcast media – the growth of media technologies, and the use and role of English, Irish and other newly introduced autochthonous community languages all provide new contexts in, and a wider range of sources for, research into language maintenance than have been previously in use.

The Official Languages Act of 2003 was signed into law on 14 July 2003. The Act is the first piece of legislation to provide a statutory framework for the delivery of services through the Irish language. Its primary objective was to ensure better availability and a higher standard of public services through Irish to be achieved by placing a statutory obligation on the Departments of State and other public bodies to make specific provision for delivery of such services in a coherent fashion through a statutory planning framework, known as a 'scheme', to be structured on a three-year renewable basis. The preparation of guidelines by the Minister for public bodies in relation to the preparation of draft schemes is presently under way. Even though the act is termed the official languages [plural] act, the role of English is skirted or ignored.

The Act also specifies some basic general provisions of universal applicability; e.g. correspondence to be replied to in the language in which it was written, providing information to the public in the Irish language or in the Irish and English languages, bilingual publications of certain key documents, etc. Among the principal provisions of the Act are:

- the right of a person to be heard in and to the use Irish language in court proceedings;
- the duty of public bodies to ensure that the Irish language only, or the Irish and English languages together, are used, on oral advertisements whether those advertisements be live or recorded, on stationery, or on signage;
- the duty of public bodies to reply to correspondence in writing or by electronic mail in the language in which that correspondence was written;
- the duty of public bodies to ensure that any communication providing information to the public in writing or by electronic mail is in the Irish language only or in both the Irish and English languages;
- the duty of public bodies that are also State bodies to publish certain documents that would be of interest to the public in Irish and in English simultaneously;
- the duty of public bodies to prepare a scheme detailing the services that they will provide through the medium of Irish, through the medium of English, and through both Irish and English, as well as the measures to be adopted to ensure that any service not presently provided through the medium of the Irish language will be so provided in the future;
- the duty of public bodies to ensure that an adequate number of its staff are competent in the Irish language and that the particular Irish language requirements associated with the provision of services in areas are met; and
- the duty of public bodies to ensure that the Irish language becomes the

working language in their offices situated in the areas within a certain timeframe to be agreed upon between the public body and the Minister.

A language ombudsman's office staffed by a Language Commissioner has already been established to supervise and monitor the implementation of the Act, so that beginning in March, 2005, only the Irish version of official place names in areas would be used in signs, official documents and maps and so that English place names would be erased; equal emphasis would be given to the Irish and English language versions of official place names in other parts of the country. The Language Act, therefore, represents the first stage of new centralised language planning aimed at ensuring the inclusion of appropriate provision for the needs of Irish speakers and of *Gaeltacht* communities in all legislation, at a time when language planning is becoming more decentralised.

The story of language in Ireland is a story about what the masses do (class power) rather than what is planned for the masses to do. There was a mass shift to English from the 17th century onwards. Status planning for the Irish language by governmental agencies mainly through education has met with continual 'mass' resistance and has had only modest success. After failing to engage the masses through centralised language planning activities from 1922 to 1960, a new realism of the hegemony of language practice led to a distancing of the State from language issues. The Irish language has survived rather than being restored. While returns from census and surveys of Irish speakers tend to be interpreted polemically, the fact that school-going children continue to conflate percentages of users shows the precarious position of Irish bilingualism. While some shift to Irish has occurred as a result of language-in-education policy and planning, that activity has not secured home bilingual reproduction and inter-generational transmission. Favourable attitudes towards the language do not appear to translate into motivation for active use or for deliberate language shift in the home domain. In spite of the positive attitudes to the language and the momentum of individuals, families and voluntary organisations involved in the language movement, unlike in Wales (Francis, 2005), home bilingualism does not appear to be gaining ground.

It could be argued that further studies of language planning in Ireland might concentrate exclusively on the *Gaeltacht*, where bottom-up language planning has impacted on and evoked a centralised-type of planning – i.e. state reactive response to pressure groups masks a new devolvement of central responsibility. In this instance, the state may succeed by working in tandem with, rather than in opposition to, class power. It is only in recent times that the languages of minorities are becoming legitimated and institutionalised in the public domain, and it is through local planning and local decision-making that planning has its ultimate impact (see, e.g., Chríost, 2006).

It has been noted recently that the only true bilingual areas in Ireland are in the *Gaeltacht* and that the concept of a language revival outside the *Gaeltacht* is illusory. In the *Gaeltacht* the Irish language, as well as the new immigrant home languages, may over time preserve only a ritual function in what may be a continuing long-term *durée*. Future status planning may be driven more by an ecological desire to maintain an important place for Irish in the linguistic diversity of a multicultural Ireland. It is likely, in a broader global context, that efforts at language revitalisation focusing on language rights and human development will continue to co-exist and survive more easily in concert with globalisation than in concert with national states; hence, the re-creation of identity and the motivation to chart language planning for Irish in this changing context may extend for many years in the future.

Italy

This monograph presents an account of multilingualism, linguistic diversity, social variation, educational confusion and the phenomena of language contact both within and outside Italy. The four main threads are:

(1)　the current linguistic profile of Italy,
(2)　the factors of language spread in the past,
(3)　the current issues in language planning and language policy,
(4)　the prediction of future developments with an eye to speaker innovations and language prospects.

Italian is the official language of the Republic of Italy (57.6 million inhabitants), the Republic of San Marino (13,000) and Vatican City (860), and it is one of the official languages of the Swiss Confederation, spoken in the Ticino Canton (195,000). Outside this area, standard Italian and/or other languages of Italy are also spoken in the region of Nice, the Principality of Monaco, Corsica, Istrian and Dalmatian towns, and in Malta. The language survives in Ethiopia and Somalia as a relic of Italian colonisation. Italian is also one of the heritage languages of immigrant communities in Australia, in the United States, and in North and South America. Emigrants who left Italy to seek employment in the industrial regions of central and northern Europe have transmitted Italian to their offspring.

In Italy, multilingualism is widespread as the result of complex historical circumstances; several historical minorities of the north are situated in areas where borders have fluctuated (Bavarian, Cimbrian, Franco-Provençal, French, German, Mocheno, Provençal, Slovenian and Walser), while those populations in the centre and south have preserved ancestral languages of old foreign settlements (Catalan, Greek, Albanian, Serbo-Croatian). In addition, Italy has three domestic minority languages – Friulian, Ladin and Sardinian – traditionally recognised as autonomous languages existing in conditions of extreme isolation from neighbouring linguistic areas.

Multilingualism in Italy is not, however, related only to the coexistence of Italian and minority languages, it is rooted in the historical background of a country whose late unification maintained a situation of linguistic diversity unique within Europe. The number of Italian speakers at the time of unification (1861) amounted to 2.5% of the total population (some 600,000 including 400,000 Tuscans and 70,000 Romans), while for 97.5% of the population Italian was a foreign language. Several unofficial languages (still ambiguously called 'dialects') are widely spoken in everyday life and have interpenetrated the national language giving it a strong regional flavour in different areas of the Peninsula. In the north, there are Piedmontese, Ligurian, Lombard, Emilian and Venetian; the central area, in addition to Tuscan dialects, also includes Umbrian and the dialects of northern Latium and the Marches; further south, the most prominent dialects are Abruzzese, Neapolitan, Pugliese, Calabrese and Sicilian. These linguistic differences provide evidence of the heritage of some ten centuries of political division and cultural diversity, which could not be eradicated by the official recognition of Tuscan as Italy's national language in 1861. Since then, the interaction between different sectors of the national community has involved a process of language change that is more complex than that found in other European countries.

Political unification was a dream when Dante wrote his *Commedia* in the Florentine vernacular at the beginning of the 14th century; it became a real possibility a century later in Machiavelli's time, in the 15th century, when Italy came very close to changing from a 'geographical expression' to a united state. But the peninsula was coveted by foreign powers, and the Church had no intention of giving up her secular possessions. Once again internal political events prevented unification; the peninsula remained fragmented for four more centuries during which time Florence lost her cultural and political supremacy. Florentine, the basis of literary Italian, inspired the literary tradition that continued to be based on the model prose and the poetry of the three great Tuscan writers, Dante, Petrarch and Boccaccio. Italian élites shared a cultural tradition but not a national community, a situation unique in Europe. It was literature that provided the model for the language to use and not the more common situation in which a standardised language becomes the vehicle for literature. At the same time, in the absence of a nation, the language common to Italians could only be learnt through study, like Latin or a foreign language. Finally, the fact that the debate on the common language in the Italian peninsula was dominated by literary rather than educational considerations also meant that the written models of classical literature have transmitted to contemporary usage a classical language, but one that is not highly standardised compared to other European languages. The fact that the Italian 'geographical expression' did not evolve into a national community until the 19th century is responsible for the survival of Italy's current linguistic diversity.

The spread of the national language – and of the literary models promoted by schools – resulted in a number of variations, due to contact with the dialects, that Italian linguists have divided into varieties or strata, depending on the main components and the characteristics of speakers. While there was virtually no contact between literary language and local dialect – the extreme ends of the continuum – the intermediate varieties increasingly influenced one another, and the rapidly changing situation made it difficult to draw the line between the different strata. Many linguists adopt *architecture* as a metaphor when describing the components of standard Italian. The complex system of forms and norms that regulate its ordinary everyday use is still polymorphic and in rapid evolution. Once the retrospective rules of the literary tradition were abandoned, it was difficult to determine 'good models' or 'acceptable norms'. Interaction between varieties is constant and, in addition, even the most inaccurate and improvised forms of language became prestigious when promoted by the most popular of the mass media – television. A major challenge became, therefore, to describe standard and nonstandard variations in a society where standardisation is still largely in progress.

At present, the typology developed by the linguist Berruto for this purpose is widely accepted:

(1)   **Literary standard Italian** is the Italian of the written literary tradition.
(2)   **Neo-standard Italian** is the variety including some innovations of the spoken language that is used by most people in formal situations.
(3)   **Colloquial Italian** is the spoken variety of informal everyday conversation.
(4)   **Popular regional Italian** is the (mainly) spoken variety of the less educated social groups.
(5)   **'Sloppy' Italian is the spoken variety of very informal situations.**
(6)   **Slang** is a spoken variety that marks one's membership of a special (age or sub-cultural) group.
(7)   **Solemn, very formal, Italian** *(italiano aulico)* is a spoken and written variety for the most formal events.
(8)   **Techno-scientific Italian** is a spoken and written variety used in professional circles;
(9)   **Bureaucratic Italian** is a (mainly) written variety used by public officials.

The status of dialects varies across the country, but their diversity is so marked in Italy that it usually prevents mutual intelligibility – unless speakers live in bordering areas – because Italian dialects differ from literary/standard Italian, and from one another, as much as one Romance language differs from another. Indeed 'dialects' in Italy are not varieties of Italian, they are separate and distinct Romance vernaculars that developed from Latin at the same time as Florentine – a unique situation in Europe. Italian is unique in Europe in that there are relatively few monolinguals and it is the first language of only about 50% of its speakers

The influence of Spanish on Italian, from the second half of the 16th century until the Spanish War of Succession (1702–1714), was not especially significant, whilst that of French in the following two centuries was far more pervasive in the philosophical, political, economic and military domains. The vocabulary that French brought into Italian hinted at innovations that were beginning to affect everyday life. The industrial revolution brought English rather to the fore as the production of industrial commodities for mass consumption was centred on Britain. Some terms were Italianised, others were adopted in their original form. Other major contributions came from the spread of popular sports and other social entertainments, and from the expansion of the new food and clothing industries. At the turn of the century, lexical contributions began to arrive from the exciting new world of the United States; however, the real impact of American English on Italian does not come until after the World War II, reaching considerable proportions during the 1970s and 1980s, and consequently leading some scholars to announce that anglicised Italian could be considered a variety of the national language. A few years later another linguist (Dardano, 1986) modified this picture to note that the impact of English on Italian society was much wider and involved a broader social spectrum of speakers and different areas of language use.

Many Italian words were integrated into English without altering their original form. The early foreign borrowings illustrate the activities and traditions that Italian people brought into Britain over the course of history. Music terminology has been greatly influenced by Italian ever since Italian composers, musicians and singers dominated the European scene. The spread of Italian art and architecture in Renaissance Europe had a similar impact. In the 16th and 17th centuries, the *Commedia dell' Arte* tradition spread throughout Europe. In the 19th century, new imports show an increasing interest in Italian everyday life – one of the favorite themes of popular fiction. At the turn of the century, the greatest impact came through contact with emigrants in the new English-speaking world, where large communities of southerners settled, bringing with them also a new taste for life in general, and eating in particular. Most culinary vocabulary relating to Italian food comes into the language through America. Post-war Italian cinema began to make the country's warmth and vitality internationally known. The Italian way of life was to become extremely seductive, especially among young people. Sometimes borrowed words maintain their original meaning but sometimes either meaning or form, or both are altered. The most interesting of stereotyped borrowings is *al fresco*. To many British people this term vividly describes life Italian style. In Italian it has survived almost exclusively with its metaphorical meaning: 'in prison'.

In Italy, over the centuries, Latin has evolved into Italian and the other romance languages spoken in Italy, but Latin has long been the language of the Church. Italy is substantially a Roman Catholic country (i.e. 98% of the population is Catholic) so the use of Latin is a significant issue. Latin did not become the language of Christian ritual until the 6th century. The effect of using Latin through the centuries when its spoken varieties gradually became distinct languages was to make the liturgy the preserve of the clergy, so that the participation of non-clericals in the religious functions was purely passive. The views of Popes on the Latin language even in recent times are exemplified by the following declarations:

- Pope Pius X (*Moto Propio on the Restoration of Church Music*, November 22, 1903) 'The language of the Roman Church is Latin. It is therefore forbidden to sing anything whatever in the vernacular in solemn liturgical functions.'
- Pope Pius XI (*Officiorum Omnium*, 1922) 'The Church – precisely because it embraces all nations and is destined to endure until the end of time – of its very nature requires a language which is universal, immutable, and non-vernacular.'
- Pope Pius XII (*Mediator Dei*) 'The use of the Latin language affords at once an imposing sign of unity and an effective safeguard against the corruption of true doctrine.'
- Pope John XXIII (encyclical *Veterum Sapientia*, 1962) 'Of its very nature, Latin is most suitable for promoting every form of culture among peoples. It gives rise to no jealousies. It does not favour any one nation, but presents itself with equal impartiality to all and is equally acceptable to all.'
- But even Pope John XXIII spoke of the special value of Latin which had proved so admirable a means for the spreading of Christianity and which had proved to be a bond of unity for the Christian peoples of Europe. Yet, to initiate renewal in the Roman Catholic Church, he convoked a general

council, the Second Vatican Council (1962–1965). The chief reforms in church practices included changes in liturgical language, from Latin to the vernacular. Since then standard Italian has been used instead of Latin except in areas inhabited by official linguistic minorities. The abandonment of Latin as a result of the second Vatican Council excited deep antagonism; one sees in the Latin liturgy an image, cherished by many, of the timeless and changeless Roman Catholic Church. Yet, it was argued that the restoration of the vernacular should restore to the liturgy two functions that it had had in the early centuries: to instruct converts and to confirm members in their faith.

- However, Pope John Paul II told an international group of pilgrims in Rome on July 28, 1999: 'We strongly encourage you all that, by diligent study and effective teaching, you may pass on like a torch the understanding, love and use of this immortal language in your own countries.'

In short, the recent history of Italian (c. 1860–2005) is marked by a massive attempt to Italianise the many 'dialects' spoken across Italy, but the relative success of that effort in turn led to the dialectalisation of Italian. At the end of World War II, Italy was still far from being able to rely on a common language among its nearly 50 million people, most of whom were still employed in the agricultural sector. The education effort required for the transition to a modern industrial society was enormous, because (officially) 13% of the population were illiterate in 1951 and, of the remaining 87%, a high proportion of adults were only semi-literate. An approximate estimate indicated that, apart from the 13% of illiterate people who were monolingual in dialect and the 18% who were monolingual in Italian, the remaining 69% were diglossic, alternating dialect and the national language for diverse purposes and with different people. By 1961 more Italians were working in industry (37%) than in agriculture (33%). By the same date only half of the population was urbanised. Compulsory education was another important factor in the transition between the pre- and post-1968 phases. In the 1970s illiteracy virtually disappeared, with 95% of children completing compulsory schooling, and the number of pupils achieving high school qualifications doubled (839,995 in 1961–1962 vs. 1,732,178 in 1971–1972) and trebled ten years later (2,433,705 in 1981–1982). This ended the role of universities as training institutions for the élites and, from the early 1970s onwards, the universities functioned as centres for intellectual debate and academic achievement open to a much wider spectrum of society.

After the monarchy was outlawed by a referendum that introduced the republic (1946), a Constituent Assembly, with representatives of all political forces, issued a Constitution that came into effect on 1 January 1948. 'Language rights' are dealt with directly in Articles 3 and 6 and, indirectly, in Article 9 and in Part 1 of Article 21. The spirit of the new democratic Constitution intended to secure two fundamental principles: the principle of 'language rights' secures the legal equality of the citizens 'without distinction of sex, race, language, religion, political opinions and personal conditions' (Article 3), and another principle safeguards 'language rights' in the sense of freedom of speech (Article 21, Part 1). Article 6 refers explicitly to minorities: 'The Republic protects linguistic minorities with appropriate measures'. Four linguistic minorities have benefited most from the spirit of the Italian Constitution, but other French, German and Occitan speakers outside these areas were not accorded the same language rights, notably because they are not in historically contested areas, nor were domestic minorities living geographically close to these areas like Ladin and Friulian speakers. Recent legislation, however, has modified the legal situation with an ad hoc norm inspired by a European Directive that Italy needed to respect. Law 15, December 1999 n. 482, on the protection of 'historic linguistic minorities' reiterates that 'The official language of the Italian Republic is Italian'.

The new legislation, declared the intent 'to safeguard the language and culture' of Albanian, Catalan, Germanic, Greek, Slovene and Croatian people and of those speaking French, Franco-Provençal, Friulian, Ladin, Occitan and Sardinian'. The limits of the legislation have been recognised and discussed: the strict reference to the two principles precludes the recognition as a 'minority identity' to communities of new settlers who might engage in language and culture maintenance activities. The principles of the Constitution, though more generic and less binding, reflected a more politically progressive approach, when they identified the 'equality' of Italian citizens in the eyes of the law, 'without distinction of . . . language'. Moreover the new legislation defined the same conditions and applied the same criteria to all listed minorities, without distinction or even consideration between the quality and quantity of language maintenance activities and their impact on minority identities. The generalisation of rights and facilities to use these languages in nursery, primary and lower-secondary education as well as in the municipal debates and in the administration of local municipalities have been seen as rather problematic. The legislation should have introduced a differential treatment of the rights of the most committed communities living in large areas, those with a historic loyalty to an old minority language of the Italian peninsula and the minorities of ancient origin but including few speakers without significant commitment to their linguistic heritage. Many linguists have exhibited less than enthusiastic reactions to the legislation partly because their expertise and advice was not adequately taken into account, partly because of the confusion which would probably ensue in schools and society from this legislative text, marked by demagoguery and approximation.

Some language planning challenges and developments in Italy are comparable to those faced by other European languages. However, many scholars have argued that Italy, either because of its recent unification or because of institutional reluctance, has never been inclined to invest much energy in language policy, with the exception of the nefarious Fascist attempts. Within Italy there are now some growing concerns in a number of areas: i.e. the new rights of domestic minorities and the fact that there is neither sufficient awareness nor sufficient informed discussion about the education of the new ethnolinguistic minorities. Language planning and support policies are urgent in order to secure a more effective promotion of Italian culture outside Italy. The need for coordinated policies to support Italian abroad has been much debated in the past. Two specific areas where the needs of Italian outside Italy require special support concern: (1) the spread of Italian in the New World – especially in English-speaking societies, and (2) the position of Italian in multilingual Europe.

At the present time, language policies to transform interest into investments are needed to maintain a role of this language in areas as far apart as Australia and North America, where Italian is spoken by large communities of Italian origin, and in the European Union, where multilingual communication requires the constant updating of national languages for international communication and for European affairs. Such diverse challenges show that at a time of increasing globalisation the fortunes of Italian will depend on its role within the national community, as much as on the changes due to contacts and interplay with other languages.

Conclusions

These studies show clearly that language planning cannot be accomplished successfully entirely through the education sector, although the education sector has a major role to play in the dissemination of language changes throughput the population. Further, these studies show the importance of involving speakers of the language(s) being planned in the planning process. Indeed, the active involvement of the population is essential because language policy development and implementation is inherently a political activity (see, e.g., Kaplan & Baldauf, 2007). These studies show the extent to which the actual writers of policy, the legislators – as well as the linguists – must understand:

- the general desirability for and the public approval of the policy;
- the need for adequate funding so that the policy may be implemented;
- the various biases of all the key players and the means by which those biases may be offset;
- the need for sufficient time to permit the policy to survive beyond any particular political cycle;
- the reality that outcomes are not likely to be immediate; and
- the ways in which the policy fits both the economic situation and other legislation that may inadvertently be at odds with the objectives.

Note

1. The studies in this volume were previously published as follows: Tosi, A. (2004) Language situation in Italy. *Current Issues in Language Planning* 5 (3), 247–335; Ó'Laoire, M. (2005) The language planning situation in Ireland. *Current Issues in Language Planning* 6 (3), 251–314; Hogan-Brun, G, Ozolins, U., Ramonienė, M. and Rannut, M. (2007) Language politics and practice in the Baltic States. *Current Issues in Language Planning* 8 (4), 469–631.

References

Chríost, D.M.G. (2006) Micro-level language planning in Ireland. *Current Issues in Language Planning* 7 (2&3), 230–250.

Francis, N. (2005) Democratic language policy for multilingual educational systems. *Language Problems & Language Planning* 29 (3), 211–230.

Kaplan, R.B. and Baldauf, R. (2007) Language policy spread: Learning from health and social policy models. *Language Problems & Language Planning* 31 (2), 107–129.

Kaplan, R.B., Baldauf, R.B., Jr., Liddicoat, A.J., Bryant, P., Barbaux, M.-T. and Pütz, M. (2000) Current issues in language planning. *Current Issues in Language Planning* 1, 135–144.

Further Reading

The Baltic States

A Report on the Activities of the State Commission of the Lithuanian Language [Valstybines lietuviu kalbos komisijos prie lietuvos respublikos seimo 2001 metu veiklos ataskaita]. (2002) *Gimtoji Kalba,* 4 (418), 28–32.

Activities of the Valstybine Commission on the Lithuanian Language. September 1997 to August 1998 [Valstybines lietuviu kalbos komisijos veikla. 1997 m. rugsejis–1998 m. rugpjutis]. (1998) *Gimtoji Kalba,* 11 (379), 21–29.

Activities of the State Language Commission: September 1997 to August 1998 [Valstybines lietuviu kalbos komisijos veikla: 1997 m. rugsejis–1998 m. rugpjutis]. (1999) *Gimtoji Kalba,* 1 (379), 23–31.

Chepiga, I.P. (1985) Vsuperech unii ta ezuits'kii ekspansii [In defiance of the Unia and Jesuit expansion]. *Movoznavstvo* 19 (4 (112)), 35–40.

Clachar, A. (1998) Differential effects of linguistic imperialism on second language learning: Americanisation in Puerto Rico versus Russification in Estonia. *International Journal of Bilingual Education and Bilingualism* 1 (2), 100–118.

Decision No. 1 [77] of the State Commission of the Lithuanian Language. Rules of Approbation of Terminology Dictionaries [Valstybines lietuviu kalbos komisijos prie Lietuvos Respublikos Seimo nutarimas nr. 1 (77) Terminu zodynu aprobavimo taisykles]. (2001) *Gimtoji Kalba,* 5 (407), 27–28.

Decision No. 4 (80) of the State Commission of the Lithuanian Language. Names of the Capital Cities of the States [Del valstybines lietuviu kalbos komisijos prie lietuvos respublikos seimo 1996 m. Geguzes 2 D. nutarimo nr. 54 'del valstybiu sostiniu' dalinio pakeitimo]. (2001) *Gimtoji Kalba,* 11 (413), 24–29.

Decisions of the State Commission of the Lithuanian Language [Bendrieji terminu zodynu rengimo reikalavimai]. (2000) *Gimtoji Kalba,* 3 (393), 22–24.

Druviete, I. (1992) Language policy in the Baltic States: A Latvian case. In K. Sagatavojis (ed.) *Valodas Politika Baltijas Valstis* [*Language Policy in the Baltic States*]. Riga: Official Language Bureau of Latvia.

Druviete, I. (1994) Etnopsihologisko faktoru nozime valodas situacijas analize [Ethnopsychological factors in language situation analysis]. *Lietuviu kalbotyros klausimai* 31, 4–10.

Druviete, I. (2000) Sociolinguistic aspects of bilingual education in Latvia. *Sociolinguistica* 14, 153–157.

Druviete, I. and Rayas, L. (1995) Politica del lenguaje y derechos humanos linguisticos en los Estados balticos [Language policy and linguistic human rights in the Baltic States]. *Alteridades* 5 (10), 105–120.

Erelt, T. (1991) La Terminologie en Estonie [Terminology in Estonia]. *Terminogramme: Bulletin D'Information Terminologique et Linguistique* 59, 1–3.

Gaivenis, K. (1994) Tarptautiniu terminologijos principu taikymas musu terminijai [The adoption of international terminology principles for Lithuanian terminology]. *Lietuviu kalbotyros klausimai* 31, 11–17.

Gaivenis, K. (1996) Apie du terminu norminimo principus [On two principles of terminological standardization]. *Lituanistica* 1 (25), 75–79.

Garliauskas, V. (2002) Pirmasis bandymas norminti Lietuvos vietovardizius 'Ausroje' [A first attempt at Lithuanian placename standardization in the newspaper 'Ausra']. *Gimtoji Kalba,* 5 (419), 7–10.

Geistlinger, M. (1997) Die russischsprachige Minderheit in Estland, Lettland und Litauen [The Russian-speaking minorities in Estonia, Latvia, and Lithuania]. *Europa Ethnica* 54 (1–2), 1–11.

Girciene, J. (1998) Naujosios svetimybes: kas kelia neaiskumu kalbos praktikams [New loanwords: A problem for language practitioners]. *Gimtoji Kalba* 11 (379), 19–21.

Grenoble, L.A. (2003) *Language Policy in the Soviet Union.* Dordrecht: Kluwer Academic.

Haarmann, H., and Holman, E. (1997) Acculturation and communicative mobility among former Soviet nationalities. In W. Grabe *et al.* (eds) *Annual Review of Applied Linguistics,* 17 (pp. 113–137). New York: Cambridge University Press.

Hint, M. (1991) The changing language situation: Russian influences on contemporary Estonian. *Journal of Multilingual and Multicultural Development* 12 (1–2), 111–116.

Hint, M. (1999) Is a linguistic theory needed for successful applied linguistics? The Estonian experience. In D. Cram, A.R. Linn and E. Nowak (eds) *History of Linguistics 1996: From Classical to Contemporary Linguistics* (Vol. 2, pp. 233–240). Amsterdam: John Benjamins.

Hirsa, D. (1998) Latvijos valstybines kalbos istatymo projektas-stabdantis ar skatinantis visuomenes integracija veiksnys? [The Latvian State legal language and integration project] *Gimtoji Kalba,* 6 (374), 24–28.

Housen, A. (2002) Contextual, output and operational variables in bilingual education in Latvia. *Intercultural Education* 13 (4), 391–408.

Keinys, S. (1994) Lietuvos valstybe, tauta ir kalba [The Lithuanian state, nation and language]. *Lietuviu kalbotyros klausimai* 31, 57–66.

Kerge, K. (2003) Standard Estonian as a space for thought. *Emakeele Seltsi Aastaraamat* 49, 7–22.

Kirkwood, M. (1990) *Language Planning in the Soviet Union.* New York: St Martin's Press.

Kirule, I. (2000) Naujasis latvijos valstybines kalbos istatymas [New law of the State language of Latvia]. *Gimtoji Kalba* 10 (400), 26–28.

Klimavicius, J. (1999) Geras, tik plonas ir ne be spragu [Nine answers-reflections on standard Lithuanian]. *Gimtoji Kalba* 1 (379), 1–4.

Knabikaite, V. (2002) Lingvistines stilistikos uzuomazgos Prano Skardziaus ir Petro Joniko darbuose [Pranas Skardzius and Petras Jonikas: Two views on stylistics]. *Acta Linguistica Lithuanica* 46, 49–57.

Kreindler, I. (1997) Multilingualism in the successor states of the Soviet Union. In W. Grabe *et al.* (eds) *Annual Review of Applied Linguistics* 17 (pp. 91–112). New York: Cambridge University Press.

Kvasyte, R. (1994) Latviu dalykine kalba kalbos kulturos aspektu [Latvian business language in its language cultivation aspect]. *Lietuviu kalbotyros klausimai* 31, 73–77.

Ladyzhenskaya, B.Y. (1988) Russkiy yazyk v Litve [The Russian language in Lithuania]. *Russkii yazyk v shkole* 75 (1), 81–84.

Laitin, D.D. (1992) Language normalization in Estonia and Catalonia. *Journal of Baltic Studies* 23 (2), 149–166.

Lazauskaite Ragaisiene, V. (2001) Kalbos programos-parama valstybinei kalbai [Language Programs – State Commission of the Lithuanian Language]. *Gimtoji Kalba* 10 (412), 3–6.

Leemets, T. (1994) Terminoloogia arengusuunad Eestis [Trends in terminology development in Estonia]. *Lietuviu kalbotyros klausimai* 31, 78–82.

Lithuanian in the Information Age – The 2000–2006 State Program [Lietuviu kalbos informacineje visuomeneje – 2000–2006 metu programa]. (2000) *Gimtoji Kalba* 4–6 (394–396), 1–4.

Malek, M. (1994) Sprachenpolitik im Baltikum. *Osteuropa: Zeitschrift fur Gegenwartsfragen des Ostens* 44 (10), 926–937.

Mikuleniene, D. (1999a) Lietuviu kalbos komisijos nutarimai Nr. 71, 72, 73 [Decisions No. 71, 72, 73 of the State Commission of the Lithuanian Language]. *Gimtoji Kalba* 11 (389), 20–23.

Mikuleniene, D. (1999b) Valstybines Lietuviu Kalbos Komisijos prie Lietuvos Respublikos seimo nutarimas Nr. 1(70) [Lithuanian Language Commission Declaration No. 1 (70)] *Gimtoji Kalba* 3 (381), 28.

Mikuleniene, D. (2000) Valstybines lietuviu kalbos komisijos nutarimas nr. 2 (76) [Decision No. 2 (76) of the State Commission of the Lithuanian Language] *Gimtoji Kalba* 11 (401), 32.

Mikuleniene, D. (2001) Valstybines lietuviu kalbos komisijos prie lietuvos respublikos seimo nutarimai [Decisions No. 2 (78) and No. 3 (79) of the State Commission of the Lithuanian Language]. *Gimtoji Kalba* 6 (408), 32.

Mikuleniene, D. and Palionyte, J. (1997) Valstybines lietuviu kalbos komisijos veikla

(1996 m. rugsejis–1997 m. rugpjutis) Lithuanian Language Commission Activities (September 1996-August 1997)] *Gimtoji Kalba* 11 (367), 22–27.

Musteikis, K. (1989) Zur Sprachkultur in der Litauischen SSR [On language cultivation in the Lithuanian Soviet Socialist Republic]. *Zeitschrift fur Slawistik* 34 (2), 278–281.

Myhill, J. (1999) Identity, territoriality and minority language survival. *Journal of Multilingual and Multicultural Development* 20 (1), 34–50.

Oispuu, J. (1998) Vahemmistokansat ja muunkielinen sivistys: montako kielistrategiaa Virolle [Minority populations and foreign-language education: The Estonian language strategy]? *AFinLAn vuosikirja* 56, 303–308.

On the juridical status of the municipalities' language officials [Kreipimasis del savivaldybiu kalbos tvarkytoju teisines padeties]. (2001) *Gimtoji Kalba* 11 (413), 29–30.

Ozolins, U. (1994) Upwardly mobile languages: The politics of language in the Baltic States. *Journal of Multilingual and Multicultural Development* 15 (2–3), 161–169.

Pajusalu, K., Velsker, E. and Org, E. (1999) On recent changes in South Estonian: dynamics in the formation of the inessive. *International Journal of the Sociology of Language* 139, 87–103.

Palionis, J. (1997) Del kalbos kulturos lietuvoje sovietines diktaturos metais [On the Lithuanian language during the Soviet dictatorship]. *Gimtoji Kalba* 6 (362), 1–3.

Pedersen, K.M. (2002) A search to merge. *Intercultural Education* 13 (4), 427–438.

Pirockinas, A. and Cizikiene, A. (1996) The Lithuanian language – Hostage of foreign powers: 1940–1991. *Lituanus: Baltic States Quarterly of Arts & Sciences* 42 (2), 44–59.

Protassova, E. (2002) Latvian bilingual education: Towards a new approach. *Intercultural Education* 13 (4), 439–449.

Pupkis, A. (1998) Didziosios ir 'mazosios' kalbos klaidos [The largest and 'smallest' mistakes in language]. *Gimtoji Kalba* 6 (374), 1–3.

Pyall, E. (1979) Mezhnatsional'nyy yazyk i dvuyazychie (na materialakh Estonskoy SSR) [International language and bilingualism (in the Estonian Soviet Socialist Republic)]. *Izvestiya Akadmii Nauk Estonskoi SSR, Obshchestvennye nauki* 28 (4), 347–360.

Raadik, M. (1994) Oskussonastike koostamisest muutuvas keeleolukorras [On the compilation of terminological dictionaries in a changing linguistic situation]. *Lietuviu kalbotyros klausimai* 31, 83–87.

Raag, R. (1996) Karl Bernhard Wiklund and Estonia [Karl Bernhard Wiklund und Estland]. *Acta Universitatis Upsaliensis: Studia Uralica Upsaliensia* 26, 399–411.

Raag, R. (1999) One plus one equals one: The forging of standard Estonian. *International Journal of the Sociology of Language* 139, 17–38.

Raag, V. (1998) The effects of planned change on Estonian morphology. *Acta Universitatis Upsaliensis: Studia Uralica Upsaliensia* 29, 1–156.

Rannut, M. (1990) Linguistic policy in the Soviet Union. *Innovation* 3 (3), 437–447.

Rannut, M. (1991a) Beyond linguistic policy: The Soviet Union versus Estonia. *Rolig Papir*, 23–52.

Rannut, M. (1991b) Influence of ideology in the linguistic policy of the Soviet Union. *Journal of Multilingual and Multicultural Development* 12 (1–2), 105–110.

Rannut, M. (1994) Language policy in the Baltic States. In R. Phillipson and T. Skutnabb-Kangas (eds.) *Papers from the Round Table on Language Policy in Europe, April 22, 1994* (pp. 25–26). Roskilde: Lingvistgruppen Roskilde University.

Rau, T.U. (1985) Language development and policy in Estonia. In I.T. Kreindler (ed.) *Sociolinguistic Perspectives on Soviet National Languages: Their Past, Present and Future* (pp. 13–35). Berlin: Mouton de Gruyter.

Raun, T.U. (1995) The Estonian SSR language law (1989): Background and implementation. *Nationalities Papers* 23 (3), 515–534.

Report on the Activities of the State Commission of the Lithuanian Language for 2000 [Valstybines lietuviu kalbos komisijos prie lietuvos respublikos seimo 2000 metu veiklos ataskaita]. (2001) *Gimtoji Kalba* 4 (406), 25–28.

Rosinas, A. (1997) Valstybines Lietuviu Kalbos Komisjos prie Lietuvos Respublikos seimo nutarimas No. 60 [Lithuanian Language Commission Declaration No. 60]. *Gimtoji Kalba* 8 (364), 18–30.

Rosinas, A. (1997) Valstybines Lietuviu Kalbos Komisjos prie Lietuvos Respublikos seimo nutarimas No. 61 [Lithuanian Language Commission Declaration No. 61]. *Gimtoji Kalba* 8 (364), 30–31.

Rosinas, A. (1997) Valstybines lietuviu kalbos komisijos prie Lietuvos Respublikos Seimo nutarimas Nr. 62 [Lithuanian Language Commission Declaration No. 62]. *Gimtoji Kalba* 11 (367), 17–20.

Rosinas, A. (1997) Valstybines lietuviu kalbos komisijos prie Lietuvos Respublikos Seimo nutarimas Nr. 63 [Lithuanian Language Commission Declaration No. 63]. *Gimtoji Kalba* 11 (367), 21–22.

Rosinas, A. (1998) Valstybines lietuviu kalbos komisijos prie Lietuvos Respublikos Seimo nutarimas Nr. 68 [Lithuanian Language Commission Declaration No. 68]. *Gimtoji Kalba* 2 (370), 1–36.

Ross, K. (2005) From algkmes to infinity: The curvy ways of language reform. *Keel ja Kirjandus* 7, 521–525.

Rykliene, A. (1998) Kalba, integracija, tvarkyba [Language, integration, regulation]. *Gimtoji Kalba* 4 (372), 15–17.

Schmid, C., Zepa, B. and Snipe, A. (2004) Language policy and ethnic tensions in Quebec and Latvia. *International Journal of Comparative Sociology* 45 (3/4), 231–252.

Senkus, J. (1997) 90-osioms gimimo metinems: Lietuviu kalbos tarties normalizacija [For the ninetieth anniversary of his birth: The normalization of Lithuanian orthoepy]. *Gimtoji Kalba* 7 (363), 19–26.

Shmelev, Y.A. (1989) Leninskaya kontseptsiya mezhnatsional'nykh otnosheniy i dvuyazychie v SSSR [Lenin's conception of international relationships and bilingualism in the USSR – 2]. *Russkii yazyk v shkole* 76 (4), 90–95.

Silova, I. (2002) Bilingual education theater: Behind the scenes of Latvian minority education reform. *Intercultural Education* 13 (4), 463–476.

Skujina, V. (1994) Valsts valoda Baltijas republika [State language in the Baltic Republics]. *Lietuviu kalbotyros klausimai* 31, 88–95.

Smalinskas, D. (2002) Kalbos inspekcija, visuomenes rastingumas ir mokykla [Lithuanian language inspection, community, literacy, and education]. *Gimtoji Kalba* 9 (423), 7–9.

Spires, S. (1999) Lithuanian linguistic nationalism and the cult of antiquity. *Nations and Nationalism* 5 (4), 485–500.

Taylor, S. G. (2002) Multilingual societies and planned linguistic change: New language-in-education programs in Estonia and South Africa. *Comparative Education Review* 46 (3), 313–338.

The program for the protection of the dialects and ethnic placenames for 2001–2010 [Tarmiu ir etniniu vietovardziu issaugojimo 2001–2010 metu programa]. (2000) *Gimtoji Kalba* 12 (402), 21–23.

Urneziute, R. (2002a) Kalbos tvarkybos kasdienybe: dokumentu kalba ir viesieji uzrasai [Everyday problems of language policy. The language of official documents and advertisements]. *Gimtoji Kalba* 5 (419), 15–19.

Urneziute, R. (2002b) Kalbos ir kulturos reikalai: butina ugdyti kompleksiska poziuri [Language policy and culture policy: An integrated approach is required]. *Gimtoji Kalba* 11–12 (425–426), 3–9.

Valiukenas, V. and Smilgevicius, A. (1999) Del technikos priemoniu pavadinimu [On the names of technical means]. *Gimtoji Kalba* 2 (380), 7–9.

Veisbergs, A. (1994) Latvian, an ancient language at the ethnic and political crossroads. *Geolinguistics* 20, 140–154.

Veisbergs, A. (1995) Latvian in the post-Soviet Republic. *Paralleles* 17 (Spring), 87–97.

Veisbergs, A. (1999) The new identity in a different world: The case of Latvian. *Geolinguistics* 25, 89–101.

Verschik, A. (2003) An outsider's support of Yiddishism in the Baltic States: The case of Paul Ariste. *Language Problems & Language Planning* 27 (2), 115–136.

Viikberg, J. (1990) The Siberian Estonians and language policy. In D. Gorter, J.F. Hoekstra, L.G. Jansma and J. Ytsma (eds), *Fourth International Conference on Minority Languages, II: Western and Eastern European Papers* (pp. 175–180). Clevedon: Multilingual Matters.

Wysoczanski, W. (1993) O sytuacji jezykowej mniejszosci etnicznych w bylym Zwiazku

Radzieckim [On the linguistic situation of ethnic minorities in the former Soviet Union]. *Studia Linguistica* 16, 87–100.

Ireland

Ahlqvist, A. (1993) Language conflict and language planning in Ireland. In E.H. Jahr (ed.) *Language Conflict and Language Planning* (pp. 7–20). Berlin: Mouton de Gruyter.

Antonini, R., Corrigan, K. and Li, W. (2002) The Irish language in the Republic of Ireland and in Northern Ireland. *Sociolinguistica* 16, 118–128.

Barbour, S. (1996) Language and national identity in Britain and Ireland. *New Language Planning Newsletter* 11 (2), 1–4.

Benton, R.A. (1986) Schools as agents for language revival in Ireland and New Zealand. In B. Spolsky (ed.) *Language and Education in Multilingual Settings* (pp. 53–76) Clevedon: Multilingual Matters.

Blake, J.J. (1998) Language planning and policy in Ireland, 1960–1998. *New Hibernia Review/Iris Eireannach Nua: A Quarterly Record of Irish Studies* 2 (4), 147–154.

Blyn-LaDrew, R. (2003) The Irish language: Past, present, and future. *Geolinguistics* 29, 40–49.

Bressan, D. (1976) Bilinguismo ufficiale e bilinguismo effettivo nella repubblica irelandese [Official bilingualism and effective bilingualism of the Republic of Ireland]. *Quaderni per la promozione del bilinguismo* 12–13 (Sept), 3–17.

Coleman, M.C. (1998) 'Some kind of gibberish': Irish-speaking children in the national schools, 1850–1922. *Studia Anglica Posnaniensia* 33, 93–103.

Cotter, C. (1999) Small languages and small language communities 30: Raidio na Life: Innovations in the use of media for language revitalization. *International Journal of the Sociology of Language* 140, 135–147.

Davis, R.L. (1990) Don't disturb the ancestors. *Teangeolas* 27.

Day, R. (2000) The Irish language and radio: A response. *Current Issues in Language and Society* 7 (2), 159–168.

Dorian, N.C. (1987) The value of language-maintenance efforts which are unlikely to succeed. *International Journal of the Sociology of Language,* 68, 57–67.

Doyle, T. (1990) English as a foreign language – Preparing for 1992. *Teangeolas* 27.

Edwards, J. (1984) Irish: Planning and preservation. *Journal of Multilingual and Multicultural Development* 5 (3–4), 267–275.

Edwards, J. (1986) Did English murder Irish? *English Today* 2 (2), 7–10.

Edwards, J.R. (1977) The speech of disadvantaged Dublin children. *Language Problems & Language Planning* 1 (2), 65–72.

Effemey, J. (2001) Treading softly and dreaming: Frisian and Irish in education. *Dutch Crossing* 25 (1), 53–77.

Ellis, P.B. (1984) Irish: An EEC language. *Incorporated Linguist* 23 (4), 220–227.

Gruenais, M. P. (1986) Irish-English: No model; A case. *Language Problems & Language Planning* 10 (3), 272–281.

Hansen, K. (1992) Zur Sprachsituation und Sprachpolitik in Irland [On the language situation and linguistic policy in Ireland]. *Wissenschaftliche Zeitschrift der Martin Luther Universitat Halle Wittenberg, Gesellschafts/Sprachwissenschaftliche Reihe* 41 (2), 91–95.

Harris, J. (1988) Spoken Irish in the primary school system. *International Journal of the Sociology of Language* 70, 69–87.

Howell, W.J., Jr. (1982) Bilingual broadcasting and the survival of authentic culture in Wales and Ireland. *Journal of Communication* 32 (4), 39–54.

Hudson-Edwards, A. (1990) Language policy and linguistic tolerance in Ireland. In K.L. Adams and D.T. Brink (eds) *Perspectives on Official English: The Campaign for English as the Official Language of the USA* (pp. 63–81). Berlin: Mouton de Gruyter.

Jucquois, G. (2000) The cost-effectiveness evaluation of minority language policies: Case studies on Wales, Ireland and the Basque Country. *Cahiers de l'Institut de Linguistique de Louvain* 26 (1–4), 400–401.

MacKinnon, K. (2004) Reversing language shift: Celtic languages today – Any evidence? *Journal of Celtic Linguistics* 8, 109–132.

Macnamara, J. (1971) Successes and failures in the movement for the restoration of Irish.

In J. Rubin and B.H. Jernudd (eds) *Can Language Be Planned? Sociolinguistic Theory and Practice for Developing Nations* (pp. 65–94). Honolulu: University of Hawai'i Press.

McCoy, G. (ed.) (2000) *Gaelic Identities: Aithne Na Ngael*. Belfast, NI: Institute of Irish Studies, Queen's University.

Ni Neachtain, M. (2000) Competence and minority language broadcasting: A response. *Current Issues in Language and Society* 7 (2), 155–158.

Ó Cinneide, M.S., Keane, M., and Cawley, M. (1985) Industrialization and linguistic change among Gaelic-speaking communities in the West of Ireland. *Language Problems & Language Planning* 9 (1), 3–16.

Ó Ciosain, S. (1988) Language planning and Irish: 1965–74. *Language, Culture and Curriculum* 1 (3), 263–279.

Ó Donoghue, T.A. (1994) Bilingual education at the beginning of the twentieth century: The bilingual programme of instruction in Ireland 1904–1922. *Journal of Multilingual and Multicultural Development* 15 (6), 491–505.

Ó Flatharta, P. (1989) The teaching of Irish as a first language in primary schools in the *Gaeltacht*. *Teanga: Bliainiris na Teangeolaiochta Feidhmi in Eirinn/The Yearbook of Applied Linguistics* 9, 75–83.

Ó Gadhra, N. (1988) Irish government policy and political development of the *Gaeltacht*. *Language, Culture and Curriculum* 1 (3), 251–261.

Ó Gliasain, M. (1988) Bilingual secondary schools in Dublin 1960–1980. *International Journal of the Sociology of Language* 70, 89–108.

Ó Huallachain, C. L. (1978) Languages of instruction in Ireland 1904–1977. *International Review of Education / Internationale Zeitschrift fur Erziehungswissenschaft/Revue Internationale de pedagogie* 24 (4), 501–510.

Ó hIfearnain, T. (2000) Irish language broadcast media: The interaction of state language policy, broadcasters and their audiences. *Current Issues in Language and Society* 7 (2), 92–116.

Ó Laoire, M. (1995) An historical perspective on the revival of Irish outside the *Gaeltacht*, 1880–1930, with reference to the revitalization of Hebrew. *Current Issues in Language and Society* 2 (3), 223–235.

Ó Laoire, M. (1996) Hebrew and Irish: Language revival revisited. In T. Hickey and J. Williams (eds) *Language, Education and Society in a Changing World* (pp. 63–72). Clevedon: Multilingual Matters.

Ó Laoire, M. (2000) Language policy and the broadcast media: A response. *Current Issues in Language and Society* 7 (2), 149–154.

Ó Murchu, M. i. (1988) Diglosia and interlanguage contact in Ireland. *Language, Culture and Curriculum* 1 (3), 243–249.

Ó Murchu, H. (1990) A language policy for Irish schools. *Teangeolas* 27, 15–20.

Ó Riagain, P. (1988) Bilingualism in Ireland 1973–1983: An overview of national sociolinguistic surveys. *International Journal of the Sociology of Language* 70, 29–51.

Ó Riagain, P. (1991) National and international dimensions of language policy when the minority language is a national language: The case of Irish in Ireland. In F. Coulmas (ed.) *A Language Policy for the European Community: Prospects and Quandaries* (pp. 255–277). Berlin: Walter de Gruyter.

Ó Riagain, P. and Ó Gliasain, M. (1990) Formulating a national language policy in the emerging European context: Some preliminary considerations. *Teangeolas* 27, 36–39.

Paulston, C.B., Peillon, M., Verdoodt, A., and De Freine, S. (1989) Review symposium. The Irish language in a changing society: Shaping the future. *Language, Culture and Curriculum* 2 (2), 135–152.

Tovey, H. (2001) The politics of language in Ireland 1366–1922. *Discourse and Society* 12 (3), 405–406.

Ureland, P.S. (1993) Conflict between Irish and English in the secondary schools of the Connemara *Gaeltacht* 1986–1988. In E.H. Jahr (ed.) *Language Conflict and Language Planning* (pp. 193–261). Berlin: Mouton de Gruyter.

Wall, P.J. (1995) Some issues regarding Irish. *Teanga: the Irish Yearbook of Applied Linguistics*, 167–175.

Italy

Arcaini, E. (1984) Multilinguismo, multiculturalismo, problemi, proposte [Multilingualism, multiculturalism, problems, proposals]. *Studi italiani di linguistica teorica e applicata* 13 (1), 7–22.

Arcaini, E. (2001) Prospettive linguistiche della Nuova Europa. Il ruolo della traduzione [The Linguistic prospects of the new Europe. The Role of Translation]. *Studi italiani di linguistica teorica e applicata* 30 (3), 425–434.

Arntz, R. (1997) Sprachenrecht und Sprachenpolitik im dreisprachigen Sudtirol [Language rights and language politics in three language-speaking South Tyrol]. In W.W. Moelleken and P.J. Weber (eds.) *Neue Forschungsarbeiten zur Kontaktlinguistik* (pp. 10–20). Bonn: Dummler.

Bochmann, K. and Brumme, J. (1991) Der Export der nationalen Sprachpolitik der Franzosischen Revolution nach Italien und Spanien. [The export of language politics of the French Revolution to Italy and Spain]. *Lendemains: Etudes Comparees Sur la France/Vergleichende Frankreichforschung* 16 (62), 6–14.

Brezigar, B. (1999) Post-Communist linguistic problems in the North Adriatic area. *Nationalities Papers* 27 (1), 93–101.

Brezigar, B. (2001) Zakon za zascito slovenske manjsine v Italiji [Laws on the protection of the Slovene minority in Italy]. *Razprave in Gradivo Treatises and Documents* 38–39, 110–117.

Casapullo, R. (2000) Qualche appunto su norma e uso nell'italiano contemporaneo [Some approaches to norms and usage in contemporary Italian]. *Franco British Studies* 30 (autumn), 19–31.

Castellani, A. (1982) Italiano e toscano [Italian and Tuscan]. *Studi Linguistici Italiani* 8 (1), 105–106.

Cavalli, M. (1997) Representations sociales et politique linguistique. Le Cas du Val d'Aoste [Social representations and linguistic planning: The case of Val d'Aoste]. *Travaux neuchatelois de linguistique (TRANEL)* 27(Oct), 83–97.

Cavanaugh, J.R. (2004) *Ideologies of Language Shift in Bergamo, Italy*. New York: New York University.

Chiocchetti, F. (1990) Il Ladino tra famiglia e scuola [Ladin between family and school]. *Europa Ethnica* 47 (4), 190–191.

Collu, I. (1991) 'Il servizio di interpretariato': aspetti giuridico-amministrativi [The Interpretational Service: Legal-administrative aspects]. *Effeta* 84 (1), 17–20.

Coluzzi, P. (2005) Language planning for the smallest language minority in Italy: The Cimbrians of Veneto and Trentino-Alto Adige. *Language Problems & Language Planning* 29 (3), 247–269.

Cordin, P. (1994) La 'discordante concordia' e gli anni dell'attesa nel Trentino dell'Ottocento [The discordante concordia and the expectation years in nineteenth-century Trento]. *Archivio Per L'Alto Adige: Rivista di Studi Alpini* 88–89, 37–50.

Cortelazzo, M., Marcato, C. and Rizzolatti, P. (1996) I problemi della grafia unitaria friulana [The problems of a unified Friulian script]. *Rivista Italiana di Dialettologia* 20, 175–180.

Coveri, L. (1981) Dialetto e scuola nell'Italia unita [The dialect and school in united Italy]. *Rivista Italiana di Dialettologia: Scuola Societa Territorio* 5–6 (1 (5)), 77–97.

Czernilofsky, B. (1997) Sprachpolitik und Sprachwirklichkeit im Aostatal [Language policy and language reality in the Aosta Valley] *Europa Ethnica* 54 (3–4), 137–153.

Czernilofsky, B. (2001) Die slowenische Sprachgruppe in der Region Friaul-Julisch Venetien-Gegenseitige Einflussnahme von Grenz- und Sprachenpolitik [The Slovenian linguistic group in the region Friaul-Julisch Venetien: Mutual influence growth between border and language politics]. *Europa Ethnica* 58 (3–4), 172–196.

Damis, C. (2001) Sprachregelungen italienischer Akademien [Language regulations in Italian academies]. *Abhandlungen zur Sprache und Literatur* 137, 89–98.

De Mauro, T. and Vedovelli, M. (1994) La diffusione dell'italiano nel mondo: problemi istituzionali e sociolinguistici [Italian language spread policy in the world: Institutional and sociolinguistic problems]. *International Journal of the Sociology of Language* 107, 25–39.

De Witte, B. (1991) The position of linguistic minorities in Italy (1972–1988). *Plural Societies* 21 (1–2), 51–65.

DeMartino, G. (1986) L'insegnamento precoce della lingua straniera nella scuola elementare [Early instruction of a foreign language in elementary school]. *Ricerche interdisciplinari di glottodidattica* 11 (May-Aug), 45–70.

Denison, N. (1989) Twixt the Scylla of total assimilation and the Charybdis of suicidal purism. *York Papers in Linguistics* 13 (special issue), 101–113.

Egger, K. (1990) Zur Sprachsituation in Sudtirol: Auf der Suche nach Konsens. [On the language situation in South Tirol: In search of a consensus]. *Deutsche Sprache* 18 (1), 76–88.

Falchi, G. (1980) Indicazioni per un'educazione dei figli dei migranti permanenti, con particolare riferimento alle lingue [Indications for permanent migrants' children education with special reference to languages;]. *Studi Emigrazione/Etudes Migrations* 17 (57), 77–90.

Foresti, F. (1983) Lessici tecnici tra norma e storia: l'esperienza di La unita della lingua (1869–73) [Technical lexicons between the norm and history: The experience of La unita della lingua (1869–73)]. *Studi orientali e linguistici* 1, 191–205.

Freddi, G. (1979) Bilinguisme et plurilinguisme en Europe et en Italie [Bilingualism and plurilingualism in Europe and in Italy]. *Quaderni per la promozione del bilinguismo* 23–24 (June), 2–12.

Freddi, G. (1982) Maggioranze, minoranze e plurilinguismo nella provincia di Bolzano (Sudtirol-Alto Adige) [Majority, minority, and plurilingualism in the Province of Bolzano (South Tyrol-Alto Adige)]. *Quaderni per la promozione del bilinguismo* 31–32 (June), 29–52.

Freddi, G. (1989) La lingua straniera nella Scuola Elementare: chi, dove, quando [A foreign language in the elementary school: Which, where, when]. *Lingue del Mondo* 54 (2), 120–122.

Gensini, S. and Dodd, C. (1995) The 'imperfect' language. Notes on Alessandro Manzoni's linguistic ideas. In L. Formigari and D. Gambarara (eds) *Historical Roots of Linguistic Theories* (pp. 151–169). Amsterdam: John Benjamins.

Hametz, M.E. (2002) 'To have what was mine': Reclaiming surnames in Trieste. *Names* 50 (1), 3–22.

Heraud, G. (1982) Les Slovenes d'Autriche et d'Italie [The Slovenes of Austria and Italy]. *Language Problems & Language Planning* 6 (2), 137–153.

Hilpold, P. (1996) Die rechtliche Stellung der Deutsch-Sudtiroler in Italien [The legal position of German South Tiroleans in Italy]. *Europa Ethnica* 53 (3–4), 117–130.

Joseph, J.E. (1980) Linguistic classification in Italy: Problems and predictions. *Language Problems & Language Planning* 4 (2), 131–140.

Klein, G. (1982) Zur italienischen Sprachpolitik: Der Normbegriff des Italienischen wahrend des Faschismus [On Italian language politics: The concept of norm in Italian during fascism]. *Linguistische Berichte* 79 (June), 53–62.

Klein, G. (1984) La lotta contro l'analfabetismo e il posto del dialetto nei programmi scolastici: sulla politica linguistica del fascismo [The struggle against illiteracy and the place of dialect in school programs: On the linguistic policy of fascism]. *Rivista Italiana di Dialettologia: Scuola Societa Territorio* 8 (1 (8)), 7–40.

Kramer, J. (1983) Language planning Italy. In I. Fodor and C. Hagège (eds) *Language Reform: History and Future*, II (pp. 301–316). Hamburg: Buske.

Lampis, A. (1994) Der Gebrauch der italienischen und deutschen Sprache in der Verwaltung Sudtirols, als Beispiel einer rechtlich geregelten Losung der Zusammenlebensprobleme unterschiedlicher Sprachgruppen [The use of the Italian and German languages in the government of South Tirol, as an example of a legally regulated solution to the cohabitation problems of different languages]. *Europa Ethnica* 51 (3–4), 121–132.

Lepschy, G. (1987) Sexism and the Italian language. *Italianist* 7, 158–167.

Lusebrink, C. (1986) Moglichkeiten und Grenzen des rechtlichen Schutzes von Sprach-minderheiten am Beispiel Sudtirol/Burgenland [The possibilities and limits of the legal protection of linguistic minorities: The case of South Tirol and Burgenland]. *Deutsche Sprache in Europa und Ubersee* 11, 57–81.

Malfatti, E. (2004) The protection of linguistic pluralism in Italy between 'dialects' and 'minority languages'. Stocktaking and prospects. *Lingua e Stile* 39 (2), 249–287.

Maraschio, N. (1988) La norma oggi e ieri [The norm today and yesterday]. *Lingue del Mondo* 53 (3), 5–10.

Marcato, G. (1998) Sappada/Plodn. Un'esperienza linguistica interessante in una comunita germanofona delle Alpi venete [Sappada/Plodn. An interesting linguistic experience in a German-speaking community of the Venetian Alps]. *Rivista Italiana di Dialettologia* 22, 169–187.

Marcato, G., and Thune, E.M. (2002) Gender and female visibility in Italian. In M. Hellinger and H. Bussmann (eds) *Gender Across Languages: The Linguistic Representation of Women and Men*, Vol. 2 (pp. 187–217). Amsterdam: John Benjamins.

Maurer-Lausegger, H. (2004) The diversity of languages in the Alpine-Adriatic Region I: Linguistic minorities and enclaves in Northern Italy. *Tidsskrift for Sprogforskning* 2 (1), 5–23.

Migliacci, N. (2002) Language and society in a changing Italy. *Language Policy* 1 (3), 291–293.

Minardi, G. (1986) Il linguaggio giuridico italiano: considerazioni sulla sua evoluzione storica [Italian judicial language: Remarks on historical evolution]. *Ricerche interdisciplinari di glottodidattica* 11 (May-Aug), 83–94.

Mioni, A. M. (1995) Confini dialettali e nuove proposte di assetto territoriale in Italia [Dialectal borders and proposals for a new territorial division in Italy]. *Lingua e Stile* 30 (1), 243–252.

Pagliai, A. (1981) La legislazione regionale a tutela del patrimonio linguistico-culturale [Regional legislation for the protection of the linguistic and cultural heritage]. *Rivista Italiana di Dialettologia: Scuola Societa Territorio* 5–6 (2(6)), 295–317.

Panti, M. (1994) Oralismo e inserimento scolastico come peculiarita dell'educazione dei sordi in Italia. Analisi critica e prospettive concrete di fuoriuscita 'bilinguistica' [Oralism and scholastic immersion as a peculiarity of the education of the deaf in Italy. Critical analysis and concrete proposals for a bilingual approach]. *Effeta* 87 (11), 206–208, 209–213; *Effeta* 87 (12), 224–234.

Pockl, W. (1995) Franzosische Form, italienisches Recht, deutsche Sprache. Uber Verordnungen in Sudtirol [French form, Italian law, German language. On ordinances in South Tirol]. *Grazer Linguistische Monographien* 10, 307–313.

Poggeschi, G. (2003) Language rights and duties in domestic and European courts. *Journal of European Integration* 25 (3), 207–224.

Posner, R., and Rogers, K.H. (1993) Bilingualism and language conflict in Rhaeto-Romance. In R. Posner and J.N. Green (eds) *Trends in Romance Linguistics and Philology Volume 5: Bilingualism and Linguistic Conflict in Romance* (pp. 231–252). Berlin: Mouton de Gruyter.

Price, G. (1976) Language standardization in the Romance field: A survey of recent work. *Semasia* 3, 7–32.

Rae, M.G. (1983) 'La Lingua media': Unification of the Italian language. *Incorporated Linguist* 22 (3), 151.

Riehl, C.M. (2002) Mehrsprachigkeit an der deutsch -romanischen Sprachgrenze: Auswirkungen der Sprachpolitik auf die mehrsprachige Kompetenz der Sprecher [Multilingualism on the German-Romance border: The impact of language policy on speakers' multilingual competence]. *Sociolinguistica* 16, 74–83.

Rifesser, T. (1992) Die Schulordnung an den Schulen der zwei ladinischen Taler der Provinz Bozen/Sudtirol [Rules governing schools of the two Ladin valleys of the Province of Bolzano in Alto Adige]. *Europa Ethnica* 49 (2), 75–89.

Rifesser, T. (1995) Internationale Tagung uber die ladinische Schule [International conference on the Ladin school]. *Europa Ethnica* 52 (2–3), 127–133.

Rundle, C. (2000) The censorship of translation in fascist Italy. *Translator* 6 (1), 67–86.

Sandrini, P. (1993) Die Rolle des Ubersetzers im mehrsprachigen Umfeld. Zum Berufsprofil des Ubersetzers im multikulturellen Umfeld am Beispiel Sudtirols [The translator's role in a multilingual area. On the professional profile of the translator in a multicultural area using the example of South Tirol]. *Lebende Sprachen* 38 (2), 54–56.

Santerini, G. (1982) Lingua e dialetto [Language and dialect]. *I Problemi della Pedagogia* 28 (1–2), 39–45.

Scalia, G.M. (1996) Minoranze linguistiche ed ambiente: la diversita culturale come risorsa [Linguistic minorities and the environment: Cultural diverstiy as a resource]. *Archivio Per L'Alto Adige: Rivista di Studi Alpini* 90, 5–15.

Scalia, G.M. (1996) Norme in materia di tutela delle minoranze linguistiche in Italia: analisi e prospettive [The norms of the protection of linguistic minorities in Italy: Analysis and prospects]. *Archivio Per L'Alto Adige: Rivista di Studi Alpini* 90, 17–36.

Sonino, E.Z., and Dehn, S. (1987) Muttersprachunterricht in Italien: Theoretische Perspektiven und Tendenzen der Praxis [Native-language instruction in Italy: Theoretical perspectives and the tendencies in practice]. *Deutschunterricht* 39 (2), 69–73.

Soulas de Russel, D.J.M. (1994) Les Problemes de la francophonie du Val d'Aoste [Problems of Francophony in Valle d'Aosta]. *Lebende Sprachen* 39 (1), 22–23.

Spaventa, L. (1981) Le minoranze linguistiche nei censimenti dell'Italia prefascista (1861–1921) [Linguistic minorities in the censuses of prefascist Italy (1861–1921)]. *Rivista Italiana di Dialettologia: Scuola Societa Territorio* 5–6 (1 (5)), 37–59.

Street, J. D. (1992) Teaching in French in the primary schools of the Valle D'Aosta, Italy. *French Review* 65 (6), 901–907.

Videsott, P. (2000) On the standardization of Ladin place-names in South Tyrol. *Onoma* 35, 289–317.

White, P. (1991) Geographical aspects of minority language situations in Italy. In C.H. Williams (ed.) *Linguistic Minorities, Society and Territory* (pp. 44–65). Clevedon: Multilingual Matters.

Woelk, J. and Palermo, F. (1995) Sprache und Recht im Gerichtswesen Sudtirols. Das Recht auf Gebrauch der eigenen Sprache im Prozess auf dem verfassungsrichterlichen Prufstand [Language and law in the judicial system of South Tirol. The right to use native language in a legal proceeding tested by the Constitutional Court]. *Europa Ethnica* 52 (2–3), 65–80.

Zuanelli, E. (1991) Italian in the European Community: An educational perspective on the national language and new language minorities. In F. Coulmas (ed.) *A Language Policy for the European Community: Prospects and Quandaries* (pp. 291–299). Berlin: Walter de Gruyter.

Language Politics and Practices in the Baltic States

Gabrielle Hogan-Brun
Graduate School of Education, University of Bristol, Bristol, UK

Uldis Ozolins
School of Social Sciences, La Trobe University, Victoria, Australia

Meilutė Ramonienė
Department of Lithuanian Studies, University of Vilnius, Vilnius, Lithuania

Mart Rannut
Department of Estonian Studies, Tallinn University, Tallinn, Estonia

This monograph provides an overview of the language situation in the three Baltic countries: Estonia, Latvia and Lithuania. It examines the recent change in language regimes that the Baltic States have deliberately brought about since the restitution of their independence, the nature of these changes, the opposition they have engendered and the linguistic, political and social consequences of these policies, both locally and internationally. First, an overview is provided on the historical background to contextualise and present language policy issues in the Baltic. Then attempts to overturn major aspects of Soviet language policy and to re-institute the national language are highlighted. Aspects of the current language situation covered include a special focus on bilingual and multilingual language use in the Baltic multiethnic settings. Detailed attention is also paid to language provision in the diverging educational settings, as well as to methods of assessment. This is followed by a discussion of attitudes to language use, standardisation, testing, languages and language variants. In conclusion the scholarly treatment of Baltic language policy issues is examined, concluding with an evaluation of the contribution of the Baltic States to our overall understandings of language policy and its complexities.

Keywords: Estonia, Latvia, Lithuania, language policy, minorities, national languages, language education

Part I: Introduction
The Baltic States and the challenge of language policy

The Baltic States, three small independent countries that re-emerged from the wreckage of the Soviet Union, have gained a prominence in language policy issues over the past two decades that belies their relatively modest place on the map of Europe. Concerned to undo the political, demographic and social legacies of half a century of Soviet rule, language issues became one of the key features of separation from the Communist past, but also a key point of controversy and at times, of conflict. The conflict has been almost entirely with Russia, whose policies have included a linguistic element in defence of 'Russian speakers'. But important differences can also be seen

31

between the Baltic States – particularly Estonia and Latvia – and European and other international bodies with their own views of language, language conflicts and interpretations of language rights.

At the extreme, language issues have threatened relations with neighbours, and threatened the accession of Estonia and Latvia to desired European bodies – the European Union (EU) and North Atlantic Treaty Organisation (NATO). At a lesser extreme, all three Baltic States in varying ways have been able to alter significantly the previous language regimes, and internal relations have often been far more marked by accommodation and agreement on the part of language minorities and populations generally than by overt hostility. This apparent contradiction between external strife and internal accommodation alerts researchers to the importance of clearly identifying perceptions and assumptions in analysing any language policy situation.

Recent language issues in this region, however, also represent a continuation of a much longer historical context of changing language regimes: over the course of the 20th century alone, no fewer than six different major language regimes can be identified as having held sway. These range from:

(1) The intense Russification and then brief liberalisation in Tsarist times.
(2) The assertion of national languages in the first period of independence of the Baltic States.
(3) The return of a different version of Russification tendencies in the first period of Soviet occupation in 1940–1941.
(4) The imposition of German during Nazi occupation in 1941–1944.
(5) The return of Soviet Russification under the mantle of 'the socialist equality of languages' from 1944 to the late 1980s/early 1990s.
(6) The subsequent reinstatement of the three Baltic languages as the sole national languages in their respective territories.

This shifting history of language regimes – not totally unique in its diversity but certainly at the extreme end of Eastern European experience – makes the Baltic States a remarkable laboratory of linguistic change, persistence and language fractures. Additionally, these three countries are small enough to trace changes in the linguistic environment with some chance of accurately delineating their complexity.

This monograph examines the recent change in language regimes that the Baltic States have deliberately brought about, the nature of those changes, the opposition they have engendered, and the linguistic, political and social consequences of these policies both locally and internationally.

Two crucial perspectives for understanding Baltic language polices are intertwined in this monograph. First, it is fundamental to understand the *specificity* of the conditions in the Baltic emerging from a long period of Soviet occupation. This period was characterised from the beginning by deportation, repression and the annihilation of their nation-states' institutions and civic life. This was followed by the full force of totalitarianism in the context of World War II and its immediate Stalinist aftermath. As the 50 years of occupation changed from overt repression to political, cultural and ideological control and the desire by the Soviet Union to create an atomised *homo sovieticus*, denying national or other cultural identity, the threats changed to incessant demographic shifts and the steady limiting of the scope of national language use. While many of these features are shared with other non-Russian parts of the former Soviet Union, other Warsaw Pact Eastern European states that did not have their national identity threatened did not share them. The specificity of the Baltic States reveals a most tenacious desire to overturn the social, cultural and institutional ravages of Soviet rule, and the actual reconstitution of national life, identity and languages that were threatened.

Second, in addition to understanding specificity, the way Baltic language policy is not only of relevance to this region of the world is illustrated. Several critical issues can be identified arising from Baltic language policies that raise wider implications for other language policy contexts:

(1) The situation in the Baltic States represented the defence and political reiteration of *national* languages that had, in the context of Soviet language policy, lost significant sociolinguistic status and functions from what they had enjoyed in their countries' first period of independence between the World Wars. This situation was not a situation of revival, or of defence of small minority language, but rather one that raises the interesting question of how national languages can be threatened, and how they can regain their status.

(2) Languages are spoken by people, and a significant part of the loss of status of the national languages in the Baltic States was due to the massive influx of immigrants, particularly into Estonia and Latvia, from other republics of the Soviet Union. Few of these immigrants learnt the republican language. The Baltic situation raises the question of whether demographic changes do or do not justify particular language polices – and justify other policies as well – not least, questions of citizenship. An additional issue here is the associated loss of linguistic privilege of previously dominant groups, and much of the politics surrounding Baltic language concerns has been to mobilise against loss of privilege; interestingly, such mobilisation has usually been restricted to a very small fraction of the Soviet-era minorities in the Baltic States, though they have at times received intense support from abroad. The issue of how loss of privilege in language status – real or perceived – acts as a source of language conflict is of relevance in many situations beyond the Baltic.

(3) Genuinely new questions of language entitlements are raised in the Baltic. In contrast to a much more common issue for language policy – situations where state institutions or officials cannot speak a particular minority language or do not provide education in those minority languages – the Baltic States show a radically different linguistic profile. The point is that a full set of immigrant minority (Russian) language institutions continued into the new regime, while many employees (state or otherwise) could not communicate in the national language. All significant state institutions and employees could communicate, however, in the minority language (Russian). Such situations are not common, nor are they easily equated to that of other linguistic minority/majority situations.

(4) The local language situation in the Baltic has also seen intense internationalisation, with a variety of governments (most prominently of Russia) and

a host of international organisations involved in an international battle over the status of languages, often cast in terms of language rights. The at times overwhelming interest of international organisations in the Baltic language situation and the stubborn adherence by the Baltic States to their intention to change their language regime significantly has the potential to bring about some profound refinements of understandings about human rights, national rights, and citizenship as well as about discrimination and related areas. Moreover, such issues have at times become central to international processes of integration of states (into the EU) and debates on legitimate roles of governments and rights of minorities and majorities. These issues thus also raise significant questions of the relation between international organisations and local and national language imperatives.

(5)   No less important has been the intellectual and academic response to the Baltic situation. The range of opinions on Baltic language policy has been arguably more extensive than it has for any other language situation anywhere in the world, with even more intense debate for and against than in the situation in Quebec (with which the Baltic States are sometimes compared), and certainly with greater institutional and human rights ramifications. The Baltic situation now has a significant literature with contributions even from authors not otherwise concerned with language policy, sensing crucial issues that need to be addressed.

(6)   Beyond the macro issues of rights and legitimacy of particular language regimes are the details of language initiatives and a range of technologies that are now closely scrutinised in an almost transparent laboratory situation – how small languages can be taught, how testing for languages can and should be carried out, how language streams in schools can be maintained or altered or abolished, how streetscapes can be linguistically altered.

(7)   Further, the altered status of the national languages and the broader political questions this entails often overshadow more sociolinguistically observable issues of language change, language use and language attitudes. The Baltic States reveal intriguing shifts in language attitudes and practices of populations sometimes considered unyielding or embedded in ethnic divisions. Despite repeated accusations of extreme nationalism among the titular populations, there is a marked degree of linguistic tolerance on their part; and parallel to this, while some immigrant minority leadership with its international supporters cries extreme discrimination, most of the minority population has come to be pragmatic and often supportive of Baltic policies. Viewing language attitudes as unchanging can often be misleading in language policy discourse.

(8)   And finally, returning to a broader historical dimension, while several aspects of the turmoil around language policy and minorities in the Baltic appear novel, in fact the Baltics have a longer history of coping with minorities, most significantly as independent nations between the World Wars when they, more than anywhere else in Eastern Europe, supported policies of cultural autonomy of minorities. This history, long forgotten by others, still informs Baltic public policy today. But it is a history not merely forgotten but overlaid with Soviet and post-Soviet views of minorities of a

completely different and much more vociferous kind. Regaining independence for the Baltic States has meant reclaiming a history often still denied by others.

In these eight ways, Baltic language policy raises issues that can resonate far beyond the borders of these republics. Numerous countries are concerned with issues of linguistic minorities as well as of immigrants, yet for some the issues may not so clearly involve minorities, but indeed rather may involve how to support their national languages against threats, either local or global. Many nation-states, interestingly, have linguistic criteria for citizenship, either limiting or promoting certain aspects of languages in their territory. Some subscribe to, and several are wary of, international instruments prescribing aspects of language policy. A whole range of issues – from broadcasting to language services, to details of school systems – raise language policy issues in countries around the world. In this context, the language issues that arise in the Baltic are certainly not all unique. However, the detailed documentation, argument, involvement of international organisations and sheer range and intensity of language policy issues in the Baltic offers an extraordinarily comprehensive reference point for understanding complexities that, from time to time, may echo elsewhere in the world.

Part Two initially provides an overview on the historical background to present language policy issues in the Baltic, including brief accounts of pre-World War I policies under German, Tsarist or Polish influence. The first period of independence between the two World Wars is also covered to give a background to the policies of cultural autonomy and of national languages that obtained then. An account of the languages themselves is provided – the Finno-Ugric Estonian, and the two Baltic languages proper, Latvian and Lithuanian, which are small and ancient Indo-European languages, neither Germanic nor Slavic – nor Finno-Ugric.

After an account of Soviet language policy, the third part looks at the attempts to overturn major aspects of Soviet language policy and to reinstitute the national language. The ensuing policy battles have an international dimension (particularly in relation to Russia on the one hand and European institutions on the other) as well as a local dimension of language use, language change and language conflict. All of the non-Russian republics of the Soviet Union instituted language laws either while still part of the USSR in the late 1980s, or as independent successor states. Detailed attention is given to the Baltic language laws and reactions to them, and in the case of Estonia and Latvia to citizenship laws as well. The burgeoning debate fostered by international institutions on language rights issues and their resonances in the Baltic is discussed.

Moving from policy to practice, the fourth part covers the current language situation, with a special focus on bilingual and multilingual language use in the Baltic multiethnic settings. Detailed attention is also paid to language provision in the diverging educational settings, as well as to methods of assessment. A discussion of attitudes to language use, standardisation, testing, languages and language variants will round off this part.

The monograph concludes by examining the scholarly treatment of Baltic language policy issues, and by evaluating the contribution of the Baltic States to an overall understanding of language policy and its complexities

Implications of Baltic developments for broader areas of language policy

Despite the very specific historical, political and demographic situation of the Baltic States, language policy that has developed in this context also has broader relevance. Several critical issues can be identified as arising from the Baltic context, and they carry wider implications for other language policy situations. These key concerns are referred to throughout the monograph, and the discussion returns to these broader issues in the final part, where the extent to which Baltic language policy can be seen as a special case, an exception, a copycat of other situations or indeed a path-breaker in language policy considerations is assessed.

Six ways in which Baltic language policy issues can help illuminate other language situations have been identified. These considerations make the Baltic experience of far greater relevance to language policy debates everywhere and not only to their small corner of Europe:

(1) *Defending national languages.* In the Baltic States the still unusual situation is apparent in which it is precisely national languages that can be threatened and that need policy support, thus raising the interesting question of how national languages can be threatened, and how they can regain their status.

This concern bifurcates the discussion. First, it re-energises a sporadic debate over national languages, one best exemplified by Coulmas' title of his 1988 book *What Are National Languages Good For?* Second, this issue has been almost overwhelmed in the literature and in policy discourse by the implications that immediately arise regarding the status of *minority* languages (Hogan-Brun & Wolff, 2003; O'Reilly, 2001). Questions of minority and majority language are central (and often paradoxical) in the Baltic situation, but will also be vital in language policy debates elsewhere. In what is a period of revival of nationalism and majoritarian thinking in many parts of the world, both minority and majority concerns in language policy are clearly back on the agenda (Brubacker, 1996; Coulmas, 1998; Crawford, 2000; Phillipson, 2003).

(2) *Language rights, demographic change and linguistic privileges.* A good portion of this monograph deals with the politically volatile issue of how language rights are to be interpreted and the correctness (or otherwise) of overthrowing a previous language regime. The Baltics have always seen themselves as presenting a situation in which an imposed ruling language took over many of the functions of the previous national languages, and for the national languages to reclaim their status it is legitimate to restrict the former dominant language. Whilst some have seen these restrictions as endangering more universally held linguistic rights, others again question the validity of some pronounced linguistic rights regimes (Druviete, 1997; Kymlicka & Grin, 2003; May, 2001; Skutnabb-Kangas & Phillipson *et al.*, 1994).

At the sharp end of politics, the renewal of independence in these countries raised the issue of how a formerly linguistically privileged group during the Soviet occupation – and a generally monolingual group, as with Russian-speakers in the Baltic – is treated and in turn reacts to a situation in which that privilege is overturned. This has wider implications for other situations (particularly of decolonisation) but has scarely been looked at in literature outside the Baltic States (Knowles, 1999; Maurais, 1997; Racevskis, 2002; Skutnabb-Kangas, 1994).

The loss of privilege is also related to the new citizenship regimes, and the question of whether demographic and political changes (such as the termination of occupation) do or do not justify restored citizenship practices (Chinn & Truex, 1996; Smith, 2001).

(3) *International organisations and concerns with ethnic conflict.* A major imperative for the involvement of international organisations in the Baltic situation was a concern to avoid what was seen as the potential for ethnic conflict, and a range of literature now looks at the significance of international organisations as against local factors in ensuring a relatively peaceful resolution to conflicts in the Baltic States and in some cases in other similar situations in Europe (Budryte, 2005; Galbreath, 2005; Kelley, 2004; Pettai, 2006). Yet from the perspective of the Baltic States the issue was never ethnic conflict, but rather a foreign affairs conflict with Moscow. The Baltic case raises important questions on the extent to which neighbouring states can or should influence language and other policy, and the possible role of international organisations in such instances. A final issue regarding international organisations is the stipulation of various criteria on language and related matters by the EU for candidature to that body. The involvement of international organisations is covered in detail in part three of this monograph, and this has been exhaustively backgrounded in available literature (de Varennes, 1996; European Commission, 2002a, 2002b; Hogan-Brun, 2005a, 2005b, 2005c; OSCE, 1998; Pettai, 2001).

(4) *Intellectual perspectives.* Intellectual interest in the Baltic States has been apparent from the early 1990s, showing a startling variety of views regarding Baltic policies, ranging from strong support to outright hostility. Some commentators from Fukuyama (1992) to Dobson (2001) have unreservedly argued that discrimination is the basis of Baltic policies, a view strongly contested by Maurais (1997) and Rannut (1994, 2004a, 2004b), Blommaert (1999), Deets (2002) and Kymlicka and Patten (2003) all of whom give more theoretical perspectives on the complexities of linguistic considerations in political theory, in an unfolding arena of critical debate. The symbolic value of Baltic policies may have an enduring currency far beyond any immediate issues on the ground.

(5) *The devil is in the detail of language policy.* Changing linguistic regimes impact at the micro-level, whether on people in employment, or in the media, or on those seeking citizenship or on students in schools. The range of technologies and micro-polices introduced in the Baltic States shows:

(a) how small languages can be taught to speakers of big languages;

(b) how testing for languages can be carried out in such areas as employment or citizenship;

(c) how language streams in schools can be maintained or altered or abolished;

(d) how streetscapes can be linguistically altered;

(e) how such minor issues have been properly addressed in many other countries (Piller, 2001; Zuicena, 2005).

Also at the sociolinguistic level, we can find new ways of studying complex language situations, measuring linguistic attitudes among populations facing change and dealing with the often complex accommodations and resistances encountered (Laitin, 1998; Priedīte, 2005; Romanov, 2000).

(6) *History and language policy.* Finally, the Baltic States have insisted on showing again the importance of historical understanding in assessing contemporary language policy, a not always comfortable position when there are frequent urgings to forget that history or to put it aside in the name of ethnic harmony or international acceptance. For the Baltic States, escape from the occupational regime of the Soviet Union represented more than a twist or turn in their history, but rather a fundamental return to values and orientations previously denied, encapsulated in the oft-use phrase 'a return to Europe'. In concrete terms, this return meant:

(a) a shift from a socialist to a capitalist socio-economic order;

(b) a willingness to undergo the considerable trauma of transition;

(c) a shift, most fundamentally, from a dominating Byzantine European to Western European cultural space, with the clinging Soviet language regime seen as one of the major obstacles to such a return.

The experience of the first period of inter-war independence – when this alliance with the values of the West was first clearly asserted – is still a real touchstone on how these states should act today. Regaining independence for the Baltic States has meant reclaiming a history still often denied by some, a situation not unknown for other countries and populations (Hiden & Salmon, 1991; Järve, 2002; Loeber, 1993).

In these many ways, Baltic language policy raises issues that can resonate far beyond the borders of these republics. Numerous polities are searching for ways to provide appropriate linguistic support for minorities and other vulnerable groups. In some cases the central concern may lie in how to scaffold their own national languages against perceived threats, either local or global. Interestingly:

- many polities have linguistic criteria for citizenship;
- others limit and promote certain aspects of languages in their territory;
- yet others subscribe to or are wary of international instruments prescribing aspects of language policy.

A whole range of issues then, from the macro level of status planning to micro level policy aspects of broadcasting, language services or details of school systems, can lead to language policy debates in countries around the world. In this context, the language concerns that arise in the Baltic are certainly not all unique. However, the detailed documentation, argument, involvement of international organisations and the sheer range and intensity of language policy developments in the Baltic provides an extraordinarily comprehensive reference point for understanding complexities that from time to time may be echoed elsewhere in the world.

Part II: Historical and Linguistic Contexts: From the Beginnings to Soviet Occupation

Language policy in the Baltic States is indelibly linked to the history of this region. While language policy as an object of study has only emerged properly in the late 20th century, and while international debate and the instruments relating to this field are even more recent, for the Baltic States many aspects of present policy have longer historical precedents (see Figure 1). Whether it be:

- the former Lithuanian empire of the 15th–16th centuries;
- the long German domination of Estonia and Latvia;
- the policies of Russia in its various incarnations over the past 300 years.

All of these have left a mark on national life and language attitudes.

As well as these longer historical influences, the Baltic States also have a very clear historical link to their first period of independence between the two World Wars. Of crucial historical and political importance currently is the stance of the Baltic States to the effect that their independence from the Soviet Union *de facto* from 1991 is actually a *regaining* of independence and a renewal of national, political and civic life of these countries that were formerly independent between the two World Wars. Language policy is seen to be primarily a restitution of the place their national languages enjoyed in this period, taking into account the influence of the years of Soviet rule and demographic change, but not being determined by these latter factors. Opposition to Baltic policies is often linked to different interpretation of past history, and in some cases to a goal to leave such history behind.

The first section of this part contextualises the Baltic setting by examining briefly the political history of this region. It looks at the various successions of domination in the Baltic area from the 13th to the 18th centuries, and subsequently dwells on the division of Poland, and on Russian rule in this region. The second section presents a concise titular language history of Estonian, Latvian and Lithuanian from their beginnings to the first period of independence. It also shows how the development of these languages has been affected by historical events, leading to a basis for a discussion of recent language policy processes in the subsequent parts. A focus on language policy in the first period of independence (1918–1940) rounds off these brief histories. This is followed by an account of demographic and linguistic consequences of the Soviet occupation, that critically examines Soviet language policy and the way in which immigration and evolving asymmetric bilingualism led to the proliferation of Russian in the public domain, stemming from ignorance of – or even hostility to – the Baltic nations, their peoples and their languages.

Historical background to the first period of independence

There is an extensive standard literature on the Baltic, including Gimbutas (1963), Kirby (1990, 1995), Clemens (1991), Hiden and Salmon (1991) and Urban (2003). Lieven (1993) perhaps gives the liveliest account of the dynamics of Baltic history over the centuries, leading to the restoration of independence in 1991.

The three Baltic States historically comprise two distinct language groupings –
the Finno-Ugric Estonians, related to the Finns both in ethnic origin and language, and the Indo-European Latvians and Lithuanians. The two groupings
had established a more or less enduring dividing line by about 1000 BCE, with
Estonians and related groups occupying the area of current Estonia and the
sea coast of the Gulf of Courland, while a number of related Indo-European
language-speaking tribes occupied the inner reaches of present day Latvia,
Lithuania and an area that at the time constituted part of Prussia.

This region had been known to the outside world from Roman times, particularly for its amber found plentifully along the eastern Baltic coast, and for the

(a)

Figure 1 The Baltic Republics: Estonia – *Eesti*, Latvia – *Latvija*, Lithuania – *Lietuva*.

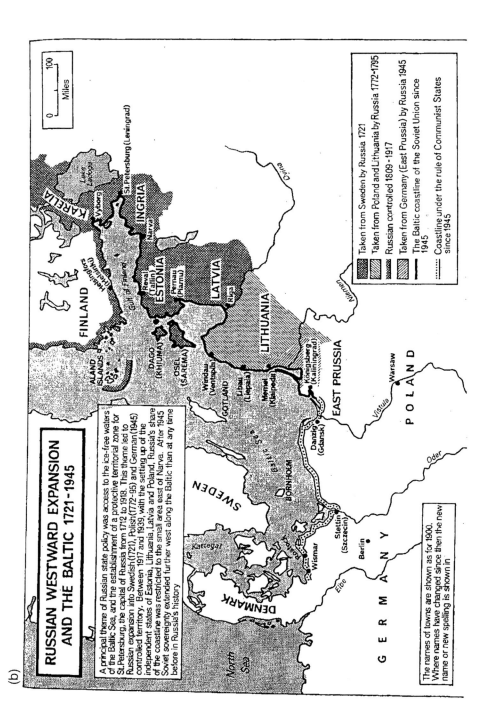

(b)

RUSSIAN WESTWARD EXPANSION AND THE BALTIC 1721–1945

A principal theme of Russian state policy was access to the ice-free waters of the Baltic Sea, and the establishment of a protective territorial zone for St.Petersburg, the capital of Russia from 1712 to 1918. This theme led to Russian expansion into Swedish (1721), Polish (1772–95) and German (1945) controlled territory. Between 1917 and 1939, with the setting up of the independent states of Estonia, Lithuania, Latvia and Poland, Russia's share of the coastline was restricted to the small area east of Narva. After 1945 Soviet sovereignty extended further west along the Baltic than at any time before in Russia's history.

The names of towns are shown as for 1900. Where names have changed since then the new name or new spelling is shown in

Taken from Sweden by Russia 1721

Taken from Poland and Lithuania by Russia 1772–1795

Russian controlled 1809–1917

Taken from Germany (East Prussia) by Russia 1945

The Baltic coastline of the Soviet Union since 1945

Coastline under the rule of Communist States since 1945

international trade that was most strongly reconstituted later by the Vikings, from the 8th century CE. However, it was religious and expanding population issues rather than trade that resulted in greater Western interest. By the 13th century, this area was the last space in Europe that was not Christian, surrounded by Roman Christianity to the west and south and Orthodox Christianity to the east, the latter having established itself in what is present-day Russia from the 10th century.

Thirteenth to eighteenth centuries: Two different histories for the Baltic

Focus on the Baltic area was heightened by the end of the Crusades, as religious orders previously preoccupied with the Middle East now turned their attention to these last pagan territories closer to home, and by a growing desire on the part of this same Western church to challenge the spread of Orthodoxy after the Great Schism of the 11th century. After some activity by earlier missionaries, the powerful Teutonic Orders gained permission from the Pope to mount a crusade in this region from the beginning of the 13th century.

Despite the intentions of the Teutonic Orders, however, their ambitions were only partly fulfilled: from the 13th century onwards, the territory of the Baltic saw two very different powers emerge, resulting in divergent histories through the late 18th century.

During this period, Lithuania enjoyed its own Empire. During the 13th century it successfully fought off the Teutonic Knights, becoming united in the process and developing an effective ruling dynasty. However, understanding all too well the forces against it, Lithuania eventually adopted Christianity in the strategic union in 1386 with the nascent Polish kingdom, an action which enabled it to arrest the Teutonic Order more effectively, and eventually to annihilate it and hold at bay Germanic influence, while steadily expanding the joint empire to the southeast. The Polish–Lithuanian confederation, formally established in 1569 with Lithuania having the status of a Grand Duchy, became the great power in this region for the next three centuries. At the height of Polish–Lithuanian commonwealth in the 16th and 17th centuries, its rule stretched to the Black Sea. This empire was also crucial in another battle over territory – between Catholics and the Reformation. When Lutheranism spread through the Germanic lands in the West and in Estonia and Latvia in the north, Lithuania became one of the strongholds of the counter-reformation, with Vilnius University being founded by the Jesuits in 1579.

However, losses to Sweden in the north, the growing power of Czarist Russia to the east, and the newer bordering Prussian and Austro-Hungarian empires, led to constant external wars and to a steady loss of territory from the 17th to the 18th centuries. Meanwhile, internally the relation with Poland also brought a continual jousting between Polish and Lithuanian elements in political life and in culture. The ruling Lithuanian elites were slowly Polonised through the centuries of the union, creating enduring cycles of national cooperation and national rivalry that lasted well into the 20th century.

By contrast, from the 13th century Estonia and Latvia were essentially colonised areas until their brief period of independence in 1918–40. They had no empire of their own nor did they enjoy independence; rather, they were continually under the rule of colonisers or of surrounding empires. For Estonia, this condition emerged with the Danish invasion in 1219 (the name of Tallinn, the capital city, is an Estonianisation of 'Dann-linn' – Danish city); the Danes ruled until 1346 when they yielded to the Livonian Order – the German religious – military – landowning caste already occupying Latvian territory and southern Estonia, excepting only the Setu territory in South-East Estonia, which was under the control of the Principality of Pskov, where the language and culture bear traces of Russian and Orthodox influence. In Latvia, the Teutonic knights, who founded Riga in 1201 and spread their influence – by conquest or negotiation – throughout the territory, overran the existing loose assemblage of independent tribes. They were thwarted from expanding further by the Lithuanians in the south, aided by still resistant Latvian groups, in the decisive battle of Saule in northern Lithuania in 1236; while sporadic attempts to invade Lithuania continued, there was no further consolidated advance.

The Teutonic Knights and other Western Christian invaders were also stopped from expanding further east, when Alexander Nevsky of Novgorod, a third generation noble Viking immigrant from Sweden, defeated both Scandinavian and Teutonic forces in turn during 1240–1241. Thus, the Baltic states constitute one of the enduring borderlines of Europe – in this case, the northeastern dividing line between Western and Eastern Christianity, seen by some commentators as being, for political as well as religious reasons, one of the defining divisions of European experience (Applebaum, 1994). Despite extensive sovereignty over this area by Russia in its various incarnations over the past few centuries, Orthodoxy gained little purchase on the native population of the Baltic, although repeated attempts were made to impose it.

As the missionaries, land-seeking aristocracy and the merchants were constrained both in the east and south, and under the combined influence of the German church, the Livonian Order turned from expansion to consolidation in both present-day Estonia and Latvia. A social and economic system was established that survived for some 700 years until World War I, despite repeated changes of political regimes over that time. In the cities, enterprising merchants fostered trade, and by the late 13th century both Riga and Tallinn became members of the Hanseatic League, enjoying safe trade in the Baltic for the next 300 years. In the countryside, German barons controlled most of the land, increasingly instituting serfdom which arrived in this part of the world much later (15th-16th centuries) than in Western Europe. Several peasant revolts in the 13th and 14th century were not able to shake off this succession of foreign rulers.

The Livonian Order (*Deutscher Orden to Lyffland*, 1237–1562), though nominally subordinated to the High Master of the German Order and a vassal to several bishoprics in the area (in reality quite the opposite due to the Order's army of up to 4000 men, most of whom were of local origin) was nevertheless an independent political body. Although the share of these outsiders (knight brethren, top clergy, etc.) comprised less than five per cent of the total resident population, the lower elite too (village chieftains, priests, part of merchants and minor landlords) who were of local (Estonian and Latvian) origin had shifted to the more prestigious

(Low, or later, Baltic) German language, as there existed no official standard for the Estonian and Latvian dialects. Thus, in its core, the Livonian Order could be considered as some form of an Estonian–Latvian state organisation that used non-local language(s) for higher functions by its apparatus, while the native languages were used in the lower social sphere.

Despite changes in sovereignty, the Germanic social structure persisted in Estonia and Latvia, as each ruling power granted renewal of existing privileges, including control of land. In the cities, the administration, guilds, religion, education and virtually all important social functions were carried out by Germans (or those who passed as Germans) and in the German language. The Reformation came swiftly to this area, and Estonia and Latvia have been nominally Lutheran from the 1520s onwards. However, unlike the Lithuanians who had chosen their own religion and remained Catholics and close to their church, Latvians and Estonians have generally had less enthusiasm for their German-brought churches.

The Livonian Order was defeated in 1561, but German privileges were maintained by the Swedes in the 17th century (albeit with some unease about serfdom which was not practised in Sweden itself), by Poland/Lithuania which controlled some of the southern regions of Latvia after the Livonian Order, and by Czarist Russia when it defeated Sweden in the Great Northern War of 1700–1721 ruling for the next 200 years. The Germans in Estonia and Latvia welcomed Czarist rule in particular, as it continued their privileges which had long since been eroded for the nobility in Western Europe with the earlier ending of serfdom; indeed the 'Czar's loyal Germans' (Henricksson, 1983) constituted an important administrative, economic and military resource to the Czarist regimes. In turn, when national sentiment developed in the 19th century in Estonia and Latvia, it was as critical or even more so of German overlords as of the Czarist regime (see additional discussion later).

The division of Poland, and subsequent Russian rule

Peter I of Russia defeated the Swedes to take possession of Estonia and Latvia after 1721. For the rest of the 18th century Czarist Russia, aided by both Prussia and Austria–Hungary, steadily battled the Polish–Lithuanian Empire until Poland was dismembered between 1772 and 1795. Lithuanians, however, subsequently joined with Poles in several unsuccessful revolts against Czarist rule, leading to repressions that included a broad-scale Russifying language policy in the second half of the 19th century, described later. In Lithuania, this involved the closure of Vilnius University in 1832, a conversion of Lithuanian to Russian-medium schools (accompanied by a prohibition on speaking Lithuanian), and a ban on printing Lithuanian books in the Latin script.

The common history of the Baltic states under Czarist rule until World War I must not deny the locally quite different attitudes to this rule, and persisting differences between Lithuania on the one hand and Estonia and Latvia on the other in understanding their history. For Lithuania, the loss of prominence and a former empire remained deeply felt, and resistance to the Czarist regime, as previously mentioned, was very pronounced. Consequently, in 1905, Lithuania was the first of the Russian provinces to demand autonomy, but independence was not granted. Lithuanian opposition was to be repeated later in another historical form in the persistent, if at first subtle, resistance to the Soviet regime, and later in Lithuania's path-breaking open opposition to that regime.

Estonia and Latvia however had a far more complicated power situation, with German overlords, Russian administrators and organised local national groups increasingly vying for influence. In some ways, Estonian and Latvian nationalists supported attempted Russian restrictions on German power which came with the expansion of the Russian bureaucracy from the mid-19th century, seeing some hope for themselves in clipping German autocracy, but they also resisted later Czarist Russification tendencies. Nevertheless, there was, at a cultural level, a good deal of respect for both German and Russian culture, and greater intermixing and cosmopolitanism in terms of a western orientation. Thus, for example, in the 19th century strong nationalist movements existed alongside significant social-democratic movements as industrialisation developed more swiftly in these two countries, and political divisions could be as acute as national divisions. On some occasions, however, national and political cleavages reinforced one another: the German barons became even more unpopular when they enthusiastically supported Czarist repressions after the 1905 revolution in Estonia and Latvia. This more complicated structure of allegiances and divisions, and a more complex demographic mix as well, has also tended to persist over time in these two countries.

National Awakening movements were common to all three Baltic States as they were for the whole of Eastern Europe in the 19th century. In the Baltic, this development demonstrated an emphasis on language, reflected in two distinct linguistic undertakings. First, a massive collection of the folkloric elements of the language, contained in the hundreds and thousands of songs, rhymes, proverbs, chants and anecdotes of the folk cultures still very much intact in this period, intended to document the linguistic and cultural richness of this heritage. Second, there was an interest in developing a standard national literary language based on this rich folkloric past that would also be capable of serving as a means for modern literary expression. One part of this activity was to provide vernacular literature – novels, poetry and drama – that could match and in fact replace the largely German, Russian or Polish high cultures of that period. This striving for a literary language remains crucial for language policy developments to the present day, with correctness of orthography, use of original roots as against borrowings and the place of dialect matters being the subject of frequent public debate, and often, official stipulation.

Titular language histories of Estonian, Latvian and Lithuanian from the beginnings to first independence

Estonian, Latvian and Lithuanian are all written in Latin script, and are, in each case, legislated as the sole national language (or official state language) in their titular territory. They represent two distinct language families, and they have at times been subject to different influences and threats in their development. However, their common fate since the end of the 18th century, and particularly during the 20th century, has in sum produced remarkably similar outcomes in terms of language development and language use, and ultimately of language policy.

Estonian belongs to the Finnic branch of the Finno-Ugric languages, close to Finnish, which has its antecedents in the large Finno-Ugric migrating population that spread across northern Europe and Siberia and largely arrived in the territory of contemporary Estonia at the beginning of the 3rd millennium BCE. The Finnic precursors to the contemporary Estonian language extended a little south of the present territory of Estonia itself.

The features of Estonian include a complex grammar of 14 noun and adjective cases, no gender markings, and for speakers of Indo-European languages an entirely distinct lexis, not made easier by general conservatism in adopting internationalisms and borrowings. This characteristic has often made the language relatively inaccessible not only for linguists but for residents speaking other first languages. Significantly, as noted in what follows, rates for learning and understanding Estonian by first language speakers of other languages are and have been somewhat lower than for Latvian in Latvia and Lithuanian in Lithuania.

Within Estonia's territory, Estonian remained the language of the peasants until well into the 19th century. Some of the local German clergy – often active in linguistic research and translating scripture – had produced partial grammars and wordbooks of Estonian from the 17th century. Besides its gathering of folklore and new literary output, the National Awakening of the 19th century also led to a significant linguistic realignment, with German-based orthographies and grammars being superseded by an awareness of the closeness of Estonian to Finnish, and a reconstituting of linguistic principles along Finnish lines. While the number of Estonian writers and literati was small in the 19th century, literacy in Estonian was relatively widespread, even among the peasantry. Two distinct standards of the languages (based on northern and southern dialects) had evolved over the previous centuries, but the standard chosen was that of northern Estonia, becoming the basis of the Estonian literary language. However, as with Latvia and Lithuania, it was not until the period of independence after World War I that a full range of social, administrative, educational, literary and political functions could be carried out in the national language. [For accessible introductions to the Estonian language situation historically see Erelt *et al.* (2003), Estonica (2006), Hennoste (1999), and Verschik (2005a, 2005b)].

Latvian and Lithuanian are Baltic Indo-European languages, closely related but not mutually intelligible, neither Germanic, nor Slavic – and not Finno-Ugric like Estonian. While displaying some typological characteristics related to Slavic, and some shared lexical items, they are thought to have separated from a common stem in the seventh century. Unlike Norwegian, Swedish, and Danish, these languages are, as noted earlier, not mutually intelligible. Only a few words are recognisable for speakers of both languages, but this is not enough to hold a conversation. Other Baltic languages, Old Prussian and its surrounding variants, were effectively eradicated by the 18th century through the increasing assimilation to German invasion in Prussia, leaving Lithuanian and Latvian as the only two extant Indo-European Baltic languages. Both Lithuanian and Latvian have a system of declension (but with far fewer cases than Estonian) with some complex phonological and morphological features. Latvian has also been influenced by Finno-Ugric elements, both in loan words and in articulation, with a typical Finno-Ugric stress on the initial syllable as opposed to the more common Indo-European floating stress as found in Lithuanian.

The distinctive features of Lithuanian have given it a prominent place in linguistics over the last century and a half, as it is seen as the most archaic of the European branches of Indo-European languages, and this is perceived as an important indicator of the nature of much discussed and theorised Proto-Indo-European. Since the 19th century, when the similarity between Lithuanian and Sanskrit was discovered by historical linguists (Dini, 2005: 471), Lithuanians have taken a particular pride in their native language as the oldest living Indo-European language.

The work of the Italian linguist Dini (2000), translated into Estonian, Latvian and Lithuanian but not yet into English, is the most comprehensive single study of the languages of the Baltic. An accessible English language introduction to Latvian can be found in Plakans (1993) or Nau (1998) and for Lithuanian a review of Baltic sociolinguistics is available in Hogan-Brun (2005b) and in Zinkevičius (1998).

As the brief history of the Baltic States given above has foreshadowed, all three languages have been adversely affected by political and related sociocultural factors. Lengthy spells of foreign rule led to the imposition of superstrate languages – Polish, German and, twice, Russian – and have seen at times the relegation of Estonian, Latvian and Lithuanian to semi-public and private settings.

Significantly, despite the typological distinctiveness of Estonian from the two Baltic languages proper, and the historical difference of Lithuanian having been (part of) an Empire while Latvia and Estonia were continually colonised, the historical development of the languages in terms of finding standard varieties, having grammars and literature, as well as living through a period of national awakening and stress on the language as a national symbol, are remarkably uniform.

The Use of Lithuanian in its Empire. From the 13th century several different languages were used as written and spoken language codes in the old, multi-ethnic Lithuanian state. The Lithuanian language was spoken only in the western, ethnically Lithuanian, Grand Duchy, whilst the inhabitants of the eastern regions were Slavs, communicating in Slavonic languages. Two written languages were used at that time. As in other European countries in the Middle Ages scribes used Latin which was the written means of the church and of science, and of state governments (on the Humanists' strivings to use Latin in the Grand Duchy of Lithuania see Dini, 1999). Latin also served for international communication, together with German. In addition, the Lithuanian state adopted the Slavonic chancellery language as a second official written language for the affairs of the eastern regions, such as state acts and various legal entries. The first historical works and chronicles were produced in that language. Later, from the end of the 14th century onwards, Lithuanians came into contact with Polish, and during the long-term union with Poland (1569–1795), Polish became the language of the dual state, with Lithuanian being relegated to the lower classes.

Of crucial historical importance is the geographic distinction in Lithuania between Lithuania Major or *Didžioji Lietuva*, comprising the southeastern section including Vilnius, and Lithuania Minor or *Mažoji Lietuva*, an area stretching westward as far as Kaliningrad (Germ. *Königsberg*, Lith. *Karaliaučius*). Eastern Lithuanian Major became most Polonised; the western part had less Slavic input but also had more contact with increasingly Germanised parts of then Königsberg, bringing a number of influences to bear on language, including from the Reformation and Enlightenment that were absent in Lithuania Major, and also bringing a robust consistency to the history of language development from Lithuania Minor to Estonia.

Common elements: Records of writing and grammars. The Estonian, Latvian and Lithuanian written languages evolved relatively late, partly as a result of such historical factors as the late adoption of Christianity, and partly as a result of the effects of dominant colonial or empirial languages. Elements of the three languages were embedded in place names and in some personal names from the earliest written records in the 13th century in Latin, Danish or German. In Estonia for example, the Danish taxation list *Liber Census Daniae* compiled between 1219 and 1220 contained some 500 Estonian place names, nine-tenths of which have survived to the present (Estonica, 2006: 2).

As a result of the 13th century crusades, the predominantly Low German-speaking nobility and burghers became established on the territory of Old Livonia, which covered areas of present-day Estonia and Latvia. Although the rulers of those territories changed several times during the 700 years of foreign occupation – that is, the territories were at various times ruled by Danes, Poles, Swedes, or Russians – the strongest influence on the local languages was exerted by Low and High German, and by the local Baltic German dialect that developed from them. In medieval times the local languages, though numerically dominant, were in a diglossic situation by being relegated to vernacular functions:

- the language used in the municipal administration was Baltic German, based on Low German (*Niederdeutsch*);
- the clergy predominantly used Latin;
- the language of land supervisors depended on the language of the conquerors – that is (Low) German, Swedish, Russian, and in places Danish and Polish.

The Reformation was influential in accelerating the evolution of the written languages. As previously mentioned, this activity spread quickly through German-controlled Estonia and Latvia, and, while the church continued to do much of its work in German, the Lutheran emphasis on vernacular led to the first serious efforts to spread religion in the local languages. The first printed books, including South Estonian, date from 1525, when they were destroyed in Lübeck due to their Lutheran content. Altogether, more than two dozen volumes were printed in Estonian and in Latvian in the 16th century, written or compiled mostly by local German-speaking pastors. Thus, a literary standard was developed on the basis of a local oral vernacular, carrying a strong grammatical impact of German and Latin, the latter seemingly providing 'the ideal model' for the structure of the local languages. The number of users of those books was modest, as in the 16th century, literacy within the population did not exceed 2% (Erelt & Laanekask, 2003). But this was not the strategy of Lutherans alone – the Roman Catholic Church also published in the vernacular to spread its message. Thus, the *Estonica* scholars have found:

> [that] [t]he first continuous Estonian text still extant, the *Kullamaa Manuscript*, dates from 1524–1528. This Catholic text contains two prayers– the Lord's Prayer and the Hail Mary, and the Creed. When the Reformation shook Northern Europe, arriving in Estonia in the early 16th century, preaching in the local languages bought about an even more pressing need to translate religious literature [...]. (Laanekask & Erelt, 2003)

The Reformation also became the deciding factor in the Lithuanian written language being initially established in Lithuania Minor. The first Lithuanian book, a catechism, appeared in 1547. In a variant of Lithuanian formed in Prussia, this book became the first written public pronouncement to Lithuanians in their own tongue (Zinkevičius, 1998: 73). The translation of the entire Bible followed in that century, and a book of sermons and some other Protestant texts were rendered into Lithuanian or originally written in this language at the end of the 16th century. Lithuanian was not used solely for religious purposes in 16th–17th century Prussia; it was also used to announce governmental decrees. Its official functions expanded when it became a chancellery language. Subsequently, it was increasingly used in a range of domains:

- Lithuanian oaths were inscribed in court records;
- Lithuanian rhymed verse was written for various occasions;
- some Lithuanian folklore was transcribed.

In Lithuania Major, literacy in Lithuanian was encouraged when Jesuits were invited to Vilnius. They produced printed Lithuanian texts to counter the progress of the Reformation. Hence, it was used in Lithuania Major for a purpose at odds with the aim that had been instrumental in Lithuania Minor. The founding of the University of Vilnius in 1579 led to the evolution of Lithuanian as a language of academic discourse. Latin served as the *lingua universalis*, preventing the spread of Polish in the academic sphere. Lithuanian on the other hand had an important function in the University as it was used for religious purposes and to propagate Catholicism in the country. Theoretical and practical knowledge of Lithuanian increased as a result of lectures on rhetoric, poetics, philosophy and theology.

The first grammars and dictionaries in all three languages were published in the 17th century, written by German scholars/clergymen. Dini relates that the first grammars of Latvian (by Rehehusen) and Lithuanian (by Klein) appeared in 1644 and 1653 respectively, showing the proximity of language recording developments (Dini, 2005: 470). The first Estonian grammars (by Stahl), and dictionaries were also compiled in the 17th century. From that time onwards, abundant Estonian-language literature has survived to the present.

Literacy and the evolution of a standard language from several options. In each language a process of standardisation went hand in hand with the development of a literature and with increasing literacy in the language. The spread of literacy was particularly evident in Estonia during the 17th century with the publication of several Estonian-language handbooks (in German and Latin), together with German–Estonian dictionaries. The first of the handbooks appeared in 1637 compiled by a German pastor, Heinrich Stahl, who used an irregular spelling system based on High German. Johan Hornung and Bengt Gottfried Forselius were mainly responsible for making a start at reforming the Estonian literary language in the late 17th century. At various Bible gatherings, they proposed a simplification of the system that had hitherto been in use, and the so-called *old spelling* developed. This period may be regarded as the beginning of conscious language standardisation in Estonia, attempting to devise a uniform usage of Estonian derived from the provision of descriptions of language structure. A strict spelling system was adopted which still relied on German orthography, although some German constructions were abandoned. Thanks to the network of folk schools and teaching in the domestic language under Swedish rule, literacy improved considerably in the 17th century, possibly reaching 10–12% (Liivaku, 1995). Raun (1979) describes the extensive literacy movement among peasants during the early 18th century, noting a slightly slower spread of this skill in Latvia. Until the mid-18th century, two language versions competed to achieve the status of standard Estonian: the North Estonian (Tallinn) and the South Estonian (Tartu) languages. Between 1601 and 1703, 87 books were published in Estonian, 23 of those in the Tartu language. The New Testament in South Estonian appeared in 1686. In 1739, the first complete Estonian-language Bible followed in a translation by a pietist Lutheran pastor, Anton Thor Helle, and his colleagues. Since the task was completed in the Northern language, this version of Estonian gained a dominant position, especially among pietist communities (the *Herrnhuter Brüdergemeinde* was very popular at that time). Other reasons for the decline of the South Estonian language were the burning down of Tartu, the centre of Southern Estonia, and the deportation of people to Russia in 1708 during the course of the Northern War waged between the Russians and Swedes, as well as the introduction of compulsory reading skills in 1729. By the end of the 19th century, the South Estonian language as a literary means had practically become extinct. Most recently, in the 1990s, a gradual revival of the South Estonian literary means started to take place, based on the *Võru* dialect, which currently claims around 50,000 speakers.

In Lithuania Major, two variants of writing evolved with distinct dialectal differentiation that complicated the formation of a unified written language. One was the so-called central (Samogitian) mode, which was the first to appear and was comparatively close to the Prussian Lithuanian written language; the other was the eastern variant, formed on the basis of the language spoken in Vilnius and its environs. Grammars and dictionaries were written in each of these two versions (see e.g. Dini, 2000: 302–305; Palionis, 1995: 101–116). The first Lithuanian book in Lithuania Major, a catechism, was printed in 1595. This publication was followed four years later by a book of sermons. The author Mikalojus Daukša urged the use of Lithuanian instead of Polish in all domains of life (Zinkevičius, 1998: 246). Some other religious texts and a few secular ones were also produced in Lithuania Major. However, the overall output was sparser in Lithuania Major than in the Duchy of Prussia. Ongoing Polonisation finally led to the extinction of the eastern variety, paving the way for central Samogitian to become firmly established in Lithuania Major as the basis for writing. Numerous borrowings from Polish flushed into Lithuanian writings, particularly in the 17th century, which also affected Lithuanian names, surnames and place names. The Polonisation of Lithuania continued strongly in the succeeding centuries: in Plasseraud's words '*la Lithuanie sera politiquement russe mais socialement elle deviendra de plus en plus polonaise*' (2003: 49) ['Lithuania was to become politically Russian, but socially it became more and more Polish'].

In Latvia, two varieties of the language became literary languages and continued to co-exist until the present day. The dominant one, from the central region, became modern standard Latvian, and it serves as the basis of the present national language. Meanwhile, the less often used Lattgallian variety, from the southeast of Latvia, a variety showing somewhat greater influence from the Lithuanian language, also developed as a literary language in the 19th century, but with greater difficulty. Historically, this area of Latvia which had been more closely tied to Lithuania and Poland since the end of the Livonian Order in the 16th century, was Catholic rather than Protestant, and produced its own literature from the beginning of the 19th century. It was also, however, subject to the same restrictions on it as a written language as was Lithuanian (see additional discussion). Stafecka (2003) and Metuzale-Kangere and Ozolins (2005) describe the solidification of standard Latvian as well as the continuing debate over the status of Lattgallian – as a language, dialect or variety.

Largely similar national awakening processes in the 19th and early 20th centuries. The standardisation process went hand in hand with, and indeed was a principal reflection of, the central role of language in the National Awakening processes in the 19th century, briefly described previously. Initially, the foreign-flavoured language of religious literature was gradually superseded by more popular usage, which also acquired secular functions. Subsequently, from the 1850s, the local languages moved rapidly from peasant vernacular to cultural status. By this time, the literacy level was significantly above the average of that found in other parts of Europe, reaching between 70 and 80% in Estonia and Latvia, where the 'three Rs' were required for compulsory confirmation in church. The local languages began to be used in literature and science.

The growth of literature based on a literary language was, during the 19th century, part of a flowering of national writers, journalists, artists, linguists and academics who started to identify themselves as nationals rather than continuing the earlier custom of 'passing' as Germans, Russians or Poles. This movement in the Baltics has been widely studied (see particularly the collections by Loit, 1985 and Raun & Plakans, 1990, as well as a seminal article by Thaden, 1985). These typically Gellnerian movements (Gellner, 1983) saw the rise of a small educated elite, looking to rural areas for its sustaining national myths and folklore, but slowly vying for power with imperial elites through the medium of schools, literature, national romantic art and, in some cases, modernising political movements such as social democracy. Of great importance were the spread of literacy, the increase of scientific societies and the growing journalism in the national languages.

External influences creating distinct issues in the three Baltic States in their National Awakening. While the national movements are seen as generally local drivers, international elements have played an important part. Although all three Baltic territories were at the time of National Awakening part of the Russian Empire, the internal politics of those national movements were quite different in the three countries, with particular difficulties experienced by Lithuania.

The fierce resistance by both Poles and Lithuanians to Russian rule in the 19th century evoked a strong reaction in language policy. Following the rebellions of the early 1860s, the Czarist regime issued an order – lasting from 1864 to 1904 – banning the use of the traditional Latin alphabet for Lithuanian books, resulting in the exclusive use of the Cyrillic alphabet for such publications. Similar restrictions applied to Lattgallian in southeast Latvia. Unexpectedly for the Czarist regime, such a ban actually led to a surge of literacy in Lithuanian and an increase in the forbidden output in the Latin alphabet. Lithuanian nationalists set up a thriving publication industry in nearby *Lithuania Minor* (then German East Prussia), producing many volumes with false dates (i.e. before 1864) that were then smuggled into the country and passed from hand to hand (Senn, 1980). The image of a peasant mother with one hand on a spinning wheel and the other holding a book and reading to her children became a symbol of Lithuanian resistance. After the abolition of this ban in 1904 the language was brought back into Lithuanian schools, stimulating the writing of textbooks and popularising Lithuanian literature.

Estonia was subject to somewhat different external influences. Beside its gathering of folklore and new literary output, the National Awakening of the 19th century also led to a significant linguistic realignment, with German-based orthographies and grammars being superseded by an awareness of the closeness of Estonian to Finnish and a reconstituting of linguistic principles along Finnish lines. By the mid-century, Eduard Ahrens had worked out a new Finnish-style orthography, the so-called *new spelling* (as distinct from *old spelling*) that became widespread within a few decades and is still used at the present time. The Finnish connection was also to be very useful during the period of attempted Russification from the 1880s, when Russian in part replaced German in administration and higher education, and Russian was also taught more extensively in the primary school system. Estonian writers, academics and linguists then often pursued their work at Helsinki University, for although Finland was also part of the Czarist Empire, it had greater legal autonomy, and the Finish language had been able to develop to a far greater extent than Estonian in Estonia (Verschik, 2005b: 283–284). This activity of Finish-based Estonian linguists in turn fed back into the standardisation of Estonian based on the northern variety.

The period of Russification in Estonia and Latvia previously referred to came in the early 1880s, as St Petersburg increased the centralisation of power over all its territories. Russification came later and more generally than its specific repressions in Poland and Lithuania, and was concerned more with administration, though it also restricted schooling in German, Estonian and Latvian (Thaden, 1981; Weeks, 1996). As previously outlined, however, Estonian and Latvian nationalists saw these changes as additionally helpful to them in undermining German hegemony. Russian became the language of instruction in schools, state services were provided in Russian and law-courts operated in it. This led to the immigration of Russian speakers who were able to compete for privileged jobs. The new situation dealt a serious blow to the German language, as it lost its previous position of official language status. As Estonian and Latvian were not restricted in publications, readership grew. In addition, various local language-medium societies, choirs, drama circles, firefighting brigades, dairy and credit unions were organised, making them competitive in business and entertainment.

Blinkena (1985) has studied the role of the 'Neo-Latvians' – Latvians who attended universities, particularly in Tartu or St Petersburg, and who declared themselves to be Latvians rather than Germans or Russians; they developed Latvian literature and journalism. As with Estonia and Lithuania, Latvian nationalists also sometimes found more congenial environments *outside* their home territory, a striking example being the publication in the Russian capital of the *Peterburgas Avīze* (St Petersburg Newspaper) by leading Latvian nationalists from the 1860s; the publication had a wide circulation in Latvia. Above all, there was a growing self-consciousness of the national language itself as being valuable for the nation:

> Many of the activists of the national awakening period stressed to the public that linguistic issues were markers of identity and that it was a national mission to collect and systematise linguistic materials. This was the period when the production of Latvian grammar passed from the Baltic German clergy to teachers and then, in the early 20th century, to educated linguists. (Metuzale-Kangere & Ozolins, 2005: 320)

Considerable standardisation of language by the first period of independence. Restrictions on publishing in Lithuanian in the Latin alphabet were lifted in 1904, and the aftermath of the 1905 revolution saw an easing of Russification generally and a flowering of literary and linguistic work in all three Baltic countries.

In Lithuania, for example, an especially important stage in the development of Lithuanian as an academic language is linked to the establishment of the Lithuanian Science Society (*Lietuvių mokslo draugija*) in 1907 and its publication *Lietuvių tauta* (Lithuanian Nation), in which scientific papers and historic resources were compiled according to rules pertaining to scientific language use (Palionis, 1995: 266–268). The activities of the Society initiated a sustained phase in the cultivation, expansion and intellectualisation of Lithuanian. As a result, a standard literary language based on a southwestern dialect evolved (Dini, 2000: 353–354; Zinkevičius, 1992; 1998: 294–296). This period also saw an unprecedented blossoming of the Lithuanian press (Zinkevičius, 1992: 299). The first Lithuanian newspapers (*Aušra*: 'Dawn', 1883–1886 and *Varpas*: 'The Bell', 1889–1905) were published in Lithuania Minor, giving a fresh impetus to written Lithuanian.

Similar literary, journalistic and scientific development characterised Estonia and Latvia, sometimes with uncanny synchronicity: the Estonian Literary Society too was founded in 1907 (Verschik, 2005b: 285). The Society organised four conferences in 1908–1911, where a substantial number of decisions on the norm of the Estonian literary language were adopted. These and other decisions were published in the Estonian Orthographic dictionary (1918). The first terminological committees were set up and, as a result, various specialised dictionaries in mathematics, physics, chemistry, geography and other fields were published (Kull, 2000). Since 1906, Estonian-and Latvian-medium schooling was allowed again, becoming the main option for achieving education. As Estonians and Latvians won majorities in county and city councils, theirs also became the languages of communal, and later, of state politics.

However, it was not until the period of independence after World War I that a full range of social, administrative, educational, literary and political functions could be carried out in the national language. For example in Estonia in 1919:

> Estonian officially became the language of instruction at the University of Tartu. In the following year, the Academic Mother Tongue Society (*Akadeemiline Emakeele Selts*) was created in order to facilitate systematic research in the Estonian dialects and to elaborate upon principles of language planning. (Verschik, 2005: 286)

Path-breaking linguistic work was undertaken by a small number of outstanding linguists in each country. In Latvia it was Kārlis Müllenbachs and after his death Jānis Endzelīns, while in Lithuania the prominent figure was Jonas Jablonskis. In Estonia there was no single pre-eminent linguist, but a gathering of influential colleagues including Johannes Aarvik, Voldemar Veski, Andrus Saareste, Paul Arise, Julius Mägiste and later Valter Tauli.

In the Lithuanians' case, replicated almost exactly in the other two countries, the first grammars of standard Lithuanian, written by Jonas Jablonskis, were published between 1901 and 1922. In his efforts to improve standard Lithuanian, Jablonskis demanded that the foundation of its continued growth should be *žmonių kalba*: 'the living speech of the people' of *Vakarų aukštaičių* (the western High-Lithuanian dialect area) (Dini, 2000: 355; Zinkevičius, 1998: 295). Jablonskis also postulated that Lithuanian should be untainted by foreign elements – as the literary language of the period suffered from heavy admixtures of foreign, especially Slavic, elements – thus guiding the evolution of written Lithuanian in a new direction.

Also important in all three countries was the increased study of dialects and varieties, undertaken in the new national universities and producing a corpus of work that continued into the Soviet period and has gained renewed impetus today. While Baltic linguists were familiar with European philological work and newer linguistic advances in the first half of the 20th century, their links to the international field have been little studied. Such connections also were generally lost during the Soviet period, and researching the development of Baltic linguistics in its wider international context remains an important task in Baltic linguistic historiography (Dini, 2005).

In the period between the two world wars, the three Baltic languages thus were able to become fully standardised and to undertake the often daunting national functions in administration, education, literary and commercial life, bolstered by the particular language polices that defended and extended them as national languages.

Inter-war independence (1918–1940)

The three Baltic States gained independence in the extraordinary confusion at the end of World War I, when the two great contesting powers on the Eastern

Front – Wilhelmine Germany and Czarist Russia – both suffered different forms of crushing defeat. The German attack on Russia in August 1914 advanced to a front across central Latvia where it stayed until the Russian revolution of 1917 and the eventual peace settlement between the newly formed Soviet Russia and Germany at Brest-Litovsk in March 1918. Over this period Baltic populations (including many of the Baltic Germans) had supported Czarist Russia against the German invaders, but the Russian Revolution changed many allegiances. The Baltic States again became a front line for new conflicts. After Brest-Litovsk the Germans quickly occupied all of the Baltic States. But White Russian forces, opposed to the Bolshevik regime, were organised in this region too, assisted after the defeat of Germany by some western military forces also seeking an overthrow of the Bolshevik regime. However, while the White Russian forces saw the Baltic as an integral part of a greater Russia, the Allies eventually favoured independence for the Baltic states to guarantee a *cordon sanitaire* between Russia (of whatever hue) and western Europe. German forces were also still present after November 1918, ostensibly to oppose the Bolsheviks but in fact with the intention of reinstating German control of the region. Against all odds, the three Baltic nations were able to take advantage of this confused situation, militarily defeating both German and Bolshevik forces and disarming the White Russian forces; Estonia and Latvia achieved this with the help of the Allies and Poland, Lithuania also with help from Poland.

Emergence of the three Baltic States was based on the principle of the self-determination of the peoples, brought to the fore in international politics and law as a result of the First World War. Consequently, through the increasing acceptance of this norm, the incompatible right of conquest was recognised less. As a reflection of the declaration by the Soviet government that all nation-alities had the right to establish independent states, Lithuania declared its independence on 16 February, 1918, Estonia on 24 February, 1918 but Latvia – bearing the full brunt of the several occupying forces – not until 18 November, 1918. Such steps in the former Czarist Empire found support outside. Among the Fourteen Points programme announced in 1918 by President Woodrow Wilson of the United States there were also demands for self-determination for the peoples of the Russian Empire. However, this was not the will of the new rulers of Russia who attempted to invade the territories pursuing sovereignty. The turmoil ended with signed treaties between each of the three Baltic States and Soviet Russia: in Estonia's case, for example, the Tartu Peace Treaty of 2 February, 1920 supporting the principle of self-determination. Article 2 of this Treaty stated:

> On the basis of the right of all peoples freely to decide their own destinies, and even to separate themselves completely from the State of which they form part, a right proclaimed by the federal Socialist Republic of Soviet Russia, Russia unreservedly recognizes the independence and autonomy of the State of Estonia, and renounces voluntarily and forever all rights of sovereignty formerly held by Russia over the Estonian people and terri-tory by virtue of the former legal situation, and by virtue of international treaties, which, in respect of such rights, shall henceforth lose their force. (Hough, 1985: 357)

In addition, article 7 prohibited the use of either nation's territory as a base for armed aggression against the other, and article 5 stated that Soviet Russia agreed to join in an international recognition of Estonia's neutrality. Virtually identical treaties were signed with each of the three Baltic States.

However, another specific shock awaited Lithuania. The historic Lithuania – Polish alliance had been revived to repel the Bolsheviks and to secure Lithuanian independence, but in 1920, after all hostilities had ceased with Soviet Russia, Polish General Zeligowski's forces rode into Vilnius and took control of what he proclaimed to be a Polish city. Despite Lithuanian protests, the Polish government would not order a withdrawal, and superior Polish military force and lack of international involvement in this issue meant Lithuanians were not able to have their historic capital for the whole of the inter-war period. Lithuania declared Kaunas to be its temporary capital, and set about post-war reconstruction without Vilnius.

The Peace Conference at Versailles respected the principle of self-determination of peoples, and from the Treaty of Versailles of 28 June, 1919, 12 new states were created and nine plebiscites were held on the territories of the Central Powers. Together with fading hopes of collapse of the 'Red' Soviet power and restoration of 'White' power, support for the independence of the Baltic States increased. On 22 September, 1921 the Council of the League of Nations recognised the three countries on condition they provide minority guarantees (Peters, 1988: 285). The states that emerged were poor, in debt and devastated by the war. Latvia had lost a million of its population in this period, while in smaller Estonia the number of casualties was about 100,000. In Lithuania similar war losses were compound as it had to relinquish the population and infrastructure of the Vilnius region.

Despite this, the countries were able to recover significantly in the inter-war period, and to became full members of European life in a very short period of time. A strong rural sector developed on the back of land reforms dispossessing the German, and to a smaller extent, Polish and Russian landed aristocracy. Latvia in particular – but also Estonia – was able to develop considerable light industry (e.g. electrical goods, manufactured goods, pharmaceuticals), and there was a rapid expansion of education in the national languages, with very high rates of participation in higher education in both Estonia and Latvia. Lithuania retained a more rural character, with less industrialisation. Nevertheless, during the short period of the inter-war independence, Lithuania's economy began to develop, and its currency (the *Litas*) stabilised quickly. General education in Lithuanian was introduced in the whole country, and the University of Kaunas was established whilst Vilnius was still on Polish occupied territory. Research in many fields was initiated, and national arts and music flourished.

In all three countries, the political regimes started out as parliamentary systems, on the typical Eastern European model of proportional representation, but the plethora of parties, economic difficulties and populism in all three states led to the coming of authoritarian regimes – as early as 1926 in Lithuania, when Smetona assumed autocratic power, but only in 1934 in Estonia and Latvia, where respectively Päts and Ulmanis ruled as relatively mild authoritarian leaders. Estonia and Latvia in fact were among the last democratic states in Eastern Europe in this inter-war period to fall into authoritarian rule, leaving

Czechoslovakia as the only democracy in Eastern Europe for a brief few years (see e.g. Neustupný́y & Nekvapil, 2003).

External geopolitical relations were also problematic. The revolutionary nature of the Soviet state and its professed claim of spreading revolution abroad were soon experienced in the Baltic in the form of an attempted Communist coup orchestrated by Moscow on 1 December 1924 in Estonia, in stark contrast to the wording of the Treaty of Versailles. Thus the Baltic States were initially unenthusiastic concerning commitments with Russia, restricting these initially to economic domains such as free transit, trade and railway agreements. But Soviet overtures to sign more political agreements covering non-aggression or mutual assistance persisted during the entire inter-war period.

In his history of Europe, Davies argues that this feature of persuading small nations to sign non-aggression treaties had decisively aggressive motives:

> For those states that intended no aggression, such pacts were irrelevant. For those intending aggression they provided excellent cover: both Hitler and Stalin were fond of them. (Davies, 1997: 949)

Treaties of non-aggression or neutrality were signed between Soviet Russia and Lithuania as early as 1926, and with Estonia and Latvia, together with several other countries including Finland, in 1932. All these treaties were seen by the Soviets as complementing the more practical trade and economic agreements in bringing greater influence in the foreign affairs outlooks of the signatory states. Particular attention was paid to the Baltic States by Maxim Litvinov, the Head of Soviet Foreign Policy from 1930 to 1939, who had worked there before and who encouraged relatively productive economic relations. His replacement by Molotov in the middle of 1939 signalled a radical turn in Soviet policy, to be discussed presently.

Language policy in the first period of independence 1918–1940

Language has been central to the National Awakening movements in all three Baltic states; in many ways, it is possible to see these countries as essentially lingua-centric in their self-identity and indeed in political and social priorities. At the same time, the newly emerging nations were acutely aware of being multi-national states, containing significant national and linguistic minorities. The ethnic spread in the three inter-war states at that time was complex but not large in absolute terms. Russians formed the biggest group (3.9%) in Estonia, followed closely by Germans (1.7%) (Hiden & Salmon, 1991: 46ff). The number of Russians in Latvia was more substantial (10.6%), and significant percentages of Germans (3.5%), Jews (4.8%) and Poles (2.5%) were settled there too (Hiden & Salmon, 1991: 46ff). In Lithuania the pattern was different since both its most multi-ethnic regions, Klaipéda and Vilnius, were occupied by Germans and Poles respectively. Jews constituted the largest minority (7.6%), followed by Poles (3.2%), Russians (2.7%) and Germans (1.4%) (Hiden & Salmon, 1991: 46). These figures and the demands of the Versailles Peace Treaties/League of Nations prompted leaders of the fledgling inter-war republics to address minority rights in their constitutions; however, the practical implementation of these rights varied under the ensuing authoritarian regimes in the Baltic (Hiden & Salmon, 1991: 46ff). No major changes in the numerical composition of the minority population took place during the inter-war period until late 1939 when, in response to an order from Hitler, most Germans left the Baltic region.

Lithuania's minority figure would have been considerably higher if Vilnius and Klaipėda had been considered to be part of its territory. Vilnius, if anything, was as much a Jewish as a Polish or Lithuanian city, with estimates of up to 40% of the population being Jewish, many gravitating there to avoid harsher treatment elsewhere in Czarist Russia. The city of Klaipėda (the German Memel) on the Baltic coast with its significant German population had an international status from 1924, but after threats from Germany it was eventually ceded back to that country in 1939. Lithuania was thus above all preoccupied with regaining its national territorial integrity, especially from Poland, and while formally agreeing to equitable treatment of minorities, this remained a secondary issue for the country. It satisfied the League of Nations in its declarations of minority rights, but it evolved no significant policies towards minorities and resisted any activity by the League of Nations in responding to petitions on minority issues since it was concerned that this channel could be used above all by Poland to interfere in Lithuanian affairs (Peters, 1988).

The historical similarity of Estonia and Latvia in relation to their minorities again saw those facing common problems when the coming of independence brought international as well as local attention to this issue. Subsequent policies towards minorities were worked out in quite complex circumstances. Clearly arising from concerns above all in the 'powder keg' Balkans, the League of Nations requirements imposed conditions for the treatment of minorities in the new Eastern European countries, but as has often been pointed out, this entailed requirements that were never imposed on members in western Europe or elsewhere (Burgess, 1999: 51; Peters, 1988).

The situation was further complicated by the fact that two groups at least – Germans and Russians – were former rulers and were widely seen as oppressors. There was particular concern over extensive German land-holdings, and concern too over the attitudes of some Russians sceptical of Baltic independence as they saw these as part of a greater – though Monarchist – Russia (Alenius, 2004). On the other hand, some minorities (such as the Poles) had clearly supported Baltic independence and in particular helped to defeat Bolshevik power, but now Poland was at odds with Lithuania.

From a social and cultural viewpoint, many minorities, particularly the Russians, were very much internally divided. Some of the older established Russian groups, such as the Old Believers who had come in past centuries, were totally integrated into the new national life with a long history of bilingualism. Some newer anti-Bolshevik 'White' Russians, however, were interested only in recovering their former status as rulers. A tiny group of Bolshevik-oriented Russians in both countries opposed Estonian and Latvian independence entirely, as witnessed in their participation in the attempted 1924 coup in Estonia (Forgus, 1992). The majority of Russians lived in eastern rural areas. Other major ethnic groups, Germans and Jews, lived mostly in towns and townlets.

The particularly divisive issue within the Baltic states concerned former ruling elements, where debates over revenge or accommodation were carried out with some heat but in the end with a firm agreement on the part of all major parties on a policy of citizenship for all, granting certain rights to minorities and pursuing restitution matters separately to questions of minority rights. This latter course was not easy, as economic power in particular was strongly concentrated in German hands, but the desire to avoid open ethnic conflict and to become members of the League of Nations was strong. So too did the awareness of the smallness of the Baltic populations and a wish to settle matters through negotiation rather than through force – an important Baltic principle which was to reappear.

Eventually a three-part settlement was reached:

(1) An extensive land reform was carried out through which all German barons had their land ownership severely reduced, the ground being redistributed to those who had worked it for the barons. While the barons used their extensive diplomatic contacts at the League of Nations to try to overturn such expropriation, they were unsuccessful. Many moved to the cities but others emigrated, and in a few cases the émigrés continued to push for renewal of their former power, eventually supporting Hitler's *Ostpoltik*.

(2) Estonia and Latvia introduced policies of cultural autonomy, through which minority groups could have their own (state-financed) school systems, some use of minority languages in districts of high minority populations, and freedom of expression in media and cultural life. In terms of East European standards, the Baltic states were widely regarded as being in the forefront of national minority recognition, and a number of minority members – particularly Werner Hasselblatt and Ewald Ammende from Estonia and Paul Schiemann from Latvia were well known in Europe and were major organisers of the ground-breaking Conference of Nationalities from 1925, which brought together national minorities from across Europe.

(3) There was extensive work on expanding the role of the respective national languages, so they would become the dominant ones in administration, public life, education and social intercourse. The scale of this was daunting. The three Baltic States had been subject to Russification in education and public life in the decades before the World War; consequently, everything from the language of higher education, to new terminologies, to ensuring use of national languages in public administration had to be tackled. In higher education all universities moved to teach in their titular languages, while continuing to use texts in German, Russian and to a lesser extent French and English. Multilingualism remained a norm for all educated Balts, but the national languages were strengthened through extensive new linguistic work and the completion of significant standardisation projects that underpinned national schooling.

The scope of language laws was considerable and complex, as described by Loeber (1993). In Estonia and Lithuania, the status of the titular language as the official state language was enshrined in the constitutions, but in Latvia it was merely the subject of legislation. In all cases, the use of other languages was mentioned in the plethora of rules and regulations covering different aspects of public life:

- In parliament, deputies could use their native language, but records of speeches were generally made in the state languages, and usually the state language was used in committees. Legislation was published in the state language, but in a few cases official translations were also published for laws particularly affecting minorities.
- In courts, accused persons and witnesses could use other languages if understood by the judge; otherwise interpreters could be used. Counsel and agencies generally had to make submissions and present documents in the state language, but documentation in other languages usually accompanied by a translation was allowed from parties.
- In government agencies the state language was to be used, but citizens could petition or write in any language known to officials. Gradually this was restricted under the more authoritarian and nationalist conditions of the 1930s, when translations were increasingly required. All correspondence from government agencies was in the official language. The armed forces used the titular language exclusively, and military service was compulsory for all males. The official language was used in such venues as railways and by the postal services. In the latter, the state language was increasingly demanded for addresses since corresponding place names and address formats had changed to the titular norm. This provoked some opposition, and in one significant case Poles in Lithuania included in a petition to the League of Nations complaints that Lithuanian railway officials spoke Lithuanian exclusively; in practice minority languages were used by railway staff if necessary (Loeber, 1993: 230).
- Municipal agencies could variously adopt other languages for their internal work and relations with the public, a provision taken up in several Russian-dominant areas in all three countries, but some countries specified particular protection for the state language: For example, Estonian citizens living in self-governing areas, in which a non-Estonian language had been adopted as the official language, were explicitly granted the right to use Estonian when dealing with local authorities. This rule reversed, as it were, the principle of protecting national minorities in favour of safeguarding the state language (Loeber, 1993: 232).
- Language testing of public officials was introduced very early after independence, given the preponderance particularly of German officials in Latvia and Estonia. Public servants, teachers, attorneys and judges and notaries were covered by these requirements, but testing was often postponed as more time was given to acquire competence. In Latvia, a number of German municipal officials were eventually dismissed for not having competence in the state language. In Klaipėda particular measures were introduced to ensure public officials (again Germans) could also master Lithuanian.
- Personal names became an object of contention as all three Baltic States demanded conformity to national orthographic traditions – in Latvia and Lithuania names are declined and usually gender marked, and non-Latvian names were officially written with endings conforming to this pattern. Original spellings could usually be included in parentheses and always

used in signatures. Cyrillic-written names were Latinised in conformity with these principles.

In Latvia, the Lattgallian language, widely spoken in the southeast of the country, was declared in legislation to have equal status to Latvian and available to be used in all official circumstances.

As can be seen, the scope of language laws and related regulations was considerable, and in many ways foreshadowed precisely the issues of language policy to be confronted in these countries second period of independence, where the imposition of Russian through the years of Soviet occupation was redressed.

The relationship between language policy and issues of cultural autonomy is worth assessing. The principle of cultural autonomy was best exemplified in Estonia, where a legislated system of 'cultural self-government' operated through a corporate body for the German and Jewish communities, with extensive control over their schools and other cultural activities; meanwhile the more geographically compact Swedish and Russian communities used local government provisions to achieve similar ends (Alenius, 2004). Such provisions continued even after authoritarian rule and became the norm from 1934, though various tightenings of language laws and stricter education policies reduced their scope. In Latvia, a tougher version of cultural autonomy focused on the school system, with national minorities exercising control through independent boards over their publicly-funded school systems; again, some restrictions came after authoritarian rule in 1934, abolishing the boards and restricting attendance at these schools (particularly academically prestigious German schools) to pupils actually from the national minority.

Finally it should be said that the programme of cultural autonomy has had many diverse interpretations (Crols, 2005; Housden, 2005; Smith, 2005). The policy could be judged a success in terms of international recognition, and certainly there open conflicts of an ethnic kind did not occur in Estonia or Latvia. However, two important caveats need to be added concerning this judgement. First, in this case Germans saw cultural autonomy as a way of almost creating a state within a state, and devoted considerable resources to ensuring that Germans could live in complete self-sufficiency – for example, financing higher education opportunities in German through German lectureships at Tartu University or being able to have a complete higher education in German at the – ironically named – Herder Institute in Riga. A German economic sphere was also well maintained, so that there was little need for any involvement in national life of an Estonian or Latvian kind. Schiemann, Haselblatt and Ammende respectively spoke little Latvian or Estonian. Strongly based on views of the elevated nature of German culture and its 'civilising' function, the German minority at times could demonstrate an almost serene superiority to the embedding national life, and detachment from it.

Second, geopolitical pressures, whether from Stalinist Russia or from the Nazi regime in Germany, were able to seriously distort internal attempts at minority relations. In his incisive look at the Estonian situation, Housden (2004) argues that, while cultural autonomy was based on clearly liberal principles in its inception, increasingly it was used for other geopolitical purposes, and labels

Hasselblatt and Ammende 'ambiguous activists' since they eventually succumbed to National Socialist projects that held cultural minorities hostage to aggressive international demands, as in the steady German undermining of the Conference of Nationalities. Where Hitler could, he demanded direct control of German minorities, as he engineered reunification with the Reich in Sudetenland, or Klaipėda; where he could not, he encouraged a return 'home', and pursued this through well-organised activist networks throughout Eastern Europe from 1938. After the signing of the Molotov–Ribbentrop pact in August 1939, Hitler called all remaining *Volksdeutsche* in the Baltic to return to Germany, and most obeyed, including Hasselblatt and Ammende.

Hiden's (2004) account of Schiemann in Latvia relates his very different end. Steadfastly refusing to succumb to National Socialist pressure, Schiemann stayed in Latvia and continued to try to promote interethnic harmony. He maintained a view that enjoyment of minority rights also obligated a loyalty to the state, a view in which he became increasingly isolated in the diminishing German community. During the World War II Nazi occupation of Latvia, he was distrusted and sidelined by the Nazi authorities, and only years later was it shown how he had hidden a young Latvian Jewish girl in his house (Freimane, 2000). He died in 1944 before the Soviets returned to occupy Latvia once more.

In response to such historical experiences, Baltic thinking on minorities since this time has been formed around two principles: (1) that notions of minority cultures and languages need to be fused with an emphasis on integration into the national culture and language; questions of commitment to the titular nation and language must be put alongside notions of minority rights; and (2) that internal minority relations must never be used for international intimidation by threats, or *chantage*. The consequences of such an approach to minority and language issues are examined in the remainder of this monograph.

Soviet occupation (1940–1990)

The political situation of the Baltic States changed for the worse with the appointment of the new People's Commissary of Foreign Affairs, V. Molotov, representative of expansionist Soviet policy. He gave the green light to Nazi–Soviet talks that reached their climax in the Molotov–Ribbentrop Pact of 23 August, 1939, with a confidential protocol establishing respective spheres of influence, determining the Baltic States and Finland to be in the Soviet sphere (Hough, 1985: 370).

The protocol was put to use immediately, paving the way for the Second World War to begin, for the Baltic states to be incorporated into the Soviet Union, and historically for another multiparty division of Poland. Hitler had wanted a secure eastern frontier and a free hand to attack Poland and then turn on France and England if they supported Poland. After Hitler's attack on Poland and the start of World War II, Stalin delivered *ultimata* to each of the countries designated as in the Soviet sphere of influence, demanding the right to establish military bases in their territories and garrisoning Soviet troops twice as numerous as local armies. This was enforced in the form of offered Pacts of Mutual Assistance in September 1939. The Finnish Parliament rejected these demands, which led to the Winter War of 1939–1940 between the Soviet Union and

Finland. The three Baltic countries however, less able to defend their territory, ceded to Soviet demands.

In a cynical move, Stalin 'returned' Vilnius to Lithuania after having latterly participated in Hitler's war on Poland. But such largesse was short-lived: on 14–16 June, 1940, when Nazi Germany occupied Paris, Moscow simultaneously demanded the replacement of the governments of the Baltic States and admission of additional troops that eventually outnumbered the local armies several times. Since resistance was considered futile, the Baltic governments complied with these demands. As a result, the occupying Soviet Army took over power. The end of local independent national governments and the occupation of the Baltic States by the Soviet Army led to mock elections of the newly formed puppet regimes. In August 1940, the Baltic States were proclaimed a part of the Soviet Union in the administrative form of Soviet Socialist Republics. The Baltic countries fell under the rule of the Soviet governmental apparatus, and Communist Party Soviet functionaries took over all aspects of administration and of the economy. As Stalinist policy was introduced in full, the three republics experienced drastic demographic changes from 1940, including its ethnic composition, resulting firstly from extra-judicial killings and mass deportation in June 1941 of around 50,000 persons from across the three Baltic States, and secondly from the first influx of colonists in the wake of the invading foreign troops. According to Hough (1985: 381), most members of the respective Governments and Parliaments, and a greater part of military officers, senior police officers and top civil servants were imprisoned and executed. The same fate befell the Presidents of Estonia and Latvia, who were arrested and deported, though Lithuanian President Smetona found exile in the West. Soviet policy of individual arrests began from the first day of occupation on 17 June 1940.

Firms were nationalised and proclaimed to be Soviet property. Non-Communist parties and organisations were banned; all schools, societies and clubs of the ethnic minorities were closed, and the system of cultural autonomy was eliminated. Freedom of the press was terminated as most journals and newspapers were abolished. Those few that survived were made heralds of Communist ideas. Access to information was channelled through the Soviet official information agency, ITAR, TASS, and through Radio Moscow. The foreign press was prohibited, and foreign contacts were terminated. The population was squeezed into the Soviet societal framework with political, and especially ideological features of identity taking priority. This resulted in massive executions of the structural (political, military) and spiritual native elite of the (former) power in order to curb their resistance.

Stalinist deportations were followed by extensive Nazi bloodlettings of Jews, Gypsies, Communists and others, in some cases assisted by local collaborators, in other cases opposed by local partisans. The German occupation had as a long-term aim the dislocation of the local populations in favour of new German populations, but the defeat of Germany on the eastern front brought back Soviet power in 1944, and further repressions. Significant numbers – around 10% – of the Baltic population went into exile. Tens of thousands died en route. The Baltic States suffered heavy population losses during World War II from repressions and deportations, extermination, war casualties and flight to other countries. Furthermore, Estonia and Latvia were also deprived of small areas of territory on their eastern borders that became part of the Russian Socialist Republic.

Soviet control of the Baltic was acknowledged *de facto* at the Allies' Yalta meeting in February 1945, but Western powers did not acknowledge the incorporation of the Baltic States into the Soviet Union *de jure*. However, they were not prepared to take action, being unwilling to confront the Soviet Union. Estonia, Latvia and Lithuania were the only countries whose independence was not restored at the end of the war, not even in the form of the so-called people's democracies of the Soviet Union's Central and East European satellite states. While the Baltic States in a sense were lost from view as small republics of the USSR, the absent acknowledgement of their incorporation ensured a continual simmering of this issue internationally for the next 45 years, and was to become a powerful driving force again internally when national movements emerged in the mid-to-late 1980s. Among the strongest demands for these national reform movements were those to restore the national languages to the predominant place they had during inter-war independence. This monograph charts these demands and their eventual realisations.

The Soviet system was introduced in the Baltic states on four levels: political, economic, sociocultural, and through demographic changes (Zamascikov, 1983, 1987).

Political control was exerted in the form of hegemonic control (Lustick, 1979). Besides massive violence and the introduction of loyal personnel brought in from Russia, decision-making was taken away from the local population and transferred to newcomers from Russia. Several top positions were reserved for ethnic Russians. The appointment of Russians in the form of functionaries second in command in Party and Government offices was a rule. Among such offices the most important one was that of the Second Secretary of the Central Committee, who supervised the activities of the cadre and administrative organs which managed the activities of all lower-level Party bodies as well as the militia and the KGB (Zamascikov, 1990: 87–89). Thus the changes were:

- penetration of the local Party organisations by Russians and Russified members of the respective nations;
- appointment of Russified and 'reliable' Balts to important positions of power;
- appointment of Russian functionaries as second in command at every party committee and local government body.

Individuals in these positions influenced the ideological pressure and provided direct subordination to Moscow. Army recruits being stationed far away from their home republics were subjected to the extraterritoriality principle, with the KGB and the Communist Party (CP) mutually controlling each other.

Economic control was exerted by a central planning system that nationalised all the land. Most industry was subordinated under central planning, and rapid extensive industrialisation, large-scale heavy industries as well as enforced collectivisation of agriculture where introduced. Largely inefficient collective farms were established in areas where the land was not left to lie fallow. The Baltic States in their new form as parts of the Soviet Union suffered unequal economic costs, indeed exploitation of their ecologic and economic potential since most produce, including energy, was exported from the Baltics to other parts of the Soviet Union; that is, the action of the Soviet Union as such could be regarded as discriminatory redistribution (Demuth, 2000).

Those strict political and economic measures, enforced throughout the entire period of occupation, were supported by demographic and cultural control of the population in the Baltic States. Different approaches were adopted with respect to the Baltic issue, usually dependant on the views of the incumbent (First, and later) General Secretary of the Communist Party as the main holders of power in the Soviet Union. Thus, the occupation may be divided into four periods:

(1) the Stalinist period, roughly ending with the years after Stalin's death and the subsequent condemnation of his genocidal policies in 1956;
(2) the period of Nikita Khrushchev and the first phase of Leonid Brezhnev's period up to the end of the Prague revolution that resulted in a tightening of ideological screws;
(3) the period of *stagnation* starting in the mid-1970s and ending with the death of the last Kremlin geriatric General Secretary of the Communist Party Konstantin Chernenko in 1985;
(4) the period of *perestroika* started by Mikhail Gorbachev and ending with the termination of the Soviet Union in 1991. This phase entailed certain characteristic constituents, leading to some sort of permanent transition, searching for a point of balance in society to keep the state together.

Throughout the entire period of Soviet occupation, there was also a trend towards applying softer methods in controlling society. Thus, genocide and deportation of whole ethnic groups during Stalin's reign were replaced by policies regulating first language education. Reduced access to native language media and culture was introduced during the subsequent periods on a gradually expanding scale, and ending up in conflicts with the demands of democratisation in the period of *glasnost*.

Demographic control was achieved through a variety of methods. First, the end of World War II resulted in another wave of Red Terror on the population of the Baltic including arrests, executions, deportations and other brutal violations of human rights. This time, the main pretext for persecution was any alleged connection with Germans during the German occupation period. During the following decade of occupation, oppressive methods were used to create favourable social and demographic conditions for the destruction of titular ethnic groups and their languages as well as of the remnants of indigenous minorities, replacing them with imported Russian-speaking, 'trustworthy' personnel. The ideological rationale for such actions was the elimination of non-proletarian classes. This policy was implemented mostly during the first post-war decade, when Stalinist policy was at its height. According to the ruling ideology of the time, the 'people's enemies' were to be crushed, with brute force being used against persons of the 'wrong' social background or class. Between 1945 and 1959, almost half a million people suffered from repressive measures, and around 100,000 of them were executed or perished. In March 1949, during one single campaign, over 70,000 persons were deported to the Far East and

Siberia, including many farmers suspected of resisting collectivisation, and numerous women and children. Many died en route (Kiaupa *et al.*, 2002: 181; Tiit, 1993). Subsequently, most of the civil servants who had collaborated with the occupiers in 1940 were arrested, and their jobs taken by 'trustworthy' workers with a Russian background. These methods of genocide and deportations produced a threat of extinction (Demuth, 2000). Post-World War II, Stalin's rule of terror with mass deportations, arrests, torture and enforced collectivisation triggered armed resistance, which led to guerrilla movements in each republic that started in1944 and were finally crushed in 1953 (Laar, 1992).

Another technique used included high in-migration of non-natives in order to strengthen ties to the Soviet Union. Soviet policy of heavy industrialisation in the Baltic region involved planned mass immigration of (mainly) Russians, particularly to Estonia and Latvia. The Soviet settlers consisted chiefly of the military and of blue-collar workers, living in urban areas, whilst the rural parts remained inhabited mostly by titular nationals. Between 1945 and 1950, over half a million mostly Russian-speaking immigrants arrived in the Baltic States, with 50,000 to 70,000 people to follow later. The resulting demographic shifts experienced by Estonia and Latvia were dramatic; in Lithuania the change was less dramatic. By 1989, the indigenous population had sunk to 61.5% from 92.4% in Estonia, to 52% from 73.4% in Latvia and to 83.45% from 84.2% in Lithuania. The situation in Latvia was particularly drastic, the country having come to the verge of losing its ethnic majority (see Table 1 below).

Cultural control was exerted by ideological means, the second main component in maintaining hegemonic control. There were two waves of ideological brainwashing during the period of occupation, one starting directly at the onset of annexation, and the other at the end of the 1970s: the first wave was designed to reform society in accordance with the new ideology, thus, throughout the occupation several attempts were made to destroy societal integrity and continuity as well as collective ethnic memory, covering most of the daily spheres of life. The past too was 're-arranged' in line with Soviet thinking. Ideologically motivated modification of history was based on two fundamental principles: the friendship of Russians and the Baltic people, and the class nature of every event in history. Recent history was falsified accordingly, and differing opinions on the part of Baltic people who themselves had experienced many of these reinterpreted events were prohibited. The occupation of the Baltic States was depicted as their admission to the Soviet Union by 'free will', proceeded by a proletarian revolution. Alongside a provision of a 'new past', national symbols were either abolished or modified according to the demands of the new governors. To make the new version of history more easily memorable, such public places as streets, squares and parks, as well as institutions and factories and even towns were renamed in honour of various revolutionaries and prominent Russian figures presiding over this 'new history'. Simultaneously, monuments and statues glorifying the past were demolished and replaced by statues that were to be important in this 'new past'. Under the USSR policy, the Balts were forcibly socialised into Soviet norms and behaviour (Vardys & Sedaitis, 1997: 60f). 'Culture' was re-interpreted as being 'national in form but uniformly socialist in content' (Vardys & Sedaitis, 1997: 93). A new cultural policy demanded that history be rewritten at the expense of local traditions: many

Table 1   Changing ethnic composition in the Baltic States from 1923 to 2000

	1923–34	*1989*	*2000/1*
Estonia			
Estonians	92.4%	61.5%	67.9%
Russians	3.9%	30.3%	25.6%
Others	3.7%	8.2%	6.5%
Latvia			
Latvians	73.4%	52.0%	57.7%
Russians	10.6%	34.0%	29.6%
Others	16.0%	14.0%	12.7%
Lithuania			
Lithuanians	84.2%	79.6%	83.50%*
Russians	2.5%	9.4%	6.31%
Poles	3.2%	7.0%	6.74%
Others	10.1%	4.0%	3.50%

*The minor change in the national percentage of ethnic Lithuanians is explained partly by the fact that the Republic's southeastern part, including Vilnius, which was under Polish occupation during the inter-war period, had been re-absorbed into state territory; the borders in the Klaipėda region too had been shifted back in favour of Lithuania by then. But also important was the Lithuanian Communist Party (composed mainly of ethnic Lithuanians) which strenuously resisted the rapid industrialisation that was taking place in Estonia and Latvia, thus avoiding the need for imported labour.
Sources: Gerner and Hedlund (1993: 74); Latvian Census (2000); Estonian Census (2000); Lithuanian Census (2000).

library books were locked away or purged, school textbooks were recast in the Soviet mould, and millions of older books were burnt. Any protest against the prevailing ideology was labelled nationalistic and severely punished: opponents were often either shot or sent to Siberian prison camps, while family members were deported to Siberia, and their relatives denied access to higher education and to certain jobs. Those who survived the GULAG were deprived of the right to live in their area of origin.

The second wave, in the form of Russification policy, found in the language and education policies of the Soviet Union, was started in 1961 by Khrushchev (a policy known as the 'second mother tongue' concept) and reinforced under Brezhnev from 1978 onwards, when another aggressive promotion of the Russian language ensued. In the second half of the 1970s, the pressure of Russification and the propaganda of the 'united Soviet people' intensified. The Russian language and its speakers were favoured. Russian was termed as 'the language of friendship of nations'. Bilingualism increased and the learning of local languages by immigrants was considered unnecessary. Cultural and educational policies were geared for Russification. Their real aim was to destroy the native language/ medium educational system as the basis of national identity.

To make conditions more acceptable for Soviet immigrants, several functional areas were Russified, and in order to keep their jobs, local people had to learn the Russian language. Russian was made the second language in education (not a *foreign* language), and in several areas, the first. The newcomers did not tend to learn the local language of the occupied states, and there were no stimuli for them to respect the local culture. It has been remarked elsewhere that these migrants had 'little sense that they were living in a foreign land and little desire to acculturate; rather [they] expected indigenes to behave as if they were in the Russian environment' (Hiden & Salmon, 1991: 97). They did not think of themselves as a minority in a 'host' country since they were treated by Moscow as the dominant group. This caused resentment on the part of the local populations.

Thus every language in the Soviet Republics was under the influence of Russification. Although Russian was not elevated to the status of state language, and whilst there was no explicit language policy, Russian was dominant. It served as the *lingua franca*, and members of the populations in all the Soviet republics regularly developed one-sided bilingualism in their own language and in Russian. In the words of Skultans (1998: 176), the moral superiority of Russian was perceived by many as 'painful'. As the spheres in which the national languages were being used contracted, their functionality also began to decrease (Zinkevičius, 1998: 320f). Vocabulary and grammatical structures were influenced by Russian. The native tongue became the language of the home and the schools. Russian was taught as a second language to non-Russian children in kindergartens, and in all primary and secondary schools and in higher educational establishments. A federal law stipulated that all non-Russian medium schools had to teach Russian as a second language. Although a subsequent 1958 law granted liberty of choice with reference to the language of education, the Russian language remained mandatory in all schools (Leclerc, 1991: 119–120).

The assimilation of third nationalities was one of the key elements in creating a Russian language environment. For non-Russian minorities in the Baltic, no possibilities were left to foster and maintain their own ethnic culture and language. All their institutions were abolished, including media, schools, clubs, etc. Though in principle the same rules applied to the Russian minority, the network of Russian-medium schools and clubs was enlarged considerably, along with all-Union socialist culture and its heavy ideological component, while local ethnic culture was not promoted. The fate of all other immigrants was to be assimilated to Russian. This new group of people, 'cleansed' of their ethnic culture, were idealised as *homines sovetici* who were expected to form a new and better type of socialist nation. Moreover, under their 50 year-long regime, the Soviets had succeeded in shifting the ethnic balance even more acutely since not only people of Russian nationality, but also many members of other ethnic communities, ended up declaring Russian as their first language. As a result, Russian was considered to be the first language in all three Republics by a sizeable proportion of Belarusians, Ukrainians, Jews and Poles who used it as a *lingua franca* in both public and private life. Of those who did not consider the national language to be their first language, some (mostly Russians) were monolingual; others were bilingual (first language/Russian) or trilingual first language/titular language/Russian). These facts and subsequent data in this monograph point to the complex nature of language loyalties, as there is no overall congruence between ethnicity and language use in the Baltic (Druviete, 2000: 40).

Language policy during the Soviet period

Language policy during the Soviet period may be viewed diachronically as well as directionally. The latter enables one to differentiate top-down (according to the command line from the Kremlin) and bottom-up policies, with the activities of local linguists having popular support and with inertia carrying over from the pre-occupation period. On a timeline, one may split top-down language policy into two segments, with a (quite vague) breaking point occurring during the 1970s. The first period had explicitly followed a laissez-faire language policy model (Phillipson, 1992), where a rearrangement of the language environment as a direct goal was secondary. Subsequently, this official position was gradually changed to direct intervention in language matters, aiming for Russification.

Bottom-up language policy followed a similar timeline. During the years of the Soviet occupation (1940–1991) standardising the local language and closely following its set norms became a form of national resistance; for example, Latvian linguists used the official rhetoric that recognised bilingualism (albeit as an intermediary phase) for the purposes of language maintenance. Insistence on a tolerant view of national cultures in a bilingual situation became the strategic basis on which to propagate the rights and wrongs of a 'pure' form of Latvian (Metuzaľe-Kangere & Ozolins, 2005: 325). This was a way of opposing the Soviet ideology, as symbolised by the Russian language. Language remained one of the most powerful tokens of identity for the Balts. Since neither the scientific study of the republican language, nor its use in most spheres of public life (including higher education) were prohibited by the Soviet authorities, the titular languages of the republics were able to survive both Russification and colonisation. During this period, the prevailing ultra-conservative position of adhering strictly to the linguistic heritage of the 1930s gave way as much as possible to a broader outlook in the 1970s that regarded language as a tool suited for the needs of an ever changing society rather than as an end product.

Status planning: Laissez-faire and the policy of Russification. Together with the influx of newcomers, territorial and functional language shifts started to take place. In several public domains, the local languages, due to their direct subordination to Moscow, were replaced by Russian – for example, in banking, statistics, the militia (Soviet police), railway, naval and air transport, mining, energy production, etc. Such changes were accelerated through the nomenclature of privileged positions in certain trades where local people were not trusted – such as navigation and aviation (an opportunity to flee abroad), the railways (the risk of sabotage), communications (state secrets). Some functional activities were completely new, having no corresponding terminology and were therefore carried out in Russian – for example, *Gosplan* (state planning) and the KGB. In other documents (e.g. those connected with military purposes) the local languages were eliminated entirely and replaced by Russian. An ancient Baltic industry, offshore fishing, was forbidden, and the boats were broken up and burnt. Instead, a Russian-medium marine fishing and transport system was created, with special attention paid to ideological alert. As a result, at the beginning of the 1980s, local speakers made up less than half of those employed in industry and transport, resulting in a marginal and informal use of the titular languages. The local ruling organs of the Estonian and Latvian Communist Parties operated solely in Russian (the Lithuanian CP proved an exception), the Governments of the Baltic republics and several ministries shifted to Russian with the pretext that there was somebody in the collective who did not speak the local language (see more in Sinilind, 1985).

Together with the functional re-allocation of languages, territorial language shifts began to occur. During the occupation, immigrants (who might not have been aware of their status, but moved, according to their opinion, to another part of the Soviet Union) settled mainly in areas where the Russian language was needed and promoted at the expense of that of the local population. This situation developed especially in various locations:

- the Baltic capitals, Riga, Tallinn and Vilnius, where the non-titular groups comprised about half or even more of the residents, as in Riga;
- cities and towns with military significance (Liepaja, Paldiski, Haapsalu, etc.);
- towns with industry under direct all-Union subordination (Ventspils, Klaipėda, Ignalina, Kohtla-Järve, Sillamäe);
- eastern regions of the Baltic territory as a result of expanding Russian-speaking neighbouring areas (Narva, Daugavpils, etc).

This trend was further supported through the establishment of closed territories where the local population was often expelled from their lands without compensation (and where access was prohibited or restricted for military purposes to almost 10% of these spaces), with preference given to newcomers in providing housing after wartime destruction.

The decrease of the functional as well as regional areas where local languages were used was paralleled by the rapid rise of the status of Russian, caused by several factors: the compulsory deployment of Russian as the sole language in several functional spheres; the establishment of a parallel Russian-medium network of plants, factories, offices, institutions and service bureaus as well as entertainment facilities and residence areas; the provision of services and full-scale education (including higher education and vocational schooling) in Russian, next to the already operating titular language-medium system. Alongside a regular, large-scale influx of immigrants, a Russian-speaking environment having no access to local cultures and languages was created in the Baltic, thus effectively hindering possible integration.

As was the case in several other domains, language policy in official documents was discussed implicitly, under the guise of ideology. The only exception seemed to be acquisition planning, which will be elaborated on later. Soviet language policy goals in the occupied Baltic States seemed to be:

- full-scale Russian monolingualism for Russians, with local titular language learning as an option, backed by cadre rotation (for military personnel, Communist Party bureaucrats);
- minority bilingualism for titular nationals, with Russian-medium functional domains in expansion;
- assimilation of 'third nationalities', mostly to the Russian language.

In order to consolidate immigrants on the basis of the Russian language, Soviet language policy was implemented in three steps:

(1) creation of a parallel Russian-medium environment that prevented integration into the local languages;
(2) continuous transfer of territorial and functional domains from the local languages to Russian;
(3) ideological incentives to encourage a preference for Russian over the local languages.

These steps also threatened to affect the integrity of the local languages (Kreindler, 1990: 242), through:

- the expanding usage of Russian in administration and mass communication;
- the development of an extensive programme of translations from Russian;
- the introduction of a massive Russian language teaching programme.

On the one hand, Article 36 of the Constitution of the USSR had stated that:

> Citizens of the USSR of various races and nationalities enjoy equal rights. Implementation of these rights is guaranteed by politics of comprehensive development and the convergence of all nations and nationalities of the USSR, the cultivation of citizens in the spirit of Soviet patriotism and Socialist internationalism, and the provision of the option to use the mother tongue and languages of other nationalities of the USSR.

However, these rights were not implemented due to the fact that the rule of law was not practiced. Constitutional and international human rights instruments ratified by the Soviet Union were not regarded as legal documents acceptable in court, and interference in delivering justice by the KGB, or Communist Party officials, was common. Several documents affecting language policy were classified, thus preventing the possibility of demanding linguistic human rights.

Language policy and its implementation. Russification amounted to implementing an asymmetric hegemonic position. Non-Russian groups were assimilated by being completely submerged by the Russian culture, and their inherent non-Russian culture was modified as being a carrier of Russian identity. The economic basis of the totalitarian regime that was introduced developed through state proprietorship, genocide of the Baltic elites and the termination of the rule of law. The mass media had exclusive rights to present one political view, that of the Communist Party of the Soviet Union. Belonging to the modernist category of imperialism, as represented in industrial societies, Russification required territorial contact for success. This success was achieved by colonising ethnically non-Russian territories, and ensuring:

- control of the language environment through a diglossic structuring of languages, with Russian at the top;
- pressure on cultural traits of ethnicity;
- disintegration of territorial identity.

Among the factors causing psychological resistance to these Russification activities mentioned by Ruutso (1998) were:

- ethnic defence mechanisms based on collective memory;
- the perceived low status of Russian-Soviet culture among the Baltic population;
- the differing boundary positions between their historical types of civilisation (*cf.* Galtung, 1996).

Other factors included:

- the goal of nation-building that was almost achieved by the beginning of occupation in 1940;
- the influence of emigré cultures;
- broadcast Western mass media (especially Finnish TV stations in Estonia);
- resistance of Baltic-minded officials in implementing Soviet policy.

The creation of a Russian language environment was successfully supported by continuous immigration flows. The second task that entailed making Russian the second language for non-native speakers seemed to falter, as previously noted. Therefore, at the 1979 Tashkent Conference, it was agreed that the promotion of Russian was an important component of the ideological push forward (Grechkina, 1981: 201). Several decisions were reached regarding the way to improve proficiency in Russian, at the cost of the local languages. As a result, the republican languages were gradually either limited or pushed out of the media by prescriptions of the Communist Party and the state apparatus.

Corpus planning.   Soviet corpus planning activities that focused on linguistic quality were based on the principle that language was mainly a tool for communication (and thus, suitable for ideological ends); all other functions were neglected. The prevailing trend was to promote 'popular usage' and reject 'useless' parallel forms (Erelt & Laanekask, 2003). Furthermore, the republican languages adopted a multitude of terms and everyday words that related to the new ideology, the new system of government and the new way of life. Simultaneously many words in use became obsolete (e.g. *Mr* and *Mrs* were replaced by *Comrade*), and numerous Soviet-related words were added, with 'bourgeois' ones being dropped.

Apart from this overtly political domain, however, corpus planning researchers in the non-Russian Republics enjoyed relative freedom. The main constraints were insufficient financial and material resources and sophisticated and ineffective publishing. From the mid-1960s, a number of terminological committees, consisting of both linguists and subject specialists, were created in various professional and technical fields. Hundreds of dictionaries of special terminology were published between 1960 and 1990. The importance of this was also based on the fundamental aims of evolving terminological work that would largely ignore the principle of minimal discrepancies from Russian (this was promoted by top-down policy, *cf* Desheriyev, 1981) and instead recommend a linguistically comparative approach in order to find the best solution for the target language.

Baltic linguists and lexicographers put a great deal of stress on following the literary norm – that is, they encouraged 'correct popular usage'. Erelt *et al.* (1997) have described this situation as being marked by a normative trend taking precedence in general corpus planning, thus obstructing the influx of Russian loanwords and other phenomena of language contact. Name policy was harmonised with international standards based on the resolutions of the 1967 1st Geneva International Conference for standardising geographical names. From the 1970s the efforts to marginalise various sub-varieties (e.g. slang, regional and dialectical varieties, youth language) faded, as these started to be recognised as a source of enrichment for the literary language. In the 1980s, prescriptive black-and-white codification with a totalitarian scent was abandoned as Soviet linguistics generally moved away from an ideologically-driven agenda, and a number of innovations were made that eased a transition to a descriptive language model.

According to Kreindler (1990: 242–243), the main features underpinning Baltic corpus planning during the occupation period were the different alphabets used (Latin for the local languages versus Cyrillic for Russian), advances in terminology, and a large corps of linguists who presented constraints to Russian-based and propagandistic Soviet language policy.

Acquisition planning. For years, Estonia and Lithuania remained the only two republics in the Soviet Union that did not begin with Russian lessons in the first grade (Kreindler, 1990: 240). Across the Baltic Republics, a new school structure was introduced for native language pupils that had one additional year of titular language-medium education (11 years instead of 10), ostensibly for the extra time it took them to master Russian. That practice constituted the first wave of re-arranging acquisition planning.

According to law, pupils in the Baltic republics had the right to study either through the medium of their native language or of another language of the Soviet Union (*cf.* USSR Law on Education, 1974). In reality, the choice was between the titular language and Russian. The children of immigrants in general attended Russian-medium schools, which further strengthened assimilationist tendencies. The number as well as the relative share of pupils attending Russian-medium establishments increased continuously.

The second wave of re-arrangement in acquisition planning focused on the teaching of Russian in non-Russian-medium schools. For this purpose, a powerful ideological system was implemented together with additional economic resources. The process was based on several top-level legal documents, such as Decree No 835, which was issued on 13 October 1978 by the USSR Council of Ministers. For implementation in the constituting republics of the Soviet Union, this decree prescribed a considerable increase in the quantity as well as quality of the Russian to be taught in the 'national schools' at the expense of other subjects (Hint, 1989; Rannut & Rannut, 1995; Sinilind, 1985: 167-169).

As a result, the teaching of Russian received a considerable amount of additional material support; pilot programmes were planned and the collective positive experience was to be ever more widely implemented. This enabled the authorities to raise the salaries of Russian language teachers and, in order to increase efficiency, to reduce the number of students in Russian language classes by dividing them into parallel groups. The plans foresaw the teaching of Russian at kindergarten level as well as Russian-medium teaching of subjects. Publications promoting Russian, such as the new Russian methods journals, were produced, without the logical counterpart for balanced bilingualism (Hint, 1987), as well as propagandist writings eulogising the Russian language as Lenin's mother tongue and a language studied with great interest by Marx and Engels.

The decisions on the political level were reflected in the USSR Law on Education, adopted in 1982, which foresaw the free mastery of Russian as the language of interethnic communication in all non-Russian-medium educational institutions. Non-Russian schools required to teach Russian as a 'second native language', were in charge of producing totally bilingual graduates, whereas the curricula of the Russian-medium schools, contained little teaching of local languages, and no Baltic history or geography. In national schools, more time was devoted to Russian than to the native tongue (*Pravda*, 1 August 1984, quoted in Zamascikov, 1990: 95).

Local language proficiency was not included in the priorities of the Russian-medium school system, and such teaching was never knowingly discussed by the government or in Party circles. Hence, in Russian-medium schools, titular language lessons were fewer in number than foreign language ones. Indeed, titular language lessons eventually became optional, and were absent as a subject in the 1956 curriculum. From 1965 to 1972, no local languages were taught at the secondary school level. This kind of language policy was characteristic of the education system in the Baltic until 1988.

Together with the massive promotion of unilateral bilingualism that focused on local language speakers, this system produced a monolingual society of speakers of Russian that was separated from the rest of the Baltic population (Rannut & Rannut, 1995: 183). Due to this unbalanced education system, two separate language communities whose mutual understanding was deficient both linguistically and culturally developed. Other (so called 'third') minority communities were not allowed to use their native language in education, and their schooling was mostly in Russian.

In Soviet acquisition planning, one can see two different periods. The first period, at least in its rhetoric, reflected the historic Leninist support for national languages, but resulted at the end of the 1970s with a powerful campaign that promoted the Russian language. This was then substituted with a transition model, which however was never fully implemented, due to the passive resistance of the population (and bureaucracy). Thanks to the former model, the high internal status of the local languages was maintained among their native speakers, and this attitude was passed on to the next generation.

Simultaneously, a monolingual Russian-medium educational structure which also maintained a high language status was created, thereby promoting the separation of these two linguistic groups. Thus, the goal of *sblizhenie*, according to which indigenous populations should have increased their understanding of the Russian language and culture, was not reached. Dellenbrant comments on this matter:

> It is obvious that the present educational system, with separate schools for the indigenous and the Russian population groups, does not promote any integration among cultures. On the contrary, it tends to reinforce the separation of the two communities in the Baltic republics. (Dellenbrant, 1990: 119)

The period of occupation ended officially on 20 August 1991, when the Baltic States renewed their independence. This political declaration led to sovereignty and new language policies. The initial steps of restitution will be analysed in subsequent part of this monograph.

Part III: The Development of Baltic Language Policy from the End of the USSR to Membership in the European Union and NATO

The origins of recent Baltic language policy are closely linked to the era of *glasnost* ('openness') and *perestroika* ('restructuring'), promoted by Gorbachev in the Soviet Union from the mid-1980s. Specifically, Baltic aspects of this period are covered by Trapans (1991), Thompson (1992), Lieven (1993), Taagepera (1993), Vardys and Sedaitis (1997) and Jubulis (2001), while Pryce-Jones (1995) and an exhaustive study by Dallin and Lapidus (1995) give accounts of these wider processes in the Soviet Union.

For our purposes, two features of this period are crucial for understanding subsequent language policy.

First, *perestroika* and *glasnost* were intended by Gorbachev and his allies as processes that would fundamentally change and reform the Soviet structure into a more efficient and rational society and economy, overcoming the stagnation that was the legacy of the Brezhnev era. These reforms were never intended to take on any national character, but from the beginning the non-Russian republics all used these processes to promote national interests, perhaps camouflaged at first but increasingly insistent as the 1980s drew to a close. Language policy was one of the clearest manifestations of this trend.

Second, however, the very structure of the Soviet Union and its own language policy facilitated this move, divided as it was into titular republics, reflecting the avowedly international nature of the 1917 revolution, but bringing about eventually a 'revenge of the past' (Suny, 1993). Rannut (2004b: 75) captures this intersection of federalism and *perestroika*:

> Together with the weakening of other military, economic and ideological power grids, the importance of federal ethnic structure increased, and the new conditions created enabled the processes of ethnic mobilisation to gain more freedom. This resulted in the restoration of independence of [the Baltic States] in 1991 and the establishment of a new power balance. However, this political declaration was one of the final steps towards sovereignty and new language policies. The crumbling of the Soviet Union started from the republics whose population still preserved high inherent self-value, by making use of the principles of *perestroika*.

The main societal result of the period of Soviet occupation in the Baltic was, as previously noted, the gradual generation of potential ethnolinguistic conflict by creating a new privileged linguistic elite based on the preferential use of Russian, supported by the artificially created Russian language environment. Meanwhile, the high inherent status of local Baltic languages among their speakers was maintained; it had not been threatened during the *laissez-faire* period of Sovietisation, and was able to withstand and eventually mobilize against the Russification of the 1980s. The central value it had was also a product of the relative shortness of the Soviet occupation in the Baltic – starting only in 1940/44, not 1917 as elsewhere in the Soviet Union – so the living memory of the inter-war period of independence persisted. Thus, two linguistic groups with high inherent native language status and opposite linguistic goals were maintained simultaneously in the Baltic: a mostly Russian-speaking community of mainly immigrant origin, and a group of titular language-speaking communities, the latter powerless at that time, due to the effective mechanisms of hegemonic control. The inevitable conflict was postponed by state violence or threat of it. Levits, writing while the Soviet Unions still existed, argued:

> Despite the formal equality of Soviet citizens, their division into two politically and socially uneven groups is an important domestic political factor which destabilizes the entire ruling system. The constantly growing need of the non-Russian part of the population for political emancipation is also increasing the significance of the national factor. (Levits, 1990: 53)

Leninist language policy had celebrated the linguistic as much as the national diversity of the Soviet Union, and the Russian language had gained its place as first among equals not through legislation and an imposed official status; rather, its dominant place had come about for two reasons – one functional and one demographic. Functionally, Russian was always promoted as the 'international language' – international *within the Soviet Union itself*, providing the essential *lingua franca* for the diverse nationalities of the Soviet Union. It thus became the understood and used language of the elite in each Soviet republic, and it was taught to all in the school system. It also displayed an international character in often serving as the model for the numerous less well-developed languages throughout the USSR. Some smaller languages that had no written scripts before the Revolution adopted the Cyrillic alphabet; terminological development – especially for a technological lexicon – was often Russian-based (Comrie, 1981; Lewis, 1972). But this strategic advantage was reinforced by a stronger factor – the demographic influence of a considerable population shift as described in the previous section, bringing about the increase of Russian-language infrastructure (school systems, broadcasting, languages in public life throughout the non-Russian republics) and together with this infrastructural change the previously described asymmetric bilingualism, a condition in which relatively few settlers learned the local titular languages, and in which the frequent Russification of non-Russian settlers who moved into other republics occurred.

Emerging from Soviet hegemony

Concern in the Baltic over language came hand in hand with that over demography, as the Soviet system was seen to be a threat to the very existence of these relatively small cultures. This concern supported the long-standing but officially long-hidden desire of many in the Baltic States to regain their former independence, with independence being ultimately seen as a *sine qua non* for saving their threatened cultures. The notion of cultural identity has been a central issue in shaping political practice to redress half a century of ethnic engineering endured under Communist rule, but it rode on the back of *perestroika*. The Baltic republics took the avant-garde position in being most receptive to *perestroika*; however, the Baltic peoples wanted to go much further than Moscow reformers were prepared to allow (Smith, 1994: 139). Thus, having no powerful control at its disposal, this move took two main directions, neither wanted by the incumbent political leaders; namely, the restitution of the national sovereignty of the Baltic Republics, and the restoration of the right of the languages and cultures of titular nations and other discriminated ethnic groups to exist. *Glasnost* and *perestroika* enabled the return to democracy.

The year 1987 marked a crucial breakthrough in the Baltic where at first vaguely structured groupings of individuals began to demonstrate publicly – as in a 14 June demonstration in Riga to commemorate the Soviet deportations on that date in 1941, and the subsequent open display of Baltic flags, insignia and national cultural displays (Trapans, 1991: 26ff). In the Baltic States, these popular manifestations became known as the 'Singing Revolution', as they were accompanied by chanted folk songs, symbolising national reawakening (Thompson, 1992). An elaborate description of the issues surrounding these marches towards independence can be found in Vardys and Sedaitis (1997: 124–160). While there were still occasional repressions against some of the individuals engaging in such activities, the lack of overall control led to an avalanche of further national activities: intellectual and creative groups, professional associations, education groups and others, all hitherto part of an obedient Soviet infrastructure, swiftly made demands for greater autonomy and in some cases for national independence, and organised themselves in mass movements, most notably *Sajūdis* in Lithuania, the People's Fronts in Estonia and Latvia, and a Citizens' Congress in Estonia. All of these movements then pressed demands that were in varying ways taken up by the republican governments – in Lithuania and Estonia, the Supreme Soviets used their pre-war national days in February 1989 to declare they had been illegally incorporated into the Soviet Union, and to assert their sovereignty. The issue of reasserting the place of the titular language was a foremost concern.

By 1989, monuments were replaced, streets renamed, national flags and anthems were legalised, and language became a symbol of national rebuilding. Most significantly, within an astonishingly brief period, over 1988–1989, various language laws or regulations were passed in *all* the non-Russian republics of the Soviet Union (Grin, 1991; Maurais, 1991), with the Baltic States, and particularly Lithuania, setting the pace. The provisions of these early language laws in varying ways embodied a series of aims:

- legislating the official status of the republican language;
- ensuring that the republican language has at least equal status with Russian in administration, education, broadcasting and other significant functional spheres;
- attempting to reverse asymmetric bilingualism by promoting bilingualism among those who did not know the republican language;
- ensuring that certain personnel (always public officials, sometimes others in contact with the public) have capacity in the republican language;
- changing aspects such as signage, language of documentation, broadcasting schedules etc. in favour of the republican languages.

Republican legislation differed in terms of timelines and details. The most strongly worded law was that of Lithuania adopted in 1988, with a timeline that demanded a demonstrated competence in Lithuanian within two years by all public officials, together with a host of other measures to reinstate Lithuanian as the sole official state language, while still giving a place to Russian for its position in inter-Union communication. In Estonia and Latvia, as in most other republics, the laws were hard fought through Supreme Soviets with still strong pro-Moscow elements; they could only attempt to bring about equality between Russian and the titular language and express a demand for competence in the titular language among personnel. The Chair of the Estonian Supreme Soviet, Arnold Rüütel, expressed this in terms of equal rights:

> The slogan 'balancing language and people' was promoted long ago. This is the ideal to which we must strive. The underlying principle of the Estonian SSR Language Act is to resolve the language rights of citizens who have Estonian as their mother tongue with the language rights of citizens who have Russian as their mother tongue (cited in Rannut, 2004b: 22–23).

The desire to ultimately leave the USSR became more openly expressed during 1989, symbolised by the 'Baltic chain' demonstration of August 23, in protest of the Ribbentropp–Molotov pact signed on that date in 1939, and its consequence of illegal incorporation of the Baltic States into the USSR. The fall of the Berlin Wall in October provided further impetus to separatism.

These moves however also began to evoke strong opposition from elements in the Communist Parties and elsewhere, criticising such moves as separatism and nationalism: *Interfronts*, organised by Communist functionaries and so named as to underline the international and unitary aspects of the Soviet Union, began to oppose such moves publicly and called for an end to potential separatism in Estonia and Latvia. In Lithuania a specific appeal to national minorities came from the similar *Yedinstvo* organisation, which was 'a product of conservative Communist forces seeking to mobilize the country's largest minorities for the purpose of continuing the orthodox Communist system' (Vardys & Sedaitis, 1997: 116; see also Ilves, 1991, for these elements in Estonia).

Separatist moves also began to be more seriously confronted by the Soviet establishment. Gorbachev himself flew to Lithuania in January 1990 to thank the people in this republic for their support of the reforms, but strenuously tried to persuade Lithuanians not to think of leaving the Soviet Union. Nevertheless, the popularity of *Sajūdis* and the People's Fronts was quickly demonstrated by their success in the 1990 Supreme Soviet elections, when the hegemony of the Communist Party in elections was broken. In all three republics elected members from *Sajūdis* and the People's Fronts gained more than a two-thirds majority in the legislatures, thus enabling them to propose changes to republican constitutions. In Latvia and Estonia such success was also significant in that the support for the People's Fronts came not only from the titular nationalities, who constituted less than two-thirds of the population in both countries; significant numbers of those not from the titular nationalities also supported the People's Fronts, who had made it clear in their programs they were not seeking to pit nationalities against each other, but rather to consolidate a broad reform-minded alliance from all sides (Taagepera, 1993: 193–194).

Strategically, the popular movements saw it as important to attract national minorities to their cause, but also to break down the view that there were only two nationalities – the titular one and Russians, or 'Russian-speakers'. Well aware that during the Soviet period other minorities had been completely side-lined in public policy in favour of the development of a *homo sovieticus*, there were now opportunities to support other cultures, in part by reasserting some of the principles of pre-war cultural autonomy. Hence, cultural centres and some schools teaching in languages other than Russian or the titular language began to be established. Various measures were also taken to reassure the rights of national minorities. In Lithuania, for example, to alleviate fears surrounding the preservation of ethnic identity, culture and development, a Law on National Minorities was passed in 1989, guaranteeing all citizens of the Republic, regard-less of ethnicity, equal political, economic and social rights and freedoms. This law *inter alia* assured the right to public education in the minority languages and the right to receive information in their language in areas with high ethnic populations (Kaubrys, 2000). On assuming office in March 1990, Lithuanian leader Vytautas Landsbergis invited Lithuania's national minorities to join in a 'brotherly endeavour whose purpose is to return Lithuania to the family of Europe's democratic states and to serve the rights of all national communities in Lithuania for the fostering of their own language, culture and customs' (quoted in Vardys & Sedaitis, 1997: 158).

It was in Lithuania that the new majority worked most radically; in March 1990 the Supreme Soviet (hastily renamed the 'Supreme Council' in translation) declared that independence was restored in Lithuania, and that Lithuania would no longer recognise the authority of the Soviet Union. This caused an immediate conflict with Moscow, which imposed a blockade, subverted by other republics that came to Lithuania's aid. Lithuania's independence thrust however was not recognised by the international community, and a long drawn-out stand-off developed between Lithuania and Moscow; Gorbachev's earlier positive stance towards these reform movements hardened as Moscow sought to break the moves to independence; after considerable pressure, Lithuania declared a mora-torium on its independence drive. By late 1990 Gorbachev was clearly siding with the forces striving to defeat separatism and to keep the USSR together at all costs, while the leading separatist politicians in the Baltic States made common cause with the rising President of the Russian Federation, Boris Yeltsin, who also began to push for increased autonomy for Russia from the Soviet Union.

Significantly, Western support for the Baltic movements varied according to changing perceptions of Gorbachev. Most Western countries had not recog-nised the incorporation of the Baltic States into the Soviet Union, a stance that irritated the Soviets without ever becoming a major point of conflict. Thus, bodies such as the US Congress or the Europarliament and its predecessors had from time to time made declarations about this state of affairs, and particularly opposed policies of Russification; earlier these were formal declarations as part of cold war politics, but interest increased rapidly from the time of *perestroika*. On 7 July 1988 the Europarliament adopted a resolution in support of demo-cratic developments in the Baltic Republics that called for the Soviet leadership to stop Russification, among other things, and to recognise the titular languages of the Baltic countries as state languages (PL 120.863/1, quoted in Vares & Osipova, 1992: 311). On 19 January 1989, a day after the adoption of the Estonian Language Law, the Europarliament accepted a resolution that supported the reinstitution of the republican languages in the Baltic as state languages (B2-1247/88, quoted in Vares & Osipova, 1992: 314). At the same time, some western governments became fearful of Baltic separatism in particular, potentially destabilising Gorbachev, and in 1990, the US administration had warned the Baltic States not to move ahead too quickly in order not to jeopardise Gorbachev's *perestroika* ideology (Vares & Osipova, 1992: 322).

Several Western leaders and diplomats called for restraint, warning that decisive steps regarding Baltic strivings towards sovereignty might harm relations with the central government in Moscow ('Upheaval in the East: Washington; Tough Choice for the U.S.: Baltic States or Gorbachev' *New York Times*, 13 January 1990). On the suggestion by Gorbachev, Mauno Koivisto, the incumbent President of Finland, reminded Baltic politicians of the importance of obedience and humility. The Swedish Minister of Foreign Affairs totally rejected the idea of re-establishing sovereignty, even in 1990, differing in his attitude from the active proponents of sovereignty, Denmark and Iceland, which points to heterogeneity of approaches in the West.

The sharpest side of resistance to Baltic moves was seen in January 1991 in Vilnius, when Soviet tanks crushed protesting civilians at the TV tower, and several civilians were also shot by Soviet forces in Riga. Hundreds of thousands of persons throughout the Baltic States in this 'barricade' period guarded strategic locations against possible attacks from Soviet troops, and large demonstrations were held in Moscow protesting against the use of force, revealing strong support even within other parts of the Soviet Union for the Baltic States. Western opinion swung strongly against the Soviet attacks, with criticisms from the USA, NATO, and several European bodies.

Despite this widespread support, including from many national minorities and numerous Russians, the Baltic movements were increasingly criticised as nationalist and anti-Russian, as for example in the 1991 essay 'Suffering from self-determination', in *Foreign Affairs* by the Latvian KGB colonel, Viktor Alksnis, who argued that the early desire for reform had been subverted by nationalism and anti-Russian revenge, themes that have endured in Moscow criticisms of the Baltic States to this day.

Independence and a heightened language agenda

The Baltic States achieved independence in extraordinary circumstances as the USSR broke up in late 1991. In the August coup of that year all three took advantage of the confused situation to declare independence, and unlike Lithuania's attempt to re-assert independence the previous year, which had not been recognised by the international community, this time their independence was supported not only by western governments, which had always seen their incorporation into the USSR as illegitimate, but also by Yeltsin's Russian Federation, and by the now depleted Soviet Union, soon itself to cease to exist at the end of 1991.

As previously noted, the movements for local autonomy during the *perestroika* period were in part directed towards the re-establishment of the practices and policies of the inter-war independence period, and among these was the re-consolidation of the status of the national languages. When post-Soviet independence was achieved – a circumstance almost as surprising to the

Baltic States themselves as to the rest of the world – the urgency was to complete the process of reinstating former institutions and policy in the political system and in all areas of public life, as well as ensuring the existence of a vibrant civil society, but all needing to be accomplished in the context of a crumbling economy, massive social distress and continuing criticism of the Baltic from Moscow and from some – but certainly not all – sections of the Russian community.

Specifically for language policy, the desire to restore the national languages to their pre-war status now had to be realised – particularly in Estonia and Latvia – in a situation of massive demographic shift, and its consequential imposition – linguistically of asymmetric bilingualism, and structurally of an entire Russian-language based infrastructure, from education systems to media to streetscapes. For language policy, independence also meant the need to reshape the language laws of the late 1980s. Lithuania's language law needed little changing after independence, and its major provisions – conducting all administration in Lithuanian, and imposing language tests on all public officials who had not had an education in Lithuanian – could be steadily introduced, even though the initial two-year stipulation was softened to five years (Mikulėnienė, 1997: 199–200). In Estonia and Latvia, however, where the laws of the late 1980s were essentially compromise laws bringing the national languages up to equality with Russian, independence now led to a strengthening of the laws along the lines taken in Lithuanian, but with an even stronger ambit, as legislation was also applied to the private economic sector.

The fundamental concern in promoting these language laws was that the Baltic States explicitly rejected a vision of themselves as being official two-community states along the lines of, say, Canada, where each of the two main population groups had its own language dominant in its territory, and an official two-language policy was strictly observed. Many had urged such a two-official language policy, often as being a solution to ethnic problems (e.g. de Varennes, 1996; Dobson, 2001). The Baltic States saw themselves as unitary states that were indeed multilingual (as they had always been) but as states in which the national language would be the language in which all essential social functions were to be conducted; accordingly, a population introduced by an illegal occupation could not claim equal status and must not determine language policy.

Yet the desire to strengthen the language laws immediately became entangled with a number of other post-Soviet issues. The first was the continuing argument over the status of the Soviet-period settler minority in all three countries, with the relentless criticism of Baltic nationalism, already stirred up in the late 1980s, gaining renewed emphasis when the issue of citizenship came to be decided in Estonia and Latvia.

Moreover, at the moment of independence, the Baltic States still had a massive Soviet military presence – indeed, because of their westward and strategic location, these republics had always been a focal point of military watchfulness, with large army and naval bases, airfields, command centres and extensive military-industrial enterprises. Immediately, as soon as talks began between the three Baltic States and the Soviet Union (then Russia) about troop withdrawal and ownership of military facilities, Moscow insisted on tying the question of withdrawal of its troops to the question of minority rights, particularly in Estonia and Latvia. The stakes now became very high, as the presence of Soviet military in these independent countries was to become a point of international concern and international pressure from the West as well (Simonsen, 2001).

The convergence of attention was to be focused on Estonia and Latvia; for Lithuania the still present Soviet military raised another issue. To the southwest of Lithuania, on the Baltic sea coast, was the Kaliningrad oblast (the former Könisberg), east Prussian capital, and famously the city of Immanuel Kant. At the end of World War II, this German province was taken over by the USSR, its former German population and infrastructure virtually eradicated, and the renamed Kaliningrad became a massive military and oil base. With the oblast formally part of the Russian Federation, Lithuania's independence now meant the Kaliningrad oblast was cut off from the rest of the Russian federation. Moscow was determined to keep a land supply line open to Kaliningrad, which could only go through Lithuania. Thus, the post-Soviet military presence now made more urgent and more contentious both citizenship and language issues, but even more significantly touched on the very issues of sovereignty of these re-emerging, renewed states.

Citizenship: One breaking point

The issue of citizenship had already started to be discussed in Estonia, Latvia and Lithuania during the late 1980s. Concerns over citizenship were clearly tied to the view that the Baltic Republics were illegitimately occupied, and that the demographic influx itself during the Soviet period was also illegitimate. Whilst no open claims could be made when the area was under Soviet control, this point was subsequently impressed on the international community, with mixed success. The question of who would form the political community now had to be decided with a large contingent of Soviet-era settlers still in place, and criticism of any idea of limiting the political community was quick to come from Moscow and later from some Western countries and institutions as well. As already noted, Lithuania had most radically challenged Soviet hegemony, and part of this challenge involved declaring its own version of Lithuanian citizenship in its fight for independence. In an argument over territory and sovereignty, the republic could bank on the far less dramatic demographic shift in its territory than in the other two Baltic States, with over 80% of its population ethnically Lithuanian. Having so firmly enunciated a citizenship policy during the difficult years of struggling for sovereignty despite some debate, Lithuania thus adopted what became widely known as the *zero option*: it declared all permanent legitimate residents as citizens, excluding military, (the then) KGB and other temporary units, and it defined its political community as the entire permanent population (Vardys & Sedaitis, 1997).

This policy brought an immediate and favourable response from Moscow, which turned its attention now to securing access to Kaliningrad through Lithuania. In terms of citizenship, focus was now directed at Estonia and Latvia, where the situation was far more complex, and hence more controversial.

In Estonia, where an initial desire for independence was expressed less radically than it had been in Lithuania, citizenship issues assumed centre stage in the period 1989–1990. A group of activists, distrustful that enduring Soviet structures would assure Estonia's future, started taking matters into their own hands, forming citizens' committees and eventually a Citizens' Congress (Taageperra, 1993: 158ff). This citizens' movement asserted that the pre-war Estonian republic that had been forcibly and illegally incorporated into the Soviet Union needed to be recognised anew. Accordingly, its political community also had to be recognised as a continuation of that community: hence, only those who had been citizens in 1940 (when annexation to the Soviet Union took place) or their descendants would now automatically have the right to become citizens. They could be of any ethnic group or background or language group, since the issue was only whether they or their forebears had been citizens in 1940. This position constituted a direct challenge to the Supreme Soviet, who (as in the case of Latvia) had tried to negotiate an agreement with the Russian Federation's Boris Yeltsin, according to which recognition of Estonia's independence should entail inclusive citizenship, along the lines of the definition followed in Lithuania. But faced with pressure from the citizens' committees, it became impossible for the Estonian government to consider citizenship for all residents upon independence. During 1990 and 1991, the Supreme Council and the Citizens' Congress vied for power, disagreeing particularly on the point of whether a process of naturalisation should accompany restricted citizenship. After the sudden restitution of independence in August 1991, the Supreme Council maintained its authority by agreeing to a restricted citizenship (based on the 1940 criteria), but it was also able to decide on a naturalisation process, a major requirement of which would be basic competence in Estonian. For those who were not citizens in Estonia, two measures were introduced in 1993: an Alien Law stipulating that non-citizens needed to re-register regularly in order to continue their residence in Estonia; and a naturalisation procedure that allowed non-citizens to become citizens by demonstrating a basic writing, reading and speaking level of competence in Estonian together with a basic knowledge of Estonian history and the constitution (Toomsalu & Simm, 1998: 45ff; see also part 4). This language requirement for citizenship and its present features are presently examined in detail in Part 4.

In Latvia, a similar citizenship movement had also gained impetus but had not been formalised into a Citizen's Congress. However, the Popular Front, which was the major vehicle of political change in Latvia from 1998, indicated early on that Latvia agreed with the principle of a 1940-based citizenship and stipulated a naturalisation process. The latter was strongly opposed by two citizens' parties in particular (Jubulis, 2001: 112ff) and led to a protracted stand-off. While the Supreme Council confirmed the 1940 basis of Latvian citizenship after independence was regained in October 1991, Latvia did not adopt a citizenship law until 1994, more than a year after Estonia, with a corresponding delay in beginning any naturalisation procedures at all. Moreover, the compromises over the citizenship law introduced a system of 'windows'; that is, naturalisation would not be available to all settlers at once, since this was considered likely to overwhelm administration, but would be organised according to the time when immigrants had arrived in Latvia. Those born in Latvia could apply immediately; those who had lived longest in Latvia could do so in the next several years, but those who had come most recently would have to wait up to nine years for naturalisation.

The political struggle to define citizenship within Estonia and Latvia led to sharp and often quite hostile reactions to these processes from outside. Russia continued to demand the zero option for all concerned, and Western observers viewed these processes with some alarm. Within Estonia and Latvia, however, there were different reactions from the non-citizen populations. In Estonia, the Alien Law which demanded that Soviet period settlers regularly register and be allowed to stay in the country only on a renewable short-term basis, created deep fear among the settler population, and a significant number, over 80,000 as reported in the 2000 Census (Euromosaic, 2004a: 2.3), took out Russian citizenship, hoping thereby for greater protection from Russia, but also to escape from the situation of being stateless after the Soviet Union ceased to exist. Partly to allay such fears, partly in response to considerable international criticism of such a policy of constant renewal of residence permits, the government amended the harshest aspects of the Alien Law, making permanent residence the norm for non-citizens. In recognition of the significant concentrations of Russians, particularly in eastern Estonia, the government also decided to allow non-citizens to participate in local government elections and to stand for local office.

In Latvia there was no Alien Law, and the in-principle agreement of naturalisation, despite delays in implementation, did not result in a huge uptake of Russian citizenship. Unlike Estonia, however, Latvia did not grant non-citizens the right to participate in local government elections, and this exclusion, together with the delays in implementing naturalisation, was to bring continued criticism – from both East and West.

This at times confusing elaboration of citizenship processes has brought a variety of responses from commentators, analysed subsequently. In many ways, the kinds of citizenship issues posed in Estonia and Latvia had a unique character since they were the only two post-Soviet countries to introduce restricted citizenship. The difference regarding this issue between Lithuania on the one hand and Estonia and Latvia on the other also created a contrast that has been endlessly exploited by Moscow: after having firmly opposed Lithuania's independence thrust in 1990–1991, the period immediately after independence in 1991 saw a complete turnaround in relations between Moscow and Lithuania. Negotiations over guaranteed access to Kalinigrad were relatively quick and successful. With Kaliningrad access guaranteed, Moscow now praised Lithuania's approach to citizenship, contrasting it with what it regarded as the recalcitrant policies of Estonia and Latvia. Significantly, while language demands continued to be made on Estonia and Latvia, Moscow was silent on Lithuania's language laws, which in fact differed little from those of the other two Baltic States.

Strengthening language laws

Latvia and Estonia refined their 1988/1989 laws after independence, establishing the groundwork for language policy which has served to this day. The revisions cut away the previous provisions of demanding both Russian and national language competence, relegating Russian to the status of a foreign language alongside other foreign languages, and stipulating a range of measures to ensure competence in the national languages.

To the surprise of many who had perhaps doubted the ability of these new states to organise such an ambitious enterprise, systematic language attestation for employment purposes was begun, showing that the governments were determined to change their linguistic landscapes. These attestation procedures had a common core: all those persons who had not undergone an education in the respective national language (Estonian, Latvian or Lithuanian), and who were employed in defined occupations, needed to demonstrate a level of knowledge of the national language appropriate to their level of employment. In Lithuania, this requirement targeted only those in the public sector; in Estonia and Latvia this requirement extended to all personnel in employment, public or private, who had contact with the public. All the language laws of the late 1980s, even before independence, had stipulated target dates by which such attestations must be complete – 1991 in Lithuanian (subsequently extended to 1995), and 1993 in Estonia and Latvia. If a person were not able to pass an attestation, this failure could constitute grounds for dismissal from a position, though in fact such measures were rarely invoked.

Language requirements were graded according to profession, so that, for example:

- a caretaker needed to demonstrate the lowest level of capacity of speaking, writing and reading;
- a nurse or police official required a medium level;
- a teacher or doctor or member of parliament required the highest level (Druviete, 1998, for Latvia; Mikulėnienė, 1997 for Lithuania; Toomsalu & Simm, 1998, for Estonia; for Lithuania).

To supervise the attestation, all three countries established central State Language Offices to oversee attestation procedures and to certify language proficiency, as well as to supervise and inspect other requirements of the laws. This central requirement of proficiency certification under the language laws has raised controversy from time to time, but the process has proved to be enduring, with several hundred thousand successful accreditations in each of the countries (see details in part 4.) In examining this phase of language policy, Druviete (1998) argues that the language attestation requirement was the single most significant step in altering the linguistic capacities of the population. Surveys showed that the need to gain language attestation was the most significant reason for those who had no proficiency in the national language to learn that language, and this proved to be an even more significant objective than learning the language for gaining citizenship (see also Järve, 2002).

The laws also stipulated a number of other language measures of greater or lesser magnitude, often recalling similar moves described as pertaining during the inter-war periods of independence in the previous section:

- Signage was changed from generally bilingual or Russian-only into the national language only. Where bilingual signs were used, the size of text in the national language was prescribed as larger than that of the other language.
- Official and public communication was to be in the national languages, with various transition periods and arrangements made for documentation and translations.

- National orthography rules were to be followed in official writing of personal names and of geographic place names.
- A system of language inspections was organised under the various State Language Centres to monitor conformity with the language laws.

A number of points should be made about what the language laws did not do. First, except for certain areas of official communication, the laws did not prescribe what language must be spoken or chosen in person to person contact, for example between a shopper and a shop assistant. Rather, the Estonian and Latvian laws that did go into the private economic sphere were only interested that shop assistants in contact with the public have the *capacity* to communicate in the national language. This distinction was crucial, as there was no intention to police actual linguistic interactions, as existed at one time in some other Eastern European situations; for example, Slovakia (Driessen, 1999).

Second, the language laws did not stop publication or broadcasting in languages other than the national language. Publications were unregulated, while state-owned radio and television increased transmitting in the titular language, maintained and in some cases determined the amount of broadcasting in Russian, and also promoted broadcasting in other minority languages.

Third, the language laws did not abolish the extensive infrastructure of Russian-language schools, a matter to be commented on presently. However, there was continuing concern over the ability of a divided school system to equip all school leavers adequately with a suitable level of competence in the national language, given the poor record in the past. Further reforms were foreshadowed and gradually introduced, as subsequently discussed.

Other laws also impinged on language. In all three Baltic States, all higher education changed to delivery in the national language, abolishing the system common in many faculties of having two streams – for example, having a Russian stream and an Estonian stream in Mechanical Engineering. By the end of the 1990s, this changeover was essentially accomplished. However, to some extent it was overtaken by another linguistic development in higher education, that is, the advent of a number of private tertiary institutions, particularly business and law schools that sprang up using English as their language of instruction.

The three republics also introduced legislation specifically covering the use of minority rights and financed minority languages in various spheres. Thus, there was a continuation of the Russian-language school system, with more prominence given to the teaching of the titular language. Finances were also found for schools and other cultural activities in several languages, which had not been made available during the Soviet period, when schools were run only in Russian or the titular language while other cultures were not recognised. This move also implicitly contested the view that all those not of the titular nation were 'Russian speakers' and, symbolically, it led away from the tendency toward Russification of other minorities. In Estonia, for example, languages of other minorities had been recognised in the 1988 language law, leading to the revival of the 1925 Law on Cultural Autonomy in 1993, that provided the basis for the development of non-Estonian cultural and educational endeavours for a number of minorities (Rannut, 2004a: 8).

Human rights as Moscow's strategy towards Estonia and Latvia

After renewed independence in the Baltic States, the earlier positive relationship with Yeltsin slowly changed, given:

- an assertive military ensconced in all the former republics of the Soviet Union;
- the growth of anti-western nationalism in Russia itself;
- the creation of the Commonwealth of Independent States (CIS), a body formed from most of the previous republics of the Soviet Union, largely to continue Russia's leading role in what it termed the 'near abroad' – that is, those areas that Russia saw as the area of its historic hegemony.

The Baltic States did not join the CIS. From late 1992, Moscow intensified the earlier Soviet period theme of accusing Estonia and Latvia of denying human rights, and subsequently appealed to a variety of international institutions to bring Estonia and Latvia into line. Russia's demands were unequivocal and remain essentially the same to the present day: that is, that citizenship should be granted to all permanent residents, and that Russian be recognised as a second official language. Moscow's stance, casting itself as the defender of all 'Russian-speakers', became increasingly lingua-centric.

Paradoxically, Russia's insistence on tying military withdrawal to human rights issues drew fire from international organisations, which demanded that such a connection was inappropriate. Rejecting Moscow's claims that it should be the guarantor of security in former Soviet territories, the West postulated withdrawal of the Russian army from independent countries (Laitin, 1998). Subsequently however, after complaints had been received from Russia and some local organisations, the United Nations and European institutions began to send delegations to investigate the case of the Baltic States. Possibly, this was also spurred by growing violence in the former Yugoslavia – at times even a confusion in the minds of the public of the 'Baltics' with the 'Balkans' – and other instances of what was, or was perceived to be, ethnic unrest in parts of the former Soviet Union.

Karklins, in her interviews with Russian foreign ministry officials in 1992, found that they stressed this deliberate use of human rights as a strategy – that is, in the words of one such official:

> The question of human rights is a very strong weapon. The West is highly sensitive to this issue, in contrast to us. As a result of our diplomatic activities, the reputation of the three Baltic countries could be undermined more and more [...]. (Karklins, 1994: 122)

A key point in understanding conflict over local language policy and the reactions to it is that, in the Baltic, these conflicts have always been seen as essentially a *foreign relations* issue between the Baltic states and Russia, and not primarily as an internal matter. From the Baltic perspective, there was little open conflict over language within their countries, though a small but voluble and largely militarist group of pro-Moscow activists and local politicians did raise objections that Moscow often took up. In addition, the conviction was that this activist group did not represent the opinions and dispositions of the vast majority of Russians and of others among the non-titular nationalities; some of the sociolinguistic evidence for this will be presently examined. The view held by the Baltic states was that there was wide support for the idea of a unitary state with one national language, and that pursuit of an official two-language policy would entrench ethnic divisions rather than 'solve' supposed ethnic conflicts that did not in fact exist.

Nevertheless, some international organisations and European bodies have tended to see the Baltic situation as essentially an issue of the treatment of a given minority. They reacted accordingly and, during the decade following the restitution of independence, the story of language policy in Estonia and Latvia was essentially one of continual interplay with international institutions, with repeated visits of missions, delegations and enquiries. In 1994, according to Rannut, some 15 human rights missions from the UN and European bodies had visited Estonia since independence in 1991 'none of which has found any gross or systematic violations of human rights' (1994: 208).

One body that became prominent over the ensuing decade – one that was critical in determining Baltic outcomes – was the Conference on Security and Cooperation in Europe (CSCE), renamed from 1995 as the Organisation for Security and Cooperation in Europe (OSCE). This body originated during the Cold War, out of the 1970s process of détente, culminating in the Helsinki Accords of 1975 and also out of attempts to lessen the tensions between East and West through processes of consultation and monitoring of potential conflicts, including issues of border tensions, security and human rights. Somewhat paradoxically, the CSCE found its most extensive work precisely after the end of the Cold War, when conflicts in Eastern Europe threatened European security. The CSCE also had a mandate to look at both international and internal causes of conflict, but with an emphasis on international tensions. In January 1993, CSCE created a new office, the High Commissioner for National Minorities (HCNM), whose brief was to look specifically at minority issues that may have cross-border implications, particularly in relation to minorities in one country that constituted majorities in a neighbouring state (CSCE Annual Report, 1993).

Given that Russia repeatedly claimed discrimination and infractions of human rights in the Baltic, the CSCE also responded to these. The activities of the CSCE coincided with a number of other significant events in the Baltic in the mid 1990s – events that to some extent quieted earlier fears of ethnic conflict and human rights problems. In 1993, the then CSCE HCNM, Max van der Stoel, made his first visit to Estonia and Lavia and reported on his findings. His report was not the damning indictment Russia had hoped for; on the contrary, while expressing some concerns over details of citizenship laws and minor concerns over language matters, he echoed all previous reports in finding 'no evidence of persecution of the Russian-speaking minorities in the Baltic States' (CSCE, 1993: 109). Van der Stoel did, however, advocate a number of measures that Baltic governments should consider in speeding up integration and improving minority relations, calling for 'a visible policy of dialogue with and integration of national minorities' (CSCE, 1993: 109).

Prior to van der Stoel's report, a CSCE delegation in 1992 had given a descriptive account of the reasons for Russia's concern in relation to Estonia:

> Estonia tries to develop a comprehensive language policy that offers Russian-speaking citizens sufficient opportunities to fully identify with Estonia and live as loyal citizens while using their own language [...]. For various reasons, many Russian-speakers perceive the policy presently followed by the government as insufficient or unreasonable. This explains to a great extent the concerns expressed by some residents regarding the human rights situation in Estonia. (quoted in Druviete, 1997: 169; see also Huber, 1995)

Russia had not expected such reports, and several authors warned that their contents could have far-reaching consequences in Russian politics: Konovalov and Evstaviev explicitly cited the 1993 report in arguing that 'this should be remembered as an example of the kind of approach that produced internal turmoil in the Russian political establishment' (1995: 178). Linked to the international agitation over the continuing presence of the Russian army, this message signalled that a reversal of Russian Baltic policies would be needed.

Van der Stoel's report also established an important benchmark for future language policy. After its seemingly favourable nature, subsequent policy involvement from the CSCE/OSCE can be seen in part as a continuation of, but also in part a retreat from, this position, with more stringent and interventionist monitoring and policy recommendations gradually being made for Estonia and Latvia through the 1990s. Yet at the same time there was no overt support for Moscow's demands of automatic citizenship or for the development of a policy to establish Russian as a second official language. Thus, other commentators (Burgess, 1999; Chandler, 1999; Deets, 2002) have interpreted the role of the CSCE/OSCE variously.

The second significant event of this period occurred in August 1994 when Russia did complete the withdrawal of its military from Estonia and Latvia. This move was not looked upon favourably in Russian ruling circles, as was their inability to have this issue tied to that of the fate of 'Russian speakers', a view that was also revised subsequently by Moscow. Some Russian commentators were sceptical of the attempted link between military withdrawal and the rights of the Russian minority, but this resulted in a rebuke of Russian policy in allowing the Baltic States to gain independence without any conditions at all. This provides another example of the positions of Russian officials:

> Having recognized the independence of Estonia, Latvia and Lithuania without any reservations or conditions (such as the status of the sizeable Russian minorities there), Russia eventually dropped its ineffectual attempts at linking their status to the withdrawal of forces [...]. In a display of enlightened internationalism, Moscow decided to take the case of the Russian minorities in the area to the UN, CSCE/OSCE and the Council of Europe. (Trenin, 1998: 181)

However, other Russian authors have stressed the complexity of the issue of the Russian diaspora and of Moscow's inability to clearly define a policy towards the Russian minorities. Zevelev (1996) for example stresses the fact that the Soviet Union fell apart without marked violence, the Transdienestra region of Moldova being the only exception. The absence of violence was due, he argues, to Russia's refusal to fan ideas of ethnic separation in the Near Abroad for fear of its rebounding via separatism in the Russian Federation itself, and also to the nature of the diaspora itself. Shocked at losing its status and completely unused to political mobilisation and its overall weakness, Russia made its own choice to go a peaceful way. As Konovalov and Estaviev had predicted, this policy would bring a reaction, and duly the mid 1990s saw the spectacular rise of Vladimir Zhirinovsky in Russian politics, marked by his desire to recreate the original extended Russian Empire – from Finland to Alaska – emerged. Interestingly, some of the more militant views on this issue came from Western authors. Smith *et al.* (1998: 117) find, similar to Zevelev, that Russia effectively turned its back on the diaspora, and that this let discrimination develop in such places as the Baltic. They also argue that more should have been done to guarantee the rights of minorities by linking this issue more closely to the withdrawal of troops. The heat of this issue, even years later, is clearly palpable.

The third significant event occurring in this 1993–1994 period was of a different kind altogether. While it may be considered a little extraordinary for an academic article to influence policy and even to influence international organisations directly, the publication of Maley and Rose's much cited 'European Barometer' study of attitudes in the Baltic States drew considerable attention. The article from the Glasgow Centre for the Study of Public Policy was accompanied by a press release, claiming that the survey showed a significant diminution of ethnic conflict in the Baltic States (Maley & Rose, 1994). Amid several results showing little ethnic hostility, items on language were among the most significant: a central question 'People like us should not be made to learn a Baltic language' drew a perhaps unexpected response from Russian respondents in the three Baltic States – a majority *disagreed* with this statement (Table 2).

In Estonia and Lithuania, a clear majority of Russians surveyed opposed such a proposition (i.e. Estonia: agree 33% vs. disagree 58%; Lithuania agree 33% vs. disagree 55%), while in Latvia where opinion was more divided, almost

Table 2   'People like us should not be made to learn a Baltic language' (%)

	Russians in Estonia	*Russians in Latvia*	*Russians in Lithuania*
Strongly agree	11	13	9
Agree	26	21	24
Disagree	36	25	30
Strongly disagree	22	22	25
Don't know	5	19	12

Source: Maley and Rose, 1994: 56.

one-fifth of respondents were unsure about a response (agree 34% vs. disagree 47% vs. undecided 19%). Similar attitudes were evinced on a question asking whether citizenship should also include a language examination – again, a majority was not opposed to this proposition. Such findings were beginning to be supported by other literature, particularly that of Laitin (1996, 1998), Hough (1996) and such Baltic authors as Druviete (1995, 1997) who reported on general individual support for, and accommodation to, the demands of language and citizenship laws.

Two planks in the Baltic states' view of their language policy and criticisms of it have already been identified:

- The situation, rarely envisaged in hitherto language policy and rights formulations, of a *national* language being under threat, not the language of a *minority*.
- The view that conflict over language in the Baltic is primarily to be understood as a foreign relations issue, particularly as a conflict with Moscow and its desire for influence in this region, than as any internal ethnic conflict.

The sociolinguistic findings give essential support to the second of these claims, in buttressing the view that the local population of whatever nationality broadly shores up Baltic language policy and language citizenship requirements. Moreover, they also back a view that actual relations between nationalities and speakers of various languages are generally accommodating and not confrontational, and that the demand to remain monolingual on the part of Russians (or of Russian speakers) was not being sustained in the overall community, however stridently this was being proclaimed by Moscow and some political activists in the Baltic.

Ina Druviete, Latvia's leading sociolinguist and later Education and Science Minister, argued that:

> [t]he present process of change in the linguistic hierarchy is slow but satisfactory and must not be artificially interrupted due to an incorrect interpretation of linguistic human rights. (Druviete, 1997: 183)

These sociolinguistic findings however, while significant in helping to understand the Baltic situation, were not to determine ongoing international response to Baltic language policy; rather, the issues were increasingly to deal with a mix of legalistic and political responses from European institutions, and continued hostility from Moscow.

Language policy gains and reactions by the late 1990s

The mid- to late-1990s saw several processes occurring in parallel. Overall, there was some bedding down of the language laws and cumulative changes to the language situation – in some cases rapid, in others much slower. Streetscapes changed radically in the Baltic over these years – Cyrillic signage disappearing almost completely; personnel in contact with the public increasingly had the capacity to speak the national language, and learning of the national language in schools started to become more widespread in practice while universities completely modified their practice to teaching in the republican language, interspersed in some cases with instruction in English (see also part 4). More attention was paid to the mechanics of language policy, particularly in terms of introducing comprehensive teaching programmes of the national languages both in schools and for adults. While competence in the national language was required for both citizenship application and for employment purposes, there was at the time of regained independence and for several years after little direct language teaching for these groups of people, a situation from time to time pointed out by international delegations. The Baltic states were offered assistance to begin financing such teaching from the mid 1990s from a number of European organisations, particularly through the PHARE programme, an EU-funded assistance packet to candidate countries to prepare the way for accession (Jurado, 2003); this became a steadily growing programme financed at first by international organisations but eventually receiving state support (see part 4 for additional discussion). In schools, long-term school reform programmes were flagged in Estonia and Latvia, with the intention of moving all secondary schooling to the national language as the principle language of instruction. This move was deferred in Estonia from the intended introduction in 2000 to 2007; in Latvia however such a move was introduced in 2004. At the same time when these developments were occurring, there was growing OSCE vigilance over language policy and citizenship policy; after the initially positive early response of van der Stoel, signals from OSCE became increasingly critical of specific aspects of policy. Citizenship issues, largely not related to language issues per se, became a particular focus of attention but, as the 1990s wore on, the OSCE and other European organisations targeted specific items of language policies in Estonia and Latvia, and in some cases brought political pressure to change aspects of the policies of the early 1990s.

European pressure on citizenship and language laws

The close interconnection of language policy with citizenship policy in Estonia and Latvia has brought continual interest from international organisations, keen to impress their views of citizenship on the Baltic. Many in Europe were puzzled over why Estonia and Latvia adopted restricted citizenship, when all other post-Soviet states including Lithuania had chosen the zero-sum option. Yet there are no international conventions on citizenship – (of all aspects of government policy, this remains probably the area most often determined by each sovereign state) – and the Baltic states were seen to present quite novel situations for which no extant international law could be called upon to raise clear objections (Skolnick, 1996). Citizenship policies around the world range the full spectrum from welcoming and liberal to entirely exclusionary, and this broad palette is present within Europe itself. There were some procedural concerns that had international outreach, particularly provisions to the effect that state actions should not deliberately leave people stateless and that individuals should understand clearly what is required for naturalisation, provided this was possible (de Varennes, 1996). There have been intense differences in views about citizenship in situations of *restoration* of states as opposed to creation of new states (Brubaker, 1995). While the international community (apart from Russia) definitely saw the Baltic situation as a case of renewed states, the entire question of recognising the Soviet period as an occupation remained a sensitive one, even though the OSCE and other international organisations did apply political pressure. This was the case in Latvia where the slow take-up of citizenship led the OSCE to urge very strongly two changes in the law – that the graduated system of citizenship 'windows' be abolished, and that automatic citizenship be available to young people who were born in the country even though their parents were not citizens. The basis of this campaign and its eventual success, after a referendum in Latvia to decide the issue narrowly backed this proposal, has been extensively covered elsewhere (Jubulis, 2001; Ozolins, 1999).

The testiness of Latvia and Estonia to this pressure was revealed in the build-up to the referendum when Latvia directly questioned the OSCE as to whether this would be the last demand that the OSCE would make on Latvian's citizenship laws. The OSCE, after some consideration, replied this would be its last demand, and also repeated this to Estonia when the parliament there was considering an amendment on stateless children (RFE/RL Baltics Newsline, 22 and 23 October, 1998). In a bizarre footnote to the battle over citizenship in Latvia, Russia – after a long period of silence on the subject – began to criticise Lithuania for its treatment of its Russian and Polish minority, contrasting this to what it argued was now a more welcoming attitude on the part of Latvia, a rare interlude in Russia's attacks on Latvia (RFE/RL Baltics Newsline 18 December, 1998). Such battles over citizenship as those witnessed in Latvia were never arguments over what international law prescribed; even the OSCE, while attempting particularly to link the treatment of minors to international conventions, clearly was applying political rather than legal pressure. Many other countries, including some in Europe, do not grant citizenship to children of non-citizens; all are free to place whatever restrictions on citizenship they see fit. Nor had the situation of former Soviet citizens in some cases now being technically stateless caused particular consular or other problems; the matter was easily accommodated through standing consular and documentation processes, or by the availability of, for example, Russian citizenship if desired. But from the mid-1990s the overwhelming concern of the Baltic states was to get approval to join the significant European institutions – the EU and NATO. As a result, an entirely different logic began to operate in respect to the way these bodies may or may not respond to particular Baltic policies, and whether Baltic policies met 'European standards', in many instances not explicit, and subject to change over time. In other cases measures were applied to candidate countries that had never been invoked in relation to other member states (Johns, 2003). Despite this context, European bodies continued to show clear disapproval of aspects of Baltic citizenship practices.

Other matters of citizenship and language included, from time to time, some recommendations to soften the language requirements of the citizenship test, such as reducing the language threshold or abolishing it altogether for the elderly. Accommodations were made for the elderly or disabled, but no other concessions have been introduced to date (Rannut, 2004a: 10). There are no international conventions that mandate any particular approach to these questions – a number of countries include language requirements as part of naturalisation, but again the nature and extent of such requirements differ widely, from detailed provisions of tests to be taken and standards to be achieved to requirements that have no indication at all as to how language competence will be assessed (Blackledge, 2006; Piller, 2001). The Baltic states, with relatively explicit requirements – basic conversational, reading and writing skills, with a clear process before a testing body – are very much at the detailed end of the spectrum, as elaborated further in part 4.

On some significant language issues, there was also an increase in critical responses from international bodies over the 1990s; that is, in several cases practices that were deemed to be in accord with international norms earlier were judged not to be so towards the end of that decade. From 1992, in accordance with a number of agreements signed with various European bodies, the Baltic states – along with a number of other Eastern European countries – agreed to submit intended legislation on crucial areas of policy to various European organisations for commentary. The three most significant examples are discussed.

Language in the private economic sphere

The regulation of language use in the private economic sphere evolved slowly in the 1990s. The earlier language laws in Estonia and Latvia had stipulated outreach into the private economic sector, including a demand that all internal and working documents of enterprises and all communication with government authorities be in the state language, and a demand that all personnel, in particular those who were in public contact positions, need competence in the national language to the extent required in their profession or occupation. While Lithuania's language laws applied to public sector personnel only, this difference needs to be seen in its context: the Lithuanian Language Law of 1988 came about in the context of the then Soviet Union, where public sector employment covered almost all economic activity; significant *private* economic activity in fact only spread after this time. Lithuania did not amend this aspect of its law; Estonia and Latvia specifically mentioned generic enterprises, many of which in time came to be privatised however, on the principle that competence in the state language should be guaranteed in all enterprises, and the question whether they were state or privately owned, or indeed whether they were entirely new economic ventures, should not make any difference.

By the mid 1990s Estonian and Latvian government representatives were concerned over the many loopholes that the earlier legislation had left, and over the still widespread lack of use of the state language, which clearly demonstrated the need for revised language laws. In European circles on the other hand there was a growing consolidation of views that regulation of language in the private economic sector was undesirable, as represented in the Oslo Recommendations on language policy.

When Estonia reconsidered its language law in 1995, there were repeated visits to Estonia by delegates from the OSCE and other European bodies to promote the idea that language use in the private economy should not be regulated (see, for example, OSCE Annual reports – Estonia, 1995–1996). This pattern was repeated in the context of the deliberations in the revised Latvian Language Law passed in 1999. In both cases, earlier drafts of the law contained provisions that were objected to, in the strongest possible terms, by European bodies:

> During March 1998, representatives from the European Commission, OSCE, and the Council of Europe issued another very disparaging report

on the draft law, observing that it did not take sufficient account of the distinction between public and private spheres and was in risk of contravening internal legal standards of human rights, particularly the freedom of expression [...]. In April 1999, Van der Stoel wrote a letter pointing out that Latvia would have potential problems in terms of accession to the EU, particularly relating to the functioning of the single market. (Schmid *et al.*, 2004: 243)

These contests became three-sided, with legislatures wanting the strongest possible laws, European delegations pressing for maximum liberalisation, and the Presidents of Estonia and Latvia, able to delay but not defeat legislation, being heavily pressured by both sides. Both the Estonian and Latvian Presidents asked their Parliaments to reconsider aspects of these laws, taking into account the reactions from Europe – Lennart Meri in Estonia had a running battle with his legislature over this, as did Latvia's President, Vaira Vīķe-Freiberga, who interestingly had spent most of her life in Quebec and now found herself facing considerable political pressure over language laws that some compared to those of Quebec (Fennel & Lambert, 2000). Parliaments did change their legislation after Presidential objections, but introduced provisos that maintained significant aspects of language reach into the private economic sector. In Latvia for example, the final 1999 law amended the regulation of private economic activity:

> The use of language in private institutions, organisations and enterprises (or companies) and the use of language with regard to self-employed persons shall be regulated in cases when their activities concern legitimate public interests (public safety, health, morals, health care, protection of consumer rights and labour rights, workplace safety and public administrative supervision) and shall be regulated to the extent that the restriction applied to ensure legitimate public interests is balanced with the rights and interests of private institutions, organisations, companies (enterprises). (Section 2, Article 2, quoted in Poleshchuk, 2002: 4)

In Estonia, there were similar moves to amend their Language Law in 2000, with a strong insistence on retaining a list of occupations that required levels of language proficiency in areas of 'justified public interest' (Section 2, Article 2, quoted in Poleshchuk, 2002: 3).

While outwardly satisfying European bodies, such formulations have, as Poleshchuk argues, only shifted ground to the murkier interpretation of what such justified public interests are. One may legitimately ask whether the tortuous formulations in the Latvian law – essentially a repetition of European mantras about what might count as a legitimate public interest – are any clearer, or easier to follow, than Latvia's much more general 1992 law demanding republican language capacity of any personnel in any enterprise whose professional responsibilities involved communication with the public. A more detailed critique of the EU's approach, including the problematic nature of drawing distinctions on the public/private sphere and doubt on the interpretation of international conventions often cited, is provided elsewhere (Ozolins, 1999; 2003).

Language requirements for publicly elected officials

This requirement in the Estonian and Latvian Language Laws was integral to the view that all personnel needed to know the State language at a level appropriate to their work, and members of Parliament were deemed to require competence in the State language at the highest level, with correspondingly lower levels for other representatives, professions, trades and personnel. The push from European bodies to change this came on the heels of the private economic activity push and led to changes both in laws and regulations and also in some significant legal decisions. Commentaries from delegations and advisory notices from the OSCE and other bodies stressed that electors should have anyone they wanted representing them, irrespective of their language abilities. This time there was a threat that this requirement could lead to rejection of candidature to desired European bodies:

> [...] leading Statesmen (including US Secretary of State Colin Powell, US President George W. Bush and NATO Secretary General Lord Robertson) have called upon Latvia to remove the restrictions. (Holt & Packer, 2001: 22, fn. 39)

Under this pressure, Estonia agreed to change this law in 2001, but introduced legislation to make Estonian the language of parliament, and Latvia made a similar decision in May 2002. In Estonia, the decision was forced through its own court system:

> The Supreme Court has twice considered the legality of the requirement for proficiency in Estonian – which under the Language Act of 1995 applied to individuals running for the *Riigikogu* [Parliament] and local self-governments – and declared them invalid in 2001. (Euromosaic, 2004a: 3.3)

Meanwhile, in April 2002, the European Court of Human Rights decided the case of *Podkolzina v Lettonie*, where a Latvian citizen of Russian origin had been denied candidature for the Latvian parliamentary elections for alleged lack of competence in Latvian, even though she had previously gained a language attestation certificate at the highest level (European Court of Human Rights, 2002a). This fascinating case has been commented on at length elsewhere (Ozolins, 2003). The court found that the applicant had been wrongly treated, through the actions of a single language inspector who arrived unannounced to give an impromptu language test, which the applicant refused to undertake, leading the inspector to report negatively on the candidate and the candidate being declared ineligible for election. However, the case raised an intriguing paradox as the Court did not view a language requirement for a parliament as being an illegitimate aim:

> The Court found that the purpose of the legislation on parliamentary elections barring citizens without an advanced degree of proficiency in the national language from standing for election was to ensure the proper functioning of the Latvian institutional system. It added that it was not for the Court to determine the choice of the working language of a national parliament, as that choice was dictated by historical and political considerations and, in principle, was exclusively for the State concerned to

determine. Requirements of that kind pursued a legitimate aim (European Court of Human Rights, 2002b, *Press Release*: 2).

This part of the judgment goes quite against a view that a language requirement for candidature must per se be an infringement of rights. That 'requirements of that kind pursued a legitimate aim' was the opposite of what had been claimed by those urging Estonia and Latvia to change such requirements. The Court, as in other such cases, decided the matter much more narrowly, on 'whether the measure removing the applicant's name from the list of candidates had been proportionate to the aim pursued' (European Court of Human Rights, 2002b, *Press Release*: 2). Part 5 considers some of the complexities of rights approaches to language issues, and the extensive debate about such approaches.

The Oslo Recommendations

These instances of European pressures on the Baltic produced a continual reworking of what constituted international standards; faced by Baltic protests that these norms were not relevant to their case, European bodies became increasingly legalistic, in the hope of finding formulations that could ensure compliance, and international standards continued to be expanded.

The OSCE instituted a number of projects that sought to define acceptable international norms in minority rights and languages. The *Oslo Recommendations Regarding the Linguistic Rights of National Minorities & Explanatory Note* (OSCE, 1998), drawn up by a small committee, specifically addressed 'those situations involving persons belonging to national/ethnic groups who constitute the numerical majority in one State but the numerical minority in another (usually neighbouring) State, thus engaging the interest of government authorities in each State...' (OSCE 1998; Introduction). Similar to the mandate for the OSCE HCNM itself, both international and internal dimensions are relevant, but the recommendations that emerged dealt particularly with internal issues of minorities. As has already been argued, the question of the very definition of such a situation being one of a 'national minority' rather than of a neighbouring State utilising some population aspect to impose foreign relations demands also needs to be considered. In this case, to address minority relations alone would ignore contexts in which national minorities are used as a pretext in dealing with international conflict.

In terms of treatment of minority languages, the question of appropriateness of these Recommendations to the Baltic situation immediately arises, for example, on use of languages in relation to Judicial Authorities:

> *Recommendation 18.* In regions and localities where persons belonging to a national minority are present in significant numbers and where the desire for it has been expressed, persons belonging to this minority should have the right to express themselves in their own language in judicial proceedings, if necessary with the free assistance of an interpreter and/or translator.

Similar recommendations cover all other significant aspects of public administration. Yet despite an apparent reasonableness of wanting public sector personnel to speak the minority language, the situation in the Baltic is the reverse of that envisaged in such a Recommendation. There, it is not a problem of finding staff competent in the minority language (Russian); staff in the judiciary, police, prisons or their related administration who do not speak this language do not exist, nor has anyone been unable to address a court or police officer in Russian, whichever region they live in. Rather, the problem is that these authorities under the Soviet regime increasingly conducted their business in Russian and employed many who could not speak the now national language. Part of the issue is thus the necessity to turn around situations dominated by monolingual Russophone officials who have insisted on being able to continue to serve through this language only (Karklins, 1994:157–158).

The Oslo Recommendations on language in private economic activity were among its most cryptic, encompassing only one single paragraph:

> *Recommendation 12.* All persons, including those belonging to national minorities, have the right to operate private enterprises in the language or languages of their choice. The State may require the additional use of the official language or languages of the State only where a legitimate public interest can be demonstrated, such as interests relating to the protection of workers or consumers, or in dealings between enterprises and governmental authorities.

It can be observed that such recommendations lead precisely to the kinds of legal entanglements embodied in the Baltic legislation to guard against private enterprises ignoring social needs altogether. In the Oslo document, no examination is made of any possible complexities in this field; for example, what happens in small markets where commercial enterprises may in fact be dominated by a particular linguistic group, or the peculiar status of privatised functions which can be in the public sector one day but in privatised functions subsequently. At the same time as battles were going on over language, other European initiatives were persuading Eastern European countries to privatise more and more of their enterprises.

Despite their at times questionable relevance, the Oslo recommendations *were* nevertheless recommendations with force – not because of their (disputable) relevance in law, but through their subsequent adoption by other European organisations, not least as criteria for candidature. This gave the recommendations an entirely different political force: a set of recommendations became a set of demands, deemed to represent 'international standards'.

The European dimension: Criteria for access to the EU and NATO

The Baltic States perceived accession to European bodies, particularly the EU and NATO, as both practically and symbolically crucial to their future development and indeed to their very survival. Whatever their envisaged material benefits, joining the EU was also symbolically seen as a long-awaited 'return to Europe', to be accepted as European nations among others and to rejoin the mainstream of European life and history. The formal process of EU enlargement to the Baltic countries started in 1995, when each of them signed a Europe agreement with the EU, and concluded with their acceptance into the EU on 1 May 2004. They had become members of NATO in March 2004.

To be accepted by these bodies, candidates needed to negotiate a wide range of admission criteria, and to deal with a variety of European institutions besides the one to which acceptance was sought. European institutional architecture is complex and intertwined, but for the purposes of this monograph, in the context of language policy, a clear division of labour can be identified among the European institutions:

- The Council of Europe (CE), only a high-order deliberative body, having no executive power, has largely confined itself to overall frameworks and human rights definitions, such as the Framework Convention for the Protection of National Minorities.
- The CSCE/OSCE has been mostly concerned with conflict prevention, and its role and functioning has already been extensively discussed.
- The EU and NATO have been mostly concerned with the issue of criteria for membership, and – while feeding off the other two bodies – have also clearly pursued their own interests, particularly the establishment of permanent and appropriate institutions and processes that facilitate openness in government and respect for human rights and minorities (see Jurado, 2003 for an insightful theorising of this division of labour).

The intertwined nature of this division of labour becomes apparent when it appears that the OSCE was often asked by other organisations such as the EU or European Commission to carry out detailed negotiations with countries on points concerning which disagreement with European norms was perceived; in turn, these norms often derived from the more general CE frameworks, and a push to ratify various such agreements became part of candidature discussions. In very specific cases, the OSCE would itself turn to making broader framework recommendations such as in the Oslo Recommendations in which CE norms were seen to need supplementation for more detailed issues. As van der Stoel's warnings to Latvia about threats to acceptance by the EU showed, OSCE activities were at times closely tied to EU candidature issues. The OSCE missions were wound up in Estonia and Latvia at the end of 2001, despite Russian protests, and from that time on it was EU criteria alone that would determine outcomes. Accounts of the EU accession process can be found in Ozolins (2003), Adrey (2005), and Hogan-Brun (2005a, 2005c).

As previously argued, the road to accession for the Baltic states has seen a continual shifting of the goalposts, as witnessed in the quite different responses to Estonia's EU candidatures in 1997 and in 2002. In 1997 the European Commission did not accept Estonia's candidature, seeing it premature largely on grounds of infrastructure development and financial issues. The questions of language and citizenship barely rated a mention in the European Commission's report; they were not seen as problematic. The report gave a positive evaluation of Estonia's human rights record (European Commission, 1997). Yet, as previously noted, the late 1990s saw an intensification of demands on those issues when Estonia was under the impression that its house was in order. The 2002 Report on Estonia (European Commission, 2002a), devotes considerable space to language and citizenship issues. While applauding some measures taken – such as changes to laws on language requirements for public office – the report regrets the slow rate of naturalisation, and points to what it perceives as some still existing incompatibilities with international norms (especially signage issues). The report is concerned with how Estonia is pursuing integration of its Russian-speaking minority largely through the teaching of Estonian in schools, and urges that 'the Estonian authorities should ensure that emphasis is placed on a multicultural model of integration as stated in the aims of the state integration programme' (European Commission, 2002a).

Meanwhile the final report on Latvia (European Commission, 2002b) remained watchful and uneasy, suspicious of inappropriate application of legislation, and even hectoring:

> As emphasised in previous Regular Reports, it is important that the competent authorities, including the State Language Centre and the judicial system, only apply and enforce the Language Law and its implementing regulations to the extent required by legitimate public interest, having regard to the principle of proportionality, as contained in Article 2 of the Language Law, and in view of Latvia's obligations under international human rights instruments and the rights and freedoms guaranteed under the European Agreement. (European Commission, 2002b: 33)

NATO candidature has presented perhaps even more emphatic mistrust, as in the requirement for language knowledge of those publicly elected, as previously discussed. The irony of European pressure on the Baltic has not been lost on some commentators. In an article 'Saying Nyet to Russian', *Newsweek International* looked at the declining situation of Russian in the now independent former Soviet Republics, and came up with a surprising Baltic outcome:

> Russia has won some improbable allies in the fight to save its language. Both NATO and the European Union have pushed the Baltic countries to drop what critics say are discriminatory laws [...]. In February, NATO Security-General George Robertson told the Latvian Parliament that its language laws might affect NATO's decision to invite Latvia into its ranks. The reason was that the issue was a contentious point with Moscow. 'It is not in our interest to admit countries that don't have good relations within their borders or with their neighbours', one NATO official explained. (*Newsweek International*, 1 July, 2002: 30)

Leaving aside the historically curious reference to good relations with neighbours – NATO was established precisely because countries felt *threats* from their neighbours – once more, the international relations aspect is vital to an understanding of the situation, but as the work of OSCE, NATO and others has shown, only solutions that refer to local national minorities and local legislation are proposed.

If European institutions continue to mistrust the Baltic, then a degree of mistrust is also entertained by the Baltic states of attempts to show them how to solve their problems. Occasional gaffes by European bodies show that many issues that might have been deemed settled – such as having only the national language as the official language in each Baltic country – are not always settled in the minds of European bodies. The March 2002 intervention by Gerard Stoudmann, OSCE's Director of its Office of Democratic Institutions and Human Rights, when he suggested that Latvia adopt Russian as a second official language, then hastily retreated from this opinion, shows the extent to which such perspectives are alive, and not in Moscow alone (MINELRES, 2002; OSCE, 2002).

Finally, while EU and NATO acceptance has now ceased active European intervention on Baltic language policy, this has not been the end of conflict over language issues. With Russia continuing to exert its influence on such matters, a sustained offensive became particularly evident when Latvia was preparing to reform its secondary school system.

Secondary school reform

The issue of reforming the education system, while an object of some concern in the previous decade, gained international attention most prominently in Latvia throughout 2004 when a proposal to modify the language of instruction in the Russian stream secondary school system to 60% in Latvian was widely publicised and criticised in the media and through demonstrations and appeals for international intervention (Hogan-Brun, 2006).

As previously described, the Soviet system left behind a two-stream school system in the Baltic, that is, a Russian-stream and a national-language stream in primary and secondary school education as well as in much of tertiary education, a system that has been maintained almost intact to the present day, though there has been a steady decline of Russian-medium schools, particularly outside major cites and concentrations. One traditional shortcoming of the Russian-medium system had been its failure to teach the local national language, while all republican-language schools taught Russian intensively. Moves in Estonia from 1993 having intent to shift the language of instruction in all secondary education to Estonian by 2000 have been previously noted. In addition to aspects of citizenship and pertinent language laws, the issue of the secondary education reform had also been a point of contention with European bodies. Jurado (2003) in her comprehensive coverage of this point in Estonia has analysed the effects of the Council of Europe, OSCE and the EU (through its European Commission and membership application procedures) in gradually altering the stance of the Estonian government. In 1997, under considerable pressure, Estonia postponed the introduction of this education law; while Jurado stresses European intervention as being significant in this postponement, equally important were logistic issues, particularly the problems of teacher supply and teacher training, as well as curriculum and materials development, in the heavily Russian-concentrated areas in east Estonia. The government also introduced a wide-ranging Integration Program 2000–2007, which *inter alia* provided for much of the necessary infrastructure improvement in the education system and allowed for a steady increase in Estonian materials and teaching during this period, both inside the education system and in the wider community. In 2000, the Estonian government revisited the issue and changed the law from demanding total instruction in Estonian by 2007 to having 60% of the curriculum taught in Estonian while the rest might be taught in Russian. This 60/40 arrangement was perceived as more realistic in terms of infrastructure and teacher provision but also, Jurado argues, as closer to a multicultural mode of integration fostering both Estonian and Russian mother tongues. This integration constituted a signal of the way the

Estonian government had moved in relation to European standards and to an understanding of minority protection (Jurado, 2003: 420ff).

However, the view that such a 60/40 arrangement would be viable initially received a hostile response in neighbouring Latvia. After making laws similar to those of Estonia for a full transfer of secondary school instruction by 2004, Latvia amended its law, adopting the 60/40 proposal as well, though not without considerable internal politics and several attempts to amend this compromise and to retain a larger proportion of instruction in Latvian (Euromosaic, 2004b: 3.8). But the intended introduction of this arrangement from September 2004 was steadily criticised, leading to some spectacular street actions and to wider appeals by an organised movement calling for hands off Russian schools. While several Russian organisations contributed to this action, a never-registered and shadowy military-styled 'Headquarters' took the most public actions for the Defence of Russian Schools, with 'Headquarters' clearly used in the military sense (in Russian, '*shtab*' [штаб]). The action of this group included the repeated appearance of pickets in Riga and the sending of delegations to the European Parliamant; most seriously, the 'Headquarters' called for a boycott of all Russian medium secondary schools by Russian parents until the law was repealed. Hogan-Brun (2006) has analysed the media coverage of this campaign, Ikstens (2004) has examined the opposition movement, while Galbreath and Galvin (2005) have looked at the shortcomings of politicisation and implementation from the Latvian government's side that led to a stand-off and open confrontation.

By coincidence, but a coincidence that radically affected the publicity surrounding these actions on the most vital day, 1 September 2004, which was the start of the new school year and of the intended boycott, but this date also marked the beginning of the Chechen rebel initiated siege at a school in Beslan in southern Russia, diverting international attention from the Latvian school reform issue. In the end, the overwhelming proportion of Russian parents did not join the boycott on September 1, and the boycott quickly petered out in the ensuing days (Latvian Centre for Human Rights and Ethnic Studies, 2004: 31). Once again, while very strident opposition to a Baltic language policy was expressed, thereby gaining an international audience, the overwhelming majority of Russian parents accepted the thrust of the policy and did not support radical action; they sent their children to school. The reasons for these dispositions, and the varying interpretations of them, are looked at again in parts 4 and 5.

Part IV: The Current Language Situation

Language policies and planning

Language legislation in the Baltic Republics: A comparative overview

The complex ethno-demographical situation, which the Baltic Republics inherited as a legacy of long-term Soviet immigration, necessitated the conception of long-term language and integration policies, with constitutionally anchored legal backing. In each republic, over time the central criteria evolved into the creation of social conditions that would ultimately ease accession to the European Union and provide adequate facilities for the fostering of additional individual bilingual capabilities amongst the minority representatives.

The means to re-establish the constitutionally anchored official status and sociolinguistic functionality of the titular languages after the restitution of independence are strikingly similar across the Baltic and have emerged out of a centralist approach. The main objective of national language policy in this region is to guarantee the status of Estonian, Latvian and Lithuanian as the only official language in each republic, respectively, as enunciated in each Constitution and detailed in the several language laws. This has been a complex process, involving an inversion of the Soviet period language hierarchy. As earlier versions of the State Language Laws were gradually refined, additional language knowledge demands were introduced, especially in the laws relating to education and citizenship.

State language legislation

The restitution of independence led to the reinstatement of Estonian, Latvian and Lithuanian both *de jure* and *de facto*. As described in part 2, language laws had already been adopted before independence by the three Supreme Soviets (Supreme Councils), but after independence various transitional arrangements (in the case of Lithuania) or residual elements giving status to Russian (in Estonia and Latvia) were removed, leaving the national languages as the ones used in administration and public life, and ensuring that personnel in various professional categories were competent in their respective titular language. Further amendments ensued, and current language policies are implemented through national State Language Laws: Estonia's was passed in 1995, Latvia's in 1999 (both with subsequent amendments) and Lithuania's in 1995. (The texts of these State Language Laws are available online and can be accessed via the websites listed in the reference section to this monograph). These laws regulate the use of the state language in the main spheres of public life and stipulate its status as well as stating the legal implications for violations of the law. They are supplemented by a number of by-laws, strategic documents and lower-level legal and normative acts that define the standing of the titular languages and of other languages used in the republics and specify their status, teaching and use within the educational system as well as in society at large. This legislative apparatus has worked as a means to secure the status of the titular languages and has radically expanded their sociolinguistic function.

The purpose of these laws has been to assure that the national language can be used freely and authoritatively within the national territory – a situation that increasingly did not obtain during the latter Soviet period. Typical of this is the central provision of the Estonian language law, which in Article 4 stipulates:

> Everyone shall have the right to use the Estonian language in dealing with administration in state institutions, local government, cultural autonomy bodies, as well as in institutions, enterprises and organisations. All employees of institutions, enterprises and organisations must be guaranteed work-related, Estonian-language information.

Debates and conflicts over the most salient points of the language laws have already been discussed in Part 3.

Citizenship legislation

Lithuania's citizenship legislation diverges from that in its sister republics. Though theoretically Lithuanian legislation could have emulated that of the other Baltic Republics, it has been in a position to opt for inclusive citizenship policies since it hosts a relatively small percentage of ethnic communities that already tend to have an adequate command of the state language. The majority of Lithuania's ethnic population was, therefore, able to acquire citizenship through a naturalisation process offering the so-called 'zero option' which permitted all individuals normally resident in the republic at the time of the restitution of independence to become Lithuanian citizens (de Varennes, 1996: 244). In contrast, the neighbouring Baltic Republics introduced stricter citizenship criteria pertaining to the immigrant population that had settled there during the Soviet occupation. After the restoration of independence in 1991, citizenship was granted in Estonia and Latvia to persons who had been resident in those states in 1940 (the year of Soviet occupation of the Baltic), and their descendants. The regulation of the status of those people (about 400,000 in Estonia and 700,000 in Latvia) who had settled in the country after that date was accompanied by heated and emotional debates. Whilst many of these immigrants requested citizenship, discussions revolved around the issue of how to impose restrictions in this context. It was feared – especially in Latvia – that a sudden surge in naturalisation would result in an organised vote to reunite with Russia (Priedīte, 2005).

Estonia's citizenship law was first passed in 1993 (revised into the current version in 1995), Latvia's in 1994, and Lithuania's in 1991. Naturalisation Boards with nationwide administrative branches were also established. As detailed in Part 3, debates continued in Latvia because of the (so-called 'windows') quota system, which set a timetable for eligibility for naturalisation according to length of residence in Latvia. In 1998, following recommendations made by the OSCE, a referendum leading to the deletion of the 'window' restrictions was held. Simultaneously, and on the basis of the same recommendations, all children born in Latvia after 1991 were to be granted citizenship if their parents applied for it. Estonia introduced a similar provision for children born in Estonia after 1991. Subsequently, the legal status of those immigrants who were permanent residents in Estonia and Latvia but who had not been naturalised was 'non-citizens' (Estonian: *mittekodanikud*; Latvian: *nepilsoņi*). In Lithuania, on the other hand, the adoption of the 'zero option' has meant that very few non-citizens reside there. At present, these groups of people have almost the same rights as citizens, except they are not allowed to vote or to become state employees (school teachers are not State employees). Additionally, they do not have to serve in the army. (In Estonia, they can vote in local government elections). They can naturalise at any time after five years of permanent residence. Apart from payment of an administrative fee, the naturalisation requirements in all three republics involve the successful completion of a test measuring lower intermediate level competence in the state language and one on the Constitution; a test on the history of the country is additionally required in Latvia.

Estonia and Latvia have very similar naturalisation requirements, and those in Latvia are described here in some detail. A handbook for applicants specifying both linguistic and historical/constitutional knowledge has been prepared and translated into English – largely for the sake of monitoring bodies who from time to time still take an interest in local citizenship arrangements. These requirements, together with the other Baltic equivalents, are among the few examples anywhere in the world of language requirements for citizenship being explicitly stated (Latvia, Naturalisation Board, 2000).

To pass the language test in Latvian, an applicant for citizenship must undertake an oral and a written component (persons over 65 need only do the oral part). The *written* section, for which 90 minutes is allowed, consists of a listening and reading comprehension test, an item requiring completion of a form, and an item requiring the writing of a letter on an everyday topic. Texts are drawn from topical media pieces of a non-technical nature or equivalent, or standard bureaucratic forms. The *oral* section is based on a 15-minute interview on an everyday topic.

An additional knowledge-based examination (based on the principles of the Constitution of Latvia, the history of Latvia, and the text of the National Anthem) takes place either in written or oral form (as chosen by the applicant). The two forms of this test are counted equally. Applicants are asked to (re)cite the text of the National Anthem and answer 10 questions on the history of Latvia (eight of them being multiple choice) and eight questions on the Constitution of Latvia (six of them being multiple choice). The entire test takes 45 minutes.

From the inception of naturalisation until April 2006, some 108,655 persons had been granted citizenship in Latvia. Around 90% of all candidates pass the naturalisation test. Free language tuition is offered to people applying for citizenship, and around 40% of applicants are granted reduction of or total exemption from the 20 Lat (equivalent to about €30) full examination fee, with significant reductions of from 50% to 90% for such categories of candidates as the unemployed, the disabled or students.

Despite this process, citizenship uptake in Latvia is only slowly reducing the significant numbers of non-citizens in the country. Just over 19,000 persons gained citizenship in 2005, the highest number for any year but, as can be seen from Table 3, there are still over 400,000 non-citizens in the country, amounting to nearly 19% of all permanent residents; many of them will never gain citizenship. Significantly, the groups showing the lowest citizenship rates are Belarusians and Ukrainians – they had tiny pre-war numbers in Latvia since they only came during the Soviet period; as a consequence, few of them could claim citizenship dating back to 1940. By contrast, at present over half of the Russians in Latvia have become citizens, constituting the largest group, proportionately, to gain citizenship.

However, one factor which will continue to increase the proportion of citizens will be the various coordinating measures that are being taken to align citizenship language tests with other language teaching and testing. In particular, when the secondary school reform (that started in 2004) is complete, those students who are not citizens will be exempt from the language component of the citizenship test if they successfully complete their secondary education including passing the final year Latvian language subject.

Table 3   Breakdown of the residents of Latvia by nationality and citizenship

	Citizens of Latvia	Non-citizens	Aliens*	Total	%
Latvians	1,348,354	2,053	1,082	1,351,489	59.0
Lithuanians	17,828	11,799	1,680	31,307	1.4
Estonians	1,532	630	374	2,536	0.1
Belarusians	29,238	55,254	2,102	86,594	3.8
Russians	351,876	278,213	22,115	652,204	28.5
Ukrainians	14,637	39,633	3,905	58,175	2.5
Poles	40,685	14,385	612	55,682	2.4
Jews	6,452	2,704	369	9,525	0.4
Others	23,680	13,769	5,804	43,253	1.9
Total	1,834,282	418,440	38,043	2,290,765	100.0

*Aliens: holding another citizenship.
Note: In Eastern European generally and in the Baltic States, nationality has always been distinguished from citizenship, and censuses (going back to the Tsarist times and continuing through Soviet or independence periods) have categorised all people by nationality, and 'non-territorial' groups such as the Jews or Roma (gypsies) have been categorised as nationalities along with Russians, Latvians, Ukrainians, etc. In the specific case of citizenship in Latvia (and Estonia), all those who were citizens in 1940 at the time of Soviet occupation, and their descendants, automatically became citizens when independence was re-established in 1991. Those of whatever nationality who came during the Soviet period can gain citizenship through naturalisation. The 'citizenship' figure in the table thus include both those whose citizenship dates from 1940, and those who have been naturalised in recent years.
Source: Board for Citizenship and Migration Affairs (1 January 2006).

Regulations for occupational language use

In addition to the above described language laws, other language regulations specifying the required levels of language proficiency were also instituted in the professional and occupational fields. As detailed in Part 3, these requirements (ranging from basic listening comprehension to full proficiency in the titular language) for various professional categories were introduced for individuals who held relevant positions but who had not attended titular language education institutions; that is, who had been schooled through the Russian education stream during the Soviet period. Since these requirements were applied without reference to the individuals' ethnicity, Estonians, Latvians and Lithuanians who had attended Russian stream education also needed to sit these language attestation tests. The original ambit thereof in Estonia and Latvia pertained to all those who were in positions of contact with the public, whether in private or in public institutions; in Lithuania this requirement only concerned officials in public institutions. Ensuing from international pressure deriving from the OSCE and the EU, these laws in Estonia and Latvia were amended by introducing the principles of public interest and proportionality, so that language restrictions would be proportionate to the communicative needs involved (Adrey, 2005: 460). Details on assessment are provided in the ensuing discussion.

Language institutions: Remit and objectives in each Baltic State. Governmental institutions were set up in order to supervise the implementation and observance of language legislation. In Estonia this role fell to the State Language Board (in 1995 renamed the Language Board). Latvia's central body responsible for the legislative aspect and the implementation of the State Language Laws was the Latvian State Language Centre; Lithuania's State Lithuanian Language Commission was responsible for this there. A range of additional special commissions was created nationwide for the certification of the level of titular language skills of speakers of languages other than Estonian, Latvian or Lithuanian. Furthermore, State Language Inspectorates (Estonian: *Keeleinspektsioon*; Latvian: *Valsts valodas inspekcija*; Lithuanian: *Valstybinė kalbos inspekcija*) were established as national controlling agencies to oversee the extent and the means of the national language laws, and other legal acts regulating language use were implemented and adhered to. The language supervisory institutional landscape in each republic at the present time is described in the ensuing discussion.

Lithuania. There are several institutions in Lithuania acting as national agents in charge of the planning, modernisation, regulation, administration and supervision of Lithuanian: these include the State Lithuanian Language Commission (*Valstybinė lietuvių kalbos komisija*), the State Language Inspectorate (*Valstybinė kalbos inspekcija*), and a county-wide language service (*Savivaldybių kalbos tvarkytojai*) with municipal responsibilities for the local supervision and inspection of Lithuanian use in the public and semi-public spheres, and for providing consultation via electronic and written media on language-related matters. Since the early 1990s, the primary concern has been the re-infusion of a sense of 'language culture' throughout the population. The regulation and implementation of norms for oral and written usage of Lithuanian were advanced through the publication of various grammars and dictionaries (for a summary see Hogan-Brun & Ramonienė, 2002, especially Appendix 1 and 2; see also Dini, 2000: 423–426). Lexical means, grammatical forms and especially syntactic constructions remain the focus of attention, and clarity of expression as well as the use of neologisms *inter alia* are being monitored. The Institute of the Lithuanian Language, and Lithuanian language studies university departments are involved in work on language standardisation and terminology development.

The State Lithuanian Language Commission, guided by the State Language Law, was formed to succeed the Lithuanian Language Commission, which had operated intermittently from 1961 until the restoration of independence of Lithuania in 1990. The membership of the language commission is composed of researchers from the Lithuanian Language Institute, university professors and representatives of other institutions. Legally, the Commission's remit is to deal with issues of codification, the use of language norms and questions relating to the implementation of the Law on the Official Language. Initiating and financing programmes for the development of Lithuanian, it supports:

- the teaching of the language;
- the preparation and publication of bilingual and multilingual dictionaries;
- the publication of books for educational purposes and for public use;
- the publication of grammars, monographs and other linguistic volumes;
- the promotion of language research generally.

The Commission is also involved in the standardisation of place names and other proper names, and in approving standard technical terms. The latter work deals with concept formation and with the systematisation and differentiation of codes, especially in the area of scientific and technological terminologies. This interdisciplinary endeavour necessitates the collaboration of linguists and subject specialists as well as logicians for the generalisation, categorisation and classification of concepts necessary for the modernisation of the Lithuanian scientific language, which contributes to the development of appropriate registers for academic discourse. The Commission's resolutions, which are published regularly on its website (http://www.vlkk.lt), are compulsory for all companies, offices and organisations. Fines are imposed for neglect of these rules.

The Commission is increasingly involved in matters of broader language policy and planning. It has initiated the development of the State Language Policy Guidelines (see State Lithuanian Language Commission, 2003: 49–50; Valstybės Žinios, 2003: 15–19), approved by the Seimas of the Republic of Lithuania in 2003. This document sets out the strategy for the promotion and the development of Lithuanian. Under the changing conditions of political, economic and cultural life, the guidelines highlight the most important and inter-related goals of the state language policy, which are:

(1) to ensure the functionality of Lithuanian in all spheres of public life;
(2) to meet the new needs of a knowledge-based society as determined by the EU;
(3) to exert a planned and creative influence on the development of Lithuanian;
(4) to promote its creative use amongst the public whilst adapting it to new functions in a rapidly changing society.

The key objective lies in the strengthening of the public trust in the value and effectiveness of its own language. This involves the preservation of Lithuanian as a heritage language as well as the promotion of its development.

Several years after the inception of the Commission, some of its decisions began to be disputed by researchers as well as by ordinary language users. One such example is its 1993–1997 codification policy dealing with new (post-1991) word borrowings in Lithuanian. The influence of incoming English terminology was felt especially in computer science and other spheres of new technology, and concerns were raised regarding the impact of English on the scientific and public language (Kniūkšta, 2001: 198–212). Although no quantitative or qualitative analyses were performed at that time, the Commission developed and approved a list of 'unacceptable borrowings' (*Nevartotinos naujosios svetimybės*) whilst simultaneously supplying replacement words. This list was prepared inconsistently and unsystematically, and the opinions of language experts often diverged as to the selection of such loans. Whilst the decisions passed by the Commission are still presently valid, they will need to be reconsidered according to a new codification strategy. Research on codification theory and practice is under way to carry out a needs analysis and an evaluation of society's new demands for this purpose (see Miliu¯naite˙, 2000; Vaicekauskiene˙, 1998, 2000, 2004).

Latvia. Latvia has successively introduced several language institutions in relation to its language laws. The original institution set up under the Language Law of 1989 was the State Langue Centre (*Valsts valodas centrs*, VVC), which was initially charged with administration, implementation, linguistic advice to institutions and individuals, policy advice and all related matters to ensure the operation of the Language Laws. Its most time-consuming work was language attestation for all personnel (in public or private employment) in contact with the public to ensure competence in the state language, as has previously been explained in part 3. The Language Centre also established an Inspectorate, which investigated breaches of the law. However its location in the Ministry of Justice meant it was quite restricted in its activities, particularly in terms of education or publicity, and the highly politically charged environment in relation to the language laws, as has been described in part 3, made its policy advisory role difficult.

On assuming office in 1998, President Vīķe-Freiberga created a Commission of the Official Language (*Valsts valodas komisija*) in her office; the commission was intended to advise on ways of strengthening the state language, as well as on policy through representative advisory groups, paying particular attention to educational and technological aspects of language policy (www.president. lv/pk.content/?cat_id = 8&lng = eng   or   www.president.lv: Commisions; Commission of the Official Language).

Further refinements have been achieved by moving language attestation away from the VVC in 2001 to the newly created Centre for Curriculum Development and Examinations which conducts such tests at the present time. A primary reason for this move was to align these language examinations with the various educational levels of the school sytem, so that students achieving a particular level of education (which must now include the appropriate level of competence in the national language) can be deemed to have satisfied language attestation requirements for employment (http://isec.gov.lv/en/history.shtml).

The linguistic advisory function of the VVC was also moved to another newly created body, the State Language Agency (www.vva.lv), in 2004. Among the various kinds of advice the Agency gives, for example, are rules on orthography and terminology and, additionally, rules for the writing of names in Latvian orthography in official documents. Terminology itself has been a vexed area of policy, again with several institutions involved. The main role concerning terminology has been in cooperation with the long-standing Terminology Commission of the Academy of Sciences, charged with mainstream language corpus planning; occasionally terminological items attract public attention with respect to recommendations on usage, for example how to render the term *Euro* in Latvian (www.termnet.lv).

Finally, the VVC itself – whose main work remains that of the language inspectorate – has been relocated from the Ministry of Justice to the Ministry of Education and Science from January 2007, a move which consolidates policy implemenation and monitoring. This move also symbolically marks a shift from a strictly legalistic approach in language law matters to a wider educational approach concerning language issues.

Estonia. Language policy in Estonia is conducted through various governmental and non-governmental institutions as well as through national research and support programmes. The Ministry of Education and Research has the main responsibility. Its objective in language policy is to preserve the Estonian language and its various dialects within the country by setting up standards for national examinations, by formulating requirements for experts and specialists working in the country and by establishing programmes and publications to offer language support. Outside Estonia, the ministry encourages the learning of Estonian in language schools and institutions of higher education through educational and cultural cooperation. Work in this area is supervised, coordinated and carried out by the Language Department (http://vana.hm.ee/uus/hm/client/index.php?13526230132363950). Under the auspices of the Ministry, an Estonian Language Council has been established. This expert body advises on policy matters.

Language supervision and control is conducted by the Language Inspectorate under the jurisdiction of the Ministry of Education. Its primary task is to ensure that the Language Act and other legal acts regulating language use are followed. Depending on supervisory actions and the extent of the non-observance, warnings or written orders, as well as fines, may be issued.

In July 1993, the President of Estonia, Lennart Meri, set up the Presidential Roundtable, a permanent Assembly in which representatives of non-citizens and national minorities participate together with members of the Estonian Parliament. According to its statute, the objective of the activities of the Roundtable was to prepare recommendations and proposals concerned with:

- establishing a stable, democratic society in Estonia and integrating into Estonian society those people who have connected their lives with Estonia or who wish to do so;
- solving problems concerning aliens and non-citizens permanently residing in Estonia, as well as problems concerning national minorities;
- supporting applicants for Estonian citizenship;
- solving problems relating to the learning and use of Estonian;
- preserving the cultural and linguistic identity of national minorities;
- creating conditions and opportunities for persons of Estonian origin, born abroad, to return to Estonia.

According to the opinion of foreign experts, the results of the actual functioning of the Roundtable were found highly satisfactory. The Rapporteur of the Council of Europe stated in his report (Council of Europe. Political Affairs Committee, 1994: 2):

> This political forum has opened the door for permanent dialogue between the Russian-speaking minority and the Estonian majority on a number of

crucial issues (conditions of citizenship, the situation in North-East Estonia; local elections, etc.) and has contributed to appeasing inter-ethnic tensions.

Subsequently, as a consequence of increased representation of various ethnic Russian politicians in the *Riigikogu* (Parliament) and local governments, the importance and functions of the Roundtable have diminished.

Besides various language institutions with political and administrative agendas, several non-governmental organisations (NGOs) and research institutions are active in corpus planning. According to the bylaws, the main providers for the literary norm are the Mother Tongue Society and the Institute of the Estonian Language (the norm-setting Orthological Dictionary is compiled and published by the Institute of the Estonian Language). Language experts at the universities of Tallinn and Tartu also carry out extensive research in these areas.

Bilateral and multilateral agreements

In the extraordinary politics at the end of the Soviet period during the late 1980s and early 1990s, the Baltic states were keen to re-establish their international credentials as one tactic in their demand for greater autonomy and finally for independence from the USSR. Over the period 1989–1991, the various Supreme Councils wished to sign a number of international covenants, particularly those of the United Nations (e.g. the International Covenant on Civil and Political Rights, on the Elimination of all Forms of Racism), moves that were repeatedly blocked by the Soviet Union. Upon independence, the status of the Baltic States was recognised by the international community and these multilateral agreements came into effect.

In its commitment to promote good citizenship relations, Lithuania has, to date, become party to the following European agreements:

- the European Convention on Human Rights;
- the Convention for the Protection of Human Rights and Fundamental Freedoms (including the Law on Petitions under Articles 25 and 46 which recognises the competence of the European Commission on Human Rights to accept petitions from individuals or groups of persons whose rights under the Convention have been violated);
- the Framework Convention for the Protection of National Minorities.

Lithuania has also recognised the jurisdiction of the Court of Human Rights in all cases related to the interpretation and application of the Convention (http://www.is.lt/tmid/anglo/minorities.htm). Bilateral political agreements implementing effective co-operation as regards national minorities have been signed with Poland and Russia (the texts to these agreements are supplied in de Varennes 1996: 365f) as well as with Belarus and Ukraine. These achievements and the national legal protection of minorities that guided Lithuania's inclusive citizenship policies met with the approval of the EU during the early phase of accession negotiations in 1997 (http://europa. eu.int/comm/enlargement/dwn/opinions/lithuania/li-op-en.pdf).

However, in the politically charged language policy environment of Estonia and Latvia, some issues of multilateral agreements have themselves become fiercely contested. While both states quickly adopted the mass of UN and European agreements on various political and civil rights mentioned above for Lithuania, one agreement was initially resisted: the Council of Europe's Framework Convention for the Protection of National Minorities. After much debate this agreement was ratified by Estonia (1996) and most recently by Latvia (2005) but with particular provisos – as the Convention does not itself define a minority, both countries restricted the definition of a national minority to those who were citizens, who differed on the basis of ethnicity, religion, culture or language from the titular nation, who had a long-standing connection with the country and who are motivated to maintain their heritage. The provisions are also deemed to apply to non-citizens identifying with a national minority unless otherwise prescribed by law. Latvia added a further proviso specifying that minority language use must be consistent with the Constitution and legislation regarding national language management policies (see Rannut, 2004b, for Estonia; Latvia Ministry of Foreign Affairs, 2006).

Less controversially, it should also be noted that a good deal of the work related to language attestation, language teaching and language for citizenship has been undertaken with substantial international assistance, including assistance from the UN Development Program and from the PHARE programme associated with entry into the EU, as well as from a number of instances of philanthropic assistance. Details may be found in Ministry of Foreign Affairs and Ministry of Education websites.

Language-in-education

Educational settings across the Baltic

Due to the differing national demographic compositions in the three Baltic countries, education policies vary considerably, and decisions are made with respect to the existence of a hybrid school population. Whilst higher education is provided in the titular languages, new school curricula were drawn up over the years in order to find adequate and useful solutions for these societies in transition. Across the Baltic, students from the main minority and immigrant communities are offered schooling in the medium of their first language, where the titular language is a compulsory subject. Whilst supporting first language instruction for children from those communities, all education models derive from a progressive change to the national language as the predominant one at university level. In each republic, pupils of non-mainstream schools are also required to take an exam in the titular language when graduating. As has been previously explained, these tests have been integrated with general language proficiency certifications that are a requirement for job seekers and for those wishing to pursue further education. A comparative study of various models of minority and immigrant language-medium education and the challenges and implications of bilingual schooling in the three Baltic Republics is provided in Hogan-Brun (2007b).

Attitudes of parents from the minority and immigrant communities towards the choice of schools for their offspring have changed gradually over the years. Seeing their children's future directly linked to success in the total society, they have increasingly started to send their offspring to mainstream schools

(Hogan-Brun, 2007a). As will be further elaborated, this move is stronger in Lithuania, but it is also found in Estonia. This trend has brought about a number of unexpected challenges, necessitating the formulation of appropriate educational policies to address particularly the need of teaching the national languages as second languages, or in mixed first language settings. Subsequently, new models of bilingual – and in Estonia, immersion – schooling at the primary and secondary levels were introduced as additional educational options. Teachers were offered training, curricula were formulated and textbooks were written to provide the necessary infrastructure. Minority schools, where instruction is chiefly held in the community languages, were retained alongside this new scheme. The nature of evolving educational provisions in each of the Baltic Republics is summarised in the ensuing paragraphs.

Lithuania. At present there are over 173 minority schools in Lithuania, located mainly in the densely multi-ethnic southeastern part of the republic and in the largest cities, especially in the capital, Vilnius, in the seaport, Klaipėda, and in Visaginas (a development next to the Ignalina nuclear power station). These community schools currently make up approximately nine per cent of all educational institutions in Lithuania: at present, 64 are Polish, 54 are Russian, 17 are Russian–Polish, 16 are Lithuanian-Russian, 13 are Lithuanian-Polish, six are Lithuanian-Russian-Polish, and one each are Belarusian, German and Jewish (see Table 4).

The medium of instruction in these schools has been, and in many cases continues to be, the minority languages, with some institutions offering a few subjects (geography, history or mathematics) in Lithuanian, plus Lithuanian as a compulsory subject. In Klaipėda's German school, some subjects are taught in German. The Jewish minority private religious school referred to in Table 4, Menachem

Table 4　Types of minority schools in Lithuania in 2004–2005

Number of schools	Type of school
64	Polish
54	Russian
17	Russian-Polish
16	Lithuanian-Russian
13	Lithuanian-Polish
6	Lithuanian-Russian-Polish
1	Belarusian
1	German
1	Jewish

Source: http://www.tmid.lt/index.php?page_id = 360.

Home, teaches mainly in Russian, with some Lithuanian, and Hebrew as a subject. The State Jewish school in Vilnius, established in 1989 and named after the Yiddish writer Sholom Aleichem, offers the general curriculum in Lithuanian, with additional explanations in Russian when required, alongside Judaic subjects (on the Torah, on Jewish history and traditions) as well as in Hebrew.

The rising demand amongst the minority population for speedy language acquisition as a means to integrate into the overall society has, however, entailed a number of unexpected educational challenges across the Baltic. In Lithuania's south eastern region where parents from ethnic communities have increasingly started to send their children to mainstream schools, numerous establishments found themselves with 60 to 70% non-Lithuanian speaking pupils per class. Such heterogenous environments turned out to be unsatisfactory for both students and their teachers. In response to this trend, Lithuania's Ministry of Education and Science took steps to promote the trialling of different models of schooling. In September 2001 it launched the project 'Development of Bilingualism' with the aim to provide for open multicultural education where the learning content is chosen to enhance pupils' bilingual development. Five bilingual models with some different directions and priorities were proposed for adoption by schools (see Table 5).

Table 5   Proposed models for bilingual schooling in Lithuania in August 2001

Model	Type of school	Educational aim	Number of schools
1	Lithuanian mainstream primary schools with a high proportion of pupils from ethnic minority communities	Initially offering some subjects in the ethnic language; plus lessons in the ethnic language and in Lithuanian as a second language offered.	5
2	Mixed secondary schools (Russian-Polish, Lithuanian-Polish, Lithuanian-Russian-Polish classes) with a small number of pupils	Where the language of instruction varies in the classes; aim: to offer some subjects in Lithuanian when the communicative competence in Lithuanian as a second language is sufficient.	3
3	Minority secondary schools	Offering 1–3 subjects in Lithuanian (up to 7 subjects in some schools).	14
4	Minority secondary schools	Offering 1–3 subjects in Lithuanian (up to 7 subjects in some schools), plus covering out-of-school activities.	10
5	All schools	Option to develop their individual model.	2

Source: Ministry of Education, Vilnius (unpublished data)

Table 5 shows that altogether 34 (Russian) schools have adopted a bilingual programme. Models 3 and 4 have proved particularly successful. Every establishment is free to adjust the chosen model according to staff qualifications and pupil needs. As yet, only two Polish schools have officially decided to embark on developing their own models, although, in practice, bilingual teaching is being practiced more widely (Kasatkina & Beresnevičiūtė, 2006: 31–48; for more information on bilingual education against a Baltic-wide perspective see Hogan-Brun & Ramonienė, 2004). About 24% of students from the minority communities study in Lithuanian-stream schools (Kalbų mokymo politikos aprašas, 2006: 67).

Post-1991 language related education policy reforms in Estonia and Latvia. In Estonia and Latvia, one central conflict has revolved around post-1991 language-in-education policies. The divided school systems inherited from the Soviet period both reflected and fuelled socio-political segregation. Education reforms were, therefore, launched in 1993 (Estonia) and 1995 (Latvia), planning the progressive introduction of Estonian and Latvian in Russian-medium elementary and secondary schools. As will be explained, implementation of the 'official-language-medium-only' policy is envisaged in both countries, with a transitional phase of *at least 60%* of subjects to be taught in the state language and *up to 40%* in the minority language, though subsequent events have made it probable this will be a permanent rather than transitional arrangement. These proposed changes raised severe protests amongst the Russian-speaking population, as was detailed in Part 3. Criticisms emerged in both countries regarding the feasibility of this reform *inter alia* on the grounds that secondary schools would not be ready to implement the law, for lack of proficiency in both Estonian and Latvian among Russian-speaking teachers and for lack of teaching material in those languages, and also because forced implementation would be detrimental to the quality of education. Estonian and Latvian authorities responded in various ways. Whilst in Estonia the proposed language-in-education changes were postponed until 2007, Latvia proceeded with this reform in 2004, fuelling protest actions from Russian-speaking movements and severe criticisms from Russia. Latvian society remained polarised on this issue: whilst some regarded the latest education reform as appropriate, others disagree with it fundamentally. The European Community appears to have tacitly acknowledged the specific post-communist 'situatedness' of Latvia by not objecting to its reform plans during the time of EU accession negotiations (see also Adrey, 2005: 465).

Latvia. Latvia's education system remained divided until the mid-1990s, and children attended either Latvian- or Russian-medium schools. Russian-speaking children were not expected to integrate into Latvian classes. Instead, Russian classes were created in Latvian establishments. As the number of Russophone students grew during the Soviet period, two-stream institutions were introduced, with Russian-medium and Latvian-medium classes respectively. Once demand had further increased, a switch to all-Russian schools was made (Priedīte, 2005: 409). During the Soviet period, Russian students attended school for 10 years, and Latvian pupils for 11 years, to learn Russian properly. The choice of establishment tended to categorise students and divide society.

Children who attended a Russian school (in Latvia) had more chances of success in the Soviet Union. If, on the other hand, parents chose a Latvian school, they and their offspring were labelled as 'narrow nationalists'. This separate Russian education system was perceived to be disengaged from the newly independent Latvian state and consequently to be located in a different informational and linguistic space. Hence the stabilisation of the language-in-education system in Latvia was and continues to be a politically explosive issue (Priedīte, 2005: 409).

In 1995 first steps were made to adapt the educational system to the changing post-Soviet situation. The existing legislation on education was amended, and clause 5 of the Education Law of the Republic of Latvia was revised, envisaging the teaching in the state language of two subjects at primary and of three subjects at secondary level in non-mainstream schools (these institutions amount to 40% of all educational establishments in total). In a subsequent revision of Article 9 dealing with the 'Language of Acquisition of Education', adopted on 29 October 1998, the position of Latvian was further strengthened. It was stated that '[...] each educatee shall learn the official language and take examinations testing his or her knowledge of the official language to the extent and in accordance with a procedure set by the Ministry of Education and Science' (*sic* in translated online version of the Law). Kersh (1997, 1998) offers detailed accounts of these early phases of educational transition in Latvia.

In 1998, the Law on Education and General Education was enacted and, in 1999, models for bilingual education in Russian-medium schools were approved. This programme was meant to ensure the teaching of 50% and more of the education contents in Latvian and bilingually from Grade 9 onwards. The overall aims of the bilingual education system are to provide Russians and other minority ethnic groups with an opportunity:

(1) to access the government's general education programme;
(2) to learn the official state language;
(3) to maintain other (minority) languages and cultures.

Such elaborated educational programmes in all the state and local government schools could be implemented in Latvia once the Ministry had licensed them. The initiation of a transition to bilingual education for primary schools was approved by Latvia in 1999 and also by internationally recognised experts. Five models of bilingual education are currently in use (see Table 6).

Methodological and language support for institutions that have adopted a bilingual approach has been provided through the National Program for Latvian Language Teaching (NPLLT; www.lvavp.lv), created in 1996. Over the years, NPLLT have produced a range of innovative teaching aids for various educational levels and types of specialisation. Apart from teacher and language training, and the development of bilingual methodologies, they also organise theme-based mixed (Russian/Latvian) camps, which have helped to reduce inter-ethnic tensions to some extent.

According to Priedīte (2005: 422), discussions tend to polarise around two extremes regarding bilingual education, offered at the lower levels of minority schooling. On the one hand, many parents, quoting official state policy statements, claim that bilingual education is needed to promote the Latvian language,

Table 6 Latvia's models of bilingual education in 2004/2005

Model	Type of school: primary/middle grades	Educational aim	Adopted by schools
1	1–9	In Grade 9 most subjects are taught in Latvian, but minority language and literature as a special subject must be guaranteed.	15%
2	1–9	In Grade 9 both Latvian and minority languages are used, the students are guaranteed to use the language of their choice in exams; minority language and literature as a special subject must be guaranteed.	13%
3	1–9	In Grade 9 a transition from minority language to Latvian is realised; minority language and literature as a special subject must be guaranteed.	42%
4	1–9	In Grade 9 at least 10–11 subjects are taught in Latvian or bilingually, all subjects in Grade 1–4 are taught only in the minority language.	11%
5	All schools:	Option to develop their individual model.	19%

Source: Ministry of Education and Science http://www.izm.lv:8080/en/default.htm.

integration and equal opportunities in Latvia, thus providing all inhabitants with the same starting positions and access to the labour market (see also Hogan-Brun & Ramonienė, 2004: 71f). On the other hand, bilingual measures have been developed to discriminate against minorities, or implemented to solve problems relating to the teaching of the Latvian language in minority schools. Some parents generally approve of bilingual education, but not in their own children's classes. This position suggests that, for their own offspring, parents are asking for the continuation of a general education in Russian as before, an attitude that has been reinforced by opponents of the education reform.

Overall, there has been an increase of Russian-speaking children attending Latvian schools (from 22% in 2002 to 32% in 2003; see also Table 7). According to a survey carried out amongst families with school-age children, the most significant factor influencing their decision regarding the choice of school for their offspring was linked to their own competence in the state language. The higher the level of respondents' knowledge of Latvian, the greater the probability that their children will be registered in a Latvian school (Priedīte, 2005: 419).

From 1997 to 2003, consultations were held with Latvian scholars, teachers and international institutions, including the OSCE and EU language policy bodies, with regard to the Latvian experience and international practice in implementing the policy of minority education. The programme that was elaborated in this preparation phase was meant to ensure the teaching of 50% and more of the education contents in Latvian and bilingually from Grade 9 onwards.

Table 7   Number of students by language of instruction

Academic year	1995/1996	1999/2000	2002/2003	2005/2006
Latvian	203,607	239,163	237,425	205,189
Russian	132,540	120,925	101,486	77,471
Other minorities*	1,513	1,344	1,397	1.287
Total	337,660	361,432	340,308	283,947
Percent learning in Latvian	60.3	66.2	69.8	72.3

Note: in some minority schools the language of instruction is predominantly either Latvian or Russian.
Source: Ministry of Foreign Affairs of the Republic of Latvia http://www.am.gov. lv/en/policy/4641/4642/4643/).

This consideration subsequently led to a widely discussed education reform and a revision of section 3 of article 9 of the Education Law, which remains controversial for many to this day. According to this amendment, acquisition of the study curriculum in the official language had to be effected according to the proportion of three-fifths (60%) of the total study load in all state education establishments at upper secondary school level (Grades 10–12, that is from 16 to 18 years of age) as from September 2004 onwards.

- The subjects to be taught in Latvian were specified in a programme with the aim to divide the curriculum into three groups as regards the language of instruction: the first group includes subjects that are mandatory for all schools. These subjects (e.g. mathematics, economics, informatics, history) should be taught in the state language.
- The second group covers subjects that are mandatory according to the specialisation of the school (e.g. science, humanities, vocational, or general). These subjects can be taught in the minority language as determined by the school concerned.
- The third group entails subjects that are optional for all schools and allows for the language of instruction to be a matter of free choice.

An interim phase was foreseen, during which pupils of Grades 11–12 would continue their studies according to the demands of the previous regulations entailing three subjects taught in the state language. These schools were then offered three more years to prepare for education according to the 60/40 pattern at the upper secondary level (from Grades 10 to 12), which will come into force in all grades by 2007/2008.

These new rules became the subject of heated debate in Latvia, which produced an increase in inter-ethnic tensions. In their analysis of the reform, Galbreath and Galvin (2005: 453) argue that the style in which the policy was implemented was partly the result of the Soviet legacy of 'show politics' on post-Soviet policies. According to the Latvian government, however, the reform, which it had to legitimate, was necessary to ensure that the numerous Russian-speaking residents learned Latvian and integrated (Galbreath & Galvin, 2005: 453). These Russian-speaking residents were mostly Soviet-era immigrants from Russia, but also from Ukraine and Belarus, who together amount to approximately 36% of the overall population. Resident Russians, who maintained that these changes would undermine their culture and language, contested the amended law. During EU accession negotiations, resident Russians seized the opportunity to appeal for minority rights in Brussels, demanding Latvia's ratification of the Council of Europe Framework Convention. Moscow's attempts to instrumentalise the situation further inflamed exchanges between Latvians and Russians.

The debates surrounding the recent (largely politicised) education reform in Latvia have been discussed in part 3, and covered in an extensive literature (Adrey, 2005; Galbreath & Galvin, 2005; Hogan-Brun 2006; 2007a; Priedīte, 2005).

Estonia. Educational transition in Estonia, analysed by Kreitzberg and Priimägi (1997), lasted until the mid-1990s. By then, and with EU support through the PHARE programme, the curriculum had been reviewed and revised, and special programmes in school management had also been developed. As had been observable in Latvia and Lithuania, the desire for more, and better, education had grown extensively during the period of these initial reforms.

The use of the language of education in Estonian schools has been a concern for both speakers of the titular language as well as those of other languages, and this concern is inherently linked to conflicting interests of state language promotion and minority language maintenance. This dilemma is reflected in the Constitution where Article 37(4) states that all persons have the right to instruction in Estonian, whilst also granting the right of educational institutions established for ethnic minorities to choose their own language of instruction. Article 6 of the Language Law guarantees education in, and acquisition of, a foreign language, according to the procedures prescribed by law. A similar principle had been adopted earlier in the Law on Education in 1992.

The use of a language as the medium of instruction in other types of schools is regulated in the corresponding laws:

- The Law on Private Schools gives the owner of a school the right to determine the language of the school (Article 14), and requires that Estonian be taught from the third grade onwards.
- The Law on Vocational Schools prescribes Estonian as the language of education (Article 18/3) with some exceptions.
- The Law on Universities prescribes Estonian as the language of instruction (Article 22/8), leaving the use of other languages to be determined by the University Council.

The demand for Estonian-language learning opportunities among Russian-speaking communities is increasing. Currently Estonian as a second language teaching strategy implemented in Russian schools has not brought about the required returns. In particular, the majority of high school graduates from

Russian-language schools do not have sufficient Estonian language skills to be competitive in the job market or to continue their studies in institutions of higher learning (Verschik, 2005b: 304). Therefore, Estonian-medium schools are now highly valued among Russian parents who seek opportunities to help their children become bilingual.

In order to facilitate better acquisition of Estonian, language immersion schooling has been introduced as a national program. This programme follows the Canadian model (Swain & Johnson, 1997) and is implemented and coordinated by the Language Immersion Centre (http://www.kke.ee/index.php?lang=eng). Around one-third of non-Estonian schools (26 schools in 2006–2007), with approximately 2000 children enrolled, apply language immersion methods. One school offers partial immersion. Two models operate side by side: early immersion, introduced in 2000, and late immersion, following four years later. In early immersion, the amount of instruction in Estonian exceeds 50% of the total curriculum. Late immersion starts in Grade 6, where one third of instruction is conducted in Estonian, with the overall proportion rising to three quarters of instruction in the ensuing grades. The aim of language immersion is for pupils to acquire equally good skills in their native and the titular language. Enrolled pupils will tend to acquire successfully the knowledge and skills set in the national curriculum (http://www.hm.ee/index.php?047187).

The language of instruction in pre-school childcare is Estonian in 78% of the total number of institutions. Since 2000, kindergartens (for children of 5–6 years of age) and Grade 1 levels are obliged to teach Estonian. Of these establishments 78 (half of which are situated in Tallinn and the remainder mostly in other urban areas) work in Russian, while 50 operate in both languages. Some personnel in Russian-medium pre-school educational institutions have low competence in Estonian and are offered extensive in-service training. Nine kindergartens have adopted the Estonian early immersion programme. In other kindergartens and pre-school courses a Russian-medium language environment is maintained, with Estonian as a subject. In one institution in Tallinn the language of instruction is English. Three-quarters of preschool children attend Estonian-medium childcare institutions. An increasing number of them have Russian as their home language, reflecting parental attitudes approving immersing them in the mainstream from an early age.

Primary schools face similar challenges. Currently, some 5% of children with a first language other than Estonian are enrolled in Estonian-medium institutions. To prevent a potential educational impasse, the number of Russian-speaking pupils in Estonian-medium educational institutions has now been limited, and alternative programmes are being started for these children. In 2006–2007, 15% of all primary schools are Russian-medium, while 5% are mixed language establishments. The former are mainly situated in and around the capital (Tallinn), and in northeastern Estonia. In other areas such establishments are rare or entirely absent, due to the marginal number of pupils with ethnic Russian backgrounds (http://www.hm.ee/index.php?047183). Several Russian institutions have been closed down, arguably because the number of Russian-speaking pupils is said to have been almost halved since independence due to decreasing birth rates in that population, but also due to increasing parental choice of Estonian-medium schools. The Soviet time monolingual Russian-medium educational system with Estonian taught mainly as a subject has been maintained. Some Russian-medium establishments use Estonian for teaching certain subjects (history, geography), in partial immersion.

At the secondary level, about 23% of pupils study through the medium of Russian. Many of these end up with an insufficient knowledge of Standard Estonian on leaving school, mostly because of the scope and methods of teaching Estonian used and because of a lack of relevant language competence amongst teachers. It is estimated that, at present, 83% of these Russian-based institutions provide bilingual teaching of sorts in Estonia, but with varying quality. To support the learning of Estonian in non-Estonian language-medium schools, state and local governments are obliged to create conditions for an eventual transition to teaching up to 60% of the total curriculum at the secondary level in the titular language. It was originally planned to introduce such measures (mirroring those recently introduced in Latvia) in 2004. However, in response to heavy public criticisms, the reform was postponed to 2007 in line with the Basic School and Upper Secondary School Act. It is hoped that this interim period will allow for the curricula of the Russian-medium and Estonian schools to be brought to the same standard (Korts, 2002: 40). The implementation of this reform is likely to present some considerable challenges since 78% of teachers employed in Russian-medium general education schools are Russians, a number of whom will still be likely to lack the necessary language skills to carry out quality tuition in Estonian by then. On the other hand, considerably fewer teachers (about 2000 fewer) will be needed in the forthcoming years than are those currently involved in teaching (3200), thus supply seemingly exceeds demand in this employment market. During this phase of preparation, Russian teachers are, however, entitled to receive support for extra curricular activities and additional teacher training.

The objective of this reform is to offer opportunities for language practice and to provide the pupils whose native language is not Estonian with equal opportunities for acquiring higher education and for succeeding in the labour market. Estonian was specified as the language of instruction for five subjects, using a gradual transition from previous languages to Estonian. In addition, schools were required to select two more subjects to be mediated through the titular language. The transition commences with the teaching of one subject in Estonian, with another one to be added annually. Teaching begins with Estonian literature, geography, music, social theory and Estonian history in Estonian, the latter subjects having been selected because the subjects are essential in the preparation for applying for citizenship.

The action plan for the transition was approved by the Government in 2006, covering the following main activities:

- training of teachers and school management for those upper secondary schools where the language of instruction was Russian;
- development of a motivation system for teachers;
- preparation of teaching materials;
- information for the public;
- coordination of activities;
- assessment of the results.

According to this plan, several hundred employees from Russian-language schools will be trained in the short run (http://www.hm.ee/index.php?047181).

A national programme for the education of new immigrant children has also been drafted, adding a new perspective to emerging educational considerations. Linguistic integration of new immigrants into Estonian society will be arranged according to a special program, including teacher in-service training and language materials for students (cf. Rannut *et al.*, 2003) and teachers, in the form of a methodology handbook (Rannut, 2003).

Under the law, Estonian is the language of tuition in vocational schools. However, as an exception, vocational training may also be carried out in Russian, in about a third of all these establishments. In Russian-language vocational schools or in Russian-language study groups there, Estonian is compulsory only for students studying during the years of compulsory education. The state does not regulate the teaching of Estonian in Russian-language vocational training. The bulk of school-leavers from Russian-language vocational schools, however, find it difficult to work and to communicate in the Estonian-language environment; thus, they become vulnerable to employment changes. Plans, among other things, foresee a considerable increase in the scope of teaching Estonian and Estonian-medium teaching, and a transition to integrated teaching in institutions with two languages of tuition.

Language as a subject

As previously mentioned, the titular languages of all three Baltic states now are compulsory through all levels of schooling to the end of the final secondary education or the vocational qualification examinations. In addition, all public tertiary education is only in the titular language, with a small number of international higher education institutions (e.g. some business schools) offering courses mainly in English. The introduction of the titular languages into the Russian stream schooling system has been a particular challenge in terms of conceptualisation of second language methodology (an entirely new experience in this region), materials preparation, teacher education and curriculum organisation.

At the same time, the necessity to learn other languages has been widely recognised and encouraged, echoing the situation before World War II when more than one foreign language was the usual fare in education. Across the Baltic, students are now offered a greater range at schools such as English, French and German as a first choice (and English, French, German, Russian, Italian or, in some establishments, some other languages as the first choice). In the mid-1990s, a policy decision was taken not to offer Russian as a first foreign language any longer. In popularity it now lags behind English, which enjoys high prestige amongst students. Russian is, however, still provided as a second foreign language, as it will no doubt continue to be a *lingua franca* in the Baltic and among all people from the former Soviet republics. The future range of schooled bilingualism among the population is therefore sure to expand – albeit mostly on a diglossic level – and involve a promotion of Western-oriented language and cultural sensitivity (Kaplan & Baldauf, 1997: 219).

Latvia. As can be seen from the previous description, the titular language is now taught as a core subject in all mainstream school systems, Russian school or other minority schools, with a requirement for a pass in the final Latvian language examination to complete secondary education. Latvian is also the exclusive language of public higher education, though a limited number of non-government or foreign higher education institutions use other languages, mostly English (as in the Stockholm School of Economics in Riga).

In Latvia, foreign languages are taught from the first year of the nine-year primary school curriculum, with a second foreign language introduced in mid-primary school. These two languages are then continued throughout general secondary education (years 10 to 12). Russian has not disappeared, but now is arrayed alongside other choices.

In Grade 3, approximately 12.5% of the time in the curriculum is spent on a foreign language, compared to the EU average of 15.7%. By Grade 6 this figure rises to 20% on a foreign language (as opposed to 12.3% in the EU) and, in Grade 9, 14.7% of time is devoted to a foreign language, compared to the EU average of 13.2%. This strong language learning pattern is continued to the end of secondary education: in 2002/2003, a massive 92.3% of pupils in Year 12 were learning English, with negligible difference between those in Latvian-stream schools and those in Russian-stream schools. Also 49.7% of students were studying German, 3.9% French and 44% Russian (Latvia, Department of Education and Science, 2004). These figures reflect the fact that many pupils tend to choose more than one foreign language at school so figures can be greater than 100%.

A crucial practice in Latvia, as in all three Baltic states, has been the development of a titular language-as-second-language methodology, materials and support. As the discussion of school systems shows, the steady increase in the number of Russian-medium schools during the Soviet period resulted in no significant teaching of the titular languages in these schools, leading to a divided educational and linguistic space. This resulted in an overwhelming need to retrain teachers and to introduce new materials and methodologies to achieve the intended educational reforms. The National Program for Latvian Language Teaching (NPLLT), introduced in 1996, worked on several different objectives:

- developing professional training activities for teachers;
- producing Latvian as a second language methodologies and materials for schools;
- teaching Latvian as a second language (LAT2) to individuals in various occupational groups who have not attended Latvian-medium education but who are none the less required to meet standards of language competence as part of language attestation procedures;
- stimulating public debate and contact with community groups on language issues.

For its first four years, the NPLLT operated under UN Development Program (UNDP) supervision, then it was fully administered by the Department of Education and Science. This work had to be carried out under circumstances far more politicised and antagonistic than is the norm with second language programmes. Despite this difficulty and the political clouds that still surround school reform in Latvia, the programme has achieved some notable international recognition; both the Council of Europe and the OSCE have commented favourably on its achievements, and the model it constructed is being used in other post-Soviet states, including Georgia and Moldova (Latvia Ministry of Foreign Affairs, 2006). The National Agency of Latvian Language Training (NALLT) (www.lvava.lv) is now continuing this work.

Estonia. Since 1992, Estonian as a second language has increasingly been taught in the educational system. The goal is to promote competence in Estonian on the Common European Framework level B2 by the end of primary education and level C1 at the outset of secondary schooling. A compulsory national examination has been introduced for secondary education. As has been the case in the sister republics, this objective has necessitated the development of curricula for Estonian as a second language and relevant teaching methods and materials. Teacher training has also been made available (mainly in the shape of in-service provision) to enable qualified teachers to upgrade their teaching.

Compared to Latvia, national programmes for the implementation of these goals have been introduced only partially; thus, the results have been modest. During recent years, however, attitudes have changed and the Estonian Ministry of Education as well as several municipalities (e.g. the capital Tallinn) have proposed detailed plans, provided financial support and actively supported the retraining of teachers at Russian schools in order to launch bilingual programmes.

At the present time, Estonian is the main medium of instruction across all levels in over 500 schools in the country. During the last 15 years, however, the overall amount of the teaching of Estonian as a native language has gradually decreased. This decrease has produced a concern among teachers of Estonian with respect to quality loss in relation to the literary standard of Estonian as well as to functional and critical literacy. Hence, a new curriculum that offers an increased focus on orthography, text comprehension and literature was introduced from the academic year 2002/2003. The number of lessons per week has been set at 19 for primary education in Grades 1–3, with a decrease to 15 in Grades 4–6 and to 12 in Grades 7–9. At the secondary school level (Grades 10–12), six courses, each consisting of 35 lessons respectively, are offered both on the subject of the Estonian language and also on literature in Estonian.

As already mentioned, Estonian is also the main medium of instruction in higher education. Some educational programmes are taught in English, and several private higher education institutions use Russian. In order to improve the quality of language used in management and business, a course on practical Estonian (involving tasks linked to text creation and processing) will shortly be made mandatory for all students. For those coming from secondary schools with a language of instruction other than Estonian, an introductory course on academic Estonian language is provided.

Lithuania. Lithuanian is taught as a compulsory subject in all schools throughout Lithuania. In primary education, 34% of the time in the curriculum is spent on Lithuanian; in basic schools 18%, and at the secondary level 11–16% (depending on student choice). The curriculum for ethnic minority schools sets the percentage of time to be spent on Lithuanian-as-a-second-language at a lower level; respectively 11%, 10% and 10–12% (Kalbŭ mokymo politikos aprašas, 2006: 84). According to the Law on Higher Education, the only language of instruction in public higher education institutions is Lithuanian, with some exceptions for special study programmes (e.g. English or other foreign languages) and courses for foreign/exchange students.

The newly emerging needs have encouraged reform in the teaching of Lithuanian-as-a- second-language at all levels. A shift from a hitherto predominantly structural focus to one that emphasises the importance of language in use has taken place and changed general principles of teaching, learning and assessment. The hitherto locally little known communicative approach, based on the premise that the language to be taught should be related to the learners' immediate and future needs and that students should be prepared for authentic communication, has taken root and has had a widespread effect on classroom practice and on language testing throughout Lithuania.

These insights have led to the development of specifications of learning objectives for Lithuanian-as-a-second-language at the following three levels: Threshold (*'Slenkstis'*: 1997), Waystage (*'Pusiaukelė'*: forthcoming) and Vantage (*'Aukštuma'*: 2000). This terminology, initially developed by van Els, and the specifications were elaborated within and published under the Council of Europe's programme for the promotion of language learning. The series offers guidance for effective learning of Lithuanian-as-a-second-language relevant to the needs of students who want to acquire the Lithuanian language for communicative purposes.

The Threshold level is the key element in the series, since it attempts to identify the minimal linguistic level that enables a learner to deal with the more predictable situations of daily life, both transactional and interactional as an independent agent. A lower level specification, Waystage, is intended as an early learning objective and provides the learner with a broad range of resources at a very elementary stage of survival Lithuanian in the most predictable situations. Vantage is the third and highest level within the programme series.

These three levels are now in place; they offer a three-tiered approach to language teaching for learners from basic to advanced stages. The guidelines have been used for the design of new curricula and for writing language-learning materials. A new set of textbooks for all grades of minority schools (at primary, lower-secondary and upper-secondary level) is currently being developed. Most of these textbooks have already been published and are being used in schools. Additional textbooks and other teaching materials are currently being developed for adult teaching (see Hogan-Brun & Ramoniené´, 2004).

Since 1992, foreign language instruction in the Lithuanian school system has undergone some important transformations. At present, the first foreign language (English, German or French) can be taught from the second grade, but becomes compulsory as of the fourth grade. A second choice (English, German or French, Russian or other) is compulsory from Grades 6–10, but is not required beyond that, except for the 'humanities' profile, which maintains the language in secondary school (Grades 11 and 12). A third language choice is optional at secondary school level. The number of hours allotted to a foreign language can vary from 2–4 hours per week, depending not only on the level of studies, but also on local administration and students' preferences.

The number of schools introducing early foreign language teaching on a voluntary basis in the second year of primary school is constantly increasing.

In 2005–2006, 47.3% of all schools were already implementing non-compulsory early foreign language teaching. The Lithuanian Ministry of Education and Science has initiated research in order to determine whether Lithuanian schools are ready to introduce early foreign language teaching. As a result of the findings, an action plan for the implementation of compulsory early foreign language teaching beginning in 2008 has been developed.

In basic schools and in gymnasia, English is the most widely chosen first foreign language. Russian ranks in second place. Though the status of Russian in Lithuania has been drastically modified, it has, up to the present, retained a strong position as a foreign language in the Lithuanian general education schools. Given the fact that a second foreign language is a compulsory element in the programme at the basic school level (from the sixth to the tenth grade), the dominant pattern for the school population is to choose English as a first and Russian as a second foreign language. This placement of Russian may be due to various factors:

- the availability of teachers;
- the fact that a generation of parents who have learned Russian can help their children with the language;
- the still occasional use of Russian as one of the working languages in some trades and firms;
- the awareness that contacts have been redefined with a powerful neighbour.

Numbers for the optional third language are low, since they represent choices made only by students from the 'humanities' profile. These choices concern almost exclusively the same four languages (English, German, French, Russian). Other languages, whether Romance (Spanish, Italian) or Scandinavian (Danish, Swedish), geographically close (Polish, Latvian) or distant (Chinese, Japanese) are not very common.

Titular language assessment

Proficiency assessment systems for the titular language as a second language to be used both at schools and in adult teaching institutions have been developed and introduced in all three Baltic states. Access to the state language is considered a prerequisite for equality in social and economic participation. Since the titular language is now the means of all (oral and written) communication in all public institutions, industry and public service establishments, its mastery has become vital for those who hold a professional position or wish to acquire a new one.

In Lithuania in 1992 the government approved three qualifying categories of state language competence for adults as well as the mechanisms for applying them to prospective public and state employees. A system of adult language testing was created and later approved by the State Commission of the Lithuanian Language. Since 1993, a total of 92,720 citizens have taken the State Language Tests at various levels, and 80,714 (87%) have passed the test they have taken (see Figure 2). A relatively large number of people who finished non-Lithuanian-medium schools before 1991 have since learnt the state language and received certificates of proficiency in Lithuanian.

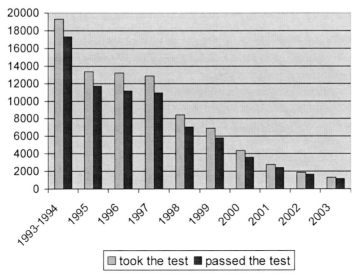

Figure 2 Dynamics of state language testing since 1993 in Lithuania
Source: http://www.pprc.lt/vkm/duomenys/chart.asp

At the secondary level, school examinations in Lithuanian as the State Language have been introduced, and students who pass the appropriate test receive certificates equivalent to those of State Language Competence for adults. In 2001 the examination in the State Language was, for the first time, administered at the centralised national level. Language proficiency of candidates is tested in four areas of language activity: listening, speaking, reading and writing. The purpose of this examination is to assess the communicative competence of the learners. Candidates of non-Lithuanian origin who pass such an examination are able to use Lithuanian in all Lithuanian higher educational establishments, universities, and in all fields of study: humanities, social sciences, natural sciences and technologies. School and adult proficiency levels are shown in Table 8.

A new idea recently proposed by the Ministry of Education and Science is to introduce a single examination of Lithuanian as a state language both for minority and mainstream language schools in 2008. Guidelines for this reform are

Table 8 Lithuanian language assessment

Ethnic minorities schools		Adult learners
	A 2 *Pusiaukelė*	1st Category of State Language Competence
Final examination of the basic school	B 1 *Slenkstis*	2nd Category of State Language Competence
Final examination of the secondary school	B 2 *Aukštuma*	3rd Category of State Language Competence

currently being prepared, and it is planned to implement this change by 2007. However, a number of complex problems relating to differences in the curricula of teaching Lithuanian as a Native Language and Lithuanian as a State Language still need to be addressed (Ramonienė, 2005: 227). Results from research initiated by the Lithuanian Ministry of Education and Science in 2005-2006 concerning the single examination of Lithuanian as a state language for both ethnic minority and mainstream schools point to the fact that students who attend minority schools are probably not ready for a single common examination of proficiency in the Lithuanian language.

The situation in Estonia and Latvia in respect to titular language competence requirements for occupations has already been covered in Part 3; consequently, only a brief recapitulation seems necessary. Interestingly, while larger quantities of political discussion surrounded this area of language attestation in Estonia and Latvia, there is great similarity in language policy among the three Baltic States. The levels, profile and pace of language attestation as reported for Lithuania is almost exactly identical with those of the other two states. The only material difference is that in Lithuania such language attestation was only for personnel in the public sector, while in Estonia and Latvia it initially covered all persons having public contact in both the public and private sectors.

A number of similarities across the board in occupational language competence can be observed:

- The identification of personnel needing to pass such occupational language tests was based not on ethnicity or citizenship criteria but on whether or not personnel had attended the titular language education system; those who had gone through the Russian school system had to provide proof of their competence in the national languages, even if they were members of the titular group.
- In all three Baltic states, the period of most extensive testing occurred from the early to the mid-1990s when over 200,000 tests were taken and passed in Estonia, more than twice as many in Latvia and about 25,000 in Lithuania. More recently, the numbers have decreased significantly; for example, in Latvia by 2005 only around 5,000 tests were being administered each year (see the Centre for Curriculum Development and Examination at http://isec.gov.lv).
- Initially the three Baltic States did have slightly different formulations of the levels of language proficiency required for various grades of personnel (Estonia tested at six levels, Latvia and Lithuania at three levels); however, the occupations identified for testing at the various levels were similar across the three countries. In Estonia, for example, the six levels ranged from A (basic listening comprehension of the 800 most common words and expression) to F (full proficiency in the Estonian language) (Verschik, 2005: 300). More recently, all three states have adopted the Common European Framework proficiently levels as described for Lithuania.
- Matching the Lithuanian experience, there have also been moves in each country to strengthen titular language learning in Russian stream schools, including success in the final secondary school examinations; those passing this final examination in the titular language subject are seen as having the equivalent of the occupational language attestation.

Language practices

The preceding language management practices have resulted in drastic changes in the linguistic situation across the Baltic since the early 1990s. In addition to their official status, the titular languages have gradually regained their prestige, and hence have regained their place in the political and social life respectively in each of the countries. The range of language laws that were introduced during the transition years across the Baltic states effectively redressed the Soviet-time language hierarchy, expanding the sociolinguistic function of the titular languages while at the same time providing protection for the languages and cultures of the national minorities. Overviews of emerging language practices in each republic are presented below.

Native language practices
Estonian as a native language. Estonia has a population of 1.35 million. Estonians comprise the bulk (about 70% in 2005) of the society. As language loyalty among Estonians is around 98%, that number roughly corresponds to the number of speakers of Estonian as a native language. (Some people from other ethnic groups have also switched to Estonian). Other major communities include Russians (almost a quarter of the total), Ukrainians, Belarusians and Ingrians (Finns). Altogether there are 145 different ethnic groups. Most (97%) of the non-Estonians residing in Estonia are immigrants who came to live in the country after World War II and their families. More than 60% of them are settled in and around Tallinn, the capital, and almost 30% live in northeastern Ida-Virumaa, adjacent to Russia. Autochthonous ethnic minority groups are small in size, comprising of:

- Russians (mostly of Old Orthodox roots) on the shore of Lake Peipsi (*ca* 39,000),
- Ingrians (8000),
- Tatars (3000),
- Jews (2500),
- Germans (1700),
- Roma (600–1500), and
- Swedes (300–1500).

According to 2000 census data, the number of people belonging to third nationalities has decreased considerably during the last 10 years, comprising 81,000 persons. Fewer than 40% have sustained the language of their ethnic affiliation, with most others shifting to Russian and, during recent years, to Estonian. Thus the number of Russian mother tongue speakers is almost 400,000, which is considerably higher than that of ethnic Russians (330,000), at the cost of third nationalities. Knowledge of the Estonian language too has increased modestly. According to the results of the census, the share of non- Estonians who are able to speak Estonian has increased steadily over recent years, from 14% in 1989 to 37% in 2000.

The various language communities are distributed unevenly throughout the country. Estonian, which is spoken everywhere, functions in four different types of language environment (Rannut, 2005, Rannut, Ü., 2002, 2005):

- Estonian provides the sole linguistic environment across the greater part of Estonia's territory, with the exception of major cities, the urban areas of Harjumaa and Ida-Virumaa and the western shore of Lake Peipsi.

- Estonian competes with Russian in the environment of stratified linguistic pluralism in most cities where Russian immigrant communities are situated (Tallinn, Tartu, Pärnu, Haapsalu, Kehra, Loksa, etc.) and where there are modest contacts between the two communities, with slowly emerging Russian-speaking ghettos.
- On the western shore of Lake Peipsi (Mustvee, Kallaste) where a traditional Russian minority is situated, the Estonian and Russian language environments tend to co-exist harmoniously.
- Estonian is marginalised (with less than 20% of speakers) in some towns of Ida-Virumaa (Narva, Sillamäe, etc.) where immigrants constitute a majority. Altogether, Estonians form a minority in six towns and four rural communes.

Both Estonian and Russian cover most functional domains, with the exception of state administration, which has moved entirely to Estonian. (Since 1992, the Estonian parliament, *Riigikogu*, has ceased to provide translations in Russian). A concise overview of language practices in different social spheres is presented:

- In the courts of law, Estonian is used in most instances. Interpretation is provided for Russian-speaking individuals who have broken the law. Sometimes Russian is used, usually depending on the locality (or language environment) and the language preference of the charged person. If a third language happens to be an individual's first language, an interpreter is provided. Proficiency in Estonian is required of all the judges, prosecutors and lawyers. The National Court operates only in Estonian.
- In education, Russian is represented at primary, secondary and tertiary level (mostly in private institutions) and also in vocational and special schools. As noted previously, the Russian-medium educational system has been shrinking because of the diminishing number of pupils.
- In industry, the language used among blue-collar employees depends on the linguistic environment, while white-collar employees generally communicate in Estonian. In the primarily Russian-speaking Ida-Virumaa region as well as in some other urban areas, Russian is used among the white-collar staff to a significant extent, as the provisions of the Language Law apply to the working language of an enterprise only in such areas as book-keeping for external audit, communications with shoppers and external communications in Estonia.
- In the service sector, requirements demand sufficient proficiency in Estonian for interaction with clients. However, language use is somewhat flexible as service staff are supposed to switch to the preferred language of a customer if at all possible.
- In agriculture, which employs an essentially Estonian-speaking rural population, the language used is Estonian.
- In research and higher education, Estonian is the main means of communication for domestic use. English is used in science globally, while Finnish and Russian regionally. Russian has lost its primary position. This situation is also reflected in scientific publications.
- In addition to Estonian, Russian is also widely used in unofficial communication in such functional spheres as rail and sea transportation,

communication, and the corrections system, where a substantial part of lower-level workers and clerks are of Russian ethnic background. As a consequence, Russian remains a major communicative vehicle for the greater part of the Russian-speaking population.

In general, the Estonian language is used in all spheres of life. In some domains, its position has weakened somewhat against the background of globalization and the development of an information based society. There is also a decrease in the number of native speakers of Estonian as a result of lower birth rates and emigration.

Latvian as a native language. The degree of attention given to the politics of language and the measures taken to safeguard the national language in Latvia have tended to draw attention away from diversity within Latvia itself, resulting in a consequent sidelining of attention to dialects and linguistic diversity. The Language Law prescribes the standard of Latvian in one single instance as 'the existing norms of the literary language'; norms of orthography and correctness are strongly adhered to. This conservatism is both historical, being a marked feature of pre-war Latvian linguistics (and not of that language alone), but also political, as a strong adherence to literary norms was an important means of limiting the influence of Russian during the Soviet period (Metuzāle-Kangere & Ozolins, 2005: 324–326 & 334). Spoken language has always been judged in light of this norm, and only recently has there begun to be an interest in actual first language usage in a descriptive rather than a normative sense (Lauze, 2004). The first intergenerational studies of spoken language are beginning to appear, but such studies still have had limited circulation (Ernstone, 2001).

In contrast to this stress on standard Latvian literary language, those concerned with dialects and variation have enjoyed little of the limelight in the post-Soviet period, and research, public policy and citizens' movements have only lately begun to address issues concerning the neglected dialects.

Latvia previously had a strong tradition in dialectology, maintained even during the Soviet years. A good deal of the traditional attention was paid to the Latgalian language in the south-east of Latvia, a region that often shared Lithuanian and Latvian influences; for example, this area is largely Catholic (as is Lithuania, and as opposed to the rest of nominally Lutheran Latvia), and the language spoken here has some features of Lithuanian orthography and phonetics. The Language Law supports 'the maintenance, protection and development of the Latgalian written language as a historic variant of the Latvian language' (Section 3 (4)), a formulation that can be worrying because of its stress on *written* (i. e. literary) language, and the mention of its being a 'historic variant' paying more attention to its past than to its present status as a lived and spoken language. Indeed, Latgalian has struggled to have even this limited legislative support realised, given little curriculum or other support for Latgalian schools, and no official enthusiasm for Latgalian becoming recognised as one of the regional languages of Europe. (See the sharp exchanges on this in 'Latvia: Tongues Wag At Riga Conference' www.minelres.lv/minelres/archive/05022001-18:08:48-25382.html). Latgalian author Cibuls (2004) refers to his language as being ground between the millstones of educational and language politics.

Lithuanian as a native language. Lithuanian is now the dominant language in Lithuania. It has several regional variations, and the majority of the country's resident population consider it to be their first language. Standard Lithuanian, which dates back about one hundred years, has regained the level of a modern and multifunctional language. It is used in all spheres of public life, in education, and in the media. (For more information on the standardisation and modernisation of Lithuanian see Dini, 2000: 353-356; Hogan-Brun & Ramonienė, 2002; Palionis, 1995; Zinkevičius, 1992).

In informal and semi-formal contexts, regional and urban variants are also used. Two major dialect groups are distinguished: *Aukštaičių* (Highlanders' dialect) and *Žemaičių* (Lowlanders' dialect or Samogitian). Some major linguistic differences exist between these varieties diminishing their mutual intelligibility. All regional dialects and sub-dialects are widely spoken by people of differing ages and social groups, particularly in rural areas and in smaller towns. Regional dialects and sub-dialects are also used in the private and semi-public spheres, in bigger towns and by more than 10% of Vilnius residents, according to the Survey of Vilnius (2004).

The last 10 to 15 years have seen marked changes as regards the perceived status of dialects in Lithuania. Initially, following the restitution of independence, there was a strong focus on corpus planning, and on the protection and further development of standard Lithuanian. The learning and teaching of Lithuanian was pitted against dialects generally, but favoured the *Vakarų aukštaičių* variant as the basis of the standard. This dialect was reputed to be 'the most correct Lithuanian dialect' and that view has put native speakers of other varieties at a slight disadvantage.

Recently, there have been growing movements among some people who practise and disseminate information about local cultures and traditions, and also about dialects, whose covert prestige is beginning to consolidate. In some Samogitian schools, the local dialect is taught as a subject, and this approach is being promoted. Since the cultural and linguistic self-consciousness of the Samigotians (Lowlanders) tends to be stronger than that of the representatives of the other Lithuanian dialects, the idea of *Žemaičių* being a regional language is gaining ground (Grumadienė, 2004). Currently, there are some attempts to produce a modern common *Žemaičių* written language. (See the website of the Samogitia Cultural Society http://samogitia.mch.mii.lt/kalba.lt.htm; Girdenis & Pabrėža, 1998; Pabrėža, 1991).

Bilingual and multilingual language practices
State language competence. Once independence was regained, and the languages Estonian, Latvian and Lithuanian were reinstated to official status, knowledge of the state language became an important factor for the integration of ethnic minorities into a changing society. Persons who were not able to communicate in the national language of their country of residence were faced with the challenge of having to learn it in order to adapt to the new social and political situation. As previously noted, all public (and some private) sector employees must be proficient in their state language according to specific language knowledge categories. The same requirement applies to all students

from these communities wishing to pursue further studies that are offered in the titular language. For a considerable number of such people, what is mandated now is a form of integration that involves both the acquisition of the state language as a second language and the preservation of their first language and culture.

The increasing use of the national languages in the Baltic republics, then, was largely propelled by legal requirements that demanded the deployment of the respective languages in the public sphere – an idea strongly supported by the growing prestige of the languages. State programmes exist to provide the population with adequate language learning opportunities. Many minority representatives are instrumentally motivated to learn their state language in order to gain status and economic success, others display integrative orientations, seeking to identify with their overall society (see Hogan-Brun & Ramonienė, 2005b). Table 9 displays data on the steadily increasing levels of bilingualism in the titular language amongst speakers of minority languages: The trend shown is particularly evident amongst the members of the younger generation who have acquired appropriate linguistic knowledge at school. (More detailed accounts can be found in Hogan-Brun & Ramonienė, 2005a, b; Metuzāle-Kangere & Ozolins, 2005; Verschik, 2005a, 2005b).

Whilst this trend is clearly continuing, one must not overlook the fact that limited data have so far become available on actual (as opposed to reported) levels of state language competence and practice.

Observations point to the fact that language habits in localities with greater, largely self-sufficient ethnic densities are changing at a somewhat slower rate (Hogan-Brun & Ramonienė, 2005b; Metuzāle-Kangere & Ozolins, 2005; Verschik, 2005a). Sizeable (mainly Russophone – consisting chiefly of Belarusians and Ukrainians, but also some Russians) minority language communities remain, particularly in Latvia and Estonia, and to a lesser extent in Lithuania. These communities exist mostly in the larger towns, and in some country locations (northeastern Estonia; eastern Latvia; southeastern and eastern Lithuania which also hosts a large Polish community). In these environments, Russian is still widely shared as a means of communication.

Overall, there is no direct connection between language preferences and ethnic affiliation amongst the so-called third ethnicities in the Baltic. Many non-Russians are competent in Russian and even have Russian as their first language; the vast majority of both titular nationals and Russians have their

Table 9   Competence in the titular languages amongst total populations

	1989	*2000*
Estonia	67%	80%
Latvia	62%	79%
Lithuania	85%	94%

Sources: Census 2000 (Estonia and Latvia), 2001 (Lithuania).

respective language as a first language, but a majority of titular nationals have competence in Russians and a majority of Russians in Latvia and Lithuania report competence in the titular language, with Russians in Estonia appearing to be somewhat behind. The nature of language loyalties remains complex in the wake of repeated phases of assimilation in the past.

Language practices in Estonia.   In their comprehensive analysis of the Estonian language situation, Vihalemm (1999, 2002a, 2002b) and Verschik (2005) give detailed outlines of the various bilingual and multilingual practices that still need to be properly researched. While the language situation in Estonia has sometimes been characterised as a simple Estonian–Russian clash, Verschik points to the complex and sometimes paradoxical relations among Estonia's 142 different identified ethnic groups and distinct language use patterns.

Despite the demographic changes brought about by the period of Soviet occupation, Estonia has reasserted its pre-war recognition of cultural autonomy for ethnic groups, and has ratified the Framework Convention for the Protection of National Minorities. In both cases it makes a crucial reservation that only people who are citizens can be regarded as a national minority, thus clearly differentiating the autochthonous groups from recent Soviet settler arrivals. This has been made more difficult by the fact that several of Estonia's traditional minorities (Germans, Jews, Roma and Swedes) were almost wiped out by events during World War II. Further, Soviet policies denied national status to these groups and instituted only an Estonian/Russian divide in education, in media and in all domains of pubic life, leading to Russification of other Slavic settlers and some indigenous groups; Swedes, Finns and Roma had to maintain their languages without support:

> By contrast, the current state policy allows these ethnicities to openly identify themselves as such, and to promote their languages and cultures, factors which have served to further undermine any notion of a homogeneous 'Russian-speaking' identity. (Verschik, 2005b: 294)

While the wider teaching of Estonian remains the prime objective of all Estonian integration policies, a number of initiatives have been taken to foster minority languages. In 2004, the Estonian Bureau of Lesser Used Languages (EstBLUL) was founded to promote language and cultural activities among the autochthonous groups (www.estblul.ee). The small size of these groups means that it is difficult to establish and maintain such schools, but some progress has been achieved through Sunday schools, summer language camps and other cultural activities that have revived these so-called 'third ethnic groups'.

The distinction between an older autochthonous group and the Soviet period arrival is well illustrated with reference to two groups – Russians and Jews. Some Russians have lived in Estonia since the 14th century, and roughly three hundred years later significant numbers of Old Believers, protesting against the then reforms in the Orthodox Church, moved to Estonia, around Lake Peipsi, where their descendents still live. This autochthonous group, all citizens and perfectly integrated into the society, are largely

Estonian-Russian bilinguals, and their Russian language is characterised by substantial borrowings and morphosyntactic convergence towards Estonian. By contrast, the Soviet era Russians have low levels of proficiency in Estonian and often little knowledge of the country they came to; in this latter group, however, clear generational differences are emerging between younger cohorts more fluent in Estonian and an older generation of Soviet settlers still isolated from Estonian life.

An even more striking linguistic contrast occurs among the Jewish population, in which the very small group of surviving pre-war Jews and their descendents contrasts in language use with their Soviet era counterparts. Verschik (2005: 298) reports that, of just over 2000 Jews in Estonia in the 2000 Census, 124 spoke Yiddish. Because those Jews who came during the Soviet period overwhelmingly did not speak Yiddish, of the Yiddish speakers, 107 were Estonian citizens. The Yiddish speakers with a direct connection back to the pre-war Yiddish-speaking minority in Estonia are also mainly bilingual with Estonian, like the Russian Old Believers.

Focusing further on the Russian group and its practices, many authors have commented on the fragmentation within the Russian population and its diverse orientations. Vihalemm and Masso argue that the Russians are 'actually not a community but a relatively diffuse assemblage of people differentiated by their future aims, social capital, and cultural and political allegiances' (2002: 185). Sociolinguistically, it is precisely this group that is undergoing considerable change. While language loyalty remains high (98.2% of Russians speak Russian as a first language), some 44% of Russians claimed competence in Estonian in the 2000 Census, as against 15% in the 1989 census, showing a significant shift towards bilingualism. Vihalemm (1999) earlier traced this trend among the Russian population in Estonia. Moreover, some research highlights that shifting patterns of use and interaction, particularly in Tallinn, are beginning to appear. The main observations are:

- Greater lexical borrowing from Estonian can be found amongst Russians than vice versa.
- In place of the characteristic Soviet period encounter in which an Estonian would always address a Russian speaker in Russian, highly diverse encounter strategies are emerging, including reverse politeness (using each other's major language), or greater common initiation in Estonian.
- Among younger Russians fluent in Estonian there is more morphosyntactic convergence and a playfulness with Estonian forms in Russian that can appear puzzling for Russian speakers from Russia.
- Third-language influence has been noted, such as in the heavy Finnish-tourist areas around Tallinn where Russians and Estonian service personnel work out communication strategies. In some cases, Russian personnel become more fluent in Finnish than in Estonian, an implicit judgment on the 'market value' of Estonian.
- Interestingly, the above strategies seem to be far more common than Laitin's (1996) predicted greater use of English as a lingua franca because of the difficulty for Russians to learn Estonian.

Vihalemm (2002b) argues that:

- the instrumental value of Estonian still remains ambivalent;
- Estonian and Russian communities are still highly segregated;
- most Estonian-Russian interaction is still in Russian.

Verschik finds that more research needs to be carried out on actual language interaction and points to greater flexibility in interaction:

> ... while various scholars in the social sciences attest to the sociocultural stratification and fragmentation of the Russian-speaking population, the relationship between these processes and contact-induced language change remains to be investigated. Preliminary empirical data, however, confirm that linguistic creativity, code-switching, a deliberate use of convergent forms, and compromise strategies are all gaining ground in Russian-Estonian communication. (Verschik, 2005: 306)

Language practices in Latvia. The 2000 Census in Latvia demonstrated that 79% of the population now assessed themselves as having competence in Latvian, a significant increase of 17% over the 1989 Census figure. Yet the peculiarity of the Latvian situation, as in the other Baltic States, is that the national language is not necessarily the most widely spoken language. As pointed out in the State Language Agency's report on *Guidelines of the State Language Policy for 2005–2014*:

> Many residents of Latvia (81%) still have a command of the Russian language, which often prompts the choice of the language for communication. English, according to the self-appraisal of the respondents, is mastered by 14%, but German by just 8% of residents. The number of people speaking other languages (French, Swedish, Norwegian, Polish) does not exceed 1%. (Latvia, State Language Agency, 2005: 24)

The political nature of language policy in Latvia has ensured that studies of attitudes about bilingualism remain at the forefront of public attention as well as of scholarly investigation. Previously, reference has been made in part 3 to the influence of the 'Eurobarometer' studies from 1994 showing the far more positive attitudes among Russians to the Baltic languages as the official languages than political protests would have suggested (Maley & Rose, 1994). These findings echoed Druviete's detailed landmark work on the Latvian sociolinguistic situation (Druviete, 1995, 1996).

Studies undertaken more recently (i.e. from 1996 to 2003) by the Baltic Social Research Institute (BSZI) provide the most comprehensive overall tracking of reported monolingual and bilingual use in large representative samples (http://www.bszi.lv/downloads/resources/language/Language_2003.pdf).

The surveys show both steady increases in knowledge of Latvian among minorities, supporting the census findings, and in the far more complicated dynamics of the situational uses of Latvian or Russian in various domains. Asked to self-evaluate their level of knowledge of Latvian, in studies conducted between 1996 and 2003, the percentage of non-Latvians saying they had no knowledge of Latvian dropped from 22 to 10%; there was also a corresponding increase in those rating their knowledge of Latvian at the highest level.

These tendencies were strongly correlated to age, showing a growing bifurcation between youth and the older group. The younger groups showed continual improvement in their knowledge of Latvian, with successive increases each year among those claiming fluency in Latvian at the higher levels. There were also steady but smaller increases among those between 35–49 years of age. For those over 50, however, there was no decrease in the number reporting no knowledge of Latvian over the last five years of the surveys, the figure staying at 20%.

In terms of knowledge of Russian by Latvians, on the other hand, there was a continuing high level of competence, with only about 3% claiming no knowledge of Russian. However, more recent work is starting to detect a situation where a number of young Latvians do not have competence in Russian, as a result of the removal of compulsory Russian from the school curriculum. Figure 3 shows knowledge of Latvian by Russians and knowledge of Russian by Latvians. In every age group over 15, more Latvians know Russian than Russians know Latvian, but this is not the case for the youngest school age groups, indirectly attesting to the effectiveness of the new second language learning educational strategies, and of the consequence of removing Russian as a compulsory language from Latvian-stream schools.

However, the BSZI studies also show the other side to this steady rise of Latvian competence and invalidate any thought that Russian is losing its relevance in Latvia. In relation to the Latvian spoken in the workplace, for example, there was a steady increase between 1996 and 2002 of Russophones reporting using more Latvian than Russian at work (from 9% in 1996 to 26% in 2002), but in 2003 this trend was reversed, the figure for Latvian declining from 26 to 20%: 'Accordingly, 78% of Russian speaking respondents *use mostly*

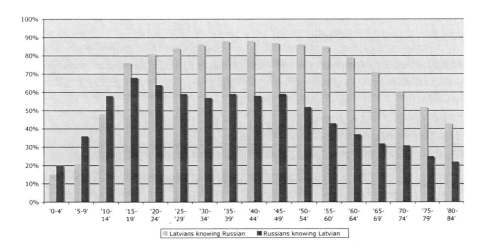

Figure 3 Lativa Census (2000): Latvians knowing Russian and Russians knowing Latvian, by age group
Source: Commission of the Official Language, from Census 2000: www.vvk.lv/print.php?id − 170.

Russian at work' (BSZI, 2003: 6). An increasing tendency of both Latvians and Russians to have media exposure in their own language was reported, reinforcing the existence of a markedly divided information space. The authors of the reports venture that the heightened politicisation of language issues around the matter of secondary school reform may be impacting both language attitudes and language use.

Interestingly, the surveys also offer a glimpse of the different ways in which Latvians learn Russian and Russians learn Latvian. In responding to questions about the level of their four macro skills, Latvians place their listening and speaking skills in Russian highest; that is, they have learnt Russian in the classic language acquisition mode, placing hearing and responding to spoken interaction above other skills. Russians, on the other hand, are more competent at reading Latvian rather than speaking it, showing that much of the learning of Latvian has not been through personal interaction in the language but through formal instruction in written communication – at school or in documentation in other aspects of life. This contrast accurately reflects the situation of the two languages in the Soviet and post-Soviet periods, a situation in which Latvians will generally respond in Russian to spoken Russian.

The BSZI studies report quite different attitudes on the part of Russians and Latvians to the question of how language should be learnt. Latvians believe strongly that Russians should learn and use Latvian; they see that the most important means of learning the language for Russians lies in using it more frequently in personal interactions. The surveys confirm that Russians overwhelmingly see the importance of learning Latvian, but Russians see the main means of learning Latvian to be the provision of Latvian in school including more language classes for adults, and the reduction of all fees associated with such classes; they do not prioritise using more interaction in Latvian on their own part. Moreover, this attitude carried a political sting: in the view of Russians, it is the state that has demanded knowledge of Latvian (for work, for citizenship, for integration more broadly), so it is up to the state to guarantee an appropriate level of Latvian for all who need it. It is assumed that such instruction is best provided through more state-financed language courses.

Besides the BSZI studies there have been copious investigations into language attitudes in Latvia, but sociolinguistic work on actual language use is still underdeveloped. Metuzāle-Kangere and Ozolins (2005) point to a number of smaller studies in more obscure sources; essentially studies that look at specific aspects of usage in different localties.

Poriņa (2001a, 2001b) has done the initial pioneering work on code-switching among bilinguals in Latvia, but there has generally been surprisingly little interest in these sociolinguistic details, and Latvian studies have not had any of the depth that Laitin's work on Estonia was able to achieve through qualitative studies of Russians and their negotiation of the Estonian language environment (Laitin, 1998).

Gender issues are often underexplored in larger surveys, but again Poriņa (2000) has lead in showing the importance of gender, with Russian females in Latvia generally having more positive attitudes to the learning of Latvian than Russian males have, and seeing the acquisition of Latvian as essential both for themselves and for their children. Volkovs' (2000) studies support this view, his work looking at the fracturing of Russian youth identities, in class terms as well as in gender terms and the resulting often confused search for identity in this group.

Finally, all of the rhetoric on language policy in Latvia, as well as some of the research, assumes a binary Latvian/Russian split, but there has been a growing salience of other minorities in Latvia, sometimes categorised in the 'Russian speaking' group but increasingly asserting their own view on language policy. The BSZI studies found, for example, that the 'other' nationalities – that is non-Latvians and non-Russians – tended to differ from Russians in some aspects of language use. For example, by 2003 some 10% of 'others' cited Latvian as their first language, and were closer to Latvians on such policy issues as the necessity to reform secondary education. As argued by sociologist Vēbers:

> The changes in linguistic patterns in Latvia are, step by step, breaking down the stereotype that all non-citizens in Latvia are Russian language speakers only. The number of non-Russian non-citizens who speak both their own ethnic language as well as the Latvian language is increasing steadily. (Vēbers, 1997: 69)

On the other hand, the State Language Agency, in its *Guidelines of the State Language Policy for 2005–2014*, points to the continuing two-language block view that prevails among minorities:

> Currently more than 90% of representatives of Latvian minorities recognise the status of the state language and the necessity to master the Latvian language, however, one can observe that they wish the status were more symbolic than real. About 70% of the minority respondents consider also that the Russian language should be granted the status of the state language. (Latvia, State Language Agency, 2005: 25)

The State Language Agency's *Guidelines* also point to the double-edged consequences of the generally conflict-avoiding handling of communication, where Latvians will often defer to Russian when encountering non-Latvians:

> Passivity of Latvians in the choice of the communication language can be observed. On the one hand, it shows the linguistic and ethnic tolerance, but on the other hand, it hinders the integration of the society on the basis of the Latvian language. (Latvia, State Language Agency, 2005: 25)

In summing up this complex picture of language attitudes and practices, a number of salient points suggest themselves. First, competence in Latvian continues to increase steadily among younger and middle-aged non-Latvians, but it remains static among older residents. Second, other indicators, especially of language use, are more ambiguous: after the relatively swift changes in language regime over the 1990s, and despite the turmoil over secondary school reform in the middle of this decade, a more stable linguistic situation is emerging than existed in either of these periods of change. Despite a seemingly irreducible hard core of those who will never learn Latvian among the older age group of Russophones, the limits of language learning and of language policy more broadly may have been reached. Just as an irreducible minority shows little interest in citizenship and can live without it, so the persistence of an extensive Russian speaking working environment allows a degree of self-sufficiency in that language, particularly for the older workforce.

Language practices in Lithuania. The 2001 census data indicate that the majority of Lithuanians and Russians declare the language of their own nationality as their native language. This, however, is not the case among Poles, many of whom declare Russian as their first language.

The inclusive nature of Lithuania's language policies has positively helped to alter the process of evolving levels of societal bilingualism/multilingualism through the simultaneous promotion of linguistic and cultural diversity and societal integration. The 2001 census data shown in Table 10 provide information on additional language knowledge by the various ethnic groups within Lithuania. For each group inserted in each row, the percentages refer to the group itself (not to the whole population of Lithuania). If a row adds up to less than 100%, it means that this group contains members who may only know one language. Where the total is more than 100%, this indicates that some members of the group are proficient in more than two languages. In the last line of the table, the figures are given as a percentage of the population of Lithuania as a whole. According to these figures, over half of the minority population (50–66%) now declare Lithuanian to be their second language. Two thirds of Lithuanians and three quarters of Poles use Russian as their second language. In some other ethnic groups, Russian is used by less then half of the population. Polish in general is not very popular as a second language.

Results from research on the adaptation of Lithuania's language groups (Kasatkina & Leoncikas, 2003: 271) point to the fact that many (mainly Russian) members of the minority communities consider a good command of Lithuanian to be a necessary precondition to pursue a career. Whether these people will be able or willing to retain their additive bilingual and bicultural identities alongside their native-like proficiency in the state language will remain to be seen.

Table 10   Knowledge of an additional language (2001 Census data)

Ethnicity	Additional languages (in percent)					
	Lithuanian	Russian	Polish	Belarusian	English	German
Lithuanians	0.3	64.1	7.8	0.1	18.0	8.6
Russians	65.8	5.9	14.4	0.6	15.9	6.1
Poles	61.6	76.9	10.9	3.1	6.9	5.8
Belarusians	54.0	40.3	31.4	10.4	7.9	4.9
Ukrainians	58.2	39.7	12.9	1.1	14.5	6.0
other	51.0	48.6	13.1	0.7	17.3	1.8
Total	10.2	60.3	8.8	0.5	16.9	8.2

Source: 2001 Census data cited in Kalbų mokymo politicos aprašas (2006: 47).

Whilst the use of Lithuanian predominates in the country as a whole, there is evidence that a growing number of residents in the densely multilingual and multi-ethnic region in eastern and south-eastern Lithuania are also adopting the state language, both in the public and in the semi-public spheres. Findings from a recent major survey on language attitudes and use in eastern and south-eastern Lithuania (Rytų ir Pietryčių Lietuvos Gyventojų Apklausa, 2002) show that, although language loyalties are complex in these regions, attitudes towards Lithuanian are positive overall. In this intensely multilingual setting, Russian (still) figures as the most widely shared language (by 90% of the local population); Lithuanian now closely follows Russian (by 83% of the local population). Only 6% of respondents reported no proficiency at all in Lithuanian. Just over half the residents also claim to use (local) Polish as a means of communication; 14% use Belarusian and 15% of the respondents report speaking in local vernaculars called *Tuteišų* ('language of locals') or *Po Prostu* ('simple language'). According to Zinkevičius (1992: 254–255), these varieties are mainly Belarusian with a strong linguistic impact of Polish, Russian and Lithuanian; these vernaculars are sometimes treated as local Polish with a strong linguistic input from Belarusian dialects, of Russian, and of Lithuanian. However, it may be more correct to treat these as varieties of the same Slavic dialect continuum (see Trudgill, 2002: 117–121). In this plural linguistic environment, many individuals, particularly Poles, possess several (bilingual/trilingual) language competencies to varying degrees, with a fairly fluid boundary between languages, where one language (formerly Russian, now increasingly Lithuanian) in the various settings is widely shared.

Findings from the survey on self-reported language use among eastern and southeastern Lithuania's inhabitants confirm that in this region (primarily inhabited by Russians and Poles), Lithuanian is now more frequently the medium of communication both in the public and in the semi-public spheres than was the case 10 years ago. The figures in Table 11 show that, over the span of a decade, the use of Lithuanian by Russians has increased by 17.2% in interactions with officials and by 18.5% in communication with salespersons, and the use of Lithuanian by Poles has increased by 19.9% in interactions with officials and by 19.5% in communication with salespersons.

Interestingly, compared to ten years ago, a greater number of Russians and Poles report to be increasingly interacting in Lithuanian in the private sphere too (Table 12), although this domain is not regulated by law.

Table 11 Use of Lithuanian in the public and semi-public sphere

Use of Lithuanian	*By Russians*		*By Poles*	
	10 years ago (%)	*At present (%)*	*10 years ago (%)*	*At present (%)*
With officials	45.7	62.9	54.4	74.3
In the shops	45.7	64.2	48	67.5

Source: Rytų ir Pietryčių Lietuvos Gyventojų Apklausa [Survey of Eastern and Southeastern Lithuania Inhabitants], (2002).

Table 12   Use of Lithuanian in the private sphere

Use of Lithuanian	By Russians		By Poles	
	10 years ago (%)	Now (%)	10 years ago (%)	Now (%)
With neighbours	41	52	44	56
With friends	38	52	49	54
With acquaintances	47	61	52	65

Source: Rytų ir Pietryčių Lietuvos Gyventojų Apklausa [Survey of Eastern and Southeastern Lithuania Inhabitants], (2002).

Table 13   Use of Lithuanian in family settings in percentiles

Use of Lithuanian (%)	By parents with their children	By grandparents with their grandchildren	By children with their brothers and sisters	By children with their parents and grandparents
By Russians	27	33	12	3–8
By Poles	32	40	14	4–5

Source: Rytų ir Pietryčių Lietuvos Gyventojų Apklausa [Survey of Eastern and Southeastern Lithuania Inhabitants], (2002).

When considering family settings, some Russians and Poles report communicating in Lithuanian with the younger generation (i.e. with children and grandchildren), as shown in Table 13. For respondents of Russian nationality this amounts to 27% and 33% respectively in interactions of parents or grandparents with their children and grandchildren, whilst the youngsters themselves appear to be communicating less in Lithuanian with their brothers and sisters (12%) or parents and grandparents (3–8%). Polish elders also claim to be using Lithuanian more frequently when interacting with their children (32%) and grandchildren (40%) as opposed to the youngest generation in communications with their siblings (14%) or parents and grandparents (4–5%).

These inter-generational enactment differences (Fishman, 1977: 29) show a clear shift to Lithuanian in interactions between parents and (grand)children. This tendency is reinforced by the fact that many parents from these communities tend to send their offspring to Lithuanian-medium schools to further their chances for success in the mainstream.

Vilnius is also located in Lithuania's most multicultural southeastern area, where Lithuanians constitute 58% of inhabitants. The remaining population consists of Poles (19%), Russians (14%) and other ethnicities (9%). An overview of Lithuania's ethnic populations is provided in Table 14.

All minority groups in Vilnius tend to indicate Russian and not the language of their ethnicity as their first language more often than people living in other regions. According to data obtained from a 2004 survey of language

Table 14   Population by ethnicity in Lithuania (%)

	Lithuanians	*Poles*	*Russians*	*Others*
Lithuania	83.5	6.7	6.3	3.5
Southeast	45.0	33.0	13.0	9.0
Vilnius	58.0	19.0	14.0	9.0
Visaginas*	14.9	8.6	52.4	24.1

*Visaginas is the town servicing the Ignalina nuclear power station, serviced largely by Russian personnel since the Soviet period.
Source: Lithuanian Census data (2000).

behaviour and language attitudes of Vilnius inhabitants, 59% of Lithuanian residents declare Lithuanian as their first language; for 22% Russian is their first language and for 13% Polish is their first language. This points to a shift mainly towards Russian but also towards Lithuanian, with a parallel move away from Polish.

On the other hand, all minority groups in Vilnius have better knowledge than their counterparts in the provinces of other languages as second-languages including Russian, Polish, English and German (Kalbų mokymo politikos aprašas, 2006: 52–54).

People who report having no knowledge of Lithuanian amount to 1% of Vilnius inhabitants (6% in southeastern Lithuania); Vilnius inhabitants with no knowledge of Russian constitute 1% (1% also for southeastern Lithuania), and those with no knowledge of Polish constitute 34% of Vilnius inhabitants (26.5% in southeastern Lithuania).

Media languages

The mass media landscape in Latvia, Estonia, and Lithuania has undergone fundamental changes since the early 1990s, and a new structure of national daily press has emerged. Television and radio have expanded most. These developments were regulated by numerous laws adopted by the national Parliaments, ensuring basic freedoms and allowing mass media to function according to the rules of a democratic society. More recently, broadcasting legislation has been modified to conform to the rules of the European Union. Politically and economically, media has established itself as an independent social structure. The media's impact on culture and its role in shaping cultural values are yet to be investigated.

Language use in Estonia's media is regulated through the 1995 Language Law and in the Law of Consumer Protection. The main focus of language regulation in the media pertains to practices on television (TV). According to the law, foreign language texts are to be accompanied by an adequate translation into Estonian except for immediately retransmitted material or foreign language learning programmes. In the 1990s, stations were frequently fined for contraventions of the law but, after adoption of amendments in 1997, the situation began to stabilise. Language use on radio is virtually unregulated. There is one national radio programme in Russian and a few in other languages. The language of local radio stations depends on the language used by the local population who comprise their listeners and who provide financial support through advertising.

In Estonia, media are available both in Estonian and in Russian, though outlets in Estonian are vastly more common. Media in Russian include three newspapers and one radio station with national coverage, plus several local stations. There is one commercial Russian-medium television program (plus local programs). In addition, Estonian national TV broadcasts a minimum of one hour in Russian daily. During recent years, Russian-language news on Estonian national TV has gradually become more popular. However, the relative share of the local media in Russian is too small to meet the needs of the population. This is partly conditioned by the higher production cost involved per unit to cover a smaller readership, and it means that the Russian-speaking population turns to TV programs from Russia offered by cable-TV operators.

The situation in Latvia almost exactly parallels that in Estonia. No regulations have ever been made in relation to the print media. But regulations as part of the Language Law from the early 1990s have limited broadcasting in languages other than Latvian. This policy was formalised in the 1995 Radio and Television Law which stipulated that no more than 25% of a station's broadcasts could be in a foreign language, with a consequent decrease of Russian language programs (Euromosaic, 2004b). Occasionally, stations were fined for contravention; consequently, legal action taken by Russian stations was ultimately successful in 2003 when the Constitutional Court declared this regulation to be unconstitutional as contravening freedom of speech. However, by then the issue of regulating language in the media had lost much of its relevance with a plethora of Russian language and other television channels appearing through cable or satellite means. The overriding concern in the media, however, is with the very separate information spaces shared by Latvians and by part of the Russian-speaking populations, with views hostile to Latvia (as with Estonia) often emanating from Russian media. The two groups, as a result, often receive radically different interpretations of events both in Latvia and outside. These very segregated information spaces were well demonstrated in the media campaigns on secondary school reform in 2004 (Hogan-Brun, 2006).

Lithuania's media landscape is somewhat more varied and caters in the first instance for speakers of Russian and Polish. In 2004, there were approximately 14 periodicals published in minority languages. The largest group of these consists of six newspapers and two journals in Russian. Three newspapers and one magazine exist in Polish. Publications for other minorities include a Germans newspaper, a monthly publication for Belarusians and one each for Jews, Tartars and Greeks.

Radio, as one of the most important mass outlets, broadcasts news and various thirty-minute informational programs in the languages of the main national minorities. The first Lithuanian radio programme transmits a daily information programme in Russian. Channel Two has a daily programme in Polish, and one for other national minorities grouped under the common name *Santara*. Broadcasts for Ukrainians, Tartars, Jews and smaller national communities such as Latvians, Germans, Estonians, and Karaites are broadcast twice a month for half an hour each within this programme. The second Lithuanian radio broadcasts a weekly programme in Byelorussian. Daily 30 minute programmes in Polish and Russian and 10-minute news programmes in Belarusian are transmitted in the regions of Vilnius and Visaginas. A private Polish radio station, *Znad Wilii*, 24 hours a day in Polish, and the Russian radio station, *Russkoje* radio, 24 hours a day in Russian.

Lithuania also receives and re-broadcasts some programmes from neighbouring countries. These are TV Polonia, a TV programme from the Republic of Poland, certain Russian TV programmes and TV stations from some other countries. At present, some private TV companies, such as Vilniaus TV, and Channel 11, also have programmes in the languages of Lithuania's minorities. (For more information see http://www.tmid.lt/index.php?page_ id=364.)

Besides the Constitution, which guarantees freedom of expression and the right to obtain or disseminate information, the Mass Media (Implementation) Law adopted by the Parliament in 1996 regulates the mass media in Lithuania.

Minority language communities and their attitudes to language and integration

Attitudes to language use have changed to varying extents in each republic over the years. Maley and Rose's (1994) large-scale Baltic survey, referred to in Part 3, reflects an overall shift in attitudes.

Over half the Russophone respondents disagreed with the proposition 'People like us should not be made to learn the titular languages' whilst agreeing with the statement 'Should people who want to become citizens have to pass an examination in the national language?' (Rose, 2000: 48f).

Some people seem to have accepted the legitimacy of the language laws, and a degree of (linguistic) accommodation appears to have evolved across the entire Baltic. In part it could be argued that this is the result of competitive assimilation, spurned by supporters of extrinsic motivation as a means to obtain material benefits and better jobs through the mainstream society.

Whilst overall positive signs of the consolidation of society have been observed in Lithuania, the picture continues to be more complicated in Estonia and Latvia as explained in the following text.

The situation in Estonia. Attitudes and values of Estonian speakers still differ significantly from those of Russian speakers. Attitudes toward the process involved in joining NATO, the fears concerning Russia's foreign policy and the evaluation of historical events are examples of these differences. In sports competitions, ethnic Russians tend to support Russia against Estonia, even if ethnic Russians are present on the latter team. Simultaneously, the Russian community in Estonia has begun to encounter problems such as high dropout rates from the educational system, unemployment, homelessness, drug use and HIV issues, and a rising juvenile crime rate. Several residential areas with speakers of Russian that used to be fashionable just 15 years ago have become ghettos. As a result, these communities have begun to recognise the status shift of Russian although the perception of Estonian as a less significant language still persists among some. These changes are accompanied by a psychological barrier towards Estonian, resulting in the formation of monolingual Russian communities and in diminishing contacts with the Estonian environment (Osipova, 1997: 30–32). Different information spaces and value systems can also impact on such diverging developments. More merging contacts however have been observed with a slightly rising pattern of mixed marriages. The younger generation has on the whole adopted an integrative attitude.

The social environment of Estonian speakers tends to be marked by a higher educational level and, correspondingly, better average salary. There are for instance four times as many highly rated specialists and twice as many directors among speakers of Estonian than of Russian. Also, Russian speakers are represented marginally on Estonia's unofficial list of millionaires. It has been observed that there is a strong connection between Estonian language proficiency and competitiveness, and school leavers with high grades in Estonian at Russian schools tend to be better off financially five years after graduation.

The weakest motivation for Estonian language acquisition occurs in the eastern border areas of northeast Estonia, where the Russian-speaking population virtually outnumbers the native population (e.g. in Ida-Virumaa, Sillamäe there are just 4.2% Estonians, in Narva 4.9%). The Estonian language skills of Russians in this district are considerably weaker than they are in Tallinn, because in this region the basic language of communication is Russian, in which both Russians and Estonians are fluent. In the areas surrounding Tallinn, where the percentage of settlers is high (37% Russians, 9% others), specific immigrant-dense areas of Russian-speakers have developed. In these areas, the Estonian language is not used among Russians in daily life, but it functions as a vehicle for achieving promotion and a higher income. In other areas, where the number of Russian-speakers is small, the Russian-speakers have gradually merged into the Estonian mainstream. Since Estonian is on the whole widely spoken, the children of assimilated Russian-speakers sometimes acquire mastery of Estonian on the playground before entering school. In those environments, the Estonian language is valued and used in everyday situations (Rannut, Ü., 2005).

The situation in Latvia. Many of the aspects of language attitudes are intertwined with the details of language use in bilingual environments; these matters have been covered earlier. At this point, some larger issues that confront different minorities in Latvia are discussed.

First, with reference to 'other 'nationalities (i.e. those who are non-Latvian and non-Russian), data from the 2000 Census presented in Table 15 illustrates some of the effects of Soviet period Russification of these other minority groups. The census enquired into competence in Latvian, Russian and other languages. The question about first language produced the results in Table 15.

This table shows that there is great language loyalty among Latvians and Russians, the two largest groups in the population, who each overwhelmingly speak their first languages. However, in the other communities relatively low proportions of speakers use the first languages corresponding to nationality – only 18.8% of Belarusians claimed Belarusian, 27.2% of Ukrainians claimed Ukrainian, and 19.4% of Poles claimed Polish as a first language. These groups

Table 15 Latvia (Census 2000): First language identification among selected national groups (rounded to nearest tenth)

Nationality of the person	Population total	With the first language of their nationality	Percent of the total population	With Latvian as first language	Percent of the total population	With Russian as first language	Percent of the total population
Population–total	2,377,383	2,050,763	86.3	—	—	—	—
Of which							
Latvians	1,370,703	1,311,093	95.7	—	—	48,242	3.5
Russians	703,243	664,743	94.5	31,141	4.4	—	—
Belorussians	97,150	18,265	18.8	6,347	6.5	70,717	72.8
Ukrainians	63,644	17,301	27.2	2,309	3.6	43,159	67.8
Poles	59,505	11,529	19.4	11,727	19.7	34,340	57.7
Lithuanians	33,430	13,187	39.4	14,203	42.5	5,437	16.3
Jews	10,385	825	7.9	918	8.8	8,211	79.1
Roma	8,205	5,637	68.7	1,670	20.4	574	7.0
Germans	3,465	541	15.6	854	24.6	1,970	56.8
Tatars	3,168	867	27.4	70	2.2	2,162	68.2
Estonians	2,652	720	27.2	1,041	39.3	840	31.7

Source: Central Statistical Bureau www.csb.lv; Census 2000, press release, 25.01.2002.

overwhelmingly reported shifting to Russian (72.8%, 67.8% and 57.7% respectively); Poles demonstrated slightly less shifting to Russian than either Ukrainians or Belarusians. These data attest to the degree of Russification these populations had undergone (not only in Latvia) and suggest that these individuals' first language does not often coincide with their nationality. Of these three groups, the Poles had been in Latvia in significant numbers for the longest period of time, dating back to the pre-war years. About 19.7% of Poles claimed Latvian as a first language.

However, the post-Soviet period has allowed a degree of language revival for these minorities, with schools now providing the following range of languages of instruction besides Latvian and Russian: Belarusian, Estonian, Hebrew, Lithuanian Polish and Ukrainian. A small number of schools also offer optional classes in Roma. Such other educational activities as weekend schools are slowly increasing in numbers. Many of these minorities, as reported previously, also strongly support various aspects of Latvian language policy including the issue of secondary school reform. For Belarusians and Ukrainians in particular, their situation in Latvia also reflects the previously (and in Belarus continuing) processes of Russification, which at present they often desire to reverse.

It may be useful to take one more look at the Russian minority proper. A constant theme in the literature, from whichever quarter, is the high degree of fragmentation in this community; in addition, it is an object of continual politicisation both by Moscow and by local Russian politicians, as well as by local Baltic nationalists. Romanov (2000), in a wide-ranging discussion, draws on fragmentation to explain the, on the whole, rather passive and conforming individual behaviour of Russians in the Baltic – rarely mobilising in politics, taking individual and pragmatic decisions on language or citizenship issues. The atomisation of this group as a result of Soviet socialisation makes it difficult for them to see themselves as a unified ethnic community or one that shares common interests over the long term. Moreover, the fragmentation of this group also occurs very distinctly along class lines, since Russians include some of the richest business entrepreneurs and speculators in the Baltic as well as a mass of the least skilled, least educated and poorest marginal workers. In many cases this division has led to a profound identity crisis among the group, since solutions referring to their situation are perceived entirely in individual terms, whether the solutions refer to language learning, to citizenship or to issues concerning their children (as illustrated in the steady increase in the proportion of Russians sending their children to Latvian schools – the BSZI survey reported 32% of parents pursuing this alternative in their last survey (BSZI, 2003: 19). Despite the attempted politicisation from various quarters, such pragmatic attitudes to language and integration are likely to continue, while the stability of the language situation and the existence of a good deal of divided linguistic space, as reported above, is also likely to continue.

The situation in Lithuania. Lithuania's minority communities are free to establish their own educational, cultural and religious institutions. Their rights are enshrined in Articles 14, 29, 37, 45 and 117 of the Lithuanian Constitution, in its Preamble, and in the Law on the State Language (*Valstybine˙s kalbos i˛statymas*). Additional legislation also exists on National Minorities

(*Tautinių mažumų*), on the Official Language of the Republic of Lithuania (*Valstybinės kalbos*), on Citizenship (*Pilietybės*), on Education (*Švietimo*), on Non-Governmental Organisations (*Nevyriausybinių organizacijų*), on Public Information (*Viešosios informacijos*), on Religious Communities (*Religinių bendrijų*) and on Political Parties and Political Organisations (*Politinių partijų ir politinių organizacijų*). The Department of National Minorities and of Lithuanians Living Abroad (*Tautinių mažumų ir išeivijos departamentas*) was established in Vilnius to implement the state national relations harmony policy. Its task is to assure the satisfaction and fulfillment of legal interests and the requirements on all inhabitants of the Republic (including ethnic minorities), and to create conditions for their universal and comprehensive participation in the public, political and cultural life of the country.

The demographic composition of the population in Lithuania is more homogenous than elsewhere in the Baltic Republics. It differs from that in Latvia and Estonia in that the percentage of non-Lithuanians is smaller (amounting to only 16% of the total population) and almost equally split between Russian (6.31%) and Polish (6.74%) residents (Lithuanian Census 2001). Other communities include: Belarusians (1.5%), Ukrainians (1%), Germans, Jews, Latvians, the Roma, Tatars, amongst others. Nearly all indigenous Lithuanians speak Lithuanian as, increasingly, do members of the other groups.

Ethnic diversity has a distinctly regional dimension in Lithuania. While most counties host 90% or more Lithuanians, the country's eastern and southeastern regions have a significant multiethnic population (55% non-Lithuanians, consisting primarily of Russians and Poles; see also Kaubrys, 2002: 215–216). This is an area with a complex history, which has long been inhabited by a mixture of (predominantly Slavic) groups of people: besides Lithuanians these are mainly Russians and the Belarusian and Polish border minorities (Kasatkina & Leoncikas, 2003: 43). In addition, being a border region, it has sustained a number of boundary changes over different periods of Lithuania's history (Plasseraud, 2003: 49f, 103 & 145f). After the 1795 division of the joint Polish–Lithuanian state, Lithuania's territory became a part of the Russian empire. The formation of the state borders occurred in the 20th century with the revival of an independent Lithuania in 1919/1920. Subsequently, Lithuania's eastern borders were shifted several times, and the territory became variably attached to Lithuania, Belarusia or Poland (Žepkaitė, 1992). This situation has resulted in long and intense periods of Russification and Polonization, which further affected the demographic make-up and cultural mixture in this region. The capital, Vilnius, Lithuania's historically most multi-ethnic and multicultural city, also forms part of this region. It hosts 42% non-Lithuanians, followed by Klaipėda (29% non-Lithuanians). Visaginas, the town near the Ignalina nuclear power plant is 85% non-Lithuanian. Table 16 juxtaposes the overall population data of Lithuania with those of its eastern and southeastern regions.

Although eastern and southeastern Lithuania stand out as Lithuania's most multiethnic, multilingual and multicultural rural regions, they are not uniformly so. On the one hand, this region hosts pockets of predominantly Polish (Šalčininkai, Vilnius regions) and Lithuanian (Utena region) groups. Visaginas, on the other hand, a new town next to the Ignalina nuclear power station, is

Table 16 Population by nationality in southern and southeastern Lithuania compared to overall national figures.

Nationality (%)	Entire Lithuania (%)	Surveyed area of eastern and southeastern Lithuania (%)
Lithuanians	84	45
Poles	6.7	33
Russians	6.3	13
Belarusians	1	5
Others or not indicated	2	4
Total	100	100

Source: Lithuanian Census (2000); Rytų ir Pietryčių Lietuvos Gyventojų Apklausa [Survey of Eastern and Southeastern Lithuania Inhabitants], (2002).

85% non-Lithuanian and mainly populated by Soviet immigrants. Most of these people, having applied for citizenship after the restitution of independence, are Lithuanian citizens, which has generated overall positive attitudes towards integration amongst these groups, providing motivation to work towards a common goal.

Data from the survey on eastern and southeastern Lithuania (Rytų ir Pietryčių Lietuvos Gyventojų Apklausa, 2002) show that attitudes towards Lithuanian in rural areas with a high percentage of multi-ethnicity are favourable overall. The majority of respondents (93%) report that it is important/very important to know the state language. The reasons that are given are first of all integrative in nature. In descending order of importance the results show that:

- 'A citizen of Lithuania has to know Lithuanian' (68%).
- A knowledge of Lithuanian is important 'in order not to be cut off from society' (18%).
- A knowledge of Lithuanian is important 'in order to be treated equally' (15%).
- A knowledge of Lithuanian is important 'in order to be accepted by society' (9%).

Instrumental orientation falls in second place in this context, as evidenced by the small percentage of respondents providing such answers as:

- 'I want to live and work in Lithuania' (0.9%).
- 'I want to get a job, and for interaction at work' (0.7%).

The overall figure of respondents who claim to have speaking/reading/writing knowledge of the official state language is 69%. According to this data, 6% indicate having no proficiency at all in Lithuanian. Of the latter, only 13% report being intent on learning it. The remainder admit that they 'do not need to learn Lithuanian' (29%), that 'it is hard to learn it' (24%), that they 'have no conditions for learning' (17%) or that they are 'too old' (17%). The main obstacles to learning appear to be linked more to a lack of motivation than to time available to do so. Amongst the variables that seem to reduce the motivation to learn Lithuanian are:

- age (87% are more than 40 and 58% are above 60 years old);
- education (half of these respondents have only completed primary education);
- gender (68% of those with no knowledge of Lithuanian are women).

Language attitudes amongst Lithuania's two major minority communities, the Russians and Poles, however have been observed to differ. Their diverging behaviour carries echoes of their varying historic origins.

The Russian minority is comprised of two segments, as is also the case in Estonia and Latvia: some (mainly Old Believers) arrived centuries ago; they tend to be well integrated though not assimilated; others are less well integrated Soviet-era settlers, many of whom live in the region around Visaginas (a town specially built for incoming workers of the Ignalina power plant), but also in other towns, mainly Vilnius and Klaipėda (Kasatkina & Leončikas, 2003: 37–47; Plasseraud, 2003: 330). Around half of them (49.7%) were born in Lithuania, and are well educated (they constitute the highest proportion of university graduates amongst the ethnic groups). During the period when Soviet Lithuania existed, most Russians did not need to speak Lithuanian, but they have now acquired reasonable proficiency and use it in both their social and private lives more often than do the Poles. The Russians also have some of their own cultural associations or centres in Vilnius, Kaunas, Klaipėda, Visaginas, Šiauliai and Šilutė, and there are numerous Russian Orthodox and an Old Believers' churches (45 Orthodox and 51 Old Believers religious communities altogether). Most of Lithuania's Poles are autochthonous citizens and have older ties with Lithuania than the Russians. They are either descendents of ethnic Lithuanian families who were Polonised during the long-term union with Poland (1569–1795) or later, during the interwar period, when eastern and southeastern Lithuania belonged to the Polish state, or else they are from Polish families who have been resident in Lithiania for generations. The vast majority of them (87.2%) were born in Lithuania and live predominantly in the southeast of the country. About 14.5% of them were Russian-speaking during the period when Soviet Lithuania existed. The most common criterion of Polish identity and a marker of their nationality, claimed by Russian-speaking and Lithuanian-speaking Poles, is the Catholic religion and the Polish church where they tend to use Polish mainly for ritual purposes without understanding the language.

Whilst both the Russian and Polish communities are generally well disposed towards Lithuanian society, the latter tend to emphasise their belonging to the Polish tradition (Hogan-Brun & Ramonienė, 2003; Kasatkina & Leončikas, 2003; for earlier observations see also Juozeliuñienė, 1996: 200; Savukynas, 2000: 67–84; Trinkuñienė, 1996: 188). Findings from two surveys (Rytų Lietuva ir valstybinė kalba, 1997; Survey of Eastern and Southeastern Lithuania Inhabitants, 2002) show that Poles are on the whole not inclined to use Lithuanian much in their private and public life and that they prefer to send their children to Polish-medium schools. The resident Russian community, on the other hand, whilst tending to foster its own culture and language, shows more signs of wanting to integrate. This is reflected in their marked desire to choose mainstream schools for their offspring. Seeing their children's future directly linked to success in the overall society, these parents do not want education to limit the children's chances by offering them too much accommodation (i.e. education in Russian). In their pragmatic attitude, they perceive integrative learning as being of instrumental value, and they favour their children's accommodation to the majority society as a necessary process for success in life in today's changed environment (Hogan-Brun & Ramonienė, 2004: 71). These observations echo those presented previously with reference to Estonia and Latvia.

Part V: A Political Conclusion: Responses to Baltic Language and Citizenship Policies

Part 5 looks at and responds to, the many interpretations that have been made of Baltic language policy by a variety of commentators, and revisits some of the contested notions about language, language rights and language outcomes that have implications reaching far beyond the Baltic states.

Intellectual responses to Baltic language policy

Soviet language policy attracted attention from numerous western scholars during the life of the Soviet Union (Knowles 1989, Kreindler, 1985, Lewis 1972), all of whom were interested in the spread of Russian, in the varying resilience of the republican languages and in the consequences of managing a multilingual empire.

The first hints of change in language policy in the Soviet Union was eagerly commented upon, for example by Knowles (1989) in his analysis of growing assertiveness of the Baltic populations, coinciding with the first wave of language laws that reasserted the status of the republican languages. Other active scholars in this period included the Quebecois, Maurais (1992), surveying the range of language initiatives throughout the non-Russian republics of the USSR, and Grin (1991) who concentrated on Estonia.

More political perspectives, however, quickly overshadowed such interest on the part of language scholars. A significant intervention which set the tone for much subsequent commentary came from Soviet author Viktor Alksnis (1991) in an article for *Foreign Policy* entitled 'Suffering from self-determination', written at a time when the Soviet Union still just managed to retain control over the Baltic republics. He argued that well-founded movements for reform in the Soviet Union had been essentially derailed in the Baltic States by strident nationalism and an avowed anti-Russian objective, attempting to displace the Russian language in favour of the republican languages, and discriminating against those who had come to live in those republics. Professing his love for his homeland (Latvia), he appealed for condemnation of such nationalist extremism and its threat to human rights. Alksnis himself, known as the 'Black Colonel', was privy to military and security decision-makers and to the local Interfronts seeking to retain Soviet domination; he never returned to the Baltics after their independence, staying in Russia and aligning himself with those military and political forces seeking to reassert Russian control over the 'near abroad'.

Yet, despite Alksnis' imperialistic stance, his charge of discrimination gained wide attention and, as noted in Part 3, it was this charge that was to be the focus of future Russian attempts to discredit the Baltic states and to appeal for international intervention. Alksnis' views also found resonance with some Western commentators. Most notably, Fukuyama (1992) wrote, in almost identical terms to those invoked by Alksnis, in an article, 'Trapped in the Baltics', in which he saw revanchist nationalism denying people automatic citizenship, and restricting their language. He appealed to the US government not to allow such discriminatory policies. Fukuyama had not previously been known for his interest in things Baltic; yet the demise of the Soviet Union and the historic changes in regimes in Eastern Europe promised much for his thesis of the 'end of history' and for the assertion that forms of liberal democracy and capitalism were an inevitable end-point for all developed societies. In this context, what he saw as aggressive nationalism was an atavistic throwback, an intolerable detour from this liberal democratic pathway.

Such views were also shared by some other European-watchers – for example David Arter, a Professor of European Integration in the UK, who argued:

> In the Baltic states, the principal obstacle to national integration has stemmed from the imperialistic attitude of the political class representing the indigenous majority towards the ethnic minorities of the former Imperial power (Russians, Byelorussians and Ukrainians) [...] Hardline nationalists held that citizenship should be conferred only on those who lived in the Baltic republics before 1940, along with their descendants. (Arter, 1993: 247)

Writing at a time when debates over citizenship were heated, and when there were fears of overt ethnic conflict, such descriptions seemed widely held by European commentators (see Smith, 1994, for a similar analysis). Yet, as was shown by the processes that led to citizenship laws in Estonia and Latvia, such legislation was supported not by 'hard-line nationalists' but in fact by almost the whole spectrum of political opinion, from the right through dominant centre parties to Social Democrats. The only groupings opposed were the small, overtly pro-Moscow parties and Interfronts. This characterisation of hard-line nationalism however has persisted.

In an ensuing and more theoretical study, Smith *et al.* (1998) trace a number of discourses that have been effectively used by the nationalising governments of Estonia and Latvia to limit the inclusion of the Russian diaspora. They argue that the use of 'draconian' language laws has enabled these states to create structures favouring the majority group in areas like employment, thus bringing instrumental rewards as well as persuasive discourses of core nation, de-Sovietisation, a scientific standardising state and a return to Europe. In their words, Estonia and Latvia are

> [...] aspiring to the idea of the 'one nation-state community', one in which all residents are expected to speak the same language and in which the national culture will therefore be secure throughout the political homeland. (Smith *et al.*, 1998: 103)

Such descriptions as 'all residents are expected to speak the same language' will be commented on further below.

Yet despite the militancy of Smith *et al.* and their closeness to many Russian accounts of the issue, not even all Russian authors shared the view that irreparable discrimination was occuring in the Baltic or elsewhere. Shamshur (1994) and Rudensky (1994) for example refer to the impact of Estonian and Latvian legislation on the insecurity felt by the non-indigenous people, even if this apparatus meet the letter of international law. They find that dissatisfaction over such issues as proposals for repatriation, or uncertainty over their status, meant the Baltic states could be faced with greater alienation from this sector of the population, as well as from heightened and increased calls for regional autonomy. Both believe that absence to date of violent confrontations on the other hand would give some prospect of resolving these issues through moderate leadership. Konovalov and Evstaviev, while warning of the negative consequences of the OSCE taking a soft approach to Estonia and Latvia, as we saw in Part 3, nevertheless at the same time accepted language requirements for certain positions, because 'the necessity to know the native language of the title nationality as a condition for occupying official positions seems normal' (1995: 177).

One point raised by many Russian and Western authors, however, was to note the low degree of mobilisation on these issues by local Russians. Smith *et al.* (1994), for example, advance several possible explanations for this, including the lack of recognized elites, the discrediting of the Interfronts, and – most of all – the heterogeneity of the Russian community, having few common features except a language and (a problematic) self-identification as Russians living outside their former home. The authors quote Semyonov's description of the Baltic Russians as a' ... motley, unorganised mass, which in a political sense does not represent movements and parties but a crowd' (Smith *et al.*, 1994: 203). Despite this low level of mobilisation within the Baltic States, however, criticism from Russia continued unabated (e.g. Ramishvili 1998).

The former conservative Swedish Prime Minister Carl Bildt provided quite the opposite tone in his (1994) paper entitles 'The Baltic Litmus Test'. He argued that the Baltic states have often been betrayed by Europe in the past, and indeed that they can be seen as a 'litmus test' for greater European troubles. When the Baltic states have lost their freedom, so too has much of the rest of Europe, and Europe must support them now in evolving rapidly out of the Soviet system, and in re-asserting their values (including language and citizenship requirements) which are essential for their own development and in no way in conflict with broader European values.

Specifically on matters relating to language, several authors have given strong support to Baltic language policies. Laitin's work has been many-faceted, including leading theoretical commentaries (Laitin, 1996), and giving a detailed and sensitive ethnographic account of Russians in Estonia's East accommodating to the new language requirements with little overt anger towards the state or overt desires for separatism (Latin, 1998). Laitin also provides a crucial argument that seeks to resolve the apparent contradiction between the fierce opposition to Baltic language policies evinced by a number of Russian leaders and the relatively accommodating and non-protesting stance of most Russian residents: at elections (non-citizen residents can vote in local government elections in Estonia) they will often support the more fire-branding leaders who promise to protect their ethnic interests, but in their everyday behaviour they see Estonian policies as legitimate and they want their children to learn Estonian and they use it themselves, inverting their behaviour during the Soviet period. Laitin has posed many possible outcomes of present Estonian language policy, including that English may become the language of intercultural communication in many instances. His view of 'competitive assimilation' will be examined further.

Similarly, Romanov (2000) has looked at Russian-speakers in Latvia, showing the often indecisive response of this fractured Russian group to language policy, again stressing the lack of overt mobilisation and the overall orientation of individual accommodation. Nørgaard captures the essential dynamics of Baltic language politics when he observes that the 'adoption of pro-Baltic language laws in 1989 led to pressure by the Russophones to maintain the language privileges they had held in the Soviet era' (1996: 178). This identification of the issue as loss of privilege, both for Russophones within the country and arguably for Russia more broadly, indeed points to a crucial division within commentaries: (1) whether Baltic language policy should be seen as an issue of human rights for a discriminated minority or (2) whether it should be seen as the redressing of a former imperialistic privileged-language situation. This distinction represents the two incompatible views of the Baltic linguistic situation. In contrast to Nørgaard's emphasis on dynamic responses, the unquestioned assumption of discrimination is often encountered in many authors' work. Dobson (2001) unreservedly entitles his paper 'Ethnic discrimination in Latvia' and goes through a familiar recounting of restrictions on employment and citizenship without language credentials, seeing each instance as discrimination. Some other recent writings continue to perpetuate such stereotypes:

> In the Baltic States, schools are required to use only the national languages, while not being proficient in these languages affects eligibility for citizenship and acceptance in the workplace. (Shohamy, 2006: 28)

Yet, as previously noted, these are not requirements for schools: there are intact Russian primary educational systems in all the Baltic States, and there have been steady reforms in secondary education to move to a 60 : 40 situation (qv). Moreover, Baltic citizenship and language practices can be argued to reflect those elsewhere and indeed can be argued to be more liberal, more explicit and clearer than in many other countries. Despite such assertions about the workplace as these or Dobson's, there are no significant economic status differences between titular nationals and others (Aasland, 2002; Aasland & Tyldum, 2000). Russian continues to be a useful language for employment, and the overwhelming majority of those who needed to demonstrate Baltic language skills for employment purposes have in fact already done so.

Contested notions

Confounding analysis of the Baltic language situation and marking seemingly permanent incompatibilities between various perspectives is the use of several terms imported from descriptions of other language situations that will often require a quite different understanding in the Baltic context. Two prominent pairs of such terms are minority/majority, and assimilation/monolingualism.

Minority/majority

What is a minority? The Baltic situation turns on its head several often taken for granted assumptions of the status of national languages and minority languages. In May's (2006) article on Minority Rights in Ricento's excellent anthology on language policy, May recounts the standard (conscious or unconscious) characterisations found in language policy debates:

- The majority or national language is the language of progress, modernity, and above all mobility; the minority language is the language of senti-ment, but also of backwardness and limitations on mobility.
- Majority languages are lauded for their 'instrumental' value, while minor-ity languages are accorded 'sentimental' value, but are broadly construed as obstacles to social mobility and progress [...]. If minority-language speakers are 'sensible' they will opt for mobility and modernity via the majority language (May, 2006: 263).

Druviete (1999: 266) points out, however, that no such assumptions can be made about majority and minority languages in the Baltic states. Crucially, this view of a majority language is precisely the one that held sway during the Soviet period – that is, that Russian was the language of modernisation, progress and 'international' communication. Russian-speaking settlers living comfortably anywhere in the Soviet Union using only Russian could safely ignore the repub-lican languages.

Overturning these assumptions lies at the heart of Baltic language policy. Skutnabb-Kangas places Baltic language policy in the context of wider strug-gles over minority language and linguistic discrimination, and comes to an extremely important insight into the situation in Estonia and Latvia, based on the previous era of linguistic imperialism. At the present time in these countries:

> Russian is thus a majorized minority language (a minority language in terms of numbers, but with the power of a majority language), whereas the Baltic languages are minorized majority languages (majority languages, in need of protection usually necessary for the threatened minority languages). (Skutnabb-Kangas, 1994: 178)

Such a paradoxical situation gives the Baltic language scene a particular flavour: that speakers of both the largest language groupings in each territory can each see their languages as being in a threatened 'minority' situation and in need of defending.

However, the reminder of lost privilege is central to understanding that the attitudes of Russian-language activists and defenders are nothing like those of traditional minorities elsewhere, as they still see their own language as the language of importance, international usefulness and therefore, arguably, of dominance. The restricted nature of languages in the Baltic (Estonian, Latvian and Lithuanian are little used except in their own territories) contrasts with the international, cultural and language-of-wider communication importance of Russian. Moreover, Karklins (1994: 157–158) has pointed to the decidedly non-minority outlook of a number of Russian language leaders who insist that they do not wish to live as a separate enclave but be fully integrated into the host

Baltic societies, but that this should be on the basis of Russian – that is, the host society should communicate with them only in Russian so they may live self-sufficiently as Russian-speakers, thereby continuing to exercise all privileges of the dominant language group.

The loss of particular linguistic privileges – having all non-Russians deal with one in Russian – rather than the defence of an endangered language or a weak minority is the key to both local objections to Baltic language policy and objections from Russia. Among these privileges, the most important was the 'right' to remain monolingual – in Russian. As noted in part 3, however, many Russian speakers do not mourn such loss of privilege, contrary to a number of spokespersons. This understanding of 'loss of privilege' also undermines one other critique of Baltic language policy – that it represents a 'reverse of the previous dispensation' (Knowles, 1999; see also Björklund, 2005). Knowles argues that previously in the Soviet Union the spread of Russian marginalised the local Baltic language; presently, the titular languages in the Baltic are trying to do the same to Russian. Yet the continual international lobbying for Russian interests and the localised remit of these languages show that the present situation is quite different from, and not simply the opposite of, the Soviet policy. In this regard Maurais speaks of 'regional majority languages'; that is, of languages that may have a majority of speakers in a particular region, but may be subject to any number of pressures internally from powerful minorities and externally from more powerful neighbours. Such languages may need particular assistance to retain their functions:

> If the goal is to achieve a situation where two unequal languages would finally be equal, then this cannot be achieved through granting similar rights to the languages. Hence the need for some sort of affirmative action programs [...]. (Maurais, 1997: 150)

Assimilation/monolingualism

Equally misleading are notions of assimilation and monolingualism. May argues that a widespread assumption in descriptions of minority languages and majority policies holds that 'language policies aimed negatively at minority languages or restrictive of minority languages will lead to assimilation and monolingualism' (May, 2006: 263). Again, the Baltic states show a situation quite at odds with what is commonly assumed regarding monolingualism and assimilation; indeed these notions very often describe the opposite of their usual denotation. The empirical evidence presented in Part 4 shows very strong and reproducing language communities on the part of both titular majorities and Russians, marked only by a glacial shift in first language together with a steady increase in functional bilingualism. Järve (2002: 92ff) uses such evidence to suggest the Baltic languages are in a stable situation and are not as threatened as they make out. Also, Russian first language figures are equally strong, and Russian first language transmission is not at all threatened in the current changed linguistic climate.

The issue of monolingualism is a quite specific one in the Baltic, where a shrinking but determinedly hard-line minority of Soviet-period settler activists insist on their right to monolingualism:

> The demand for the right to stay monolingual is the background and the essence of the linguistic human rights problem of the Russian-speaking population in all the Baltic States. (Druviete, 1997: 181; see also Rannut, 1991: 1994)

Meanwhile, the majority of 'Russian speakers' – of whatever national back ground – confirm their own and their children's growing proficiency in the national languages. This practice is also perfectly in line with the long-standing multilingualism of the titular population, historically stemming from repeated periods of foreign overlordship. While to some extent dependent on education, it was extremely common for Balts up until World War II to be multilingual, with all educated Estonians and Latvians generally having a command of Russian and German and often other languages, and Lithuanians' repertoires encompassing these languages and often Polish. There are in fact virtually no monolingual titular nationals in the Baltic States. As previously shown, the Baltic language policies requiring competence in the national languages are basically additive, in extending the repertoire of monolinguals rather than subtractive in their intention and operation. With a fully functioning Russian-language primary school system, a generally 60 : 40 teaching division in second-ary school in Latvia (and the likelihood of a comparable one in Estonia) and a fully functioning Russian language maintenance system in publications, media, the arts and public discourse, one language that is not under threat in the Baltic States is Russian.

The concept of assimilation, however, has also been used in other ways in recent scholarship. Laitin has argued that, in the Baltic States, one sees a situation of 'competitive assimilation', where the question of whether one group could assimilate into another was largely dependent upon economic conditions; the clearly superior economic performance of the Baltic states was a major factor in Russians not mobilising as an aggrieved nationalist movement, but rather seeking accommodation to the new regimes (Laitin, 1996; 1998). More recently, the accession to the EU showed parallel movements of 'dual integration' – Russians integrating more into Estonian society, but both Russians and Estonians integrating more into Europe (Laitin, 2003). Specifically on questions of assimilation, Laitin surveyed Russians in four post-Soviet countries – Estonia, Latvia,

Table 17 Attitudes towards titular languages and assimilation: Russian respondents in different republics (% agreeing)

	Estonia	*Latvia*	*Kazakhstan*	*Ukraine*
'All permanent residents should be fluent in the titular language'	58.2	70.6	23.0	36.9
'Titular language should be a required subject in school'	95.8	95.2	64.4	84.7
'The best future for Russians in this republic is to assimilate'	7.9	48.4	7.7	23.1

Source: Laitin (1996: 7).

Kazakhstan and Ukraine. It should be noted that the language proficiency in the titular language of Russians in these various republics differed greatly: based on the 1989 Census, 33.3% of Russians in Ukraine and just 0.86% of those in Kazakhstan spoke the titular languages.

As shown, there is overwhelming support for having titular languages as compulsory school subjects, and strong support in both the Baltic Republics for residents achieving fluency in the titular language. The low level of knowledge of Kazakh on the part of Russians clearly influences views on this point. Interestingly, even on the very hard question of assimilation, almost half the Russians responding agree that assimilation in Latvia will lead to the best future for them. The figure for Estonia is much smaller, reflecting the far greater local concentrations of Russians, particularly in the eastern part of Estonia where a viable Estonian surrounding in which assimilation would be possible is lacking.

However, Laitin's use of the term 'assimilation' here is very revealing in unexpected ways, particularly of the Russian respondents in Latvia. They over-whelmingly favour Latvian language teaching in school and substantially agree that fluency in Latvian can be a legitimate expectation of permanent residents. But first language retention among Russians is very high: nothing like 47% of them are likely to give up their language or to shift to Latvian only; language maintenance among Russians will remain closer to the 100% mark. Yet, as noted in Part 4, the rate of Latvian knowing among Russians is constantly increasing. For the 47% of Russian respondents who favoured the 'assimilation' option, the closest fit of the varying opinions and behaviours of this population is that they will maintain Russian, be reasonably fluent in Latvian, and that their children will master Latvian completely without giving up their first language and will become functionally bilingual. For these respondents, 'assimilation' means functional bilingualism.

> Baltic titular nationals have historically demonstrated a permanent stable bilingualism. A successful outcome of Baltic language policy would be to have all other groups also achieve a permanent stable bilingualism. Such an outcome would illustrate the virtually total incoherence of trying to use such notions as assimilation and monolingualism in the Baltic context, and the irrelevance of assimilation and monolingualism as a critique of Baltic language policy.

Arguments over language rights

In the landmark collection *Language Rights and Political Theory*, edited by Kymlicka and Patten (2003), the eruptions in Eastern Europe in the late 1980s and 1990s are seen as the greatest single stimulus for the rapid growth of inter-est in language rights. While other language situations around the world had previously led to attempts to define such rights, it was the sharpness of conflicts in Eastern Europe that brought language rights into clear focus. However, such attention to Eastern Europe '...quickly led to the realisation that linguistic issues are far from being 'resolved' in the West either' (Kymlicka & Patten, 2003: 4); from Western perspectives, previous views of language differences as being divisive or as needing to be eradicated have softened into acceptance of multicultural or regional autonomy alternatives. The authors argue that' ... the shift towards official language rights in the West, therefore, is intimately tied up with increased acceptance of the legitimacy of minority nationalism ...', but this is not the case in Eastern Europe 'where the idea of minority nationalism remains anathema [... as] language conflicts are inextricably related to nationalist conflicts' (Kymlicka & Patten, 2003: 5–6).

They describe the several European conventions that have been adopted regarding minority languages as 'declarations of minimum standards and best practices' (Kymlicka & Patten, 2003: 4), thus with a far less exalted legal status than their advocates would accept. Yet such bodies as the EU, OSCE and others have explicitly argued that recognition of language rights is fundamental to being acceptable European states. The stakes, as a consequence, become very high in seemingly technical arguments over the legal or political force of particular requirements. A number of other contributions to the anthology also point to the very limited basis of what can be identified as language rights, leading to the most lively contribution from Stephen May (2001), who protests that his colleagues are 'misrecognising' language rights and are still assuming monolingualism as a norm, therefore sanctioning the failure of political states to recognise language issues.

The limited remit of language rights

Despite the confidence of European institutions in espousing views of human rights and language rights, the actual basis for such rights in the international law literature is shakier than is often asserted. A feature of international law literature is that it almost universally bemoans the lack of clear international norms in relation to language issues. Dunbar (2001), from a legal perspective, gives a concise overview of such limitations, while more recently Skutnabb-Kangas (2006), from a linguistic human rights activist perspective, also points out such limitations, and she also argues that many claims by rights proponents are extravagant and are never likely to be recognised in law. One example of trying to define the scope of language rights is de Varennes (1995/1996, 1996), whose works have been widely used by European institutions much attracted to his argument that a positive appreciation of minority language rights can be a useful tool in diminishing ethnic conflict. de Varennes goes on to show, however, that relevant international instruments have often been interpreted in restrictive ways. His proposed way forward is to argue for more liberal interpretations on such questions as:

- When do certain citizenship requirements become discriminatory?
- How should a sliding scale be handled to look at where minority languages are used by official bodies?
- What ways are available to limit state legislation on language?

He uses a series of hypothetical examples of what courts might hold to be discriminatory in various cases, including some Baltic examples in which he favours a two-official languages policy. While the conclusions he draws from his specifically Baltic examples have been questioned (Druviete, 1997), and will be commented on further, de Varennes has usefully demonstrated the often limited nature of language-related legislation and international norms.

Such limitations are pointed to by a number of other authors. In Kymlicka and Patten's (2003) collection, Rubio-Marin argues that linguistic human rights advocacy must be restricted to 'ensuring a person's capacity to enjoy a secure linguistic environment in her/his mother tongue and a linguistic group's fair chance of cultural self-reproduction which we will call language rights in a strict sense' (Rubio-Marin, 2003: 56). She argues that only if this capacity and self-reproducing chance is infringed does a policy become clearly one of linguistic human rights, or non-instrumental language rights. This line of interpretation follows closely the few 'hard law' requirements of treatment of language, as in the influential Article 27 from the International Convention on Civil and Political Rights:

> In those states in which ethnic, religious or linguistic minorities exist, persons belonging to such minorities shall not be denied the right, in community with other members of their group, to enjoy their own culture, to profess and practice their own religion, or to use their own language. (ICCPR, 1966)

In this case, the private realm of language is stressed, and it has led to little claim on public policy. Rubio-Marin, however, raises two further considerations. First, the state must ensure lack of discrimination in terms of instrumental rights, particularly where lack of the majority language prejudices individuals' interests, such as in due process of the law (providing interpreters), or in blocking pathways to certain work on the grounds of unjustifiable linguistic criteria. Second, Rubin-Marin argues that refusal to treat linguistic diversity with sympathy in pubic policy can itself affect the democratic legitimacy of states, particularly where there are large minorities:

> When the numbers of people affected by linguistic obstacles to access are sufficiently broad, the reality becomes troubling not just from the perspective of the enjoyment of their individual rights, but also from that of the overall commitment of the state to legitimisation principles such as the rule of law or a democratic form of government. (Rubio-Marin, 2003: 79)

This argument extends far beyond the more restricted issues of language rights law, and identifies one of the main areas of strenuous debate over Baltic language policies and the even more hotly contested issue of citizenship. Yet, perhaps to the surprise of many commentators, citizenship law is an even more restricted area of international norms than is supposed language legislation.

For the Baltic situation, in de Varennes' view, the crucial factor again is that of the proportion of the population negatively affected. Considering the size of the excluded population, and the objective difficulties faced by Russian speakers in learning Latvian or Estonian, he argues that it could be held that the language requirements in these citizenship laws become onerous:

> The exclusive preference given to Latvian and Estonian seems disproportionate and unreasonable as an attempt to rectify past Soviet practices, bearing in mind the number of permanent residents [...]. A better approach may be to have both the official language and Russian included as part of the naturalization process. (de Varennes, 1995/1996: 137–138)

This seemingly law-based conclusion in fact makes a political jump to an assumption that the zero-option on citizenship and two official languages constitute the only 'solutions 'to conflict, whereas it might be argued that this conclusion is precisely a perpetuation of 'past Soviet practices', politically as well as linguistically. Moreover, if implemented, such a continuation of Soviet practices would, in turn, lead to an ongoing mobilisation against such policies by the titular nationals and many others from minorities, as was demonstrated in the late 1980s and early 1990s. The conflicts would continue.

Relatively absent from most commentaries on language rights, either narrowly conceived or more broadly conceived as part of liberal political philosophy, is a concern with the restitution purposes of language policy (cf. Blake, 2003: 222–224 who argues the strongest case for minority national and indigenous languages is precisely to recover from past injustices). The recovery from past injustices and the overturning of past privileges accruing to outside forces is also at the centre of post-colonialist perspectives, particularly in the third world. Some commentators, however, see this as also directly relevant to the Baltic states: Racevskis (2002) argues that the Baltic states fit all the criteria for having been occupied and colonised by the Soviet Union, but this situation is rarely accorded the status it deserves in broader post-colonial analysis. The point has not been lost on a number of other Eastern European observers. The prominent Hungarian commentator Gyorgy Szépe, in looking at East European language situations, states specifically with reference to Estonia:

> This is a very complex issue; we have to admit that human rights (and linguistic human rights) are very important and central issues, but they are not adequate tools to solve the problems of an entire historical age. The invasion of the new coloniser – exemplified by the Russian immigrants to Estonia after the occupation of that small country in 1940 – can endanger the existence of the linguistic community of the country. Estonia's reaction in requiring a positive attitude to the language of the country by the (former) colonisers is not novel aggression but the restitution of the previous peaceful stage. (Szépe, 1994: 47)

Szepe ends by offering one reminder: 'Without interfering in the dispute, may I remark that human rights are meant to protect the underdog rather than the (past, present or potential) overdog' and in his view there are no doubts as to who has been (and very much still is) the underdog in this context (Szépe, 1994: 47).

The strongest Baltic advocates of their language policies support this view. Druviete argues against de Varennes and others who conclude that peaceful integration of the large Soviet settler population can only be achieved by having two official languages and granting automatic citizenship. She argues this would perpetuate Russophone monolingualism and asymmetrical bilingualism for the titular nation. Integration, she maintains, must precede citizenship, and any proposed granting of citizenship to all before a satisfactory level of integration was achieved 'would have been dangerous for national statehood' (Druviete, 1997: 169). Integration must be based on ensuring that the national language becomes part of the repertoire of all minorities, and points to the considerable advances that had been made in this regard by the mid-1990s in language attestation, use patterns, and attitudes of minorities towards the official state language:

> The present process of change in the linguistic hierarchy is slow but satisfactory and must not be artificially interrupted due to an incorrect interpretation of linguistic human rights. (Druviete, 1997: 183)

In her view, however, such sociolinguistic considerations seem rarely to be taken into account in the debate, and advocacy for a two official languages policy, when the alternative is now clear and appropriate, in fact can only undermine linguistic human rights:

> The Baltic countries represent a unique case, probably not taken into consideration when universal declarations on linguistic human rights are written. Their situation shows that the linguistic human rights of state language speakers can also be infringed and that the official state language in an independent country may be an endangered language at the same time. (Druviete, 1997: 183)

A critique of rights as a basis for policy

Independent of considerations of the Baltic, but of great relevance to the language conflicts there, Deets (2002) has provided a radical critique of views of language rights and ethnic rights, pointing out quite the opposite point of view espoused by de Varennes; that is, an emphasis on language rights has the potential to intensify ethnic conflict and to prevent viable language or other equitable outcomes in multi-ethnic situations. Like de Varennes and Dunbar, Deets (2002) stresses the hitherto limited interpretations of minority education and language rights in international law, and agrees that moves to write more explicit minority rights into international instruments has often failed. But his reaction to this is the opposite of de Varennes': Deets argues that such unwillingness to countenance minority rights has often been highly perceptive and beneficial, precisely because it limits rights-based conflicts that often become intractable. He argues his case from the perspective of the long-standing debate in liberal political theory over whether group rights exist (as against individual rights) and how they should be treated in social policy. For Deets, a group rights perspective is flawed:

> This is not to argue that policies promoting minority identity and culture should be abandoned, but perhaps much of the discourse on minority rights should be. The language of rights has a seductive power. Its logic often cascades in unexpected directions, and the unavoidably increasing gap between perceived rights and actual policy is potentially explosive. (Deets, 2002: 52)

Focusing on Central Europe, he details the success of some minority policies which did not espouse a rights rhetoric in Hungary and Romania, and argues a point of great relevance to the Baltic situation: that the basis for Hungary's very liberal policies for its small minorities is precisely to be able to pressure surrounding countries in their treatment of Hungarian minorities; that is, as an instrument of international relations.

On the issue of rights, Deets argues that in Eastern Europe 'some of the more successful policies in balancing liberalism and collective minority interests have avoided acknowledging a rights claim' (Deets, 2002: 52). Macedonia is a case in point from the late 1990s, where the OSCE adopted a particular approach to the conflict over the Albanian language university set up clandestinely in Tetovo, but opposed by the Macedonian government. Rather than asserting group rights and valorising an Albanian right to such a university, the OSCE transformed this into an international university, which operated in a number of languages including Albanian. But Deets then contrasts this successful approach to what he considers the disastrous approach by NATO in handling the 2001 conflict in Macedonia, where armed Albanian forces demanded that Albanian be made an official state language and also demanded a number of other language and equity measures including a six-fold increase of Albanians in the police force. Faced with the threat of violence, European organisations hastily pressured Macedonia to accede to these demands, even though previously they had accepted Macedonia's policy of one official language – Macedonian. In pressing such demands, Deets argues, Western governments were directly responsible for legitimising armed threats to gain minority rights:

> Their own failure to effectively communicate the rationale for [...] NATO intervention in Bosnia-Herzegovina and Kosovo fostered a broad array of interpretations over when minorities could legitimately use force to effect those changes in policies that could not be achieved through the democratic institutions. (Deets, 2002: 52)

The Macedonian case also had consequences in the Baltic, through the stance taken by Russia. Interestingly, at the height of the 2001 conflict, Russia urged Macedonia to resist such Albanian demands, arguing that such concessions should not be made to insurgents. But, when the Macedonian government was forced to accede to the demands, Russia quickly drew parallels with the Baltic states, arguing that

> [w]hile less than 30% of the population in Macedonia demand that the language should be accorded the status of state language, this problem is not being solved in the Baltic and not taken into account in their accession to the EU. (ITAR/TASS News Agency, 2001)

Consequently, Russia used the Macedonian example to continue to berate the Baltic States ('Russian-Baltic benevolent dialogue possible – Putin' ITAR/TASS News Agency, 3 September 2001).

The different perspectives espoused by de Varennes and Deets point to a central issue at stake for language policy: whether rights-centred approaches to minority conflict have the potential to diminish such conflict (de Varennes) or to increase it (Deets). Moreover, these would seem to be empirical claims, and attention to the actual mechanisms employed – legal or otherwise – in different contexts may yield useful (and usefully limited) results. The Baltic States present one such case, and the evidence presented in this monograph points to the overall strong legitimacy of Baltic policies and the ability of the Baltic States to move relatively calmly away from Soviet linguistic and political patterns.

International pressures, organisations and local language policy

The role of international organisations in Eastern Europe more generally, and the Baltic States in particular, has spawned a large but often contradictory literature. Bratt Paulston and Heidemann (2006), writing on language education policy after accession to the EU, stress the force of European strictures on language policy and predict greater support for Russian speakers:

> In Latvia, the driving force behind the language legislation is fear of impending language shift to Russian and the loss and death of the Latvian language forever [...]. [But] the more control, the more enclosure, the more likely such language policies are to result in conflict and contestation. In addition, the minority-language policies of the European Union (Latvia became a member in 2004) are likely to support the Russian speakers' demands (Bernier, 2001), and no one can predict the future consequences with accuracy. (Bratt Paulston & Heidemann, 2006: 299)

Spolsky (2004), writing just on the cusp of accession to the EU, takes a far more laconic approach and expresses mild surprise at the limited remit of international organisations. He sees the EU accession process as being dominated by an interest in ensuring linguistic readiness on the part of officials of the candidate countries to participate in EU work, giving little attention to the more conflicted issues of language rights:

> The nature of the intervention makes very clear the limits that the European Community sets on its interpretation of language rights. It sees no fundamental problem with the goal of the three Baltic nations to switch from Russian-dominated bilingualism to national – language monolingualism, provided that the process avoids infringing the individual human rights of speakers of the minority languages, including Russian. (Spolsky, 2004: 152)

Spolsky notes that, apart from some concern about Romany, European institutions do not identify which languages need protection, or in which languages education is mandated, as long as there is opportunity to study a relevant minority language; he sums up Europe's stance as a contrast between rhetoric and bureaucracy:

> For all its rhetoric of European multilingualism, the European Community appears comfortable with the maintenance or even establishment of national monolingualism, provided only that appropriate officials have plurilingual proficiency in other European languages. (Spolsky, 2004: 153)

These divergent views of international institutions and norms may reflect different expectations of authors, but also they may to some extent reflect the fact that these institutions were faced by novel situations, not least in the Baltic states, and normative guidelines were not always apparent. Nevertheless, as the 1990s wore on, European institutions often gave very emphatic directives on language policy.

In her comprehensive study, Kelley (2004) builds on Brubaker's widely-cited triad model of interethnic relations in Eastern Europe, which identified three main players: the nationalising state, the national minority, and the minority's external homeland (Brubaker, 1995, 1996). Kelley also incorporates the later additions to the models by Smith (2002) and Tesser (2003) to see international organisations as constituting a fourth player that can drive policy outcomes. Her study centres on the question of what mechanisms are most effective in reducing ethnic conflicts: normative approaches and persuasion on the one hand, or conditionality (usually access to European organisations) on the other. She analyses in depth some 64 cases occurring between 1990 and 1999 in Estonia, Latvia, Romania and Slovakia, arguing that conditionality was a superior approach in gaining compatibility with international standards in such areas as citizenship, electoral issues, language laws and educational provisions. This exhaustive data set covers 21 Latvian and 18 Estonian cases, backed by interviews with policy makers, and includes cases where the OSCE, the Council of Europe (CE) or the EU were involved, but interestingly also cases in which they were not involved, exploring whether compatibility with international norms could be achieved by internal opposition or external homeland pressure alone. The study confirms that cases of non-involvement by European institutions rarely resulted in outcomes compatible with international norms – in no cases were internal opposition or external homeland pressure capable of overturning policies of the nationalising states. Thus, engagement by international institutions was crucial; beyond that, Kelley argues that conditionality, particularly accession to the CE and EU, provided greater incentives to Estonian and Latvian lawmakers to comply with international standards than did the merely normative approach of the OSCE but that cooperation between the OSCE and other bodies enhanced effectiveness, even when domestic opposition to suggested reforms was high.

Problems arise from Kelley's study because of her assumptions, in many cases unexamined, of what international norms are in various matters. Thus, she asserts, without any argument, that such language education proposals as requiring minority schools to teach some subjects in the national language, or as having higher education in the national language, are contrary to international norms. On citizenship, she acknowledges the lack of international agreement about requirements, but argues that both Estonia and Latvia consistently defied international norms until conditionality pressures were brought to bear. It is certainly true that international organisations were concerned with citizenship in these countries, but it was overwhelmingly the desire to reduce the number of non-citizens, a clearly political aim, rather than any international norms being at stake. On citizenship, only the issue of stateless children could be argued to have some broader basis in international agreement.

In 1994, as previously noted, Latvia worked out its naturalisation law granting automatic citizenship only to those who were citizens in 1940 and to their descendants, and initially favouring a strict quota system of naturalisation which meant that few non-citizens could attain citizenship. European bodies did object to this proposal, and the legislation was changed, with assistance from European experts, to a system of 'windows': non-citizens were grouped according to how long they had resided in Latvia. People under 20 years of age who had been born in Latvia could apply for naturalisation starting from 1996. The final cohort – consisting of the most elderly born outside Latvia – became eligible from 2003. By 1998, however, the pace of naturalisation was perceived to be too slow in the eyes of the OSCE and others, giving rise to a campaign to overturn the windows provision, which European bodies themselves had helped Latvia devise a few years earlier. The tautologous conclusion must be that international standards are whatever international institutions demand, even if these norms are subsequently changed. This, interestingly, is exactly how European pressure was often felt by the Baltic states, and by Macedonia as well.

A second problem lies in the fact that the influence of Russia on the situation in the Baltic has been given inadequate attention. Curiously, as Pettai (2006) points out in his review of Kelley's work, most authors discount the influence of the minority's homeland – in this case, Russia advocating for all 'Russian speakers' – as they cannot see clear outcomes on Brubaker's model of an external homeland playing a significant part in interethnic outcomes. Kelley (2004: 113, 166–170) does, however, acknowledge Russia's crucial role not in determining outcomes but in setting agendas, repeatedly insisting on international intervention, and sometimes causing Baltic leaders to presume that international organisations were working at Russia's bidding (Kelley, 2004: 105). Such agenda-setting can have long-term consequences on the way situations are defined by third parties, including international organisations, yet this constraint in no way influences Kelley's main analysis showing that international norms are regarded as axiomatic and that European institutions simply demand compliance to these axiomatic norms.

Arguably, Kelley's set assumptions regarding international organisations are that:

- International organisations have evolved their stances through a solid basis of accepted law; international organisations have a vital role in spreading ideas particularly of rights and obligations to countries whose level of political development may hinder their understanding of such rights and obligations.
- Disagreements with international organisations are usually narrowly nationalistically based, attesting to political intransigence.
- Solutions to such disagreements and conflicts more generally lie in ensuring better local laws that affect minorities, rather than in international efforts to change the agenda-setting behaviours of other states.

Equally problematic are some of the outcomes themselves and of the ways those outcomes have been viewed by international organisations. Almost invariably, when Baltic countries have agreed in some way to international pressure, profuse praise has emanated from various international bodies, and assertions have been made that these countries are now 'essentially in conformity' with international norms and agreements (e.g. Kelley, 2004: 216, n72), only for another aspect of that same issue to be raised again in future negotiations. Even more ironic were situations in which European institutions went in different directions as, for example, when the CE issued a statement in 1993 that Estonia's law on citizenship 'is extremely liberal' and abstained from setting conditionality requirements on this or any language legislation, while the OSCE was starting to lobby Estonia on precisely this law (quoted in Kelley, 2004: 104). Johns (2003) has more broadly pointed to European organisations' inconsistency in stipulating for the Baltic countries measures on citizenship never demanded of Western European members.

On some occasions actual changes to laws or regulations by Estonia or Latvia did not meet the demands being made of them. Kelley lists a number of cases where only partial agreement was reached. As one Estonian politician stated – after an agreement in which several points that had been insisted upon by European bodies earlier had not been included in final legislation – 'the international institutions wisely understood not to ask for too much' (Kelley, 2004: 89). In this case, clearly, international organisations ostensibly promoting democracy come up against firm views of legislatures as democratic representatives. The hollowness of such statements as being in conformity with international standards in areas where there are in fact few international standards (as in citizenship issues) is frequently overlooked. The mantra of being in accord with international standards may also have had another objective for international organisations – to get Russia and its complaints off their back.

Two further critiques – one theoretical and one surprisingly practical from the field of economics – can be made in regard to international institutions and rights approaches. First, at some distance from a focus on the Baltic, more critical theoretical perspectives have also been directed at language rights theory. Such authors as Stroud (2001), Blommaert (2006) and Pennycook (2006) have argued that standard approaches to minority language situations have been essentialist, seeing an iron link between groups and their languages and between languages and identity, often failing to understand the flux in which individuals live. Blommaert argues that the relation between a language and national identity is not fixed but is, above all, an ideological relation: 'Singular projections of language onto national identity do not work any more .... Language policy, consequently, should best be seen as a niched activity, and the same goes for its desired product, national identity' (Blommaert, 2006: 249).

Echoing from a different perspective some of Deets' concerns, these authors argue that strict identification of groups with their language by international institutions or rights claimers can in itself intensify group conflict and fail to recognise the true language situation which can be very complex as is the case across the Baltic. Stroud points to numerous problems of rights approaches, centrally because:

> [A] rights perspective for all practical purposes assumes a specific understanding of language, identity and group rights. This is one whereby languages are commonly projected to be in 'monovalent' relationship to identity as markers of ethnicity, and as indexically tied to the emotions and social values supposedly attached to the ethnicity. Furthermore, identity is viewed as something fixed, a permanent feature of Self. (Stroud, 2001: 347)

Stroud's own argument for 'linguistic citizenship' stresses the negotiating and empowering possibilities of recognising the diversity of languages and linguistic patterns, rather than of rigid categories, and encouraging cooperation based on the recognition of flux between all minority languages. Pennycook's (2006) more abstract approach dwells on the phenomenology of self in linguistic acts, but also homes in on the valorising and essentialising link that is often too easily assumed between language and groups. For the purposes of this monograph, such approaches stressing individuals and flux may seem far from the mark in the Baltic, where nationalising states have clearly essentialised (to say the least) their national languages, and a clearly oppositional block (and, even more, its external sponsor) has essentialised its position as a fight for one language against the nationalising states. Yet the social does eventually determine the political, and attention to the sociolinguistics and the tell-tale lack of mobilisation behind either extreme nationalist or oppositional leadership means that people are making individual decisions and accommodations, having many different relations to 'their' language and to those around them, and in many cases feeling a linguistic citizenship that belies overt politicisation. Druviete (2002) usefully points to the way in which, in the Baltic region, languages are used and interchanged for any number of instrumental, situational, personal or group reasons, and growing bilingualism only encourages such interchanges. This also reflects the already noted phenomenon of relatively relaxed personal language relations in the Baltic, little marked by hostility towards speakers of other languages.

Kymlicka and Grin (2003), in their insightful survey of language politics in Eastern Europe, also question legalistic approaches to language, in the context of trying to establish clearer criteria of revaluating what policies can be effective in such situations. They observe, first, that language diversity poses problems for liberal political theory: a state cannot be neutral to language as it can, say, to religion; there has to be a language or languages of administration, legislation, education, etc. Liberal approaches that, on other matters, stress freedom and equality cannot give such wide 'hands off' latitude to all possible languages in a state. For Kymlicka and Grin, liberal theory has come to a 'conceptual dead-end in the area of language policy' (Kymlicka & Grin, 2003: 12). Notions of justice and liberalism have not been dominant in the way states go about their language policy in Eastern Europe, as attested to by the need for international pressure on these countries at various points, interventions which 'reveal repeatedly that the underlying concern behind state language polices is not justice, but security' (Kymlicka & Grin, 2003: 13), and this concern for security must be addressed through attention to normative issues for both majorities and minorities. Moreover, attempts to define linguistic human rights fall into difficulty when trying to make universal claims for vastly different minority situations. A multidisciplinary approach is seen to be necessary to comprehend all the factors that affect language politics, among which is taking historical circumstances and nationalism seriously:

> We cannot begin to understand language politics without a sense of how these historical and geopolitical factors are perceived and interpreted through the lens of nationalist ideologies. (Kymlicka & Grin, 2003: 22)

This perception needs to be supplemented, in their view, by a much cooler look at policy analysis and a working out of effectiveness in policy – given certain objectives, what are the policy steps that can most clearly deliver this outcome, regarding both effort and cost, be acceptable to nationalising states but also gain the consent of minorities? Thus, Kymlicka and Grin call for a two-pronged response: better understanding of historical and symbolic context, and more realistic technical appraisals of policies that have a chance of implementation and acceptance.

Almost as if to answer the suggestion by Kymlicka and Grin for a better historical and geopolitical approach, Budryte, in her landmark work, *Taming Nationalism* (2005), takes up themes of historical memories in analysing nationalist ideologies and the convoluted relation between these ideologies and the efforts of international organisations to bend such seemingly illiberal nationalism in a liberal direction. She brings two particular emphases to bear: first, to look at the unintended consequences as well as the well-publicised 'successes' of international intervention; and second, to argue that the reason such unintended consequences were so frequent was precisely because there was a deliberate avoidance of the historical issues that underpinned this nationalism. She quotes approvingly Schöpflin's claim that 'the West has not been prepared to engage with symbolic and historic dimensions of European enlargement so vital to Central Europe's sense of self-esteem' (Budryte, 2005: 192). Budryte's book is an analysis of all three Baltic states, usefully including considerations of Lithuania, which has been unjustifiably neglected in most language policy work on the Baltic, but in which she sees problematic issues arising from nationalism even though there has been little international attention devoted to it. After a compellingly comprehensive review of literature on nationalism, Budryte highlights the issue of historical memory, particularly that of the Soviet period, as underpinning Baltic nationalism and giving it an enduring sense of threat. The emphasis by international organisations on minority rights and their neglect of past national traumas had negative effects: 'Excessive use of minority rights discourse thus became a source of insecurity, especially in Latvia and Estonia', for example in 1998, as a result of European pressure on citizenship requirements, which had the result that "many Latvians perceived this pressure to liberalize the Citizenship Law to be the direct result of Russian influence" (Budryte, 2005: 202). But this effect did not apply only to the Baltic titular nation majority: Budryte cites the widespread perception by both Baltic nationalists *and* Russian minority members that the OSCE High Commissioner for National Minorities was a 'defender' of ethnic Russians in these countries. She concludes that:

> [T]he liberalization of laws on language and citizenship probably did little to help build bridges between the Baltic and Russian communities [...]. The case studies suggest that another unfortunate consequence of international intervention in political community building in Latvia and Estonia was an increase in feelings of victimhood among ethnic Balts and Russian speakers. (Budryte, 2005: 202)

This perception also explains why the eventual Baltic agreements to change legislation at least partially were undertaken for entirely strategic reasons, for access to the CE, EU or NATO, rather than as the result of some 'transformation' of an illiberal nationalism. Every such change was the result of a calculation:

> Latvia and Estonia made concessions related to their citizenship laws and rights of minorities only when they became convinced that these concessions would directly affect their chances for membership in these organizations. (Budryte, 2005: 201)

Moreover, Budryte challenges the view that exclusionary policies in language or citizenship were inimical to the development of democracy. On the contrary, she argues, such exclusion often helped to establish a democratic basis and also slowly to build trust in the regime among the Russian minority, for 'this separation has been part of the solution and a reason why Estonia has managed to maintain a functioning political community' (Budryte, 2005: 91). In relation to the ethnic Russian enclave in the eastern area of Estonia

> the state has tolerated a virtual cultural autonomy in the ethnic enclave and has extended a high degree of self-governance for local communities. Together with the rights to use the state as a 'service station' (i.e. social and economic benefits and the ability to be a member of civil society), these arrangements have probably contributed to the growing acceptance of the Estonian state by Russian speakers'. (Budryte, 2005: 91)

A similar approach was taken by Lithuania to its mixed ethnic enclave in its southeast. This approach also reflects the work of other Baltic scholars who have argued that the restricted citizenship in Latvia provided the basis of a functioning democracy; a zero-option would have led to endless political stalemates and possibly to a constitutional crises as well as an intense ethnic mobilisation (Broks *et al.*, 1996/1997).

Echoing Schöpflin, Budryte argues that 'international actors interested in promoting minority rights and human rights have to be ready to engage the symbolic dimension of nation building' (Budryte, 2005: 200). Even in Lithuania, with citizenship available to all, with much greater knowledge of the official language by minorities and certainly with less intervention by international organisations, she finds persistent anxiety over the loyalty of its Russian and Polish minorities, as witnessed in ongoing arguments over minority language schools and strong ethnic voting patterns (Budryte, 2005: 168–170). Again, the basis of such differences can only be understood by reference to historical relations between these groups.

If a better understanding of historical aspects is required of international organisations, then so too, in Budryte's view, is a democratisation of history needed in the Baltic states and in Eastern Europe more generally. Following the work of Onken, the victimhood narratives she identifies still serve as 'dominant narratives', used officially and endlessly by the respective groups (whether leaders of a nationalising state or leaders of a minority), consequently assuming a ritual status. On the contrary, what is needed is to provide a history that looks at variation in experience and at paradoxes of personal and group involvement, understanding one's nation as sometimes collaborators or sometimes bystanders, as well as sometimes victims. Budryte concludes that such a process will only be really successful if it is also carried out in the minority's 'homeland' – Russia in the case of the three Baltic states, and Poland in the case of Lithuania (Budryte, 2005: 192). While such a process has begun in Poland, the still dominant narratives emanating from Russia give little hope for such a process there in the near future. In the meantime, international efforts to influence Eastern European national states will only have limited outreach, particularly at the normative level:

> International influence can affect government policies and legislation, but it is unrealistic to expect that the international actors pursuing

'Europeanization' are going to re-shape the identities of nation-states and affect societal norms and prevalent attitudes. (Budryte, 2005: 202)

Budryte's work thus provides one path towards basing language policy upon more realistic and more historically and geopolitically attuned approaches to majority/minority relations. The other line of argument, deriving from Kymlicka and Grin, recalls the detail of language policy and the way language change can be encouraged or thwarted by international organisations.

Such authors as Skutnabb-Kangas (2006) and such international instruments as the Hague Recommendations Regarding the Educational Rights of National Minorities have stressed the need for minorities to learn majority languages, and not to refuse bilingualism and a share in the national culture. This notion of bilingualism has been a bedrock of Baltic approaches to language policy and integration, but the approach has received only partial recognition in the work of European organisations, largely through the support for various language teaching programs for Russian speakers, as described in parts 3 and 4. However, European interest in language teaching has been, arguably, a purely political concern for raising citizenship rates, while paradoxically vetoing other requirements to promote use of the language. A substantial critique of such approaches comes in the work of Grin (1999), who argues that much language policy is often excessively concerned with 'supply-side' issues – that is, with the inputs into language education or other areas – rather than with looking analytically and historically at more fundamental issues of language use, language attitudes and end-user incentives.

In the Baltic case, a particular version of this supply-side approach is evident, with the emphasis from international organisations on formal language learning, and with the material support of numerous language learning initiatives. Yet while financing some language teaching programs, and making hopeful statements about minorities learning the Baltic languages (Holt & Packer, 2001: 4), much more European effort has gone into limiting demands by the state for official language capacity; as previously noted, international organisations have moved against some of the clearest incentives that could be built into a system for language learning and language use – for example, their objection to ensuring language capacity in the private economic sector. Druviete criticises such moves:

> If there is no incentive to use the language for practical purposes, [then teaching] it is simply like pouring water into a leaking bucket – a vicious circle. (quoted in Budryte, 2005: 121)

The fundamental understanding of language pedagogy and language psychology – that language learning depends critically upon opportunity to use the target language in meaningful contexts – has been ignored. The evidence that the requirements for language attestation has been a major stimulus to improving capacity in the language (an even greater stimulus than gaining citizenship) has been demonstrated in both Estonia and Latvia (Druviete, 1998: 141; Järve, 2002: 93), and has provided the basis for changing the linguistic ecology in these countries. The seeming view of some international organisations that only supply-side measures can be taken to affect language capacity thus lies squarely at odds with language realities, weakening the credibility of these organisations while not necessarily weakening their political clout.

Part VI: A Language Planning Conclusion

The relatively short intellectual history of language planning has constantly struggled to formulate more or less general principles of planned language change in the face of the extreme variety of historical language situations. The politics of language in Eastern Europe in recent decades has led language planning to become much more alert to issues of language ideology and the structuring of language regimes, bringing the realm of values and power into understandings of language that may in the past have been seen in more technical or apolitical ways.

In the Baltic states, emerging controversies have often been defined as issues of minority rights, with an implicit assumption of a powerful and even predatory official state language, which is far from the case. Curiously, in the evolution of language planning as a field of study, the nature of the link between official state language and minorities is often assumed rather than made an object of study and theory building: not the least contribution that an understanding of the Baltic states' language situation can make is to provide us with much more sensitive awareness of the interplay and complexity of majority/minority language relations.

From a language planning perspective, in this section a brief summary of two phases of Baltic language policy is offered: (1) the early post-Soviet years witnessing the overthrow of the Soviet language regime; and (2) a more recent phase of heightened internationalisation of language and related issues is also considered. Identifying some of the current tasks for language planning in the three Baltic states together with a brief recapitulation of the broader international implications of the Baltic states' language planning experience is provided by way of conclusion.

Factors making for success or lack of success in planned language change: The 'early years' of Baltic language policy

The early period of renewed Baltic language policy – from the late 1980s to the mid-1990s – provides a particular vantage point for looking at how changes to a language regime are promulgated and broadcast in a complex historico-linguistic setting, and what language changes can or cannot be expected to occur quickly. Maurais (1991, 1997) points to a number of features of the Baltic language situation that, on the one hand, contributed to successful implementation, and on the other hand, contributed to delay and opportunities foregone.

Language laws as power redistributors

Language laws caused the mobilisation of groups based on linguistic interests. However, anxiety lies not only in the content of the law, but also in the political factors behind the law. Maurais analysed the Estonian Language Law in comparison with Quebec's law and with the laws of four other Soviet Republics, noting that the language question conceals power struggles in a given society; that is, extralinguistic factors play their part in language planning (Maurais, 1991: 119).

*Language laws were intended for propagandistic purposes
as well as for implementation*

The centrality of language to Baltic national identity meant that, to some extent, the language laws of the late 1980s acted as *de facto* statements of independence, being largely symbolic and declarative. Thus, they should be considered to be signals for power change and broader regime realignment. Implementation of the laws was secondary, and it was also politically sensitive, demanding postponement into the future. This factor may provide an explanation of why, in all three Baltic states, the language laws were the focus of attention from 1988 but the various offices for implementation of the laws were only established slowly and with some considerable time lag. Maurais (1997: 158), observing these problems, regards as a major flaw the lack of a state agency charged with all the practical aspects of implementing the change-over from Russian in particular contexts at the initial stage.

Visible signs of the new language policy

Maurais, (1997: 152) emphasises the necessity for perceptible change in some language policy domains, in order to reduce uncertainty about the future of the language concerned through visible, concrete manifestations of the language. In the Baltic case, despite the lag in establishing state agencies to supervise implementation, the process worked out well:

(1)   through initially public bilingual signs rapidly becoming monolingual in national languages;
(2)   through public information being delivered in the national languages – even in minor areas such as announcements about public transport;
(3)   through language requirements for employment which were, as previously noted, the most potent motivators for learning and using the national languages.

Language requirements instead of ethnic criteria

In the Baltic case, language as a vital element of national identity and national survival was non-negotiable. At the same time, the issue of ethnicity was less significant. Thus, no ethnic preferences in legislation and administration were introduced; instead, however, language requirements were the most significant means of signalling the change from the Soviet regime, while simultaneously providing clear language rights – but no longer hegemonic rights – for speakers of other languages. Significantly, however, both opponents of these changes and, in some cases, international bodies wanting to play a mediating role often characterised (or assumed) the desired changes to be ethnically based, as a move against one ethnic group in each country, rather than as a strategy for preserving a threatened language. Moreover, this concern over ethnicity came in a confused way, employing the concept *Russian speakers* almost as a substitute ethnic category. There is a particular tenacity required on the part of any movement desiring language change to show what its real motivations are and to overcome the accusation of ethnic preference; threats to a language are often seen or valued only by that language group.

In this way, the adoption of the Laws signalled the redistribution of power and the formation of new elites in the Baltic. However, due to the limited formal changes for most of the Russian-speaking population (the Laws did not concern most of them directly or immediately), the ambiguity of the situation with the two endo-majorities remained, thus causing several additional conflicts to emerge and offering grounds for outside political interference. Greater salience of the language laws only came with the delayed attestation of titular language skills for those in public contact situations from around 1992. Fundamental school reform was, however, another decade away. Maurais thus identifies a number of missed or delayed opportunities, as well as a number of successful initiatives in the Baltic case, with an implicit reference to the more structurally thorough language policy in the Quebec situation.

One contextual difference of great significance in comparing Quebec with the Baltic States, however, is that, in the Quebec case, the issue of a language law and Francophone reorientation was seen as the most critical issue the Quebec legislature adopted and the main focus of a controlled and well-planned implementation strategy. In the Baltic states, on the other hand, the language laws were propagated in contexts of huge social turmoil, economic downturn, catastrophic decline of governmental budgets and all the other salient features marking the end of the Soviet Union, thus language laws were far from the only concern of policy makers who were responding to often astonishingly rapid changes of events. Nor was the Baltic situation one where the more subtle, patient but relentless Catalonian drive for 'normalisation' could be emulated in a relatively peaceful context. Both Quebec and Catalonia must ultimately be seen in language planning terms as essentially federalist struggles. Significantly, the period of the late 1980s was one during which the Baltic states were themselves in a 'federalist' situation, albeit one very different to federalism in liberal democracies; thus, the comparisons made by Maurais are of great value. But upon independence this situation changed as international pressures from both East and West bore heavily on the new States. Whatever federalist struggles Quebec or Catalonia had to fight, they did not have to face significant international opposition.

The changing context of Baltic language policy: International attention and local priorities

The period of the late 1990s and the early 2000s has seen the substantial internationalisation of language and related issues in the Baltic, detailed in Part 3 and subsequently. The historic concern of Western Europe to monitor Eastern European minority situations, from as far back as the Versailles Treaty of 1918, has taken on new aspects, particularly in the context of various human dimension and human rights concerns of a number of European bodies, backed by conditional criteria for acceptance into European institutions. If the 'early years' of Baltic language policy were a direct expression of the Baltic States' intention to undo a Soviet linguistic heritage, then the more recent period can be seen as a period of greater negotiation of norms and closer international scrutiny, and while tactical changes have been made by the Baltic States in some areas of language policy, it is argued that the original intentions have been largely maintained.

Yet significantly, despite the appeal to rationalism and the attention to legal norms, this latter phase has seen if anything an even stronger enunciation of language ideologies, both from the Baltic states and their advocates on the one hand, and from international and European organisations on the other often needing to articulate their own assumptions, critically examined in Part 5. Blommaert (1999) uses the concept of language ideologies to analyse the sometimes unspoken, sometimes loudly proclaimed assumptions that underpin language policies and that often arise from concerns far removed from language per se. Assertions of universal values or agreed frameworks on language issues, particularly in this case to persuade Eastern European countries of their merits, often reveal the incommensurability between these Western European normative assertions and the continuing lived experience and ongoing post-Soviet situation in Eastern Europe.

Smith (2001) has described this approach as the 'Western project', promoting policies of human rights and multiculturalism in a context where Eastern European countries with alternative belief systems and experiences are often seen as recalcitrant if they are reluctant to adopt suggested approaches. Yet as Kymlicka (2002) has argued, most Western European countries have only recently come to adopt multicultural policies and ideologies with respect of their own populations, and these policies and ideologies themselves remain highly varied, and they are not systematically applied.

Along lines similar to Blommaert' position, May argues that many approaches to language issues through international frameworks adopt a synchronic or, using Bourdieu's term, a *presentist* stance, emphasising egalitarianisms, thus 'under-emphasising the specific socio-historical and socio-political processes' (May, 2003: 126). As argued in the previous chapter, such *presentist* stipulations provide an air of universality, but at the cost of relevance to particular situations. From a wider language planning perspective, this stance emphasises the need to replace earlier models of language planning as social engineering (or some current perspectives of language planning as legalistic maxims) with what Blommaert sees as a more critical and diachronic analysis taking account of the diverse factors of human agency, political intervention and power relations in the way they construct strong but also changing national ideologies (Blommaert, 1999: 7). In the light of such concerns Hogan-Brun argues:

> the transferability of Western models of minority rights and multicultural citizenship is limited by the effects of diverging sociohistorical and socio-political configurations on the structure and outlook of society in applicant countries in Central and Eastern Europe. (Hogan-Brun, 2005c: 374)

Yet while recognising the importance of values and ideologies in these contexts, language planning must not constitute only politico-historical analyses, but must attend to issues that are often equally ignored in *presentist* or legalistic formulations: that is, actual language use, language attitudes, language interaction and the myriad ways in which these are changing and evolving. Most critically, this approach enables language planning to move beyond sometimes assumed mechanistic links between language and ethnic groups, or between languages and identity; the valorisation of these links, assumed to be unchanging entities through legalistic approaches or defences of rights, can entrench rigidity and division that such approaches claim to want to overcome in the name of promoting integration or human rights.

In terms of actual language use, facility and attitudes, the Baltic states have:

- been able to alter radically their streetscapes and townscapes in signage;
- brought about a steady and continuing increase of proficiency in the national languages among non-titular nationals;
- witnessed largely positive attitudes to their language policy developing in the non-titular populations;
- started to effect a transition to a significant proportion of teaching in the national languages in minority secondary schools;
- brought about a virtually total proficiency in the national language in the service sector;
- refined national language teaching and language testing for adults to a world standard;
- significantly entrenched their languages in the structures of the EU.

At the same time, minority languages have not been extinguished; rather, a particular emphasis has developed on providing elementary education in a number of non-Russian minority languages, thus beginning to reverse the previous Russification of other minorities. In terms of Russian, there has been a continuation of a broad Russian linguistic environment with high language maintenance through a system of schooling, appropriate media and cultural institutions, aided of course by the proximity of Russia itself. These achievements have occurred in a context of extreme economic pressure, the need to alter radically many aspects of the Soviet heritage, and incessant pressure from Russia and from various international players.

Current agendas in Baltic language planning

The at times divergent histories of language policy in Lithuania on the one hand and in Estonia and Latvia on the other mean that there are some differences in agendas in current language planning in the three countries. In the more politicised situations in Estonia and Latvia, secondary school reform remains the most watched issue; particularly as Estonia is due to introduce a larger number of subjects to be taught in Estonian in Russian medium secondary schools in 2007. The Latvian experience of such a move in 2004, with relatively quiet consolidation after intense initial politicising, augers well for the Estonian situation, but the lack of an Estonian linguistic environment in the Eastern border area will make this plan perhaps harder to achieve than it was in Latvia. The issue of language use in official institutions in areas of high minority concentration will continue to smoulder, though the steadily greater facility in the national languages among all but the oldest of the Soviet period settlers will likely slowly dissipate this contention as an issue.

The overt politicisation of many aspects of language policy has meant there has been inadequate attention to what may be considered the 'normal science' of language planning – in particular corpus planning and terminology – but also the historical philological attention to issues such as dialects and variation. While the issue of dialects in Estonia and Latvia has certainly fallen into the shadows, it can be predicted that a greater attention will be brought to bear on the particular issues of Võro (southern Estonian) in Estonia and Lattgallian in Latvia, despite scarcity of resources.

Lithuania has avoided some of the sharper conflicts in forcing change to language regimes by adopting a more *laissez-faire* attitude to its much smaller minorities – for example, by making no formal changes to the curriculum of Russian medium secondary schools, but rather by allowing demographic change (particularly the miniscule Russian birth-rate and the increasing tendency of Russian parents to send their children to Lithuanian medium schools), gradually to reduce the number and salience of Russian schools.

The Polish community, the largest of all non-Lithuanian communities, has shown a keen interest in retaining and actively promoting their Polish identity, while at the same time (like other ethnic minority communities) they have become increasingly proficient in Lithuanian. The majority of ethnic minority population is bilingual, and some – particularly Poles – are trilingual. This development suggests that language policy should be directed towards the maintenance and support of bilingualism and multilingualism.

Standard Lithuanian enjoys high status and prestige, but it is based on one dialect, whereas other dialects are at a disadvantage, as they are considered to be inaccurate and inappropriate for the public domain, although they are not only used in rural areas but also in towns and cities. The low prestige of regional varieties puts them at risk of deterioration or death. Therefore, one of the challenges for the present and the future is the promotion of dialects and the improvement of their status.

A number of language planning activities and needs can, however, be identified as common across the three Baltic states. These include:

- increasing use of the Common European Framework to set standards and methodologies for teaching the titular languages as second languages, and for teaching foreign languages, along the lines of the first language +2 formula;
- early teaching of a first foreign language in primary schools together with introducing a second foreign language also in later primary school is now becoming widespread;
- attention to orthographic issues, particularly in light of the common historical practice in all three countries to titularise the orthography of foreign names, a very strong principle in all three languages but one that creates negative responses from some;
- greater attention to foreign language needs and impacts; above all the predominant student and market preference for English that needs to be balanced with other foreign language needs, while Russian, though losing popularity as a foreign language in schools, is still very widely used as a language in business and commerce;
- greater corpus planning and terminological development, particularly in areas of technology, and again much related to the increasing salience of English as a source language;
- finally, a need for continuing monitoring of the effectiveness of language requirements and equally a watchfulness over political processes that may weaken the titular languages: some political parties are currently more aggressively targeting naturalised citizens and promising changes to language or citizenship requirements. For a certain section of the political

elite in all three Baltic states, despite their occasional national rhetoric, language issues are of little concern and could become one more pawn to barter for political gain internally or externally.

Implications of the Baltic examples

This monograph began by outlining a number of ways in which the Baltic language policy record may have implications for many other language situations around the world. Given the detailed analysis of the Baltic situation, some of these implications can be pointed to more generally.

First, the Baltic states stand as a significant exemplar in language planning of previously marginalised languages regaining their national status. Notwithstanding the sociopolitical differences that attend each distinct language situation, if languages are to change their status systematically, then many of the processes will be similar to what has occurred in the Baltic states. Forced language change brought about by massive demographic shifts, and fostered by external forces can be ameliorated and reversed – to what ultimate extent remains the unanswered question for the Baltics. The case of the Baltic states constitutes a testament to determined language planning, showing how national languages can defend themselves. While not threatened by any direct invasion or colonisation, many countries are equally concerned to defend their national languages against potentially newer and perhaps more subtle threats, such as the influence of English or a deteriorating speaker base for their language. As well, the Baltic states experience shows a considerable resistance to language policy initiatives from a small but well-supported part of the Russophone population arguing for the right to remain monolingual, and it raises the important issue of language planning often leading to loss of privilege for a particular linguistic group.

Second, the growing attention to, and at times enforcement of, legal and rights-driven frameworks by European bodies, extensively commented on previously, has brought its own reaction, with a growing critique as detailed in the work of Blommaert, Kymlicka and others previously cited, often reflecting the particular counterarguments to European imperatives espoused by Baltic authors. The Baltic case provides some suggestive implications for what is increasingly seen as the need to temper universalist approaches with a sound understanding of local history in language policy, particularly for cultures with a strong allegiance to their language as the bedrock of their culture and existence. The radically divergent interpretations that exist of the Baltic situations in their legal as well as their political aspects underline this point.

Third, the technologies of change in Baltic language situations are well documented, providing a particular range of approaches likely to be included in the repertoire of any nation, region or group seeking to overturn a previous language regime. As an illustration, the situation in the mid-2000s when a number of Western European countries are seemingly hastily adopting measures for testing national language competence of immigrant populations, or testing their immigrants' knowledge of the ways of the host country, present an ironic commentary on previous criticisms of the Baltic countries for adopting seemingly similar measures. After a slow start in the post-Soviet climate, technologies ranging from second language teaching to language testing to language inspection and changes in school curriculum and methodology have been developed at times with significant European or other international help but increasingly from local resources.

Fourth and finally, the Baltic states have adopted an unreservedly historical approach to both a national language and to multilingualism, taking as their reference point a previous statehood and a civil society overthrown by the Soviet regime and consequently needing to regain their former status. The particular language policy initiatives have not been narrowly ethnically based but rather have recognise a long-standing tradition in the Baltics of multilingualism and a degree of cultural autonomy that is difficult to re-establish after the atomising experience of Soviet occupation. While the Baltic states seem to have effectively re-established their national languages, present and foreseeable language policies will enable the Baltic states to continue both their national and multilingual traditions.

Correspondence

Any correspondence should be directed to Gabrielle Hogan-Brun, Graduate School of Education, University of Bristol, Bristol, England (g.hogan-brun@bristol.ac.uk).

References

Aasland, A. (2002) Citizenship status and social exclusion in Estonia and Latvia. *Journal of Baltic Studies* 33 (1), 57–77.
Aasland, A. and Tyldum, G. (2000) *Better or Worse? Living Conditions Developments in Estonia, Latvia and Lithuania 1994–1999.* Oslo: FAFO, Report No. 334 On WWW at http://www.fafo.no/norbalt/index.htm. Accessed 17.09.07.
Adrey, J-B. (2005) Minority language rights before and after the 2004 EU enlargement: The Copenhagen Criteria in the Baltic States. In G. Hogan-Brun (ed.) Language and Social Processes in the Baltic Republics Surrounding EU Accession, Special Issue. *Journal of Multilingual and Multicultural Development* 26 (5), 453–468.
Alenius, K. (2004) Under the conflicting pressures of the ideals of the era and the burdens of history: Ethnic relations in Estonia 1918–1925. *Journal of Baltic Studies* 35 (1), 32–49.
Alksnis, V. (1991) Suffering from self-determination. *Foreign Policy* 84, 61–71.
Applebaum, A. (1994) *Between East and West.* New York and Toronto: Random House.
Arter, D. (1993) *The Politics of European Integration in the Twentieth Century.* Aldershot: Dartmouth.
Baltic Institute of Social Research (2003) *Language 2003.* On WWW at http://www.bszi.lv/downloads/resources/language/Language_2003.pdf
Bernier, J. (2001) Nationalism in transition: Nationalizing impulses and international counter-weights in Latvia and Estonia. In M. Keating and J. McGarry (eds) *Minority Nationalism and the Changing International Order* (pp. 342–362). New York: Oxford University Press.
Bildt, C. (1994) The Baltic litmus test. *Foreign Affairs* 73 (5), 72–85.
Björklund, F. (2005) Ethnic politics and the Soviet legacy in Latvian post-Communist education: The place of language. In W. Safran and J.A. Laponce (eds) *Language, Ethnic Identity and the State* (pp. 105–134). London and New York: Routledge.
Blackledge, A. (2006) The magical frontier between the dominant and the dominated: Sociolinguistics and social justice in a multilingual world. *Journal of Multilingual and Multicultural Development* 27 (1), 22–41.
Blake, M. (2003) Language death and liberal politics. In W. Kymlicka and A. Patten (eds) *Language Rights and Political Theory* (pp. 210–229). Oxford: Oxford University Press.

Blinkena, A. (1985) The role of the neo-Latvians in forming the Latvian literary language. Acta *Universitatis Stockholmiensis–Studia Baltica Stockholmiensia* 2, 341.

Blommaert, J. (ed.) (1999) *Language Ideological Debates*. Berlin: Mouton de Gruyter.

Blommaert, J. (2006) Language policy and national identity. In T. Ricento (ed.) *An Introduction to Language Policy* (pp. 238–254). Malden, MA: Blackwells.

Board for Citizenship and Migration Affairs (2006) On WWW at http://www.np.gov.lv/index.php?en=fakti_en&saite=residents.htm. Accessed 17.9.07.

Bratt Paulston, C. and Heidemann, K. (2006) The education of linguistic minorities. In T. Ricento (ed.) *An Introduction to Language Policy* (pp. 292–310). Malden, MA: Blackwells.

Broks, J., Ozolins, U., Ozolzile, G., Tabuns, A. and Tisenkopfs, T. (1996/1997) The stability of democracy in Latvia: Pre-requisites and prospects. *Humanities and Social Sciences Latvia*. Double edition: no. 4 (13) 1996; no. 1 (14), 1997.

Brubaker, R. (1995) Aftermaths of empire and the unmixing of peoples: Historical and comparative perspectives. *Ethnic and Racial Studies* 18 (2), 189–218.

Brubaker, R. (1996) *Nationalism Reframed: Nationhood and the National Question in the New Europe*. New York: Cambridge University Press.

Budryte, D. (2005) *Taming Nationalism? Political Community Building in the Post-Soviet Baltic States*. Aldershot: Ashgate.

Burgess, A. (1999) Critical reflections on the return of national minority rights regulations to East/West European affairs. In K. Cordell (ed.) *Ethnicity and Democratisation in the New Europe* (pp. 49–60). London and New York: Routledge.

Chandler, D. (1999) The OSCE and the internationalisation of national minority rights. In K. Cordell (ed.) *Ethnicity and Democratisation in the New Europe* (pp. 61–76). London and New York: Routledge.

Chinn, J. and Truex, L.A. (1996) The question of citizenship in the Baltic. *Journal of Democracy* 7 (1), 133–147.

Cibuļs, J. (2004) Latgaļu valoda starp izglītības un valodu politikas dzirņakmeņiem (The Latgalian language between the millstones of education and language politics). In *Valodas politika un sociolingvistiskie jautājumi* (Language Policy and Sociolinguisitcs) 1, *Proceedings of the Conference 'Regional Languages in the New Europe'* (pp. 31–43). Rezekne: Rezekne University, Department of Philology.

Clemens, W. (1991) *Baltic Independence and the Russian Empire*. New York: St. Martin's.

Common European Framework of Reference for Languages: Learning, Teaching, Assessment (2001) Cambridge: Cambridge University Press.

Comrie, B. (1981) *The Languages of the Soviet Union*. Cambridge: Cambridge University Press.

Coulmas, F. (1988) *With Forked Tongues: What are National Languages Good For?* Ann Arbour: Karoma.

Coulmas, F. (1998) Language rights – interests of state, language groups and the individual. *Language Sciences* 20 (1), 63–72.

Crawford, J. (2000) *At War with Diversity. U.S. Language Policy in an Age of Anxiety*. Clevedon: Multilingual Matters.

Crols, D. (2005) Old and new minorities on the international checkboard: From League to Union. In D.J. Smith (ed.) *The Baltic States and their Region: New Europe or Old?* (pp. 185–209). Amsterdam: Rodolphi.

CSCE [Conference on Security and Cooperation in Europe]– see OSCE.

Dallin, A. and Lapidus, G.W. (eds) (1995) *The Soviet System: from Crisis to Collapse*. Boulder: Westview.

Davies, N. (1997) *Europe. A History*. London: Pimlico.

Deets, T. (2002) Reconsidering East European minority policy: Liberal theory and European norms. *East European Politics and Societies* 16 (1), 30–54.

Dellenbrant, J.A. (1990) The Integration of the Baltic Republics into the Soviet Union. In D.A. Loeber, V.S. Vardys and L.A. Kitching (eds). *Regional Identity under Soviet Rule: The Case of the Baltic States* (pp. 101–120). Hackettstown, NY: Publications of the Association for the Advancement of Baltic Studies, 6.

Demuth, A. (2000) Politics, migration and minorities in independent and Soviet Estonia. Dissertation im Fach Geschichte zur Erlangung des Grades Dr. Phil. vorgelegt von

Andreas Demuth. Graduiertenkolleg Migration im modernen Europa. Osnabrück: Institut für Migrationsforschung und Interkulturelle Studien (IMIS).

de Varennes, F. (1995/6) The protection of linguistic minorities in Europe and human rights: Possible solutions to ethnic conflicts? *Columbia Journal of European Law* 2 (1), 107–143.

de Varennes, F. (1996) *Language Minorities and Human Rights*. International Studies in Human Rights (Vol. 45). The Hague/Boston/London: Martinus Nijhoff.

Dini, P.U. (2000) *Baltų kalbos. Lyginamoji istorija* (The Baltic Languages. Comparative History).Vilnius: Mokslo ir enciklopedijų leidybos institutas.

Dini, P. (1999) The dispute among Vilnius humanists regarding Latin, Lithuanian and Ruthenian. *Historiographia Linguistica* XXVI (1/2), 23–36.

Dini, P. (2005) Towards a Baltic linguistics historiography? *Journal of Multilingual and Multicultural Development* 26 (5), 469–473.

Dobson, J. (2001) Ethnic Discrimination in Latvia. In C.C. O'Reilly (ed.) *Language, Ethnicity and the State* (Vol. 2), *Minority Languages in Eastern Europe Post-1989* (pp. 155–188). Houndmills & New York: Palgrave.

Driessen, B. (1999) The Slovak State Language Law as a trade law problem. In M. Kontra, R. Phillipson, T. Skutnabb-Kangas and T. Varady (eds) *Language, A Right and a Resource: Approaching Linguistic Human Rights* (pp. 147–165). Budapest and New York: Central European University Press.

Druviete, I. (1995) *The Language Situation in Latvia* (Part I) [in Latvian]. Riga: Latvian Language Institute.

Druviete, I. (1996) *The Language Situation in Latvia* (Part II) [in Latvian]. Riga: Latvian Language Institute.

Druviete, I. (1997) Linguistic human rights in the Baltic States. *International Journal of the Sociology of Language* 127, 161–186.

Druviete, I. (1998) La situation sociolinguistique de la langue lettone. In J. Maurais (ed.) *Les Politiques Linguistiques des Pays baltes*. Special number of *Terminogramme* (pp. 105–149). Quebec: Office de la langue française.

Druviete, I. (1999) Language policy in a changing society: problematic issues of implementation of universal linguistic human rights standards. In M. Kontra, R. Phillipson, T. Skutnabb-Kangas and T. Varady (eds) *Language, A Right and a Resource: Approaching Linguistic Human Rights* (pp. 263–276). Budapest and New York: Central European University Press.

Druviete, I. (2000) *Sociolinguistic Situation and Language Policy in the Baltic States*. Riga: Mācību apgāds.

Druviete, I. (2002) The future of the Latvian language in the enlarged European Union. *Humanities and Social Sciences in Latvia* 1 (34), 34–46.

Druviete, I. (2003) Sociolinguistic Processes and Language Policy Latvia. Baltic Language and Integration Network. *1st BLaIN Workshop*, Vilnius, 16–18 June 2003. On WWW at http://www.blain-online.org/abstracts.doc. Accessed 17.9.07.

Dunbar, R. (2001) Minority language rights in international law. *International and Comparative Law Quarterly* 50, 90–120.

Education Law. On WWW at http://www.legaltext.ee/en/andmebaas/ava.asp?m=022. Accessed 17.9.07.

Education Law. On WWW at http://www.aic.lv/rec/Eng/leg_en/LV_lik/ed_law.htm. Accessed 17.9.07.

Erelt, T. and Laanekask, H. (2003) Written Estonian. In M. Erelt (ed.) *Estonian Language* (pp. 273–342). Tallinn: Linguistica Uralica.

Erelt, M., Sedrik, M. and Uuspõld, E. (eds) (1997) *Pühendusteos Huno Rätsepale: 28.12.1997 keeleteadlase 70. sünnipäevaks* (Festschrift for Huno Rätsep on the occasion of his 70th birthday). Tartu: Tartu Ülikool.

Ernstone, V. (2001) Paaudžu komunikācija ikdienā: Sociolingvistiskais aspects (Communication across generations in everyday life: Sociolinguistic aspects). *International Conference on Communication and Community* ('Komunikācija un kopība') 17–18 May, Abstracts (pp. 5–6) Jelgava: Institute of Humanities, Jelgava Agricultural University.

Estonian Census (2000) On WWW at http://pub.stat.ee/px-web.2001/I_Databas/Population_Census/Population_Census.asp. Accessed 17.9.07.

Estonica (2006) *The Estonian Language.* On WWW at http://www.estonica.org/eng/lugu. html?menyy_id=1090&kateg=38&nimi=&alam=101&tekst_id=1091. Accessed 17.9.07.
Euromosaic (2004a) Estonia – Country profile. On WWW at http://ec.europa.eu/ education/policies/lang/languages/langmin/euromosaic/lat5_en.html#. Accessed 17.9.07.
Euromosaic (2004b) *Latvia – Country profile.* On WWW at http://ec.europa.eu/ education/policies/lang/languages/langmin/euromosaic/lat5_en.html#. Accessed 17.9.07.
European Commission (1997) *Commission Opinion on Estonia's Application for Membership of the European Union.* Luxembourg: European Commission.
European Commission (2002a) *Regular Report on Estonia's Progress Towards Accession.* Brussels: Commission of the European Communities. On WWW at http://ec.europa. eu/enlargement/archives/enlargement_process/past_enlargements/eu10/ estonia_en.htm. Accessed 17.9.07.
European Commission (2002b) Regular Report on Latvia's Progress Towards Accession. Brussels: Commission of the European Communities. On WWW at http://ec.europa. eu/enlargement/archives/enlargement_process/past_enlargements/eu10/latvia_ en/htm. Accessed 17.9.07.
European Court of Human Rights (2002a) *Podkolzina v. Lettonie.* Case 46726/99.
European Court of Human Rights (2002b) *Press Release issued by the Registrar. Chamber Judgment in the case of Podkolzina v. Latvia.* 9 April. On WWW at www.echr.coe.int/ Eng/Press/2002/apr/PR%20Podkolzina%2009042002E.htm. Accessed 17.9.07.
Fennell, T. and Lambert, B. (2000) Calming the Baltic waters: Latvia's president, who spent 44 years in Canada, wrestles with the language issue. *Maclean's*, 7 February, 26.
Forgus, S. (1992) Soviet subversive activities in independent Estonia (1918–1940). *Journal of Baltic Studies* 23 (1): 29–46.
Framework Convention for the Protection of National Minorities. On WWW at http:// conventions.coe.int/Treaty/EN/Treaties/Html/157.htm. Accessed 14.01.07.
Freimane, V. (2000) Remembering Paul Schiemann. *Journal of Baltic Studies* 31 (4), 432–437.
Fukuyama, F. (1992) Trapped in the Baltics. *New York Times*, 19 December, 15.
Galbreath, D.J. (2005) *Nation-Building and Minority Politics in Post-Socialist States.* Stuttgart: Ibidem Verlag.
Galbreath, D.J and Galvin, M.E. (2005) The titularization of Latvian secondary schools: The historical legacy of Soviet policy implementation. *Journal of Baltic Studies* 36 (4) 449–466.
Galtung, J. (1996) *Peace By Peaceful Means: Peace and Conflict, Development and Civilization.* International Peace Research Institute; Oslo, London, Thousand Oaks, California, and New Delhi: SAGE Publications.
Gellner, E. (1983) *Nations and Nationalism.* Oxford: Blackwell.
Gerner, K. and Hedlund, S. (1993) *The Baltic States at the End of the Soviet Empire.* London: Routledge.
Gimbutas, M. (1963) *The Balts.* New York: Frederick A. Praeger.
Girdenis, A. and Pabrėža, J. (1998) *Žemaičių rašyba* (Orthography of Samogitian). Vilnius-Šiauliai: Žemaičių kultūros draugijos redakcija.
Grin, F. (1991) The Estonian language law: Presentation with comments. *Language Problems and Language Planning* 15 (2), 191–201.
Grin, F. (1999) Supply and demand as analytic tools in language policy. In A. Breton (ed.) *Exploring the Economics of Language* (pp. 31–61). New Canadian Perspectives Series. Canada: Canadian Heritage.
Grumadienė, L. (2004) The Sociolinguistic situation of the Samogitians. In *Language Policy and Sociolinguistics.* Proceedings of the Conference on *Regional Languages in the New Europe.* International Scientific Conference, 20–23 May 2004, Rezekne. Vol. 1, 104–110.
Hennoste, T. (ed.) (1999) Estonian sociolinguistics. *International Journal of the Sociology of Language* 139, 1–16.
Henricksson, A. (1983) *The Czar's Loyal Germans.* Boulder: East European Monographs.
Hiden, J. (2004) *Defender of Minorities: Paul Schiemann, 1876–1944.* London: Hurst & Company.

Hiden, J. and Salmon, P. (1991) *The Baltic Nations and Europe. Estonia, Latvia and Lithuania in the 21st Century.* London and New York: Longman.

Hogan-Brun, G. (2003) Baltic national minorities in a transitional setting. In G. Hogan Brun and S. Wolff (eds) *Minority Languages in Europe: Status – Frameworks – Prospects* (pp. 120–135) Houndmills: Palgrave/Macmillan.

Hogan-Brun, G. (guest ed.) (2005a) Language and social processes in the Baltic Republics surrounding EU accession (Special Issue). *Journal of Multilingual and Multicultural Development* 26 (5).

Hogan-Brun, G. (guest ed.) (2005b) Baltic sociolinguistic review. (Special Issue). *Journal of Baltic Studies* 36 (3).

Hogan-Brun, G. (guest ed.) (2005c) The Baltic Republics and language ideological debates surrounding their EU accession, in language and social processes in the Baltic Republics surrounding EU accession. (Special Issue). *Journal of Multilingual and Multicultural Development* 26 (5), 367–377.

Hogan-Brun, G. (2006) At the interface of language ideology and practice: The public discourse surrounding the 2004 education reform in Latvia. *Language Policy* 5 (2), 313–333.

Hogan-Brun, G. (2007a, in press) Contesting social space through language education debates in Latvia's media landscape. In M. Krzyzanowski and A. Galasińka (eds) *Discourse and Social Change – Post-Communism and Beyond.* Houndmills: Palgrave/Macmillan.

Hogan-Brun, G. (2007b) Education in the Baltic States: Contexts, practices and challenges. *Comparative Education* 43 (4), 553–570.

Hogan-Brun, G. and Ramonienė, M. (2002) Locating Lithuanian in the (re-)intellectualisation debate. *Current Issues in Language Planning* 3 (1), 62–75.

Hogan-Brun, G. and Ramonienė, M. (2003) Emerging language and education policies in Lithuania. *Language Planning* 2, 27–45.

Hogan-Brun, G. and Ramonienė, M. (2004) Changing levels of bilingualism across the Baltic. *International Journal of Bilingual Education and Bilingualism* 7 (1), 62–77.

Hogan-Brun, G. and M. Ramonienė (2005a) The language situation in Lithuania. In G. Hogan-Brun (guest ed.). The Baltic Sociolinguistic Review (Special Issue). *Journal of Baltic Studies* 36 (3), 345–365.

Hogan-Brun, G. and Ramonienė, M. (2005b) Perspectives on language attitudes and use in Lithuania's multilingual setting. In G. Hogan-Brun (guest ed.) Language and Social Processes in the Baltic Republics Surrounding EU Accession (Special Issue). *Journal of Multilingual and Multicultural Development* 26 (5), 425–441.

Hogan-Brun, G. and Wolff, S. (eds) (2003) *Minority Languages in Europe: Status – Frameworks – Prospects.* Houndmills: Palgrave/Macmillan.

Holt, S. and Packer, J. (2001) OSCE developments and linguistic minorities. *MOST Journal on Multicultural Societies,* 3 (2). On WWW at http://www.unesco.org/most/vl3n2packer.htm. Accessed 18.9.07.

Hough, W.J. (1985) The annexation of the Baltic States and its effect on the development of law prohibiting the forcible seizure of territory. *New York Law School Journal of International and Comparative Law* 6 (2), 303–533.

Hough, J.E. (1996) Sociology, the state and language politics. *Post-Soviet Affairs* 12 (2), 1–19.

Housden, M. (2004) Ambiguous activists. Estonia's model of cultural autonomy as interpreted by two of its founders: Werner Hasselblatt and Ewald Ammende. *Journal of Baltic Studies* 35 (3), 231–253.

Housden, M. (2005) Cultural autonomy in Estonia: One of history's curiosities? In D.J. Smith (ed.) *The Baltic States and their Region: New Europe or Old?* (pp. 227–249). Amsterdam: Rodolphi.

Huber, K.J. (1995) Preventing ethic conflict in the new Europe: The CSCE High Commissioner on national minorities. In I.M. Cuthbertson and J. Leibowitz (eds) *Minorities: The New Europe's Oldest Issue* (pp. 285–310). Prague: Institute for East-West Studies.

Ikstens, J. (2004) Latvia. *European Journal of Political Research* 43 (7–8), 1054–1058.

Ilves, T.H. (1991) Reaction: The intermovement in Estonia. In J. Trapans (ed.) *Towards Independence: The Baltic Popular Movements* (pp. 71–84). Boulder: Westview.

International Convention on Civil and Political Rights (ICCPR) (1996) United Nations.

ITAR/TASS News Agency (2001) Macedonia should not make concessions to separatists – Foreign ministry. 18 July 2001. On WWW at www.itar-tass.com.

Järve, P. (2002) Two waves of language laws in the Baltic states: Changes of rationale? *Journal of Baltic Studies* 33 (1), 78–110.

Johns, M. (2003) 'Do as I say, not as I do': The European Union, Eastern Europe and minority rights. *East European Politics and Society* 17 (4), 682–699.

Jubulis, M.A. (2001) *Nationalism and Democratic Transition: The Politics of Citizenship and Language in Post-Soviet Latvia.* Lanham: University Press of America.

Juozeliūnienė, I. (1996) Individual and collective identity. In M. Taljūnaitė (ed.) *Changes of Identity in Modern Lithuania. Social Studies* (pp 194–213). Vilnius: Lithuanian Institute of Philosophy and Sociology.

Jurado, E. (2003) Complying with European standards of minority education: Estonia's relations with the European Union, OSCE and Council of Europe. *Journal of Baltic Studies* 34 (4), 399–431.

Kalbų mokymo politikos aprašas (2006) [The description of Language Education policy]. Vilnius: Švietimo aprūpinimo centras.

Kaplan, R.B. and Baldauf, R.B. (1997) *Language Planning from Practice to Theory.* Clevedon: Multilingual Matters.

Karklins, R. (1994) *Ethnopolitics and Transition to Democracy. The Collapse of the USSR and Latvia.* Washington: Woodrow Wilson Center Press; London: John Hopkins University Press.

Kasatkina N. and Beresnevičiūtė V. (2006) Ethnic structure, inequality and governance of the public sector in Lithuania. In Y. Bangura (ed.) *Ethnic Inequalities and Public Sector Governance* (pp. 31–48). UNRISD; Houndmills: Palgrave/Macmillan.

Kasatkina, N. and Leončikas, T. (2003) *Lietuvos etninių grupių adaptacija: Kontekstas ir eiga* (The Adaptation of Ethnic Groups in Lithuania: Context and Process). Vilnius: Eugrimas.

Kaubrys, S. (2002) *National Minorities in Lithuania.* Vilnius: Vaga.

Kelley, J.G. (2004) *Ethnic Politics in Europe: The Power of Norms and Incentives.* Princeton and Oxford: Princeton University Press.

Kersh, N. (1997) Aspects of privatisation of education in Latvia. *Oxford Studies in Comparative Education* 7 (2), 35–46.

Kersh, N. (1998) Current developments in education in Latvia: Difficulties of renewal. *Oxford Studies in Comparative Education* 8 (2), 35–48.

Kiaupa, Z., Mäesalu, A., Pajur, A. and Straube, G. (2002) *The History of the Baltic Countries.* Tallinn: Avita.

Kirby, D. (1990) *Northern Europe in the Early Modern Period: The Baltic North 1492–1772.* London: Longman.

Kirby, D. (1995) *The Baltic World 1772–1993.* London: Longman.

Knowles, F. (1989) Language planning in the Soviet Baltic Republics: An analysis of demographic and sociological trends. In M. Kirkwood (ed.) *Language Planning in the Soviet Union* (pp. 145–173). London: Macmillan.

Knowles, F. (1999) Ethno-linguistic relations in contemporary Latvia: Mirror image of the previous dispensation? *Current Issues in Language and Society* 6 (1) 48–56.

Kolstoe, P. (1995) *Russians in the Former Soviet Republics.* Bloomington: Indiana University Press.

Konovalov, A.A. and Evstaviev, D. (1995) The problem of ethnic minority rights protection in the newly independent States. In I.M. Cuthbertson and J. Leibowitz (eds) *Minorities: The New Europe's Oldest Issue* (pp. 157–183). Prague: Institute for East-West Studies.

Korts, K. (2002) Estonian and Russian-language press on Russian schools and Russian-language education. In R. Kõuts (ed.) *Estonian Press about Integration, Media Monitoring of Integration of the Russian-Speaking Population* (pp. 40–49). Tartu: Tartu Universit Press.

Kreindler, I. (ed.) (1985) *Sociolinguistic Perspectives on Soviet National Languages.* Berlin: Mouton de Gruyter.

Kreindler, I. (1990) Baltic area languages in the Soviet Union: A sociolinguistic perspective. In D.Λ. Loeber, V.S. Vardys and L.A. Kitching (eds) *Regional Identity under Soviet Rule:*

The Case of the Baltic States (pp. 233–248). Hackettstown, NY: Publications of the Association for the Advancement of Baltic Studies, 6.

Kreitzberg, P. and Priimägi, S. (1997) Educational transition in Estonia 1987–1996. *Oxford Studies in Comparative Education* 7 (2), 47–59.

Kull, R. (2000) Kas kindel või lagundatud kirjakeel? (Fixed literary language or disintegrated language?). *Keel ja Kirjandus* 2000 (1), 1–9.

Kulu, H. and Tammaru, T. (2004) Diverging views on integration in Estonia: Determinants of Estonian language skills among ethnic minorities. *Journal of Baltic Studies* 35 (4), 378–401.

Kymlicka, W. (2002) Multiculturalism and minority rights: West and East. *Journal of Ethnopolitics and Minority Issues in Europe* 4 (1), 1–25.

Kymlicka, W. and Grin, F. (2003) Assessing the politics of diversity in transition countries. In F. Daftary and F. Grin (eds) *Nation-Building, Ethnicity and Language Politics in Transition Countries* (pp. 1–27). Series on Ethnopolitics and Minority Issues; Budapest: LGI Books.

Kymlicka, W. and Patten, A. (Eds) (2003) *Language Rights and Political Theory*. Oxford: Oxford University Press.

Laar, M. (1992) *War in the Woods: Estonia's Struggle for Survival 1944–1956*. Washington: Compass Press.

Laitin, D. (1996) Language and nationalism in the post-soviet republics. *Post-Soviet Affairs* 12 (1), 4–24. Latvia: Commission of the Official Language [Valsts valodas komisija].

Laitin, D. (1998) *Identity in Formation: The Russian Speaking Populations in the Near Abroad*. Ithaca: Cornell University Press.

Laitin, D. (2003) Three models of integration and the Estonian/Russian reality. *Journal of Baltic Studies* 34 (2), 197–222.

Latvia, Department of Education and Science (2004) Skolēnu skaits LR vispārizglītojošajās dienas skolās, kuri mācās svešvalodas [Number of students in general education day schools learning foreign languages]. On WWW at http://izm.izm.gov.lv/upload_file/Izglitiba/Vispareja_izglitiba/Statistika/2003/kopeja%20svesvalodu%20apguve.xls. Accessed 18.9.07.

Latvia, Ministry of Foreign Affairs (2006) *Integration Policy in Latvia: A Multi-Faceted Approach*. On WWW at http://www.am.gov.lv/en/policy/4641/4642/4649. Accessed 17.9.07.

Latvia, Naturalisation Board (2000) *Examinations as Prescribed by the Law on Citizenship*. On WWW at http://www.np.gov.lv/en/faili_en/history.rtf. Accessed 17.9.07.

Latvia, State Language Agency (2005) On WWW at http://vva.valoda.lv/index.php?sadala=76&id=96. Accessed 17.9.07.

Latvian Census (2000) On WWW at http://data.csb.gov.lv/DATABASEEN/tautassk/databasetree.asp?lang=l. Accessed 17.9.07.

Latvian Centre for Human Rights and Ethnic Studies (eds) *Integration and Minority Information Service Reports*. On WWW at http://www.humanrights.org.lv/html/. Accessed 17.9.07.

Lauze, L. (2004) Ikdienas saziņa: vienkāršs teikums latviešu sarunvalodā (Everyday communication: The simple sentence in spoken Latvian). Liepaja: Pedagogy Academy LiePA.

Law on the Estonian State Language. On WWW at http://www.legaltext.ee/en/andmebaas/ava.asp?m=026. Accessed 17.9.07.

Law on the Latvian State Language. On WWW at http://www.ttc.lv/New/lv/tulkojumi/E0120.doc. Accessed 17.9.07.

Law on the Lithuanian State Language. On WWW at http://www3.lrs.lt/pls/inter3/dokpaieska.showdoc_e?p_id=275246. Accessed 17.9.07.

Leclerc, J. (1992) *Language et société*. Laval, Canada: Mondia.

Levits, E. (1987) National elites and their political function within the Soviet system: The Latvian elite. *Journal of Baltic Studies* XVIII (2), 176–190.

Lewis, E.G. (1972) *Multilingualism in the Soviet Union*. The Hague: Mouton.

Lieven, A. (1993) *The Baltic Revolution*. New Haven, CT: Yale University Press.

Liivaku, U. (1995) *Eesti raamatu lugu* (History of the Estonian book). Tallinn: Monokkel.

Lithuanian Census (2000) On WWW at http://www.stat.gov.lt/en/pages/view/?id=1503. Accessed 17.9.07.

Loeber, D.A. (1993) Language rights in independent Estonia, Latvia and Lithuania, 1918–1940. In S. Vilfan (ed.) *Ethnic Groups and Language Rights* (pp. 221–249). Aldershot: Dartmouth.

Loit, A. (ed.) (1995) *National Movements in the Baltic Countries during the 19th Century.* Stockholm: Acta Universitatis Stockholmiensis, Studia Baltica Stockholmiensia, 2.

Maley, W. and Rose, R. (1994) *Nationalities in the Baltic States: A Survey Study.* Glasgow: Centre for the Study of Public Policy.

Maurais, J. (1991) A sociolinguistic comparison between Québec's Charter of the French Language and the 1989 Language Laws of five Soviet Republics. *Journal of Multilingual and Multicultural Development* 12 (1&2), 117–126.

Maurais, J. (1997) Regional majority languages, language planning and linguistic rights. *International Journal of the Sociology of Language* 127, 135–160.

Maurais, J. (1998) (ed.) *Les Politiques Linguistiques des Pays Baltes*; Special number of *Terminogramme.* Quebec: Office de la langue française.

May, S. (2001) *Language and Minority Rights.* London: Pearson.

May, S. (2006) Language policy and minority rights. In T. Ricento (ed.) *An Introduction to Language Policy* (pp. 255–272). Malden, MA; Oxford; Carlton, Victoria, Australia: Blackwells.

Metuzāle-Kangere, B. and Ozolins, U. (2005) The language situation in Latvia from 1850–2004. In G. Hogan-Brun (guest ed.) The Baltic Sociolinguistic Review. (Special Issue), *Journal of Baltic Studies* 36 (3), 317–344.

MINELRES (2002) *Minority Issues in Latvia,* no. 47. On WWW at http://www.minelres.lv/MinIssues/info/2002/47.html. Accessed 17.9.07.

National Program for Latvian Language Teaching (NPLLT) On WWW at www.lvavp.lv. Accessed 17.9.07.

Nau, N. (1998) *Latvian. Languages of the World 217.* Munich: Lincom Europa.

Neustupný, J.V. and Nekvapil J. (2003) Language management in the Czech Republic. *Current Issues in Language Planning* 4 (3&4).

Nørgaard, O. (Ed.) (1996) *The Baltic States After Independence.* Cheltenham: Edward Elgar.

O'Reilly, C.C. (Ed.) (2007) *Language, Ethnicity and the State* (Vol. 2). *Minority Languages in Eastern Europe Post-1989.* Houndmills and New York: Palgrave.

OSCE [Organisation for Security and Cooperation in Europe] *Annual Reports.* On WWW at www.osce.org.

OSCE (1998) *The Oslo Recommendations Regarding the Linguistic Rights of National Minorities & Explanatory Note.* The Hague: Foundation on Inter-Ethnic Relations.

OSCE (2002) Press statement, Gerard Stoudmann, Director of the Office for Democratic Institutions and Human Rights, 21 March. On WWW at http://www.osce.org/item/6620.html. Accessed 17.9.07.

Ozolins, U. (1999) Between Russian and European hegemony: Current language policy in the Baltic States. In S. Wright (ed.) *Language Policy and Language Issues in the Successor States of the Former USSR* (pp. 6–47). Clevedon: Multilingual Matters. (also in *Current Issues in Language and Society* 6 (1), 6–47).

Ozolins, U. (2002) Post imperialist language situations: The Baltic Republics. *World Congress on Language Policies,* Barcelona. On WWW at http://www.linguapax.org/congres/taller/taller1/Ozolins.html. Accessed 24.06.04.

Ozolins, U. (2003) The impact of European accession upon language policy in the Baltic States. *Language Policy* 2, 217–238.

Pabrėža, J. (1991) *Žemaičių rašybos patarimai* (Recommendations for Samogitian Orthography). Šiauliai: Titnagas.

Packer, J. (2001) The protection of minority language rights through the work of OSCE institutions. In *Minority Rights in Europe. European Minorities and Languages* (pp. 255–274). The Hague: T.M.C. Asser Press,

Palionis, J. (1995) *Lietuvių rašomosios kalbos istorija* (History of Written Lithuanian). Vilnius: Mokslo ir enciklopedijų leidykla.

Pennycook, A. (2006) Postmodernism in language policy. In T. Ricento (ed.) *An Introduction to Language Policy* (pp. 60–76). Malden, MA; Oxford; Carlton, Victoria, Australia: Blackwells.

Peters, R.P. (1988) Baltic States diplomacy and the League of Nations minorities system. In J. Hiden and A. Loit (eds) *The Baltic in International Relations between the Two World Wars*. Stockholm: Acta Universitatis Stockholmiensis – Studia Baltica Stockholmiensia 3, 281–302.

Pettai, V. (2001) Estonia and Latvia: International influences on citizenship and minority integration. In J. Zielonka and A. Pravda (eds) *Democratic Consolidation in Eastern Europe* (Vol. 2) *International and Transnational Factors* (pp. 257–280). Oxford: Oxford University Press.

Pettai, V. (2006) Explaining ethnic politics in the Baltic States: Reviewing the triadic nexus model. *Journal of Baltic Studies* 37 (1), 124–136.

Phillipson, R. (1992) *Linguistic Imperialism*. Oxford and New York: Oxford University Press.

Phillipson, R. (2003) *English-Only Europe? Challenging Language Policy*. London: Routledge.

Piller, I. (2001) Naturalisation language testing and its basis in ideologies of national identity and citizenship. *International Journal of Bilingualism* 5 (3), 259–278.

Plakans, A. (1993) From a regional vernacular to the language of a state: The case of Latvian. *International Journal of the Sociology of Language* 100–101, 203–219.

Plasseraud, Y. (2003) *Les Etats Baltiques. Les Sociétés Gigognes. La Dialectique Minorités-Majorités*. Crozon: Editions Arméline.

Poleshchuk, V. (2002) *Estonia, Latvia, and the European Commission: Changes in Language Regulation in 1999–2001*. On WWW at http://www.eumap.org/articles/content/40/402/index_html?print +/.

Poriņa, V. (2000) Indivīda un sabiedrības multilingvisms Latvijā: Situācija un prognozes (The multiligualism of individuals and society in Latvia: The current situation and future prospects). In E. Vēbers (ed.) *Integrācija un Etnopolitika* (Integration and Ethopolitics) (pp. 282–297). Riga: Jumava.

Poriņa, V. (2001a) Code switching as a social marker in Latvia. *Baltic States and Societies in Transition: Continuity and Change*. 4th Conference on Baltic Studies in Europe. University of Tartu, 27–30 June.

Poriņa, V. (2001b) Code switching between bilinguals in Latvia. *International Conference on Language Development 'Estonian in Europe'*. Tallinn, 12–14 March, 69–71.

Priedīte, A. (2005) Surveying language attitudes and practices in Latvia. In G. Hogan-Brun (guest ed.) Language and Social Processes in the Baltic Republics Surrounding EU Accession (Special Issue). *Journal of Multilingual and Multicultural Development* 25 (6), 409–424.

Pryce-Jones, D. (1995) *The War That Never Was. The Fall of the Soviet Empire*. London: Weidenfeld & Nicolson.

Racevskis, K. (2002) Towards a Postcolonial Perspective on the Baltic States. *Journal of Baltic Studies* 33 (1), 37–56.

Ramishvili, T. (1998) Latvia and Estonia: Human rights violations in the center of Europe. *International Affairs* 44 (4), 116–127.

Ramonienė, M. (1997) *Valstybinės kalbos mokymo programa* (The Curriculum of Lithuanian as a State Language for Adults). Vilnius: Danielius.

Ramonienė, M. (2006) Teaching Lithuanian as a second/foreign language: Current practices. In *Eesti Rakenduslingvistika Ühingu aastaraamat 2, Estonian Papers in Applied Linguistics* 2, 219–230.

Rannut, M. (1991) Linguistic policy in the Soviet Union. *Multilingua*, 10 (3), 241–250.

Rannut, M. (1994) Beyond linguistic policy: The Soviet Union versus Estonia. In T. Skutnabb-Kangas and R. Phillipson (eds) *Linguistic Human Rights: Overcoming Linguistic Discrimination* (pp. 179–208). Berlin: Mouton de Gruyter.

Rannut, M. (2003) Framework of the Estonian Language Policy. Baltic Language and Integration Network. *1st BLaIN Workshop*, Vilnius, 16–18 June 2003. On WWW at http://www.blain-online.org/abstracts.doc.

Rannut, M. (2004a) *Language Planning in Estonia: Past and Present*. Ciemen-Mercator Working Paper 16. On WWW at http://www.ciemen.org/mercator/index-gb.htm. Accessed 17.9.07.

Rannut, M (2004b) *Language Policy in Estonia*. Noves SL. Revista de Sociolingüística, Spring-Summer. On WWW at www6.gencat.net/llengcat/noves/hm04primavera-estiu/docs/rannut.pdf. Accessed 17.9.07.

Rannut, M. and Rannut, Ü. (1995) Bilingualism – a step towards monolingualism or multilingualism? In T. Skutnabb-Kangas (ed.) *Multilingualism for All* (pp. 183–198). European Studies on Multilingualism 4. Lisse: Swets and Zeitlinger.

Raun, T. (1979) The development of Estonian literacy in the 18th and 19th centuries. *Journal of Baltic Studies* 10, 118–124.

Raun, T. and Plakans, A. (1990) The Estonian and Latvian national movements: An assessment of Miroslav Hoch's model. *Journal of Baltic Studies* 21 (2), 131–144.

RFE/RL [Radio Free Europe/Radio Liberty] Baltics Newsline. On WWW at http://search.rferl.org/. Accessed 18.9.07.

Romanov, A. (2000) The Russian diaspora in Latvia and Estonia: Predicting language outcomes. *Journal of Multilingual and Multicultural Development* 21 (1), 58–71.

Rose, R. (2000) *New Baltic Barometer IV: A Survey Study*. Studies in Public Policy. Glasgow: University of Strathclyde.

Rouillard, R. (2005) Between east and west is north: The loyalties and allegiances of Russian authors and painters living in EU Estonia. In Hogan-Brun, G. (guest ed.) Language and Social Processes in the Baltic Republics Surrounding EU Accession. (Special Issue). *Journal of Multilingual and Multicultural Development* 26 (5), 391–408.

Rubio-Marin, R. (2003) Language rights: Exploring the competing rationales. In W. Kymlicka and A. Patten (eds) *Language Rights and Political Theory* (pp. 52–79). Oxford: Oxford University Press.

Rudensky, N. (1994) Russian minorities in the newly independent states. An international problem in the domestic context of Russia today. In R. Szporluk (ed.) *National Identity and Ethnicity in Russia and the New States of Eurasia* (pp. 58–77). Armonk: M .E. Sharp.

Ruutsoo, R. (1993) In A. Matsulevitš (ed.) *Eessõna. Vähemusrahvuste kultuurielu Eesti Vabariigis 1918–1940: Dokumente ja materjale* (Foreword to Life of Minorities in the Republic of Estonia 1918–1940: Documents and Materials). Tallinn: Olion.

Rytų ir Pietryčių Lietuvos Gyventojų Apklausa (Survey of Eastern and South-Eastern Lithuania Inhabitants) (2002) (unpublished).

Savukynas, V. (2000) Lietuvos lenkai ir rusai: Dvi skirtingos laikysenos (Lithuania's Poles and Russians: Two different perspectives). *Politologija* 2 (18), 67–84.

Schmid, C., Zepa, B. and Snipe, A. (2004) Language policy and ethnic tensions in Quebec and Latvia. *International Journal of Comparative Sociology* 45 (3–4), 231–252.

Senn, A.E. (1980) Tsarist authorities and Lithuanian book-smuggling. *Journal of Baltic Studies* XT (4), 334–340.

Shamshur, O. (1994) Current ethnic and migration issues in the former USSR. *Current Issues in Language and Society* 1 (1), 7–27.

Shohamy. E. (2006) *Language Policy. Hidden Agendas and New Approaches*. London and New York: Routledge.

Simonsen, S.G. (2001) Compatriot games: Explaining the 'Diaspora Linkage' in Russia's military withdrawal from the Baltic States. *Euro-Asian Studies* 53 (5), 771–791.

Sinilind, S. (pseudonym of Juhan Talve) (1985) *Viro ja Venäjä. Havaintoja Neuvostoliiton kansallisuus-politiikasta Virossa 1940–1984*. (Estonia and Russia. Observations on the Soviet national policy in Estonia 1940–1984. In Finnish). Jyväskylä: Alea-Kirja.

Skolnick, J. (1996) Grappling with the legacy of Soviet Rule: Citizenship and human rights in the Baltic States. *University of Toronto Faculty Law Review* 54 (2), 387–417.

Skultans, V. (1998) *The Testimony of Lives. Narrative and Memory in Post-Soviet Latvia*. London and New York: Routledge.

Skutnabb-Kangas, T. (1994) Linguistic human rights in education. *Language Policy in the Baltic States. Conference Papers*. Riga: Gara Pupa.

Skutnabb-Kangas, T. (2006) Language policy and linguistic human rights. In T. Ricento (ed.) *An Introduction to Language Policy: Theory and Method.* (pp. 273–291). Malden, MA; Oxford; Carlton, Victoria, Australia: Blackwells.

Skutnabb-Kangas. T. and Phillipson, R. (eds) (1994) *Linguistic Human Rights: Overcoming Linguistic Discrimination.* Berlin: Mouton de Gruyter.

Smith, G. (ed.) (1994) *The Baltic States: The National Self-Determination of Estonia, Latvia and Lithuania.* London: Macmillan.

Smith, D.J. (2001) *Estonia: Independence and European Integration.* London and New York: Routledge.

Smith, D.J. (2002) Framing the national question in Central and Eastern Europe: A quadratic nexus? *The Global Review of Ethnopolitics* 2 (1), 3–16.

Smith, D.J. (Ed.) (2005) *The Baltic States and their Region: New Europe or Old?* Amsterdam: Rodolphi.

Smith, K.E. (2001) Western actors and the promotion of democracy. In J. Zielonka, and A. Pravda, (eds) *Democratic Consolidation in Eastern Europe* (Vol. 2) *International and Transnational Factors* (pp. 31–57). Oxford: Oxford University Press.

Smith, G., Aasland, A. and Mole, R. (1994). Statehood, ethnic relations and citizenship. In G. Smith (ed.) *The Baltic States: The National Self-Determination of Estonia, Latvia and Lithuania* (pp. 181–205). London: Macmillan.

Smith, G., Law, V., Wilson, A., Bohr, A. and Allworth, E. (1998) *Nation-Building in the Post-Soviet Borderlands: The Politics of National Identities.* Cambridge: Cambridge University Press.

Spolsky, B. (1998) *Sociolinguistics.* Oxford: Oxford University Press.

Spolsky, B. (2004) *Language Policy.* Cambridge: Cambridge University Press.

Stafecka, A. (2003) Izloksne, dialekts, valoda [Variety, dialect, language]. In J.Kursīte and A. Stafecka (eds) *Latgale: Valoda, literatūra, folklora* [Latgallia: Language, literature, folklore]. Rēzekne: Lattgallian Cultural Centre.

State Language Policy Guidelines. On WWW at http://www.vlkk.lt/legal-framework. htm. Accessed 17.9.07.

State Lithuanian Language Commission. On WWW at http://www.vlkk.lt. Accessed 17.9.07.

Stroud, C. (2001) African mother-tongue programmes and the politics of language: Linguistic citizenship versus linguistic human rights. *Journal of Multilingual and Multicultural Development* 22 (4), 339–355.

Suny, R.G. (1993) *The Revenge of the Past: Nationalism, Revolution, and the Collapse of the Soviet Union.* Stanford: Stanford University Press.

Swain, M. and Johnson, R.K. (1997) *Immersion Education: International Perspectives.* Cambridge: Cambridge University Press.

Szépe, G. (1994) Central and Eastern European language policies in transition (with special reference to Hungary). *Current Issues in Language and Society* 1 (1), 41–64.

Taagepera, R. (1993) *Estonia. Return to Independence.* Boulder: Westview.

Tesser, L.M. (2003) The geopolitics of tolerance: Minority rights under expansion in East-Central Europe. *East European Politics and Societies* 17 (3), 483–532.

Thaden, E. (ed.) (1981) *Russification in the Baltic Provinces and Finland 1855–1914.* Princeton: Princeton University Press.

Thaden, E. (1985) *Russia's Western Borderlands 1710–1870.* Princeton: Princeton University Press.

Thompson, C. (1992) *The Singing Revolution: A Political Journey through the Baltic States.* London: Michael Joseph.

Tiit, E. (1993) Eesti rahvastik ja selle probleemid [Estonian population and its problems]. *Akadeemia*, 8, 1654–1679; 9, 1847–1866; 10, 2112–2132.

Toomsalu, M. and Simm, L. (1998) Les exigences linguistiques pour obtenir la citoyenneté et occuper un emploi en Estonie (Language postulations for citizenship and employment in Estonia). In J. Maurais (ed.) *Les Politiques Linguistiques des Pays Baltes.* Special number of *Terminogramm* (pp. 37–61). Quebec: Office de la langue française.

Trapans, J. (ed.) (1991) *Towards Independence: The Baltic Popular Movements.* Boulder: Westview.

Trenin, D. (1998) Russian and western interests in preventing, managing and settling conflicts in the former Soviet Union. In B. Coppieters *et al.* (eds) *Commonwealth and Independence in Post-Soviet Asia* (pp. 171–190). London: Frank Cass.

Trinkūnienė, I. (1996) Ethnic relations and stereotypes. In M. Taljūnaitė (ed.) *Changes of Identity in Modern Lithuania. Social Studies* (pp. 183–194). Vilnius: Lithuanian Institute of Philosophy and Sociology.

Trudgill, P. (2002) *Sociolinguistic Variation and Change.* Edinburgh: Edinburgh University Press.

Urban, W.L. (2003) *Tannenberg and After: Lithuania, Poland, and the Teutonic Order in Search of Immortality* (3rd ed.). Chicago: Lithuanian Research and Studies Center.

USSR Law on Education. On WWW at http://www3.lrs.lt/pls/inter2/dokpaieska.showdoc_e?p_id=21110&p_query=&p_tr2=. Accessed 17.9.07.

Vaicekauskienė, L. (1998) Svetimbiu vertinimas Lieturoje: Sociolingvistine kalbos vartotojų požiūrio analizė. *Kalbotyra* 47 (1), 143–152.

Vaicekauskienė, L. (2000) Lietuvių kalbos leksikos gryninimo tradicija ir dabarties tendencijos. *Lietuvių kalbotyros klausimai* XLII, 200–208.

Vaicekauskienė, L. (2004) Codification theory and practice of new borrowings in Lithuania Summary of doctoral dissertation. Vilnius: Vilnius University.

Valstybės žinios (2003), Nr 57 (document 57–2537) 15–19.

Vardys, V.S. and Sedaitis J.B. (1997) *Lithuania. The Rebel Nation.* Boulder & Oxford: Westview Press.

van Ek, J.A. and Trim, J.L.M. (1991) *Threshold Level 1990.* Strasbourg: Council of Europe Press.

van Ek, J.A. and Trim, J.L.M. (1995) *Waystage 1990.* Strasbourg: Council of Europe Press.

van Ek, J.A. and Trim, J.L.M. (1996) *Vantage Level.* Strasbourg: Council of Europe Press.

Vēbers, E. (1997) *Latvijas Valsts un etniskās minoritātes* (The Latvian State and Ethnic Minorities). Riga: Academy of Science, Institute of Philosophy and Science, Centre for Research on Ethnic Relations.

Verschik, A. (2005a) Research into multilingualism in Estonia. In G. Hogan-Brun (guest ed.) The Baltic Republics and Language Ideological Debates Surrounding their EU Accession. (Special Issue). *Journal of Multilingual and Multicultural Development* 26 (5), 378–390.

Verschik, A. (2005b) The language situation in Estonia. In G. Hogan-Brun (guest ed.) Baltic Sociolinguistic Review (Special Issue). *Journal of Baltic Studies* 36 (3), 283–316.

Vihalemm, T. (1999) Estonian language competence, performance and beliefs on acquisition among the Russian-speaking inhabitants of Estonia 1989–1999. *International Journal of the Sociology of Language* 139, 69–85.

Vihalemm, T. (2002a) Theoretical perspectives on the formation of new civic identity in Estonia. In M. Lauristin and M. Heidmets (eds) *The Challenge of the Russian Minority. Emerging Multicultural Democracy in Estonia.* (pp. 165–173). Tartu: Tartu University Press.

Vihalemm, T. (2002b) Usage of language as a source of societal trust. In M. Lauristin and M. Heidmets (eds) *The Challenge of the Russian Minority: Emerging Multicultural Democracy in Estonia.* (pp. 199–217). Tartu: Tartu University Press.

Vihalemm, T. and Masso, A. (2002) Patterns of self-identification among the younger generation of Estonian Russians. In M. Lauristin and M. Heidmets (eds) *The Challenge of the Russian Minority. Emerging Multicultural Democracy in Estonia* (pp. 185–198). Tartu: Tartu University Press (also in *Journal of Baltic Studies* (2003) 34 (1), 92–116).

Vilniaus miesto gyventojų kalbų vartosenos įpročiai (Survey of Vilnius Inhabitants) (2004) (unpublished).

Volkovs, V. (2000) *Krievi Latvijā* [Russians in Latvia]. Riga: Academy of Science, Institute of Philosophy and Science, Centre for Research on Ethnic Relations.

Weeks, T. (1996) *Nation and State in Late Imperial Russia: Nationalism and Russificiation on the Western Frontier 1863–1914.* DeKalb: Northern Illinois University Press.

Zaagman, R. (1999) *Conflict Prevention in the Baltic States: The OSCE High Commissioner on National Minorities in Estonia, Latvia and Lithuania.* European Centre for Minority Issues. Flensburg: ECMI, Monograph #1. Flensburg: ECMI.

Žepkaitė, R. (1992) Lietuvos rytų sienos klausimas (1920–1940) (The question of eastern border of Lithuania (1920–1940)). In V. Milius (ed.) *Pietryčių Lietuva: Istorija, kultūra, kalba* (South-Eastern Lithuania: History, culture, language). Vilnius: Mokslas.

Zevelev, I. (1996) Russia and the Russian diaspora. *Post-Soviet Affairs* 12 (3), 265–284.

Zinkevičius, Z. (1992) *Lietuvių kalbos istorija 5, Bendrinės kalbos iškilimas* (*History of the Lithuanian Language 5, Emergence of Standard Lithuanian*). Vilnius: Mokslo ir enciklopedijų leidykla.

Zinkevičius, Z. (1998) *The History of the Lithuanian Language*. Vilnius: Mokslo ir enciklopedijų leidykla.

Zuicena, I. (2005) Scales of language proficiency levels in learning and assessment for Latvian. In D. Cunningham and A. Hatoss (eds) *An International Perspective on Language Policies, Practices and Proficiencies*. Belgrave, Australia: FIPLV.

The Language Planning Situation in Ireland

Muiris Ó Laoire
Senior Lecturer, Department of Humanities, Institute of Technology, Tralee, Ireland

Language planning for the Irish language in the Republic of Ireland has featured prominently in international language policy and planning literature over the years. Researchers in the field may not be up to date, however, with recent developments in the area of Irish language planning and their impact on the language ecology. This monograph describes the language planning situation in the Republic of Ireland in its historical and social contexts as well as delineating language policy and planning for the Irish language implemented over the past number of years, showing developments in education, community, media, religion and local politics.

Keywords: Ireland, language planning, language ecology, language policy, language pedagogy

Introduction

Article 8 of the Irish Constitution, *Bunreacht na hÉireann* of 1937 makes the following affirmation:

1. The Irish language as the national language is the first official language.
2. The English language is recognised as the second official language.

The official languages of Ireland, therefore, are Irish (Gaelic) and English. Ireland, apart from officially being a bilingual country, has firm multilingual foundations (Cronin & Ó Cuilleanáin, 2003). An array of myths bedevil discussions of languages in Ireland, conjuring up a monoglot and monolithic English-speaking or a pristine Gaelic-speaking island, disillusioned by the call towards bilingualism and multilingualism and refusing to change from humdrum monolingualism. The debunking of these myths is coming from a call for a more up-to-date representation of the language situation in the increasing climate of multilingualism and multiculturalism in contemporary Ireland.

The story of language policy and planning for the languages of Ireland, in particular the story of the Irish language has been retold on too many occasions to require rehearsal here (see, for example, Hindley, 1990; Ó Huallacháin, 1994; Ó Laoire, 1997; Ó Riagáin, 1988, 1997). In brief, the government's strategy for the revival of Irish between 1922 and 1960 comprised a dual policy of maintenance and restoration; that is, maintenance of the spoken language in areas where it was still a community language (the *Gaeltachtaí*) and its restoration through reversal of language shift in all other areas. The latter involved, in particular, a reintroduction of the language into domains from which it had been excluded since the 17th century. The education system was designated as the major institutional means by which such a reversal would be achieved. Over time, this dual policy was overridden by a third, concerned with providing the necessary infrastructure for maintenance and revival. This three-part policy was subject to considerable modification as its implementation was pursued with a consider-

193

able deal of determination and commitment and with varying degrees of success.

The overall result of this language strategy by the early 1960s was an increase in the ratio of Irish speakers outside the Gaeltacht (Irish language speech community) and a decrease in the number of indigenous Irish speakers and users in the Irish-speaking regions. To speak about results in terms of increase and decrease, however, is an oversimplification masking important spatial and social shifts in the designation of what was to constitute an Irish language speech community. The sociopolitical contextualisation of efforts of Irish language maintenance and revival competing against the predominance of English has formed the general discourse for language planning in Ireland.

There has never been an official policy in the Irish State as regards the English language. English began to replace Irish as the language of business, trade, administration, education and daily communication in Ireland from the 18th century onwards. Today, Ireland is almost universally English-speaking, with no recorded remaining monolingual speakers of Irish. While the Irish language mainly gives access to cultural identities, the powerful certainty of the English language as a gateway to all forms of social and economic access is known to all the residents of Ireland, to both citizens and to immigrants (Ó Laoire, 2004). While one may argue that this duality is a consequence of colonisation or unequal power relations, the reality is that ideas, perceptions and tensions around the competing English–Irish power struggle have influenced percep-tions about language status and informed and continue to inform decision making about the Irish language in particular.

Language planning in Ireland is still largely about the protection and regener-ation of Irish, rather than about the implementation of a given articulated and well-labelled language policy that incorporates English, Irish and the other languages of Ireland. Language policy tends, therefore, to be ad hoc and haphaz-ard rather than being subject to any 'new' sociopolitical, laden ideology. If such a policy existed in the past, recent attempts to apply a more instrumental perspective to cope with language education diversification in the new Ireland of immigration and increasing multiculturalism have shown its shortcomings. There is a call now for a language policy, based on an extensive analysis of Ireland's present and future language needs (Little, 2003: 14). Such a call for the articulation of a language policy is coming only from educational and curricu-lum policy sectors, where an implicit 'acquisition' policy already exists (e.g. Irish and English are taught in schools for x number of hours per week, are taught from the beginning of primary education right through to the end of post-primary education, etc.) and not from other sectors such as the private sector.

There is evidence, on the other hand, of a growing consciousness of a new rights-based linguistic mobilisation in the *Gaeltachtaí* with the articulated demand that housing in these regions be available to only Irish speakers (*Foinse*, 24 November 2004). This policy appears to have a conscious underlying ideology and discourse in which politicians are beginning to engage in local-ised contexts.

There is also evidence of more overtly declared policy with an institutional-ised and conceptualised language planning in The Official Languages Act 2003, which was signed into law on 14 July 2003. The act is the first piece of legislation to provide a statutory framework for the delivery of services through the Irish Language (www.pobail.ie/en/Irishlanguage/officialLanguagesAct 2003/) The objective of the act is to ensure better availability and a higher standard of public services through Irish and will be principally achieved by placing a statutory obligation on Departments of State and public bodies to make specific provision for delivery of such services in a coherent and agreed fashion through a statutory planning framework, known as a 'scheme', to be agreed on a three-year renewable basis. Even though the act is termed the Official Languages Act, the role of English is skirted or ignored.

If, however, we take a language policy description to involve a setting out of a network of conceptualised ideas on language beliefs, practices and management (Spolsky, 2004) rooted in the traditions of national policy, then Ireland currently lacks such a statement. The strategy and statements of politicians at a local level are not emanating from any fully and centrally conceptualised policy. The decisions confronting curricular policy makers regarding diversification (should we include other languages on the curriculum and if we should, which languages?) are not informed by a policy constituted by inherent attitudes and practices towards linguistic diversity. Language planning has been excluded to date from national development planning. Even though Ireland is a member of the European Union which espouses a policy of mother tongue plus two other languages, the implications of this in national policy are not yet worked out.

With this background in mind, the present study explores the language profile of Ireland, the background to Irish language revitalisation, language spread, the role of education, religion, the media in status planning, and charts corpus planning in efforts towards modernisation and standardisation.

The approach taken throughout this study is to interpret the data of accounts of the main actors, agencies and practices at the macro level embedded in a language ecological framework as evolutions of sociopolitical and socio-economic interconnections often reflected in actions, inactions or motivations at the micro level. It is hoped to situate language planning, therefore, in its correct context of natural development and human resources development planning (Kaplan & Baldauf, 1997: 4–5) and to interpret centralised and non-centralised language planning activities as efforts at management of the language ecology. In adopting this approach, it is hoped to avoid taking a linear model of event interpretation holding all change to be triggered by central political ministration. To take such an approach to the study of language planning in Ireland, which has featured rather prominently in the international polity literature to date, would be to distort and idealise the effectiveness of political decision or *événement* on social change or to view language planning as a monolithic activity. To study language planning in Ireland, rather, is to understand the power and potential of niche growth in a language- environment ecology and its 'ripple-type' effects.

The Language Profile of Ireland

It would be safe perhaps to assume that more than 95% of the population of Ireland speaks English as a first language. In the absence of official data and records, one can only assume this. English, however, is the second official language of the Irish State. The 2002 Census does not record the number of native and other speakers of English currently in the State. The emphasis in most questions about language is generally on the Irish language. Irish, an autochthonous language, is the first official and national language spoken habitually by only about 5% of the population. Preliminary figures for the 2002 census, which included questions as to competency and use of the Irish language, reveal that 1.57 million people have some knowledge of the Irish language with 9.05% of the population professing to use Irish on a daily basis. When school-going children are omitted from this statistic, however, the number of people who habitually use the language drops to 2.6% of the population (Ó hÉallaithe, 2003). These figures generally point to an increase from the 1996 census in which 1.43 million self-reported 'some' competence in the language. This competence, however, may often reflect activation of receptive rather than productive skills (Ó Murchú, 2001). These skills are garnered, in the main, through the education system where students experience at least 11 years of exposure to the language.

The majority of primary Irish speakers who use the Irish language on a daily basis are located in the Irish-language speech communities or *Gaeltachtaí* situated in fragmented groupings along the western seaboard. These primary Irish speakers are all bilingual (Irish and English) with few, if any, remaining monolinguals. There are a growing number of Irish speakers located in Irish-speaking networks outside the *Gaeltachtaí* who have made Irish their language of choice. A significant number of these speakers are to be found in hinterlands and catchment areas of all-Irish-medium playgroups and schools, which have increased significantly in number in recent years. This presents what could be termed as an over-simplification of a language situation that is, in reality, much more complex.

Firstly, Irish is used to a greater or lesser degree by more than 5% of the population. In the 1996 National Census, 1.43 million speakers, or 43% of the total population, returned themselves as Irish speakers. The 2002 Census reveals that this figure has risen to 1.57 million. Nonetheless, in percentage terms this represents a slight decline from 43.5% to 42.8%. Ability to speak Irish was again highest among the school-going population. In 1996, 76% of the population aged 3 years and over were recorded as Irish speakers. This dropped to 73% in 2002 (www.cso.ie). The Census question, on which this data are based, while eliciting self-report on ability and frequency in speaking Irish, did not distinguish categories of proficiency with which informants could really identify. If this category of school-going respondent is removed, for example, as mentioned above, the real figure for regular users is between 3% and 5% of the population. In any event, it is well known that estimating levels of usage and proficiency may be unreliable, when one bears in mind that language students in general tend to overestimate ability (Clyne, 1982) when self-reporting on language proficiency.

Secondly, although Irish could be classified as being a 'minority' language in terms of numbers of speakers, because of its official status it cannot be considered a minority or lesser-used language. Since the 1920s, State policy of reversing language shift has sought to re-establish this minority language as a national language. Like Maori in New Zealand, therefore, Irish in Ireland as a minority language is espoused as a state national language.

Thirdly, since the mid-1990s, the unprecedented economic growth experienced by the Republic of Ireland has meant that from being a country of emigration, Ireland now has net immigration. The language situation is necessarily affected by this change, as new linguistic minorities are being constituted, with heretofore unexamined situations of bilingualism and multilingualism.

Historical overview of Irish in Ireland

Irish belongs to the Celtic branch of the Indo-European family and is estimated to have been brought to Ireland between 500 and 300 BCE by invading Celts (Ó Siadhail, 1989: 1). Subsequently, the language extended through the processes of colonisation to Scotland and to the Isle of Man. The earliest form of the language is preserved in *ogham* inscriptions, which date mainly from the fourth and fifth centuries CE. The inscriptions found mainly on commemorative stones and gravestones contain little more than personal names but reveal a form of Goidelic much older than Old Irish, the earliest documented variety of the language. Old Irish, generally assigned to the period 700–850, evolved into Middle Irish, the language of the Viking and post-Viking period.

By the mid-11th century, Irish was the primary language of Ireland and Scotland, with both regions sharing a common tradition of literacy and learning. In Scotland, the language began to decline and contract from the end of the 11th century (Ó Murchú, 1988: 79), although the Irish-speaking areas of Ireland and Scotland continued to share a standardised literary language until the 17th century.

The language endured its first decline in the 11th and 12th centuries as a result of colonisation by the Anglo-Normans. While some language shift to French and English occurred in Ireland (Picard, 2003; Risk, 1968), the Anglo-Norman linguistic impact was at first absorbed and a predominantly Irish-speaking Ireland emerged with its cultural traditions remaining distinctive and viable until the English conquest of Ireland in 1603. This conquest led to the dispossession of the native aristocracy and to the demise of native social, political and cultural institutions. From that period, the decline of Irish from majority to minority status can be delineated.

Following the demise of the native cultural institutions, the gradual Anglicisation of the Irish-speaking middle classes followed and was completed largely by end of the 18th century (Wall, 1969). Although the demise of the language was well under way before the mid-19th century, the economic collapse led to a decimation of the Irish-speaking masses by sustained emigration and by death from famine in 1845–1848. The famine was most severe in western and poorer regions with its impact greatest among the Irish-speaking communities (Wall, 1969). The result was that by the late 18th and the beginning of the 19th century, there was a very rapid abandonment of the language by the remaining poorer classes in rural areas (Ó Murchú, 1988).

The shift to English was particularly rapid in the decades following the famine (Nic Craith, 1994). Between 1851 and 1891 the statistics of Irish speakers in the under 10 age group for Ireland as a whole was as shown in Table 1.

The post-famine figures of 5.33% and 3.47% of speakers have predominantly represented the size of the Irish speech community to this day. The retreat of the

Table 1 Irish speakers under 10 years old

1851	166,839	12.66%
1861	96,568	8.44%
1871	60,783	5.28%
1881	58,269	5.33%
1891	30,785	3.47%

speech community to a scattering of separate areas (*Gaeltachtaí*) around the western seaboard was already determined in these figures.

Ironically, while the 19th century witnessed sustained shift to English in the number of its speakers, the status of Irish was gradually being restored in international linguistic scholarship, which stressed the language's significance as a part of the European linguistic and cultural tradition. Its position within the Indo-European family of languages was being researched and published, and Old Irish and Middle Irish texts were becoming available in printed form.

At the end of the 19th century, these academic developments partially merged with a growing language maintenance movement, which reflected the growing cultural nationalism elsewhere in Europe (Ó Laoire, 1999). In 1893, the Gaelic League (*Conradh na Gaeilge*) was founded to become a most effective force for the maintenance and promotion of the Irish language. As well as gaining recognition for the language in the education system and for matriculation purposes, it popularised the ideal of Irish revival, establishing a network of Irish language classes throughout the country. As a result of the League's ideology, Irish was designated 'the national language' in the constitution of the new State in 1922 when competence in the language was stipulated for admission to the civil service, police (*Gardaí*), and army.

The leaders of the separatist Irish-Ireland (Ó Laoire, 1999) movement propagated the view that Irish, being the ancestral language of the country, was *ipso facto*, the most distinctive mark of Irish ethnicity. The language was also projected significantly as belonging predominantly to parts of rural Ireland and appeared to be dislocated from the growing urban consciousness of the 1960s, 1970s and 1980s. This was the predominant essentialist view that fuelled the revitalisation movement. Successive surveys since the mid-1970s continue to show a considerable majority of respondents favouring the use of Irish and the provision for the language in education, and significantly, 65% or more of the population regarding Irish as essential to the maintenance of a distinctive cultural identity.

Historical overview of English in Ireland

English was introduced into Ireland in the aftermath of the Anglo-Norman invasion in 1169 by descendants of Flemish colonists who were settled by Henry I in the 12th century around South Wales and South Pembrokeshire. Interestingly, there is no evidence of either Flemish or Welsh being introduced, even though there were large numbers of Welsh and Flemish soldiers in the invading forces. It appears that English, French, and Latin were the main languages of the colonists

(Kallen, 1988). One view is that the first colonists were exclusively French speaking. However, there is no general agreement on the status of English and French among these earliest Anglo-Norman settlers (Kallen, 1988). French was used in various H functions, and there is a fragmentary literature including poetry and prose. More significant perhaps was the use of French in Anglo-Irish law, as Kallen (1988: 128) points out. English, however, started to replace French as the language of the Irish Parliament in the late 15th century.

Within the first hundred years, the Anglo-Normans had, in fact, become Gaelicised with a concomitant language shift from Latin and French to Irish. Laws, known as the Statutes of Kilkenny, were passed in 1366 with the aim of maintaining the linguistic and cultural unity of the Anglo-Normans. Legislation was enacted so that '[e]very Englishman use the English language, and be named by an English name' (Berry 1907: 435, cited in Kallen, 1988).

English, therefore, gradually came to vie with French and Latin as prestige languages within Anglo-Norman society, and with Irish and Latin as the prestige languages of traditional Irish society. As Kallen (1988) rightly points out, this early period of the English language in Ireland is significant in that it laid the foundation of the ideological value underpinning both English and Irish. English became associated quickly with colonial administration, with Irish being associated with native political structures and culture. Kallen (1988: 130) writes:

> Although the concrete aspect of language use was to change dramatically from the early colonial period to the time of the modern Irish nation state, the ideological values which were established in early times did not change in the same way.

From the 13th to the 17th century, the Irish language was strongly assimilative, which means that the number of monoglot English speakers was relatively small. The pattern emerging from the 17th century, however, indicates that English had started to dominate in the core of towns and urban centres with suburbs and the countryside remaining predominantly Irish speaking.

The 19th century was pivotal in the shift to English. In the decades after the Great Famine (1845–1848), the steady pattern of language change emerged. By 1911, 17.6% of the population was reported to be Irish speaking, with 82.4% English speaking. The shift in Ireland to 100% English-speaking continued rapidly in the following years (Kallen, 1988). Some of the phonological features of Irish English, known also as Hiberno-English, coincide with the fact that the language started to be adopted as a vernacular in the 18th and 19th centuries. The more noticeable phonological, syntactical and morphological features of Hiberno-English are largely due to influence of the Irish language it replaced.

In this crucial period of language shift between 1850 and 1920, the language for upward mobility was English – the language already in place for this social function in Britain. Thus the native population came to need English more and more for commerce, education, politics and emigration.

There was no support system or social infrastructure to meet the needs of Irish speakers who were emigrating mainly to English-speaking countries. On the other hand, there was a cultural support system which met educational, economic and political supports if one were to function in English. Upward mobility demanded English. Gradually the cultural model for the Irish became the Anglo-Irish culture, despite the existence of the Irish language culture as a minority movement. The two cultures, the majority and minority, have existed side-by-side since the foundation of the State to the present day.

The Irish language gathered momentum as a cultural force against colonialism, but this interpretation was largely the work of middle-class elites who manipulated cultural nationalism to serve their political aims. For the vast majority, Irish was bound up with the narrative of identity. From the 17th century onwards, the language lost its important daily communication register as a mass shift towards the English language occurred. This shift to English was more marked in the 19th century in the wake of the Great Potato Famine. It has been estimated that 1.5 million people died during the famine and between 1846 and 1851 and 1 million emigrated. It is not unreasonable to assume that a great proportion of these were Irish speakers (Wall, 1969: 87). Irish to this point has assimilated the language of the Viking and Norman invaders. Henceforth, this 'unplanned' language feature (i.e. mass shift to English) altered and perverted the language planning processes. It was difficult, as the following sections will show, to recapture (Kaplan & Baldauf, 1997: 237) that language register or to artificially recreate an ecological niche for it.

Status Planning: Reversing Language Shift

As stated in the introduction, initial language planning on a macro level was fuelled by a dual policy of maintenance and restoration; i.e. maintenance of the spoken language in areas where it was still a community language (the *Gaeltachtaí*) and its restoration through reversal of language shift in all other areas. The following gives an account of planning for the restoration of Irish outside the Gaeltacht areas in the period from 1922 to 1990 to reverse the shift to English initially towards Irish monolingualism (1922–1960) and towards the establishment and fostering of some form of stable bilingualism (1970–2004).

Irish language revitalisation: The foundations of language planning

If the writings of the early proponents of a language restoration in the new state were examined, it appears that there was a lack of clarity about what exactly constituted language restoration or revitalisation. The rather amorphous concept of a linguistic restoration was inherited from a certain confusion among the Gaelic League (*Conradh na Gaeilge*) propagandists themselves regarding the exact nature of language revival. The Gaelic League was seen to influence the thinking on revival in the new State (Ó Tuama, 1991), and leaders of the movement, like Eoin Mac Néill, who assumed the significant and potentially very influential position of Minister for Education in the first Government, played key roles.

Whatever aspirations the founders of the Gaelic League may have had about how the language should be restored, they did not formulate any working definition of what they meant by a revival. They certainly did not write anything definite into their constitution about having Irish spoken by *all* the people of Ireland, nor was there any declared intention or objective about the total replacement of English by Irish (Ó Cuiv, 1969: 128). The Gaelic League's language ideology was not anti-English, the antithesis of the picture popularly presented. The contours of their construct of a bilingual Ireland can be retraced indicating a non-sectarian approach to the Irish language, seeing it as an expression of unification of the two cultures and traditions of the island of Ireland. The movement was pluralist with marked social objectives and had a well-developed vision of the role of the languages and culture of Ireland in economic progress (Kirby *et al.*, 2002: 25), pointing to an inclusive imagined community to which the majority could owe allegiance.

In outlining his vision for a bilingual Ireland, one of the founding members of the organisation, Douglas Hyde, for example posited the unbroken and pristine continuation of the Irish tradition as an ideological base for the restoration of the Irish language but vacillated in his understanding of what exactly constituted a language revival (Ó Laoire, 1996: 53). In an article entitled 'A Plea for the Irish Language' which appeared in *The Dublin University Review* in 1886, Hyde showed that he did not envisage a language revival occurring outside the Gaeltacht as a viable option; that is, reversing language shift. He advocated a social and economic restoration of the Gaeltacht rather than the revival of the language in the country as a whole:

> There is no use arguing the advantage of making Irish the language of our newspapers and clubs because this is and ever shall be an impossibility. But for several reasons we wish to arrest the language of its downward path and if we cannot spread it (and I do not believe we very much can) we will at least prevent it from dying out, and make sure that those who speak it now will also transmit it unmodified to their descendants. (Hyde, 1886, cited in Ó Conaire, 1986: 36)

Had Hyde persisted in this policy, which was apparently aimed at language maintenance in the Gaeltacht, the Gaelic League would have continued perhaps in quite a different course of action from that which it historically pursued: the aim being the social and economic development of the Gaeltacht areas rather than the restoration of the language throughout the country as a whole (Ó Laoire, 1996).

In a later speech given to the *Cumann Gaelach* (The Irish Society) in the United States, published in *The Irish American*, 27 June 1891, he referred again to what he visualised in a language revival:

> I do not for a moment advocate making Irish the language of the country at large or of the National Parliament. . . . What I want to see is Irish established as a living language for all time among the million or half-million who still speak it along the west coast, and to ensure that the language will hold a favorable place in teaching institutions and government examinations. (Hyde 1891, cited in Ó Conaire, 1986: 45)

It is clear, therefore, that Hyde never envisaged the Irish language actually supplanting English as the dominant language of the country. Even in his celebrated *Necessity for the De-Anglicisation of Ireland* oration in 1893, he reinforced the overriding importance of language maintenance over reversal of language shift. He wrote:

> [b]ut in order to keep the Irish language alive where it is still spoken, which is the utmost we can at present aspire to, nothing less than a house-to-house

visitation and exhortation of the people themselves will do. (cited in Ó
Conaire, 1986: 151–2)

Eoin Mac Neill, who with Hyde was a founding member of the Gaelic League,
and who was, to a large extent, the inspirational force behind the movement,
believed that the revival could not be achieved through the agency of the school
alone. His theory underpinned the importance of intergenerational transmission, a crucial element in achieving language revitalisation. In his blueprint for
the regeneration of the language, entitled, *Toghairm agus Gleus chum Oibre* (*A
Summons and a Method Towards Work*) in 1893, Mac Neill spelled out the significance of achieving linguistic transformation in the home, seeing it as being the
key to revival (Ó Laoire, 1996). He wrote:

> A language has never survived, when it has not survived beside the hearth.
> Even though teaching Irish is important, it is not the most important thing.
> The first thing we need to do is to keep the language alive at the hearth.
> (Cited in Ó Laoire, 1996: 54)

If we look, therefore, at the theories and ideologies such as these of the protagonists of the revival movement, quite conflicting ideas of what exactly constituted a revival are in evidence. While the Gaelic League in its earliest activities
seemed to target the non-Gaeltacht population, it is interesting to note that the
revival was associated more with language maintenance in the Gaeltacht and
with achieving some kind of English–Irish societal bilingualism rather than
reverting to an Irish monolingualism.

These theories of achieving a societal bilingualism were lost sight of in the
context of early planning for the language after independence in 1922. The Gaelic
League was undoubtedly a successful cultural movement in that, within a short
period, it had won wide support in particular for its educational programme.
However, MacNamara (1971) refers to the fact that the Gaelic League, nonetheless, failed to muster significant support among the working classes, with the main
support for its 593 branches coming from the middle-income group. It was this
group that formed the vanguard elite of the Irish revival for many succeeding
decades. With the founding of the Free State in 1922, the thrust and nature of the
ideology of language revival remained closely influenced by the cultural nationalism model. Proposals to revive the language on the basis of that model were
largely alien to the culture and aspiration of the vast majority of the population.
The national political factors were less successful in the case of Irish; from then
onward economics competed with culture for the main ideology of the new State.

Ó Doibhlin (no date) has commented, in fact, that it was the native government which dealt the greatest blow to the revival movement by leaving it without its *raison d'être*. Successive governments have formulated strategies through
the years aimed at promoting the extension of Irish outside the Gaeltacht, and the
survival of the Irish-speaking areas, along the western seaboard, as distinctive
speech communities has become a primary focus of policy intervention to maintain the language.

Language planning: A megapolicy

Ó Buachalla (1994) states that the State's policy for the Irish language from

1922 onwards became a 'megapolicy' – a master policy, which determined the main guidelines and approach to be adhered to in developing specific language or education policies. The Government of the new State, while initially espousing wholeheartedly the Gaelic League's agenda, which had become more political in the years prior to independence, lost sight of some of the theories of the early enthusiasts. The notion of a revival was associated with promoting Irish monolingualism, or reversing language shift rather than achieving the bilingualism that the Gaelic League proponents had envisaged.

This was due in no small measure to the Irish-Ireland movement that endeavoured to foster a culture and a concomitant image of a self-sufficient Ireland, diametrically opposed to all British influence. The centrality of intergenerational transmission of Irish was not emphasised, and education became the main agency in revitalisation.

The vision from which the earlier megapolicy derived its energy started to evaporate in the new State. Eventually it was espoused only among a few influential politicians. The declining political support for the language matched a corresponding decline in the use and presence of the language in the State administrative system. By the end of the 1950s, planning efforts had lacked the cohesion and clarity-thrust of the early planning strategies and responses in all State sectors. The 1950s, 1960s and 1970s lacked contemporary versions of the earlier enthusiasts. The policy eroded over time, became fragmented with modern development and in places disappeared almost completely.

Ó Buachalla (1994) sees the potential re-emergence of a megapolicy in the context of sustained popular support for the language in recent decades as evidenced in the language surveys of the mid-1980s and mid-1990s. To reconstruct such a megapolicy would require a coherent and clear set of policies being brought forward by politicians in the main political parties with a recreated idealism and conviction that fuelled and drove early revivalist policies in the new State.

The megapolicy for acquisition planning

A particular feature of language planning in Ireland has been the centrality of the education system as an agent of maintenance and revitalisation. Since the inception of the Irish Free State in 1922, the education system has been seen as a cornerstone of the movement for the revitalisation of Irish. In fact, the espoused planning policies for revitalisation devolved almost entirely on the schools. Announcing its policies on Irish in the schools in 1922, the Government's aim for the immediate inclusion of Irish as a core curriculum subject, simply stated, was to gradually replace English with Irish as the sole medium of instruction in all subjects (Ó Buachalla, 1984, 1988; Ó Domhnalláin, 1977). This meant that Irish in primary and post-primary education became, what Flynn (1993: 79) has termed, a 'politically-based curriculum subject', that is, a subject taught to bolster the Government's aim of fostering an Irish-speaking identity on behalf of the nation. Thus programmes for Irish in the primary schools introduced in the 1930s specified that Irish be the sole medium of instruction and of in-school activities during the first three years of schooling. Further policies in primary education underlined a positive discrimination approach as emphasis was put on increasing provision of Irish-medium schools in English-speaking areas. Examples of these included additional funding per pupil taught through the medium of Irish and a lower pupil-to-teacher ratio.

The influence that the political system exerted on the status of the national language was also evident in the post-primary curriculum. Here, as in primary education, there was a positive discrimination for using Irish as the medium of instruction. For example, the 1923–1924 *Rules and Programmes* specified that candidates in the State examinations answering through Irish could benefit from excess marks not exceeding 10% of the total marks awarded (Department of Education, 1924: 9). Similarly, in the 1932–33 Report, Irish became a compulsory subject for all students in the State examination, with a pass grade being a requisite for award of the final Leaving Certificate (Ó Domhnalláin, 1977: 89). This policy, in turn, impacted on, and was reinforced by, policies regulating entry to the professions and public service (Ó Riagáin, 2001: 207). Additional funding was also given to schools in which all or part of the work was conducted through the medium of Irish (Battersberry, 1955: 290). It was clear, therefore, with the exceptional status being accorded to it, and the added incentives for its use, that the educational system was targeted as being instrumental in the restoration and expansion of the language.

Very shortly after the establishment of native government, not only was Irish introduced as a subject at primary and post-primary levels, but also financial incentives were used to promote the teaching of other subjects through Irish. It was decided in 1921 that the first aim of the new syllabus in schools would be the furtherance of the policy for the restoration of Irish. In the wake of enthusiasm and idealism generated by the Gaelic League and by nationalism, it was hoped to achieve a national restoration of the Irish language. The Government saw the educational system as the essential machinery for its philosophy of national building – that is, for building up a national competence in the language. The belief was widespread that an Irish-speaking Ireland would emerge within a very short period. The fallacy in State policy, however, was that the burden or task of a restoration was laid totally on the shoulders of the educational system. In other words, this meant that since it was politically impossible to begin on the road to a restoration, the job of preserving Irish was turned over to the schools; and that is where the problems about to be examined in the present study are rooted.

Planning developments in education between 1922–1960

From 1900 onwards, the teaching of Irish had been allowed in primary schools, subject to special limitations. From 1878 to 1900, in response to the efforts of the Society for the Preservation of the Irish Language (SPIL), Irish was taught to the fifth and sixth-class pupils outside official class time. However, even when the 10 shilling fee attached to the extra tuition was lifted in 1899 at the request SPIL, Irish was being taught in a mere 1% of schools.

The Commissioners of the National Board, in a report in 1905–1906, announced provision for the teaching of Irish in 25 Gaeltacht schools. In the school year 1906–1907, there were 36 bilingual schools in which Irish was taught. By 1920 this figure had risen to 234. It was being taught as a subject in 1261 out of 7947 (15.8%) schools excluding the Gaeltacht during the same period (Battererry, 1955: 213–14). So the Gaelic League's ideal was in no uncertain terms being palpably felt within the educational system before the foundation of the Free State.

Ó Domhnallin (1977) reports that only a small proportion of primary teachers, however, had any knowledge of the Irish language. In 1926, the Government established preparatory colleges for the training of national teachers. Special provision was given for entrants from the Gaeltacht (places reserved), and all teaching was through the medium of Irish in the colleges. Colleges were set up in Cork, Dingle, Donegal, Dublin, Galway and Mayo. Crash courses were given during the vacation periods to equip every teacher for the teaching of Irish. By 1929, 50% of all teachers had some qualification in Irish for these courses. Each teacher was expected to obtain a bilingual certificate within a fixed period.

Perhaps the most salient feature of the teaching of Irish at primary level was the 'immersion' approach. A new programme early in the 1930s laid down that Irish be the sole medium of instruction and activities during the first three years of schooling. This meant that English-speaking children throughout Ireland on commencing attendance at primary schools were immersed in an Irish language environment for all classroom interactions in infant and early classes (grades). English reading was introduced in second class. Teachers were urged to teach through the medium of Irish in higher classes and it was hoped that schools gradually would be teaching all subjects – except English language – through Irish. Between 1930 and 1940, all-Irish primary schools thrived. In 1930 there were 228 all-Irish primary schools, thus representing 4% of the national primary schools. This percentage was trebled by 1940 when there were 632 such schools.

The language was taught intensively, therefore, and used as the sole medium of instruction and of in-school activities wherever feasible during the first years of schooling. The methodology employed by primary teachers was generally based on the direct method (Ó Mathúna, 1974) with little or no resort to translation into English. The syllabus being implemented was a content-type syllabus. The assumption underlying the content-type syllabus (widely implemented in language teaching elsewhere until replaced by the audio-visual and communicative type programmes in the 1960s and 1980s) was that language consisted of a finite set of rules which could be combined in various ways to make meaning (Nunan, 2001). The task for the language teacher was to present each rule, and to ensure that learners mastered it through practice before moving on to the next rule. Eight years of concentrated teaching using the direct method and content-type syllabus, however, was not yielding effective results.

In the mid-1940s the immersion programme began to witness the shifting of support from under its feet. Teachers seemed to have become anxious about teaching through the medium of Irish as is witnessed in the Report by the Irish National Teachers' Organisation (INTO) in 1941. In 1939, the Irish National Teachers' Organisation carried out a survey among its members concerning teaching through the medium of Irish in schools in which English was the dominant language in their hinterlands. Questionnaires were issued to over 90,000 teachers of whom only 1347 (1.5%) replied. The Report of 1941 indicated that the majority of teachers were not in favour of teaching through Irish only in junior classes, nor of teaching through the medium of Irish in higher classes. Ó Domhnalláin (1977: 86) says of these findings:

There is no doubt that this Report had effect on the extent to which Irish was used as a medium of communication in schools from that time onward and that it also had some effect on public opinion in the matter.

Later, MacNamara (1966) documented the adverse effects of a bilingual programme on the primary learners' academic progress and cognitive development. MacNamara's study associated negative cognitive and (negative) academic outcomes with bilingualism. Maintaining a 'balance effect' in language learning, he found that Irish children from English-speaking homes paid for their Irish-speaking skills by a decrease in the first language (English) speaking skills and secondly by a retardation in problem arithmetic. While international research has long since disproved these findings and dispelled fears, the context of the power imbalance between the prestigious English and Irish created a context of distrust.

Ó Domhnalláin (1977: 86) assessing the impact of such findings on the educational system at primary level stated that they probably accelerated a reduction in the amount of time devoted to Irish-medium teaching in schools; he stressed that they were not a major factor in that reduction. It is more likely that the reduction was caused by a general feeling that the whole of the restoration of Irish as a daily language was being left to the schools and that there was little evidence of effort towards that end in other sectors of society.

Policy and planning since 1960: The Commission on the Restoration of the Irish Language

It has been remarked that the 1960s marked the beginning of a new era in government policy towards the languages of Ireland. Already in 1958, the Government had understood the need for some new research and evaluation. In that year the Commission on the Restoration of the Irish Language (A*n Coimisiún um Athbheochan na Gaeilge*) was established by the Government to secure the restoration of the Irish language, and to consider and advise as to the steps that should be taken by the community and the State to hasten progress to that end.

The Commission's Report was comprehensive, including some interesting background consideration on the entire issue of language restoration: the demographic decline and decay of the Gaeltacht, the high rate of emigration and the socioeconomic attractions of the English language. The lack of any real coordinated policy, and the social and quantitative expansion of an Anglicised media, were both seen by the Commission as decisive factors militating against an effective societal goal of preservation and extension of the Irish language.

Against this uncompromising pessimism on one hand, the Commission made explicit reference, on the other hand, to the considerable knowledge of the language in the English-speaking part of the country, where it had been practically unknown at the beginning of the century. The proportion of Irish speakers given (on a national basis) was 26%, a figure based in no small measure on the 1961 Census, which recorded 27.2% of the Irish population as Irish speaking.

The State, in its revival movement up to the early 1960s, had little by way of definitive success. Yet the lack of apparent success was not equated with failure in the Commission's view. It saw the efforts from 1922 to 1962 as being concentrated largely on a promotion of the language through the educational system.

This represented a first stage in State planning. The Commission called for State support to be placed behind a second stage of putting the great amount of Irish in the community to general use. In discussing the role of the State, the Commission elicited other interesting facts. For example, it showed that expenditure incurred in promoting Irish was marginal, being only 0.2% in 1962 and 0.3% in 1963 of the total State expenditure. It was only one-sixteenth of the cost of the army and one-twelfth of the cost of the *Garda Síochána* (police force).

The kernel of the Commission's concern was the successful implementation of three basic conditions:

(1)   That ordinary Irish youths leaving school will have a sufficient command of the language to enable them to understand it, speak it and read it without difficulty.
(2)   That all around them during later life, enough Irish will be heard and seen by them to ensure at least that they will retain their command of it and if possible will be adding to it all the time without any conscious effort on their part.
(3)   That they will be certain that, if they use the Irish language in any normal circumstances in their daily lives, their use of it will be understood, welcomed responded to and not considered odd.

The Commission stated that, up to the early 60s, these conditions had not been fulfilled. The translation of these conditions into reality was the main objective in the recommendations, which broadly outlined a policy in the educational system to ensure later-life usage in the professional sphere in the social sphere (culture, entertainment) and in the media.

It also called for an examination in Irish for those who had already been teaching it without a degree and for the finance of in-service summer courses in the Gaeltacht for teachers during the first three years of teaching. The Commission was pessimistic on the whole regarding the then position of the language. It was seen to be declining in the Gaeltacht, the victim of apathy because of the absence of any coordinated policy. The language was compulsory in the educational system and had extraordinary status in the curriculum in the sense that certificate candidates had to pass Irish to ensure the conferring of the certificate – yet the position in the school with regard to speaking the language warranted drastic change.

The report was perhaps the first important synthesis of undercurrent feelings and attitudes on an apparent regression in the use of the language, which was taking place at all levels of society. The report of the Council of Education in 1961–62 had dealt exclusively with the educational system, and the curriculum of the secondary school including Irish as part of its report. However, this report aimed at setting up overall coordinated planning for the language, because the Commission seemed to understand that to achieve progress in one area of society would necessarily mean achievement in all other areas as well. So it brought the question into the arena of public concern, and, in so doing, went beyond leaving the issue to civil servants and to teachers. The report uncompromisingly evoked government policy to implement its recommendations, which concentrate on an extension of the use of the language in governmental, educational and social spheres as well as calling for a government-supported cogent, coordinated, over-all policy for the language.

The 1960s, therefore, witnessed a new direction in government planning for the Irish language. The Government, faced with researched reports and continued criticisms on the state of the language, was forced to renew its policy. In its new policy, the Government aimed at getting people to use the Irish they had learned at school in ordinary everyday situations. They also aimed at introducing new measures for counteracting the social, economic and thereby the linguistic erosion of Gaeltacht areas. This meant in effect a new direction in government policy outside the education system. Many who received their primary or secondary education (from the foundation of _Saorstát Éireann_ to the 1960s) sometimes may refer to the 'pushing of Irish' that went on in the school. In the 1960s, all this seemed to end. Government policy now tended to minimise 'the all important agency of the school' which it stressed in its earlier policies on restoration.

The 1965 White Paper on the Restoration of Irish embodied a new planning – a new conception of language use and maintenance. One cannot but feel that the Government, in supplying reasons for a restoration, was being unrealistic when it stressed the need for the same pristine idealism of the earlier years. The Government's appeal therefore was to this idealism as the prime motivating factor in the restoration. This would lead one to question whether government policy was based on a somewhat naive and unrealistic idealism, an idealism that was characteristic of historical events and earlier political developments.

The White Paper of 1965: The Restoration of the Irish Language

The Government published its response to the Commission's Report in a White Paper entitled '_Athbheochan na Gaeilge: The Restoration of the Irish Language_'. The body of the paper delineates the response to the 288 recommendations of the Commission. In its introduction, the White Paper restated its aim of restoration of the Irish language, specifying that the national effort would take longer to achieve than originally envisaged. The beginnings of a change of a decentralised and 'distancing-delegation' policy are evident, where it is stated that the responsibility and planning can not be discharged by the Government on its own. The need for public support was apparent. There was recognition, therefore, of the contribution of class power to successful planning enterprises and the importance of change at the micro level. There was a need for '[a] sustained personal effort to achieve the national aim' (White Paper, 1965: 6).

The sense of urgency to revive the language was not evident. There was a feeling that regeneration might be more _durée_ than _événement_. There was, rather, a tacit acceptance that class power had shifted to and adopted English, and the drive to supplant English by reversing language shift was not present. English would remain and would now be included in planning (albeit reluctantly).

> Irish must have primacy as the national language and every effort will be made to extend and intensify its use. Nevertheless, for a considerable time ahead, English will remain the language chiefly used outside the Gaeltacht for various purposes. To assume otherwise would be unrealistic and detract from appreciation of the effort needed to achieve the national aim in regard to Irish. (White Paper, 1965: 10)

This represented a new approach in State policy, one that was to signal a new thinking in terms of Irish–English bilingualism that would emerge within a decade. The Irish State was at this time looking towards development of a new economy incorporating wider markets and multinational companies.

The Government decided to issue an ongoing and up-to-date consistent account of the progress achieved towards meeting the recommendation. It was recommended that a report should be issued annually by the Government detailing the work done by the State, written directly or indirectly for the preservation of the Gaeltacht and for the revival of the language outside the Gaeltacht during the previous year. This report should also indicate the objective to be aimed at during the following 12 months. Only two such reports ever appeared, however – one in 1966 and the second in 1968.

It is intended here to present some of the Government's recommendations and to review the progress achieved at the end of two years. It is in the relation between the 'ideal' (the recommendation – the overt statement of intention) and the 'concrete' (the progress achieved) that one can perceive the overall effectiveness of Government policy. It is intended, secondly, to examine how the Government policy in the White Paper showed a new direction emphasising language use and maintenance rather than the promotion of the language solely through the educational system.

The Commission's recommendation that the main aim of teaching Irish in the primary school should be to give the student a functional command of the language was endorsed by the White Paper. Regarding conditions governing the education and training of primary teachers, the Commission had demanded that a high standard of oral fluency be exacted from entrants into training colleges and that they should be given adequate training in modern methods of language teaching. The White Paper stated that arrangements were being made in accordance with these recommendations, Articles (134–136). In general, the response of the Government was favourable on the proposed implementations and changes suggested by the Commission. In the White Paper, the Government accepted the recommendations that the primary purpose of Irish in the secondary school system should be orally oriented with secondary emphasis to be placed on the literary aspect of the subjects. The White Paper reported that school authorities had been asked to pay particular attention to entrants into the larger secondary schools who showed considerable lack of proficiency in Irish. This was in response to a proposal by the Commission, and again there was no apparent follow-up.

Towards a new type of status planning

A new type of planning emerged, therefore, concerned with providing the necessary infrastructures for maintenance and revival. The State had finally come to terms with the fact that the schools alone were unable to restore Irish as the language of the people. The Commission had pointed out that the restoration of the language, as a vernacular, would be inevitably retarded until such time as a practical day-to-day use of the language outside the schools was encouraged and fostered. It had also pointed out that failure to arrest the decay of the Gaeltacht (i.e. failure to maintain the Gaeltacht as a prosperous, economic social community) would inevitably result in the annihilation of 'the last pockets where

Irish is the language of an organic community'. The White Paper and subsequent progress reports reveal that the Government had taken serious measures to encourage use of the language and to arrest its erosion. Newspapers were to cover Dáil (government) proceedings in Irish. An extension of the use of Irish was promised in interdepartmental work in the civil service. Specialised courses were proposed to meet the needs of civil servants who wanted to increase their proficiency in Irish. There were also new ambitious policies for the Government aims for rural development, to ensure the more intensive use of land within the limits set up by market possibilities so that the maximum number of people could be retained in agriculture consistent with social and economic progression. The Government devoted most of its attention, however, to the prevention of the demographic, economic and linguistic erosion of the Gaeltacht. A brief look at some of the isolated proposals would suffice to give an overall understanding of intended policy.

Here the apparent direction in government planning began to coincide with the proposals of two other contemporary reports, *The Inter-Departmental Committee on the Problems of Small Western Farms* and *The Second Programme for Economic Expansion*. The progress reports revealed that government policy was in action. Schemes for improvement of houses, operated by *Roinn na Gaeltachta* (Department of the Gaeltacht) were increased from £400,000 in 1964–65 to £575,000 in 1965–66. *Roinn na Gaeltachta* prepared a booklet outlining schemes for improvement in land projects, farm buildings, water and sewerage amenities and secondary schools. New factories were set up by *Gaeltarra Éireann* (see section on Gaeltacht). Irish-speaking agricultural advisors were éipointed, and grants for 'Summer Holidays Schemes' under *Roinn na Gaeltachta* were increased.

With its policies of language use and maintenance, the White Paper and Progress Reports operated at the level of commendation and acceptance of the Commission's findings. It became apparent in the Progress Report that the Government had understood how a restoration was contingent, among other factors, on the continued use and extension of the language in all spheres of society. Government policy was now to concentrate more on the Gaeltacht, since it had become apparent that language promotion through the schools alone was ineffectual without sufficient back-up in all areas of society and by maintaining and strengthening the language.

Towards bilingualism

In response to the sometimes adverse but constructive criticisms of the Commission on the Restoration of Irish and in response also to the White Paper, *Comhairle na Gaeilge* (an advisory body for Irish) was set up. This body was to have a dual function, 'to help in reviewing policy on the Irish language and to advise on future implementation of this policy' (*Comhairle na Gaeilge*, 1970: v). It was to 'prepare reports and recommendations for the government on general policy matters and on measures which should be taken to extend the use of Irish as a general medium of communication' (*Comhairle na Gaeilge*, 1970: v). It was set up in 1969, and over the following years it began to point to areas in which government policy should be developed. The first and most important of these areas of guidelines was 'bilingualism'. The *Comhairle*'s study of the different aspects of bilingualism was a direct response to the request of the then Minister for Finance, Mr Haughey, for a 'broad and comprehensive study of the complex question of bilingualism' for the benefit of the Government and of the general public. To help in its analysis of bilingualism, *Comhairle na Gaeilge* prepared a paper setting out some concepts of the science of linguistics with particular reference to bilingualism and to the associated pattern of language use and diglossia. The first paper, *Urlabhra agus Pobal, Language and Community*, written by Máirtín Ó Murchú, appeared in 1970. The paper was largely devoted to the clarification of the concepts of linguistics and bilingualism, but the latter part looked at the (then present) position of the language and made some predictions as to its future in terms of a diglossia. The central concern appeared to be the imminent attainment of an Irish–English diglossia. Fishman (1967) envisaging a situation where Irish would no longer be the traditionally weaker language, had already asserted that planned research and experimentation would be foremost in affecting a diglossia. Ó Murchú (1970) adopted and developed this idea of Fishman's by laying the theoretical foundations which a societal shift to diglossia would entail. *Comhairle na Gaeilge* took up Ó Murchú's outlined concept of a diglossia and bilingualism and illustrated how the diglossia concept might be exploited for the greater use of Irish. *Comhairle na Gaeilge* saw its function primarily as advisor to the Government on how the Irish language could be restored as a general medium of communication. It, therefore, suggested a policy of 'diglossia' to the Government in the 1970 document, *Language and Community*. In attempting to describe procedures necessary for a diglossic society, *Comhairle na Gaeilge* hoped that the Government would help to bring about their desired aim (Ó Murchú, 1970: v). It became clear to *Comhairle na Gaeilge*, following Ó Murchú's elaboration of a stable bilingualism, that their desired aim could be brought about, not by shifting to a monolingual Irish situation but by a situation whereby Irish would be a partner with English in a bilingual situation.

In a diglossia, Irish would be presented as the language to be associated at a given time with a range of domains. The choice of sociolinguistic domains where a diglossia situation would prove the most favourable for the extension of the use of Irish would have to be identified by research. *Towards a Language Policy* issued a clear directive on the need for coordination and support for a diglossia. It envisaged support in four main areas – a support which, if forthcoming, would be indicative of a well-coordinated and consolidated State policy for the development of a diglossia.

(1) Support in the communications media. Full support could be drawn from this valuable resource to present the new approach to the public to familiarise them with the selected domains.

(2) Support in the educational system. The diglossia approach would entail a comprehensive programme for the development of teaching aids to provide learners with the minimum of proficiency required in a diglossic situation.

(3) Since the Gaeltacht gives special insights into the attributes of an already operative diglossic community, it should be socially and economically strengthened to make an important contribution to the development of a diglossia in the rest of the country.

(4) Effective and coordinated planning and organisation by the State would be tantamount to the successful, even if gradual, adoption of the diglossic

approach. The State would have to be actively responsible for the overall supervision of the plan.

A report which followed in 1972, *Implementing a Language Policy*, recommended guidelines for an effective implementation of the new approach should it be adopted by the Government. The key recommendations were stated in an introduction to the report by the chairman of *Comhairle na Gaeilge*:

(1) that the general function of extending the use of Irish throughout the country be assigned to a new statutory board to be called *Bord na Gaeilge*;
(2) that all the Gaeltacht development functions be assigned to a separate statutory board to be called *Udarás na Gaeltachta*;
(3) that both these boards should be the responsibility of a department called *Roinn na Gaeilge* (The Department of Irish).

Underlining from the outset that the sociolinguistic patterns of diglossia could only be achieved in Ireland after a considerably long period (a tentative target being the increase from 5% to 20% Irish in the proportion of conversations carried out by the average Irish person daily by the year 2000), the report emphasised the vital necessity of planning, organisation and evaluation in government policy. After indicating in broad terms the practical implications of developing a strategy of diglossia in areas where English was the sole medium of communication, in church, in education, at work – the report stressed again that all language efforts would need to be guided and supported by constant research, review and evaluation with a view particularly to identifying the efforts which are successful and capable of development.

Comhairle na Gaeilge felt that the identification of a department which would have primary responsibility for Irish language policy rested with the Government. The report emphasised that *Comhairle na Gaeilge* did not deem it very fitting to locate responsibility for Irish in a department, which would have responsibility for policy relating to the arts and creation. The White Paper of 1965 had located the responsibility for the implementation of its recommendations with the Minister for Finance. In fact, the staff of the Irish language section of the Department totalled six, and most of their duties were secretarial or at best concerned with the organisation of Irish language courses for the public service. This lack of personnel was hardly conducive to an effective coordinating and supervisory function. What was needed was the location of a department and minister whose function would be clearly defined with responsibility for Irish. Allied to the unsatisfactory equipment of the Department of Finance, the Department of Education had no officer on the administrative side whose full-time concern was the general language policy within the educational system.

What *Comhairle na Gaeilge* stressed was needed was to set up a body or agency readily identifiable for the organisation, planning and direction of societal bilingualism.

Secondly, it called for a government department with a skilled, full-time staff bearing primary responsibility for the implementation of all necessary measures. This is what they meant by a radical reorganisation of the administrative structures at present dealing with the Irish language. The use of the words 'radical reorganisation' not only revealed their dissatisfaction with the policy, but it showed that they understood the clash of ideologies, the growing disparity between theory and practice (research proposals and effective implementation) that had been hindering progress.

Comhairle na Gaeilge arrived at these recommendations from a review of the recommendations made in turn by the Devlin Report. The Devlin Report (1966–1969) had stipulated that the promotion of the Irish language be assigned to a separate minister, other than *Aire na Gaeltachta* (Ministry of the Gaeltacht). In accordance with its thesis that the function of government on behalf of the community be split as between policy and execution, the report suggested that development policy (up to the responsibility entirely of *Roinn na Gaeltachta*) be assigned to a separate executive agency, *Bord na Gaeilge*, and that the execution of preconcerted policies be assigned to another executive agency, *Bord na Gaeilge*, with a reporting arrangement between the minister's department and the chief officers of the executive. This meant that the Department for the Gaeltacht, *Roinn na Gaeltachta*, which had as its goal the promotion of the Irish language and culture, and the Department of Finance, which had as its goal the promotion of the Irish language, a supervisory and coordinating function in the implementation of policy, should hitherto shed responsibility for the implementation or execution of this policy, and that this responsibility would be transferred to two executive agencies in the certificate examinations – *Bord na Gaeltachta* (Board for Gaeltacht Development) and *Bord na Gaeilge* (Board for Language Restoration). *Comhairle na Gaeilge* reiterated the Devlin thesis and stressed that the execution of Irish language policy be the central concern of the two new executive agencies: (1) *Bord na Gaeltachta*, which would perform the Gaeltacht development functions, and (2) *Bord na Gaeilge*, which would perform the function relating to the extensions of the use of Irish throughout the country.

In 1978, *Bord na Gaeilge* was established with the task of promotion of the Irish language, particularly promotion of its use as a living language and as an ordinary means of communication. No clear demarcation was established between this agency and other agencies other than that of a watching brief on the activities of State organisations in general and on any proposed legislation that might affect the position of Irish (Tovey, 1988). The *Bord* has over the years embarked on a number of promotional initiatives and provided a range of community schemes to extend the use of Irish and of supports, including financial assistance to groups within the voluntary language movement. In particular, it has supported the preschool language (*naíonraí*) and the immersion schooling (*Gaelscoileanna*) movements. In its promotional campaign it has aimed at the creation of positive vibrant and sophisticated images for the extension of the language aimed at the Irish people as a whole. It has also embarked on a series of community scheme projects working with local voluntary groups devoted to language change in their local areas. These schemes reflected the then current thinking that local development rather than State intervention represented the path to progress. It must be said, however, that many of the local groups failed to sustain the planning efforts (beyond organisation of day events or festivals) that would effect a language shift.

In 1983, *Bord na Gaeilge* published *An Action Plan For Irish*, which was a strategic plan with targets to be met after a 10-year period. Its goal was realistic compared with previous reports in that it aimed not for the restoration or revival of the language, but for its survival into the 21st century as one of the functioning languages of a bilingualism (*Bord na Gaeilge* 1983: 2). It appealed to the nationally attested positive attitudes to the language in a survey on language attitudes in 1975 and set out agreed targets for the provision of certain basic State services such as schools, television and radio services. A large part of the action plan involved the establishment of coordinating committees between the *Bord* and other agencies. The action plan represented further evidence of a new rethink on planning and of erecting a growing distance between the State and revivalist efforts.

Some commentators observed the role of *Bord na Gaeilge* as reductionist in its representation of a language movement, opting to represent the State to the language. Tovey (1988: 67), for example, writes:

> Nearly a century ago Irish became the focus of a strong populist and antistate movement. If a similar social movement were to arise today, and some argue that this is the only way the language could survive into the next century, it could hardly occur under the auspices of *Bord na Gaeilge*.

There is evidence that the populist and right-based movement has in fact started to mobilise the State to legislate, but the work of *Bord na Gaeilge* has shown that language issues must be taken out of the realms of political argument and moved into the realm of community and human development. The *Bord* has worked largely within the consensus of support for the language. Its work continues within the context of that broad support which, while significant, will not necessarily translate into active use unless a niche for such use pre-exists or is created in the language environment.

In December 1999, *Bord na Gaeilge* was replaced by *Foras na Gaeilge* which became the body responsible for the promotion of the Irish language throughout the whole island of Ireland (The Irish Republic and Northern Ireland). In the Good Friday Agreement, it was stated that a North/South Implementation body be set up to promote both the Irish language and the Ulster Scots language. Under the auspices of *Foras na Gaeilge*, all the designated responsibilities regarding the Irish language are being carried out. This entails facilitating and encouraging the speaking and writing of Irish in the public and private arena in the Republic of Ireland, and in Northern Ireland where there is appropriate demand, in the context of Part Three of the European Charter for Regional and Minority Languages.

Foras na Gaeilge has a role in advising administrations, North and South, as well as public bodies and other groups in the private and voluntary sectors, in all matters relating to the Irish language, and it also undertakes supportive projects and grant-aiding bodies and groups throughout the island of Ireland.

Acquisition planning for Bilingualism 1970–2000

An important report entitled *Irish in Education* was issued by *Comhairle na Gaeilge* in 1974. The rationale of the report was based on a reaction by *Comhairle na Gaeilge* to the changes made by the Minister for Education regarding Irish. *Comhairle na Gaeilge* set a high premium on the necessity of retaining compulsory Irish. The decision to study Irish should be enforced and not left to the discretion of the individual parent or pupil. Central to *Comhairle na Gaeilge*'s anxiety was the conviction that, since a pass was no longer required for the certificate examinations, a sharp drop might occur in the numbers applying themselves seriously to Irish in the schools in the future.

The findings of the Committee on Irish Language Attitudes Research (1974) showed that there were serious failure rates in Irish in State examinations, where in fact it was conceded that the relation between failure in Irish and failure in other subjects was very high. *Comhairle na Gaeilge* advocated that a better system than the inducement arrangement envisaged would be one whereby marks gained well in excess of the pass-grade requirement in Irish could be transferred to another subject in which marks slightly below the pass-grade were obtained. The report also recommended that, in a situation where an individual school had shown an inordinately low standard in Irish, the Department demand a satisfactory standard in Irish from that school as a condition for departmental recognition as a school.

Referring to immersion education, the report stated that one of the most important ways in which the Department of Education could help in the task of encouraging the use of Irish throughout the community was by establishing and adequately maintaining well-equipped Irish schools. The report outlined the decline in the all-Irish schools, which had been established in the 1930s and 1940s. Many factors contributed to the decline, for example, the lack of essential texts and reading matter for courses, the inadequate arrangements for providing teachers' competence to teach Irish, and above all the fact that financial inducements offered to the managements of all-Irish schools to encourage them to overcome the special difficulties associated with teaching Irish have now only a marginal value within the new scheme of free post-primary education. *Comhairle na Gaeilge* stressed that a new approach was needed. It was proposed that all-Irish post-primary schools be redistributed on a national basis, in such a way as to serve most of the country, so that anyone seeking education through Irish would have a reasonable opportunity of obtaining it. Secondly, it recommended that all-Irish primary schools be established in the catchment areas of such schools.

Comhairle na Gaeilge was concerned about the pervasive influences of a decline in the standards of Irish (especially spoken) among teachers at both primary and post-primary sectors. The teachers in need of training were in fact unable to receive it because of a definite lack of in-service training facilities available for the teaching of other subjects through Irish. Compounded with dissatisfaction with teacher training, *Comhairle na Gaeilge* was also unhappy with the lack of ancillary teaching aids and inadequate training in their use. It was *Comhairle na Gaeilge*'s contention that modern teaching aids greatly enhanced the expertise of the teacher in an age when education is dependent on modern technology and when theories indicate that instruction be given by means of pictures, illustrations, cartoons, recordings and other similar materials. It was found that there was a dearth of learning materials in Irish as well as a lack of facilities and training for teachers. Attention was also drawn to shortcomings in the syllabus. The views expressed in *Irish in Education* were endorsed in the subsequent Committee on Irish Language Attitudes Research (CILAR) report (1975). The report emphasised that the State could not remain extraneous to any Irish language policy and stressed the importance of the educational system in the implementation of any State policy, calling the school the central agency in building up competence in the language (p. 391). It summed up the role of the State as follows:

(1) Ensuring that communicative competence in the language is built up in the schools.
(2) Ensuring a minimal competence among certain crucial groups in the State apparatus.
(3) Facilitating the process by which competent speakers come into contact and facilitate links with each other. (p. 292)

Oral assessment was introduced in 1960 and was reported to have had a favourable impact on the teaching of Irish (Department of Education and Science Report, 1961: 58), although the extent of its actual success has never been established scientifically by research. Yet its effect on the teaching of Irish was generally described in terms of improvement regarding the language teaching methods and students' proficiency in the language. A newfound interest in the language by pupil and teacher alike was reported. The use of Irish in extra-curricular activities was similarly reported, such as visits to the Gaeltacht and attendance at Irish summer courses, which were seen as desirable complements to the greater attention being given to the spoken language in classroom teaching. A Department of Education Report in (1961: 55) referred to the progress as follows:

> Since the introduction of the oral test in Irish at Leaving Certificate, there has been a notable improvement in the standard of oral Irish, particularly in the senior classes. In addition many extra-curricular activities such as visits to the Gaeltacht, attendance at Irish summer courses are a desirable complement to the greater attention being given to the spoken language in classroom teaching.

Certainly, the numbers attending Irish summer courses from 1960 onwards denoted a very important side-effect of the oral Irish test. In the summer of 1959, there were 5000 attending courses in Irish colleges. This figure rose to 7317 in 1960, to 9042 in 1961 and to 10,857 in 1964. It continued to rise to 13,006 in 1967 and 12,060 in 1970 (10 years later), an increase of over 50% over ten years. These figures provide clear evidence that the introduction of oral Irish, while improving conditions regarding Irish in the school, also contributed to the growth in importance and popularity of the Gaeltacht among school goers.

The 1980s and 1990s witnessed a rise in Irish immersion programmes; some significant changes occurred as well in the emphasis in the teaching of the language and in syllabus orientation. The majority of Irish students study Irish as a school subject. Irish as a school subject is offered for one hour daily in primary schools for eight years (on average: 1600 hours) and a further exposure of 35 minutes daily on average for five days a week (over an academic year of 30 weeks for five years). This gives a total of 2300 hours on average not including homework, private tuition and courses in the Gaeltacht. This amounts to a lot of hours of input and one would expect a greater student proficiency in the language at the end of this time. This apparent mismatch between input and output was at the kernel of the findings in the first annual report issued by the Irish Language Commissioner in March 2005. This official account highlighted the fact that many pupils have not even attained basic fluency in Irish despite being taught the language for 13 years and prompted the Commissioner to call for a review of how the language is being taught in primary and secondary schools. There is some evidence that the duration of instruction cannot allow the rate of forgetting to exceed the rate of learning, the distribution of those hours over 13 years working at cross-purposes with the amount of instruction.

With the introduction of free post-primary education (O'Connor, 1986) in 1967, the traditional classical approach to the teaching of Irish became quickly outmoded and irrelevant for a large influx of students from all socioeconomic sectors. The traditional grammar translation approach used with academically oriented elite or middle-class fee-paying students who populated secondary education before the advent of free education was quickly found to be inappropriate when used with socioeconomic classes that comprised the secondary school cohort. Thus the proportion of students failing Irish language courses in public examination rose to as high as 33% in 1983 (CEB, 1985: 40).

Expansion and development in post-primary education in the 1970s and 1980s brought ever-increasing numbers of students into the system. Among these were considerable numbers of less successful or less academically oriented pupils who had difficulty in adapting to the dominant educational model (Ó Dubhthaigh, 1978; Ó Laoire, 1994, 1997). This resulted in concern about unprecedented rates of failure in Irish in the public examinations and about a general deterioration in standards. The syllabus was felt to be 'quite unsatisfactory' (CEB, 1985) and as a consequence, the failure rates in the language in the public State examinations were predominantly between 33% and 40%. For example, almost half – 47.8% – failed the State examination Day Group Vocational Certificate in 1979.

Deterioration in standards was linked with an over-emphasis on literature texts. The language of these prescribed literary texts was regarded as being too demanding for the majority of the students previously underrepresented in post-primary education (CEB, 1985: 29). As Hopkins (1984: 21) wrote:

> The prescribed literature sections of the Irish language syllabuses are possibly the one area with the greatest negative effect on motivation to acquire the language. A case can be made for having a reasonably high literary content in language courses for those whose competence in the language will enable them to appreciate and enjoy literature. Those whose level of competence is low might derive greater benefit from material designed to impart a degree of communicative competence to enable them to exchange ideas on everyday matters.

Concern centred on the way that literature texts were approached by teachers in the classroom and on their inaccessibility to some students' experience through obscure and difficult language, that is, the textual features that tend to make them difficult for non-native language users – either difficult to understand at all, or difficult to appreciate. Such concern does not, of course, detract from the obvious benefits of including belletristic material in language courses, such as cultural enrichment (Collie & Slater, 1987), or the exploration of authenticity in text types (Duff & Maley, 1990).

The Curriculum and Examinations Board, identifying language as a key area for review and development, published *Language in the Curriculum* in 1985. This document informed curriculum revision and key developments and reform that began at the end of the 1980s.

Referring to outmoded curricula in Irish, the need for new syllabi was emphasised. These syllabi were to be drafted in accordance with the then new insights into language development, which had implications for the design of new courses and materials. The intent was to counteract unsatisfactory findings with regard to the syllabi then in place. In particular, the Curriculum and Examinations Board found the aims of the Irish courses to be vague and unrealistic, with no graded objectives, and fluency in Irish is expected of students at all stages of their schooling. The Board also expressed concern about the deterioration in the standard of Irish. Dissatisfaction was also directed at the excessive prominence of reading and writing. Students and teachers were said to be frustrated by a syllabus which did not facilitate development of oral competency.

New common syllabi for immersion and non-immersion programmes alike for L1 and L2 learners, prompted by new common syllabi in French, German, Spanish and Italian espousing a communicative paradigms were introduced in the late 1980s in post-primary schools and have only recently been implemented in the primary curriculum. The shift to communicative language teaching from the old expository grammar approach has been by and large useful in language instruction for bilingualisms but the underlying potential to foster bilingualism in the English-speaking areas has been untapped to a considerable extent.

The implementation of a communicative syllabus involved a transition from 'school Irish' to everyday Irish. The term 'school Irish' denotes a certain attenuated and oversimplified type of language unrelated to a large extent to the Irish of everyday use. It is, nonetheless, the type of Irish that one encounters regularly in situations where the Irish language is used outside the Gaeltacht. With the introduction of the new communicative-type syllabus, perhaps there was a new expectation that the second-level syllabus somehow would teach students to speak everyday Irish and that this would, in turn, lead to an extension of bilingualism outside the Gaeltacht. There is no evidence, however, that this has occurred. Mac Aogáin (1990: 30–31) states in relation to this:

> The reason that school Irish doesn't survive very well in the everyday life is not because it is school Irish but because there is nothing to do with it. School Irish never stopped anybody who had a worthwhile use for the language. Those who believe that by teaching a new kind of Irish in the schools they will close the gap between the school and the world outside will be quickly disappointed. This is the old biological solution: dose the children and wait for old age to remove the others. (This method will not even change miles to kilometres.) The weaker version of the argument, that students taught everyday Irish will be more likely to participate in whatever little Irish exists outside the school is fallacious too, since it is chiefly motivational and it is social factors which determine language use outside the school, not levels of competence, and still less the kind of Irish taught. This is why we now have a growing sub-population of people who had all-Irish education and never speak a word of the language.

The problem is that there is no fully articulated explicit language policy that would bolster a vibrant acquisition policy. In the absence of such a policy, the question that needs to be answered and addressed is: to what extent does learning Irish in schools at present guarantee rates of reproduction of sequential bilinguals to ensure consolidation and extension of the speech community? This question has not yet been fully addressed, partly because the orientation of Irish language pedagogy within the framework of bilingual reproduction has been sidetracked for a considerable time now by two interrelated developments in Irish education in the 1980s and 1990s: expansion in primary and post-primary education and subsequent curriculum development.

As stated earlier, in the context of general curriculum reform, the need to introduce new syllabi arose out of such concern and was prompted by the general malaise in the area of Irish language pedagogy. Most of the 1980s and 1990s were taken up, therefore, with syllabus reform to make the language more accessible and relevant to all students and to lower the rates of failure. The adoption of communicative-type syllabi in both junior and senior cycle programmers was undertaken deliberately by the NCCA (The National Council for Curriculum and Assessment) with this background of malaise and with the objectives of accessibility and relevance in mind. But in implementing these important syllabus-related issues, curriculum planners may have been sidetracked, albeit necessarily so, and have lost sight of the central issue: how learning Irish prepares students for participation in the Irish language speech community. Unlike the Gaeltacht student of Irish who may have the support mechanism and neighbourhood domains in sustaining proficiency through use, the school alone, for the learner of Irish as L2 outside the Gaeltacht, may indeed be the only source of language learning and interlanguage development. Learning Irish in school all too often is not reinforced by participation in, and integration into, the speech community. Irish-speaking networks outside Gaeltacht have never been sufficiently numerous to form a readily identifiable and easily visible speech community to facilitate easy integration.

This reality creates its own problems for the learning of Irish as an L2 within a communicative competence framework. The communicative-type syllabus now being taught in schools implies that learners who have little or no prospect of eventually integrating into or enacting with the speech community are asked to suspend disbelief and rehearse communicative situations, which can only be authentic or valid within the Gaeltacht or in the Irish-speaking networks outside the Gaeltacht.

Such an approach is suitable if it is geared towards learners who will want to, or who will have to, or who will choose to use Irish at some stage in their lives in the language speech community in the Gaeltacht. But does Irish language pedagogy prepare learners to integrate into the Irish language speech community outside the Gaeltacht if such were their choice?

It is not always easy to communicate or even to know how and when to communicate with Irish speakers outside the Gaeltacht. Learners at a crucial integration-threshold stage at high proficiency levels often think that their command of the language is not good enough and compare their own efforts unfavourably with the standard of the target network-group. Unfortunately, such learners often give up. This points to a need not only for more research into the sociolinguistic and motivational variables of integration but also for preliminary studies of interlanguage pragmatics in the case of Irish speakers. (The latter would be to provide data, for example, on the nature of illocutionary acts among speakers belonging to the Gaeltacht and non-Gaeltacht speech communities.)

Many would contend, as did Mac Aogáin (1990), that the language tasks set within the Irish communicative framework should not always be designed to fit into some vision of an Irish-speaking community outside the school. The thinking here is that the new communicative syllabus should fit into a model of language involvement that is meaningful for the students within classroom settings.

The CEB (Curriculum and Examinations Board) document of 1985, which preceded syllabus definition, argued that the classroom itself must be used to motivate learners at least in the short term by creating a need to use Irish in the accomplishment of meaningful activities which appeal to their interests and imagination. It states that:

> the classroom is therefore a valid communicative situation, which can in itself be exploited as a valuable resource for learning. To view it merely as a rehearsal studio for the world outside is an approach unlikely to sustain the motivation of many learners of Irish. (CEB, 1985: 31)

Irish is an essential part of Ireland's heritage and a significant part of the country's life and identity. It is, therefore, entirely appropriate, some would argue, that the language should constitute an obligatory core subject of the primary and post-primary curricula. It is also clear that the study of Irish as part of the primary or post-primary curriculum espouses general educational aims that are laudable in themselves (i.e. an essential contribution to the emotional, aesthetic and cognitive development of the individual), independent of reference to learning the language for the utilitarian purposes of communication and for extending and developing bilingualism. Again, apart from the pragmatic dimension of learning language for the purpose of using it in the speech community, the Irish language is singled out in the curriculum as being an important vehicle through which students' cultural and linguistic heritage is mediated. Nonetheless, if education is concerned with extending bilingualism, the idea of learning language for language use in the context of bilingual settings and domains that characterise Ireland sociolinguistically needs to be examined.

In the absence of any systematic research, it is difficult to assess the impact of the revised syllabus on students' potential to participate in the Irish language speech community. While teachers welcomed the challenge of the new syllabus, they may also have felt that the constraints of a teacher's daily routine would render change difficult. In many ways the changing perception of how learning actually occurs in the classroom shifts responsibility from the teacher to the learners themselves. Knowledge acquisition, rather than being an instructional process, is increasingly being seen as an autonomous construction process which can only be assisted and not enforced by the teacher. I am not altogether sure, however, if teachers understood this new paradigm and took it on board in their teaching.

The wider context of economic and social change

Bearing in mind the philosophy of the methodology adopted in this study, looking at the wider context outside education is important here. Resistance to

Irish and demotivation are, of course, related to out-of-education factors. During the 1950s in particular, there was the beginning of an ideological change as successive governments struggled to deal with the national heritage of the preceding decades of the late 19th century and of the previous decades of the 20th century. As the Irish economy improved with increased exports to Britain and a marked increase on capital expenditure to secure improved infrastructure (Kennedy *et al.*, 1988), there was a change in emphasis on what constituted the new Irish identity. Passing examinations in Irish was the norm for professional advancement and for access to positions within the hierarchies of status in the State civil service and employment strata. Those who made the greatest effort with Irish were the most likely to succeed and to obtain employment. Those who failed the language were excluded. Thus, the language became associated with social exclusion.

Gael Linn was founded in 1953 and aimed to secure State support for a range of actions regarding the language, securing the necessary funding through football pools. It succeeded in a range of language planning initiatives such as:

- a scheme to send children to the Gaeltacht;
- the establishment of a film company, *Amharc Éireann* to make short films in Irish;
- the encouragement of drama;
- the production of commercial recordings of Irish traditional music; and
- the establishment of industry in the Gaeltacht.

But the reasons for learning Irish other than professional advancement were to change. As State philosophy of economic nationalism changed with the opening of trade agreements with Britain in particular, so too the cultural nationalist philosophy changed – a philosophy that had espoused the language as a salient marker of identity in the context of anti-English post-colonialism. The death in 1949 of the founder of the Gaelic League, Douglas Hyde, coincided with the new rethink and marked the end of the era of struggle for reverting to Irish monolingualism. The new language discourse and a new shift in politicisation emanated from the frustrations, dissatisfactions and cynicism accumulated over the preceding decades. The nationalist anti-English focus of reversal to an Irish monolingualism became increasingly balanced by an emphasis on realism (Kelly, 2002: 140). The linguistic and cultural issues were taking a back seat to the new economic struggle to overcome poverty and emigration. As new debates opened up about the role of the language in the continuing life and in the opening up of the State (see Commission on the Restoration of the Irish Language, 1963; The White Paper, 1965), cynicism about the language abounded, and the Language Freedom Movement (LFM) was founded in 1965 to oppose State policies to restore the language; indeed, there was open vocal opposition to the school-based revival policy, including compulsion (Kelly, 2002). Some language activists attached themselves to the language. In 1966 a group of writers went on a week-long hunger strike to focus attention on the language, and a large meeting of the LFM was broken up, jeered and heckled by language revival activists. The language issue became polarised and divisive, a condition in which modernising forces competed with traditionalist ideology at the dawning of a new Ireland where the focus shifted more and more towards the country's participation in the mainstream European economy. There was a perceived need to transform the regressive nationalist aspiration into a broader issue of achieving a societal bilingualism. The State had started to distance itself from deliberate centralised LP projects and the language became an important feature of local community identities.

Acquisition planning through immersion

As stated previously, throughout the 1940s and 1950s the State's efforts in status and acquisition planning were faltering (Ó Catháin, 1973). The Commission on the Restoration of the Irish Language pointed out that revitalisation of the language would be retarded until such time as a practical day-to-day use of the language outside the schools was encouraged and fostered, a factor that was largely ignored in the early planning policies. With renewed focus on language planning at societal level in the late 1960s, and in the wake of the Commission's Report and White Paper (1965), the Government had finally come to terms with the fact that the schools alone were incapable of restoring Irish as the language of the people.

There has been considerable debate in the literature on language revitalisation regarding the contribution of schools to language spread and change. The debate has focused typically on schools as agents of language revival, examining the concept of language planning, acquisition planning and language education policy (Spolsky & Shohamy, 2000) and discussing the potential of schools in community or in national efforts to contribute to language knowledge and language use. Huss *et al.* (2003: 4) point out, for example, that schools as well as pre-schools have shown themselves to be critical contexts for both language loss and revitalisation. Fishman (1991) claims that schools have only limited value in language revival in that restoration and successful survival of a threatened language essentially requires reinstating and relocating the language primarily in the home domain in parent–child transmission. Unless schools directly feed into and facilitate the reinstatement of home and family transmission, then they will always occupy a secondary role in language restoration. This does not always happen, however. It is a feature of many language revitalisation movements that they overlook the crucial stage of family transmission (Fishman's 1991 Stage 6 in the Graded Intergenerational Disruption Scale) in an effort to move with undue alacrity to minority language education (May, 2001: 142).

Hornberger and King (1996: 438) claim, however, that instruction can facilitate the introduction of languages into new linguistic domains and to new speakers with an associated increased status of language. In spite of the fact that education has been identified as being the most important single institutional variable in minority language maintenance (Gibbons & Ramirez, 2004: 229), schools on their own may be totally ineffective in saving threatened languages (May, 2001). Edwards and Pritchard Newcombe (2005) equally maintain that the school alone is not enough to effect language reproduction. Links with the speech community are critical. McCarthy (1998), for example, argues that schools must adopt a prominent position in language revitalisation and maintenance efforts since schools have had destructive effects on indigenous languages in the past. Education is also the site where larger political, social, ideological values are transmitted and reflected, the very values which fuel the language revival struggle. Schools can thus become awareness-raising agents, sensitising students to language use or lack of language use in community domains and influencing linguistic beliefs, practices and management of the language community. Skutnabb-Kangas (2000: 570) refers to the potential of the school in this context as agent of change. The school may also be one of the chief agents of legitimation and institutionalisation in the public domain of the language to be revitalised, a counterforce of language discrimination accruing after centuries of proscription, derogation and neglect.

Since the schools were, to a large extent, an agent in reversing language shift from 1922 to 1960, Irish language planning needed a new model. This model was to be presented in terms of a societally patterned and functionally differentiated diglossia. As was seen, *Comhairle na Gaeilge* had clear directives on the need for coordination and support for a diglossia in four main areas – communication and media, education, the Gaeltacht, and a planning agency – with the stipulation that research would identify the choice of sociolinguistic domains where a diglossic situation would prove most favourable. Its report, *Irish in Education,* contained proposals for further development of policy for language planning in education to concur with the establishment of societally patterned diglossia. Among its recommendations, which continue to inform current policy, was the re-establishment and maintenance of Irish-medium schools which had declined significantly from the 1940s onwards (*Comhairle na Gaeilge,* 1974: 7). The report, however, lacked specific guidelines and specific in-school policies for the development of bilingualism that would define attainable objectives and targets for students, teachers and parents. The teaching of Irish since has lacked a clearly defined policy (Ó Riagáin, 1997), but continues to play some role, albeit largely undefined, in the spatial structure of bilingualism in Ireland. It is against this background that one can examine the emergence and growth of the immersion schools (*Gaelscoileanna*), parent-established primary schools in which Irish is used as the medium of instruction.

As discussed earlier, by the early 1940s the number of government-induced all-Irish schools throughout the Republic had reached its peak. As well as this phenomenon, more than half of the State's primary schools were offering instruction in varying amounts in Irish for English-speaking students. Decrease in demand for all-Irish schools occurred for a variety of reasons.

Pedagogical reasons included dissatisfaction with the ineffectiveness of rote, grammar-based methods used to teach Irish (Ó Laoire, 1982, 1995; Ó Riagáin, 1997) and questions regarding the academic achievement of students being taught through Irish (MacNamara, 1966). Other reasons related to the existing social context. For example, Irish national identity gradually became disassociated from the Irish language (Baker, 1997), and the economic determinism of Ireland from the 1960s onward in which social and economic advancement became associated with English-speaking businesses also contributed to this decline. As a result of these factors, the number of primary level Irish-medium schools for English-speaking students reached its nadir by about 1970 (Ó Riagáin, 1997).

At approximately the time of the low point in the number of all-Irish schools and the 1974 *Comhairle na Gaeilge* report, a number of 'new' Irish immersion schools were being established. The schools were established as a result of parental demand for Irish-medium education and represent an example of local decentralised functional language planning. A national voluntary association, *Gaelscoileanna* (www.gaelscoileanna.ie) was set up in 1973 with the aim of providing support to the immersion schools and of advising parents who wished to establish and develop such schools. The schools grew from 11 in 1971 to 134 in 1999. Financial support from the State was generally granted after, but not before, schools were established, and schools often had to fight for recognition. In 1996, for example, when seven *Gaelscoileanna* were denied acknowledgement as primary schools by the State, those schools took the then Minister of Education to court, thereby winning recognition (*Irish Times*, 1 November 1996). There has been a gradual move away from Catholic patronage in these schools as exists in the majority of State primary schools, since the establishment of a multi-denominational and inter-denominational patronage association (*An Foras Patrúntacta na Scoileanna Lán-Ghaeilge*) in 1993.

In 1974, about 53% of the students enrolled in these schools were from English-speaking homes (Coady, 2001), and many of the parents who enrolled their children in the schools appeared to use the language in the work sphere. A study conducted in 1979 revealed that 51% of the fathers of children enrolled in Irish-medium schools were government or semi-state employees whose jobs required Irish (Ó Riagáin & Ó Gliasáin, 1979). Modern Irish-medium schools were considered to be qualitatively distinct from the all-Irish schools that existed from the 1920s to the early 1970s. Ó Riagáin (1997) explained that the modern schools were founded as a result of grass roots, parental efforts as distinct from top-down, government policy-imposed schools. The schools are, by and large, additions to the school system rather than conversions of the existing schools to bilingual teaching. Thus, any suggestion that they represent a reversal of trends needs considerable qualification. They are more accurately seen as the start of a substantially new trend (Ó Riagáin, 1997: 24). Like Ó Riagáin, Cummins (1978) described these schools as qualitatively different from their predecessors. He noted that the new wave of schools had a high degree of parental participation and support, as well as participation in national Irish cultural events (Coady & Ó Laoire, 2002).

Since the early 1970s, the number of all-Irish immersion programmes has continued to increase. Ó Laoire (1995) has attributed the growth in such schools to parents observing the advantages of an education through a second or minority language. Sometimes, however, the decision of parents to enrol their children in such programmes might have to do with choices other than linguistic or cultural ones. Location of the school or the apparently smaller pupil to teacher ratio might be more suitable or more attractive to some parents. Whatever the reasons, parental participation clearly has played, and continues to play, an important role in the establishment and ongoing growth of such immersion programmes (Ó Riagáin, 1997). Apart from language reasons, educational reasons, and both language and educational reasons underscored in the Ó Riagáin study, a fourth category for parental decision can be discerned from data obtained by Coady (2001) in which parental participation and choice in the context of the growth trend of *Gaelscoileanna* was examined.

The study consisted of the readministration of a survey conducted by Cummins in 1974 to teachers of *Gaelscoileanna*, students' writing samples in both Irish and English, and qualitative data collected from teachers, parents, and students at two participating Irish-medium schools. This data also revealed reasons that were neither language nor education oriented. Some parents stated, for example, that they sought non-traditional educational options such as coeducation and a non-Catholic (or multi-denominational) educational option. Some parents further stated that they sought an educational environment in which they could participate in the organisation and management of the schools. The growth of *Gaelscoileanna* is related to parents' desire to participate in the education of their children, having a coeducational option, and an option to avail themselves of non-traditional religious instruction (Coady & Ó Laoire, 2002).

However, despite their growth and parental support, the immersion programmes are affected by problems resulting from a mismatch between the Government's espoused policy to foster bilingualism and acquire Irish, and the supports necessary for such programmes. Some of these mismatches include adjustments made to language policies removing positive discrimination towards the language; the lack of teaching aids and textbooks in the language; and the lack of training programmes for pre-service and existing teachers in the area of language pedagogy (Coady, 2002).

Progression rates from immersion primary schools (*Gaelscoileanna*) to postprimary immersion schools (*Gaelcholáistí*) remain low, indicating that the majority of students currently enrolled in primary schools do not choose, or are unable to choose, to continue their education through Irish. The fact that there are 50 post-primary schools compared with 125 primary schools points to the contraction in choice. This difference, however, is significant since it is during secondary schooling that networks of friendships tend to be formed, which can have a permanent influence on the choice of language used in bilingual society. The oral competency outcomes in these immersion pedagogy contexts are, of course, much higher than in Irish as L2 programmes (Kavanagh, 1999) which would not normally allow for real peer-to-peer communication.

While statistically these immersion schools amount to no more than 7.35% of the total number of primary schools and 4.9% of secondary schools, nonetheless, the steady growth in demand for these schools represents an example of grass roots development and bottom-up language planning, similar to the development of *Kōhanga Reo* and *Kura Kaupapa Māori* immersion schools in Māori language regeneration (Hohepa, 1999) in New Zealand (Benton & Benton, 2001; Kaplan & Baldauf, 2003). In these contexts, the language itself is not necessarily as central an issue as is the emic rights discourse of effort, struggle and popular demand.

Language Shift and Language Spread

The shift from Irish to English

The shift from Irish monolingualism to English monolingualism to English/ Irish forms of bilingualism has been documented elsewhere (Ó Riagáin, 1997). In the context of discussing language shift and language spread within a study of current issues in language planning, the more recent public surveys on language attitudes give indications of current challenges. Considerable data on language shift have been generated from designed surveys on language use and language attitudes which have been carried out over the last 30 years. The first of these main national language surveys occurred in 1973, conducted by the Committee on Irish Language Attitudes Research, which focused mainly on the attitudes of the Irish public towards Irish and Irish language policy. The following were the terms of reference for this committee to report on:

(1) Current attitudes towards the Irish language and towards efforts to restore it as a general means of communication.
(2) The extent to which the public would support policy development which seemed to offer a greater chance of achieving the aim of restoring Irish as a general means of communication in a significant range of language functions.

The Committee on Languages Attitudes Research (CILAR) began its research in 1972 and continued until October 1975, when the Committee finally submitted a report to the Minister for the Gaeltacht. Samples were taken from the national population (N = 2443) and from the traditional Irish-speaking areas in the Gaeltacht (N = 542). This national survey, which became known as the CILAR survey, was repeated by *ITÉ* (Linguistic Institute of Ireland) in 1983 and in 1993, with a reiteration of similar questions as in the 1973 survey to give comparable data (Ó Riagáin, 1997).

By and large all the surveys reveal findings similar to various census data, that is, about 13% of the national samples unambiguously regarded themselves as competent Irish speakers, while a further 10–13% claimed to possess partial fluency in Irish. The surveys give some insight, however, into the spread of English and the reversing of language shift from English to Irish, achieved mainly through the education system. Respondents were asked, for example, about the extent and nature of their use of Irish. In general, the survey data revealed a significant differentiation in language spread between the adult and the school-going populations. Language spread occurs mainly among the latter category as the obligatory study of Irish brings students and young adults into practically daily classroom contact with Irish. Figures broadly indicative of language spread were inclusive of school-going populations and were not representative of the general adult population.

The surveys suggested discontinuity in language use during the adult life of secondary bilinguals, with usage being most intensive during school years. The surveys included a number of questions about respondents' ability in the language and give some indication, therefore, as to the extent of this self-reported usage. About half of the sample self-reported having no competence in the language, with 40% responding that they could produce a few simple sentences or parts of conversations and with 10% confirming that they were able to participate in most or all conversational situations (Ó Riagáin, 2001: 201).

Those with high levels of ability in Irish, found mainly among the highly educated, revealed a pattern of intensive use. Usage in the home domain, however, the most essential element in intergenerational transmission, remained low at 5%, even though all the survey data suggest that favourable attitudes to the language were still predominant. Positive attitudes, however, did not appear to translate to active usage. Home bilingualism on its own, therefore, is unable to sustain an acceptably secure and stable level of bilingual reproduction. In this context the bilingual reproduction capacity of school is crucial (Ó Riagáin, 1997) for sustaining a societal bilingualism.

Outside the Gaeltacht, bilingualism develops around family and social networks sometimes located around all-Irish immersion schools. Again, these networks lack the important sustained capacity to attract, recruit or reproduce new members. Favourable attitudes towards the language do not appear to translate into motivation for active use or for deliberate language shift in the home domain. In spite of the positive attitudes towards the language, which are consistently gauged in the surveys, and the momentum of individuals and families involved in the language movement, home bilingualism does not appear to be gaining ground. For these reasons, Ó Riagáin concludes that bilingualism in Ireland has somewhat shaky and vulnerable foundations. This is the case especially since the capacity of Irish-speaking networks to reproduce themselves over time is severely restricted by their size, thin distribution, and transitory character.

The spread of English

The reverse side of the shift from Irish is the spread of English. The loss of Irish was tantamount to gain for English. Between 1600 and 1900, two-thirds of the population changed its language. This shift occurred over a period of eight generations. Adams (1985) has outlined the most likely four stages of the process of the shift to English which could have occurred at any time during this period within four generations of a family, in the context of non-migration, that is, remaining in the same area.

(1) The monoglot Irish speaker who in adulthood picked up English from English-speaking immigrants and colonists but could not speak the language effectively.
(2) The Irish monoglot's children learned English at school and later improved their knowledge of the language to the point of speaking English semi-fluently, but only as second to Irish.
(3) The Irish monoglot's grandchildren spoke both languages but had more occasions to use English and failed to transmit Irish to their children.
(4) The Irish monoglot's great-grandchildren spoke only English from childhood but had limited / passive knowledge of the language derived from the grandparents.

Adams (1985) makes the points that the process could, of course, be speeded up or retarded by differential linguistic behaviour or influences on the parts of males or females within the family. Some parish reports contain documentation on local conditions for language shift. Parish reports compiled by Mason (1814–1819) quoted by Kallen (1988) attest to the transition to bilingualism. The report on one small parish in the north-east of the country, in the region where the initial shift to English was most prominent, states, for example:

> Most of the inhabitants speak the English language but they prefer the Irish among themselves. All the children speak the English language. In the west of the country, the position was somewhat different: Many persons, however are utterly ignorant of the English language; and a great

proportion of the inhabitants speak Irish in preference. (quoted in Kallen, 1988: 132)

It was during the stages of overlap, interface and contact between both languages, stage three (in particular) and stage four, that cross-influences between the languages were established. These cross-influences were to become the distinctive phonological and morphological features of Hiberno-English.

At the micro level, some of the causal features of the shift to English for the average family were no doubt socioeconomic or sociopolitical in origin. Increasing opportunities to improve family fortunes by becoming a teacher, by joining the police force (The Royal Irish Constabulary), by joining the civil service or the post office all necessitated fluency in English (Wall, 1969). At the macro level, a confluence of historical occurrences and political factors helped to speed the shift from Irish to English; the establishment of English-medium primary schools in the 19th century (1832), the institutionalisation of English in the Catholic Church outside of liturgical contexts, the use of English by Irish revolutionary and constitutional political leaders, the decimation of the Irish-speaking population during the 19th century famine and the ensuing haemorrhage of emigration.

From 1851 onwards, the nation was firmly in transition from Irish monolingualism to bilingualism. In the initial stages, the transition was from Irish monolingualism to Irish–English bilingualism, which later developed generally into English monolingualism. By 1861, a 3: 1 ratio of English to Irish speakers was recorded: 3,325,024 English speakers and 1,077,087 Irish speakers. By the end of the Famine era (1871) and at the advent of the flood of emigration, the ratio was even higher (*c.* 4: 1) given the marked decline of Irish speakers: 3,248,547 English speakers and 804,547 Irish speakers. By 1911, there were 543,511 Irish speakers compared with 2,428,481 English speakers (4.5: 1). By 1946, there were 588,725 Irish speakers compared with 2,182,932 English speakers (3.7: 1). In this crucial period of language shift between 1850 and 1920, the language for upward mobility was English – the language already in place for this social function in Britain. Thus the native population came to need English more and more for commerce, education, politics and emigration. The almost exclusive English-medium universities and colleges became leading and normative institutions in this process.

Policy and planning for English

The early period of the English language in Ireland in the 16th and 17th centuries laid the foundation of the ideological value underpinning both English and Irish, in that English came to occupy the H function once held by Irish.

English rarely features, however, in the debate and literature on language policy and planning in Ireland. This is so perhaps because the term 'language planning' in an Irish context seems automatically to imply that there was no need, perceived or otherwise, to plan for English language spread and maintenance. The rapid and successful spread of English as outlined above, was, and is, after all, the reason why status planning for Irish had to be developed. It is also the case, perhaps, because language planners in Ireland (and elsewhere) never conceived the notion of language ecology, as Mühlhäusler (1996: 77) states: 'The first manifestations of . . . linguistic imperialism is not the reduction of the quantity of indigenous languages but the destruction of the region's linguistic ecology, a fact often overlooked by those who write about language decline.'

The fact that language shift always occurs within political-ideological contexts is clear from studying the position of English in Ireland. Irish played a largely symbolic role in nation building as has been previously outlined. From the early years of the State until the 1950s, English was perceived as the 'enemy', the language which all revivalist efforts were designed to supplant. At the same time, the ideological processes in which the emerging politics and economy of the country were formed and articulated were in English. English, although it was never promoted, was the language through which the strong conceptualising and ideological processes were mediated. Ideologies are discontinuous (Blommaert, 1999), and the new economic and social forces at work were stronger than any appeal to cultural nationalism-inspired ideology of language restoration. While Irish was the language of symbol and rhetoric, English was the language of symbolic power, of marketplace and linguistic economy. This is a strong argument to show the overriding control of sociopolitical and economic contexts in which planning and policy evolve and an instantiation of power relations.

The rethink on language policy in the 1960s, for example. The White Paper (1965: 10) on the Restoration of Irish, started to take cognisance of the symbolic power of English:

> [f]or a considerable time ahead, English will remain the language chiefly used outside the Gaeltacht for various purposes. To assume otherwise would be unrealistic and would detract from appreciation of the effort needed to achieve the national aim in regard to Irish.

Thus, the emphasis was to be placed more and more on bilingualism as in a tacit acceptance that a reversal to Irish monolingualism was neither a short-term nor a long-term reality. This coincided, of course, with the growing conviction of a decreasing usefulness of nationalist ideology as the main actors looked in the direction of wider markets and multinational companies. It also shows language as a material entity not impervious to human agency and widespread popular belief. Planning interventions for Irish must be located more and more in the nexus of the relation between material instrument and popular concepts of advancement, that is, locating language planning in real socio-politically moulded space and time.

Status planning outside education

The media

The establishment of the first radio station in Ireland almost coincided with the emergence of the new State. Thus, broadcasting was seen to play a significant role in nation building. Reinforcing the ideology of national identity meant that the symbolic importance of Irish for the new State was emphasised in the new radio station, 2RN. While the amount of time devoted to broadcasting was relatively small, broadcasting itself became an act of nation building and took on a symbolic importance (Watson, 2003). The State was intent on influencing programmes in a direction that would mould listeners in the image of traditional national identity and ideology. The existence of the language continued to be of symbolic importance, and this was reflected in the broadcasting schedule and content of the new radio station. There were calls from the very inception of the new radio station for a radio station especially for the Gaeltacht (Watson, 2003: 18–19). In its role of nation building, the radio station 2RN, later called *Raidió Éireann* (The Radio of Ireland), targeted native speakers and potential speakers and included programmes over the decades to teach the language to listeners. The amount of broadcasting time devoted to current affairs, entertainment and educational programmes in the language increased from 4% of broadcasting time to 10.6% in 1945 but fell to 8.4% in 1955.

Throughout the 1930s and 1940s, when the State appeared to want to protect its people from 'foreign' influence, Irish radio played a role in attracting listeners away from these influences and continuing to disseminate symbols of Irish identity (Watson, 2003). Its perceived role, however, in being a language educator, that is, its potential to activate or reactivate receptive language competence, appears to have been less successful. Television began in Ireland in the 1960s, and coincided with a new decade of modernisation. In language policy, this was marked by engagement in a new reflection on the lack of success in language restoration and by a movement towards admitting the English language into future considerations on the direction of language planning. The era of the 1960s is marked by modernisation and liberalisation and by a shift from the earlier nation-building ideology in which the State influenced programmes in a direction that would mould listeners in the image of traditional national identity towards 'a new ideology in which the type of programmes that were most popular would survive' (Watson, 2003: 5).

In the modernism and liberalisation of the period from the mid-1950s onwards, to which television contributed significantly, and in the new national identity that emerged, de-emphasising the nationalistic nation-building symbols of traditional national identity, a new language discourse based on individual and group rights emerged in a campaign for an Irish-language radio and television station for the Gaeltacht. This new rights-based discourse was employed in the late 1960s by the Gaeltacht Civil Rights Movement.

Raidió na Gaeltachta (The Radio of the Gaeltacht) began broadcasting in 1972 as a Gaeltacht radio station, which can be received outside the Gaeltacht as well. Established in 1972, the station was intended to provide a comprehensive radio service through the medium of Irish for the people of the Gaeltacht and for Irish speakers throughout the country. Initially the station broadcast only in the afternoons, but on 1 May 1999 broadcasting was expanded from 06.30 to 23.00, seven days a week. Broadcasting is exclusively through the medium of Irish from studios situated in the main Gaeltacht areas in Galway, Kerry and in Donegal. The station adhered to, and still adheres to, a policy of not permitting English in interviews or in song lyrics, which appears to be a strong political stand on a language issue.

With the establishment of *Raidió na Gaeltachta*, the State, in effect, had reacted and responded to the pressure of the rights-based lobby group. As such, it marked a new direction in bottom-up language planning where reactive response to pressure groups underpinned and masked a new devolvement of central State responsibility. This reactionary course of action was also at the heart of the State's response to grassroots demand from parents for all-Irish immersion education, as previously discussed.

During the 1970s, increased demand for Irish language programmes on television came from language enthusiasts, and by the 1980s a Gaeltacht group had started to demand a separate television channel in Irish. Again, this demand was located within a minority rights-based ideological framework using a rights-based discourse (Watson, 2003). There was no major opposition to the idea of establishing a dedicated Irish language television channel. By the 1990s, in the wake of a national campaign, all political parties adopted it in their manifestos. A 1995 Green Paper on Broadcasting (*RTÉ* 1995) paved the way for the new channel on the grounds that the Irish-speaking population required a dedicated television channel of its own. In 1996 the channel, initially called *Teilifís na Gaeilge* (The Television of the Irish Language), started broadcasting. Unlike *Raidió na Gaeltachta*, targeting primarily a Gaeltacht audience, the new television channel sought and continues (now as TG4) to seek its share of the national audience. The station maintains that 800,000 people, or 20% of Irish viewers, tune in to the channel at some point each day.

There is a strong commitment to the production of quality entertainment on TG4. The idea is to 'serve all groups with a knowledge of or interest in Irish' (Fennell, 2001: 55). The longer-term impact of TG4 might be difficult to assess. Ó Riagáin (1997) states, for example, that the ratio of passive or receptive knowledge appears to have increased with the advent of an all-Irish TV channel in 1997. Those who now self-report passive knowledge of the language mainly in listening to radio and watching television appear to be at 20%, demonstrating a strong relationship, as might be expected, between ability and usage levels.

To understand how the broadcast media impact language planning and language use, or vice versa, it is important to bear in mind that people in general make sense of the media product in their own ways. Similarly, language planning can be understood at the micro as well as at the macro levels, but regrettably, few qualitative studies have focused on this issue to date. If language planning is examined at the micro level of the individual family, then the issue becomes one of investigating the causes and conditions whereby an individual or an individual family changes, alters or modifies language within the home or in other domains. Of particular interest here is how the broadcast media can become an agent of status planning and of acquisition planning. In other words, can the broadcast media, radio or television, effect some degree of language shift in areas where the language is the target language of revitalisation efforts, or can it consolidate language maintenance in areas where the broadcast language is the language of the speech community? The question can also be asked whether the broadcast media can contribute to, and be part of, a language-teaching and a language-learning policy.

Broadcast media have an important role to play in language planning. The evaluation of the contribution of the media to language shift and language spread involves not only a measurement of success of the media product in terms of attracting audience and compiling ratings, but must also assess its context, process and implementation within the framework of language planning itself (Ó Laoire, 2001). The responsibility for this must not devolve on the agency of State alone but must principally involve the broadcasting agency itself. It might be a useful exercise also to concentrate on, and extend the role of the broadcast media in the process of language learning itself to make it more meaningful in a minority language context.

Religion

Religion has been described as one of the most powerful forces in effecting language change and language spread (Ferguson, 1982). The use of classical Arabic in Islam, and Welsh in the Welsh chapels and Welsh religious life in the home (Williams, 2000), for example, illustrate that religion can preserve language. There is a generalised feeling that religion (i.e. the Catholic Church) is an important part of Irish identity. Given this centrality of religion to Irish social life, one would expect religion to have played a central role in language planning. Much of the sociological research into the role of religion in Irish social life in general has tended to emanate from the churches themselves and has tended to be positivist, concentrating on gathering statistical information and data through social survey and avoiding a rigorous interrogation of the role of religion in shaping Irish historical and contemporary identity. The role of religion in the historical spread of English has been well documented. Wall (1969: 81) refers to the oversimplification in describing the contributory role of the Catholic Church in the demise of the Irish language. 'Today nearly every child in Ireland will tell you that Daniel O' Connell (a 19th century politician), the Catholic clergy and the National (primary) schools together killed the Irish language' (Wall, 1969: 81). The historical truth is that during the 18th century, however, the Catholic clergy tried to persuade their flocks to adhere to their language, being aware that it provided the best possible insulation against the teachings of Protestantism (Wall, 1969: 83). There is evidence in the church records from this period that bishops and clergy were careful that priests working in the Irish-speaking communities would be Irish speakers. The clergy in Co. Kerry, for example, successfully petitioned the Pope preventing the appointment of an individual to the bishopric on the grounds that he knew no Irish. Irish was also taught in the Irish seminaries in continental Europe (Wall, 1969).

When Catholic colleges could be opened legally at the end of the 18th century, English quickly became the language of Catholic higher education. The principal seminary, Maynooth College, founded in 1795, was a royal college of the British Government, and all courses were taught in English. From it priests went to minister in Irish-speaking areas. English very quickly became associated with the ritual language. The spread of English through institutionalised and organised religious practice was not planned in an explicit or premeditated way but nonetheless played a pivotal role in producing what could be described as a linguistic-religious imperialism. There was a strong association between Presbyterians and the Irish language, and the language is, of course, seen to establish an important part of Presbyterian heritage in Ireland and Scotland. Since the language was a part of the heritage of both communities in Ireland, it was seen to have a unifying potential. Irish Catholicism in the Republic of Ireland, on the other hand, did not have language as a defining force in Irish identity, and the language never inspired the public fervour and enthusiasm which espoused Irish Catholic identity.

While the language revival movement ideology was pluralist, liberal and non-sectarian, the ideology pervading the new State was an authoritarian, conservative form of Catholicism promoting anti-intellectualism and compliance with authority (Kirby, 2004). As a result, the strong spiritual experience expressed through local ritual and language became gradually suppressed, and aspects of identity were redefined and reformulated to comply with the model of Catholicism being proposed. In time, the Irish language itself became part of the redefinition of identity. Being Irish-speaking became synonymous with being Catholic, and the Irish language was seen to lose much of its liberal and developmental forces as a result (Kirby, 2004). This association between language and conservatism did not occur as much in the English language in which dissenting critical voices were first heard. Regrettably, there have been no studies carried out in Ireland to date assessing the influence of religion in language restoration and regeneration.

Law

There was no question in the formulation of the Constitution as to the role of Irish in the State. As mentioned in the introduction, the 1937 Constitution stipulated that the Irish language should be the national language and the first official language of the State, with the English language being recognised as the second official language. In a parliamentary debate on the 25 May 1937, prior to its publication, a suggestion was made by a member of Parliament, Deputy McDermott, that both articles be amended to read: 'The Irish and English languages are recognised equally as national and official languages' (cited in Ó Riain, 1984: 25). Deputy McDermott explained that to call the Irish language the sole language of Ireland was to ignore the reality that more Irish people were able to speak English than Irish. He called the proposed constitutional declaration 'artificial and mischievous'. In reply, the *Taoiseach* (Prime Minister) at the time, Éamonn De Valera, explained that the Irish language is most associated with the nation and the traditions of the people while the English language was the language of those that came as invaders. In the vote on the amendment, no other deputy supported McDermott in his call for equal recognition for both languages. A high court pronouncement in 1934, following a legal case challenging the constitutional equality of Irish and English as 'national languages', underlined the status of Irish as the national language, on the basis that it did not have to be universally spoken by all the people. Its designation as national language rather was based on the fact that it was the historic distinctive speech of the Irish people (Ó Riain, 1994). The State was, therefore, bound to do everything within its sphere of action to establish and maintain the language in its status as the national language and to recognise it for all official purposes as the national language (Kelly, 1984: 34).

The interpretation of the constitutional position regarding the languages is that a principal of individual choice is invoked. A citizen can opt to use either official language in the courts, and interpretation facilities are made available when the courts are not in a position to understand Irish. Ó Riain (1994) has argued, however, that the principal of regionality rather than the principal of personal choice should apply, particularly in the Gaeltacht regions where English is the normal language of the courts. The new Official Languages Act

2003, however, has the potential for implementation of a coherent rights-based language planning policy in this respect.

The civil service

Given that the civil service is directly controlled by the State, it has considerable potential as a language planning agency. In the early years of the new State, the upper echelons of the civil service took over from the colonial service and were effective in discouraging the use of the Irish language (Ó Riain, 1994). The civil service nevertheless was targeted down through the years in efforts to Gaelicise the State. From 1925 onwards, for example, Irish was compulsory for entrants to the civil service, and from 1931 onwards a special examination in oral and written Irish was obligatory for all candidates. A further examination had to be sat by candidates pursuing higher grades. It was understood that each officer would do his or her own share to promote the language in his or her own department and office (Ó Riain, 1994: 33). This appears to have been a request, however, rather than a part of official policy and planning. Even though there has been a guarantee since 1929 that an Irish-speaking citizen would be entitled to conduct business and correspondence in Irish if she or he so wished, the planning and implementation of that concept were never fully realised. It was stated by 1934, for example, that little use was made of Irish (quoted in Ó Riain, 1994: 35). One problem was undoubtedly the fact that some civil servants lacked competence in the language. The other reason appears to have been lack of policy implementation. In 1936, a special committee was appointed within the civil and public service to promote the language in the different departments and to oversee implementation. While this ensured an increase in the use of the language in some departments, the overall result was not as effective as planned. Another committee, set up in the 1950s to examine the use of Irish among civil and public servants, showed that those civil servants who were proficient in the language had increased from 6.4% in 1925 to 14.1% in 1959. Overall, it was reported, however, that an increase in some sections of the civil service was balanced by a decrease elsewhere and that the amount of official business conducted in Irish was as low as 2%. The number of civil servants constantly using Irish declined to 2.1% in the 1970s. In the 1970s an organisation, *Gaeleagras*, was set up within the civil service to promote use of the language within the civil service. This was a voluntary organisation aiming to organise courses, scholarships for study in the Gaeltacht and social and entertainment occasions through the medium of Irish. In all, the use of Irish in the civil services has continued to decline, although the new Official Languages Act 2003 has the potential for developing a language planning policy in the civil service, in that demand for using Irish by the Irish-speaking public will have to be met. This means that those in the civil services with competence in the language may be called on to use it more and more in daily official transactions. This may differ from the situation that existed in the early years of the state when civil servants attested competence in the language did not translate into active language use in the absence of public demand.

Language planning in the Gaeltacht

The Irish language speech community comprises the inhabitants of the defined Gaeltacht regions as well as speakers and users of the language living outside these regions. The 2002 Census data indicate that two out of every three persons now speak the language in these regions, accounting for almost three-quarters of the population in Gaeltacht areas in 2002. However, such figures indicate a decrease from 76% in 1996. This is a higher proportion of speakers than existed at the inception of the State and is due in some measure to the successes to date in language planning. Outside the Gaeltacht, most Irish speakers are neospeakers and secondary bilinguals, who have learned Irish as a second language, or whose parents learned it as a second language and then transmitted it to them. Contemporary Irish speakers outside the Gaeltacht have a different linguistic ability. They do not usually form a cohesive visible community or network of users. The maintenance of Irish as a community language in the *Gaeltachtaí* has both a symbolic and functional importance for these speakers. The Gaeltacht is at once the reservoir from which Irish language learners and users draw inspiration (Commins, 1988) and the exemplar of the living language community. Special interventions were required, therefore, over the years to secure demographic viability in the Gaeltacht regions. In these regions, language maintenance was and is closely linked to demographic maintenance, which in turn is linked to socioeconomic development. This matter will be discussed in more detail.

The term, *Gaeltacht*, means Irish-speaking region. Naturally occurring variations in social patterns of language use do not allow for neat demarcation of a speech community. The Gaeltacht originally meant an Irish-speaking people rather than a region. At the beginning of the State, it became necessary for administrative purposes to achieve some kind of regional delimitation based on the numbers of speakers in a given area. The first boundaries of the Gaeltacht were drawn up by the Gaeltacht Commission in 1926. It recommended a regional demarcation based on demographics of 80% Irish speakers in a given area, dividing the regions into *fíorGhaeltachtaí* (authentic *Gaeltachtaí* and *breacGhaeltachtaí* (where there were ratios ranging from 25% to 80% of Irish speakers). Such identification was strategic. Hindley (1990) and Ó Riagáin (1997) have shown that these calculations and demarcations were unreliable and inconsistent with the 1926 Census data.

Over the years, the administration of the Gaeltacht has been passed from one government ministry to another. In 1956, however, a special ministry was set up, called the Department of the Gaeltacht (*Roinn na Gaeltachta*), to coincide with the official agreement on the territorial boundaries. At this time in the 1950s, census reports, however inaccurately interpreted, showed the language to be in decline in the Gaeltacht regions. This was due in part to high emigration from the regions where the lack of employment opportunities presented a continuous challenge to maintenance and reproduction of the speech community. In 1953 one Irish-speaking island, the Great Blasket, was abandoned by residents due to emigration and the *laissez faire* nature of the State response to the harsh living conditions of its population. Up to the 1950s the economy of the Gaeltacht was based predominantly on subsistence agriculture and fishing. Limited alternative employment opportunity, therefore, led to consistent emigration.

Gaeltarra Éireann was set up by the Government in 1958 to halt the decline in the population and signalled for the first time a new understanding of the social and economic dimensions to language planning. From this point on until the 1990s, language planning became synonymous with socioeconomic planning and gradually became divorced, as it were, from research on the linguistic implications of this economic planning. This meant that the necessary data on indicators of language shift as a result of, or affected by, such economic developments on a macro level and on the micro level of linguistic behaviour, were not available to monitor and guide planning. Planning, however, was to become decentralised and more localised in a response to grass roots initiatives.

Gaeltarra Éireann took responsibility for the establishment and promotion of indigenous rural industry such as tweed manufacture, knitwear, lace and embroidery. Given the difficulties of promoting industry in a peripheral region, *Gaeltarra Éireann* had quite a creditable record in employment provision (Commins, 1988: 15). This brought new challenges in terms of a threat of language shift as the change to an industrial and commercial economy introduced new English-using domains and contexts. Commins (1988: 16) argues that the use of English was common both in the activities of the personnel involved in the new commercial and industrial enterprise and in the transactional relationships between the local-level agencies and the central administration. As part of growing civil-rights based initiatives in the 1970s, there were proposals and demands from community groups for an agency that would minimise outside influence and give Gaeltacht people more democratic representation.

Gaeltarra Éireann was replaced in 1980 by *Údarás na Gaeltachta* which was founded under the provision of the *Údarás na Gaeltachta* Act of 1979 to encourage the preservation and development of Irish as a primary means of communication through economic, social, cultural and linguistic development. The *Údarás na Gaeltachta* Act allowed that additional powers could be given to the *Údarás* by the Government for the purpose of promoting the linguistic, cultural, social, physical and economic development of the Gaeltacht. *Údarás* has had appreciable success in the socioeconomic development of the Gaeltacht regions. Seeing the necessity to redefine the Gaeltacht economy in the light of Ireland's economic boom and in the context of 600–800 graduates leaving the region within a period of five to ten years to take up employment outside the region, the extra powers promised were demanded in 1999 but were refused by the Government.

Údarás na Gaeltachta today provides an attractive financial package for new and expanding businesses. This includes grants for equipment, building and training. *Údarás na Gaeltachta* assists prospective investors through all stages of start-up, from location identification to help with recruitment, training and legal requirements. *Údarás na Gaeltachta* has available a portfolio of modern industrial buildings and sites. The main business activities in the Gaeltacht are in electronics, engineering, information technology, film, television and video production, high fashion textiles and clothing, food processing, fish farming, rubber and plastics manufacturing, electronics, assembly, crafts and modern office services.

A diverse range of overseas companies from countries such as Belgium, Canada, Finland, France, Germany, Norway, the United Kingdom and the USA have made the Gaeltacht their investment destination. Businesses vary in size from small craft industries to companies employing hundreds of people. A maximum of 12.5% corporation tax applies for manufacturing industry. This is fixed to the year 2010 and has been guaranteed by the Government with the agreement of the European Commission.

Apart from attracting economic initiatives, greater emphasis is being placed on the provision of early education through the medium of Irish, increasing the number and improving the quality of the *naíonraí* or pre-school groups, the development of youth services and community arts and in general accessing all opportunities which will further the use of the language in the community (www.udaras.ie).

The report of the *Coimisiún um Athbheochan na Gaeilge* (The Commission for the Restoration of the Irish Language) in 1963 noted how the *Gaeltacht* population has been consistently pressured to use English in communication with administration and State agencies and with local government (Commission on the Restoration of the Irish Language, 1963). The report also referred to the constraining influence of other cultural forces such as the media which had contributed to turning the use of Irish by the inhabitants of the Gaeltacht into a kind of private language.

The vague and largely unqualified response by the State in the White Paper of 1965 led eventually to the emergence of a new rights-based grass roots struggle by members of the Gaeltacht community. In 1969, a special movement to seek and ensure civil rights for the Gaeltacht residents was founded. The group, calling themselves *Cearta Sibhialta na Gaeltachta* (The Movement for Civil Rights of the Gaeltacht), held public demonstrations in Galway, the nearest and largest urban centre and founded an illegal Irish language radio station, *Saor Raidió Chonamara* in 1970. The State responded to the pressure of seeming to be responding to civil rights by the establishment of *Raidió na Gaeltachta* and eventually an Irish language television channel (see section on media.)

Grass roots community active groups operating out of a civil rights ideological base continue to play a similar role in a decentralised language planning agenda. Community groups and initiatives like *Pléaraca* (Revelry) based in the Conamara Gaeltacht, for example, are seeking to eliminate social exclusion and disadvantage by celebrating an annual festival of the local culture, music, dance and traditions and thereby are creating a new self-awareness and self-confidence among Gaeltacht inhabitants. In recent times, *Pléaraca* has started to highlight various social issues that affect the Gaeltacht population, for example, the difficulty surrounding the planning for housing for residents. This new awareness of the importance of their linguistic tradition and the crucial role to be played by community groups in the safeguarding of that tradition has fueled continuing rights discourse-based initiatives (see the sections on Law and the Civil Service, above) in the context of the Languages Act 2002.

The boundaries of the official Gaeltacht as a region are under revision as confusion persists as to its extent. Recent studies (*Coimisiún na Gaeltachta*, 2002: Ó hÉallaithe, 2003, 2004b) show, for example, that the geographically defined Gaeltacht areas are no longer predominantly Irish speaking, and after 80 years of language policy, there is neither a definitive list nor a map of electoral divisions and townlands that comprise the Gaeltacht. A recent study by Walsh *et al.* (2005) has started to remedy this situation by undertaking a geographical definition of the Gaeltacht using legislative sources and Geographical Information Systems.

Education through Irish also remains a continuous challenge for language planners in the Gaeltacht. A recent study of Gaeltacht schools (*COGG*, 2005) has found that 10% of students were leaving these schools with little or no Irish. The report, commissioned by the Educational Council for Gaeltacht schools (*An Chomhairle um Oideachas Gaeltachta agus Gaelscolaíochta, COGG*, 2005) found that English was the main conversational language among pupils in Gaeltacht schools with only a quarter of pupils leaving primary school with what could be deemed a reasonable level of Irish. The report calls for a redefinition of Gaeltacht schools based on the education model (either first language educational model with Irish as medium of instruction or an immersion model with Irish as medium of instruction) used by schools rather than on the geographical location.

Corpus Planning for the Irish Language

Features of the language

As stated earlier, Irish belongs to the Celtic branch of the Indo-European languages and displays some of the general features or characteristics of the other Celtic languages, notably in inflectional morphology. Nouns are grouped into declensions and verbs into conjugations. Thus, the noun *cat*, meaning 'cat' can exist as *cat, chait, chat, gcat*. Inflection in the case of nouns usually involves initial mutation called lenition (see below) and a change in the ending of the consonantal cluster, referred to as attenuation or slendering. Thus *an post* (the post) in the genitive case becomes *an phoist* as in *fear an phoist* (the postman). Syncopation (loss of a letter or more from the main body of the word) may also occur, e.g. *Micheál* (Micheal) becomes *Mhichíl* in the genitive. Verbs inflect for number, person, mood tense and voice and exist in both analytical and synthetic forms, while the verb *tóg* (take) in the first person, in present, past, future, conditional mood appears as *tógaim, thóg mé, tógfaidh mé, thógfainn* respectively.

Central to the Irish orthographic system is the existence of two vowel groups, broad (a, o, u) and slender (e, i), phonetically back and front vowels respectively, and two consonantal groups, broad and slender. This feature is also present in Scottish Gaelic and Manx. This distinction between broad and slender consonants corresponds roughly to the distinction between hard and soft consonants in Russian and Polish and is often referred to as velarisation and palatalisation (Greene, 1966: 19; Ó Siadhail, 1989: 9). An important rule in Irish spelling is what is termed the *caol le caol, leathan le leathan* 'slender with slender, broad with broad' rule. This means that, particularly in the verb endings system where a slender vowel occurs on one side of a consonantal cluster or group, it must be followed by a slender E. Thus in *briseann* (breaks) the slender I in the root *bris* has to be followed in the present tense by the ending *-eann*, beginning with a slender E. Similarly, broad vowels must be followed by broad vowels, e.g. *glan* (cleans) – where the broad A in the root *glan* is followed by the ending *-ann*, beginning with the broad vowel.

Lenition and aspiration, which are grammatically conditioned initial mutations, are features of modern Irish most worthy of note. Lenition occurs quite frequently in nouns and verb, involving an inclusion of a H after the initial consonant, thus affecting the sonal quality of that consonant; e.g. the plosive C /k/ becomes /x/ as cat > *chat* or B /b/ becoming BH /w/ in *bhog*. Eclipsis is the other grammatically conditioned initial mutation where a letter or combination is placed before the initial consonant or vowel in nouns and verbs thus altering the initial phoneme.

The phonological variants in Irish are considerable and are attributable to the existence of three separate dialects, roughly corresponding with geographical distribution, *canúint an Tuaiscirt* (northern dialect) in the north-west region, *canúint an Iarthair* (western dialect) in the western region of Co. Galway and Co. Mayo and Connemara, and *canúint na Muamhan* (Munster dialect) in the south-west region. The dialectal variations have not been confined to phonology alone, but have also affected lexis, grammar and orthography. The differences are in evidence in the common greeting, 'How are you?'

Northern: *Goidé mar atá tú?*
Munster: *Conas tá(nn) tú?*
Western: *Cén chaoi a bhfuil tú?*

All these features give the language a complexity that made corpus planning difficult.

Norm selection

As part of its campaign for the restoration of the language, the Gaelic League secured recognition for Irish at second and tertiary level education. After 1913, when it was accepted as a subject for matriculation purposes, there was a considerable increase in the number of secondary schools that included Irish in their programme of instruction. This increase in the use of Irish for instructional and academic purposes, as well as the existence of a growing number of Irish writers, focused debate on the question of standardisation.

A controversy arose over the form of written Irish to be used. Some scholars argued for a linear continuation of the standardised written form of the neo-classical period, as exemplified in the 17th-century prose writing of Seathrún Céitinn. Others sought to establish a form of written Irish that would mirror and reproduce the colloquial Irish of the people. It was the latter group who won the debate. Ó Baoill (1988: 111) makes an important remark on the outcome of this controversy in favour of the language of the people, *caint na ndaoine*.

> Had the grammar of classical Irish (1200–1650) as used by Seathrún Céitinn and the professional poets of that period become the norm, the resulting cleft between the literary language and the speech of the Irish-speaking areas (collectively known as the Gaeltacht) would certainly have alienated native speakers of Irish and those who had already learned Irish to a proficient degree.

The fact that the written form now reflected the language spoken by the people augured well for the future of the Irish as a vibrant, modern language in tune with the thoughts, aspirations and imagination of its speech community. However, the use of the language of the people as it occurred in the three dialects across three provinces, underlined the need for standardisation and for norm selection in particular, which proved all the more difficult, since none of the three dialects possessed the prestige and status to dominate as a socially accepted norm. Had a speech community developed in any urban centre, its dialect would be expected to dictate the choice of norm. This, however, has not occurred to any extent in Ireland. The fact that no one dialect was prescribed as being normative meant that spelling followed the varying pronunciation patterns of each of the dialects. This of course is not peculiar to Irish. Ó Baoill (1988: 112) mentions a further problem with spelling at this time.

> Words in many instances looked longer than their present pronunciations would indicate, because of the retention of certain older spellings handed down from an earlier period of the language. Such spellings had changed very little since the period of classical Irish 1200–1650. In many respects it was far removed from the type of Irish current in Ireland in 1922.

When the National Government of 1922 was working towards achieving a restoration of the language and its maintenance in the indigenous speech communities, it had to confront all these problems, which arose from the lack of norm selection and standardisation. In any event, it seemed to have been taken for granted without debate that there ought to be a national standard language. This shows that corpus planning took place without consultation and dialogue with the relevant partners in the three main speech communities, a feature found in language planning situations elsewhere with planning taking place amid conflicting views and lack of discussion (Jernudd & Neustupný, 1987).

The Gaelic script

From 1600 onwards, writings in Irish mainly used the Gaelic script. When the language of the people was adopted as the norm, a decision was made to abandon the Gaelic script in favour of the Roman script. This decision not only involved an obvious change in the shape of the letters and in the way Irish appeared, but there were also morphophonemic changes to be made. A dot over the initial or internal consonant in the Gaelic script conveyed lenition. In the Roman script, this dot was replaced by the letter H following the lenited consonant. Thus C /x/ was replaced by CH, and F by FH, etc. It was hoped that the change in script would simplify and modernise the language, thereby bringing it into line with the modern languages of Western Europe. The change was decried and resisted, however, by many campaigners for the revival of language who advocated a basic and pure preservation. This purist versus modernist tension is, of course, characteristic of much corpus language planning (Fishman, 1983).

The problem of spelling

Problems had always surrounded the system of spelling in Irish. The adaptation of the Latin alphabet in the sixth century caused problems in the development of a system of orthography that would accurately reflect pronunciation. Ó Cuiv (1969: 26) explains that certain features in Irish such as lenition and eclipsis had no counterpart in Latin. This created a problem where a single letter had to represent more than one sound. The letter G, for example, represented the modern G sound as well as the lenited G sound, today spelled GH, a division of values for G not unlike that in Old English. Ó Cuiv (1969: 27) explains the outcome:

> All this is slightly puzzling to us nowadays and it does not surprise us to find that literate Irishmen eight or nine centuries ago were not altogether

satisfied with the current system of orthography. Bit by bit, the main incon-sistencies were removed and eventually a reasonably unambiguous system was available. This orthography was relevant to the sound system of spoken Irish of the twelfth century and as such it was adequate.

When the standardised literary language was established during the classical Irish period, the spelling problem was resolved. However, once *caint na ndaoine* (or the language of the people) was accepted as the norm at the end of the 19th century, the problem of spelling emerged again. While the classical literati had no problems with spelling because they ignored the spoken language, the writers of the late 19th century felt the need for a more simplified system corresponding to pronunciation.

Ó Cuiv (1969: 25) tells us that efforts at such simplification and correlation of spelling and pronunciation had already taken place in the classical era. Theobald Stapleton, author of a catechism, published in Brussels in 1639, *Cathcismus sen Adhon, an Teagasc Críostaí iar na foilsiú a Laidin & a nGaoilaig*, attempted a simplifi-cation which deviated from the classical standard. Silent letters in certain words were replaced; e.g. the DH in the word *suidhe* (sitting) was replaced by Í – *suí*, as in modern Irish. The GH and DH in *ríoghdhacht* (kingdom) were omitted to produce *ríocht*. Stapleton brought the spelling closer to the pronunciation by replacing THBH by F as in spoken Irish; *uathbhás* (terror) – becoming *uafás* as in modern Irish. It was only the authors of devotional literature, however, who followed Stapleton's lead, and the spelling system retained its classical complex-ity until official efforts at standardisation took place after 1922 and in particular after 1931.

Writers of the Gaelic League era continued to use the antiquated classical spelling. Fr Dineen's *Irish/English Dictionary*, published in 1927, did little to revise the spelling system or to align it with the current language of the people. The dictionary, in fact, had the effect of stabilising the old spelling system, although it was helpful in exposing learners and speakers to examples of lexis from the three dialects.

In 1922, the National Government had officially assigned the standardisation of the spelling and grammar to the Translation Section of the *Dáil* (Parliament). Standardisation of the spelling system essentially involved a movement towards simplification as had already been attempted by Stapleton. However, there was strong opposition, especially from the Gaelic League, the language restoration organisation, to the idea of changing the spelling. In 1928, the League passed a resolution stating that it would be better not to change the spelling of Irish until the language was out of the danger of death or destruction. Ó Cuiv (1969: 29–30) remarks as follows on the slow pace of change towards simplification:

> So powerful were the conservatives that in spite of the fact that Roman type and a more simplified form of spelling were in use in parliamentary publi-cations in Irish, the government decided to publish the new Irish constitu-tion in 1937 in Gaelic type and the outmoded spelling.

The Translation Committee, nevertheless, continued its difficult task, and, in 1931, it prepared a circular in which the new simplified spelling system was proposed. Modifications were made to the classic spelling system in Dineen's dictionary, giving consideration to dialectal pronunciation, avoidance of ambiguity, grammar, appearance of words and etymology. It is interesting to look at some of the changes suggested to the spelling system, as listed by Ó Baoill (1988: 113).

Earlier classical version (1200–1650)	*Revised (1931)*	*Modern Spelling (1957–)*
oidhch	*oíche*	*oíche* (night)
áiteamhai	*áitiúil*	*áitiúil* (local)
ochtmhadh	*ochtú*	*ochtú* (eighty)
meadhon	*meán*	*meán* (middle-average)
indiu	*iniu*	*inniu* (today)

These examples illustrate the trend of change in the revised system. One notices the efforts at simplification in effecting change in two principal ways. Firstly, the system corresponded more closely with the spoken word. One notices the substitution of internal unvoiced consonantal groupings, (e.g. MH, DH in the words listed above) by a stressed vowel, thereby reflecting a closer correlation between the written and the pronounced word. These changes tended to represent the general pronunciation pattern of all the dialects, although not fully and thoroughly. Secondly, the new spelling was also a good deal shorter. Ó Baoill (1988: 113) writes, 'The new spellings were more psychologically real in the sense that what one wrote was a lot closer to what one said than was previously the case.' However, such change was generally resisted, even though it was widely used in all government departments. Even though efforts at achieving a simplified and standardised system had begun as early as 1922, it is no surprise perhaps that it took 35 years to arrive at a final publicised accepted version. In 1945, the pace had been slow when the *Taoiseach* (Prime Minister) of the day, Éamonn De Valera, requested the Translation Section to complete its work. When the Translation Section submitted its work, *Lámhleabhar an Chaighdeáin Oifigiúil* (Irish Spelling: The Official Standard Handbook), it was found that an entire system needed to be worked out and completed.

It was not until 1957, therefore, that the standard version was finally authorised and published as *Gramadach na Gaeilge agus Litriú na Gaeilge* (The Grammar and Spelling of Irish). This is the version that has remained as a yardstick for all writing in Irish since, and has been more or less widely accepted. However, this was not the case in the beginning. One Professor of Irish of the National University called the newly published standard 'the most hateful monster that ever appeared in the language' (Ó Ruairc, 1993: 36). Since the standardised system was first used and propagated within the civil service, one still hears disparaging reference to *Gaeilge na státseirbhíse* (the Irish of the civil service). Dictionaries published since 1957, notably De Bhaldraithe (1959) and Ó Dónaill (1977) have had the effect of strengthening the standard version of spelling, but many problems still remain unresolved.

Problems and challenges

The standardised spelling system has held sway for nearly 40 years now and is used in all school textbooks and educational publications. Dialectal variations in spelling and grammar continue to appear in reprinted school texts (e.g. the works of the Donegal writer Máire), but they are generally highlighted and explained in a glossary. The general situation, however, is far from satisfactory.

Firstly, the complicated morphological and inflectional system of the language continues to present problems for the learner. The evolving standard has not gone far enough to reduce the intricate complexities that confront learners at all levels. There is evidence to suggest that some learners in Irish schools, where the study of the language is compulsory, may have little understanding or awareness of how the system differs from English, even after a period of nine years' instruction (Ó Laoire, 1995).

The greatest problem with the official standard, however, is that it does not agree in any systematic way with the spoken dialects. While some efforts were made to ensure that the spelling system should correspond with pronunciation variations, many scholars would argue that such efforts have not been sufficient. Bliss (1981: 911), for example, criticises the official standard for not taking cognisance of variation. He explains:

> As far as pronunciation is concerned it seems impossible to discern any rhyme or reason in the choice of spellings. Some changes in traditional spelling are quite inexplicable, as for instance the change of the historical *chuaidh, deachaidh* 'went' to *chuaigh, deachaigh*, a change that could not possibly be dependent on pronunciation since dh or gh were identified many hundred years ago.

There appear to be discrepancies, therefore, between the choice made in the standard system and the dialectal variations. Sometimes, the choice made in standardisation makes little sense. Bliss (1981: 911) quotes an interesting example of this discrepancy:

> . . . the word traditionally spelt *tráigh* (strand), in Northern Irish generally has the pronunciation *trái* and in Southern Irish the pronunciation *tráigh*, but the *caighdeán* (standard) spelling is *trá*, a pronunciation hardly heard outside Cois Fharraige (a localised sub-dialect of the western dialect).

The discarding of the -IGH was not carried out systematically. It was retained for some unknown reason in many verbs, for example, *dóigh* (burn) or *léigh* (read).

Some scholars also argue that simplification in spelling has led to a more complicated grammatical system (Wigger, 1979: 195). In the old spelling system the ending -(E)ANN was added to all verb roots in the present tense – e.g. *briseann* (breaks), *léigheann* (reads), *nigheann* (washes). In Modern Irish, however, while the -GH was retained in the root form *léigh, nigh*, the present tense of such verbs according to the standard spelling system introduces a new ending -ONN in the case of *nigh*, while *léigh* retains the -EANN ending. The new spelling system has *léann* and *níonn* respectively. These examples represent only some of the problems that are often cited as being attributable to the new system.

Another problem that standardisation did not address fully is the irregularity of the Irish spelling system. Irish, unlike Welsh (which is reputed for the phonographic regularity of its writing system), remains highly unpredictable. This irregularity is due to the fact that Irish has more sounds than the Latin alphabet can represent. It can be argued that efforts at standardisation to date have not gone far enough to correct this irregularity and to bridge the gap between written and spoken Irish. The rules remain too faithful sometimes to the standardised written form, which was first influenced by the way Irish was pronounced centuries ago. The spelling and pronunciation of the word *Taoiseach* (Prime minister), which has often caused problems for foreign newscasters, illustrates this irregularity. The combination AOI in *Taoiseach* is an alternative to the sound UÍ. The combination EA in *Taoiseach* corresponds to the A sound in the English word 'hat' so alternatively the word could be spelled *Tuíshach*. However, AOI at the beginning of a word has an Í /i: / quality – EE as in the word 'been' in English. Thus, the proper name 'Aoife' could be spelled as *ífe*. Furthermore, AO can be pronounced as É /e: / in Munster as in *saor* /sér/ (free), or as Í /i: / in the western dialect. Visitors to Ireland have much difficulty in pronouncing place names like Dún Laoghaoire /*doon lére* or *doon líre*/ with the silent internal GH.

The pronunciation of Irish is often not obvious from the spelling, and may be quite confusing as these examples serve to illustrate. While some scholars would maintain that the official spelling standard has done 'great harm to the cause of the Irish language' (Bliss, 1981: 912), more research needs to be done among the public, learners and writers on the level of acceptability of the present spelling system. Very little research, if any, has taken place in this area. While problems of discrepancies still continue to exist, one must recognise that great strides have already been made. Ó Murchú (1993: 60) puts the development that has taken place in context: 'Twentieth century Irish, given that it was faced with critical problems of a choice of script, a destabilised spelling, and a substantial degree of dialectal variation with no unifying form, could hardly have evaded strife and vacillation.'[1]

Terminology

Committees of Irish-language experts were set up as early as 1927 in order to provide terminology for the education system. *An Buanchoiste Téarmaíochta* (The Permanent Terminology Committee) was established by the Minister of Education in 1968. The Terminology Committee transferred to *Foras na Gaeilge* in 1999, according to the provisions of the Belfast Agreement. The Committee functions at three levels:

(1) The Permanent Committee, having 22 members appointed by the Minister of Education, consists of Irish-language experts, representatives from third-level and research institutions and related organisations. Their role is to monitor policy.
(2) The Steering Committee, comprising 15 members, mostly drawn from the Permanent Committee, attend monthly meetings. They agree terminological principles, plan and supervise the work through establishing subcommittees, and sanction miscellaneous terminological lists.
(3) The subcommittees comprise smaller groups of experts in specialised fields. They sanction substantial lists of technical terms and compile specialised dictionaries of terminology. Over 20 such dictionaries have been published, arising from the work of the subcommittees. The Committee aims to deliver standardised authoritative terminology to the public by means of the most efficient and modern communications media and thereby fulfil the terminological requirements of the educational sector, State services, and the

general public. It maintains an efficient terminological database as an integral component in ongoing corpus planning, drawing on the richness and diversity of the oral and literary tradition in the development of the terminology necessary for all modern language functions.

An Coiste Téarmaíochta has cooperated with a number of public bodies and other commmunity projects, through providing extensive terminological advice, which resulted in the publication of 10 English–Irish dictionaries or handbooks.

The achievements in corpus planning have been considerable, particularly in making Irish more accessible and more understood (Cronin, 1996). Ironically, the most significant parts of corpus planning – standardisation, simplification, etc. – were carried out at a point in time when Irish was no longer being considered to occupy the role of principal language of the State.

Present and Future Language Maintenance and Prospects

In this study, after situating language planning in its historical context, I ventured to outline some of the more significant developments in language planning, particularly in education, which was the target for language planning from the beginning of the State onwards. The period from 1990 to the present, which will be treated in this section, is characterised by a growing and mobilising awareness of linguistic rights – including the 'new' languages of migrant communities – by grass roots movements to secure these rights in the linguistic communities. This function includes the publishing of the Official Languages Act (2003). The evolving role of the media, already discussed, particularly the broadcast media, the growth of media technologies and the use and role of English, Irish and other newly introduced allochthonous community languages, provide new contexts in and a wider range of sources for research inquiry into language maintenance.

The Official Languages Act of 2003

The Official Languages Act of 2003 was signed into law on 14 July 2003. The Act is the first piece of legislation to provide a statutory framework for the delivery of services through the Irish Language. Its primary objective is to ensure better availability and a higher standard of public services through Irish, to be achieved by placing a statutory obligation on the Departments of State such as the Department of Education and Science, Department of Finance and public bodies, to make specific provision for delivery of such services in a coherent and agreed-upon fashion through a statutory planning framework. The preparation of guidelines by the Minister for public bodies in relation to the preparation of draft schemes is now under way.

The Act also specifies some basic general provisions of universal applicability, for example, correspondence to be replied to in the language in which it was written, providing information to the public in the Irish language, or in the Irish and English languages, bilingual publications of certain key documents and so on. Among the principal provisions of the Act are:

- the right of a person to be heard in and to the use the Irish language in court proceedings;

- the duty of public bodies to ensure that the Irish language only, or the Irish and English languages together, are used on oral advertisements, whether they be live or recorded, on stationery, on signage and on advertisements;
- the duty of public bodies to reply to correspondence – in writing or by electronic mail – in the language in which that correspondence was written;
- the duty of public bodies to ensure that any communication providing information to the public – in writing or by electronic mail – is in the Irish language only or in the Irish and English languages;
- the duty of public bodies, that are also State bodies, to publish certain documents that would be of interest to the public, in Irish and in English simultaneously;
- the duty of public bodies to prepare a scheme detailing the services that they will provide through the medium of Irish, through the medium of English, and through Irish and English, and the measures to be adopted to ensure that any service not provided through the medium of the Irish language will be so provided in the future;
- the duty of public bodies to ensure that: an adequate number of its staff are competent in the Irish language and that the particular Irish language requirements associated with the provision of services in Gaeltacht areas are met;
- the Irish language becomes the working language in their offices situated in the Gaeltacht areas within a certain timeframe to be agreed between the public body and the Minister.

A language ombudsman office with a Language Commissioner has already been established to supervise and monitor the implementation of the Act, and in March 2005 only the Irish version of official place names in Gaeltacht areas began to be used in signs, official documents and maps with the English name being erased, and with equal emphasis being given to the Irish and English language versions of official place names in other parts of the country. This has given rise to controversy in the town, formerly known as Dingle, now known only by its Irish name, An Daingean. The residents of the town located in the touristic south-west region have publicly expressed concern that the change in the linguistic landscape will result in a loss of business for the town and have requested a plebiscite to determine what the people of the town consider an appropriate name for the town. At the district court in Dingle/An Daingean recently, a judge had to adjourn court cases pending clarification on what exactly the court area there is to be called. Dingle written as a court area had been crossed out and replaced by An Daingean by a civil servant anxious to comply with the new Act (*The Kerryman*, 28 July 2005).

This debate appears to possess many of the features of a bottom-up resistance to top-down planning. The local English newspaper, *The Kerryman*, featured an editorial in its edition of 28 July (2005: 10) which testifies to this bottom-up/top-down divisive tension:

> As if the debate over changing the name of Dingle to *An Daingean* proved divisive enough, we now discover that Minister Ó Cuiv's [*the government Minister largely supportive of the Official Languages Act 2003*] rush of cultural

wisdom may prove to have legal and statutory requirements. Whether Dingle be called *An Daingean* or *Uíbh Rathach* sounds remotely like Iveragh to a German tourist is just one aspect of the debate. The reality is that there will never be consensus on the issue save a plebiscite or local democratic election. What the entire debate illustrates, once more, is that the heavy hand of the civil service or of political masters far removed from everyday rural life believes they know what is best for people.

The Languages Act, therefore, represents the first stage of new centralised language planning, aimed at ensuring the inclusion of appropriate provision for the needs of Irish speakers and of Gaeltacht communities in all legislation, at a time when language planning has become more decentralised.

EU working status for the Irish language

The accession of Ireland to the EEC in 1973 (now the European Union), was seen to present new opportunities for the Irish language. According to *Comhairle na Gaeilge*, there was a potential for increased realisation of a diversity and richness of language in an enlarged community that would diminish the hitherto dominant Anglo-American influence on Irish society and strengthen the desire for a greater expression of individuality among the smaller members, including Ireland (*Comhairle na Gaeilge*, 1974: 14). While it was felt that membership of the EEC would increase the need for Irish citizens to learn French and German, it was hoped that the new focus on these languages would not be used as a reason for abandoning the teaching of Irish. The fact that bilingualism was seen to be facilitative of third language learning was stressed ' . . . [t]o the extent that a degree already exists here, or people should be more receptive to a new language'.

Worries that being in the EEC would contribute to the loss of Irish were abated, and it is true that the EU has brought greater opportunity for support for regional or minority languages. In the 1980s a Bureau for Lesser Used Languages was established in Dublin, which brought information and documentation of other language policies, issues, planning and struggles from other European regions in terms of conferences, publications and general advertising. There was an important general impression given that Irish was not alone in terms of efforts to gain wider recognition and extension of use.

There was an opportunity on accession that Irish would be recognised and used as one of the EEC working languages. However, Irish became a Treaty language, and not a working language. The EEC apparently did not refuse such recognition. It was reported that the Minister for Foreign Affairs in 1973 had told the EEC that the Government did not want Irish to be a language of the community (Ó Croidheáin, 2000). The Irish Government is not a signatory to the European Charter for Regional or Minority Languages of 1992, even though Irish governmental representatives played an active role in the drafting process (Ó Murchú, 2004). The title of the Charter, emphasising minority languages, has been problematic in the context of the constitutional status of Irish as official and national language.

The accession of new states to the EU in June 2004 and the inclusion of Maltese, Lithuanian, Latvian, etc. as working languages has witnessed the re-emergence of the lobby for the recognition of Irish as an official working language of the

European Community. These circumstances may have clouded the issues of the State being signatory to the Charter, as has happened in the case of Welsh, Scottish Gaelic and Irish in Northern Ireland in March 2001.

The year 2004 was dominated by a public campaign to press for official EU recognition of Irish. In April 2004, over 5000 supporters took to the streets of Dublin, calling on the Government to seek official working status for Irish in the European Union. An on-line petition with up to 80,000 signatures was presented. Speaking at the rally, Dr Padraig Ó Laighin, spokesperson for the lobbying group called *Stádas* (Status), said that the achievement of official status was simply the will of the people who were asking for fair play for a national language and Ireland's first official language.

In November 2004, the Irish Government tabled a proposal in the EU Parliament in Brussels seeking official and working status in the EU for the Irish language. The Government's proposal required the unanimous support of Member States. The EU foreign ministers unanimously approved the Irish Government's proposal to accord official and working status in the EU to the Irish language in June 2005, with effect from January 2007. The intervening period is to enable the EU institutions to build the capacity to provide the Irish language services that flow from the Government's proposal. The possibility of extending the range of documents to be translated into Irish will be considered. Simultaneous translation from Irish will also be provided at certain ministerial meetings, and certain other practical benefits will also flow from this decision, including Irish being one of the languages taken into account for the purposes of recruitment to the EU institutions (Government of Ireland, Department of Foreign Affairs, Press Section, 13 June 2005).

Present day linguistic and cultural diversity

Since the mid-1990s, immigration has continued to contribute to language change in Ireland. During the economic boom of these years, significant labour shortages meant that the number of workers from EU countries was not sufficient to meet the economy's labour needs. As a result, work permits were issued to non-EU citizens to fill specified jobs. Since the national census of population does not include questions on spoken languages other than Irish, it is impossible to chart the extent of multilingualism in Ireland. Application records for work permits give some indication of the extent of multilingualism. Apart from EU citizens living in Ireland, significant numbers of migrant workers have come to Ireland from countries such as the Czech Republic, Latvia, Lithuania, Poland, the Philippines, and South Africa. In 2000, 8000 work permits were issued, but the figures have risen to 36,000 in 2001 and to 40,000 in 2002. In 2002, the following applications for work permits were processed: Czechs (957), Filipinos (2680), Latvians (3409), Lithuanians (3273), Malaysians (956), Romanians (2054), Poles (2676) and Russians (1,037). These figures clearly testify to a growing multilingual Ireland, and as such do not include the 'increasingly significant presence of students from China who choose to study and engage in part-time employment in Ireland' (Cronin & Ó Cuilleanáin, 2003).

Another group of recent immigrants to Ireland are those seeking asylum. The numbers of asylum seekers and refugees internationally grew during the 1980s and early 1990s. In the UK, for example, the number of asylum seekers grew from

2905 in 1984 to 22,005 in 1990 and to 44,845 in 1991. In Ireland, at the same time, the number of people seeking asylum rarely rose above 50. In 1991 it stood at 31. By 1998, this figure had risen to 4630, and by 2002 it had increased to 11,634. Asylum seekers come from many countries including Algeria, Democratic Republic of Congo, Nigeria, Romania, Republic of Moldova, Poland, the Russian Federation, and the Ukraine.

Ireland has, thus, in recent years experienced a growth in ethnic and cultural diversity. Simply listing the numbers of people and the countries from which they come does not fully represent the reality of linguistic and cultural diversity which these new communities represent. A country like Nigeria, for example, contains three major ethnic groups and perhaps more than 240 minority languages and ethnic groups. Other countries of origin may also be quite diverse.

The diversity found in contemporary Ireland contributes to the multilayered richness of Irish culture. Although the recent growth in immigration has given rise to a greater awareness of cultural diversity in Ireland, it could be argued that Ireland has long been culturally and linguistically diverse. One of the largest minority ethnic groups in Ireland is the Irish Traveller community which has its own language called Shelta or Cant (Binchy, 1994). Historically this has been a secret language available only to members of that community and inaccessible to the settled community (Kirk & Ó Baoill, 2002). There are an estimated 25,000 Irish Travellers in Ireland, a further 15,000 Irish Travellers living in the UK and 10,000 living in the USA. This cultural diversity, however, has not always been recognised in Ireland, a phenomenon characteristic of many societies, where the majority culture sees itself as holding a universal validity or norm in relation to values, meanings and identity. The freedom and celebration of cultural diversity is palpable at the micro level; one user of Irish has recently commented, for example (Mac Murchaidh, 2004: 112):

> My perception is that . . . attitudes have changed subtly in recent years. When I speak in Irish to my young son on today's Dublin bus, I no longer feel that I am stared at because these days we're surrounded by people speaking Latvian, Russian, French and Portuguese. Being different, in whatever way, is a more comfortable experience when lots of people are different too.

New immigrants and refugees whose mother tongue is not English may experience language problems when their lack of English seriously limits their access to the institutions of Irish society as well as being separated from their own language community to which they owe their sense of ethnicity and personal identity (Little, 2000). Without access to their parents' and grandparents' first languages in the curriculum, the children, being integrated into Irish society through English, may well have to pay a price in terms of estrangement from their ethnic and cultural origins as has happened elsewhere (Norton, 2000, 2001; Olshtein & Kotik, 2000; Valdés, 1997; Yelenevskaya & Fialkova, 2003).

The presence of the newer languages in Ireland is giving rise, therefore, to calls for a language policy to accommodate diversification in the language curriculum. It is perceived that such a policy would be based on an extensive analysis of Ireland's present and future language needs (Little, 2003) undertaken to international standards using a coherent approach to reduce any ad hoc decisions taken under the pressure of new events like diversification. The scientific work and cross-country approach of the Council of Europe (Beacco & Byram, 2003) may be used for that purpose.

Summary and Conclusions

In this study an attempt was made to situate language planning in its correct context of natural development and human resources development planning. The story of language in Ireland is a story about what the masses do (class power) rather than what is planned for the masses to do. There was a mass shift to English from the 17th century onwards. Status planning for the Irish language by governmental agencies mainly through education has met with continual 'mass' resistance and has had only modest success. After failing to engage the masses through centralised language planning activities from 1922 to 1960, a new realism of the hegemony of language practice led to a distancing of the State from language issues. The Irish language has survived rather than being restored. While returns from census and surveys of Irish speakers tend to be interpreted polemically, the fact that school-going children continue to conflate percentages of users shows the precarious position of Irish bilingualism. While some shift to Irish has occurred as a result of a language-in-education policy and planning, that activity has not secured home bilingual reproduction and intergenerational transmission. Favourable attitudes towards the language do not appear to translate into motivation for active use or for deliberate language shift in the home domain. In spite of the positive attitudes to the language and the momentum of individuals, families and voluntary organisations involved in the language movement, home bilingualism does not appear to be gaining ground.

It could be argued that further studies of language planning in Ireland might concentrate exclusively on the Gaeltacht, where bottom-up language planning has impacted on and evoked a centralised-type planning: that is, State reactive response to pressure groups masks a new devolvement of central responsibility. In this instance, the State may succeed by working in tandem with, rather than in opposition to, class power. It is only in recent times that the languages of minorities are becoming legitimated and institutionalised in the public domain (May, 2001), and it is through local initiatives and local decision making that planning has its ultimate impact (Kaplan & Baldauf, 2000).

It has been noted recently that the only true bilingual areas in Ireland are the Gaeltacht (Ó hÉallaithe, 2004a) and that the concept of a language revival outside the Gaeltacht is illusory. In the Gaeltacht, the language along with the new immigrant home languages may only over time have a ritual function in what may be a continuing long-term *durée*. Future status planning may be driven more by an ecological desire to maintain an important place for Irish in the linguistic diversity of a multicultural Ireland. It is likely, in a broader global context, that efforts at language revitalisation focusing on language rights and human development will continue to coexist and survive more easily with globalisation than with national states (Wright, 2004); hence, the recreation of identity and the motivation (Ager, 2001) to chart language planning for Irish in this changing context may extend for many years to come.

Acknowledgement

The author would like to acknowledge the support of an IRCHSS, Government of Ireland Research Fellowship 2003–2004, in the research, preparation and writing of this monograph.

Correspondence

Any correspondence should be directed to Dr Muiris Ó Laoire, Institute of Technology, North Campus, Tralee, Ireland (drmolaoire@eircom.net).

Note

1. Irish is, of course, not the only language dealing with such problems; similar problems exist in China (both *putonghua* in the PRC and Mandarin in Taiwan), Korea (particularly in North Korea in its attempts to use socialist principles to restructure the language) and Japan (which has struggled for many years with the split between the élite language and the common language). See, for example, Kaplan and Baldauf (2003), among other more targeted sources. In addition, in many South Asian languages, the writing system follows the classical texts making it hard for children to become literate in what is virtually a foreign language.

References

Adams, G.B. (1985) Linguistic cross-links in phonology and grammar. In D. Ó Baoill (ed.) *Papers on Irish English* (pp. 27–35). Dublin: IRAAL.
Ager, D. (2001) *Motivation in Language Planning and Language Policy.* Clevedon: Multilingual Matters.
An Coimisinéir Tearga (2005) Tuarascáil (Report) http://www.coimisineir.ie/.
Baker, C. (1997) Education in Ireland, Scotland and Wales. In J. Cummins and D. Corson (eds) *Encyclopedia of Language and Education.* Dordrecht: Kluwer Academic.
Battersberry, R. (1955) *Oideachas in Éirinn (Education in Ireland) 1500–1946.* Dublin: Stationery Office.
Beacco, J.C. and Byram, M. (2003) *Guide for the Development of Language Education Policies in Europe.* Strasbourg: Council of Europe.
Benton, R. and Benton, N. (2001) RLS in Aotearoa/New Zealand 1989–1999. In J. Fishman (ed.) *Can Threatened Languages Be Saved?* (pp. 423–50). Clevedon: Multilingual Matters.
Binchy, A. (1994) Travellers' language: A sociolinguistic perspective. In M. McCann, S. Ó Siocháin and J. Ruane (eds) *Irish Travellers: Culture and Identity* (pp. 134–44). Belfast: Queen's University Belfast, Institute of Irish Studies.
Bliss, A. (1981) The standardization of Irish. *Crane Bag* 5 (2), 908–14.
Blommaert, J. (1999) *Language Ideological Debates.* Berlin: Mouton de Gruyter.
Bord na Gaeilge (1983) *Action Plan for Irish 1983–1986.* Dublin: *Bord na Gaeilge.*
CEB (Curriculum and Examinations Board) (1985) *Language in the Curriculum.* Dublin: CEB.
Clyne, M. (1982) *Multilingual Australia.* Melbourne: River Seine.
COGG (*An Chomhairle um Oideachas Gaeltachta agus Gaelscolaíochta*) (2005) *Staid Reatha na Scoileanna Gaeltachta. A study of Gaeltacht Schools 2004.* Dublin: An Chomhairle um Oideachas Gaeltachta agus Gaelscolaíochta.
Coady, M. (2001) Policy and practice in bilingual education: Gaelscoileanna in the Republic of Ireland. Unpublished PhD Thesis. University of Colorado, Boulder.
Coady, M. and Ó Laoire, M. (2002) Dilemmas of language policy and practice in education: Gaelscoileanna in the Republic of Ireland. *Language Policy* 1 (2), 143–58.
Coimisiún na Gaeltachta (Gaeltacht Commission) (2002) *Tuarascáil/Report.* Dublin: Department of Arts, Heritage, Gaeltacht and the Islands.
Collie, J. and Slater, S. (1987) *Literature in the Language Classroom.* Cambridge: Cambridge University Press.
Comhairle na Gaeilge (1972) *Implementing a Language Policy.* Dublin: Stationery Office.
Comhairle na Gaeilge (1974) *Irish in Education.* Dublin: Stationery Office.

Commins, P. (1988) Socioeconomic development and language maintenance in the Gaeltacht. In P. Ó Riagáin (ed.) *Language Planning in Ireland. International Journal of the Sociology of Language* 70, 11–28.

Commission on the Restoration of the Irish Language (1963) *Final Report.* Dublin: Stationery Office.

Committee on Irish Language Attitudes Research (CILAR) (1975) *Report.* Dublin: Stationery Office.

Cronin, M. (1996) *Translating Ireland.* Cork: Cork University Press.

Cronin, M. and Ó Cuilleanáin, C. (eds) (2003) *The Languages of Ireland.* Dublin: Four Courts.

Cummins, J. (1978) Immersion programs: The Irish experience. *International Review of Education* 24 (3), 273–82.

De Bhaldraithe, T. (1959) *An English-Irish Dictionary.* Dublin: Stationery Office.

Department of Education (1924) *Rules and Programmes.* Dublin: The Stationery Office.

Department of Education (1961) *Report.* Dublin: Stationery Office.

Dineen, S.P. (1927) *An Irish/English Dictionary.* Dublin: Educational Company of Ireland.

Duff, A. and Maley, A. (1990) *Literature.* Oxford: Oxford University Press.

Edwards, V. and Pritchard Newcombe, L. (2005) When school is not enough: New initiatives in intergenerational language transmission in Wales. *Bilingual Education and Bilingualism* 8 (4), 298–312.

Fennell, C. (2001) Debate. In H. Kelly-Holmes (ed.) *Minority Language Broadcasting. Breton and Irish.* Clevedon: Multilingual Matters.

Ferguson, C.A. (1982) Religious factors in language spread. In R. Cooper (ed.) *Language Spread: Studies in Diffusion and Social Change* (pp. 95–106). Bloomington: Indiana University Press.

Fishman, J.A. (1967) Book reviews. *The Irish Journal of Education* 1 (1) (Summer), 79–80.

Fishman, J.A. (1983) Modeling rationales in corpus planning: Modernity and tradition in images of the good corpus. In J. Cobarrubias and J.A. Fishman (eds) *Progress in Language Planning* (pp. 107–18). Berlin: Mouton.

Fishman, J.A. (1991) *Reversing Language Shift: The Theoretical and Empirical Foundations of Assistance to Threatened Languages.* Clevedon: Multilingual Matters.

Flynn, D. (1993) Irish in the school curriculum: A matter of politics. *Irish Review* 14, 74–80.

Gibbons, J. and Ramirez, E. (2004) *Maintaining a Minority Language.* Clevedon: Multilingual Matters.

Greene, D. (1966) *The Irish Language.* Cork: Mercier.

Hindley, R. (1990) *The Death of the Irish Language.* London: Routledge.

Hohepa, M. (1999) Hei Tautoko I Te Reo [Mäori language regeneration and whänau book reading practices]. Unpublished PhD Thesis, University of Auckland.

Hopkins, M. (1984) Irish language and literature in the post-primary school. *Studies in Education* 2 (2), 7–19.

Hornberger, N. and King, K.A. (1996) Language revitalization in the Andes: Can the schools reverse language shift? *Journal of Multilingual and Multicultural Development* 17 (6), 427–41.

Huss, L., Camilleri Grima, A. and King, K.A. (eds) (2003) *Transcending Monolingualism. Linguistic Revitalization in Education.* Lisse: Swets & Zeitlinger.

INTO (Irish National Teachers' Organisation) (1941) *Report of the Committee of Inquiry into the Use of Irish as a Teaching Medium to Children whose Home Language is English.* Dublin: INTO.

Jernudd, B.H. and Neustupný, J.V. (1987) Language planning: For whom? In L. Laforge (ed.) *Proceedings of the International Colloquium on Language Planning* (pp. 71–84). Quebec: Presses de l'Université Laval.

Kallen, J. (1988) The English language in Ireland. In P. Ó Riagáin (ed.) *Language Planning in Ireland. International Journal of the Sociology of Language* 70, 127–43.

Kaplan, R.B. and Baldauf, Jr., R.B. (1997) *Language Planning: From Practice to Theory.* Clevedon: Multilingual Matters.

Kaplan, R.B. and Baldauf, Jr., R.B. (eds) (2000) *Language Planning in Nepal, Taiwan and Sweden.* Clevedon: Multilingual Matters.

Kaplan, R.B. and Baldauf, Jr., R.B. (2003) *Language and Language-in-Education Planning in the Pacific Basin.* Dordrecht: Kluwer.

Kavanagh, J. (1999) Outcomes from all-Irish secondary schools compared with schools where Irish is a single subject. Unpublished PhD Thesis, La Trobe University, Victoria, Australia.

Kelly, A. (2002) *Compulsory Irish: Language and Education in Ireland 1870s–1970s.* Dublin: Irish Academic Press.

Kelly, J. (1984) *The Irish Constitution.* Dublin: Jurist.

Kennedy, K.A., Giblin, T. and McHugh, D. (1988) *The Economic Development of Ireland in the Twentieth Century.* London: Routledge.

Kirby, P. (2004) *Pobal, Féinmheas, Teanga.* Dublin: An Aimsir Óg.

Kirby, P., Gibbons, L. and Cronin, M. (2002) *Reinventing Ireland: Culture, Society and the Global Economy.* London: Pluto.

Kirk, J.M. and Ó Baoill, D. (2002) *Travellers and their Language.* Belfast. Queen's University Belfast.

Little, D. (2000) *Meeting the Language Needs of Refugees in Ireland.* Dublin: Language Support Unit, Trinity College.

Little, D. (2003) *Languages in the Post-primary Curriculum.* Dublin: NCCA.

Mac Aogáin, E. (1990) *Teaching Irish in Schools: Towards a Policy for 1992.* Dublin: ITE.

Mac Murchaidh, C. (ed.) (2004) *Who Needs Irish? Reflections on the Importance of the Irish Language Today.* Dublin: Veritas.

MacNamara, J. (1966) *Bilingualism and Primary Education: A Study of Irish Experience.* Edinburgh: Edinburgh University Press.

MacNamara, J. (1971) Successes and failures in the movement for the restoration of Irish. In J. Rubin and B.H. Jernudd (eds) *Can Language Be Planned? Sociolinguistic Theory and Practice for Developing Nations.* Honolulu: University of Hawaii.

McCarthy, T.L. (1998) Schooling, resistance and American Indian languages. *International Journal of the Sociology of Language* 132, 27–41.

May, S. (2001) *Language and Minority Rights. Ethnicity Nationalism and the Politics of Language.* Harlow: Longman Pearson Education.

Mühlhäusler, P. (1996) *Linguistic Ecology: Language Change and Linguistic Imperialism in the Pacific Region.* London: Routledge.

Nic Craith, M. (1994) *Malartú Teanga: An Ghaeilge I gCorcaigh sa Naoú hAois Déag* [*Irish in Cork in the 19th Century*]. Bremen: Cumann Eorpach Léann na hÉireann.

Norton, B. (2000) *Identity in Language Learning. Gender, Ethnicity and Educational Change.* New York: Pearson.

Norton, B. (2001) Non-participation, imagined communities and the language classroom. In M. Breen (ed.) *Learner Contributions to Language Learning: New Directions in Research* (pp. 159–71). London: Longman.

Nunan, D. (2001) Syllabus design. In M. Celce-Marcia (ed.) *Teaching English as a Second or Foreign Language* (pp. 55–66). Boston: Heinle & Heinle.

Ó Baoill, D. (1988) The standardization of Irish. In P. Ó Riagáin (ed.) *International Journal of the Sociology of Language* 70, 109–26.

Ó Buachalla, S. (1984) Educational policy and the role of the Irish language from 1831 to 1981. *European Journal of Education* 19 (1), 75–92.

Ó Buachalla, S. (1988) *Education Policy in Twentieth Century Ireland.* Dublin: Wolfhound.

Ó Buachalla, S. (1994) Structural inequalities and the State's policy on the Irish language in the education system. *Studies in Education* 10 (1), 1–6.

Ó Catháin, S. (1973) The future of the Irish language. *Studies* (Autumn / Winter), 302–22.

Ó Conaire, B. (1986) *Douglas Hyde: Language, Lore and Lyrics.* Dublin: Irish Academic Press.

Ó Croidheáin, C. (2000) Language from below: Ideology and power in 20th century Ireland. Unpublished PhD Thesis, Dublin City University.

Ó Cuiv, B. (1969) *A View of the Irish Language.* Dublin: Stationery Office.

Ó Doiblin, B. (undated) *Aistí Critice agus Cultúir* [*Essays of Criticism and Culture*]. Dublin: FTN.

Ó Domhnalláin, T. (1977) Ireland: The Irish language in education. *Language Problems and Language Planning* 1, 83–96.

Ó Dónaill, N. (1977) *Fóclóir Gaeilge-Béarla [Irish–English Dictionary]*. Dublin: Stationery Office.

Ó Dubhthaigh, F. (1978) Múineadh na Gaeilge san Iar-bhunscoil [Teaching Irish in post-primary school]. *Léachtaí Cholm Cille* 9, 19–43.

Ó hÉallaithe, D. (2003) An daonáireamh agus An Ghaeilge [Irish and the population]. *Foinse* (29 Meitheamh), 8–9.

Ó hÉallaithe, D. (2004a) From language revival to language survival. In C. Mac Murchaidh (ed.) *Who Needs Irish?: Reflections on the Importance of the Irish Language Today* (pp. 159–92). Dublin: Veritas.

Ó hÉallaithe, D. (2004b) Cé mhéad a labhrann Gaeilge? [How many people speak Irish?]. *Foinse* (4 April), 20–21.

Ó Huallacháin, C. (1994) *The Irish and Irish: A Sociolinguistic Analysis of the Relationship Between a People and Their Language*. Dublin: Irish Franciscan Provincial Office.

Ó Laoire, M. (1982) Irish in education: Policy and problems. Unpublished MA Thesis, National University of Ireland, Maynooth.

Ó Laoire, M. (1995) Developing language awareness in the Irish language classroom. *Journal of Celtic Language Learning* 2, 54–77.

Ó Laoire, M. (1996) An historical perspective on the revival of Irish outside the Gaeltacht 1880–1930, with reference to the revival of Hebrew. In S. Wright (ed.) *Language and The State* (pp. 51–63). Clevedon: Multilingual Matters.

Ó Laoire, M. (1997) The role of instructional inputs in promoting autonomy in the second language classroom. *Teanga* 17, 43–54.

Ó Laoire, M. (1999) *Athbheochan na hEabhraise: Ceacht don Ghaeilge?* [The revival of Hebrew: A lesson for Irish?] Dublin: An Clóchomhar.

Ó Laoire, M. (2001) Language policy and the broadcast media: A response. In H. Kelly-Holmes (ed.) *Minority Language Broadcasting. Breton and Irish* (pp. 63–8). Clevedon: Multilingual Matters.

Ó Laoire, M. (2004) New speech communities in Ireland: Competitors or partners for Irish Gaelic? Talk at Language Education and Diversity Conference Waikato University, New Zealand, November 2003.

Olshtein, E. and Kotik, B. (2000) The development of bilingualism in an immigrant community. In E. Olshtein and G. Hoorenczyk (eds) *Language Identity and Immigration* (pp. 201–37). Jerusalem: Hebrew University Magnes Press.

Ó Mathúna, S.P. (1974) *Múineadh an Dara Tearga*. Dublin: The Stationery Office.

Ó Murchú, H. (2001) *Irish: The Irish Language in Education in The Republic of Ireland*. Ljouwert/Leeuwarden: Mercator Education.

Ó Murchú, H. (2004) The European Charter for regional or minority languages. *Teanga* 20, 110–43.

Ó Murchú, M. (1970) *Language and Community*. Dublin: Comhairle na Gaeilge.

Ó Murchú, M. (1988) Historical overview of the position of Irish. *The Less Widely Taught Languages of Europe* (pp. 77–88). Dublin: IRAAL.

Ó Murchú, M (1993) Some general observations. *Teangeolas* 32, 59–61.

Ó Riagáin, P. (ed.) (1988) Bilingualism in Ireland 1973–1983: An overview of national sociolinguistic surveys. In P. Ó Riagáin (ed.) *Language Planning in Ireland. International Journal of the Sociology of Language* 70, 29–52.

Ó Riagáin, P. (1997) *Language Policy and Social Reproduction: Ireland 1893–1993*. Oxford: Clarendon.

Ó Riagáin, P. (2001) Irish language production and reproduction 1981–1996. In J. Fishman (ed.) *Can Threatened Languages Be Saved?* Clevedon: Multilingual Matters.

Ó Riagáin, P. and Ó Gliasáin, M. (1979) *All-Irish Primary Schools in the Dublin Area. A Sociological and Spatial Analysis of the Impact of All-Irish Schools on Home and Social Use of Irish*. Dublin: ITÉ.

Ó Riain, S. (1994) *Pleanáil Teanga in Éirinn 1919–1985* [Language planning in Ireland]. Dublin: Carbad.

Ó Ruairc, M. (1993) Forbairt na Gaeilge-Caoga Bliain Amach [The development of Irish-fifty years later]. *Teangeolas* 32, 35–44.

Ó Siadhail, M. (1989) *Modern Irish*. Cambridge University Press: Cambridge.

Ó Tuama, S. (1991) (ed.) *The Gaelic League Idea*. Dublin: Mercier.

Picard, J.M. (2003) The Latin language in early medieval Ireland. In M. Cronin and C. Ó Cuilleanáin (eds) *The Languages of Ireland* (pp. 57–77). Dublin: Four Courts.

Public Services Organisation Review Group (1969) Report (The Devlin Report). Dublin: Stationery Office.

Risk, H. (1968) French loan-words in Irish. *Études Celtiques* 12, 585–655.

RTÉ (Radió Teilifís Éireann) (1995) *RTÉ Response to the Government's Green Paper on Broadcasting*. Dublin: RTÉ.

Skutnabb-Kangas, T. (2000) *Linguistic Genocide in Education or Worldwide Diversity and Human Rights?* New Jersey: Lawrence Erlbaum.

Spolsky, B. (2004) *Language Policy*. Cambridge: Cambridge University Press.

Spolsky, B. and Shohamy, E. (2000) Language practice, language ideology, and language policy. In R.D. Lambert and E. Shohamy (eds) *Language Policy and Pedagogy* (pp. 1–42). Philadelphia / Amsterdam: John Benjamins.

Tovey, H. (1988) The state and the Irish language: The role of Bord na Gaeilge. In P.Ó Riagáin (ed.) *Language Planning in Ireland. International Journal of the Sociology of Language* 70, 53–68.

Valdés, G. (1997) Bilinguals and bilingualism. Language policy in an anti-immigrant age. *International Journal of the Sociology of Language* 127, 25–52.

Wall, M. (1969) The decline of the Irish Language. In B. Ó Cuiv (ed.) *A View of the Irish Language* (pp. 81–90). Dublin: Stationery Office.

Walsh, J., McCarron, S. and Ní Bhrádaigh, E. (2005) Mapping the Gaeltacht: Towards a geographical definition of the Irish-speaking districts. *Administration* 53 (1), 16–37.

Watson, I. (2003) *Broadcasting in Irish: Minority Language, Radio, Television and Identity*. Dublin: Four Courts.

White Paper (1965) *Restoration of the Irish Language*. Dublin: Stationery Office.

Wigger, A. (1979) *Irish Dialect, Phonology and Problems of Irish Orthography. Papers in Celtic Phonology*: Coleraine: New University of Ulster.

Williams, C. (ed.) (2000) *Language Revitalisation*. Cardiff: University of Wales Press.

Wright, S. (2004) *Language Policy and Language Planning: From Nationalism to Globalisation*. Hampshire: Palgrave MacMillan.

Yelenevskaya, M. and Fialkova, L. (2003) From 'muteness' to eloquence: Immigrants' narratives about languages. *Language Awareness* 12 (1), 30–48.

The Language Planning Situation in Ireland: An Update 2005–2007

Muiris Ó Laoire

Introduction

In the intervening eighteen month period between the publication of the monograph and the present updated work, some developments have taken place in language planning in Ireland, and these are outlined and discussed briefly here.

Planning in the *Gaeltacht*

There are ongoing discussions and reflections on the questions and issues concerning the Irish language that have been raised and analysed in the monograph. Regarding language maintenance or sustaining linguistic vitality in the *Gaeltacht*, which has taken a centre-stage part in language planning over the past two years, concerns continue to be expressed, in particular, about curricular and education policy issues. The monograph referred to a 2005 study of *Gaeltacht* schools (COGG, 2005) which showed that 10% of *Gaeltacht* students leave school with little or no Irish. This concern has not abated. A conference in April 2007, for example, examined the way forward for a *Gaeltacht* education policy, with proposals being made for a new structure to be established – an Education Board for the *Gaeltacht*. This development would imply a more decentralised language planning structure, removing the responsibilities for education in the *Gaeltacht* from the State's Department of Education and Science. The monograph has already referred to the emergence of new, bottom-up, local, community language planning initiatives in the *Gaeltacht*. These initiatives continue, therefore, to be functioning significantly in the story of language planning in Ireland.

The threat posed by the return of native Irish speakers with English speaking families and the movement of English speakers to the *Gaeltacht* in the context of an unprecedented economic boom has resulted in housing planning restrictions being imposed in the Connemara *Gaeltacht*. Language impact statements represent a local, structured initiative to control residential, commercial and industrial developments. Galway County Council has conducted language impact studies and has produced guidelines to counteract the negative affects of uncontrolled planning (Galway County Council, 2003). The complex relation between people, place and language comes into play, and it will take a further decade to be able to assess the impact of this type of planning on the language.

A sociolinguistic study on the use of Irish in the *Gaeltacht* has been undertaken, but has not yet been published. The Irish language newspaper, *Foinse*, of 22 April 2007, reports, however, that the study will give a gloomy insight into the language use of young *Gaeltacht* residents in particular. One of the pre-reported recommendations of the report is that the status and official designation of the

Gaeltacht area will be removed from any area within the *Gaeltacht* that does not fulfil certain demographic linguistic criteria that are laid out.

The comments in the conclusion of the monograph, therefore, still appear to hold true, i.e. that in spite of positive attitudes and the momentum of individuals, families and voluntary organisations involved in the language movement, there is little evidence that home bilingualism is gaining ground.

The discourse in the *Gaeltacht* still tends towards rights and equality. Mac Giolla Chríost (2005) has recently pointed out that the recognition of language rights in Ireland has been almost exclusively associated with *Gaeltacht* residents. Language rights tend to flow largely from speakers' territorial relationship with the *Gaeltacht*. There is much less focus in rights' discourse on the conditions of individual speakers of the Irish language in any other part of the Republic. Mac Giolla Chríost (2005: 236) rightly concludes that the official *Gaeltacht* is too narrow a niche to sustain the future of the language, since the actual ecology is broader than this defined territory, including Irish-speaking networks and speakers outside the *Gaeltacht*.

Irish as a Working Language of the EU

The monograph reported that the Irish Government in 2004 had tabled a proposal in the EU Parliament in Brussels seeking official and working status in the EU for the Irish language. The EU Foreign Ministers unanimously approved the Irish Government's proposal to accord official and working status in the EU to the Irish language in June 2005 with effect from January 2007. On 1st January 2007, the Irish language became the 23rd official working language of the European Union. This means in effect that Irish MEPs (Members of the European Parliament), can speak in Irish, if they so choose, during the plenary parliamentary sessions, provided that they give prior notice to the Parliament. The final texts of EU regulations, which are approved jointly by the European Parliament and the Council of the European Union, will now be translated into Irish. After a period of five years, this situation will be reviewed, and a decision will be taken on whether Irish language services can be further extended.

One of the Irish-speaking MEPs, Seán Ó Neachtain, referred to the symbolic importance of this legislation, stating 'in the European Parliament, it is about more than communication. The majority of the MEPs speak in their native languages and when they do that, they are making a statement of identity as well as a political statement' (http://www.europarl.ie/ retrieved 11 January 2007). The Minister for Community, Rural and *Gaeltacht* Affairs, Éamon Ó Cuív TD, emphasised ' . . . the most important thing now is that people are encouraged to make use of the new rights which have been granted to them' (http://www.europarl.ie/ retrieved 11 January 2007). How often Irish MEPs will use the language remains to be seen.

Irish has always been a Treaty language, and all the EU treaties had been translated. Since the 1997 Amsterdam Treaty, Irish speakers have had the right to write to any of the EU institutions in Irish and to expect a response in their own language. The status of Irish as a Treaty language ensured that all EU Treaties had to be translated into the language. Its new status, however, will ensure that the Irish language will take its place among the multilingual family of the European Union. Among the EU institutions, it is in the European Parliament that this new status will have the strongest impact. One of the impacts of the new found status for the language has been the opportunities on offer to competent Irish language translators. Whereas previous advertisements for translators in the EU appearing in Ireland usually stipulated that applicants be proficient in what would be a third language (e.g. French, German, Spanish, and Italian) for Irish citizens, recent vacancies for positions as Irish translators require just Irish and English. There has been strong and competitive demand, therefore, for translator positions available at the institutions of the EU.

All things considered, this status legislation affords a significant insight into the complex symbiosis between top-down and bottom-up planning initiatives. In the context of the expansion of the EU with its pluralist and multilingual realities, the achievement of EU status for Irish provides an example of an ecology where constitutional top-down status planning has worked alongside community and language rights initiated actions.

A Languages-in-Education Policy 2006

The development of the curriculum for Irish as L2 and its deliberately thought-out alignment with CLT (Communicative Language Teaching) was outlined in the monograph. This process produced debate about the appropriateness of adopting an approach that originated in languages of wider communication in a lesser used or minority language context. The state of Irish language teaching and its alignment with other modern languages in the curriculum have become part of the recent seminal review of languages in the curriculum by the NCCA (National Council for Curriculum and Assessment) Review of Languages (www.ncca.ie), referred to in the monograph.

Responding to outcomes and the processes of the review, in 2005 the Department of Education and Science invited the Council of Europe's Policy Division to begin work on a national languages-in-education policy. The Language Policy Division of the Council of Europe is particularly well known for its work in developing tools and standards to help member states elaborate transparent and coherent language policies (www.coe.int/lang) and implement intergovernmental medium-term programmes with a special emphasis on policy development in this process.

The process of review, research and documentation which began in 2005 led to a final Profile Report on the current position and possible future developments in language education of all kinds in Ireland. The process of the Profile consisted of three principal phases:

(1) The production of a 'Country Report', describing the current position and raising issues which are under discussion or review (DES, 2005).
(2) An 'Experts' Report' which took into account the 'Country Report' and discussions and observations during a week's visit to Ireland in October 2005.
(3) A final report (DES, 2005) addressed many issues considered pivotal to language planning in education that was submitted to the Department of Education and Science in 2006.

One of main findings in the final report (DES, 2005) specified that a languages-in-education policy can only operate and be implemented within the wider context of national policy and societal attitudes. The fact that Ireland is a bilingual State was taken as critical consideration in the construction of a languages-in-education policy. But, importantly it also viewed attested competence in foreign languages as an essential resource for the State, with due regard to the cultural, social and economic needs of individual learners and of the State itself.

The European Council (Barcelona, March 2002) called on member States 'to improve the mastery of basic skills, in particular by teaching at least two foreign languages from a very early age'. Ireland has yet to formulate a response to this aspiration of 'mother tongue plus two'. While school-going students generally study one foreign language in addition to English and Irish, the Report expressed disquiet that the numbers studying foreign languages in the State have decreased in the post-primary terminal examination. In February 2006, the Royal Irish Academy Committee for Modern Language, Literary and Cultural Studies held a conference to discuss the need for and the role of a language policy for Ireland. In its final report (Ó Dochartaigh & Broderick, 2006) it too underlined its concern at the decreasing numbers who choose to study foreign languages not only in the terminal examination but also in courses at tertiary level. It called on the government to show leadership in addressing this trend and saw the implementation of a national language policy as a fundamental first stage solution (Ó Dochartaigh & Broderick, 2006: 2).

From Bilingualism to Multilingualism?

The presence in the education system of large numbers of students whose first language is neither English nor Irish constitutes a new phenomenon. Recent census reports record the presence of 167 languages being spoken in Ireland. Three main issues were identified in the Country Report (DES, 2005) which arise from the fact that Ireland's school-going population is likely to become increasingly multinational, multilingual and multi-ethnic:

- firstly, the need to integrate newcomers into the education system;
- secondly, the need to provide the necessary language skills for children whose first language is neither Irish nor English and
- thirdly, the question of appropriate first language support for the children of newcomers.

The fact that Ireland is becoming increasingly multilingual calls for studies of how various current states of bilingualism may be altered or developed in the years ahead. This new trend, of course, is the result of Ireland's rapid economic development and its need for an enlarged labour force. This fact increases the language resources on which Ireland can capitalise, allowing for greater space for languages in many mainstream communities – in urban areas in particular – and for altering schools from potentially bilingual to actually multilingual micro-communities. To date, little if any research has been undertaken on the linguistic and attitudinal changes that may underpin this social and sociolinguistic transformation. The ethnic homogeneity of the Irish population has always been a factor in its relationship to, and its 'claims' on, the Irish language. In the changing sociolinguistic map of Ireland, however, more attention will need to be brought to bear on the complex and transforming relationship between a more heterogeneous, pluralist society and the Irish language.

Irish in the Curriculum

In March 2007 the Minister of Education and Science announced that the percentage of marks for oral Irish would be increased from 25% to 40%. This decision was significant in that it indicated government policy for the Irish language. As referred to in the monograph, the reasons why the State wants all its citizens to learn the language for a period of twelve to thirteen years (2300 hours on average) have not been articulated in any policy document. The cultural rationale is often posited as a compelling, cogent one; i.e. children learn Irish because the language is part of Irish culture and *part* of what the Irish are. The problem with this rationale is that it is no longer completely plausible in the changing contemporary multicultural circumstances. The language can, of course, unify the diversifications at the heart of the essence of contemporary Irishness, but espousing and valuing the language as part of Irish culture will not necessarily guarantee that children will speak it. Learning a language for cultural reasons is not the same as learning a language for communicative reasons. One can legitimately cherish Irish for the insights it gives to the meaning of heritage, traditions, literature and spirituality, but one can appreciate this culture-related information without feeling compelled to speak the language at all. It might sometimes be a matter of listening to a song in Irish, or watching a programme on TG4, rather like fostering an interest in Irish music without necessarily being able to, or wanting to, play a traditional instrument. So a language syllabus designed solely for cultural reasons would have a different thrust and content than a language syllabus designed with the objective to foster communication skills among students. This is why the Minister's decision is a significant one, leaving no doubt as to what government thinking and policy are. The increased emphasis on oral proficiency contextualises and re-underwrites a State view on the language as communication.

The apparent contraction of the *Gaeltacht* community as evident in the recent census data has shifted the emphasis from native speaker as the last bastion of the language to the significance of the pivotal part to be played in the survival of Irish in the future by the neo-native speaker who acquires Irish in school. But acquiring a language as distinct from learning a language in school is not that easy. Producing students with even a moderate oral command of the language in the day-to-day classrooms is a complicated enterprise.

The question has been raised again and again as to why students appear to be unable to hold a simple conversation in the language after thirteen years of instruction. The debate up to now has centred on teachers' alleged poor standards of Irish, the need for reform of the curriculum and the removal of literature from the syllabus. The missing and vital focus of the debate has been on the lack of any clear distinction between the type of learning that occurs in the classroom and the purposeful acquisition of language. Even though the average student spends 2300 hours learning about the language and practising (mostly in writing) its structures and vocabulary, there may be little evidence that students actually *acquire* the language during this time.

Politicians and Irish language organisations that pronounce on Irish language issues and are unhappy with the teaching of Irish often miss the point. There have been references to defective or unsatisfactory teaching methods. Modern research on language teaching shows, however, that language teaching methods are flawed only if they do not facilitate some degree of language acquisition in the classroom. Rather than focus on a mechanistic model of teaching, the focus can be placed on teaching as facilitative of purposeful learning and acquisition. Learners will learn more effectively if they see a communicative purpose for the language outside the classroom. The learning of Irish as a second language – the characteristic experience of the vast majority of Irish learners – contrasts often with the more purposeful learning of the language in immersion contexts like in all-Irish programmes, where the language appears to be successfully acquired by students who use it meaningfully to communicate outside the Irish class.

Crucially, the approach to the way the testing and marking of the oral examination may have to change if standards can be expected to improve. The oral examination format consists of reading a literary passage and answering questions in a controlled interview-type conversation. This technique describes one method of oral assessment, but it may not be the most effective. Day-to-day conversational chit chat is never demanded of candidates; neither is their ability to ask questions nor their ability to express themselves naturally examined. Testing language acquisition as separate from learning reams of material by heart to feign fluency would necessarily involve a different approach with interaction being a key feature along with producing an output that would be unpredictable. So, in addition to a controlled or free interview, candidates might be expected to undergo oral presentations, verbal essays, information transfer, role-play and interaction tasks.

The developments outlined above underline ongoing status and acquisition planning efforts for Irish. While debates on the teaching and learning of the language through education continue, the main shift of focus for language planners in the future will be establishing a sustainable space for the language and other languages in the context of increasing multilingualism and multiculturalism.

References

COGG (*An Chomhairle um Oideachas Gaeltachta agus Gaelscolaíochta*) (2005) *Staid Reatha na Scoileanna Gaeltachta. A Study of Gaeltacht Schools 2004*, Dublin: An Chomhairle um Oideachas *Gaeltachta* agus Gaelscolaíochta.

DES (Department of Education and Science, Ireland) *Language Education Policy* (2005) *Profile: Country Report: Ireland.* Dublin: Department of Education and Science.

Galway County Council (2003) *Galway County Development Plan 2003–2009.* Galway: Galway County Council.

Mac Giolla Chríost, D. (2005) *The Irish Language in Ireland. From Goídel to Globalisation.* London: Routledge.

Ó Dochartaigh, P. and Broderick, M. (2006) *Language Policy and Language Planning in Ireland.* Dublin: Royal Irish Academy.

The Language Situation in Italy

Arturo Tosi
Department of Italian, Royal Holloway, University of London, UK and Scienze della Comunicazione, Università degli Studi di Siena, Italy

This monograph provides an overview of the language situation in Italy, within the framework of language policy and language planning. It presents an account of multilingualism, linguistic diversity, social variation, educational issues and phenomena of language contact both within and outside Italy. The four main threads are (1) the current linguistic profile of Italy, (2) language spread in the past, (3) the current issues in language planning and language policy, (4) the prediction of future developments and language prospects. A number of historical factors have been elaborated to account for the highly unusual conditions of Italian multilingualism. One factor is that the so-called 'dialects' of Italy are actually Romance languages and not dialects of Italian different from the standard. Another is that Italian is a far less standardised language than other Romance languages. The fact that Italian became a major European language without having had the experience of a common nation explains a wide range of issues relevant to language policy and language planning: from education to literacy. Such issues include aspects of national education and foreign language instruction, minority languages, and immigrant languages. My aim has been to provide the readers with critical guidance regarding various policy decisions.

Keywords: Italy, language policy, language planning, dialects, language spread, future trends

The Language Profile of Italy

A sketch of language diversity

Italian is the official language of the Republic of Italy (57.6 million inhabitants), the Republic of San Marino (13,000) and the Vatican City (about 900) and is one of the official languages of the Swiss Confederation, where it is spoken in the Ticino Canton by some 195,000 people. Outside Italy, standard Italian and/or other languages or dialects of Italy are also spoken in the region of Nice, the Principality of Monaco, Corsica, Istrian and Dalmatian towns, and in Malta. It survives in Ethiopia and Somalia as a relic of Italian colonisation. Italian is also one of the heritage languages of immigrant communities in the New World, especially in Australia and in the US, and in South America. Italian has also been transmitted to the new generations by the emigrants who left Italy to seek employment in the industrial conurbations of central and northern Europe. In Italy, multilingualism is widespread and is the result of complex historical circumstances. A bird's eye view of the situation suggests that several historical minorities of the north are situated in areas where the borders have fluctuated (Bavarian, Cimbrian, Franco-Provençal, French, German, Mocheno, Provençal, Slovenian and Walser), and those in the centre and south have preserved ancestral languages of old foreign settlements (Catalan, Greek, Albanian, Serbo-Croatian). In addition, Italy has three domestic minority languages (Friulian, Ladin and Sardinian), which are traditionally recognised as autonomous languages and which have grown in conditions of extreme isolation from neighbouring linguistic areas. Multilingualism in Italy is not, however, related only to the coexistence of Italian and minority languages: it is rooted in the historical background of a country whose late unification maintained a situation of linguistic diversity that is unique within Europe. Several unofficial languages (still ambiguously called 'dialects') are widely spoken in everyday life and interpenetrate the national language giving it a strong regional flavour in different areas of the peninsula. In the north, there are Piedmontese, Ligurian, Lombard, Emilian and Venetian. The central area, in addition to Tuscan dialects, also includes Umbrian and the dialects of northern Latium and the Marches. Further south, the most prominent dialects are Abruzzese, Neapolitan, Pugliese, Calabrese and Sicilian. These linguistic differences are evidence of the heritage of some ten centuries of political division and cultural diversity, which could not be erased by the official recognition of Tuscan as Italy's national language in 1861. Since then, the interaction between different sectors of the national community has involved a process of language change that is more complex than that found in other European countries, as will be seen in the next section.

A brief historical outline

Greek historians say that when their people came to set up colonies along new coasts of the Mediterranean they found a population called 'Italoi', suggesting that the name 'Italy' was given in proto-historic time to a small region in the extreme south of the peninsula. However, during the first millennium BC many different civilisations were present in the area that today we call Italy (see Figure 1). The most famous were the Etruscans, people respected by the Romans for their high levels of education and literacy; indeed, their alphabet was adopted by other populations. There were also the Latins, living in the region called Latium, and among them the Romans, whose language would soon be distinguished between the *sermo urbanus*, the language spoken in the fast expanding city of Rome, and the *sermo rusticus* of the neighbouring areas. It was the former (*sermo urbanus*) that, because of its prestige, later became the model of the language used by the Roman administration and in Latin literature. The process of 'Romanisation' of the Italian peninsula took place increasingly through consensus rather than coercion, by means of extending Roman citizenship to all its inhabitants. This was granted also to populations outside the peninsula, but those living inside benefited from jurisdictional harmony and a more homogeneous urban development that, reinforced by onomastic and toponomastic unity, laid the foundations of a first linguistic uniformity, despite the widespread language diversity. Multilingualism, however, emerged early during the Roman Empire and spread soon after its decline, because of the different regional ways of speaking Latin, although there was a common written language.

Spoken Latin evolved so differently in different parts of Italy because of the existence of many 'substrata' corresponding to the diverse linguistic origins of its speakers. To a lesser extent, the evolution of Latin is due to a 'superstratum' (contacts with foreign languages spoken by populations dominating different parts of Italy at various times). The 'substratum' theory has collected strong evidence that the multilingualism that developed within Italy, at the time of the

Figure 1 The dialects of ancient Italy (*c.* 400 BC)

formation of other Romance languages, basically coincided with the settlement boundaries of the populations of speakers of different languages before the Roman conquest. Some linguistic phenomena characteristic of regional diversity were the same in the pre-Roman and post-Roman periods: for example, Oscan 'nn' corresponds to Latin 'nd'; just as in Campano dialects it remains 'nn' and in Italian it is 'nd' (*quanno* = / = *quando*; *monno* = / = *mondo*). Many historical documents show that the awareness of bilingualism – the coexistence of two separate languages – increased substantially towards the end of the Middle Ages. Ordinary people used the local vernacular only, while the educated elite was fluent in the local vernacular as well as in Latin, which had long been the only written language and, of course, the language of prayers and all religious functions. In the 13th century, some city-states in Tuscany rapidly expanded their political prominence and economic wealth, and acted as allies of the Emperor or intermediaries between him and the Pope. Among these states there was Florence, whose cunning and resourceful aristocracy was divided between, on the one hand, local politics and international diplomacy and, on the other hand, a genuine commitment to the patronage of liberal arts, academic culture and education. A major challenge for Florence's economic elite was to secure for their local language the same cultural and political prestige other languages were acquiring at that time in other parts of Europe.

When Dante wrote his *Commedia* in the Florentine vernacular at the beginning of the 14th century, this was immediately recognised by cultural elites all over Italy as a model for a pan-Italian literary language. In addition, Dante showed lucid awareness of the main criteria for the planning of a new language in a developing nation. He said that Florentine was the only 'vernacular' (people's language) in the peninsula which had achieved high standardisation (it was 'cardinal'), which was also suitable for literary purposes (it was 'illustrious'), and had the characteristics of both 'curial' and 'aulic' (it therefore had social and political prestige). Dante explained this in his linguistic treaty, *De Vulgari Eloquentia* which he wrote in Latin to give his innovative ideas the widest possible circulation via the international lingua franca of the time both inside and outside Italy. Within Dante's lifetime and that of the next generation, a number of factors of a cultural and linguistic nature concurred to establish the supremacy of Florentine. Not only was Florentine the medium of the literary works of Tuscany's leading vernacular writers, Boccaccio and Petrarch (who after Dante had acquired international stature), but it continued to be spoken, and came gradually to be used in written texts, by the peninsula's most influential state in terms of wealth, culture and political prestige. Furthermore, its linguistic system presented morphosemantic structures and phonetic features that occupied an intermediate position between the other vernaculars that had developed in the north and the south.

If political unification was a dream in Dante's time, it became a real possibility one century later in Machiavelli's time. In the 15th century, Italy came very close to changing from a 'geographical expression' to a united state. But the peninsula was coveted by foreign powers and the Church had no intention of giving up her secular possessions. Once again internal political events prevented unification; the peninsula remained fragmented for four more centuries and Florence lost her cultural and political supremacy. Florentine, the basis of literary Italian, inspired the literary tradition which continued to be modelled on the prose and the poetry of the three great Tuscan writers, Dante, Petrarch and Boccaccio. Italian elites shared a cultural tradition but not a national community. This situation, unique in Europe, had many repercussions on the future development of the common language and culture of Italy. It was literature that provided the models of the language to use and not vice versa; and at the same time, in the absence of a nation, the language common to Italians could only be learnt through study, like Latin or a foreign language. In short, literary models rather than social use determined language transmission for several centuries, making the body of Italian language open to a multitude of norms from diverse literary traditions. This explains why Italian is still much less standardised compared to most European languages. The fact that the Italian 'geographical expression' (as it was described by the Austrian politician Prince von Metternich) did not evolve into a national community until the 19th century is responsible for the survival of Italy's current linguistic diversity (see Figure 2).

Figure 2 The dialects of modern Italy

The official language: Italian

The spread of the national language – and of the literary models promoted by schools – resulted in a number of variations, due to contact with the dialects, that Italian linguists have divided into varieties or strata, depending on the main components and the characteristics of speakers. However, while there were few contacts between literary language and local dialect – the extremes of the continuum – the intermediate varieties increasingly influenced one another, and the rapidly changing situation made it difficult to draw the line between the different strata. This is why many linguists adopt a metaphor of 'architecture' when describing the components of standard Italian (Berruto, 1987; Dardano, 1994). The complex system of forms and norms that regulate its ordinary everyday use is still polymorphic and in rapid evolution. Once the retrospective rules of the literary tradition were abandoned, it was difficult to determine 'good models' or 'acceptable norms'. Interaction between varieties is constant and, in addition, even the most inaccurate and improvised forms of language became prestigious when promoted by the most popular of the mass media: the television. A major challenge is, therefore, to describe standard and nonstandard variations in a society where standardisation is still largely in progress, while the official language is in constant interaction with other languages present in everyday Italian life:

the so-called dialects which, however, are neither Italian dialects nor dialects of Italian (Lepschy, 2002a, 2002b).

The best architecture is that proposed by Berruto (1987, 1993). Its components are taken from different varieties of Italian (but not from dialects). Berruto starts with divisions based on region (diatopic varieties), on social differences, (diastratic varieties), on domain and functions (diaphasic varieties), and on spoken or written medium of use (diamesic varieties). Berruto establishes the extreme models of each variety, and intermediate stages are placed along a continuum. On the diatopic continuum, the highest code is represented by the literary tradition, which adopts the Florentine models (with the phonetic rearrangements of northern Italian intonation, proposed by Galli de' Paratesi (1985)). The lowest code is the regional variety with the features typical of use by a dialect speaker. On the diastratic continuum, at the top end, one finds the sophisticated language spoken by highly educated groups, while at the lowest end there are forms adopted by rural communities and uneducated members of the working classes. On the diaphasic continuum, at the top end there are the formal registers and at the bottom are illustrations of very 'sloppy' language. Along the diamesic continua, that contrasts written use to spoken language, at one extreme there are formal written styles and at the other extreme unplanned colloquial styles (a distinction made by Nencioni, 1976, and developed by Berretta, 1994). Berruto comments that in normal everyday language a given variety may be placed on any of the four different continuums. For example, a diaphasic variety such as professional jargon is also confined to use by certain social groups, thus becoming part of the diastratic continuum. The diatopic and diastratic varieties are practically indistinguishable as nearly every user is a native speaker of a regional variety (of the diatopic continuum), but only those who achieve high social positions can abandon the lowest levels of that variety and reach the high levels of the standard on the diaphasic continuum. Berruto eventually reduced his typology to only three main continua (see Figure 3).

To exemplify different types of language Berruto used a sentence that, neutrally, would be the equivalent of 'We cannot come to see you'.

(1)	*Italiano standard letterario:*	*La informo che non potremo venire.*
(2)	*Italiano neo-standard:*	*Le dico che non possiamo venire.*
(3)	*Italiano parlato colloquiale:*	*Sa, non possiamo venire.*
(4)	*Italiano popolare:*	*Ci dico che non potiamo venire.*
(5)	*Italiano informale trascurato:*	*Mica possiam venire, eh!*
(6)	*Italiano gergale:*	*Ehi, apri 'ste orecchie, col cavolo che ci si trasborda.*
(7)	*Italiano formale aulico:*	*Mi pregio di informar La che la nostra venuta non rientra nell'ambito del fattibile.*
(8)	*Italiano tecnico scientifico:*	*Trasmettiamo a Lei destinatario l'informazione che la venuta di chi sta parlando non avrà luogo.*
(9)	*Italiano burocratico:*	*Vogliate prendere atto dell'impossibilità della venuta dei sottoscritti.*

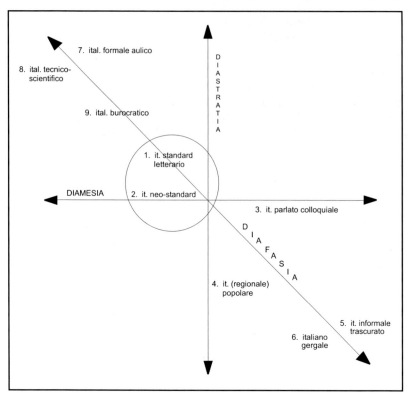

Figure 3 A three-dimensional typology of Italian varieties (Berruto, 1987, 1993)

Literary standard (1) is the Italian of the written literary tradition. The neo-standard Italian (2) is the variety including some innovations of the spoken language that is used by most people in formal situations. Colloquial Italian (3) is the spoken variety of informal everyday conversation. Popular regional Italian (4) is the (mainly) spoken variety of the less educated social groups. Casual Italian (5) is the spoken variety of very informal situations. Slang (6) is a spoken variety that marks one's membership of a special (age or sub-cultural) group. Solemn, very formal, Italian (*italiano aulico*) (7) is a spoken and written variety for the most formal events. Technical-scientific Italian (8) is a spoken and written variety used in professional circles; bureaucratic Italian (9) is a (mainly) written variety used by public officials.

The neo-standard is an extension of the standard and involves an ongoing emancipation of low-variety ('working-class', colloquial) forms and expressions, upgraded either through use by well-educated people seeking colourful effects, or by the medium of their use (for example, TV programmes and telephone interviews on the radio). Special languages are varieties that were originally developed by specific professional sectors. They are now exercising pressure on ordinary language in two ways: an increasing number of lexical items, idioms and metaphors are transferred into everyday speech, and an increasing number of people from professional sectors forget to translate their specialised jargon into ordinary language, or are no longer able to do so. As a result, the technicisms of the special languages make these varieties seem more prestigious to the general public. The emergence of slang among young people, especially in urban areas, expresses their need for external transgression and internal solidarity, now they can no longer tap the reservoir of linguistic inventions once provided by the vitality of dialects. These are the forces at national level affecting the diversification of Italian. At local level, however, the forces and resources are different. Here, the notion of 'standard' seems to reflect what Galli de' Paratesi (1985: 66) defines as the 'supraimposition of the norms of the national language on regional linguistic realities'.

Grammar: A brief summary

There is general agreement that the northern standard, that has been gaining ground in the country since the time of industrialisation, now enjoys high prestige. Strong regional variations usually make it possible to recognise speakers from the North, the Centre or the South, and some of the most recognisable features of those regional standards will be outlined in this section (see also Lepschy & Lepschy, 1977; Vincent, 1981).

Spelling

The Italian writing system derives from the Latin. The Latin alphabet was adapted to the vernacular during the Middle Ages, and the spelling conventions became gradually standardised during centuries of academic debate on the best models for literary Italian. However, since the political history outlined in the previous section prevented until recently a widespread spoken use of the literary standard, at present, there is strong regional variation rather than uniformity of pronunciation. In addition, the writing system does not render certain phonetic distinctions of Tuscan pronunciation, and the phonological system of Florentine, which is at the root of modern Italian, is no longer considered a national model – quite the opposite: certain features are seen as puristic if not parochial. This system, however, is the conventional starting point for the description of Italian phonology.

The phonological system

In Latin the difference between long and short vowels was distinctive (*mālum*, 'apple' vs malum 'bad'), but in Italian it depends on syllable structure (*fato* 'fate' with long *a* vs *fatto* 'done' with a short *a*). The Italian or, rather the Florentine, phonological system includes five vowel sounds in unstressed position [i], [e], [a], [o], [u], and seven vowels in stressed syllables, which are very similar to the cardinal ones. [i], [e], [ɛ], [a], [ɔ], [o], [u]. The oppositions of mid-high and mid-low vowels /e/ and /ɛ/ and /o/ and /ɔ/ are neutralised in unstressed syllables, and although most Italian speakers have the four sounds, the pronunciation is much varied both for the kind of mid-vowels used and the individual words in which they are used. In the vowel system [i] and [u] have two allophones which are semiconsonants and are pronounced as [j], [w]. There are 21 consonant sounds: [p], [b], [t], [d], [k], [g], [ts], [dz], [t ʃ], [dʒ], [f], [v], [s], [z], [ʃ], [m], [n], [ɲ], [l], [ʎ], [r]. All consonant sounds can be single or double apart from [ts], [dz], [ʃ], [ɲ], [ʎ] which are always long intervocalically, and [z] which is always short. Single and double consonants are pronounced according to the traditional spelling, but this is another area of little uniformity due to

Table 1 Italian borrowings with similar sounds in English

Adagio	Influenza	Ravioli
Ballerina	Libretto	Spaghetti
Cappuccino	Mozzarella	Terracotta
Dilettante	Nobile	Umbrella
Espresso	Oratorio	Villa
Fiasco	Pizza	Zucchini
Gondola	Quarantine	

regional variations. The same applies to the distinction between [s] and [z]. In initial position before a vowel all Italians have [s], while intervocalically north-ern Italians have only [z], and southern Italians only [s]. The contrast between / ts/ and /dz/ is gradually disappearing, this time following the increasing tendency from the North to use /dz/ in all words. Table 1 provides an alphabeti-cal list of words with similar sounds in English.

Italian is considered a phonetic language, as letters tend to have constant phonetic values. While it is generally true that a given letter corresponds closely to the IPA value of that symbol, there are some noticeable exceptions: - *gl* - = /ʎ/, - *gn* - = / ɲ /, - *sc* - (*i*) = /ʃ/, - *s* - = /s/ or /z/, -*z*- = / ts/ or /dz/, -*c* - and -*g*- = /k/ and /g/ before *a, o* and *u*, and / tʃ/ and /dz/, before *i* and *e*. The digraphs –*ch*-, - *gh*- represent /k/, /g/ before *i, e*, and –*ci*- and –*gi*- represent / tʃ, dʒ / before *a, o* and *u*. There is no orthographic distinction between /e/ and / ɛ / or between /o/and / ɔ /, although in stressed final position /e/ is represented normally by *è* and / ɛ / by *è*. Stress is marked only when in final position, but the position of stress is impor-tant in that it is responsible for the difference between one word and another.

Morphology and syntax

Italian morphology shows a traditional Indo-European pattern including adjectives, nouns and verbs, and with a separation of verbal and nominal inflec-tion, the latter also involving pronouns, articles and adjectives. Nouns are either masculine or feminine; the neutral gender no longer exists. Because the case system of the Latin declension has mainly disappeared and prepositions are used instead, as in other Romance languages, the great freedom of Latin word order has been much reduced in Italian.

Articles, nouns and adjectives

The articles include indefinite and definite forms, both singular and plural and masculine and feminine. A number of prepositions combine with the defi-nite article to form a single word. Nouns inflect for gender (masculine and femi-nine) and number (singular and plural). Masculine nouns ending in [o] inflect in the plural in [i], feminine nouns ending in [a] inflect in the plural in [e], mascu-line and feminine nouns ending in [e] inflect in the plural in [i], and masculine nouns of Latin or Greek origin ending in [a] inflect in the plural in [i]. The plural form by vowel alternation rather than the adding of -*s* (-*es* etc.) is one of the distinct features of Italian compared to other Romance languages such as French, Spanish and Portuguese. Adjectives, which always agree in number and gender with the noun they qualify, fall into two main categories: those which have four forms, the singular masculine [o] singular feminine [a] the plural masculine [i] and the plural feminine [e], and those which have two forms, for both masculine and feminine the singular [e], which becomes [i] in the plural. Adjectives are generally postnominal and the position can change the meaning. If placed before the noun, they tend to be part of a 'fixed phrase', of frequently used connotations. One feature peculiar to Italian is the role of suffixation in modifying the value of both nouns and adjectives. Four broad groups of suffixes can be attached to nouns and adjectives, roughly meaning 'small', 'large', 'nice' and 'nasty', but not all suffixes combine with all nouns, and this makes it difficult to predict the value without consideration of the context.

The verb system

The Latin verb pattern is basically preserved, with the three traditional conjugations, marked by the three vowels, *a, e* or *i* as in *amare, temere, sentire*, the latter two are morphologically more similar to each other than either is to *a*-verbs. One important feature is that Italian does not need to express the pronominal subject of the verb and that it can place the subject after the verb. As in any language, there are a number of irregular verb forms, mostly in the historic past and past participle, and much less in the present tense. Apart from sentences that use the indicative tenses, there are sentences with the conditional and the subjunctive whose use is made increasingly shaky by regional variations and contemporary usage. The use of the conditionals may: (1) suggest desire, intention or possibility, (2) propose something less categorically than the indicative, (3) report unconfirmed views and (4) express in indirect speech a successive or contemporary subordinate. The use of the subjunctive conveys doubt or marks subordination, but contemporary usage shows that the choice is increasingly a stylistic one. In Italian, as in other Romance languages, verb forms regulate the system of address. Standard Italian distinguishes between a familiar and a polite style. The former uses the second person singular forms *tu, te, ti, tuo* and the imperative. The latter adopts the deferential pronoun *Lei* (from a late Latin form that spread in the Renaissance due to Spanish influence) which in many parts of the South is expressed by *Voi, ve, vi, vostro* which function as polite singular forms.

Vocabulary

Word formation

The fact that literary Florentine, as used by the great Tuscan writers of the 14th century, was gradually accepted as the national standard makes Italian exceptionally 'conservative' as compared with other Romance languages. Evidence of this is that native speakers of Italian at the present time can read and understand the early classical texts (especially Petrarch and Boccaccio). At the beginning of the 16th century, the *questione della lingua* helped to codify the Florentine literary models, and later inspired the Florentine *Accademia della Crusca*, founded in 1582–3, which adopted the same theories and criteria to produce the *Vocabolario degli Accademici della Crusca*, in 1612, which was also the first modern language dictionary. Written Italian benefited from the contribution not only of academics and literati but also large numbers of writers in the fields of art, architecture, science and technology. Among the latter, Galileo Galilei (1564–1642) is often remembered both because of his polemical use of Italian, instead of Latin, to promote innovative ideas amongst the more progressive secular circles, and for his deliberate effort to deliver a scientific prose which was more codified in terms of lexis, style and argumentation.

Foreign influences

The influence of Spanish on Italian, from the second half of the 16th century until the Spanish War of Succession (1702–1714), was not especially significant, whilst that of French in the following two centuries was far more pervasive in the philosophical, political, economic and military domains. This is also because French became the first widely spoken foreign language in a modern sense. The impact on Italian, as on most other languages, was still limited to a small elite, but the vocabulary that French brought into Italian hinted at innovations that were beginning to affect everyday life: *restaurant, buffet, redingote, trousseau, cocotte*. In the 19th century, the industrial revolution brought English rather than French to the fore as the production of industrial commodities for mass consumption was centred on Britain. Some were Italianised ('tramway' = *tramvai*, 'locomotive' = *locomotiva*), others were adopted in their original form ('ferry boat', 'yacht', 'tandem', 'tunnel'). Other major contributions came from the spread of popular sports ('sport', 'rugby', 'tennis', 'football', 'goal', 'derby', 'record') and other social entertainments ('poker', 'bridge'), and from the expansion of the new food industry ('tea' *tè*; 'beef steak' *bistecca*; 'whisky'; 'sandwich', 'roast beef' sometimes spelt *rosbiffe*) and clothing ('smoking', 'plaid', 'jersey', 'waterproof'). At the turn of the century, lexical contributions began to arrive from the exciting new world of the United States: Far West, 'cowboy', 'barman', 'cocktail' and 'skyscraper', translated into *grattacielo* and in the early days *grattanuvole*. The real impact of American English on Italian does not come until after the Second World War (Migliorini, 1963). The language used to represent this new mass culture – where money meant freedom, home meant comfort and work meant wealth and satisfaction – had a dramatic effect on most European languages, including Italian: 'part time'; 'full time'; 'leasing'; 'self service'; 'supermarket'; 'babysitter'; 'hostess'; 'playboy'; 'teenager'; 'public relations'; 'relax'; 'stress'; 'sex appeal'; 'suspense'; 'beauty case'; 'minigolf'; 'bestseller'; 'show'; 'jazz'. This influence of English reached considerable proportions during the 1970s and 1980s, and some scholars announced that anglicised Italian could be considered a variety of the national language that was spoken by the upper classes with international contacts, and by company managers (Sanga, 1981). A few years later another linguist (Dardano, 1986) modified this picture. The impact of English on Italian society was, he said, much wider and involved a broader social spectrum of speakers and different areas of language use.

Italian influences on English and other languages

In the past, many Italian words were integrated into English without altering their original form. The early foreign borrowings illustrate the activities, and traditions which Italian people (whether individual artists or groups of travelling companies) brought into Britain in the course of history. Music terminology has been greatly influenced by Italian ever since Italian composers, musicians and singers dominated the European scene: *maestro, virtuoso, libretto, aria, sonata, concerto, oratorio, andante, soprano*. The spread of Italian art and architecture in Renaissance Europe had a similar impact: *portico, stucco, torso, chiaroscuro, putti, capriccio*. In the 16th and 17th centuries, the *Commedia dell' Arte* tradition spread throughout Europe, influencing popular plays and also the works of Shakespeare: *saltimbanco, dilettante, diva, ballerina, prima donna, bravura, rodomontade, fiasco, gran finale*. In the 19th century, new imports show an increasing interest for Italian everyday life as seen by travellers. This became one of the favourite themes of popular fiction and the encyclopaedic magazines: *cicisbeo, malaria, mafia, omertà, capo, bambino, mamma, carabiniere, campanile*. At the turn of the century, the greatest impact came through contact with emigrants in the new English-speaking world, where large communities of southerners settled, bringing with them also a new taste for life in general, and eating in particular. Most culinary vocabulary relating to Italian food comes into the language through America (or American English): *pizza, pasta, spaghetti, al dente, granita, maccaroni, lasagna, mozzarella*. Post-war Italian cinema began to make the country's warmth and vitality internationally known. The Italian way of life was to become extremely seductive, especially among young people: *simpatico, dolce vita, arrivederci, ciao, bella figura*. Sometimes borrowed words maintain their original meaning and sometimes they alter either meaning or form, or both. Most interesting of stereotyped borrowings is *al fresco*. To many British people this term vividly describes life Italian style. In Italian it has survived almost exclusively with its metaphorical meaning: in prison.

Unofficial languages: The 'dialects'

The status of dialects varies across the country, but their diversity is so marked in Italy that it usually prevents intelligibility, unless speakers live in bordering areas. This is so because Italian dialects differ from literary / standard Italian: and from one another, as much as one Romance language differs from another. Indeed 'dialects' in Italy are not varieties of Italian, they are separate and distinct Romance vernaculars, which developed from Latin, at the same time as Florentine. This is a unique situation in Europe and the peculiar use of the term 'dialects' in the Italian sociolinguistic context needs some clarification.

With the dismemberment of the Roman Empire, the different dialects of spoken Latin developed even more freely than before because of the lack of central focus. The rural areas remained linguistically conservative, while the trade and religious centres began to catalyse language development, acting as new cultural and linguistic foci. In feudal Italy, so much social life and cultural activity was concentrated on churches that the language historian Devoto (1953) quipped that for most of the Middle Ages in the peninsula there were as many vernaculars as parishes. In Europe the awareness of bilingualism, in the sense that competence in the native language could no longer provide access to Latin texts, and that diverse dialects of spoken Latin were becoming mutually unintelligible, emerges first for French. Because of the distance of the French vernaculars from Latin, and also because of the rapid political aggregation of the new speech communities, historical documents referred specifically to French and German as languages before the end of the first millennium, while the local vernaculars in Italy were still referred to either as 'native' or 'vulgar' forms of Latin.

In the 13th century, the artistic resurgence of many Italian cities contributed to their role as regional cultural centres and new linguistic foci. The languages of their courts, trading centres or literary circles, though acquiring new dignity, were still called *volgari*. As the prospect of political unification disappeared after the 15th century, any debate about the most illustrious of these *volgari*, Florentine, now called often the 'Italian language' was of interest only to those who were reading and writing literature. From the 16th century to the 19th century, dialects were spoken throughout Italy, but Florentine or rather 'Italian' was the only language adopted for general writing purposes, excluding of course literature in the vernacular. In the 18th century, the great Venetian playwright, Carlo Goldoni, still referred to *toscano* and *veneziano*, with no sense of stigma attached to the latter. This is so because, before unification (1861), Venetian or, for that matter, Piedmontese, Neapolitan or Sicilian, (and all the other regional languages) were not only used by peasants in rural communities or the urban working classes, but also by aristocrats and scholars. After unification, multilingualism was consolidated, while Florentine became the national language and the regional languages, now officially demoted to the status of 'dialects', survived in rural situations, especially in areas and domains which were little affected by the recent national integration. With the increased contacts between communities and individuals, after unification, monolingualism in the local language was gradually overcome, and bilingualism became the norm. In the space of 150 years the Italian situation changed from widespread monolingualism to widespread bilingualism in Italian and the regional languages, which have been transmitted with the lower denomination of 'dialects' (see Figure 4).

The main linguistic boundary of this unofficial multilingualism is the La Spezia–Rimini line, which cuts the north of Italy from the rest of the peninsula. It also separates western (French, Spanish and Portuguese) from eastern (Italian, Rumanian) Romance tongues, the former including Gallo-Italian vernaculars (Piedmontese, Ligurian, Lombard and Emilian) and Venetian (Venetian shares some features of northern dialects and some from the Tuscan dialects). Central dialects include also Umbrian and the dialects of northern Latium and Marches. Southern dialects are Abruzzese, Neapolitan, Pugliese, Calabrese, Sicilian. These divisions reflect administrative boundaries juxtaposed to natural geographical barriers, roughly corresponding to the divisions between the areas of the languages spoken in pre-Roman time (the pre-Roman substratum).

Regional varieties of Italian

If the term 'standard Italian' describes a broad set of possible variations, the term 'regional Italian' refers to Italian as it is actually spoken in everyday use, unlike the standard language that is ruled by strict conventions observed only in writing (Cortelazzo, 1977; Mengaldo, 1994). The regional varieties should not be interpreted as manifestations of a process of destandardisation (Berruto, 1985), but rather as expressions of the vitality of the dialects acting as sources of inspiration (and not just interference) for Italian speakers (Sobrero, 1974). Regional characterisation of the national language is frequent in major European languages (Telmon, 1993). It is stronger in Italian, which is unique in Europe in that there are relatively few monolinguals and it is the first language of only 50% of its speakers (Grimes, 1988). Phonetics are important in regional Italian, but

Figure 4 Boundaries of Italian 'dialect' areas

ho	*mangiato*	*troppo*	*ora*	*sono*	*sazio*	*e devo*	*prendere*
ho	*mangiato*	*troppo*	*adesso*	*sono*	*abboffato*	*e devo*	*pigliare*
sono	*mangiato*	*troppo*	*mo*	*sso'*	*abbottato*	*e ho da*	*pigliare*
sso'	*magnato*	*troppo*	*mo*	*sso'*	*abbottato*	*e tengo a*	*piglià*
sto	*magnato*	*troppo*	*mo*	*sto*	*abbottato*	*e tengo a*	*piglià*
ʃto	*magnate*	*troppe*	*mo*	*ʃto*	*abbottate*	*e teng a*	*piglià*
ʃto	*magnète*	*troppe*	*mo*	*ʃto*	*abbottète*	*e teng a*	*piglià*
'ʃtɛNg	*ma'ʃɛt*	*'trpp*	*mo*	*'ʃtNg*	*ab:o't:at*	*e 'teNg a*	*pi'a*

Figure 5 Regional variations in Abruzzo
Source: Telmon, 1993

there are also significant lexical and morphosyntactic differences. These occur more in the spoken language, while in written language they are increasingly infrequent though still acceptable (Poggi Salani, 1981).

An even more striking regional division involves the formal pronouns of address: *Lei* is normally adopted in northern / central Italy while in the southern regions, in Sicily and Sardinia, there used to be a general *Voi*, increasingly differentiated between *Lei* for formal but impersonal situations and *Voi* denoting special distance and respect. Telmon (1993) provides a full survey of phonetic, morphosyntactic and lexical variations. He says that in some areas almost every word of a sentence can be affected by regionalisms and that the most radical regionalisms can coincide with the local dialect. He exemplifies the continuum with this sentence: *Ho mangiato troppo: ora sono sazio e devo prendere (un digestivo)* as it would be uttered by eight different speakers in Abruzzo (Figure 5).

Another typical feature of marked regional differences are the specific lexical variations frequently used at work (especially in manual occupations) and for tools. Telmon exemplifies these geosynonyms with words for 'apron' (*grembiule* in standard Italian).

faudale, fodale, faldale	Piedmont
scossale	Lombardy, Canton Ticino, Liguria, West Emilia
bigarolo	West Lombardy
traversa	Venetia, Venetia Giulia
grombiale	Trento region
sinale, zinale	Marche, Umbria, Latium
parannanza	Latium
parninza	Abruzzi
mantile	Abruzzi, Molise, Salentum
mantesimo, vandevantale	Sardinia

Such variation was given as typical of the polycentrism of Italian (De Mauro, 1970), and for a long time linguists suggested that everyday vocabulary was regional, many words (88%) having more than two synonyms (Rüegg, 1953 quoted in Mengaldo, 1994). *Espresso* for 'coffee' is a rare exception, with only one form. In the interaction between these regional variations (which are often incomprehensible in other regions) and the standard language, some new trends have been recognised (Mengaldo, 1994; Telmon, 1993).

(1) Some regional expressions for characters, attitudes, habits have become incorporated in the national language: *mondezza* (rubbish), *bustarella* (backhander), *inghippo* (snag), *morosa* (girl friend), *balera* (discotheque), *burino* (boor), *racchia* (hag), *pappagallo* and *paparazzo*.

(2) Tuscan expressions are not comprehended more than other regionalisms. Many that are still common in Tuscany seem archaic (*balocco* = toy, *acquaio* = sink, *gruccia* = hanger, *mesticheria* = a household commodities store, *ciuco* = donkey, *diaccio* = icy cold) or even affected (*figliolo/figliola* for *figlio/figlia* = son / daughter; *babbo* for *papà* = daddy; *giacchetta* for *giacca* = jacket).

(3) The never-ending competition between Milan and Rome comes out here too. Milan and the north in general seem especially influential in the promotion of industrial terms (often from northern regionalisms) that oust terms referring to more traditional manual occupations. Rome as the political capital, as well as headquarters of the media, lends national prestige to regional expressions, when these are borrowed from street life and used to add colour. The follow-

ing descriptions give an idea of the main variations of regional Italian and the examples are a selection from the works of De Mauro (1970), Lepschy and Lepschy (1977), Telmon (1993) and Mengaldo (1994).

Northern varieties

The main typical phonetic features are: weakening of double consonants between vowels (e.g. *bella* is pronounced *bela*); *s* between vowels pronounced as /z/ (e.g. *casa* pronounced *caza*); double *z* is often voiceless (e.g. *razza* (skate fish) and *razza* (race) sound the same); open and closed *e* and *o* sound the same – e.g. *pésca* (fishing) and *pèsca* (peach). Some idiomatic expressions include: *avercela su* (to be angry with/mad at), *andare in oca* (to go gaga), *fare i mestieri* (to do the housework). Some typical lexical terms in these varieties are: *mollica* (soft part of bread), *secchiaio* (sink), *sottana* (skirt), *scodella* (bowl), *pianoterra* (groundfloor), *posdomani* (the day after tomorrow).

Tuscan varieties

The best known pronunciation feature is the 'aspiration' of /k/, /p/, /t/ sounds in intervocalic position (e.g. *hoha hola* for Coca Cola; *topho* for *topo* = mouse). Widespread morphosyntactic features include the impersonal (third person) *si* in lieu of the first person plural (e.g. *si va* for *andiamo*), with a frequent inclusion of the plural pronoun (e.g. *noi si va*); the pronoun *te* for *tu* ('you', nominative) and the substitution of *dassi* and *stassi* in the imperfect subjunctive for *dessi* (verb: *dare*) and *stessi* (verb: *stare*). There are many lexical peculiarities, including *punto* to emphasise a negative quality (often inflected in the plural *punti/e*: e.g. *non ci sono punte uova* = there are no eggs at all); the adjective *preciso* used instead of the adverb *precisamente*. *Codesto* is a demonstrative pronoun or adjective between the widespread standard forms *questo* (this) and *quello* (that). Likewise *costì* and *costà* (there) mean near the person spoken to, not the speaker.

Roman varieties

Phonetic features include the pronunciation as *g* of intervocalic *c* (e.g. *grego* for *greco* = Greek); the doubling of voiced bilabials and palatals in intervocalic position (e.g. *abbile* for *abile* = able). The loss of double *r* is common especially in the more rural areas (e.g. *tera* for *terra* = land, earth; *fero* for *ferro* = iron), together with the transformation of *nd* to *nn* (e.g. *monno* for *mondo* = world; *monnezza* for *mondezza* = rubbish). Much of the most picturesque Roman lexis was made popular in Italy by famous *commedia all'italiana* films (e.g. *beccamorto* = gravedigger, *caciara* = racket, *pataccaro* = swindler, *pappone* = pimp, *pupo* = baby, *sbafare* = to gorge oneself, *sganassone* = slap in the face, *menare* = to punch up).

Southern varieties

Both the Sicilian and Campanian varieties have the Roman doubling of consonants (e.g. *aggile* for *agile*; *rubbare* instead of *rubare* = to steal). The intervocalic *s* is always voiceless (e.g. *casa*) and *s* after liquid or nasal sounds is affricated like *z* (e.g. *penzare* for *pensare* = to think and, at a more 'popular' level, also voiced: *borsa* becomes 'bor[ts]a' and 'bor[dz]a'.). The sounds /t/, /k/ and /p/ and the voiceless affricate /ts/ ('ch') become voiced (e.g. *tembo* for *tempo* = time; *cambana* for *campana* = bell; *angora* for *ancora* = still, yet). Syntactic features include the addition of an indirect complement particle *a* after words not requiring one (e.g. *amico a me* for *amico mio* = my friend; *figlio a te* for *figlio tuo* = your son) and intransitive verbs may become transitive (e.g. *correre la motocicletta* for *far correre la motocicletta* = to speed the motorbike up); the use of indirect complements after transitive verbs (e.g. *vedere a Pietro* for *vedere Pietro* = to see Pietro). Verbal peculiarities include 'if' sentences constructed with the double conditional (e.g. *se vorrei potrei*) or the double subjunctive (*se volessi potessi* = if I wanted I could). Characteristic lexical features are *compare* for *padrino* (godfather); *faticare* for *lavorare* (to work); *mo'* for *ora* (now); *paesano* for *compaesano* (fellow villager); *stare* for *essere* (to be) and *tenere* for *avere* (to have).

Linguistic minorities

Minority languages at the time of unification (1861) were Catalan in Sardinia, French and Occitan in Piedmont and the Aosta Valley, Albanian and Greek in southern regions and Sicily, and their speakers formed 2.1% of a population of 38 million. With the annexation of Veneto in 1866, new communities of speakers of 'foreign languages' were added, and after the First World War (in 1918) and the Second (in 1945) more communities from the areas around Trento and Trieste became 'Italian'. The historical minority languages now include those acquired after the two World Wars (German mainly in South Tyrol, Slovene and Serbo-Croat in the provinces of Trieste and Gorizia). If, to the number of these speakers, those of the domestic minority languages were added, the present overall figure would amount to 4.8% of the Italian population (Francescato, 1993). Domestic minority languages include Ladin, Friulian, Sardinian, since they have traditionally been regarded as distinct Romance languages, rather than dialects, although only Ladin enjoys official status outside Italy.

Domestic minority languages

Ladin

Several varieties of Ladin – which is of Raetro-Romance origin – are spoken in some valleys in Switzerland (where this minority language enjoys official status), in Italy in the province of Bolzano (where it receives some support), and in the provinces of Treviso and Belluno, where it was granted official status (*Corriere della Sera*, 25 October 1999). However, it continues to be exposed to the penetration of the national language. The number of Ladin speakers in Italian territory has been calculated at about 30,000 (Francescato, 1993), but their dispersion in mountain valleys makes language loyalty and community solidarity difficult. The situation is further complicated by the writing system that is largely inconsistent since it reflects very different dialect variations.

Friulian

Friulian is the second largest domestic minority language in Italy, with approximately 700,000 speakers scattered across different parts of the Friuli Venezia-Giulia region, living more frequently in mountain areas than in cities, and often in contact with other minority language speakers (especially of German). The Friulian-speaking community strives to maintain the use of the three languages – Italian, German, Friulian (Denison, 1972). Friulian has long been granted the status of language of Raetro-Romance origin, and benefited from the 1999 official recognition granted to all historical and domestic minorities. Francescato (1991) feels that this idiom is maintained largely because of its speakers' loyalty to the rural past, even within areas that are no longer rural. This would explain the declining competence noted among most young people, as they are less interested in that past. There are two further reasons for this. Firstly, when the written forms closely reproduce the local variations, there is a high degree of inconsistency. Secondly, when teachers opt for the supra-local orthography of a hybrid koiné, the language seems artificial. Because of the rapidly developing economy of the region, people tend to adopt the national language at work. This is not true for the old steel and clockwork villages (Maniago and Pesariis), where the use of the minority language has developed a special relationship with occupational skills and family traditions.

Sardinian

Sardinian has long been recognised by linguists as a distinct language of the Italo-Romance family, and is the most widely spoken minority language of Italy with a million and a half speakers. But it has always been treated as a dialect, both in schools and in Italian society. The separate dialects (Gallurese and Sassarese in the north and Campidanese and Logudorese in the south) have distinct identities and variants, and this has not facilitated the recognition of an orthographic koiné to be adopted as the written language of all Sardinian speakers. Today, many young people are still competent in Sardinian, and use it more frequently than other Italians use their local dialects, but this circumstance is not generally expected to provide secure support for long-term maintenance of this minority language, or of the stable conditions of bilingualism in Sardinia.

Historic minority languages

With the spread of the national language, the pattern that has emerged for most minority speakers is bilingualism with Italian in compartmentalised diglossic conditions, though with a general, slight shift towards the expansion of Italian and the decline of minority languages. However, the language roles and repertoires of these bilingual speakers vary greatly even within different communities of the same minority language. Moreover, communities are often trilingual or quadrilingual rather than bilingual, for example, with two varieties of the minority language as well as of Italian, or two varieties of both.

Occitan and Franco-Provençal

Occitan and Franco-Provençal are two languages of the Gallo-Romance area that has French as its main language at present. Occitan developed from old Provençal and in present-day Italy is still spoken in the western part of Piedmont, whereas Franco-Provençal is mainly concentrated in the north-western Italian Alps, i.e. in the Aosta Valley, a region which acquired autonomous status in 1945. In these communities of speakers, these two important minority languages used to be alternated with a local French patois, whilst standard French was the traditional language in schools and churches. Italian was usually reserved for official use and for higher education. This balance has gradually changed, especially in the Aosta Valley, where political support for bilingualism and bilingual education is reinforcing French at the expense of the Franco-Provençal variety.

German

German can be found in a number of valleys along almost all of the Alpine range, but at the present time the main concentration is in the non-urban areas of South Tyrol as, in the past, Italian families from other regions were encouraged to migrate to large towns in the area. While the formation of other German-speaking communities in northern Italy dates back to the 12th or 13th centuries, the presence of German in the South Tyrol region is not due to migration but to the political incorporation of the area after the First World War. The other German dialects, like the Bavarian-Austrian dialect spoken in the mountains from the Aosta Valley to northern Friuli, were used only as the languages of religious functions, and their contemporary use is increasingly endangered by the growing dominance of Italian. Since German provides these isolated communities with far better job opportunities, it has become more attractive, particularly to the younger generations.

The German-speaking communities in South Tyrol are in favour of the preservation of German even at the cost of maintaining, or spreading, its use in domains – like education and work – which may seriously hamper the use of the national language. These communities are in the majority, and Italian-speaking families are only slightly more numerous in the main urban centres (Bolzano-Bozen, Merano-Meran, Bressanone-Brixen, Laives-Leifers). Under the 1992 agreement, separate schools were set up for the two communities. This means, effectively, that the agreed education policy for the area has not taken on the challenge of fostering better community relations, nor of using two languages in schools to develop bilingualism. This is clearly not a forward-looking solution, as the teaching of the other language as a curriculum subject in monolingual education can hardly offer the intellectual mastery of German to the Italian minority or of Italian to the local German-speaking majority. This is not a good prospect for majority–minority collaboration. Nor does it augur well according to Fishman (1977) for full socioeconomic integration of the region within the national community.

Slovene and Croation

In the Eastern Alps of Friuli, Friulian as well as Slovene are also spoken. These multilingual communities are increasingly exposed to a third language (Italian) and occasionally, but to a lesser extent recently, to a fourth language (German) (Francescato, 1993). There are 25,000 Slovene speakers in the areas around Trieste and 28,000 around Gorizia. Slovene is protected by a political agreement, which establishes the teaching of the language in schools. The Slovene-speaking villages in the areas around Udine were not included in the agreement (Aiello, 1984). Croatian is spoken further south in the Molise region, where a community of migrants settled in the 15th century after fleeing the Dalmatian coast, which was being invaded by the Turks. This minority language has been heavily influenced by local Italian dialects and has evolved independently from mainland Croatian. This makes it more difficult to teach the language. Teaching is currently undertaken on a voluntary basis to its community of 3000 people.

Albanian

The Albanian minority live in a few isolated areas in the southern regions and in Sicily. There is a total population of 100,000 speakers of a variety of Albanian. They have maintained their minority community language, although this has been heavily influenced by contact with Italian, and they have developed a flourishing literary tradition. There are currently two major difficulties concerning the educational support for this language. One is the lack of political protection (although Albanian benefits from regional government measures). Another is the distance between the communities, which has hindered the koineisation of the dialects and the identification of common models for language description and teaching purposes.

Greek

Greek is spoken in parts of Calabria and Apulia, but it is rated highly neither by the speakers themselves nor by their neighbours. It is still controversial whether these communities are descended from much larger Greek-speaking settlements pre-dating the spread of Latin (Magna Graecia) or whether they are more recent. This minority language today is, however, diversified into several dialects lacking a common focus. Greek in southern Italy is separated from Italian and its dialects, and remains the medium for informal home interaction, but it is in rapid decline because of discontinuous and fragmentary exposure to incomplete repertoires. The more privileged sectors of the communities are completely Italianised and this acts as an additional factor in the stigmatisation of the language, especially in the villages of Calabria (Sobrero, 1982).

Catalan

About half of the people living in the town of Alghero on the northern coast of Sardinia (40,000 altogether) have some competence in a Catalan variety, which is to be expected since this town was held by Catalan settlers from 1354 onwards, and for some hundred years interethnic marriages with the population of either Sardinian or Corsican origin were forbidden. Today the new generations seem less committed and sometimes have receptive competence only. Although the cultural contacts with the city of Barcelona have increased over the past years, Catalan is currently under pressure from Italian, and to some extent from Sardinian.

New ethnolinguistic minorities

Rom people

The Rom people in Italy are somewhere between the domestic minorities and the new ethnolinguistic groups of immigrants, not only because their ethnic origin from India is very distant, but also because their number has increased considerably since the wars in the Balkan area, where they used to enjoy more hospitality than in most countries. At the present time, in Italy they occupy a position that is comparable neither to that of domestic minorities nor to that of the new ethnolinguistic groups, in that their language serves a cryptic function as well as one of cultural transmission and can survive as long as the individual chooses to remain in the clan and resist all forms of eradication from its traditions. The leading specialist on the language and customs of this group (Hancock, 1979) pointed out that the corruption of the Rom heritage and identity also includes initiatives inspired in most countries by the local church and volunteers' associations that aim to teach the Roms to live differently. This is their position in Italy (De Mauro, 1987), although it is difficult to generalise a single pattern, as there are old communities that chose Italy as a territory for their travels a long time ago, while other clans have arrived after the diaspora from Eastern

Europe. With the first, the language presents substantial contacts with Italian and/ or dialects but has achieved stabilisation. With the later arrivals, the Rom variety and/or the bilingual repertoire may not include Italian, but individual adults are more vulnerable to pressure, and their children are more likely to be assimilated into conventional education. Since the Rom groups have distinct needs and aspirations, their situation is, perhaps, not comparable to that of other immigrant groups.

Foreign immigrants

Italy, which used to be a country of emigrants, has become a country of immigration over the past 20 years. Since the early 1990s, the phenomenon has reached such proportions that it has attracted the attention of several sectors of linguists and educationists (Chini, 2004). The question of the autonomy of a variety developed by immigrants exposed to Italian and dialects in Italy is still under debate, and the attention of scholars is concentrated on the range of dialects, varieties and sub-varieties of Italian with which adults come into contact in different parts of Italy (Giacalone Ramat, 1993). The multitude of first languages of diverse ethnic groups providing different linguistic backgrounds and materials for transfer suggest such a wide spectrum of linguistic variations and communicative styles that it is hard to identify common patterns of unguided second language acquisition and common forms of simplifications in immigrants' Italian. The phenomenon of contact with the dialects is more evident, but there are contradictory developments, as immigrants react to them differently in different parts of Italy and at different stages of their time in Italy. Examples of rejection of the dialects are reported when the immigrant has been in the country long enough to make conscious choices (Vedovelli, 1990). But in the first months after arrival, especially when large groups are housed in hostels situated in areas where the dialect is predominant, the dialect is assimilated and its idioms are transferred to other areas when the migrants move, often aggravating communication and relations with the local community (Chini, 2004; Tosi, 1995).

A number of new issues are emerging from the language situation of new immigrants in southern Europe, when compared to old migration to central and northern Europe. The linguistic background of the new migrants is usually far more complex than that of the old migrants, who mostly came from rural areas and were usually monolingual dialect speakers. In most cases at the present time, immigrants are not monolingual on their arrival. Besides the village dialect, they know the national language and have had substantial education and/or urbanisation in the country of origin. They often have rudimentary knowledge in an international language, which is usually English for most Asians, and French for North Africans, although competence is often far from fluency levels. When there is fluency, it is normally in a contact or creolised variety.

With regard to language maintenance, attitudes vary depending on group experiences and personal circumstances. This marks another difference from what is known about old migration. Chinese people lack the international experience of other English-speaking Asian groups but are the most likely (through their family ties and community infrastructures) to maintain the linguistic heritage necessary to transmit Chinese values and traditions. Philippine people in Italy usually have a greater experience of education, internal migration, urbanisation and use of English alongside their ethnic and standard languages. Because

Table 2 Continents of origin of immigrant populations, 2001

Continent	Number	Percentage of total	Continent	Number	Percentage of total
European Union	147,495	10.8	South and Central Asia	104,893	7.7
Central and Eastern Europe	394,090	28.9	West Asia	18,614	1.4
Other European countries	22,300	1.6	Total Asia	259,783	19.1
Total Europe	563,885	41.4	North America	46,073	3.4
North Africa	243,846	17.9	Central and South America	112,133	8.2
East Africa	25,351	1.9	Total America	158,206	11.6
West Africa	89,036	6.5	Oceania	2,461	0.2
Central and South Africa	8,365	0.6	Stateless	824	0.1
Total Africa	366,598	26.9	Not known	10,873	0.8
East Asia	136,276	10.0	Total	1,362,630	100.0

Source: *Caritas/Dossier Statistico Immigrazione* from Home Office data (2001)

of the political and linguistic fragmentation of their own community and the Roman Catholic religion they share with Italians, they normally aim at integration and make much less effort for linguistic and cultural maintenance than the Chinese. The Arabic-speaking groups from North Africa normally speak national variations of Arabic, which are not always mutually comprehensible, and are often complemented by a completely different tribal language (e.g. Berber for the Moroccans). Although the Moroccans are the largest single group of immigrants in Italy, it is difficult to generalise their attitudes and aspirations. Some wish to settle, others are used to seasonal migration. Some have a strong sense of the family; others can live long distances from their families for months or even years. Some have no wish to be identified with Western culture and values; others seek full cultural integration, for their children if not for themselves. The same heterogeneity can be found in the aspirations of Eastern Europeans, for whom immigration is usually an individual rather than a community project. A major variable in language use and attitudes towards maintenance is whether they left with the family or alone. South Americans have in common a strong inclination to accelerate their integration into Italy. They can do so better than other immigrants, either because they are of Italian origin themselves or because of their high level fluency in standard Italian.

The picture, which is summarised by continent in Table 2, is complex and does not lend itself to easy generalisations, though some clear differences emerge from the pattern of settlements of immigrants in Italy as compared to that of other countries of older immigration. In Italy, the ethnic minority communities, and their attitudes towards language aspirations and cultural maintenance, will be ruled by regional and urban factors to a much greater extent than elsewhere.

The reason for this is that Italy continues to maintain a strong polycentric structure, where cultural and emotional inclinations of people are still dominated by
features of regional and urban rather than national identity.

Italian-based lingua francas and creoles

Round the Mediterranean

The UK-based Maltese language historian Joseph Cremona (1922–2003),
who devoted his life to the study of Italian-based lingua francas around the
Mediterranean, always insisted on the plural ending -s of the term 'lingua
francas'. More specifically, Cremona distinguished between a folk and an elite
use of Tuscan-based Italian in this context. The former spread, mainly in its
spoken form, when uneducated and semi-literate people, especially sailors and
merchants, moving from one port of the Mediterranean to the next, needed to
communicate with local populations but could not speak the language. The
term 'lingua franca' relates here (the folk version) to a hybrid form of
Tuscan-based Italian. The elite version was based on a much less hybrid form of
Tuscan-based Italian which was written as well as spoken, and functioned as a
lingua franca among educated travellers, including diplomats and officers
from embassies and legations, in need of a common language for negotiations.
These low-status and high-status varieties of Tuscan Italian were regularly
spoken around the Mediterranean over a long period of time, starting possibly
with the Crusades in the less prestigious spoken forms and ending in the 18th
century, in the more prestigious written form, when French became the recognised international language for foreign affairs and was spoken and written by
diplomats of all countries. The less prestigious contact variety was less close to
Tuscan Italian, whereas the later lingua franca used by literate embassy officers
and diplomats could rely not only on the written forms of Tuscan literature, but
also on the models of administrative and diplomatic documents compiled in
the Italian peninsula, and based on this language. Cremona (2002) found, from
a wide range of reports, that the Italian-based lingua francas around the Mediterranean adopted elements of Tuscan Italian to an increasing extent, even
when travellers or diplomats were Genoese or Venetians colonising islands in
the Aegean sea or parts of the Dalmatian coast. In such cases the reference to this
Italian-based pidgin, or contact variety included terms such as *franco*, *parlar
franco*, *lingua franca* or even *italiano corrotto*. This hybrid language survived for
many centuries, and it must still have been heard in 18th century Venice if it reap-
pears, for comic effects, in the 'foreign talk' of the Turkish, Arab and Levantine
characters of Goldoni's comedies (Cremona, 2002).

The Italian-based lingua franca in its more codified form was the medium of
negotiations between the diplomacies of the Western powers and the Turkish
Ottoman Empire. It was used regularly either in oral interpretation or for direct
negotiations by delegates of different first languages, or as an interlanguage in
which contracts and agreements were initially stipulated before final translation.
Cremona examined a huge number of documents kept in the archives of Tunis
(in his words 'the Shanghai of the sixteenth century'), and found that, out of some
15,000 documents, two thirds were written in Italian and one third in French. It is
only after 1690, he says, that the proportion of French and Italian documents is

reversed. From this documented spread of Italian at the end of 17th century, with the dual role of the lingua franca for merchants and seafaring people and as a diplomatic language between the great powers around the Mediterranean, Cremona comes to a twofold conclusion. On the one hand the businessmen, merchants, heads of chancery and consuls, who needed to draft carefully their written contracts in Italian, must have been equally competent in spoken Italian; on the other hand, the knowledge of Italian as a lingua franca spoken by wider circles of the inhabitants of the Mediterranean coasts, among people whose native language was not a dialect of the peninsula, suggests that 150 years later, at the time of unification, the figure of a mere 2% to 3% of speakers of Italian, based on the literacy data, is an underestimation of the spread of the language within the peninsula itself.

Italian in the New World

Origin and first interpretations

As English is one of the most widely spoken languages, and as Italy has provided one of the largest immigrant communities, the interaction between Italian and English outside Italy was bound to produce significant opportunities for language contact. One noteworthy feature is that the geographical distance between Italian communities living in English-speaking countries has not prevented there being considerable affinities in the language spoken by people of Italian descent in places as far apart as North America and Australia. But the fact that very large numbers of speakers make use of this mixed language in their everyday communication has not led to any status recognition of this contact variety (Bettoni, 1981; Brault, 1964; Correa-Zoli, 1981; Rando, 1967, 1968, 1973; Saltarelli, 1986). Yet the strong sense of cultural identity associated with this mixed language has enabled communities around the world to maintain their 'Italianness' through this 'incorrect' but highly meaningful and expressive language, rather than through English – in which they are often competent but with which they have few emotional ties, or standard Italian for which they feel more emotional ties but in which they are rarely competent (Boissevain, 1976; Di Pietro, 1977).

Several historical and linguistic issues have been discussed in regard to the Anglo-Italian contact variety (Haller, 1993). One major feature, which makes this Italian-English mixed variety distinctive but not unique among other language contacts, is the interplay with a third language. At the time of emigration, most Italians who left the country as young, uneducated people of rural extraction, spoke a local dialect rather than the national language. Thus the mechanism of language interpenetration was further complicated by the interplay between the village dialect and standard Italian. There were two source languages: the dialect, which is the 'low' language and expresses the rural traditions of the local community; and standard Italian which is a higher status language, marked by its urban and national prestige. The interaction between the rural dialect, the national standard and English abroad is linguistically unusual, and interesting, because virtually all Italians were native speakers of dialects, and at the time of emigration they were substantially cut off from the standard language. What happened, consequently, is that the language habits and experiences which were alien to village life, and would come to be expressed by standard forms via cultural and linguistic urbanisation – as indeed happened in Italy in the second half of the 20th century – were worked into the fabric of a foreign language.

The first systematic observations of the spread of this phenomenon date back to the early part of the last century (Migliorini, 1927), as large numbers of emigrants returned to Italy especially from the US in the first half of the century. Only much later, however, did linguists look at the returning emigrants' adjusted language with regard to the adaptation of English into local dialects (Tropea, 1983; Zamboni, 1986). Menarini, looking at the contacts between English and Italian dialects overseas (1939) and at their imports in Italy (1940), came to the conclusion (1947) that the dialectal fragmentation of Italian communities in the US could not provide a solid basis for language maintenance outside Italy. He suggested that the Italo-American versions of dialects spoken in the US are creolised varieties of Italian and claimed that this Italo-American creole is conspicuously affected by English lexical elements, but that the main phonological, morphological and syntactic structures of the dialect remain substantially unaffected. He recalls these examples: *sainame la ceca* from 'sign the cheque for me', *ho brocco una legga* from 'I have broken a leg'. Following Weinreich's (1953) study on language contacts which distinguishes between interferences of *parole* and of *langue*, using Saussure's terms, other studies agreed that the two language systems should not be viewed in isolation. This approach influenced writers like Bettoni in Australia (1981), and also my own work in the Bedford urban area in England (Tosi, 1984).

Speaker competence and language status

In the Bedford study, causes other than the need to avoid dialectal differences within the Italian community, or the wish to show involvement in the English environment, seem responsible for the rapid adoption of English. For the majority of Italians who immigrated into Britain soon after the Second World War, the village vernacular could not provide the language they needed to talk about their new 'urbanised' lives. Standard Italian, of course, had the necessary repertoire, but most immigrants did not speak it. Consequently, in interaction between Italians, even if the dialects were similar and mutually intelligible, there were frequent transfers from English. These words or phrases were used to describe experiences and situations that had not been part of village life. (Similarly, fellow villagers who moved to large northern cities in Italy gradually transferred from standard Italian, which was the language of that urban environment).

Standard English	English transfers	Italian meaning
graduate	*graduato*	of higher rank
to go on strike	*straccare*	to tire

Outside Italy, when the dialect is considered inadequate for the status or the topic, a transfer from English is usually preferred, and may be used when speaking to native speakers of standard Italian. If there is an equivalent word in standard Italian, or one very similar in meaning, the transfer is successful and the speaker sounds fluent and competent. But should the meaning in standard Italian diverge from the English meaning, despite the similarity in form, then the outcome is a false cognate and this phenomenon sounds strange to a standard Italian speaker if (1) the only discrepancy concerns register, or (2) real misunderstanding occurs when it involves meaning.

Standard English	English transfers	Standard Italian
(1) list	*lista*	*elenco*
celebrate	*celebrare*	*festeggiare*
paint	*pittura*	*vernice*
desk	*desco*	*scrivania*
court	*corte*	*tribunale*
(2) library	*libreria* (bookshop)	*biblioteca*
attitude	*attitudine* (aptitude)	*atteggiamento*
pretend	*pretendere* (claim)	*fare finta*

When an equivalent word does not exist in standard Italian, the transfers from English still produce Italian-sounding forms, occasionally incorporating a similar meaning or a semantic association.

Unsuccessful transfers

affogarsi nella nebbia	(drowning in the fog)
fare l'ingheggio	(to become engaged)
prendere una ciansa	(to take a chance)

Successful transfers

cancellare un volo	(*annullare un volo*)
implementare un piano	(*realizzare un piano*)
supportare un'iniziativa	(*sostenere un'iniziativa*)

In terms of urban usage in Italy, the new borrowings can be grouped into three categories: (1) those which are considered utterly unacceptable since they are neither recognised nor understood by speakers of standard Italian; (2) false cognates that have become quite well known among Italians who are familiar with English and an English-speaking country – indeed, some may have become acceptable Anglicisms in Italy since they appeal to the jet-set and their services (e.g. cancellare un volo used by Alitalia staff); (3) paronyms which have entered scientific usage due to the influence of English associated with the lack of adequate standardised terminology in Italian. *Testare* from 'to test' is a classic example of an early borrowing whose low status has now been enhanced by technical use.

(1)	(2)	(3)
graduato	*cancellare*	*testare*
graduate	to cancel	to test

This new Italian repertoire of transfers from English is, for Italian immigrants in any English-speaking country, the result of alienation from models of urban language in Italy. But there is one ironic, though significant, issue that affects transfer evaluation. The extent to which such attempts are considered successful is determined less by the currency of linguistic contacts abroad and more by the status they carry within specialist groups and elite speakers in Italy.

When changes are in contrast with the evolution of the linguistic system in the country of origin, a purist tends to see them as language erosion. The opposite view sees them as language enrichment, since they expand the speaker's repertoire. This is actually a controversy about the status of language as much as an issue of speakers' competence. The social status of any contact variety depends partly on the societal attitudes to ethnic minorities and mixed ethnic identities. In the New World, the acceptance of a 'hyphenated' identity is welcomed as a by-product of a mixed cultural tradition. Being Italo-American, Italo-Canadian or Italo-Australian is a respectable way to represent a successful community that does not wish to be identified either with the Anglo-Celtic majority, or with their nationals in the country of origin (Child, 1943). Britain, however, like other European countries, does not recognise mixed cultural identities. Thus, the members of her minority communities still face the alternative – and the tension – between two identities typically expressed by the usual question: 'Do you feel Italian or English?' The different attitudes of European countries towards the status of this contact variety and its educational value are made clear by the debate on *italiese* (from *italiano* and *inglese*) also known professionally as 'Italian as a community language'.

This debate has occupied academics and media people in many multiethnic societies from the 1980s onwards. From a multicultural perspective, schools must take into account the true mother tongue of each child when he or she starts. The further away community organisation and school policies are from this view, the more likely it is that the language competence of ethnic minority children will not be correctly understood and this will hinder efforts for language maintenance. For example, Italian teachers and educators who may have been trained to appreciate dialect diversity in Italy often tend to stigmatise the mixed language of Italians outside Italy. They take as norms of reference the mixture of language, dialects and varieties in Italy today. In comparison, the bilingualism of a speaker who mixes a rural dialect and a foreign language is interpreted as a linguistic deficiency. The opposite view, focusing on the value of the child's mixed repertoire as the medium of communication for informal family and community relations, claims that the natural speech-community of such a child is neither Italy nor the majority environment of the new country. Thus, the contact variety adopts and mixes rules derived from the norms and vocabulary of two distinct languages and maintains its function as an effective language in the child's early development. This competence has been provocatively but poignantly defined as 'bilingualism as a first language' (Swain, 1972). Attitudes to Italian-English contact varieties in different national settings are reflected by an evolution in terminologies (Tosi, 1979). Australia was the first to pioneer the term 'community language', abandoning the notion of 'immigrant', or 'migrant language'. For a long time, the United States used the term 'non-English mother tongues', introduced by Fishman (1966). In Canada, the predominant term is still 'heritage language'. Britain, too, moved from the more traditional 'mother tongue' to the more innovative 'community language' in the mid-1980s. This term now tends to be preferred throughout the English-speaking world as it focuses professional attention on two important educational aspects: learning and use. These are different from either first language use or foreign language learning (Tosi, 1986b).

Sign languages in Italy and the Vatican

Italian is one of the 14 Deaf Sign Languages in the world. It is partially intelligible with French Sign Language but it is not intelligible with American Sign Language. In Italy there are regional differences, but signers from different regions seem to communicate fluently. Italian sign language is normally used in families and clubs but is not officially recognised in Italy, though there are a number of specific laws which include reference to the use of a sign language interpreter. The Italian Deaf Association has prepared a proposal relating to the recognition of sign language and is in the process of preparing Members of Parliament for their proposal. There is no estimate available for Italian sign language users, but in the country there are some 877,000 individuals with registered hearing problems, and 92,000 deaf-mute people.

Another sign language is that listed by the Vatican amongst its official languages (together with Italian and Latin), but it should not be confused with the language of disabled people. It is the monastic sign language used by religious communities which functions as a means of communicating while maintaining the vows of silence. The Vatican source specifies that it is used especially in Europe and as a second language only as, clearly, it does not have native 'speakers'.

Religions and their main languages

Italy is predominately Roman Catholic (98%) with established Protestant and Jewish communities and a growing community of Muslim immigrants, with a small number of converts.

Roman Catholics

Latin did not become the language of Christian ritual until the 6th century. The effect of using Latin through the centuries when its spoken varieties gradually became distinct languages was to make the liturgy the preserve of the clergy, so that the participation of non-clericals in the religious functions was purely passive. The views of Popes on the Latin language even in recent times are exemplified by the following declarations:

- Pope Pius X (*Moto Propio on the Restoration of Church Music*, 22 November 1903): 'The language of the Roman Church is Latin. It is therefore forbidden to sing anything whatever in the vernacular in solemn liturgical functions'.
- Pope Pius XI (*Officiorum Omnium*, 1922): 'The Church – precisely because it embraces all nations and is destined to endure until the end of time – of its very nature requires a language which is universal, immutable, and non-vernacular'.
- Pope Pius XII (*Mediator Dei*): 'The use of the Latin language affords at once an imposing sign of unity and an effective safeguard against the corruption of true doctrine'.

- Pope John XXIII (encyclical *Veterum Sapientia*, 1962): 'Of its very nature, Latin is most suitable for promoting every form of culture among peoples. It gives rise to no jealousies. It does not favour any one nation, but presents itself with equal impartiality to all and is equally acceptable to all'.

Even Pope John XXIII spoke of the special value of Latin which had proved so admirable a means for the spreading of Christianity and which had proved to be a bond of unity for the Christian peoples of Europe. Yet, to initiate renewal in the Roman Catholic Church, he convoked a general council, the Second Vatican Council (1962–65). The chief reforms in church practices included changes in liturgical language, from Latin to the vernacular. Since then standard Italian has been used instead of Latin except in areas inhabited by official linguistic minorities. The abandonment of Latin as a result of the second Vatican Council excited deep antagonism; one sees in the Latin liturgy an image, cherished by many, of the timeless and changeless Roman Catholic Church. Yet, it was argued that the restoration of the vernacular should restore to the liturgy two functions that it had in the early centuries: to instruct converts and to confirm members in their faith.

However, Pope John Paul II told an international group of pilgrims in Rome on 28 July 1999: 'We strongly encourage you all that, by diligent study and effective teaching, you may pass on like a torch the understanding, love and use of this immortal language in your own countries'.

Protestants

One more specifically Italian group is the Waldensians. The name comes from the founder, Peter Waldo. This movement began in the 12th century, based on the canons of poverty and preaching. There were large followings in France. Many believers were forced to flee to northern Italy, and from here the movement spread to other parts of Europe. After adhering to the Reformation in 1532, the Waldensians became strongly influenced by Calvinism. They were persecuted during the Counter Reformation. Initial tolerance came in 1848 with the Edict issued by Carlo Alberto, King of Piedmont. This was incorporated into the 1929 law that specified which religions were to be accepted in Italy. The state recognised the independence of the Waldensian Church in 1967. There has been unification with the Italian Methodist Church. The itinerant preachers were called *barbe*, a dialect Piedmont term for 'uncle', meaning a distinguished person. The number of Protestants living in Italy has greatly increased with recent immigration. One estimate is that Protestant churches have 60,000 members and that the Waldensian church is the largest. In the cities it is easy to find many different Protestant churches, for example Anglican, Church of Scotland, Lutheran and Baptist churches.

Jews

Italy has the oldest Jewish community in Europe. A large number of Jews came under the leadership of Judas Maccabaeus in the second century BCE. Later, thousands were brought as slaves to help build the Colosseum after the victory of the Romans over the Jews of Jerusalem in AD70. Their fortunes fluctuated over the following centuries. During the 13th century, for instance,

Pope Innocent III decreed that they should wear distinguishable marks on their clothing (a yellow circle for men and two blue stripes for women). The first ghetto was set up in Venice in 1516 (the word 'ghetto' comes from *gheto*, the name given to a Venetian quarter because of the foundry there). Many Jews left Italy during and after the Second World War. About 8000 were deported to Auschwitz (see for example Primo Levi's famous 1947 book *Se questo è un uomo*). Today, there are about 40,000 Jews, a large proportion of whom live in the capital. The community is mostly Sephardic. Jews have always studied Hebrew, and often they have speakers of other languages which are archaic forms of the vernaculars spoken where they lived or came from (e.g. Yiddish). In Italy, a Judeo-Italian contact variety, sometimes called Italkian, developed especially among the Jewish community in Rome: at the present time, there are only a few speakers who are able to use it fluently. Only 10% (about 4000) out of the total number of 40,000 Jews scattered throughout Italy occasionally use some elements of this contact variety in their speech which, for this reason and the lack of support, is considered nearly extinct.

Muslims and other immigrant groups

The Islamic religion is second after the Roman Catholic religion due to recent immigration, especially from north Africa. The major cities with people regularly practising the Islamic religion in recognised centres are Bari, Bologna, Catania, Florence, Genoa, Milan, Naples, Palermo, Rome, Turin and Venice. An estimate by the Caritas Association reports the distribution of religions among the immigrants with legal residence in Italy (Table 3).

Table 3 The religious affiliations of foreign residents

	No. of adherents	*Percentage*
Christians	1,281,489	50.3
Muslims	824,342	32.4
Other	441,905	17.3
Total	2,547,736	100.0

Since the 1980s, the largest group is constituted of Moroccans, but the more recent immigrants diversify substantially the common religious core, in attitudes, strictness and linguistic proximity between the native language and that of the Koran. In addition to people from the Maghreb, there are groups from Senegal, Nigeria, Egypt, Somalia, Iraq, Iran, Bangladesh, Pakistan, Bosnia, Macedonia and Albania, but there are also Kurds from Turkey and Rom people.

Among the 1,281,489 Christians from countries in Africa, South America, South-east Asia and Eastern Europe, 651,000 are Roman Catholics, 470,000 Orthodox, 114,000 Protestants and 46,000 Christians from other churches. The 441,905 foreign residents who reported other faiths (17.4%) include 60,996 Hindus (2.4%) 49,460 Buddhists (1.9%) 29,803 of other traditional faiths (1.2%), 6843 Jewish (0.3%), 297,803 with no declared religion (11.7%).

Language Spread: The Italianisation of Multilingual Italy

From unification to the Republic (1861–1946)

De Mauro (1970) was the first to suggest that the number of Italian speakers at the time of unification amounted to 2.5% of the total population (some 600,000 including 400,000 Tuscans and 70,000 Romans), while for 97.5% of the population Italian was a foreign language. Castellani (1982) claimed that there must have been a large sector of the population (some 10%) for whom Italian was neither a mother tongue nor a foreign language, who were able to understand it even without instruction and to use it as a second or additional language. Certainly, after unification the linguistic conservatism of rural communities was challenged by what became the most influential factor in the spread of the national language: internal migration. There were two major patterns of mobility. One direction of migration was across regions, mainly from the rural south to the industrialised north; the other was the urbanisation that took place in all regions, involving the general move from rural areas to small towns or large cities. If the intraregional mobility brought a challenge to the linguistic isolation of many dialect-speaking communities, inter-regional migration provided the major impulse for the promotion of the national language with the function of a true lingua franca to overcome the problems of the country's widespread linguistic diversity. For De Mauro, Italian towns modified the village vernaculars and evolved the local dialects into more regional forms. They provided the melting pots for contact between dialects that were not mutually accessible, especially when their speakers moved to different regions and from the south to the north. The adoption of Italian and the abandonment of the local language were welcomed by the literary and educated circles. Yet in the eyes of ordinary people and sometimes of the upper classes – especially where the local dialect was strongly supported by historical traditions – the affected attempt to Italianise everyday spoken language was seen as an expression of ostentation.

The role of Rome as the new capital – for centuries a centre of cosmopolitan clergy speaking Italian as a lingua franca – was not comparable to that of Paris, London or Madrid, because the polycentric structure of Italy before unification survived for so long. Indeed, regional capitals are still cultural foci at present, and they are more influential locally in matters of politics, economics or intellectual debate than is the national capital. Another area that experienced the sudden imposition of the national language was the bureaucratic state. In contrast to marked decentralisation, the first national governments imposed a highly centralised political and administrative structure. The adoption of common procedures and the appointment of administrators of different regional origin (though predominantly from the south) aimed to promote the national language, and to make employees loyal to the administration and to the national state. Schools were of course another major factor in the spread of the national language. The commitment shown by the school authorities to impose the 'good' models of the literary language led to such radical stigmatisation of the local dialects (called *malerba dialettale* or 'dialectal weeds'), that for the first 100 years the mastery of the national language in schools was used as an instrument of social selection. The national service in the unified army prescribed the sole use of the national language, and servicemen were posted to a different area, so as to encourage the development of a sense of national, rather than local, identity and so that Italy would have a supraregional army in times of social unrest or war. The national language found another major source of impulse in the First World War. The need to replace local dialects with a common language became urgent: World War I highlighted the difficulty of commanding a national army which did not share a national language, and also the dramatic disorientation of soldiers who were not supported by competent and understanding military authorities. With the rhetoric and patriotism inherited from a long war, Italy entered the most unfortunate phase of language deprivation and linguistic nationalism under Fascism.

Changes during Fascism and democracy

Though Fascism left a marked heritage in the style of communication with the public, its policies had no real strength since the dialects were still predominant among the vast majority of the population. If a language shift did take place from the dialect to the national language in these 20 years, it was limited to the upper and middle classes in the major urban centres, where the regime was able to introduce a trend of linguistic conformity via its nationalistic ideology. For the rural masses and people living in small centres, the Fascist Government reduced the opportunities of access to the national language for short-sighted motives of political propaganda. For example, emigration abroad was banned to facilitate national demographic growth, causing large communities of southerners to be confined to their linguistic isolation. Internal migration, too, was substantially reduced by new regional programmes of economic self-sufficiency. This dramatically limited the urbanisation of the rural populations, who remained confined to agricultural occupations in socially and linguistically backward environments.

The new democratic Constitution (1948) reintroduced the freedom of the press, the right of trade union and political representation and a system of general education that helped to break down the barriers that had effectively prevented many Italians from participating in the life of their national community. Once these fundamental opportunities had been re-established, the linguistic diversity of the country re-emerged as an important social and educational problem. From the early 1950s to the late 1960s, however, the national language found unprecedented impetus as a result of industrialisation and urbanisation, and by way of the new popular channel of information and entertainment, the television.

Industrialisation, urbanisation and the media

This accelerated spread of the national language through television attracted the attention of many writers and intellectuals. Pier Paolo Pasolini was among the first to recognise the new process of language change in a country that had been traditionally divided between spoken dialects and the written language of academic and intellectual elites. In a much-quoted article of 1964, *Nuove questioni linguistiche*, summing up the effect of the new socio-linguistic transformations, he provocatively announced '*l'italiano è finalmente nato!*' (Italian finally is born!). This new Italian was not, Pasolini said, based on ordinary language, nor did it show that the true culture of the masses had been integrated within the national community. It was a language created by capitalism and functional within a capitalistic society, based in the industrial areas of the North. It was gradually imposing its models derived from use in commerce, industry and the media for adoption by people who could no longer escape the impact of a new technocratic society and would become Italy's first national language. Italo Calvino (1965) replied to Pasolini, and convincingly argued that the so-called new Italian was not a common idiom, nor could it be described as 'technological'. It was rather a linguistic deterioration due to an endemic Italian tendency to complicate language and make it more abstract and obscure (an antilanguage). If Pasolini was wrong, however, about the function of language change, he was right about the origin of the new language: the technological channels of modern communication (such as television) began to have more impact on people's language than the more traditional operators in language learning and language status (such as, respectively, schools and literature). In the mid-1960s, 50% of the population listened to the radio daily, and some programmes were followed by two thirds of the nation. More importantly, by 1964, 32 families out of every 100 watched television daily, and those who could not afford a TV set usually watched with other families or in public places, such as cafés. The radio had always tended to use more formal styles of speech, based on the written models. Now suddenly large sectors of the population became exposed to a very wide variety of styles – from the controlled, concise register of the news broadcasts to the colloquialisms of films and serials, to the improvisations of showmen or of politicians. As a result, many new speakers of Italian achieved unprecedented levels of structural homogenisation and lexical standardisation. But television also promoted popular respect for a new type of eloquence, which justified Pasolini's concern about the so-called 'technological' language and Calvino's dislike of this *antilingua*. Both writers criticised the national tendency to formalise communication styles even when it was unnecessary or actually counterproductive.

With the television, however, the national language situation did not become less complex. There were marked regional variations, an increasing tendency to borrow words from foreign languages, and a fast growing new generation of special languages, which came from the widespread practice of modifying both style and terminology when discussing topics requiring specialised knowledge. Everywhere the dialects lost ground, not only because they were perceived as outdated in a modern industrial society (significantly they were frequently ridiculed on TV) but also because parents tried to provide children with a strong basis in the national language, before they would be required to use it at school. Urbanisation brought many southerners to the more industrial North, modifying the linguistic composition of many towns such as Turin, Milan and Genoa, and turning them into melting pots for the promotion of the national language. Regional centres provided regional variations that made communication in the national language more attractive. The new media became more readily available and television soon made linguistic innovations acceptable – whether these came from the new urban life, the fast expanding North or from abroad. Changes, neologisms and foreign borrowings were associated with a more adventurous and challenging lifestyle (Gensini, 1985).

A turning point: 1968

The year 1968 is remembered for the students' revolts in universities in Europe and in North America. In Italy (as in France) it is the year in which the questioning of conventions and traditions of the whole society began, and it is widely perceived as a landmark between the old world and the new. Many Italians recognise that, at the end of the 1960s, the social tensions and the widespread desire for change eventually modified established conventions, eradicated outdated traditions, and spread deeper awareness of the cultural and political life of the national community. The fear of unemployment and the protest against élitist education became the favourite topics of the 1968 student movement. This soon assumed strong ideological radical leftist connotations, and its uncompromising revolutionary character challenged middle-class traditions and institutions that aimed to preserve the privileges of a 'bourgeois' society. Much has been said about 1968, but the cultural innovation of the student movement was neither that of popularising political language nor that of promoting stereotypes so as to make speeches in universities and factories more oratorical and persuasive. The movement was instrumental in changing social conventions rather than lexis and structures: it did so by creating opportunities for questioning issues of national interest across traditional boundaries (e.g. students in factories, workers in universities) and enjoyed desecrating the status of traditional and backward institutions (e.g. political speeches in theatres, assemblies and debates in schools, in the workplace or in churches, slogans and mottoes written as graffiti on every available wall). A whole generation who were in their twenties and thirties in the late 1960s learnt to voice their views about life and their aspirations, in ways that would have been considered irreverent in the past. The social changes that came about in the 1970s – most of which emerged from referenda expressing popular opposition to governments, such as the retention of the divorce law, the right to abortion, the workers' charter, and the new family statute stipulating equality between men and women against a tradition of fundamental inequality – would have been impossible without the confidence to speak in public assemblies gained by those who were students in 1968.

Another factor that modified communication and brought increased confidence when speaking in public or taking part in open debates was the proliferation of local radio stations against the previous monopoly of the state-controlled broadcasting corporation (*RAI*). The first 'free' or 'pirate' stations were not serious competition for the national corporation, which was richer in ideas and resources, but eventually they innovated everyday spoken language in two ways. They helped to spread the new models of authentic spoken language, with all the good and bad features of improvisation, as opposed to the prepared speech that was predominant in state programmes. In addition, the free radios spread the appeal of telephone interviews and public debates that made ungrammatical simplifications and colloquialisms more acceptable. These 'question time' programmes on television with ordinary people discussing current affairs, asking questions or expressing views, acquired immediate popularity, and surprised many viewers by bringing into their homes the unexpected diversity of the country, with regionalisms in language as well as in customs and traditions. By the mid-1970s one Italian in three watched television between 7.30

and 10 in the evening, but the percentage of Italians reading newspapers did not vary much between the 1950s and the 1970s (De Mauro, 1976). As many as 46% of Italians read no newspapers at all and only 24% read at least one book per year (40% in Spain, 56% in France, 63% in the UK and 69% in Switzerland). This showed the marked preference for the spoken rather than written language even for pleasure and entertainment.

Bilingualism in the last 50 years

During the 1950s and 1960s interregional contacts increased, replacing rural conditions of isolation and fostering a more generalised use of the national language. This came to be adopted more and more widely throughout the nation, not only as a written language, but also as a spoken one. Now that the large majority had become bilingual, because of the experience of exposure to, and use of, regional dialect and national language, the alternation of these two languages in everyday life facilitated the interpenetration of the two systems; this in turn consolidated some mixed regional forms that began to be regarded as more acceptable for local use than the over-rustic rural vernacular, or the too distant national language. In other words, the increasing availability of the national language in communities where the dialect was once the only medium of communication created a phenomenon that is more complex than a straightforward 'language shift' (that is, the new generation giving up their parents' dialect to adopt the national language as their everyday tongue) for two main reasons. Firstly, the way that the spoken language entered communities and interplayed with the dialects differed widely from region to region. Secondly, language change began with one generation and involved the succeeding generations, thereby affecting the local dialect, which continued to be spoken in the local community or at home, and began to approach forms of the national language, while the national language began to develop local features. This complex interplay of languages, as was pointed out by Lombardi-Satriani (1974), is explained not only by the older generation's strong loyalty to their local language, but also by the younger generation's desire to preserve regional solidarity alongside national identity. The point is well made by De Mauro who said that the regionalisation of local dialects shows that, after 150 years of post-unification promotion of the national language, Italy was no longer plurilingual but still strongly pluricentric (1970).

The linguist Pellegrini (1960) was the first to analyse the new condition of linguistic diversity that derived from Italian and dialects in contact. He pointed out that, in most parts of Italy, one needed to draw distinctions between four strata or varieties. As well as (1) the national language and (2) the local dialect, there was (3) a more inward-looking variety of the national language and (4) a more outward-looking variety of the local dialect. This situation was exemplified by Lepschy and Lepschy (1977). They took a single sentence ('Go home boys') as it would be pronounced in a Venetian village and made the following distinction (an attempt is made to reproduce the pronunciation). The allegedly standard form in the national language would be: *andáte a kkása ragáttsi* and in the local dialect: *ve káza túsi*. But in the same village people may also use a less local, more regional Venetian form such as: *nde káza tózi* and a less national, more regional Italian form such as: *andáte a káza ragási*. In this example, the lexical choice (*ragazzo* vs. *toso*) highlights the distinction between Italian and dialect; and there are grammatical and phonological differences which allow one to differentiate quite clearly between two types of dialect (local vs. regional, with and without metaphony and with different forms of *andare*) and the two types of Italian (national vs. regional: with and without double consonant sounds and affricates [ts/dz]).

Lepschy and Lepschy (1977: 14) also add that 'one can move between the two varieties of the standard and the two varieties of the dialect in an indefinite number of stages'. This practice is quite common, and switching from one variety to another (or switching from a single element of one to those of another) is a frequent phenomenon and may be used to introduce a more friendly form of address in a more careful style of speech (*andáte a káza túzi*) or an ironic touch in a more friendly context (*ve káza ragáttsi*).

It is important, however, to realise that the four or more varieties or repertoires (defined as 'keyboards' by Pellegrini, 1960) are not equally available to all speakers in a speech community. One could say that the speaker's ability to move from one variety to another depends not only upon individual skill and age, but also upon the community's social composition: the richness of the linguistic varieties and the stabilisation of diglossic conditions. In communities which, on account of their geographical location in mountain or rural areas, have remained substantially isolated, local dialects show little movement towards regional amalgamation ('koineisation'). When speakers have had only minimum exposure to the standard, they seem unable to transfer to national forms, even in a regional variety. Up to the last major wave of internal mobility in the 1960s, a high percentage of these people lived in rural communities, and were often illiterate.

The social dimension of language repertoires

Following Pellegrini's description of the new linguistic diversity, in the 1970s Mioni discussed access to diverse repertoires and suggested a typology with three major varieties of Italian and three varieties of dialect (1975). The first (I1) is adopted only in writing.

I1	=	literary Italian
I2	=	formal Italian
I3	=	colloquial Italian
D1	=	high status regional koiné
D2	=	urban dialect
D3	=	local vernacular

He identified the use of the six varieties by different social groups and suggested the following patterns:

```
I1 ⎫
I2 ⎬ upper class ⎫
I3 ⎭            ⎬ lower middle class ⎫
D1              ⎭                    ⎬ working class ⎫
D2                                  ⎭               ⎬ peasants
D3                                                  ⎭
```

Upper and middle class people moved easily between I1 and D1, using I3 and D3 for their less formal communication and also adopting D2 and D3 for extra-group functions. Lower middle class people mastered from I2 to D2 with occasional and often unsuccessful attempts to cover also I1. Peasants normally covered all the dialect varieties, D1, D2 and D3 and were occasionally able to approach forms of colloquial informal Standard. The urbanised working class stood between the lower middle class and the peasants.

Although Mioni pointed out that this representation is only an exemplification of mutable tendencies for oral production (except for I1), the diagram is useful for a general idea of the social distribution of repertoires available to social groups during the late 1960s and the early 1970s and shows that the high language for one social group can correspond to the low language of another. By the 1970s, the process of socioeconomic transformation that turned the country into a modern and competitive industrialised society, and moved large sectors of the population from areas of poverty to urban centres, was virtually completed. This movement was one of the major factors responsible for the gradual decline of local vernaculars and the growth of three strata of varieties between these vernaculars and the national language. The three repertoires that became available to an increasing number of urbanised people with manual or middle class occupations are (1) the regional dialect koiné, (2) regional Italian and (3) 'popular' Italian, a simplification of the national language based on tangentially national, rather than regional rules. The diffusion of (3) is due to various conditions, ranging from the spread of literacy to the increased need to use the national language outside the region of origin (Berruto, 1983).

From the 1970s onwards, Italian linguists have been trying to agree upon a new typology to describe the language of the many Italians who have not achieved a full command of the whole range of repertoires in the national language but who have managed to move from the (lowest) varieties of their local dialects to the mastery of the functional repertoires of the national language. This language change has largely been supported by new conditions of socioeconomic emancipation due to wider educational opportunities and higher standards of living. Where urbanisation and invasion by the media was not accompanied by the growth of meaningful group social life, the transfer from highly stigmatised rural and under-privileged cultures to urban habits led to emotional and cultural shock (as typified in Pasolini's novel *Una vita violenta*, 1965). De Mauro reports this in isolated rural communities in the Mezzogiorno and in sub-proletarian slum areas created by the hasty expansion of many cities. In these city areas, cut off from the language of their village community, speakers not only found it difficult to adjust to the national language, but had serious problems trying to express themselves in any language (De Mauro, 1972). De Mauro says that industrialisation and urbanisation have contributed to the renewal and standardisation of repertoires across social divisions and that increased uniformity reflects the common lifestyles of socially reorganised communities.

This uniformity is expressed, according to F. Sabatini (1985) by the *italiano dell'uso medio*. This emergent variety (with some old features) is one of the four varieties in his typology. This includes (1) standard Italian, (2) *italiano dell'uso medio*, (3) regional Italian of educated groups, and (4) popular / regional Italian of less educated people. The first two varieties are characterised by national features, the latter two by regional traits. The debate on the most suitable typology to describe recent sociolinguistic developments significantly concentrates on the intermediate varieties rather than the interaction between dialects and the national language. As Grassi (1993) points out, there is little contact between the two ends of the continuum. There is most contact in everyday use between the lowest codes of the national language (popular Italian) and the highest codes of the vernacular (urban dialect and / or regional koiné).

Focusing on the stratification of the national language through pressure from the local usage, Berruto (1987) studied the spoken varieties of the national language in the same regional area and mapped the possible variables of register, morphology and phonology. He provides a typology of six distinct codes (see below) that are exemplified in a specimen sentence (as it would be pronounced by different speakers in different situations and / or with different interlocutors) (Figure 6).

As Figure 6 illustrates, some of the synonymic variables distinguish a high degree of eloquence (1–2) from the formality marked by literary styles (3–4). The latter are in turn different from more informal varieties of the ordinary standard (5–6) while the two varieties immediately below are characteristic of colloquial informality (7–8). The next variety is typical of slipshod informal language (9). Finally, the two varieties at the bottom of the chart are characteristic of popular Italian. Number 10 includes some national and number 11 some regional forms. Berruto's typology and terms are as follows:

1–2	*italiano formale aulico*
3–4	*italiano standard letterario*
5–6	*italiano neo-standard*
7–8	*italiano parlato colloquiale*
9	*italiano informale trascurato*
10–11	*italiano popolare*

Berruto also provides a diagram (see Figure 7) that shows how the varieties overlap in the bordering areas. The main divisions of the national language are called *standard allargato* (extended standard) and 'substandard'.

Since the late 1980s, linguists have agreed that dialects are showing unexpected energy. No longer spoken by monolinguals as alternatives to the national language, they were revitalised by the spread of bilingualism. Dialects are still strong within the family in most regions, and in some cities they have also provided an alternative source of invention for the language of young people. According to statistics provided by the Doxa surveys (see Table 4), the use of dialects shows a gradual decline but is still quite stable in certain domains. In 1988, 66% of Italians still used the dialect at home at least with some relatives, whilst for 23% it was the normal language both at home and outside the home. Moreover, for 40% of speakers the dialect was the exclusive language at home, and for 33% it was the preferred language with friends. According to the same 1988 sample, the most regular users are: (1) men rather women (an inversion from the 1982 sample); (2) older rather than younger people; (3) in the southern regions and in the islands rather than in central / northern Italy; (4) in the country

1	non	sono	affatto	a conoscenza di	che cosa		sia stato	loro	detto
2	non	sono	affatto	a conoscenza di	che cosa		abbiano	loro	detto
3	non	do	affatto		che cosa		abbiano	loro	detto
4	non	so	affatto		che cosa		abbian	loro	detto
5	non	so	affatto		che cosa		hanno	loro	detto
6	non	so	mica		che cosa	gli	hanno		detto
7	non	so	mica		che cosa	gli	han		detto
8	non	so	mica		cosa	gli	han		detto
9	Ø	so	mica		cosa	gli	han		detto
10	Ø	so	mica		cosa	ci	han		detto
11	Ø	so	mica		cosa che	ci	han		det'o

Figure 6 Variations in levels of formality within the national language
Source: Berruto (1987)

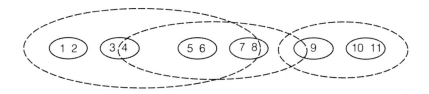

Figure 7 Possible variables within a single regional area
Source: Berruto (1987)

rather than in towns; (5) in lower class groups rather than in the middle and upper classes.

The Veneto region was in second place (after Sardinia) for the use of dialects with friends and colleagues in 1982. In the following survey in 1988, this northern region had the highest percentage of normal dialect use in the family (75%) followed by 73% in Sicily, by 59% in Abruzzo and Campania, and by 57% in Basilicata and Calabria. This high maintenance of the dialect, in a region that is economically strong, is consistent with the language loyalty noted by Lepschy (1989) in a city like Venice, where strong local linguistic traditions across the social spectrum is counterbalanced by the nationwide stigmatisation of the dialects.

The revitalisation of the dialects was confirmed by the 1991 Doxa survey, with some considerable regional variations. Excluding Tuscany and Lazio, the highest percentage for dialect use only was 28.9% in Veneto and the lowest 1.2% in Piedmont (national average 11.3%). The highest percentage of people speaking only Italian was in Lombardy with 31.6% and the lowest was 5.6% in Sicily (national average 30.2%). These data and those indicating the stabilisation of the use of dialects in certain domains, such as family and informal socialisation, suggested to Berruto (1994) that the domains of the national language and of the dialects have now reached compartmentalisation, and that the majority of bilin-

Table 4 Use of Italian and dialects

		1974	1982	1988	1991	1996
At home	dialect with everyone	51%	47%	40%	36%	34%
	Italian with everyone	25%	29%	34%	34%	34%
With friends and colleagues	only or mainly dialect	42%	36%	33%	23%	28%
	only or mainly Italian	36%	42%	47%	48%	50%

Source: Doxa data from Lepschy, 2002a

gual speakers could happily switch from one to another. This new trend was reinforced by the 1996 Doxa survey which, as Lepschy (2002a) spells out, suggests three important considerations: (1) the parallel increase in the use of Italian and the slow decline of the dialects indicates an extraordinary tenacity of the latter, both in the home and outside; (2) the use of Italian remains stable (since 1988), while the use mainly or exclusively of the dialect with friends and colleagues has increased from 23% to 28% in the period between the 1991 and 1996 inquiries; (3) the use of Italian outside the home reaches 50% of the population for the first time in Italian history, while the use in the home of the idiom of which people are native speakers shows the same figure (34%) for Italian and for the dialect. This is Lepschy's conclusion (2002a: 44):

> we can note that the main difference between today and the years of unification seems to be that then Italy was effectively a monolingual country, with the local dialect being the only idiom known to the vast majority of the population, while now it is largely a bilingual country.

New factors of diversity

The last 30 years have shown three different forces at work in the linguistic situation in Italy: (1) enduring polycentrism (of its cultural and linguistic traditions); (2) increasing homogenisation (of everyday habits and life in a mass society); and (3) international challenges (deriving from the increased power of the media in mass communications).

In this era of highly advanced technological communications, information centres can provide their owners with unprecedented opportunities to be able to condition the way news is reported, and even to influence political debates. To combat this, there must be some level of monitoring of private interest. Italy has not yet provided a model for democratic reform in this field: its media system made a rapid move from a prehistoric stage of state monopoly to Wild West competition between private networks, which may even interfere with the rules of electoral campaigns, if not with those of democracy itself.

However, if television remains the unchallenged leader of the mass media, the reading of newspapers has increased considerably since the late 1960s. The substantial increase in reading in general is consistent with statistics on the standards of education and literacy. De Mauro, speaking to the *Corriere della Sera* (1992), reported data showing that young people (under 25) now have three times as much schooling as those over 55 and that they spend much more time reading than do the older members of the population. According to De Mauro

(1994), this has led to the thorough penetration of the national language in all regions and at all social levels.

Following this great spread of the national language, features like accents assume the role of new social markers. With regard to the most prestigious accents, the survey of Galli de' Paratesi (1985) with the significant title of *Lingua Toscana in Bocca Ambrosiana* ('Tuscan Language Spoken by Milanese') concluded that national attitudes have changed in the last 50 years. Today the northern accent, particularly that of the industrially active Lombardy (St Ambrose is the patron saint of Milan) carries higher prestige throughout Italy than other regionally based varieties, including that of the capital. A decline of prestige in the Tuscan variety has been confirmed by lexical research based on the *VDB* (De Mauro, *Vocabolario di Base* Basic Vocabulary) which indicates that typical (but uncommon) Florentine terms (*acquaio* sink, *gruccia* hanger, etc.) are widely perceived as a regional degradation of the national language (Gensini, 1985). These new trends are particularly noticeable among younger people, and disc jockeys typically adopt northern accents wherever they may hail from. From a total 140,000 words of the *Lessico universale italiano*, the *VDB* lists 7000 of the most frequent words used throughout Italy, which can be assumed to form a common core repertoire for all Italians. The survey of the LIP (*Lessico di Frequenza dell'Italiano Parlato* Spoken Italian Frequency Lexis) carried out by De Mauro (1993) narrows this down to a shortlist of 500 words, which constitutes as much as 80% of the language used in everyday conversation by a representative cross-section of the population, a statistic that reflects the number of words in the most recurrent repertoire of other European languages (*Corriere della Sera*, 1993). The *LIP* survey also shows that, in the 1990s, in four major urban centres (Milan, Florence, Rome and Naples) the bulk of everyday language, 98.4%, was made up of a common lexical core while only 1.3% was derived from regional dialectal terms and a mere 0.3% covered foreign borrowings and Latinisms, contrary to the alarmist declarations of purists.

In the process of the Italianisation of the new generations, television seems to have been more influential in the 25 years after World War II than in the last 25 years of the century, simply because of the greater number of dialect speakers. Today some people are especially critical of TV's promotion of 'bad' linguistic trends, the victims of which are said to be the young generations. There is still the feeling (Castellani Pollidori, 1994) that Italian could lose its richness because the presenters and protagonists on TV programmes use a limited range of expressions. In the same vein, others criticise the proliferation of foreign borrowings, especially from English, as this is thought to 'pollute' the Italian language. Other linguists minimise the negative aspects and refer to historical precedents that increased the vitality and wealth of Europe's languages. De Mauro himself denies the negative impact of these innovations on young people's language and feels that the basic creativity of their language is not lessened. The personalised switching to and from the dialect, or (when this is not available, as in most urban situations) the invention of a slang among young people, shows that the language is in a constant state of evolution. Yet not only the general public but language scholars, too, complain about the linguistic impoverishment of the young and say that this is the fault of teachers who were too 'normative' in the past and are too tolerant at present (Dardano, 1994).

The purists have recently directed their criticism at another traditional source of models for good language use: the daily press. The rapid evolution in style affecting all the newspapers over the last 20 years is often explained as an exaggerated linguistic visualisation borrowing techniques typical of television talk shows. Another source of regular complaint is the language of politicians, which sometimes, though not always, creates meaningless stereotypes wrapped up in the language of popular sport. The mutual influence of the languages of the media is further complicated by the invasion of terms and forms from special languages. This may be positive when the aim is precision, but can have deleterious effects when people become addicted to their professional jargon, and this comes to be perceived as an inaccessible anti-language by the ordinary public. Many Italians have a tendency to adopt 'officialese', as soon as they leave their homes and/or speak with outsiders, as Calvino was the first to point out. Italian cannot be described as over-conservative or over-dynamic when compared to other European languages, but its new developments show some interesting challenges reflecting specific social tendencies within Italy. On the one hand, marked linguistic efforts have been made towards handicapped people (*portatori di handicap* handicap bearers, *non vedenti* not seeing, *non udenti* not hearing, *insufficienti mentali* mentally insufficient), but these are not accompanied by adequate services. At the same time, public administrations continue to treat women as men linguistically (an attempt to reform these old-fashioned habits can be found in *Presidenza del Consiglio dei Ministri*, 1997).

The impact of formal education

Changing approaches to diversity

After unification, the leading writer, Alessandro Manzoni, suggested spreading the use of Florentine by hiring Tuscan teachers. Once this project was abandoned, the interest in Italy's linguistic diversity, in her multitude of dialects and minority languages, gradually fell away. Most teachers of Italian insisted on rigid rules and models, and based instruction on narrative and poetry, thus turning the teaching of the national language into a foreign language course little different from that of French or Latin. After World War I, a progressive educationist, Giuseppe Lombardo Radice, proposed an innovative scheme significantly entitled *Dal dialetto alla lingua*. His aim was to raise the status of the dialects and to use the pupils' native competence in these languages as a basis on which schools could develop the teaching of Italian. This project was short-lived, partly because of the quiet resistance of conservative teachers, partly because of the overt opposition of the new Fascist Government, and its campaign against dialects. On a par with other expressions of local culture and regional diversity, the use of dialects was considered anti-Italian and, if dialects could not be stifled altogether, they were systematically ignored.

At that time language education focused primarily on patriotic literature, so as to teach young people to be good Italians and to train them to speak 'correct' Italian language. Grammar lessons were common in the language curriculum, but the teaching was prescriptive for the main purpose of selecting pupils on the basis of their mastery of the formal rules of the language. This approach had little to do with the support for the teaching of grammar, favoured by the anti-Fascist scholar and politician Antonio Gramsci. Gramsci was against both the old-fashioned normative approach to grammar teaching and the idea that schools could stand back and let language teach itself. He was in favour of 'conservative schooling for radical politics' as Entwistle (1979) put it. Gramsci's nonconformist view of language education becomes clearer when seen in the context of his long-term perspective; he felt that it was a priority for a national community to share the same language, because of the limited cultural and political value of dialects in modern society. Yet at the same time he knew that dialects provided young children with solid emotional and intellectual support.

Literacy

At the end of the World War II, Italy was still far from being able to rely on a common language among its nearly 50 million people, who were still mainly employed in the agricultural sector. The education effort required for the transition to a modern industrial society was enormous, as (officially) 13% of the population were illiterate in 1951 and, of the remaining 87%, a high proportion of adults were only semi-literate. An approximate estimate (De Mauro, 1970) indicates that apart from the 13% of illiterate people who were monolingual in dialect and the 18% who were monolingual in Italian, the remaining 69% were in a state of diglossia, alternating dialect and the national language for diverse purposes and with different people. By 1961 more Italians were working in industry (37%) than in agriculture (33%). By the same date only half of the population was urbanised. Compulsory education was another important factor in the transition between the pre- and post-1968 phases. In the 1970s illiteracy virtually disappeared, with 95% of children completing compulsory schooling, and the number of pupils achieving high school qualifications doubled: (839,995 in 1961–62 vs. 1,732,178 in 1971–72) and trebled 10 years later (2,433,705 in 1981–82). This ended the role of universities as training institutions for the elites, and from the early 1970s onwards, they functioned as centres for intellectual debate and academic achievement open to a much wider spectrum of society. (Census data – see Table 5 – about literacy were collected in different ways from the time of unification in 1861 (when the signature used to be the main indicator) until today. Italian linguists, however, have always referred to it without further analysis. In short, the term literacy has been defined differently over time, and many of the definitions lack precision.)

Table 5 Fluency in the national language, illiteracy and truancy

Year	Population	Fluency in Italian	Illiteracy	Truancy
1861	22,182,000	2.5%	75%	50%
1911	35,845,000	58%	42%	25%
1951	47,516,000	86%	13%	15%
2001	56,996,000	97%	3%	–

Source: Adapted from De Mauro, 1970 with subsequent Doxa data

From literary training to education for all

For some 15 or 20 years after World War II, apart from Gramsci's proposals, there was a general stagnation of ideas on language education. While language teaching remained hopelessly unimaginative, it was instrumental in maintaining a selective school system. For at least 15 years, language curricula taught only eloquence to those who knew the language, and failed to teach the language to those who did not. In the school year 1959–1960, only 20.4% of 13–14-year-olds successfully completed a post-elementary level of education. Almost 31% of children of the same age were still in elementary schools or in the first two years of post-elementary schools or training courses, and just under 50% had left school without completing the five years of compulsory elementary education (De Mauro, 1985).

The situation changed in the 1960s when attendance of the lower secondary school (three years in addition to primary level) became compulsory, and when this middle school became comprehensive with the reform *scuola media unica* in 1963. A debate on the national language, the treatment of dialects at school and the need to reform language courses was stimulated by the work of the linguist Tullio De Mauro. He stressed that children are cut off from reality when schools attempt to eradicate the dialects. These, as De Mauro showed, had historically been sources of linguistic creativity for individual speakers and of cultural resources for the national language. It was wrong, therefore, for a child's development, and, in terms or language and cultural loyalty, to ignore the dialects and inappropriate to concentrate the teaching of the national language based on the norms and models of the literary tradition. A passionate call not to undervalue or stifle the linguistic and cultural experiences of underprivileged communities was also made in a wonderful book written by primary school children in an isolated, socially deprived area:

> . . . we should settle what 'correct language' is. Languages are created by the poor, who then go on renewing them forever. The rich crystallise them in order to put on the spot anybody who speaks differently. (Scuola di Barbiana, 1967)

Don Milani, the teacher-priest who inspired this work, entered the controversial domain of language education in a class-divided society, and his pupils succeeded in demonstrating how everyday language teaching in the classroom is often used to select rather than to educate the new generations (Milani & Scuola di Barbiana, 1977).

Don Milani's work was influential in two ways. It appealed to many politically motivated people as it showed that education in those years was used as a mechanism of selection by the ruling classes, who wanted to keep higher education for their own children. It also made a great impression on many well-meaning (but politically unaware) teachers who felt betrayed by the school system, which had made them stigmatise the language of the poor and discriminate against the very people they felt most affinity and solidarity with. As a result there was widespread professional unrest, which culminated in a manifesto called the *Dieci tesi per l'educazione linguistica democratica* (Ten Theses for Democratic Language Education) that was published by the association *GISCEL* (Group for Action and Research in Language Education) in 1977. In the late 1960s and early 1970s, this group coordinated initiatives for school and university teachers who were interested in developing language education methods especially for social groups who had previously been excluded from schools. In a country that was finally changing from its rigid class system into a mass society with new needs and different priorities, the *Dieci tesi* set out some innovative principles for the teaching of the national language. These principles counteracted the traditional belief that language is uniform and speakers can easily conform to the most prestigious models. The manifesto helped to spread in schools new projects based on the idea of freedom to criticise, rather than conform, which was seen as a prerequisite for both teachers and learners and was essential for the success of language education. Since teachers would need training in how to elicit language awareness in pupils, reservations were advanced that, once sanctioned by the central authorities, such projects could not always be carried through, as teachers had had little or no training to help them implement the new ideas (Simone, 1979).

Teachers' attitudes and innovative schools

In 1963 the central authorities extended compulsory schooling from the age of 11 to age 14, establishing a comprehensive system, without Latin. Large sectors of young people from rural and working class backgrounds gained access to schools, but although 'native competence' in Italian was idealistically assumed in all children, teachers were often able to communicate only with pupils who enjoyed a second 'hidden curriculum at home' (Pozzo, 1985). Gradually many teachers came to feel that the institutional efforts made to direct pupils' language to good academic use were ineffectual. By following ministerial guidelines and old-fashioned curricula, they were teaching neither good everyday use to all, nor academic mastery to a few. They were simply enforcing a special jargon inside the school that was no longer relevant outside. This special language tended to replace everyday lexis with conventional 'proper' expressions. In the late 1960s and early 1970s, this was condemned by the profession as anachronistic, and their main target became the type of Italian taught (Vanelli, 1977). This became known by the derogatory name of *italiano scolastico* (school Italian), of which the following terms are some examples:

Everyday Italian	→	**School Italian**
arrabbiarsi (to get angry)	→	*adirarsi* (to lose one's temper)
fare (to do)	→	*eseguire* (to undertake)
andare a letto (to go to bed)	→	*coricarsi* (to lie down)

One reason for teachers' dissatisfaction was that remodelling pupils' language for classroom purposes was not really teaching language. Gradually three main positions emerged within the profession. An elite of extremely motivated teachers became the protagonists in later debates and changes. They were backed by a large number of progressive, sensitive teachers who were prepared to support the innovations initiated by the first group, though perhaps not always to implement them. The majority of classroom teachers were, however, reluctant to adopt any change that might interfere with their comfortable though uninspiring routine. Numbers varied from North to South and between cities and rural areas. Simone (1979) speaks of a typically Italian situation where school change is initiated by the teaching profession rather than by the education authorities.

Pozzo (1985) stresses that the aspirations of the avant-garde teachers were both political and cultural. They had been given no professional training before starting teaching but had tried to provide training for themselves while in service. There are advantages and disadvantages in this very Italian situation where graduates can become teachers of their academic subjects without professional training. Compared to other European colleagues, they are less skilled when they begin their profession, but may be also less conditioned by prejudices concerning differences of class, culture and language. In addition, it is very difficult to make a profession feel the need for any training when none has been required previously.

Pozzo also notes that Italian teachers were not given clearly defined roles and responsibilities as the education authorities deliberately left these vague. Because of a paucity of ideas or because of political impotence, for years the school authorities pursued a compromise between (1) language education as training for social emancipation (under pressure of the changes proposed by the most innovative teachers) and (2) language education as a way of exercising the mind and learning to think systematically and logically, studying the notions and models of the old literary tradition. Berruto (1983) comments that this produced two types of language teaching in Italian schools: one based on the unquestioning acceptance of the old tradition, the other limited to the classrooms of the most innovative teachers. The new innovative approach was adopted by only a small elite of the profession, because the teachers had to organise their own retraining and had to take charge of ordering equipment and materials, and of taking any measures that would prove necessary in the running of the school or in classroom management.

Publishers began to support some of the most progressive suggestions. Language teaching materials should not be limited to academic or literary use but should try to promote effective communication in different domains and for different functions. Despite this admirable aim, however, few textbooks or grammar books in the 1960s and 1970s supplied more than a new terminological presentation. During the 1970s, isolated projects and experiments initiated by very gifted and committed teachers like Bruno Ciari, Marco Lodi and Orlando Spigarelli (see Renzi & Cortelazzo, 1977) tried to base courses on the philosophy of one of Italy's greatest children's writers, Gianni Rodari ('*tutti gli usi della parola a tutti*' = 'all word uses for all'). At the same time, the most sensitive teachers gained support for educational associations that aimed to promote a new approach to language teaching, more creative in purpose and more democratic in inspiration: *MCE* (*Movimento di Cooperazione Educativa*), *LEND* (*Lingua e Nuova Didattica*), *CIDI* (*Centro di Iniziativa Democratica degli Insegnanti*) and *GISCEL* (*Gruppo di Intervento e di Studio nel Campo dell'Educazione Linguistica*).

The state's response to the new campaign, which aimed to translate the comprehensive approach to equal opportunities into more effective classroom teaching, was contradictory and inconsistent. No government took the responsibility of initiating a reform that would lead to a systematic definition of the role of language teaching in compulsory education, and above. All governments allowed pilot projects with a special programme of experimentation, which meant that the most innovative teachers were able to make important changes in their schools. There was an obvious contradiction, however, between the ruling about each *sperimentazione* (pilot project) lasting only three years, and the obligations for approved projects to be those of national relevance. In fact, the political responsibility for national reform was too big an undertaking for any government, while no government wished to be accused of suppressing the best models developed by the most innovative and successful schools.

Models of lack of models?

Currently, most Italian linguists agree that schools have generally modified their view of language, and possibly their approach to language evaluation, but have not yet really changed the methods of language teaching. (For an overview of the school system, see Figure 8.) There seems to be a compromise between general tolerance towards children's inability to comply with the norms of the standard, and basic incompetence in training children to comply with these norms (Gensini, 1985). The curriculum introduced in 1979 contributed to the spread of such notions as (1) language education is a multi-disciplinary training across the curriculum, and (2) no child should be penalised for his or her linguistic background. Beyond these vague declarations of intent, however, the vast majority of Italian teachers (who have to quantify success according to children's progress in mastering the norms of the standard) still adopt the method of parsing and the teaching of grammar. With the growth of the media and the rapidly expanding linguistic experiences of children, an increasing number of teachers found that the traditional approach was not only ineffective: it was no longer respected as many people considered its models far less authoritative than those of the streets or, more especially, of the media.

Some linguists think that the progressive teachers' associations did little to improve language teaching but a lot to expand the norms of the standard so that it included colloquialisms and popular expressions of 'substandard' varieties, thus enhancing the status of the neostandard in schools and society (Dardano, 1994). Other linguists like Bruni (1992) went even further and suggested that Italian schools had lost their traditional role as conveyors of the 'right models and proper language', and have become the major vehicle of 'substandard' Italian. Berruto (1986), however, denies that the lack of models in schools may be the source of *italiano popolare* for dialect speakers coming into contact with the standard for the first time.

If the schools have neither lowered the standards of competence nor improved students' command of 'correct' language, one might ask what exactly their social role is. At the present time, Italian linguists are still divided over this question. Some feel that language education should be adapted more to contemporary usage, especially in the streets and the new media; since these two fields are familiar to most children, this would make language learning more natural. Others believe that, as the media have contributed to the rapid deterioration of the language, the schools should take on their old task of selecting norms and teaching them firmly. The authorities should ensure that this is done. This position is held by those who think that attempts to make language education more 'democratic' have deprived schools of a clear role without providing an alterna-

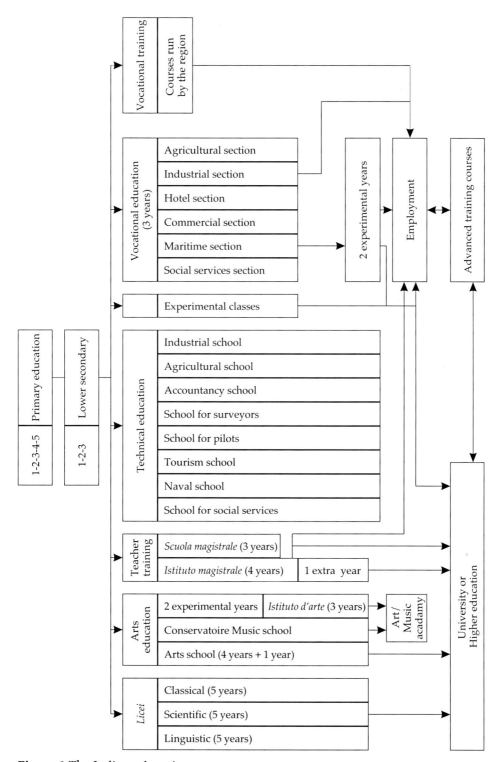

Figure 8 The Italian education system

tive one. Dardano (1994) claims that, since Italy stopped treating education as a social priority, the suggestions of progressive teachers have been invariably adopted by the Government for demagogic rather than constructive purposes. Consequently, a manifesto like the *Dieci tesi* (*GISCEL*, 1977), which included admirable declarations of principle, had only helped to spread preconceived hostility against norms and models. This, says Dardano, deprived language education of its basic purpose, which is that of teaching pupils to respect (not to criticise) the given models. One may disagree with such an interpretation, though it is more difficult to disagree about the demagogy of school policies when they adopt radical principles without measures or resources to implement them. This debate will no doubt continue, especially in view of the tendency of the national school system to pay lip service to modern trends without implementing a systematic approach nationwide. This is also the case with the new challenge for the school system: the problem of teaching Italian to immigrant children.

Italian as L2 for ethnic minorities and new immigrants

There is some confusion regarding the teaching of the Italian language to pupils of immigrant background. This is due partly to the unexpected re-emergence of the problem of non-native speakers in schools, and partly due to the fact that some teachers are trying to follow models of immigrant education from other European countries without first carefully assessing the premises and conditions for their successful implementation. This discrepancy between the ambitious principles of a few pilot projects and the reality of everyday practices in the vast majority of schools seems an unavoidable impasse for many Italian language education reforms, whether native or non-native speakers are involved.

The right to education guaranteed for all Italian nationals 'without distinction' by the 1946 Constitution was extended in 1994 to offer all pupils equal opportunities in compulsory education, including children from a non-European Community background (*MPI*, 1994a). Children from the European Union are admitted directly into the class after the last class attended in the country of origin, while children from outside the EU require translations of their medical, birth and school certificates and proof of their parents' legal residency. The ministry directive recommends that foreign children should be placed according to age. However, many pupils who are not first-language speakers of Italian are still placed in lower classes, which are inappropriate in terms of cognitive development, but appear to be suitable only because teachers train younger children in the basic skills of reading and writing. This important issue of cognitive development and language is unregulated by the legislation governing foreign children of compulsory school age. Two further directives endorsed the principle that the national language was to be taught to foreign pupils (*MPI*, 1989) and suggested that there should be no more than five in any one class, and that a pupil who is not a first-language speaker of Italian should, wherever possible, be placed in a class where there was another pupil with a similar background (*MPI*, 1990). Table 6 lists the most heavily represented groups of non-Italian citizens in Italian schools (school year 2000–2001).

While there is no specification of appropriate practices or programmes of language teaching to immigrant children, the relevant legislation makes a special

Table 6 The most heavily represented groups of non-Italian citizens in Italian schools, 2000–2001

Nationality	Number	Percentage of all foreign pupils
Albania	25,050	17.0
Morocco	23,052	15.6
Former Yugoslavia	16,225	11.0
China	8,659	5.9
Romania	6,096	4.1
Peru	4,486	3.0
Others		44.4

Source: Ministry of Education and Home Office Research (2002)

call on schools to adopt an 'intercultural approach' for the education of all pupils, and to reject outright the idea of 'special' or 'separate' classes. Great emphasis is placed on the fact that children are to be taught to understand cultural differences so they can live harmoniously in an increasingly multicultural society (MPI, 1994a, 1994b). Diversity tends to be represented as an asset for all pupils and is emphasised as a positive ingredient of a non-segregationist school policy, which is consistent with the case made in the past for socially disadvantaged and physically handicapped learners. Decisions on curriculum changes, and language courses, to meet the specific needs of pupils who are not first-language speakers of Italian are left to each individual primary or secondary school. This decentralisation allows flexibility in those schools that have high standards of professional commitment and can set up an integrated plan of curriculum change, development of materials and teacher training. But the vast majority of schools do not have high standards, often because they have not been granted the resources necessary to introduce specific innovations. This is why the lack of national policy leads to the old 'sink or swim' approach despite the official declarations of intent to offer equal opportunities to all members of the new multiethnic and multicultural society (Tosi, 1995).

The 1946 Italian Constitution stipulated that special measures should be granted to areas in which the first language was not Italian; but no ministerial directive has so far considered the extension to the new immigrants of this educational opportunity, which was introduced for domestic minorities. Italy has not had a great deal of experience in bilingual education theory or classroom research, and its limited experience is drawn mainly from domestic minorities, whose linguistic backgrounds are quite different from those of the new immigrants. Bilingual education may be unrealistic, but the most common reality is that ordinary schools have little time and few resources available to develop linguistic programmes for non-Italian speakers (one to three hours per week teaching), and that even this time is discretionary, as head teachers can decide to use it for other activities. In some towns, the local administration pays part-time teachers as a way of assisting pupils whose first language is not Italian with the problems of learning, but these experiences are neither statistically significant nor relevant in terms of innovative methodology and materials (see Table 7 for a list of initiatives funded for the reception of foreign pupils).

Table 7 Initiatives funded for the reception of foreign pupils

	Number	2000–2001 (Percentage)	2001–2002 (Percentage)
Contact with families of new pupils	3707	84.8	85.9
Informal meetings	2311	52.9	51.5
Awareness raising	1287	29.5	25.7
Supplementary language classes	635	14.5	20.4
Courses for teachers	600	13.7	13.5
Meetings with Italian families	521	11.9	28.8
Contacts with immigrant communities	433	9.9	19.6
No response	199	4.6	7.3
Italian language classes	88	2.0	3.6
Interpreters	55	1.3	2.5
Planned projects	40	0.9	1.2

Source: Ministry of Education and Home Office Research (2002)

Increasingly, Italian teachers and immigrant families feel that language diversity should be dealt with systematically to help children rather than to celebrate pluralistic philosophies. Many educators are beginning to recognise that different ethnic groups in Europe may have different priorities. Language education with a focus on the ethnic first language may be the aspiration of immigrant groups in European countries of 'old immigration'. New settlers in Italy, who are concerned about isolation and explicit discrimination, fear all forms of separate schooling and sometimes distrust any special emphasis on their cultural diversity (Tosi, 1995). In view of these differences, the concept of 'community' and 'minority language', when applied to recent immigrants, needs to be clarified, both in terms of social fabric and in terms of cultural and linguistic maintenance leading, for example, to 'ethnic first language teaching' aspirations. In Italy the national debate on these issues is relatively new, and though European-funded projects have created opportunities for transnational experiences, they have sometimes created illusions of clear solutions that in actual fact depend on practical implementation. This is certainly not the lesson to be learned from the European debate, which shows that it would be wrong to generalise solutions, curricula and even terminologies from the socio-educational experiences of other countries.

What needs to be distinguished in Italy is the education of children from well-established ethnic minority communities, and that of new immigrants who are sometimes crowded in multi-ethnic urban enclaves, with little or no community infrastructure. In established communities, if children have developed bilingualism because of the home–school switch (minority language at home; Italian at school), it is important to consider that competence in the ethnic first language is built on a wide range of experiences. Not only do the new arrivals often lack a community life, which can preserve the linguistic and cultural traditions of the country of origin, but competence in the ethnic first language of the new generations is restricted to a mere exchange of everyday basic information with the parents. This distinction has important consequences for intercultural education and language education in particular (Tosi, 1996). The well-established minority ethnic group can regard their culture maintenance not only as an individual aspiration, but also as a natural process of transmission, from one generation to the next, of diverse emotional connotations that are necessary to be able to perceive and describe the local environment. For the children of these minorities, it is true that a great part of their everyday emotional and cultural experiences is denied if a language they have learnt from birth in the local environment has no role in the classroom. One day, this may well become an issue in Italy too. But, at present, the prime responsibility is to make sure that every school is equipped to teach Italian to those who do not yet know it.

Foreign language education

Europeanisation has increased curiosity about other countries and their languages. To the popular mind, English is perceived as the world language that could make Italy more international. This preference is not perceived as conflicting with Europeanism, although in practice it leads to a general tendency to consider English as the foreign language of all Europeans.

Since 1992–93 the teaching of a foreign language as a compulsory subject has been gradually introduced for all pupils aged seven. Pupils at the *Liceo artistico* do not take a compulsory foreign language unless they enrol on an experimental course, for which the school may change the official curriculum and make the teaching of a foreign language mandatory (see Figure 9).

In the 1960s, French lost its supremacy as the most important foreign language in Italian schools. It was overtaken by English so rapidly that there was no time for teachers to be replaced gradually. At times, parents openly rejected schools that could not guarantee English classes for their children. Improved standards of living in the 1970s, and growing economic success abroad in the 1980s, encouraged many families to provide their children with extra English language tuition, such as evening classes in Italy and study holidays in Britain. (See Table 8 for language studies in Italian schools in 2000.)

Fluency in English was soon perceived not only as an advantage in life but also as a mark of social prestige. Privileged families already sent their children to study abroad, especially to Britain, which offered good boarding schools. The new elites increasingly felt that schools with full immersion in English should be provided in Italy. The Government quoted the Constitution, which sanctions Italian as the sole medium of instruction, and resisted several attempts by private organisations to set up private English-medium schools. The Italians are not the only ones in Europe to dream of making their children fluent quickly and cheaply. France and Germany, while allowing bilingual schooling, with English being used at no detriment to the national language, have taken strict measures to prevent the national languages being at a disadvantage among their own nationals. These countries took the view that school leavers should not gain access to home universities if their cognitive and academic competence in English was much better than in the first language (Tosi, 1990). In Italy there is no national model of bilingual education, although there are some regional provisions for linguistic minorities. An increasing

Table 8 Choices of foreign languages studied by pupils by levels of instruction

Type of school	English	French	German	Spanish	Other language*	Total†
Elementary	1,591,362	162,693	10,830	5,044	0	1,769,929
Lower Secondary	1,360,925	641,501	30,074	1,814	0	2,034,314
Upper Secondary	1,981,243	696,301	169,694	40,586	492	2,888,316
Total	4,933,530	1,500,495	210,598	47,444	492	6,692,559

* Usually Russian and Serbo-Croatian
† Pupils in lower and upper secondary school who study foreign languages are counted as many times as the number of languages they study; primary school pupils are counted only once.
Source: Ministry of Education, Progetto Lingue 2000

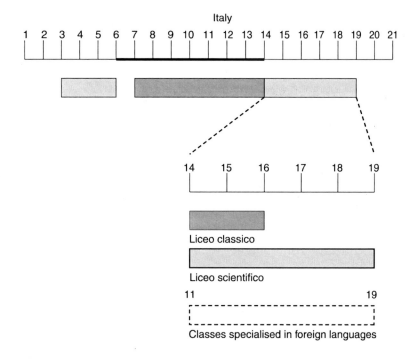

Figure 9 Provision of foreign language teaching at pre-primary, primary and general secondary levels, 1999–2000
Source: Ministry of Education, 2000

number of ordinary families, wishing to imitate the elite, seek private English tuition, investing in all sorts of language training to help their children improve their English. The dream of social mobility made a powerful impact on the spread of new Anglicisms. Italians seem more willing to accept these Anglicisms because of their status than because of their utility. English words in the media, in songs, advertisements and shop windows are perceived by the most recently emancipated social groups to denote modernity and efficiency, the end of the age of isolation and provincialism.

Language Policy and Language Planning

The national language

After unification

After five centuries of discussions and controversies on the right models for the language of literature, the first time that issues of language policy and language planning were explicitly discussed in connection with language use and education was in 1861. This was the year of the political unification of the peninsula into the state of Italy. The two major actors in the debate were the novelist Alessandro Manzoni and the distinguished scholar Graziadio Isaia Ascoli. Manzoni was an enthusiastic supporter of spoken Florentine as a national language, and author of *I Promessi Sposi* (The Betrothed), of which he wrote two versions modelled on the literary tradition before finally being satisfied with a third version based on the everyday language of well-educated Florentine middle class people. Ascoli was a linguist in modern terms, and also less passionate about the policies and politics of language planning. He simply pointed out the limitations of Manzoni's ideas, and the impracticality of attempting to use the school system to teach a language that was alien to the vast majority of Italians. Ascoli's argument – in the first issue of his journal *Archivio Glottologico Italiano* (1870) – was critical of the view that contemporary Florentine usage should be adopted by all Italians and that one main vehicle for its diffusion should be the compilation of a dictionary.

Italian linguists today tend to stress the merits of the two positions (Gensini, 1993; Lepschy & Lepschy, 1977). Manzoni's literary experience was not typically that of a writer interested in language as a social phenomenon, and his proposal that the Italian education authorities should enforce the adoption of spoken Florentine was not determined by puristic choices. He subscribed to the liberal philosophy that it was better and more practical to teach a language that was actually spoken somewhere in the national community, rather than the lifeless models of the dead language of a literary tradition. If he chose to write his novel in Florentine rather than in the pan-Italian literary language prescribed by the academics, it was not because he wished to impose a dead language on schools, but rather because he wanted to adopt the best forms used in everyday language. Ascoli argues against Manzoni's choice because some forms of the pan-Italian literary tradition had already spread nationally and contrasted in everyday use with the Florentine alternatives (that had developed only locally). He also believed that, in any case, Manzoni's recommendations could not facilitate the promotion of Florentine, as the natural spread of a national language takes place through social interaction within a national community, and could not be imposed by trying to enforce its adoption in schools, or by other similar measures.

Language changes within Italian society were later to endorse Manzoni's view that it is the everyday language that provides good models for literature and not vice versa. But Ascoli's prediction was also to be confirmed, in that Florentine (once the dialect of the cultural capital of Italy) could not be promoted to the status of national language only by operations of formal education and status planning. It was shown that a capital's dialect could become a national language only where centuries of official use have gone hand in hand with natural daily interaction, as was the case in Paris and London. In Italy, there was a wide range of different spoken languages, which actually counteracted the literary purism of a tradition which despite its linguistic excellence was confined to the cultural elites. Francesco D'Ovidio, historian and linguist, is often said to combine desire to promote a *lingua viva* and Ascoli's realistic assessment of the process of language planning, rather than idealistic, patriotic or puristic expectations. Writing towards the end of the 19th century, this scholar predicted many of the factors in the spread of a national language: for example, the focus provided by a common capital; the intellectual and political activities of the new elites; the general participation in the life of the national community. But the most progressive policies for education and literacy development were suppressed as linguistic nationalism prevailed under Fascism.

The Fascist language policy

Nationalistic tendencies predated the 21 years (1922–1943) of the Fascist regime (Raffaelli, 1984). Mengaldo (1994), amongst others, points out that, despite the explicit and noisy Fascist campaign, there was, in reality, widespread tolerance either because measures were seen as controversial or because their implementation was inefficient. There were three main objectives in the nationalistic campaign: (1) repression of the dialects; (2) opposition to the linguistic minorities; (3) purification of the national language through the exclusion of foreign words, and the prescription of selected forms considered to be more 'Italian' (the allocution *voi* instead of *lei*). The Fascist school policies date from 1923, and the first initiative was to suppress a reform (*Dal dialetto alla lingua* 'From dialect to language') designed to introduce dialects and folk literature texts into schools as a basis for better teaching. In the first ten years, the regime censored the use of dialects, and from 1933 their very existence was ignored. Even stronger measures were applied to eradicate minority languages, which gradually lost their status as media of instruction in those border areas inhabited by speakers of other languages. At first, other languages were confined to extra-curricular activities, as the Government wished to avoid tensions with some of Italy's powerful neighbours. In the second decade of the regime, they were banned from all higher state education, and Italian was imposed as the only language to be used in offices as well as in the press (Klein, 1986). By eradicating the natural channels of communication and cultural transmission, it was hoped that minority languages would eventually disappear and that minority populations would be rapidly Italianised. The campaign against foreign borrowings was also introduced in the early days of the dictatorship (1923), but it reached extreme forms in the late 1930s and finally produced a full programme of Italianisation assigned to a state academy (1940). This measure can be traced back to previous years – to the time of the Giolitti Governments (1903–1914 and 1920–1921). The Fascist approach, however, became famous for its uncompromising style that involved slogans such as *Italiani boicottate le parole straniere!* (Italians, boycott foreign words!), where the word *boicottate*, far from being Italian in origin, derived from the name of James Boycott, an Irish land agent who was a victim of this practice. Mengaldo underlines the inconsistency of these puristic interventions that allowed words clearly marked by 'foreign' consonantic endings (sport, film, tennis, tram) and imposed unnecessary neologisms, when borrowings were associated with notions allegedly responsible for anti-Fascist feelings: *non-belligeranza* (non-belligerence) was replaced with *neutralità* (neutrality). Political rhetoric more than linguistic purism was pursued by Fascism and changed the official language of the regime rather than that of ordinary people. This is shown by the unsuccessful attempt to replace *lei* with *voi*, or the substantial survival of dialects in everyday use, as well as the almost insignificant operation (based on the proverbial Renaissance slogan revived under the Fascist regime: *lingua toscana in bocca romana*, (Tuscan tongue in Roman mouth) to give spoken Italian not orthodox, Florentine pronunciation but rather that of Rome, the capital of the Empire and centre of its political life. The rhetoric of Fascism is part of a nationalistic evolution in the style of official language that predated the regime, and included the puristic cleansing of Italian from foreign borrowings. Leso (1978) suggests that at the turn of the century there was a combination of events leading to a sharp change of style in political speeches and news reporting. Colonialism, the irredentism after the First World War, the fast developing innovations (such as aircraft and cars) and their use in everyday life, generated a sense of adventure that was captured by the nationalist ideology that inspired popular writers like Gabriele D'Annunzio. The Fascist regime was quick to appropriate the technical innovations of the radio, the newspapers and the film industry, once it realised that communication via the new media could exercise great influence on people's attitudes and beliefs. Any lasting impact on the national language was achieved by way of exposure to the rhetoric of the period and not really through the attempted imposition of a Fascist language policy.

The 1948 Constitution

After the monarchy was outlawed by a referendum that introduced the republic (1946), a Constituent Assembly, with representatives of all political forces, issued a Constitution that came into effect on 1 January 1948. 'Language rights' are dealt with directly in Articles 3 and 6 and, indirectly, in Article 9 and in Part 1 of Article 21. The spirit of the new democratic Constitution intended to secure two fundamental principles. The principle of 'language rights' secures the legal equality of the citizens 'without distinction of sex, race, language, religion, political opinions and personal conditions' (Art. 3). Another principle safeguards 'language rights' in the sense of freedom of speech (Art. 21, Part 1). Article 6 refers explicitly to minorities with the sentence, 'The Republic protects linguistic minorities with appropriate measures'. Four linguistic minorities have benefited most from the spirit of the Italian Constitution from 1948: French speakers in the autonomous region of the Valle D'Aosta, German speakers in the province of Bolzano, Slovenian speakers in the provinces of Trieste and Gorizia, Ladin speakers in the province of Bolzano. Yet other French, German and Occitan speakers outside these areas were not accorded the same language rights, notably because they are not in historically contested areas, nor were domestic minorities living geographically close to these areas like Ladin and Friulian speakers. Recent legislation, however, has modified the legal situation with an ad hoc norm inspired by a European Directive that Italy needed to respect. Law 15,

December 1999 n. 482, on the protection of 'historic linguistic minorities' reiterates that 'The official language of Italian Republic is Italian' (Art.1).

The 482/1999 law on minority language rights

This legislation was introduced to conform to the principles expressed in the 1948 Constitution and also to conform to various European resolutions on minority languages (' . . . in harmony with the general principles established by European and international institutions'). The two major criteria for eligibility were: (1) identification of the minority language with a specific geographical area, and (2) the fact that the community had been settled there for a long time. Accordingly, the new legislation, referring to these communities as 'historic linguistic minorities', declared the intent 'to safeguard the language and culture' of Albanian, Catalan, Germanic, Greek, Slovene and Croatian people and of those speaking French, Franco-Provençal, Friulian, Ladin, Occitan and Sardinian. The limits of the legislation have been recognised and discussed on several grounds. The strict reference to the two above principles precludes the recognition of a 'minority identity' to communities of new settlers who might engage in language and culture maintenance activities (Orioles, 2003). De Mauro (2001) comments that the principles of the Constitution, though more generic and less binding, reflected a more politically progressive approach, when they identified the 'equality' of Italian citizens in the eyes of the law, 'without distinction of . . . language'. Moreover, the new legislation defines the same conditions and applies the same criteria to all listed minorities, without distinction or even consideration between the quality and quantity of language maintenance activities and their impact on minority identities. In this perspective, the generalisation of rights and facilities to use these languages in nursery, primary and lower-secondary education (Art. 4), as well as in the municipal debates and in the administration of local municipalities (Art. 7), have been seen as rather problematic. Orioles (2003), amongst others, argues that the legislation should have introduced a differential treatment of the rights of the most committed communities living in large areas (e.g. the German-speaking people in South Tyrol), those with a historic loyalty to an old minority language of the Italian Peninsula (e.g. Friulian and Sardinian) and the minorities of ancient origin but including few speakers without significant commitment to their linguistic heritage (e.g. Greek and Croatian). Many linguists have shown less than enthusiastic reactions to the legislation partly because their expertise and advice was not adequately taken into account, partly because of the confusion which would probably ensue in schools (Simone, 1999) and society (Renzi, 2000) from this legislative text, which appears to be marked by demagoguery and approximation. Lepschy more cautiously comments that: '[t]he practical consequences of this law remain to be seen' (2000a: 47).

European mobility and language maintenance

Mother-tongue teaching for children of migrants

After the Second World War Italian emigration started again, and took large numbers of unemployed people either to the New World, among co-villagers already settled in the large conurbations of North America and Australia, or to

the most industrialised areas of northern and central Europe. When Italian families moved to England, Belgium, Germany and Switzerland, they found that the
local schools did not offer Italian courses, and the problem of language maintenance became a major issue in the life of those communities. The teaching of Italian was perceived as a crucial factor in preserving an Italian identity. It was also a
means of strengthening family ties with relatives 'back home' and a guarantee
that a door would be kept open if they should return. In response to widespread
demand in the early 1960s, the Italian Government developed a system of provision that was expanded in the 1970s and gained substantial financial support
from the European Community, under the programme of 'internal mobility of
labour'. These measures, operating with teachers recruited in Italy and administered by Italian head teachers and officials, were designed 'to provide extracur-
ricular assistance to integrate education in the host country with knowledge of
the language and culture of the country of origin' (*Ministero degli Affari Esteri*,
1972). Since the long-term objective of the provision was to offer a linguistic
bridge in the host society and a formal qualification in the case of reintegration
into the home school system, some of the assumptions regarding the learners and
their competence were quite controversial. The directive stated that 'the teaching
of Italian must be directed specifically towards: (a) the reinforcement of the
child's relationship with family members, speakers of the national language, and
(b) the maintenance of emotional and cultural contact with the country of origin'.
These tasks should be carried out via the national language 'which children
should be able to use naturally from the first grade (age 5)' (*Ministero degli Affari
Esteri*, 1972: 4–8). Many of the sociopolitical criteria and approaches adopted to
treat language diversity in Italy served as guidelines for the elaboration of principles and the establishment of 'mother tongue' programmes for Italian migrants
abroad. In particular, the problem of native competence in dialect, ignored at
planning level in Italy, was also underestimated at both planning and organisa-
tional level abroad (Tosi, 1984).

Paradoxically, even the strong commitment of parents to the teaching of Italian in their new country was counterbalanced by a confusion concerning the
relationship of the national language to the Italian dialects. This is not to say that
there has ever been any doubt that standard Italian, and not the village vernaculars, should be taught. Rather, the confusion was in the parents' underestimation
of the children's difficulties in learning the standard when they heard dialect, not
standard, Italian at home. Most parents perceive the process of acquiring Italian
in terms of polishing up 'bad Italian' (the *dialetto*) into 'proper Italian' often
Italianised by them as *italiano proprio* (sic.). Given these circumstances, the
programmes for teaching Italian and the syllabi and materials used may at most
have served the political purposes of a welfare measure, whilst they missed the
linguistic aim of their declared educational target. Significantly, official discussions and documents on the content and aims of Italian courses have until
recently ignored the problem of language diversity: they identified immigrant
tongues as the 'national language of the country of origin', and avoided mention-
ing the term 'dialect', except in irrelevant contexts. Official syllabi, confidently
assuming that the learners in these programmes were competent native speakers
of standard Italian, left it to teachers to take the necessary measures to bridge the
gap between the child's dialect and the language of instruction. The approaches

adopted by the instructors, who were recruited among unemployed graduates from Italy who lacked linguistic training and adequate techniques, often resulted in an admirable attitude of class solidarity with their pupils and toler- ance of the dialect. Yet, as they had themselves been victims of a strict and purist use of standard Italian in their school years, they perpetuated in the classroom a language which was too distant and unpalatable to speakers of village or regional dialects. Consequently, the courses reproduced in schools a dangerous conflict between two styles of life and two systems of communica- tion: one regional, belonging to the old-fashioned rural life of the home village and felt to be inferior; the other urban and modern, presented as more presti- gious, but still distant in terms of origin and identity to young Italians born in a new country.

Since the 1980s, following a European Directive (1977), many schools in coun- tries with second and third generation children of Italian background have begun to teach Italian in the curriculum, but these courses, too, offer little support to bilingualism when they adopt a foreign language approach. This is so because the syllabi and examinations adopted by national education systems were based on assumptions relevant to the learning process typical of those who were mono- lingual native speakers of the school language. Accordingly, teacher-training institutions made teachers more sensitive to the opportunity of enforcing stan- dard models of the national language of the country of origin but did not help them to deal capably with the mixed variety developed by bilingual learners abroad. Since this foreign language approach continues to penalise the native competence of bilingual children in view of their non-standard skills, it is not surprising that national education systems, where migrant and minority languages are taught as foreign languages, still operate as agencies of language assimilation rather than language maintenance (Tosi, 1991b).

International education for mobile elites

The awareness of the previously mentioned situation explains why Italian professionals, when posted to another European country ('highly mobile' fami- lies to use a term introduced by Baetens Beardsmore, 1979) seek schools follow- ing international rather than national education systems, committed as they are to the maintenance of the Italian language, and concerned that their bilingual children should not be put in unfair competition with local monolingual chil- dren. The most popular programmes of international education are those for the European Schools and the International Baccalaureate.

The European Schools model

The system of European Schools (*Scholae Europeae*, 1973) was originally designed to reflect the principle of language equality and to meet the aspirations of the families working for the administrative and technological programmes of the European Community. The pupils who form the multilingual population of the European Schools are all nationals of member states and their languages, by constitution, enjoy the same status in all European Schools. Within a given school, students from the same member state are taught together in their national section in the official language of their country of origin. Every pupil, however, is expected to learn certain curricular subjects through the medium of another European language, and to study a third language as a foreign language. The emphasis on the maintenance of the national language and on the development of a second European language which is taught like the first language, for academic use, indicates that the European School model is designed to develop bilingualism. The policy objectives are that students should be in a position (1) to be able to reintegrate into their national community and education systems, and (2) to be able to move to another European School, or else to a national school in a different member state. The curriculum is the same in every European School, as they were founded on the principle that language equality is needed to fulfil the aspirations of all European national groups. Unfortunately the European Schools, which are open to all EU citizens, are extremely expensive to run, and this is why only very few were set up. They are all close to some major EU head-quarters (three in Brussels and one respectively in Mol (Belgium), Luxembourg, Calham (Britain), Varese (Italy), Karlsruhe, Munich and Frankfurt (Germany), Alicante (Spain) and Bergen (Netherlands).

The International Baccalaureate model

The language curriculum of the International Baccalaureate (IB) schools is very different from that of the European Schools since it adopts monolingual not bilingual education systems (only one language rather than two as media of instruction). The IB programme originated from the efforts of some schools to agree on a common curriculum for mobile students that could be recognised for university entrance in as many countries as possible. The International Baccalau-reate curriculum, which includes a two-year pre-university upper secondary course, is taught only via either English or French (with the noticeable exception of the Ecole Bilingue in Paris). Thus the major problem of language planning that the IB needed to solve was the treatment of languages other than English and French, and subsequently to provide a suitable structure for the teaching and testing of other languages. Instead of using the terms 'mother tongues' and 'for-eign languages', the IB adopted the terms 'Language A' and 'Language B'. (Inter-national Baccalaureate, 1967). The policy documents of the IB could not be more explicit about the original framework of a Language A and a Language B. Two Language A programmes were accepted but not two Language B programmes. The policy documents say 'Language A is the first language or the *adoptive* language [my emphasis] of the student which is his basic means of communica-tion and culture'. Language B, which was designed as a foreign language programme, was expected to provide a suitable examination also for its native speakers since 'their mother tongue may be taught to them as a foreign language' (International Baccalaureate, 1967, 1986). The lack of a special examination for bilingual students who have developed the academic use of two languages has consequences for the validity of the IB examination system as a whole. In one option, non-native speakers of the school language choose to enter the examina-tion of the language of instruction (Language A), but as native speakers of Language B are examined in their first language together with genuine foreign language learners. Naturally, in a system operating with norm-referenced language tests, the top marks are awarded to native competence. In the other possible option, non-native speakers of the school language ask for their native competence to be examined by a mother tongue programme (Language A), and their second language (Language B) achievement is examined by foreign language tests. In this case, the competence of students who have learnt a language within the most favourable curricular opportunity – that of using it as a medium of education – are expected to meet unrealistic standards against which are measured the achievement of candidates who have studied the language only as a foreign language, within the limited time-frame of a curriculum subject. Either option introduces inconsistencies of standards, and the situation is further complicated as the majority of IB students who are not native speakers of the school language are almost evenly divided between the two options. Their decision to take one combination or another depends on a number of personal and contextual factors. For example, some schools have a policy whereby all students are free to choose the language they wish in the Language A and in the Language B programmes. Others do not allow native speakers to enter a Language B programme. Some more or less oblige native speakers to do so, since they offer only the Language A programme in the school medium of instruction.

The two models compared

The European School model was set up in 1958 and gives all students two languages of instruction – one to develop native competence and to provide education in the national language and culture, the other to promote cognitive functioning and European identity through the academic use of a second language. The curricular cost for students is not as high as the resource cost for schools: the time spent on the second academic language does not cause the first academic language to deteriorate, and the reward is a population of educated bilinguals, equally at ease in two languages, in their own national culture and in the supranational European identity. Though European Schools are not private, because of the high cost, their curriculum is normally offered only to communities of technologists and administrators working for the EU institutions and is only made available for ordinary European families working outside their own countries if they are resident in the same district. Unlike private international schools, the European Schools charge no fees. This does not mean, however, that they are less exclusive: it simply means that children from non civil-servant families are not admitted to the schools. The high cost of these schools has not prevented this privileged European education from being made accessible to a few powerful families; but so far, the high cost has been an obstacle to the spread of this model to other areas of Europe where urban concentrations of non-nationals are made up of less fortunate and less powerful families.

Most of the International Baccalaureate schools are private, and need to be concerned primarily with resources and cost-effectiveness. Accordingly, they do not adopt expensive measures of bilingual education with two or more media of instruction; they attribute to one international language (at the present time overwhelmingly English) the exclusive role of vehicular language and culture-carrying medium. In addition, the IB schools teach one foreign language (usually French or Spanish) to all those pupils who study the school language as a Language A, including native speakers and non-native speakers alike, when the latter (for example Italians) are not offered a programme to study their first language either as a Language A or as a Language B. The risk of monolingualism or imbalanced bilingualism with cultural assimilation and cognitive operation predominantly in the English language is greater in IB than in European Schools, and this is proved by the results, though the IB schools may state different intentions. Certainly, native speakers of English have no facilities to develop bilingualism through the academic use of another language in any English-medium school. Pupils who are non-native speakers of English can study English as their adopted language, and their first language as a foreign language. If they wish to maintain and develop the academic use of their first language, however, the IB schools do not have the appropriate facilities. Thus the IB curriculum works well as an immersion programme for those who have firm grounding in any language other than English, and who wish to add the academic mastery of this language to their competence in their national language. But for those pupils who have had many years of schooling outside their own country, the IB curriculum speeds up alienation from their cultural and linguistic origins, unless the family arranges for private tuition outside the school. The IB programme was set up 10 years after the European Schools and emphasised the privilege of being educated in a world language (English) rather than the educational value of learning to function successfully in two languages and cultures.

Italian as a community language in the New World

In the late 1970s many English-speaking societies in the New World began to discuss a multicultural policy in response to the needs of the fast growing, multi-ethnic population of their schools (The 'New World' or, rather, *il nuovo mondo* from an immigrant perspective describes the countries of destination once the past or *vecchio mondo* is left behind. Its English translation, therefore, does not convey here the contrast between the New World and the Old World from the conquistadors' perspective). Immigrants' languages, which had previously been taught only through the support of community organisations and/or the authorities of some countries of origin, were introduced in the school curricula. Italian was the first community language to be taught in schools, since its ambivalent academic status was interesting both to non-immigrants and to the descendants of immigrants. This was welcomed by the community organisations, and by the Italian authorities in Italy. Giulio Andreotti, then Minister for Foreign Affairs, said that the immigrant communities abroad were the major vehicle for the promotion of Italian language and culture around the world. However, both the Italian authorities and the schools had great difficulties in setting the programmes which would teach Italian as a community language, rather than as a foreign language (Tosi, 1991a).

The Italian authorities said that the programmes needed to aim specifically for the maintenance of an emotional and cultural tie with Italy. These programmes erroneously identified the native language of immigrant children with standard Italian. Not surprisingly, pupils in these classes often found the experience as traumatic as that of learning a true foreign language. Cummins (1983: 35) made these comments in connection with Canada and the United States:

> . . . many children in heritage language classes speak a dialect of L1, and teachers sometimes feel that they must eliminate this *inferior* form. Often children are told that the forms they had learned at home are wrong and the teacher attempts to make children replace these *incorrect* forms with the

Standard *correct* form. . . . [I]t is extremely important that heritage language
teachers do not attempt to eradicate the dialect . . . (emphasis in the original)

Since the 1980s, under pressure from the international debate on bilingualism
and multiculturalism, Italy has tried to make its policies more relevant, and the
programmes more consistent (Bettoni, 1993). It was thought that since the
national standard is not the native language of the children of immigrants, and
its acquisition does not follow the patterns of a 'mother tongue', it should be
learned and taught as a foreign language. At the same time, some school authorities abroad, too, found the foreign language approach more desirable than the
first language arrangement. This was the case in Britain, for example, where
there was a widespread illusion that minority languages enjoyed a higher educational value when taught as foreign languages (Swann, 1985).

In Australia, where there was a stronger belief in the educational value of
community language teaching, an Evaluation Report of the Multicultural
Education Program (Cahill, 1986: 58) criticised 'the prevalent practice, especially in the case of Italian, of mixing language maintenance learners with
second language learners in one class' and commented that 'this practice stems
as much from naiveté about language learning processes as from funding difficulties and timetabling constraints as well as the lack of adequate commitment'. In Canada, too, the practice of making heritage language education
conform to the teaching of a foreign language was found to be widespread. The
Ontario Institute for Studies in Education was a strong opponent of this
approach: 'when the methodology of language teaching is drawn primarily
from second language literature this has the effect of turning community
language education into a foreign language course unpalatable and unhelpful
to the young bilingual children' (Allen & Swain, 1984: 11). This debate could
not fail to produce two different schools of thought, which are often unper-
ceived at classroom level but which reflect an old dilemma in education:
whether teaching methods should be adapted to children's needs, or whether
the norms of the target language should be modified to comply more closely
with the community's real usage of the language (Tosi, 1989). Accordingly, one
view suggests that minority language programmes should not choose teaching
materials, teacher training and examination criteria that adopt either first
language or foreign language methodologies. Since the former assumes that
the learners have native competence in the target language and the latter that
they have none, a specific educational policy for Italian as a community
language was required since its learners have a bilingual background (Danesi,
1986). The other reaction is more radical and recommends not an adjustment of
the methodology but a substitution of the models of the target language.

Some of those in favour regard the mixed repertoire developed by the Italian
community in Canada or in Australia as an original and comprehensive system
of norms, which they call *italiese* or *australoitaliano*. The claim is that the replacement of standard Italian by the mixed repertoire would solve many problems
encountered by second and third generation learners in heritage language
programmes, as in this way the community language could be taught as a true
first language (Andreoni, 1981). This argument, which clearly overestimates the
consistency of the spoken contact variety, is politically interesting; it aims to

promote the repertoire of speakers of Italian in multi-ethnic and multicultural societies outside Italy by enhancing the status of their new dialect. It is a drastic reaction by radical educationists against an elitist tradition in education which, they feel, is now trying to penalise nonstandard language abroad, after centuries of penalising dialect speakers in Italy. It is significant that the distinctiveness of the new Italian-English contact variety is argued for especially by those who support the cultural autonomy of Italo-Canadians or Italo-Australians from the allegedly elitist culture of institutions in Italy. And this is in sharp contrast to the view of those politicians and academics in Italy who used to say (some still do) that the language spoken within Italian communities in other countries is essentially 'incorrect'.

The promotion of Italian as a foreign language

The need for considered planning to support Italian abroad has been much debated (De Mauro & Vedovelli, 1994; Lo Cascio, 1990a). Specific areas where the interests and needs of Italian outside Italy require special policies, if it is to be able to compete with other languages, are those of multi-ethnic English-speaking societies, the Italian communities in South America and, in the EU, the teaching of Italian as a language of commerce and as a vehicle of a great cultural heritage. The lack of attention for the diverse interests, attitudes and aspirations of different target groups has diminished the status and spread of Italian as a foreign language in some – especially European – countries. This has happened in recent years when diversified approaches to foreign language teaching spread in schools as well as in the business world, and where English began to take the lion's share in all foreign language curricula. Italian authorities have sent several messages of disapproval to the EU, and to many educational authorities of EU countries. The complaint has not met with success. The trend that increased the hegemonic position of English in foreign language curricula has been present in Italy since the 1960s. But from the widespread view of English as the common foreign language of all Europeans, Italian has suffered more than French and German. Moreover, it has not been able to take the fullest advantage (as Spanish has) of its position as a language that is relatively easy for Europeans to learn, at least in the early stages, and equally satisfying to practise, for social purposes or during holidays. The reasons for this are manifold. Responsibility for Italian as a foreign language is assigned to two separate ministries, Foreign Affairs and Public Education. For ten years they attempted to establish a common policy via an inter-ministerial advisory committee whose membership drew together decision makers from Italy and linguists from abroad. The committee broke up in the 1980s, when two institutions (*Università per Stranieri* at Perugia and *Università per Stranieri* at Siena) were able to secure government resources to conduct research and development projects, teacher training, and qualifications in the field of teaching and learning Italian as a foreign language. It is a rather anomalous approach, compared to that of the British Council, Alliance Française, and indeed the more recent, but very successful, Instituto Cervantes, which are specialised in implementing abroad a coherent national policy decided at home. Italy, instead, did not pursue the route of the coherent policy initiated in the 1980s. It replaced this with fragmented initiatives and resources which were scattered across too many, and competing, agencies: the Italian Cultural Institutes directed by a cultural attaché of the embassies; the semi-governmental *Società Dante Alighieri*, active overseas especially in South America; the education offices of the consulates, with considerable resources especially targeted at Italian nationals living abroad; and the *Università per Stranieri* at Perugia and *Università per Stranieri* at Siena, generously resourced by the Government but lacking the necessary insights and contacts to negotiate policies with educational agencies in other countries. Not surprisingly, the view of many Italianists in schools and universities abroad is that the efforts and money invested in these many initiatives have not given comparable returns; and that the situation has worsened since competition became tougher after the success of Spanish.

Accademia della Crusca: Past and present

An informal organisation that is becoming quite influential in the spread of Italian in Italy as well as abroad is the *Accademia della Crusca*, which began its activities during the Renaissance, under quite different auspices. Founded in Florence in 1582–3, this academy was inspired by the theories of Pietro Bembo (1470–1547), a Venetian who felt that the best models for literary works were those of the old Tuscan writers of the *Trecento*. In 1590 its members set out to select and define the words and norms in the works of the great Tuscan writers, especially in Dante, Petrarch and Boccaccio. This project led to the compilation of the *Vocabolario degli Accademici della Crusca* (1612), the first modern language dictionary. It was produced to provide the models of the language to use: a rationale due to the paradoxical condition of Italian, a language with a great literary production but without a nation state. In the 17th and 18th centuries, the *Accademia* exercised an editorial role on the linguistic qualities of literary texts for publication based on the puristic distinction between those forms and words which could be included, and those considered impure which were to be excluded. The academy developed until 1937, when it changed its role and became a research centre into the language of literary works. Since then, the academy has developed a number of projects under the leadership of outstanding linguists such as Giacomo Devoto and Giovanni Nencioni. Among such projects were, the compilation of new editions of the *Vocabolario*, a new juridical dictionary (at present taken up by the *Istituto di Teorie e Techniche dell'Informazione Giuridica*), and the corpus of Medieval Italian (*Tesoro della Lingua Italiana delle Origini*). The current President of the *Accademia della Crusca*, the linguist Francesco Sabatini, has strengthened the language and literary projects of the *Accademia* with the support of modern technologies. In addition, he has secured for this prestigious *Accademia* the new role of leader of national awareness on issues of corpus and status planning with regard to the contemporary Italian language, both in Italy and abroad.

Concluding remarks

Some language planning challenges and developments are comparable to those faced by other European languages. However, many have argued that Italy, either because of its recent unification (Romano, 1982, 1983) or because of institutional reluctance (Avveduto, 1983), has never been inclined to invest much energy in language policy, with the exception of the nefarious Fascist attempts. Within Italy there are now some growing concerns in a number of areas. One is that of the new rights of domestic minorities (*Corriere della Sera*, 25 November 1999). Also, there is neither sufficient awareness nor sufficient informed discussion about the education of the new ethnolinguistic minorities (Zincone, 1999). Language planning and support policies are also felt to be urgent in order to secure a more effective promotion of Italian culture outside Italy. The need for coordinated policies to support Italian abroad has been much debated in the past (Lo Cascio, 1990a). Two specific areas where the needs of Italian outside Italy require special support, concern (1) the spread of Italian in the New World, especially in English-speaking societies, and (2) the position of Italian in multilingual Europe. At the present time, language policies to transform interest into investments are needed to maintain a role for this language in areas as far apart as Australia and North America, where Italian is spoken by large communities of Italian origin, and in the European Union, where multilingual communication requires the constant updating of national languages for international communication and for European affairs. Such diverse challenges show that at a time of increasing globalisation, the fortunes of Italian will depend on its role within the national community, as much as on the changes due to contacts and interplay with other languages.

Speaker Innovations and Language Prospects

New social conventions

Linguistic etiquette
   The clear marker of social distance in the Italian language is the opposition between *tu* and *lei*. *Lei* is the normal, polite form and is also the third person colloquial/neo-standard feminine subject and object pronoun – equivalent to the masculine *lui* – that is now used instead of the rare *ella* or the almost obsolete *essa*. It is now time to reassess social conventions. The reciprocal use of *tu* was traditionally restricted to people who were on terms of equality and informality. Though family and professional status used to be the criteria in the past (as is explained in any grammar book), the reciprocal *tu* has recently spread outside these circles. The opposition is now more complex and the rules of behaviour in public have changed (Renzi, 1993, 1994). It is said that, after the landmark year of 1968, the wider use of the *tu* form was a sign of greater informality, which is sometimes interpreted as bad manners. This is not quite true. To understand this apparent revolution, it is important to appreciate that diverse conventions mean different rules, not less formality. Most people perceive only the increase or decrease in informality, sometimes interpreted as better manners, or worse manners. Only the specialist can place the changes in a more general picture and show that, though the rules of address change, distance often remains the same. Renzi (1994) studied the contemporary use of the rules of address, the so-called *dare del tu* (using the *tu* form) and *dare del lei* (using the *lei* form), and the use of titles and honorifics. He identified complex patterns that contrast with the more traditional, pre-1968, conventions, and provided a typology of 'canonical' forms and 'alternative' forms.

canonical forms	alternative forms
io	*(noi)*
tu	*lei, voi (noi)*
voi	*loro*
lui, lei	*(noi)*

The normal (or canonical) form by which the speaker refers to himself or herself is *io*, and the alternative form (*noi*) is used by authorities like the President of the Republic or the Pope (as the royal 'we' in English) or by writers and critics. In the second person, the speaker would adopt the alternative form *lei* instead of *tu* when the listener is felt to be superior in status or when there is no close relationship of intimacy or solidarity. The same distance is implied by *voi*, which was more common than *lei* in parts of central Italy and in the south (but not in Sardinia). In central and southern Italy, the situation is further complicated by the fact that most dialects respect social distances by adding epithets of courtesy (like *Signoria, Vossignoria*) in sentences with *tu*. Consequently, the use of the unfamiliar *lei* is inconsistently mastered and is sometimes felt to be a more modern but less respectful allocution than *voi*. *Ella* as a form of address is, at present, either anachronistic and / or bureaucratic. The choice between *lei* or *voi* can be confusing to a foreign listener, but usually it is not for a native speaker. *Voi* is predominant in popular use in the South. It has also survived, but only in dialect, in Veneto, Emilia and Lombardia as a form of respect for parents and grandparents in patriarchal families. *Voi* also appears in translations of dialogues in foreign books or films, especially old ones. The language of advertising prefers *voi* to *lei* and at present, increasingly *tu*. The use of *voi* in advertising and public notices can of course be a deliberate ambiguity between the normal plural allocution and a more formal singular form.

In everyday life, at present, if there is a close informal relationship between speakers a reciprocal *tu* is normal, whereas if there is a distance the 'inferior' uses *lei* (or *voi*) whereas the 'superior' can choose to keep the distance and use *lei* (or *voi*) or to remove it with *tu*. Moving from a *lei* or a *voi* relationship to one based on *tu* is usually an irrevocable step and this is why it should always be suggested by the 'superior' person, that is, the older person, a woman or someone of higher (professional) status. *Ciao* is strictly for people who are friends. *Salve* is a compromise between *Buongiorno* and *Ciao*, and is frequently used in 'superior' → 'inferior' as well as 'inferior' → 'superior' contexts. *Buona giornata*, which is becoming increasingly popular, began as being more appropriate to an 'inferior' → 'superior', whilst at present it is used in both directions. The internationally popular use of *Ciao* and the US-based 'have a nice day!' (i.e. *buona giornata!*) increasingly modify their Italian versions. To sum up, the national spread of *tu* marks new values and sensitivity, rather than lack of social respect in a traditional sense. The *tu* form is increasingly used, for example, among adults to spell out membership of the same professional circle or the same social milieu, even at a first meeting. Among young or youngish people it just marks membership of the same age group, whatever differences there may be in wealth, social background or education.

Language and gender

In Italian society more traditional women still accept their husband's role and career as more dominant and see their own role as supportive (Bates & Benigni, 1975). At the same time, however, many Italian women adopt a less conventional position. They value their own careers and think their role in society is conditioned by the historical domination of men. In Italian, one obvious inequality is in the naming of professions. Often only the masculine form exists. But (1) when the feminine form is available it may signify 'wife of'; (2) when the masculine form is applied to the woman some say that it is a source of ridicule; but (3) if a neologistic feminine form is used some find it equally unacceptable.

(1)   *ambasciatore > ambasciatrice* (ambassador), *generale > generalessa* (general), *presidente > presidentessa* (president), *maresciallo > marescialla* (marshal).

(2)   *la ingegnere* (engineer), *la ministro* (minister), *la avvocato* (solicitor), *la capitano* (captain), *la cavaliere* (chevalier), *la censore* (censor).

(3)   *l' ingegnere > la ingegnera, il ministro > la ministra, l'avvocato > l'avvocata, il capitano > la capitana, il cavaliere > la cavaliera, il censore > la censora.*

As these examples show, the choice of innovative women linguists does not always coincide with the phonetic preference of many educated (male or female) native speakers. These linguists prefer *la soldata* to *la soldatessa* (the soldier) and *la sacerdote* to *la sacerdotessa* (the priest). It seems that the established feminine forms carry negative connotations developed at the time when the masculine form suggested higher status and the feminine equivalent meant lower status. For this reason, *la dottoressa* is sometimes refused. A *Dizionario Sessuato della Lingua Italiana* (Gender Dictionary of Italian Language) (Deiana *et al.*, 1994) suggests that a more dignified feminine form for the masculine *dottore* (doctor) should be *la dottora*. These terms are still highly charged, and their use is restricted mainly to dedicated feminists. Other modern women simply prefer the masculine form, which 'elevates' their position. For example, Irene Pivetti, President of Parliament in Berlusconi's Government, called herself *cittadino* (citizen) instead of *cittadina*, the conventional form. F. Sabatini (1987) recalls the negative impression that might arise on account of the pejorative connotations of the suffix *-ora*, usually used for more working class occupations (like *fattora* female land agent, or *pastora* shepardess). He would, therefore, not be in favour of *provveditora* (chief education officer), *questora* (director of police) *pretora* (type of magistrate).

He introduces the positive suggestions made in a study commissioned by the *Presidenza del Consiglio dei Ministri* and carried out by another (not related) scholar, A. Sabatini (1987). In the very detailed corpus of inbuilt sexism in Italian (*dissimmetrie grammaticali* grammatical dysymmetries), A. Sabatini identifies some obvious instances of sexist attitudes: *Il primo ministro indiano assassinato* (Indira Gandhi, Indian Prime Minister assassinated). Another tendency that A. Sabatini condemns is the use of the masculine form followed by *donna* (*il sindaco donna* the mayor woman) because an equivalent form is not adopted for men and is therefore negatively marked (e.g. *uomo casalingo* does not exist). Likewise, A. Sabatini objects to the masculine connotations of certain idiomatic expressions leading to semantic mismatches, when applied to women: *paternità di un'opera* (paternity of a work of art), *fratellanza dei popoli* (brotherhood of peoples). She feels that this incongruity is particularly objectionable in sentences like *la paternità di questo lavoro è da attribuire a Maria*. Her study includes a survey of sexist terms in newspapers, and a comprehensive section of recommendations concerning honorifics (*titoli*), official positions (*cariche*), professional jobs (*professioni*) and manual occupations (*mestieri*). It concludes that a rectification of the sexist imbalance in the Italian language should be undertaken. This message was positively received after the 1995 edition of the Zingarelli *Vocabolario della Lingua Italiana*. This edition not only lists unusual transformations of traditionally male occupations (*autotrasportatrice* lorry driver; *barrelliera* stretcher-bearer; *minatrice* miner; *stalliera* groom) but reforms the gender of nouns by denoting as 'feminine' nouns describing jobs and positions that were traditionally thought of as 'masculine' but whose form is 'feminine': e.g. *elettricista* (electrician). This lexical innovation in such a highly esteemed dictionary could not fail to attract the interest of the press. *La Stampa* (10 July 1994) pointed out another revolution: some substantives referring traditionally to women (*spogliarellista, prostituta*) are often adopted in a masculine form: (*lo spogliarellista* male stripper, *il prostituto* male prostitute).

Political correctness

The Italian debate on PC language is often perceived to be associated with Anglo-American culture, both in its positive (liberal/progressive) and negative (prescriptive/intolerant) connotations. This is evident in the English borrowing adopted by Baroncelli (1994) *Il linguaggio non offending come strategia di tolleranza* (Non offending language as a tolerance strategy). At the present time, in the US, bookshops offer great numbers of books on PC language. In its own little way, the evolution of Italian words referring to people working in other people's homes is very telling:

> *serva* (servant), *cameriera* (maid), *donna di servizio* (service-woman), *donna* (woman), *lavoratrice domestica* (domestic worker), *collaboratrice domestica* (home help), *collaboratrice familiare* (family collaborator later abbreviated into *colf*).

In the 1980s, when awareness about the male-focused, and man-made, quality of language spread through the feminist movement and stimulated political debate outside the English-speaking world, some equal opportunity activists in Italy investigated the possibility of purifying the Italian language from the 'negative' influence of the WMPS (White Male Power Structures). The lexical area where Italian PC analysts have been most active – apart from sexist language – is that of the terms describing physical handicaps and physically handicapped people. Words like *cieco* (blind) and *invalido* (disabled) came under scrutiny because they were used negatively in ordinary Italian. *Cieco* meant unwillingness to understand or discern and *invalido* was referred to a general inability to perform or conclude actions. The trend of euphemistic circumlocutions developed as a result of bureaucratic timidity to use explicit expressions. Various euphemistic circumlocutions were suddenly heralded into everyday language, especially by the institutional agencies that decided to promote them: schools, councils, the social services and transport companies. Here are some more common examples:

sordo (deaf)	> *audioleso* (with damaged hearing) *non udente* (not hearing)
cieco (blind)	> *non vedente* (not seeing)
handicappato (handicapped)	> *inabile fisicamente* (physically disable)
mongoloide (mongoloid)	> *affetto da sindrome di Down* (with Down's syndrome)
povero (poor)	> *economicamente sfavorito* (financially underprivileged)
spazzino (street-cleaner)	> *operatore ecologico* (ecological operator)
minorato (disabled)	> *portatore di handicap* (handicap bearer)
normale (normale)	> *normodotato* (of normal intelligence)
invalido (invalid)	> *non deambulante* (not walking)
paralitico (paralytic)	> *affetto da paralisi* (affected by paralysis)

In Italy the press has underlined the very wide gap between the state's willingness to adopt PC language and the lack of concrete measures to alleviate people's suffering. The expression *diversamente abili* (differently able) used to describe handicapped people by former Under Secretary Ombretta Fumagalli Carulli was discussed when the interview was published (*Corriere della Sera, Lettere a Montanelli*, 24 November 1995). Some years previously the famous novelist, Natalia Ginzburg, had been very critical of the adoption of PC language by a state that was known to do so little to help the people concerned. Many linguists in Italy agree with the linguist Noam Chomsky, who suggested that this so-called liberal trend merely unveils a lot of unresolved problems (*L'Unità*, 2 January 1995).

Linguistic racism

The Italian word *negro* was one of the words discussed in the PC context. The old Italian euphemism was *persona di colore* (coloured person), later becoming *negro* (black) (Faloppa, 2004). For most native speakers of Italian *negro* does not (or did not) carry any pejorative connotations, and it is wrong to transfer censorship of the English word 'negro' and 'nigger' to an Italian word which only looks and sounds similar. This was the final pronouncement of the authoritative daily, *L'Unità*, reported also by *Corriere della Sera* (29 November 1995) '*negro è politicamente corretto*' ('*negro* is politically correct').

The connotations that terms like *negro* are perceived to carry in present-day use was revealed shortly after this by a survey carried out by the Italian Psychological Federation and reported by *la Repubblica* (9 December 1995). Of the sample interviewed, 53% found the word *negro* 'offensive to human dignity', followed by the word *ebreo* (47%), *handicappato* (39%) and *terrone* (for Southerner) (33%). The other findings in the survey seem to suggest that the vast majority of Italians wish to combat racism and xenophobia (89%). They feel they are the result of ignorance (66.2%) and that they are becoming dangerous (78.7%). This is surprising since the only word with a pegorative meaning is the last one: the other three historically have a neutral connotation. The interviewees must have felt that all four are commonly used in an offensive way. This shows that in a PC sensitive environment changes in meaning are not universally perceived.

When mass immigration began, the state offices most sensitive to PC language introduced the clumsy expression *extracomunitari* (people from outside the European Community). The term has gained currency especially in official circles, where *stranieri* is also used, though it does not distinguish between EU citizens and those from outside the European Union. Most Italians, however, are inclined to treat them differently. One term that became popular to refer to immigrants on TV, in the press, or in general conversation is *vuccumprà*, i.e. street hawkers (from the Neapolitan dialect for 'you wanna buy?'). Today there is still scant public concern for potentially discriminatory language, as long as it does not become explicitly racist. This is confirmed not only by the widespread popularity of the term *vuccumprà*, but also by the distasteful success of a neologism invented by the Italian state TV for the name of a quiz show called *Vuggiocà?* (You wanna play?). Explicit racism has, however, its own explicit language. Today it is usually related to the neo-Nazi groups or football hooligans. Their language is typical of the violent world they live in, and their racist slogans against Jews and immigrants so far express more linguistic conformism than political ideology. Indeed, the language of the football stadiums has not always belonged to the conformism of the extreme Right. In the 1970s (called *gli anni de piombo* 'the years of lead' because of Red Brigade terrorism), violent football supporters spoke the language of the extreme Left, which gained them the name of *gli ultrà*.

The language of young people

Slang or new language?

The language adopted by young Italians is one of the most remarkable developments in Italian society in the last 30 years or so, and could not fail to attract the attention of a great number of Italian linguists. There is consensus that this form of speech has developed concomitantly with the decline in use of dialects among young people. There is also agreement that the 'new language' is not used indiscriminately by the younger generation but is an alternative repertoire that comes alive within a special peer group. It is also agreed that use is no longer restricted to these special groups when the members are speaking about certain topics within certain social circles or regional areas. This special use shows different features in different age groups, for example, early teens, late teens and undergraduates, but (as has been observed in other countries) one general characteristic is the short lifespan of most expressions, with a few surviving because of their impact on ordinary language. Neither a language variety nor a slang, this language (in a broad sense) is a special register made up of the repertoires of many linguistic varieties which are appropriate when communication takes place within the peer group. Unlike other slangs in Italian society, such as those of old handcraftmen, street gangs and the drug culture, the intention is neither cryptic nor antagonistic, because the inventions are made for fun, and their use has spread for reasons of conformism or anti-conformism. Now that the phenomenon is more or less nationwide, young people do not switch into their special register unless two conditions are satisfied: (1) they are talking about topics requiring a stronger identification of their own personal position which needs to be marked by special language, and (2) they feel part of a special group and share the feelings of membership to what they regard as their own speech community. This form is sufficiently wide-spread to have left substantial traces in the ordinary language spoken by the 'normal' or adult world.

Once established within the restricted group, the new lexis expands within the immediate circle (which could be the school, the bar, the sports club, the discotheque or the *piazza* or any other meeting point). From then on, the aggregative spirit of the gang provides a favourable ground for circulation, but the original force of the neologism consists in the individual invention of the member of the group who has found a more imaginative and witty form to capture a meaning. This form will replace the existing term that will henceforth be felt too dated for the group.

This cycle highlights what aspects of language are more exposed to manipulation, in what domain of use, and by whom and why. The answer to the first question is that the lexical variations are almost exclusively subject to frequent transformation. The domain of use is that of the most important activities of the group. The transformations are created by members of the group, often its leaders, who can impose their inventions on others. The mechanism of renewal and circulation is constantly activated by the need for identification and conformity. In Italy, at least, the great popularity of this language, and its ability to constantly renew itself, is not determined by antagonism to the world of adults but by the gratifying activity of manipulating language as one manipulates materials for a work of art.

Origins

An older slang, which originated from a similar desire to play with language, was that used by soldiers. In Italy it developed largely to initiate the new recruits to life in the camp and adopted a lingua franca repertoire that was understood across regional dialects. Unlike the *gergo militare* (army slang), early slangs that were popular among young people were socially marked and made only a local impact, such as the *parlar snob* (affected speech) of some privileged groups in Milan and in Rome (De Mauro, 1970). The first major youth slang that achieved nationwide circulation was the language of university students in the late 1960s. The initial forum was the political debate in assemblies during the occupation of universities. Trade Union terminology and metaphorical idioms were adapted to paraphrase or emphasise the correctness of ideological positions and criticise any different ones: *situazione alternativa* (alternative situation), *masturbazione mentale* (mental masturbation), *prospettiva allucinante* (hallucinating prospective), *scelta demenziale* (insane choice), *è un impegnato* (he's politically committed), *è un alienato* (he's deranged), *è un integrato nel sistema* (he's part of the system). The *sinistrese* or political slang of students involved in the 1968 revolts (*sessantottini*: i.e. '68-ers') had a short lifespan within the original group of users in universities across the country, but it inundated the language of that generation for several years to come and left some phrases that are still heard in ordinary communication.

The next period of production came a few years later with the setting up of hundreds of local radio stations that introduced among the younger generations the trend called by some Italian linguists *parlare di sé* (speaking about oneself) (Simone, 1980). This coincided with the decline in the tendency to talk politics in schools and universities. Local radio programmes provided an effective vehicle to promote reform and innovations in the colloquial language that young people adopted to talk about themselves. The major impact was on the liberation of forms of syntax that were in a borderline area between incorrect language and tolerated colloquialisms. While previous radio programmes had proposed careful models of the spoken language, often read from pre-prepared scripts, the improvisation of untrained presenters and the increasing participation by the audiences promoted a new, hyper-colloquial model that appealed because it sounded thoroughly informal and therefore more genuine. The language of this phase of gangs and groups was often marked by certain interests (social life, clothing, music, sport, etc.) and goes by the name of postmodernist trends. It is linguistically so complicated by transfers (which may or may not be ironic) that one specialist (Cortelazzo, 1994) commented that beyond pragmatic values (exclamation, insult, compliments) it was not easy to appreciate the current literal meanings of many terms. The most famous of the post-modernist slangs was *paninaro*, a fortunate expression derived from the name of a bar in central Milan, usually frequented by middle class people in their late teens. This name, adopted after a popular TV programme *Drive In*, helped to promote the linguistic inventions of this group. Films and magazines in the 1980s provided further channels for the spread of the first linguistic trend to unify large sectors of the younger generation in a single style of communication that went beyond social and regional barriers. This slang was more humorous than antagonistic, and its inventions paraphrased habits and attitudes encountered at school and elsewhere by young people. The many euphemistic and pejorative epithets seem to contain a stronger component of irony than of cynicism. The contexts reveal affective rather than aggressive purposes. Thus parents can be ironically referred to as *sapiens* and a girl as *sfitinzia*, and old people can be ridiculed with the term *semifreddo* (semicold) or *fossile* (fossil). A less attractive girl can be *una contro tutte le tentazioni* (a girl against all temptations). In this game of irony and invention, there is more social and cultural antagonism with the way of living and speaking of old-fashioned and stigmatised gangs than with the targets for jokes and mockery at home and school. For example, the slang term for 'parents' has changed over the past 30 years from *vecchi* (my old folks) to *matusa* (from 'Methuselah'), *sapiens* (from Latin 'homo sapiens'), *arterio* (from 'arteriosclerotics') and *Führer*. The *sfitinzia* produced by the *paninaro* slang was discarded by the new gangs only a few years later. Despite the very short lifespan of most recent repertoires (most observers give a limit of three to five years), some expressions of old and new slang have made considerable impact, not only on the jargon of the next age group, but also in the language spoken by adults. These are some examples: *dritto* (smart fellow), *ganzo* (cute), *gasato* (pompous), *goduria* (delight), *pizza* (drag), *sputtanarsi* (to lose face), *bestiale* (great), *pazzesco* (crazy).

Interaction with dialects and the standard

The relationship with dialects has been the source of much discussion, but linguists have now clarified its ambivalence. It was noted that the origin of the early slangs coincided with the loss of dialects among young people, who were consequently deprived of an alternative repertoire which was often much more expressive with regard to the need for creative manipulation of everyday language than could be provided by the national standard (Cortelazzo, 1994; Lavinio & Sobrero, 1991). This is confirmed by the geographical spread of *gerghi* (slangs), which tend to originate and circulate more in the less dialectophone north than in the south, and in urban rather than rural environments, where rural communities still make frequent use of dialects. On the other hand, young people's slang today is rich in dialectal influences, not only from local dialect, but also from dialects of different regions: these are adopted in the language of urban groups in the north with different connotations from those in the south and vice versa. However, the use of dialectal expressions in the speech of young people should not be considered as a revival of dialects, but rather as an attempt to increase the anticonformist components, as a protest against adults conforming to standard Italian (Radtke, 1993). Two routes have been observed in the borrowings from the dialects, and each has specific motivations and connotations.

One route goes from local dialect to local jargon. This is explained by a revived interest in semantic 'localisms' (Coveri, 1993), rather than the use of dialect as such, to characterise speech in a nonconformist way. In other words, the dialect is one of the several linguistic repertoires available to urban youngsters to find inspiration for their new inventions and manipulations. *Muchela!* (cut it out!) in Milan, and *Ciao vecio!* (in the sense of 'hey-man!') in Veneto, are just two classic examples. More often in the south than in the north, fluency in dialect offers opportunities for occasional code-switching to increase emphasis or to create caricatured effects (Lo Piparo, 1990). The second route is when dialect expressions and epithets characteristic of southern speech become adopted in northern jargons for comic connotations: *arrapare* (to turn on), *bona* (good looking girl), *frocio* (queer), *racchia* (unattractive girl), *scamorza* (wimp), *sgamato* (smart), *burino* (lout). For many young Italians these expressions have already lost their dialectal as well as southern connotations. The suffix *-aro* to modify negative personal habits or behaviour is also of central/southern origin, although it too loses the regional connotation when in neologisms invented in the north of Italy: *fricchettaro* (freak), *rockettaro* (rock fan), *metallaro* (heavy metal fan). The main centres of diffusion of all recent *gerghi* are, however, the great urban centres of the north. This testifies to the fact that the new trends of slangs develop in geographical areas where dialects have been phased out and that they grow among middle class groups who then spread the trend downwards but not upwards.

Sources and repertoires

The three contributions already mentioned (colloquialisms, dialects, classic repertoire of old slangs) form a substratum, and new trends combine this with a rapidly changing adstratum of original inventions. Today the process that dates and regenerates this adstratum moves very rapidly. The jargon that was adopted by all youngsters in their late teens in the second half of the 1980s has now been superseded by new trends that are spreading gradually from the cultural foci in the north to the less trendy centre and south of the country. A survey carried out by Cortelazzo among 1200 school students throughout Italy (reported in *la Repubblica*, 27 January 1995) indicates that the repertoire of innovations that made *paninaro* the first national slang of the new generation is considered 'out' by all those interviewed. They all reported the need to innovate everyday language to feel 'in'. Thus terms that made up the typical innovations of that trend are rejected and stigmatised for their old-fashioned connotations. Among them there are the once famous: *tamarro* (lad), *sfitinzia* (babe), *lumare* (to stare at), *cuccare* (to screw), *al brucio* (in a hurry). More recently one typical source of neologisms was the hyperbole, with exaggerations designed to describe things and people (*da Dio*: heavenly; *favoloso*: fabulous; *mitico*: mythical) sometimes magnified by prefixes of which *mega* is the favourite (*megagalattico*: megagalactic; *megafesta*: megaparty; *megadiscoteca*: megadisco; or simply *mega* to mean 'it's fantastic'). Metaphors are also frequent to describe parents, again, and friends who are quick or, alternatively, slow (*ameba*: amoeba; *mollusco*: mollusc; *sveglione*: wideawake; *mandrake, golden boy, giusto*: smart) and more or less attractive (*autostrada*: motorway; *bolide*: rocket; *gallo*: rooster). Medical sources are also used to generate metaphors that describe people's characters or their appearance (*foco* from *focomelico*; *handy* from 'handicapped'; *schizo* from *shizofrenico*; *arterio* from *arteriosclerosi*). The last four are also examples of apocope, the omission of the final part of the word. This has always been a typical feature of youth slang (*prof* for *professore* and *matusa* for *Matusalemme*).

The invention of acronyms is also a frequent trait, and started with the international OK, followed by the very Italian *DOC* ('Controlled Denomination of Origin' used for wines, meaning OK) and among the tailor-made repertoire created by the young, *CVD* (*Come Volevasi Dimostrare*, as was clear), *TVB* (*Ti Voglio Bene*, I love you), *CTF* (*Completamente Tagliato Fuori*, completely marginalised) and the famous *CBCR* (*Cresci Bene Che Ripasso* grow, I'll come back later) a witticism used by older boys to younger girls.

From the lexis of graffiti comes another spelling innovation. The hard *c* sound is written with a *k*. The intention is to attach a derogative meaning of military and authoritarian flavour, probably from the post-1968 *sinistrese* which introduced *OKKUPAZIONE, AMERIKA, KAPITALISMO* and *KOSSIGA* (Cossiga, at that time Minister for Home Affairs). This habit has not had any impact on ordinary language, but it must be widely understood among adults if the press decided to use it to spell the name of *BERLUSKONI*. A second major source of inspiration and innovation is the language of the media: in particular expressions from famous TV programmes and commercial slogans heard on TV and/or read in magazines. The first source includes expressions by people or characters that are repeated in every programme and end up assuming a pragmatic function in a conversation where the speaker is in the situation depicted in the programme or alluded to in a popular song. In the 1960s, Topo Gigio's question '*Cosa mi dici mai?*' ('What do you mean?') was used to epitomise innocent (or ironic) surprise; in the 1970s the lines '*Vengo anch'io? No tu no!*' ('I'll come too? No, you don't!') from a popular song by the singer Enzo Iannacci synthesising an unhappy relationship with the gang, and the tune '*Vamos a la playa*' obsessively repeated in one of the hits of the 1980s was transformed and still functions today to mean '*Andiamo a passeggiare in piazza!*' ('Let's go for a walk in the square!'). The obsessive repetition of some slogans in TV commercials can also inspire the metaphorical impersonalisation of the characters through their dialogue, or more simply the first part of the slogan automatically brings out the set follow-up with ironical effect: '*Silenzio!*' – '*Parla Agnesi!*' ('Silence!' – 'Agnesi speaking!'). The third, and most prolific, source of recent innovations is the lexical area of foreign imports or inventions that include several separate repertoires: true borrowings and loan translations mainly from English, Anglo-American and South American adaptations; and genuine Italian-adapted expletives from comic strips. The repertoire of true borrowings can be found especially in music, most frequently in rock, punk, pop, underground, acid, folk, or metal music. But a selection of recurrent words is found systematically incorporated in the jargon of the young throughout Italy: very, new, parents, boss, money, baby, vacation, kiss, boy, city, fantastic, television, travel, company, and their use is often comic. Loan translations can be adopted sometimes for comic or sometimes for more serious, literal, meanings (*fuori di testa*: out of his/her mind). This is often seen in the language of music and computers (see *stavamo interfacciando* we were making out and the famous *Baco del Millennio* the Millennium Bug).

Adaptations from Anglo-American and South American languages always have a clearly ironic purpose. They are promoted by comics, magazines and TV programmes, and they can take on various connotations including pseudo-transfer with international connotations. Those coined from English may end with '-ation' that can be written *-escion* (*arrapescion, inchiappetation, tentacolescion*) while a slight machismo may be obtained from those from Spanish/Portuguese (*cucador* a great lover; *cuccare* to knock off; *mucho gusto* much pleasure; *me gusta* I love it). Most of these neologisms now travel diachronically across subsequent trends and synchronically from one sector of use to another, for example from television to discotheques where the disc jockeys function as major promoters of trends and innovations. On the way, the words assume connotations that sometimes change their original meaning, sometimes denoting the fetishes and idols that symbolise the subculture of the young.

The influence of English and other languages

Dardano (1986) proposed that the influence of English on Italian should be assessed at two levels: (1) at the higher level, the enrichment of cultural lexis and of technical terminologies while (2) there is interference at middle and lower levels 'where new creations – often ephemeral – appear in the language of journalism, advertising and youth slang'. This is a useful distinction. It points to the naïve attitude of many Italians who learned bits of English at school. They think the brevity of English discourse patterns makes native speakers more pragmatic and that these patterns can be easily adapted to other languages and cultures, hence making English automatically an international language. This view is widespread, particularly in the world of advertising. Slogans completely or partially in English are believed to increase the impact of the message. Dardano recalls that the 'plasticity' of English (e.g. grammatical flexibility and the abundance of monosyllabic words) is crucial in those areas where economy of space is of extreme importance, as in the names of TV programmes, for instance. The brevity of the messages, when compared with the complexity of Italian translations, only partly explains the appeal of Anglicisms in the media. Often names, slogans and trademarks are linguistically meaningless but are presented in meaningful iconic contexts. For example: *Jolly Box, ShoppingUp, Mama's Address, Baby Style, Time Now, Pop the New*.

The exorbitant numbers of names for shops and products modelled on English words that have invaded many Italian towns have been used by some newspapers to stir up feelings of linguistic patriotism. Florence in particular was in the headlines because some feel that at least the historical centre of the Italian language should be spared the foreignisms of the anglomaniacs. One local journalist wrote an outraged report saying that Florentines could find more English than Italian in places ranging from the local job centres (product manager, application engineers, promoter, telesellers, credit manager, advertising, area sales manager, senior sales engineers, account, franchising) to cinemas with untranslated film titles such as *Clerks, Stargate, Once Were Warriors, Pulp Fiction, The River Wild, Junior, Nightmare before Christmas*, to the names of local shops such as Babychic, Food e Drink, Baby & Lady, Day Day, Dress Company, Fashion Project, Forever, Minitrend, The Guys, Trench, Barber Shop, Hard Discount and a baker's shop with the hybrid name of Pantasy. The crusade by the Florentine reporter, however, did not create much interest (*la Repubblica*, Florence edition, 17 February 1995), possibly because the institutional supervision of language use still recalls the ridiculous purism of the Fascist era. Dardano (1986) reminds his readers that an early purist policy was introduced in 1874, well before Mussolini, with a higher tax on commercial signs written in a foreign language. As a result, only a very few Anglicisms were replaced by translations, if one considers the vast number of borrowings: *miting*, originating from 'meeting', soon disappeared, leaving *comizio* and the same happened to *spice*, an adaptation of 'speech', that did not survive competition with *discorso*.

Under Fascism, the *Regia Accademia d'Italia* issued a proscription list and imposed a prison sentence on anyone using foreignisms in public notices. But even this measure had less impact than expected, and many of the banned words like *electrochoc* and *cocktail* have survived, while their prescribed translations (*elettrosquasso* and *coda di gallo*) have left no trace.

Alarmist calls by the popular press in the 1990s sparked only two brief initiatives, one by the *CCD* party and one by the Northern League. But neither found much by way of support or followers. Indeed, only a very small number of academics, such as the lexicographer Oli and the language historian Castellani, campaigned for institutional initiatives to adapt or translate foreign borrowings, as was done when 'jacket' became *giacchetta* and 'beef steak' *bistecca*. They proposed that 'bestseller', 'fast food' and 'weekend' should become respectively *vendissimo, cibolesto* and *intredima*. Most contemporary linguists think a campaign against foreignisms would be artificial and unnecessary. One of the most influential linguists, Tullio De Mauro, writing in the 1970s, described the presence of foreignisms as marginal. Although the number has since increased remarkably, the 1995 edition of the Zingarelli dictionary confirmed his view, listing only 1811 English words of some currency, within a corpus of 134,000 items. This represents 1.35%, while other estimates indicate an even lower figure (0.3%) for all foreign words used in everyday language. There are other figures, some of which raise the number of foreign borrowings (15%) and give a higher occurrence (Mini, 1994) (Table 9).

Most contemporary linguists accept foreign words in their original language form and are not shocked by 'phonetic monsters' (like *faxare, formattare*, and *softwarismo*). This view was held by Nencioni, President of the *Accademia della*

Table 9 Estimates of foreign borrowings in Italian

	Zingarelli	*Mini*
English	840	3430
French	384	1450
Spanish	146	140
German	116	140
Russian	18	55
Portuguese	–	20
Total foreign words	1811	6500

Crusca until 2000. Under the new Presidency of Sabatini, the *Accademia* offers a new service designed to 'suggest' Italian translations of most English imports.

The Europeanisation of Italian

Language contacts within the EU

The view that the voice of Europe is somewhat stifled by continental bureaucracies is quite widespread in English-speaking countries. Although in other parts of Europe, people think that it is quite normal for administrations to use obscure language – and in some countries like Italy it would be a matter of some suspicion if it were otherwise – there is, at present, a great deal of confusion about the rhetorics of the new Europe. Certainly, thus far there have been only a few systematic attempts to explain why the language of Europe is gradually turning into a new supranational Eurospeak, incomprehensible in most European countries. Consider, for example, two English and Italian passages from a white paper on Community legislation, *European Governance* (EU, 2001).

> The link between European and global governance should lead to the Union speaking more often with a single voice. The prioritisation for dealing with complaints about breaches of the Community law will maximise the impact of the Commission's work as guardian of the Treaty.

> *Il nesso fra governance europea e governance mondiale deve indurre l'Unione ad esprimersi più spesso all'unisono. Grazie ad una migliore definizione delle priorità nell'esame dei reclami per violazione del diritto comunitario, si massimizzeranno i risultati dell'azione della Commissione in quanto custode dei trattati.*

The meaning of this passage in English is clear, although the style might not reflect the best of British uses, but we cannot say the same about the Italian version. Any reader will find it difficult to understand, though it is hard to pinpoint the reasons for its obscurity. The language is not technical, the sentences are short, the syntax is simple and, apart from one foreign borrowing, there are no discrepancies with everyday language. In other words, its obscurity is not one that Italian readers are accustomed to. The awkwardness of this language does not belong to the bureaucratic excesses of Italian, but to the realm of supranational abstractions. This discrepancy must raise some questions about communication in the EU, and the often-quoted slogan that the EU speaks with a single voice in many languages. But in connection with this ambitious project, two questions come to mind. Firstly, can Europe protect its policy of multilingualism at a time of increasing hegemony by one international language? Secondly, is the EU system of multilingual communication equipped to deal with the unprecedented volume of language contacts typical of cultural globalisation, and indeed the new expanded EU itself? (See e.g. van Els, 2001.)

Considering the variety of materials presently produced by EU institutions – only a small proportion of which concern legislation – it is interesting that their style of communication has developed features which are immediately recognisable to the general public. Although writers and translators are specifically requested to be aware of different registers and diverse styles within different national cultures, EU written materials have developed two visible features: (1) a textual uniformity, whatever the topic and the readership, that makes the voice of Europe distant from ordinary use in everyday life, and (2) the fact that the 'Europeanisation' often impairs good communication, thus threatening the status if not the credibility of the voice of Europe. There are several factors involved.

In the European Parliament, all languages can be used as working languages and can be either source or target languages, depending on the circumstances. This means that, when the Union had 11 languages (until May 2004), the Parliament Translation System needed to cope with 110 combinations, each language functioning as a source for the other ten. Since this policy of full multilingualism has been applied to the recent enlargements, 380 combinations for 20 languages are now required. The justification for this massive operation of simultaneous interpretation was that, when European MPs interact within the assemblies and committees, they are speaking for the electors in the national community that they represent. The Commission has adopted a system of multilingualism with an unequal, rather than equal, status among the official languages. The justification was that this was more practical and it would not interfere with the multilingual operations of the institution. Yet since the Commission's institutional task is to serve and inform the public, European citizens must receive all documentary and legislative materials in their national languages. There are two main points to note about these arrangements.

The first is that the Commission, by limiting the combinations and reducing the problem of quantity, has introduced a problem regarding quality. This will not be easy to solve, since EU officials are not (in a rapidly increasing proportion) native speakers of English. And at the present time, English is effectively the only lingua franca, as French tends to be used exclusively for internal staff regulations and the management of the Commission offices. The second point is that whereas interpreters give impromptu oral translations in the Parliament, those in the EU who really set models and affect linguistic trends are the translators of written language, because their choices are seen by the general public. They are the true innovators in this new multilingual environment, where changes are adopted in writing long before they have been accepted in the spoken language. And this is certainly one unprecedented outcome of language contact in Europe today.

Translation and the impact of technology

All European citizens must be able to read and understand documents and legislation in their own languages, according to the 1958 Language Charter, which remains the legal basis for the EU multilingual policy. Thus, from the very beginning of the process of European unification, it was decided that the official languages would be those (initially four in number) of the member states. This principle is enshrined in Regulation No. 1 of the 1958 Charter, which is amended each time a new country joins so as to include the new language. Currently, the Regulation reads: 'legislation and other documents of general application shall be drafted in the 20 official languages . . . ' The term 'drafted' suggests that the legislator should operate with parallel and simultaneous drafting in all the languages. Indeed, this was the case in the early years. But, over time, this has gradually changed and an administrative reform introduced a system whereby a single language version was always to be the starting-point for the production of the other versions by way of translation. The multilingual transactions have at present reached such quantitative and qualitative proportions that, for many reasons, the system is becoming highly defective. First, the EU translation procedures have not been devised or analysed by language experts. Rather, some of the major operations were introduced as routine decisions, as if they were to have no impact on the policy nor on the quality of the end product. Second, in legal terms, translation was introduced in lieu of multilingual drafting by plurilingual experts and is substantially present in the Community legislative process; but it is officially absent from the legislation itself. Thirdly, since translation does not 'exist', the translators must be 'invisible'. This paradox accounts for two more controversial decisions: (1) the separation of the translation service from the decision-making divisions, and (2) the anonymous and collective (rather than individual) responsibility of translators.

As far as EU multilingual policy is concerned, the notion of 'equivalence' is crucial. For example, the various language versions of the regulations and other European laws are 'equivalent', in the etymological sense of the word, since they have the same legal value and can be invoked indiscriminately by EU citizens irrespective of their member state of origin or the country's official language. Yet two assumptions need to be tested. One assumption is that legal equivalence is supported by textual equivalence, without which there cannot be equality of message for all European citizens. The second is that all translations must be as readily accessible as the originals. Otherwise, EU citizens are not 'equal' as regards the messages they receive. It is crucial, therefore, that translators find the best linguistic choices in order to safeguard the 'equivalence' of documents and legislative materials, as these must carry the same legal value in all language versions (Tosi, 2002a).

But the multilingual system, which is in operation in the largest translation agency in the world, leads translators to believe that all translations are acceptable and equal, as long as the single units in their texts are replaced one by one, and if care is taken to ensure that the units in the new language correspond to those from the source language. The rather 'mechanistic' procedures translators are trained to adopt encourage the straightforward substitution of all items in a text. In addition, sometimes, separate sections of a text (all in one source language) are given to different translators. At other times, the sections to be translated are in different source languages and are given to different translators. This visual approach is extended to all textual features, from the graphic layout, to the typographical style, including the length of the sentences and the punctuation. The result is an impressive visual correspondence; but this surface approach clashes with the linguistic anomalies of the texts and the semantic discrepancies between the different language versions.

Moreover, the growing role of technology in the multilingual communication between the EU and its citizens shows how these exponentially increased opportunities for language contacts can take place with little, if any, cultural interaction between the communities of speakers concerned. The memory system called TWB (Translators' Workbenches) enables users not only to search translation memories for previously translated sentences but also gives access to databases for individual terms. Any text for translation that contains passages or key ideas which have been translated in the past can be consulted, and adapted, directly from the main EU server at the touch of a key, and can be recreated by simply copying old passages into the new translation by an automatic system of cutting and pasting . This translation memory system automates the process of standardisation, and it has significant consequences not only for international communication but also for language change in national contexts. Three consequences deserve further investigation. First, the choices made at the click of a mouse by translators operating under intense time pressures may become 'final' solutions when they are memorised by the workbenches; and the problem is that they may not be the best solutions. Second, the traditional distinction between the written and the spoken word is becoming increasingly blurred, because new EU ideas are coming to depend on the written language of translation rather than on the language spoken within national communities. Third, the workbenches will make it difficult, if not impossible, for speakers in the national communities to participate in the process of standardisation. All proposals for decisions, directives and regulations may be available on the Internet for everybody to read, judge and react to, but it is most unlikely that anyone will succeed in challenging the validation of the choices made by a translator's terminal once they are put in cyberspace to feed memory for years to come (Tosi, 2005b).

Certainly English and French, which have coexisted for many years as working languages within the EU institutions, have benefited from resources and opportunities for transparency and standardisation which are unrivalled by any other language. Italian, which for historical reasons is still not highly standardised, could be more exposed than other languages to this new trend (Tosi, 2002b and 2005a). In this connection, it seems appropriate to conclude this survey of the Language Situation in Italy with a prediction made by Italo Calvino in 1965. In his debate with Pasolini, he announced the urgency to switch attention from the multilingualism within the Italian peninsula to the multilingualism in Europe, and prophetically described the emergence of a new international scenario.

> Nowadays every cultural question has immediate international resonance; it needs instantaneous verification around the globe, or at least it must be checked against a worldwide series of points of reference . . . Our age is characterised by this contradiction: on the one hand we need to be able to translate everything which is said into other languages immediately; on the other we realise that every language is a self-contained system of thought and by definition untranslatable . . . My prediction is this: each language will revolve around two poles. One pole is immediate translatability into

other languages, which will come close to a sort of all-embracing, high-level interlanguage; and another pole will be where the singular and secret essence of the language, which is by definition untranslatable, is distilled. And from this distillation, systems as different as popular slang and the poetic creativity of literature will drink.

Acknowledgements

I am most grateful to Giulio Lepschy with whom I had the opportunity to discuss various sections of this monograph at different phases of its production. Professor Lepschy has been most helpful with comments and suggestions that have been instrumental in introducing many improvements. I would also like to thank Professor Robert B. Kaplan and Dr Richard B. Baldauf Jr, the series editors, who have helped me with their expert guidance and advice. Naturally I am responsible for all inaccuracies and imprecisions that have survived.

Correspondence

Any correspondence should be directed to Professor Arturo Tosi, Department of Italian, University of London, Royal Holloway, Egham, Surrey, TW20 0EX, UK (a.tosi@rhul.ac.uk).

References

Aiello, R. (ed.) (1984) *Le Minoranze Linguistiche. Stato Attuale e Proposte di Tutela* [*Linguistic Minorities. Current State and Support Proposals*]. Pisa: Giardini.

Allan, P. and Swain, M. (eds) (1984) *Language Issues and Educational Policies: Exploring Canada's Multilingual Resources.* Oxford: Pergamon Press.

Andreoni, G. (1981) Australoitalian: A community language. Introduction. In F. Leoni (ed.) *Vocabolario Australoitaliano* [*Australoitalian Glossary*]. Armidale: University of New England Press.

Ascoli, G.I. (1870) Proemio [Introduction]. *Archivio Glottologico Italiano* [*Italian Glossologic Archives*] 1, v–xxxv.

Avveduto, S. (1983) Relazione [Report]. In *L'italiano Come Seconda Lingua in Italia e all'Estero.* [*Italian as a Second Language in Italy and Abroad*] (pp. 16–20). Rome: Istituto Poligrafico dello Stato [Polygraphic State Institute].

Baetens Beardsmore, H. (1979) Bilingual education for highly mobile children. *Language Planning and Language Problems* 3 (9), 138–65.

Baroncelli, F. (1994) Il linguaggio non offending come strategia di tolleranza [Non-offending language as a strategy of tolerance]. *Materiali per una storia della cultura giuridica* [*Materials for a History of Juridical Culture*] XXIV(1, Jun.). (pp. 11–55).

Bates, E. and Benigni, L. (1975) Rules of address in Italy: A sociological survey. *Language in Society* 4, 271–88.

Berretta, M. (1994) Il parlato contemporaneo [Contemporary spoken language]. In L. Serianni and P. Trifone (eds) *Storia della Lingua Italiana* (vol. 2). *Scritto e Parlato* [*History of the Italian Language* (vol. 2) *Written and Spoken Language*] (pp. 239–70). Torino: Einaudi.

Berruto, G. (1983) L'italiano popolare e la semplificazione linguistica [Popular Italian and linguistic simplification]. *Vox Romanica* 42, 38–79.

Berruto, G. (1985) Neo-italiano o neo-italiani? [Neo-Italian or Neo-Italians?] *Sigma* 78 (1/2), 125–34.

Berruto, G. (1986) L'italiano popolare. *Italiano & Oltre* (1-4), 171–8.

Berruto, G. (1987) *Sociolinguistica dell'Italiano Contemporaneo* [*Sociolinguistics of Contemporary Italian*]. Rome: La Nuova Italia Scientifica.

Berruto, G. (1993) Le varietà del repertorio [The variations of the repertoire]. In A.A.

Sobrero (ed.) _Introduzione all'Italiano Contemporaneo: Le Variazioni e gli Usi_ [_Introduction to Contemporary Italian Language: Variations and Uses_] (pp. 3–36). Bari: Laterza e Figli.

Berruto, G. (1994) Come si parlerà domani: Italiano e dialetto [How we will speak tomorrow: Italian and dialect]. In T. De Mauro (ed.) _Come Parlano gli Italiani_ [_How Italians Speak_] (pp. 15–24). Florence: La Nuova Italia.

Bettoni, C. (1981) _Italian in North Queensland: Changes in the Speech of First and Second Generation Bilinguals._ Capricornia, 3. Townsville: James Cook University of North Queensland.

Bettoni, C. (1993) Italiano fuori d'Italia [Italian outside Italy]. In A.A. Sobrero (ed.) _Introduzione all'Italiano Contemporaneo: Le Variazioni e gli Usi_ [_Introduction to Contemporary Italian Language: Variations and Uses_] (pp. 411–60). Bari: Laterza e Figli.

Boissevain, J.F. (1976) _The Italians of Montreal: Social Adjustment in Plural Society._ Ottawa: Studies of the Royal Commission on Bilingualism and Biculturalism.

Brault, G.J. (1964) Some misconceptions about teaching American ethnic children their mother tongue. _Modern Language Journal_ 48, 67–71.

Bruni, F. (ed.) (1992) _L'Italiano Nelle Regioni. Lingua Nazionale e Identità Regionali._ [_Italian in the Regions. National Language and Regional Identities_]. Torino: UTET.

Cahill, D. (1986) An evaluation of Australia's multicultural education programme. _Journal of Multilingual and Multicultural Development_ 7 (1), 55–69.

Calvino, I. (1965) L'italiano, una lingua tra le altre lingue [Italian, a language amongst other languages]. _Rinascita_ [_Rebirth_] 5, xxii, (January). Reprinted in I. Calvino (1980) _Una Pietra Sopra_ [_A Rock Above_] (pp. 116–26). Torino: Einaudi.

Castellani, A. (1982) Quanti erano gli italofoni nel 1861? [How many speakers of Italian were there in 1861?]. _Societa' di Linguistica Italiana_ [_Italian Linguistic Society_] 8, 3–25.

Castellani Pollidori, O. (1994) La plastica del parlato [The plasticity of spoken language]. In T. De Mauro (ed.) _Come Parlano gli Italiani_ [_How Italians Speak_] (pp. 9–14). Florence: La Nuova Italia.

Child, I. (1943) _Italian or American? The Second Generation in Conflict._ New Haven: Yale University Press.

Chini, M. (ed) (2004) _Plurilinguismo e Immigrazione in Italia: Un Indagine Sociolinguistica a Pavia e Torino_ [_Plurilingualism and Immigration in Italy: A Sociolinguistic Inquiry in Pavia and Torino_]. Milano: Franco Angeli.

Correa-Zoli, Y. (1981) The language of Italian Americans. In A. Ferguson and S.B. Heath (eds) _Language in the USA_ (pp. 239–56). Cambridge: Cambridge University Press.

Cortelazzo, M.A. (1977) Dialetto, italiano regionale, italiano popolare [Dialect, regional Italian and popular Italian]. In I. Paccagnella and M.A. Cortelazzo (eds) _Lingua, Sistemi Sociali, Comunicazione Sociale_ [_Language, Literary Systems and Social Communication_] (pp. 71–87). Padova: CLEUP.

Cortelazzo, M.A. (1994) Il parlato giovanile [The language of young people]. In L. Serianni and P. Trifone (eds) _Storia della Lingua Italiana_ (vol. 2). _Scritto e Parlato_ [_History of the Italian Language_ (vol. 2) _Written and Spoken Language_] (pp. 291–317).

Coveri, L. (1993) Novità del / sul linguaggio giovanile [Novelties of / about the language of young people]. In E. Radtke (ed.) _La Lingua dei Giovani_ [_The Language of Young People_] (pp. 35–47). Tübingen: Narr.

Cremona, J. (2002) Italian-based lingua francas around the Mediterranean. In A.L. Lepschy and A. Tosi (eds) _Multilingualism in Italy: Past and Present_ (pp. 24–30). Oxford: Legenda.

Cummins, J. (1984) _Bilingualism and Special Education: Issues in Assessment and Pedagogy._ Clevedon: Multilingual Matters.

Danesi, M. (1986) _Teaching a Heritage Language to Dialect-Speaking Students._ Toronto: Ontario Institute for Studies in Education and Centro Canadese Scuola e Cultura Italiana.

Dardano, M. (1986) The influence of English on Italian. In W. Viereck and W.D. Bald (eds) _English in Contact with Other Languages_ (pp. 231–52). Budapest: Akadémiai Kiadó.

Dardano, M. (1994) Profilo dell'italiano contemporaneo [Profile of contemporary Italian]. In L. Serianni and P. Trifone (eds) _Storia della Lingua Italiana_ (vol. 2). _Scritto e Parlato_ [_History of the Italian Language_ (vol. 2) _Written and Spoken Language_] (pp. 343–430). Torino: Einaudi.

Deiana, E., Madeccia, B., Maziani, M., Novelli, S. and Pellegrini, E. (1994) *Dizionario Sessuato della Lingua Italiana* [*Dictionary of Sexual Connotations in Italian Language*]. Roma: Libera Informazione Editrice.

De Mauro, T. (1970) *Storia Linguistica dell'Italia Unita* [*Linguistic History of a United Italy*]. Bari: Laterza.

De Mauro, T. (1972) Sociolinguistique et changement linguistique: Quelques considérations schématiques. In *Proceedings of the 11th International Congress of Linguists* (Vol 11) (pp. 819–24). Bologna: Il Mulino.

De Mauro, T. (1976) Giornalismo e storia linguistica [Journalism and the history of language]. In V. Castronovo and N. Tranfaglia (eds) *La Stampa del Neocapitalismo* [*The Press of Neocapitalism*] (pp. 457–510). Bari: Laterza.

De Mauro, T. (1985) La scuola, riforme mancate e impegno dei docenti [The school, lack of reforms and commitment of teachers]. In O. Cecchi and E. Ghidetti (eds) *Profili dell'Italia Repubblicana* [*Profiles of Republican Italy*] (pp. 119–44). Rome: Editiori Riuniti.

De Mauro, T. (1987) I Rom e il linguaggio [The Rom and their language]. In *L'Italia delle Italie* [*The Italy of Italies*] Rome: Editori Riuniti.

De Mauro, T. (ed.) (1994) *Come Parlano gli Italiani* [*How Italians Speak*]. Florence: La Nuova Italia.

De Mauro, T. (2001) Premessa [Foreword]. In V. Orioles and F. Toso (eds) *Insularità Linguistica e Culturale. Il Caso dei Tabarchini di Sardegna* [*Linguistic and Cultural Insularity: The Case of the Tabarchini in Sardinia*], Proceedings of the Convegno Internazionale di Studi (pp. 11–14). Recco: Le Mani.

De Mauro, T. and Vedovelli, M. (1994) La diffusione dell'italiano nel mondo: Problemi istituzionali e sociolinguistici [The spread of Italian in the world: Institutional and sociolinguistic problems]. *International Journal of Sociology of Language* 107, 25–39.

Denison, N. (1972) Some observations on language variety and plurilingualism. In J.B. Pride and J. Holmes (eds) *Sociolinguistics* (pp. 65–77). Harmondsworth: Penguin.

Devoto, G. (1953) *Profilo di Storia Linguistica Italiana* [*Profile of Italian Linguistic History*]. Florence: La Nuova Italia.

Di Pietro, R.J. (1977) The magic of Italian in the New World. In R.J. Di Pietro and E. Blansitt (eds) *Third LACUS (Linguistic Association of Canada and the United States) Forum* (pp. 158–65). Columbia, SC: Hornbeam.

Entwistle, H. (1979) *Antonio Gramsci: Conservative Schooling for Radical Politics*. London: Routledge and Kegan Paul

European Union (2001) *European Governance*. White Paper. [Italian translation: *Un Libro Bianco Sulla Governance Europea*]. Brussels: Commission of the European Union.

Faloppa, F. (2004) *Parole Contro: La Rappresentazione del Diverso in Italiano e nei Dialetti* [*Words Against: the Representation of Diversity in Italian and its Dialects*]. Milano: Garzanti.

Fishman, J.A. (ed.) (1966) *Language Loyalty in the United States: The Maintenance and Perpetuation of non-English Mother Tongues by American Ethnic and Religious Groups*. The Hague: Mouton.

Fishman, J.A. (1977) The social science perspective: Keynote. In J.A. Fishman (ed.) *Bilingual Education: Current Perspectives* (pp. 1–49). Arlington, VA: Centre for Applied Linguistics.

Francescato, G. (1991) *Nuovi Studi Linguistici sul Friulano* [*New Linguistic Sudies on Friulian*]. Udine: Società Filologica Friulana [Friulian Philological Society]

Francescato, G. (1993) Sociolinguistica delle minoranze [Sociolinguistics of minorities]. In A.A. Sobrero (ed.) *Introduzione all'Italiano Contemporaneo: Le Variazioni e gli Usi* [*Introduction to Contemporary Italian Language: Variations and Uses*] (pp. 311–40). Bari: Laterza e Figli.

Galli de' Paratesi, N. (1985) *Lingua Toscana in Bocca Ambrosiana. Tendenze Verso l'Italiano Standard: Un'Inchiesta Sociolinguistica* [*Tuscan Language Spoken by Milanese. Trends towards Standard Italian: A Sociolinguistic Inquiry*]. Bologna: Il Mulino.

Gensini, S. (1985) Che lingua parliamo? [What language do we speak?]. In O. Cecchi and E. Ghidetti (eds) *Profili dell'Italia Repubblicana* [*Profiles of Republican Italy*] (pp. 289–329). Rome: Editiori Riuniti.

Gensini, S. (1993) *Volgar favella. Percorsi del Pensiero Linguistico Italiano da Robertello a Manzoni* [*Vulgar Tongue. Developments of Italian Linguistic Ideas from Robertello to Manzoni*]. Florence: La Nuova Italia.

Giacalone Ramat, A. (1993) Italiano di stranieri [Italian of foreign immigrants]. In A.A. Sobrero (ed.) *Introduzione all'Italiano Contemporaneo: Le Variazioni e gli Usi* [*Introduction to Contemporary Italian Language: Variations and Uses*] (pp. 341–410). Bari: Laterza e Figli.

GISCEL [Group for Action and Research in Language Education] (1977) Dieci tesi per l'educazione linguistica democratica [Ten theses for democratic language education]. In L. Renzi and M.A. Cortellazzo (eds) *La Lingua Italiana Oggi: Un Problema Scolastico e Sociale* [*Italian Language Today: An Issue in Schools and Society*] (pp. 93–104). Bologna: Il Mulino.

Grassi, C. (1993) Italiano e dialetti [Italian and dialects]. In A.A. Sobrero (ed.) *Introduzione all'Italiano Contemporaneo: Le Variazioni e gli Usi* [*Introduction to Contemporary Italian Language: Variations and Uses*] (pp. 279–310). Bari: Laterza e Figli.

Grimes, B.F. (ed.) (1988) *Ethnologue Index: Languages of the World*. Texas: Summer Institute of Linguistics.

Haller, H.W. (1993) *Una Lingua Perduta e Ritrovata. L'Italiano Degli Italo-americani* [*A Language Lost and Found: The Italian of Italo-Americans*]. Florence: La Nuova Italia.

Hancock, I. (1979) Romani sociolinguistics. *International Journal of the Sociology of Language* 19, 1–9.

International Baccalaureate Schools Examinations Syndicate (ISES) (1967) *The International Baccalaureate*. Geneva: ISES.

International Baccalaureate Schools Examinations Syndicate (ISES) (1986) *General Guide to the International Baccalaureate* (5th edn). Geneva: ISES.

Klein, G. (1986) *La Politica Linguistica del Fascismo* [*Fascist Language Policy*]. Roma: Arginato.

Lavinio, C. and Sobrero A.A. (eds) (1991) *La Lingua degli Studenti Universitari* [*The Language of University Students*]. Florence: La Nuova Italia.

Lepschy, A.L. and Lepschy, G. (1977) *The Italian Language Today*. London: Hutchinson.

Lepschy, G. (1989) Quanto è popolare l'italiano? In *Nuovi saggi di linguistica italiana* (pp. 25–36). Bologna: Il Mulino. English version: How popular is Italian? In Z. Baranski and R. Lumley (eds) *Culture and Conflict in Postwar Italy. Essays on Mass and Popular Culture* (pp. 63–75). London: Macmillan, 1990.

Lepschy, G. (2002a) The languages of Italy. In G. Lepschy *Mother-tongues and Other Reflections on the Italian Language*. Toronto/Buffalo/London: University of London Press.

Lepschy, G. (2002b) What is the Standard? In A.L. Lepschy and A. Tosi (eds) *Multilingualism in Italy: Past and Present* (pp. 74–81). Oxford: Legenda.

Leso, E. (1978) Osservazioni sulla lingua di Mussolini [Observations on Mussolini's language]. In E. Leso, M.A. Cortelazzo, I. Paccagnella and F. Foresti *La Lingua Italiana e il Fascismo* [*Italian Language and Fascism*](pp. 15–62). Bologna: Consorzio Provinciale Pubblica Lettura.

Levi, P. (1947) *Se querto e un nomo*. Forino: Einaudi.

Lo Cascio, V. (1990) Introduzione. Un programma per l'Italia nell'Europa degli anni novanta [Introduction. A programme for Italy in the Europe of the nineties]. In V. Lo Cascio (ed.) *Lingua e Cultura Italiana in Europa* [*Italian Language and Culture in Europe*] (pp. ix–xlvii). Florence: Le Monnier.

Lombardi Satriani, L.M. (1974) Dal dialetto alla lingua: Riscatto culturale e perdita di identità [From dialect to language: Cultural emancipation and loss of identity]. In L.M. Lombardi Satriani (ed.) *Dal Dialetto alla Lingua* [*From Dialect to Language*] (pp. 5–18). Pisa: Pacini.

Lo Piparo, F. (1990) Introduzione [Introduction]. In F. Lo Piparo (ed.) *La Sicilia Linguistica Oggi* [*Linguistic Sicily Today*] (pp. 15–53). Palermo: Centro di Studi Filologici e Linguistici Siciliani [Centre of Philological and Linguistic Studies of Sicily].

Menarini, A. (1939) L'italo-americano degli Stati Uniti [Italo-American language in the United States]. *Lingua Nostra* [*Our Language*] 1, 152–60.

Menarini, A. (1940) Echi dell'italo-americano in Italia [Echoes of Italo-American language in Italy]. *Lingua Nostra [Our Language]* 2, 111–15.

Menarini, A. (1947) *Ai Margini della Lingua [At the Margins of Language]*. Florence: Sansoni

Mengaldo, P.V. (1994) *Il Novecento [The Twentieth Century]*. Bologna: Il Mulino.

Migliorini, B. (1927) Lingua e dialetti italiani negli Stati Uniti [Italian language and dialects in the United States]. *Cultura [Culture]* 5, 285–6.

Migliorini, B. (1963/1990) *Lingua Contemporanea [Contemporary Language]*. Firenze: Sansoni. Reprinted in *La Lingua Italiana del Novecento [The Italian Language of the Twentieth Century]*. Florence: Le Lettere.

Milani, L.D. and Scuola di Barbiana (1977) Chiamo uomo chi è padrone della sua lingua [I call a man, he who is the master of his own language]. In L. Renzi and M.A. Cortelazzo (eds) *La Lingua Italiana Oggi: Un Problema Scolastico e Sociale [Italian Language Today: An Issue in Schools and Society]* (pp. 40–53). Bologna: Il Mulino.

Mini, G. (1994) *Parole Senza Frontiere [Words without Frontiers]*. Bologna: Zanichelli.

Ministero degli Affari Esteri (MAE) (1972) *Programmi di Insegnamento di Lingua e Cultura Generale Italiana [Programs for the Teaching of the Language and General Culture of Italy]*. Rome.

Ministero della Pubblica Istruzione (MPI) (1989) *Inserimento degli Stranieri nella Scuola dell'Obbligo: Promozione e Coordinamento delle Iniziative per l'Esercizio del Diritto allo Studio*. Circolare Direzione Generale Istruzione Elementare, Direzione Generale Istruzione Secondaria primo grado, Servizio Scuola Materna [*Insertion of Foreign Pupils in Compulsory Education: Promotion and Co-ordination of Initiatives for the Implementation of the Right to Education*. Circular by the General Division of Primary Education, the General Division of the First Level of Secondary Education and Nursery Education], No. 301/1989. Rome.

Ministero della Pubblica Istruzione (MPI) (1990) *La Scuola dell'Obbligo e gli Alunni Stranieri. L'Educazione Interculturale*. Circolare Direzione Generale Istruzione Elementare, Direzione Generale Istruzione Secondaria primo grado, Servizio Scuola Materna [*Compulsory Education and Foreign Pupils, Intercultural Education*. Circular by the General Division of Primary Education, the General Division of the First Level of Secondary Education and Nursery Education], No. 205/1990. Rome.

Ministero della Pubblica Istruzione (MPI) (1994a) *Educazione Interculturale e Convivenza Democratica: l'Impegno Progettuale della Scuola*. Circolare Ufficio di Gabinetto [*Intercultural Education and Democratic Cohabitation: The Developing Programme of Education*. Circular of the Cabinet Office], No. 73/1994. Rome.

Ministero della Pubblica Istruzione (MPI) (1994b) *Iscrizione alla scuola degli alunni non in possesso del permesso di soggiorno*. Circolare Ufficio di Gabinetto [*School Registration of Pupils without Residence Permits*. Circular of the Cabinet Office], No. 5/1994. Rome.

Mioni, A. (1975) Per una sociolinguistica italiana. Note di un non sociologo [For a sociolinguistics of Italy. Notes of a non sociologist]. Foreword to J. Fishman, *La Sociologia del Linguaggio [Sociology of Language]* (pp. 7–56). Roma: Officina.

Nencioni, G. (1976) Parlato-parlato, parlato-scritto, parlato-recitato [Spoken-spoken, written-spoken, recited-spoken]. *Strumenti Critici [Critical Tools]* 10, 1–56.

Orioles, V. (2003) *Le Minoranze Linguistiche. Profili Sociolinguistici e Quadro dei Documenti di Tutela [Linguistic Minorities. Sociolinguistic Profiles and the Framework of Support Legislations]*. Roma: Il Calamo.

Pasolini, P.P. (1965) *Una Vita Violenta [A Violent Life]*. Milano: Garzanti.

Pellegrini, G.B. (1960) Tra lingua e dialetto in Italia [Between language and dialect]. *Studi Mediolatini e Volgari [Mediolatin and Vulgar Studies]* 8, 137–53.

Poggi Salani, T. (1981) Per uno studio dell'italiano regionale [For a study of regional Italian]. *La Ricerca [Research]* 3, 249–69.

Pozzo, G. (1985) Tra il dire e il fare. L'insegnamento linguistico e la ricerca glottodidattica oggi in Italia [Between saying and doing. Language education and language education research in Italy today]. In A. Ciliberti (ed.) *Didattica dalle Lingue in Europa e negli Stati Uniti [Language Teaching in Europe and the United States]* (pp. 105–64). Milano: Edizioni Scolastiche Mondadori.

Presidenza del Consiglio dei Ministri (1997) *Manuale di Stile: Strumenti per Semplificare il*

Linguaggio delle Amministrazioni Pubbliche [*Tools for the Simplification of the Language of Public Administrations*]. Dipartimento della Funzione Pubblica. Bologna: Il Mulino.

Radtke, E. (1993) Varietà giovanili [Language varieties of young people]. In A.A. Sobrero (ed.) *Introduzione all'Italiano Contemporaneo: Le Variazioni e gli Usi* [*Introduction to Contemporary Italian Language: Variations and Uses*] (pp. 192–235). Bari: Laterza e Figli.

Raffaelli, S.R. (1984) Prodomi del purismo xenofobo fascista [Anticipations of the xenophobic purism of Fascism]. In *Parlare Fascista. Parlare Fascista e politica linguistica del Fascismo. Movimento operaio e socialista* [*Speaking Fascist-Style. Speaking Fascist-Style and the Language Policy of Fascism. Workers and Socialist Movement*] (pp. 79–86) 1, a. vii, 1984. Genova: Centro Ligure di Stocia Sociale.

Rando, G. (1967) Italiano e inglese in Australia [Italian and English in Australia]. *Lingua Nostra* [*Our Language*] 28, 115–18.

Rando, G. (1968) Influenze dell'inglese sul lessico italiano [Influences of English on Italian vocabulary]. *Lingua Nostra* [*Our Language*] 29, 17–22.

Rando, G. (1973) Influssi inglesi sul lessico italiano contemporaneo [English influences on contemporary Italian vocabulary]. *Lingua Nostra* [*Our Language*] 24, III–20.

Renzi, L. (1993) La deissi personale e il suo uso sociale [Personal deixis and its social use]. *Studi di Grammatica Italiana* [*Studies of Italian Grammar*] 15, 348–90.

Renzi, L. (1994) Egli-lui-il-lo. In T. De Mauro (ed.) *Come Parlano gli Italiani* [*How Italians Speak*] (pp. 247–50). Florence: La Nuova Italia.

Renzi, L. (2000) Il catalano si parla ad Alghero. La nuova legge e le minoranze linguistiche [Catalan is spoken in Alghero. The new legislation and the linguistic minorities]. *L'Indice dei Libri del Mese* [*The Index of Books of the Month*] 2, 38–9.

Renzi, L. and Cortelazzo M.A. (eds) (1977) *La Lingua Italiana Oggi: Un Problema Scolastico e Sociale* [*Italian Language Today: An Issue in Schools and Society*]. Bologna: Il Mulino.

Romano, S. (1982) La lingua italiana all'estero [Italian language abroad]. *Il Veltro* [*The Greyhound*] 26 (3–4), 167–77.

Romano, S. (1983) Premessa [Foreword]. In Presidenza del Consiglio dei Ministri [Presidency of the Council of Ministers] *L'Italiano come Lingua Seconda in Italia e all'Estero* [*Italian as a Second Language in Italy and Abroad*] (pp. 5–6). Roma: Istituto Poligrafico e Zecca dello Stato.

Rüegg, R. (1956) *Zur Wortgeographie der Italienischen Umgangssprache* [*Linguistic Geography of Ordinary Italian*]. Cologne: Romanisches Seminar der Universität.

Sabatini, A. (1987) *Il Sessismo nella Lingua Italiana* [*Sexism in Italian Language*]. Report for Commissione Nazionale per la Realizzazione della Parità tra Uomo e Donna [National Committee for Equal Opportunities between Men and Women]. Roma: Istituto Poligrafico e Zecca dello Stato [Poligraphic Institute and State Coinage Office].

Sabatini, F. (1985) L'italiano dell'uso medio. Una realtà tra le varietà linguistiche italiane [Italian of middle use. A reality among other Italian language varieties]. In G. Holtus and E. Radtke (eds) *Gesprochenes Italienisch in Geschichte und Gegenwart* [*Spoken Italian Language: Past and Present*] (pp. 154–84). Tübingen: Narr.

Sabatini, F. (1987) Più che una prefazione [More than a preface]. In A. Sabatini, *Il Sessismo nella Lingua Italiana* [*Sexism in Italian Language*] (pp. 13–19). Roma: Istituto Poligrafico e Zecca dello Stato [Poligraphic Institute and State Coinage Office].

Saltarelli, M. (1986) Italian in the USA: Stratification and cohesion. In C. Bettoni (ed.) *Italian Abroad. Studies on Language Contact in English-speaking Countries* (pp. 105–12). Sydney: Frederick May Foundation of Italian Studies.

Sanga, G. (1981) Les dynamiques linguistiques de la société italienne (1961–1981): De la naissance de l'italien populaire à la diffusion des ethnicismes linguistiques [Linguistic dynamics of Italian society (1961–1981): From the birth of popular Italian to the spread of linguistic ethnicisms]. *Langages* [*Languages*] 15, 61, 93–115.

Scholae Europeae (1973) *Schola Europea ex Foedere Novem Nationum*. [European Schools by the Agreement of Nine Nations] Luxembourg: Office for Official Publications of the European Communities.

Scuola di Barbiana (1967/1972) *Lettera ad una Professoressa*. Florence: Libreria Editrice Fiorentina. English translation: *Letter to a Teacher*. Harmondsworth: Penguin.

Simone, R. (ed.) (1979) *L'Educazione Linguistica [Language Education]*. Florence: La Nuova Italia.

Simone, R. (1980) Parlare di sé [Talking about oneself]. In E. Galli della Loggia *et al.* (eds) *Il Trionfo del Privato [The Triumph of the Private]* (pp. 191–230). Bari: Laterza.

Simone, R. (1999) Minoranze in minoranza? [Minorities in minority?] *Italiano e Oltre [Italian and Beyond]* 5, 195–6.

Sobrero, A.A. (1974) *Una Società tra Dialetto e Lingua [A Society between Dialect and Language]*. Lecce: Milella.

Sobrero, A.A. (1982) La grecía Calabrese (provincia di Reggio Calabria) [Greek-speaking Calabria (Province of Reggio Calabria)]. In G. Francescato (ed.) *Le Minoranze Linguistiche in Italia [Linguistic Minorities in Italy]* Sociologia della Comunicazione *[Sociology of Communication]* 1 (2), 119–22.

Sobrero, A.A. (ed.) (1993) *Introduzione all'Italiano Contemporaneo: Le Variazioni e gli Usi [Introduction to Contemporary Italian Language: Variations and Uses]* Bari: Laterza.

Swain, M. (1972) Bilingualism as a first language. Unpublished PhD Thesis, University of California, Irvine.

Swann, M. (1985) *Education for All*. The Report of the Committee of Inquiry into the Education of Children from Ethnic Minority Groups. London: HMSO.

Telmon, T. (1993) Varietà regionali [Regional varieties]. In A.A. Sobrero (ed.) *Introduzione all'Italiano Contemporaneo: Le Variazioni e gli Usi [Introduction to Contemporary Italian Language: Variations and Uses]* (pp. 92–149). Bari: Laterza e Figli.

Tosi, A. (1979) Mother tongue teaching for the children of migrants. *Language Teaching and Linguistics: Abstracts* 12 (4), 213–31.

Tosi, A. (1984) *Immigration and Bilingual Education: A Case Study of Movement of Population, Language Change and Education within the EEC*. Oxford: Pergamon.

Tosi, A. (1986b) Home and community language teaching for bilingual learners: Issues in planning and instruction. *Language Teaching* 19 (1), 2–23.

Tosi, A. (1989) Bilingual education. In R.B. Kaplan *et al.* (eds) *Annual Review of Applied Linguistics* 10 (pp. 103–21). New York: Cambridge University Press.

Tosi, A. (1990) Italiano e anglofonia in Italia e all'estero [Italian and English-speaking people in Italy and abroad]. In V. Lo Cascio (ed.) *Lingua e Cultura Italiana in Europa [Italian Language and Culture in Europe]* (pp. 51–62). Florence: Le Monnier.

Tosi, A. (1991a) *Italian Overseas: The Language of Italian Communities in the English-Speaking World/L'italiano d'Oltremare: La Lingua delle Comunità Italiane nei Paesi Anglofoni* (bilingual text). Florence: Giunti.

Tosi, A. (1991b) High-status and low-status bilingualism in Europe. *Journal of Education* 173 (2), 21–37.

Tosi, A. (1995) *Dalla Madrelingua all'Italiano: Lingue ed Educazione Linguistica nell'Italia Multietnica [From Mother-tongue to Italian: Languages and Language Education in Multiethnic Italy]*. Florence: La Nuova Italia.

Tosi, A. (1996) *Learning from Diversity: Language Education and Intercultural Relations in the Inner City*. Brussels: European Commission and Eurocities.

Tosi, A. (ed.) (2002a) *Crossing Barriers and Bridging Cultures. Towards a New Translation Culture in Support of European Multilingualism*. Clevedon: Multilingual Matters.

Tosi, A. (2002b) The Europeanisation of Italian language by the European Union. In A.L. Lepschy and A. Tosi (eds) *Multilingualism in Italy: Past and Present* (pp. 170–94). Oxford: Legenda.

Tosi, A. (2005a) Languages in contact with and without speaker interaction. In A.L. Lepschy and A.Tosi (eds) *Rethinking Languages in Contact* (pp. 160–72). Oxford: Legenda.

Tosi, A. (2005b) The devil in the kaleidoscope. Can Europe speak with a single voice in many languages? The Pit Corder Memorial Lecture, Proceedings of the British Association of Applied Linguistics 2004 Conference. In C. Leung and J. Jenkins (eds) *Reconfiguring Europe – the Contribution of Applied Linguistics*. London: Equinox.

Tropea, G. (1983) Americanismi nei dialetti italiani [Americanisms in Italian dialects]. In P. Beninca, M. Cortellazzo, A.L. Prosdocimi, L. Vanelli and A. Zamboni (eds) *Scritti Linguistici in Onore di Giovan Battista Pellegrini [Linguistic Essays in Honour of Giovan Battista Pellegrini]* (vol. 1) (pp. 179–87). Pisa: Pacini.

Vanelli, L. (1977) Italiano e veneto nella scuola (e fuori) [Italian and Veneto within (and outside) schools]. In L. Renzi and M.A. Cortelazzo (eds) *La Lingua Italiana Oggi: Un Problema Scolastico e Sociale* [*Italian Language Today: An Issue in Schools and Society*] (pp. 275–85). Bologna: Il Mulino.

van Els, T. (2001) Language planning in the European Union. *Current Issues in Language Planning* 2 (4), 311–60.

Vedovelli, M. (1990) La percezione della standardizzazione nell'apprendimento dell'italiano L2 [The perception of standardisation in the learning of Italian as an L2]. In E. Banfi and P. Cordin (eds) *Storia dell'Italiano e Forme dell'Italianizzazione* [*History of Italian and Forms of Italianisation*]. Roma: Bulzoni.

Vincent, N. (1981) Italian. In B. Comrie (ed.) *The World Major Languages* (pp. 269–92). London: Croom Helm.

Weinreich, U. (1953) *Languages in Contact*. New York: Humanities.

Zamboni, A. (1986) Gli anglismi nei dialetti italiani [Anglicisms in Italian dialects]. In *Elementi Stranieri nei Dialetti Italian* [*Foreign Elements in Italian Dialects*] (pp.79–125). Pisa: Pacini.

Zincone, G. (ed.) (1999) Primo rapporto sull'integrazione degli immigrati in Italia [*First Report on the Integration of Immigrants in Italy*]. Report by the committee chaired by G. Zincone, Presidenza del Consiglio dei Ministri [Presidency of the Council of Ministers]. Bologna: Società Editrice Il Mulino.

Biographical Notes on Contributors

Gabrielle Hogan-Brun, Swiss by origin, is Senior Research Fellow at the University of Bristol, England. Her research fields are multilingualism, language ideologies, language attitudes, and language-in-education policy, with a current focus on the Baltic Republics. She is an editor of the journal *Current Issues in Language Planning*, and of the book series *Palgrave Studies in Minority Languages and Communities*. Her published work includes the edited special journal issues 'Language and Social Processes in the Baltic States surrounding EU Accession' (in *Journal of Multilingual and Multicultural Development*, 2005), and 'Baltic Sociolinguistic Review' (in *Journal of Baltic Studies*, 2005), as well as the book *Language Minorities in Europe: Frameworks – Status – Prospects* (Palgrave, 2003). She manages the British Academy funded 'Baltic Language and Integration Network' (BLaIN; www.blain-online.org). With Meilutė Ramonienė she has carried out a survey-based British Academy funded research project on the Lithuanian language communities.

Muiris Ó Laoire (PhD) works as a senior lecturer in undergraduate language, communication and culture courses at the Institute of Technology, Tralee, and works on a consultative basis on the Review of Languages at the NCCA (National Council for Curriculum and Assessment), Dublin. He is co-editor of *Teagasc na Gaeilge* (Ireland) and *The Celtic Journal of Language Learning* (US). He is the author of textbooks, academic books and several articles on sociolinguistics, language regeneration and language pedagogy. He is outgoing president of IRAAL, the Irish Association of Applied Linguistics, the Irish affiliate of AILA and of NAACLT (North American Association of Celtic Language Teachers). He is visiting scholar at the department of Maori Studies, University of Auckland and at the University of Massey. Having organized and hosted the Third International conference on Trilingualism and Third Language Acquisition, he is currently engaged in full-time research. He was awarded IRCHSS Government of Ireland Research Fellow 2003–2004. His most recent international publications appear in the *Language Policy* (Kluwer) and in *Current Issues in Language and Society* and in *Language Awareness* (both Multilingual Matters) with forthcoming articles to appear in the *International Journal of the Sociology of Language* (Mouton) and *The Encyclopaedia of Language and Linguistics* (Elsevier Science). He is also editing a special volume of the new *International Journal of Multilingualism* and an edited book, *Multilingualism in Educational Settings* (Schneider Verlag). He has been recently appointed Chairman of the European (EU) Label for Innovation in Language Teaching and has been nominated to the Modern Languages Committee at the Royal Irish Academy in October 2004.

Uldis Ozolins was born in West Germany after World War II and came to Australia as a child, the son of Latvian refugees. He gained an Arts Honours degree in Politics and Philosophy from the University of Melbourne, and completed a PhD on Australian language policy at Monash University in Melbourne, focusing on the development of policy in relation to the languages of immigrants. The dissertation was published as *The Politics of Language in Australia* (Cambridge University Press, 1993). His interest in language policy has extended to other areas in the world and, since the late 1980s, he has spent considerable time in the Baltic States, and has published numerous articles on language policy and political issues there. He has taught in a variety of academic disciplines, including Politics, Philosophy, Education and Translating & Interpreting at various universities in Melbourne. He also manages a consultancy company 'Language Solutions'. He is currently Lecturer in Politics at La Trobe University in Melbourne, and together with his partner Kaija is raising two bilingual children, Freja and Finn.

Meilutė Ramonienė is Associate Professor and Head of the Department of Lithuanian Studies at the University of Vilnius. Her research interests include applied linguistics, sociolinguistics and onomastics, on which she also lectures at the University of Vilnius. Formerly she taught Lithuanian as a foreign language at the University of Helsinki. She is author of several textbooks and teacher reference books for teaching Lithuanian as a second language. Her published output also includes papers on applied linguistics, sociolinguistics and anthroponymics. With Gabrielle Hogan-Brun she was engaged in a survey-based, British Academy funded research project on the Lithuanian language communities, which led to a number of joint publications. She has coordinated an international Socrates Lingua 2 project entitled 'ONENESS' that produced on-line courses of five less-used and less-taught European languages.

Mart Rannut is Associate Professor at Tallinn University. Formerly he has worked as Director General of the Estonian Language Board, adviser to the President of Estonia and diplomat at the office of the CBSS Commissioner of Human Rights. His scholarly interests include language policy and planning, linguistic human rights, acculturation of new immigrant children and Estonian as a Second Language (phonetic accent). He has published extensively in Estonian (and also in Russian) on language policy, including a textbook for students and a manual for language policy specialists (in Russian). He has also co-written a textbook of Estonian for new immigrant pupils. Mart Rannut is a member of several national committees and boards. He is a co-founder of the Estonian Institute of Human Rights and its first General Secretary; subsequently he has served as a member of the Board.

Arturo Tosi was born and raised in Italy but has taught in British universities for many years, combining his teaching and research with various activities in the field of applied linguistics. He originally left Italy to pursue research on bilingualism within Italian communities in English-speaking countries (England, Australia and Canada) and he was coordinator of the first EU project on bilingual education in Bedford (1976–1980). He was appointed Chairman of the National Council for mother tongue teaching for ethnic minority communities in Britain, and he set up a programme for the training of teachers of ethnic minority languages (Royal Society of Arts, 1980–1985). During the 1980s he was a member of the Italian Ministry of Foreign Affairs Committee on Italian language planning and promotion abroad and, during the same period, he was responsible for Italian examinations and teacher training (mother tongue and foreign language) within the International Baccalaureate Examination Programme and the European Schools of the EU. In the field of language assessment, he directed the Bilingual and Language Testing Project at the Institute of Education, and the European Certificate for attainment in Foreign Languages, at the University of London School Examination Board. Over the last ten years he has led EU projects on the language education of children of immigrants in Italy and Britain, and he has been actively involved in the field of multilingual translation and the training of Italian translators within the EU Parliament and Commission. He has also acted as an external expert to the Commission in the field of language policy and language education, and since 1998 he has been a member of the BMW Foundation on Intercultural Learning in Munich.